KV-383-062

HARVARD HISTORICAL STUDIES

PUBLISHED UNDER THE DIRECTION OF
THE DEPARTMENT OF HISTORY

FROM THE INCOME OF
THE HENRY WARREN TORREY FUND

VOLUME XLII

HARVARD HISTORICAL STUDIES

I. The Suppression of the African Slave-Trade to the United States of America, 1638–1870. By W. E. B. DuBois.

II. The Contest over the Ratification of the Federal Constitution in Massachusetts. By S. B. Harding.

III. A Critical Study of Nullification in South Carolina. By D. F. Houston.

IV. Nominations for Elective Office in the United States. By Frederick W. Dallinger.

V. A Bibliography of British Municipal History, including Gilds and Parliamentary Representation. By Charles Gross.

VI. The Liberty and Free Soil Parties in the Northwest. By Theodore Clarke Smith.

VII. The Provincial Governor in the English Colonies of North America. By Evarts Boutell Greene.

VIII. The County Palatine of Durham. A Study in Constitutional History. By G. T. Lapsley.

IX. The Anglican Episcopate and the American Colonies. By A. L. Cross.

X. The Administration of the American Revolutionary Army. By Louis Clinton Hatch.

XI. The Civil Service and the Patronage. By Carl Russell Fish.

XII. The Development of Freedom of the Press in Massachusetts. By C. A. Duniway.

XIII. The Seigniorial System in Canada. By W. B. Munro.

XIV. The Frankpledge System. By William Alfred Morris.

XV. The Public Life of Joseph Dudley. By Everett Kimball.

XVI. Mémoire de Marie Caroline, Reine de Naples. Edited by Robert Matteson Johnston.

XVII. The Barrington-Bernard Correspondence. Edited by E. Channing.

XVIII. The Government of the Ottoman Empire in the Time of Suleiman the Magnificent. By Albert Howe Lybyer.

XIX. The Granger Movement. By S. J. Buck.

XX. Burgage Tenure in Medieval England. By Morley de Wolf Hemmeon.

XXI. An Abridgment of the Indian Affairs transacted in the colony of New York from 1678 to 1751. By Peter Wraxall. Edited with an introduction by Charles Howard McIlwain.

XXII. English Field Systems. By Howard Levi Gray.

XXIII. The Second Partition of Poland. By Robert Howard Lord.

XXIV. Norman Institutions. By Charles Homer Haskins.

XXV. Robert Curthose, Duke of Normandy. By Charles Wendell David.

XXVI. Bismarck's Diplomacy at its Zenith. By Joseph Vincent Fuller.

XXVII. Studies in the History of Medieval Science. By Charles H. Haskins.

XXVIII. The Origins of the War of 1870. New Documents from the German Archives. By Robert H. Lord.

XXIX. The Monroe Doctrine, 1823–1826. By Dexter Perkins.

XXX. The Franco-Russian Alliance, 1890–1894. By W. L. Langer.

XXXI. Fur Trade and Empire. George Simpson's Journal . . . together with accompanying documents. Edited by Frederick Merk.

XXXII. The Schleswig-Holstein Question. By Lawrence D. Steefel.

XXXIII. The Presbyterian Churches and the Federal Union, 1861–1869. By Lewis G. Vander Velde.

XXXIV. The Influence of the Commons on Early Legislation. By Howard L. Gray.

XXXV. The National Workshops. By Donald Cope McKay.

XXXVI. Franz Joseph and Bismarck before 1866. By C. W. Clark.

XXXVII. The Caracas Company, 1728–1784. By Roland D. Hussey.

XXXVIII. Great Britain and the Cyprus Convention Policy of 1878. By Dwight E. Lee.

XXXIX. The Fronde. By Paul Rice Doolin.

XL. French Foreign Policy during the Administration of Cardinal Fleury, 1726–1743. By Arthur McCandless Wilson.

XLI. The Genesis of Napoleonic Imperialism. By Harold C. Deutsch.

XLII. The Diplomacy of the Balkan Wars, 1912–1913. By Ernst Christian Helmreich.

HARVARD UNIVERSITY PRESS
CAMBRIDGE, MASS., U. S. A.

THE DIPLOMACY OF THE BALKAN WARS
1912-1913

ERNST CHRISTIAN HELMREICH
ASSISTANT PROFESSOR OF HISTORY AND GOVERNMENT
BOWDOIN COLLEGE

CAMBRIDGE
HARVARD UNIVERSITY PRESS
LONDON : HUMPHREY MILFORD
OXFORD UNIVERSITY PRESS
1938

PRINTED BY THE HARVARD UNIVERSITY PRESS
CAMBRIDGE, MASSACHUSETTS, U. S. A.

To my father
CHRISTIAN HELMREICH

PREFACE

TWENTY-FIVE years ago the Balkan Wars were fought only to be at once dwarfed by the World War. Primarily in order to clarify the origins of the latter conflict countless documents, memoirs, biographies, and monographs have been published. Although books without end have been written on the diplomacy of the Great War, there is no systematic treatment of the Balkan Wars based on this new material.

In addition to the printed material generally available I have made use of the rather inaccessible volumes published by the Bulgarian Parliamentary Committee of Inquiry at Sofia, 1918–19. I was privileged to consult the attaché reports, reports of the *Evidenzbureau*, and certain other material in the Vienna *Kriegsarchiv*. The many interviews which were accorded to me by eminent statesmen and scholars in 1929–30 served not only to illuminate certain points but aided greatly in general orientation. Everywhere, as a Sheldon Fellow of Harvard University, I was received with the greatest cordiality and friendliness. To the University which made possible this year of study in Europe, as well as to the many individuals who granted me interviews — they are named in the bibliographical note — I desire again to express my thanks.

This study originated in a doctoral dissertation on "The Diplomacy of the First Balkan War, 1912–1913" which was presented at Harvard in 1932. Since then this account has been thoroughly rewritten in the light of subsequent evidence and the study carried on through the Second Balkan War and its aftermath. The closing chapters, dealing with the Albanian boundaries, the disposition of the Aegean Islands, financial and railway problems, show how unsettled Balkan — and indeed European — affairs remained in the year that elapsed between the end of the Second Balkan War and the beginning of the World War. The plans for partition of Macedonia according to the Serbian-Greek agreements of June 1, 1913, shown in juxtaposition with the more familiar disputed zone of the Serbian-Bulgarian agreement of March 13, 1912, is, I believe, a new feature of a map dealing with the Balkan Wars. The proposed boundary of Albania as decided on at the foreign office in Vienna in December, 1912, has never been published before. I am indebted to Professor Ludwig Bittner, director of the *Haus-, Hof-, und Staatsarchiv* in Vienna for the photostats on which the map of Albania is largely based. The summary of the military measures taken by Austria-Hungary in 1912–13 and the translation of the Serbian-Bulgarian treaty of alliance of 1904 are published for the first time in the appendices.

Some portions of the study have appeared as articles in the *Berliner Monatshefte* (translated into German), *The Journal of Modern History*, and *The Slavonic Review*. These have been worked over and incorporated in the present text. The spelling of names when dealing with Balkan history always constitutes a problem, and the forms here used no doubt are at times open to criticism. Attempt has been made to be consistent in the text and for that reason changes in spelling and capitalisation have sometimes been made within quotations. In the footnotes names are spelled as on the title page of the book, except that Izvolsky is used as a more or less arbitrary abbreviation for Stieve's well known volumes, *Der Diplomatische Schriftwechsel Iswolskis*.

Personally I am especially indebted to Professor Willliam L. Langer who first called my attention to this field of study and who has helped me in numberless ways both while a graduate student and since. To Louise Roberts Helmreich not only her husband but every one who reads this book is deeply obligated. Her criticism and appreciation have been a constant aid. I only wish her part in the volume could be more adequately shown. To my parents and to my sister, Agnes Helmreich, I owe much for encouragement and aid during the first years spent on this study. To Cyril E. Black I am under very special obligation for invaluable aid in the study of the Bulgarian sources. I also wish to thank R. H. Moore '39 and C. E. Campbell '39 who aided in typing the final manuscript as part of the student aid program sponsored by Bowdoin College.

E. C. HELMREICH

Brunswick, Maine
June 30, 1938

TABLE OF CONTENTS

LIST OF MAPS

ABBREVIATIONS

Complete citations are to be found in the bibliography

Balkanicus [S. Protić].	*The Aspirations of Bulgaria.*
B.D.	*British Documents on the Origins of the War 1898–1914.*
Benckendorff.	*Graf Benckendorffs Diplomatischer Schriftwechsel,* ed. by B. von Siebert.
Berl. Mon.	*Berliner Monatshefte.*
Conrad [Feldmarschall]	*Aus Meiner Dienstzeit 1906–1918.*
D.D.F.	*Documents diplomatiques français 1871–1914.*
Diplomaticheski dokumenti.	*Diplomaticheski dokumenti po namesata na Bŭlgariya v evropeĭskata voĭna* [Bulgarian Orange Book].
Diplomatist.	*Nationalism and War in the Near East.*
Doklad.	*Doklad na parlamentarnata izpitatelna komisiya* [Report of the parliamentary commission of inquiry].
Driault [E.] and Lhéritier [M.].	*Histoire diplomatique de la Grèce de 1821 à nos jours.*
G.P.	*Die Grosse Politik der Europäischen Kabinette 1871–1914.*
Gueshoff [I.E.].	*The Balkan League.*
Izvolsky	*Der Diplomatische Schriftwechsel Iswolskis 1911–1914,* ed. by F. Stieve.
K.A.	*Krasny Arkhiv.*
Ö–U.A.	*Österreich-Ungarns Aussenpolitik 1908–1914.*
Ö–U.K.A.	*Österreich-Ungarisches Kriegsarchiv in Vienna.*
Lončarević [Dusan]	*Jugoslaviens Entstehung.*
Poincaré [Raymond]	*Au service de la France.*

R.D. — *Die Internationalen Beziehungen im Zeitalter des Imperialismus. Dokumente aus den Archiven der Zarischen und der Provisorischen Regierung.*

S.D. — *Die Auswärtige Politik Serbiens 1903–1914*, ed. by M. Boghitschewitsch.

Toshev [A.]. — *Balkanskite voĭni* [The Balkan Wars].

THE DIPLOMACY OF THE BALKAN WARS
1912–1913

CHAPTER I

SERBIAN–BULGARIAN RELATIONS, 1904–1911

IN OPENING the discussions for an alliance with Serbia in the fall of 1911, the Bulgarian statesmen harked back to the Serbian-Bulgarian agreement of 1904. Rizov, who had negotiated that instrument, was sent to Belgrade to make the first soundings and the proposed alliance was looked upon as a sort of renewal of the earlier agreement. In fact, the first Bulgarian memorandum drawn up in 1911 epitomised the program as, "The renewal of the treaty of 1904, *mutatis mutandis*: instead of reforms we shall ask for autonomy; if that should prove impossible we shall divide Macedonia." [1]

It thus is essential to start a study of the Balkan League of 1912 with this treaty of 1904, for although attempts at a Balkan league can be traced in other centuries, there was no connection between these earlier diplomatic efforts and the actual conclusion of the alliances. On the other hand, between 1904 and 1912, although negotiations may have stopped temporarily, the idea and plan persisted; the final alliance was but a climax to these eight years of diplomatic fencing.

Strangely enough, although both Gueshov and Protić referred to these agreements of 1904 in their books on the Balkan Wars,[2] other writers have paid little attention to them. This is no doubt to be explained by the fact that until very recently only a part of the agreement of 1904 was known. This was the treaty of friendship between the principality of Bulgaria and the kingdom of Serbia, published from the Russian archives after the collapse of

[1] I. E. Gueshoff, *The Balkan League* (London, 1915; hereafter cited as Gueshoff), p. 14, see also p. 10; Dr. M. Boghitschewitsch, *Die Auswärtige Politik Serbiens 1903–1914* (3 vols.; Berlin, 1928–31; hereafter cited as S.D.), I, no. 152.

[2] Gueshoff, pp. 10, 14; Balkanicus, *The Aspirations of Bulgaria* (London, 1915; hereafter cited as Balkanicus), pp. 78, 80. Balkanicus is the pseudonym for Stojan Protić, Serbian finance minister 1909–12, minister of the interior 1913–14.

the tsarist regime.[3] This treaty is devoted entirely to cultural and economic matters and does not mention reforms. Obviously this could not be the treaty referred to by the Bulgarian memorandum quoted above. Nor does it measure up to the references made by Protić to the 1904 agreement. Toshev, former Bulgarian minister to Belgrade, was the first to publish the remainder of the agreement of 1904. This consists of a "Treaty of Alliance" dealing with political and military matters, and a "Final Protocol" containing explanatory material for both treaties.[4]

With the overthrow of the Obrenović dynasty in Serbia the Old Radical party came to power. They favored an agreement with Bulgaria, for it would strengthen their government and enhance the economic welfare of the country.[5] King Peter, with an uncertain crown upon his head and still unrecognised by various European powers, was also eager to strengthen his position by an alliance. The outbreak of the Russo-Japanese war, which withdrew the possibility of Russian aid and apparently left the Balkan Peninsula open to Austro-Hungarian advance, was the deciding factor in bringing about the conclusion of the treaties. Moreover, Italy, full of mistrust of the Dual Monarchy, lent the rapprochement every possible encouragement.[6]

[3] Narodni komissariat po inostrannym dielam, *Sbornik sekretnikh dokumentov iz arkhiva bivshavo ministerstvo inostrannykh diel* [Collection of secret documents from the archives of the former ministry of foreign affairs] (2d ed.; Petrograd, 1917–18), no. 2, pp. 34–35; E. Laloy, *Les documents secrets des archives du ministère des affaires étrangères de Russie publiés par les Bolchéviks* (Paris, 1920), p. 18; S.D., II, no. 420; Bulgarian text in A. Toshev, *Balkanskite voĭni* [The Balkan Wars] (2 vols.; Sofia, 1929–31; hereafter cited as Toshev), I, 155–56; see below, Appendix II, pp. 465–66.

[4] Toshev, I, 153–55, 156–58. The texts were obtained from General Racho Petrov, Bulgarian minister-president 1903–06. See below, Appendix II, pp. 463–64, 466–68.

[5] *Ibid.*, I, 41; M. Boghitschewitsch, *Serbien und der Weltkrieg* (Berlin, 1931), p. 29; Herman Wendel, *Der Kampf der Südslawen um Freiheit und Einheit* (Frankfurt am Main, 1925), p. 567; Dusan A. Lončarević, *Jugoslaviens Entstehung* (Vienna, 1929; hereafter cited as Lončarević), pp. 116, 132.

[6] Francesco, Tommasini, *L'Italia alla vigilia della guerra. La politica estera di Tommaso Tittoni* (3 vols.; Bologna, 1934–7), I, 109–10; V. Corović in the Belgrade *Politika*, May 1–4, 1937, as reported in *Berliner Monatshefte*, XV (1937), 529–30; Paul Herre, *Die Kleinen Staaten Europas und die Entstehung des Weltkrieges* (Munich, 1937), pp. 334–6.

In a conversation with the Bulgarian attaché, Hesapchiev, on February 1, 1904, King Peter discussed the question of an agreement. The suggestion was favorably received by the Bulgarian government and they soon dispatched Rizov, at that time minister at Cetinje, to Belgrade to aid the attaché in carrying on the negotiations. The result was the two treaties of March 30/April 12, and the Final Protocol of March 31/April 13, 1904, referred to above.

The treaty of friendship dealt with cultural and economic matters and was couched in general terms. In fact it was but a preliminary agreement enumerating the principles and questions which should be dealt with in later treaties and conventions. It provided that common postal and telegraph rates be established, that the cyrillic alphabet be introduced in telegraphic communications between the countries, that passport requirements be abolished, and that all hindrances to travel between the two countries be removed.

Conventions were to be drawn up providing for the extradition of criminals, and for a common circulation of coinage. Trade was to be encouraged by a reduction of freight and passenger rates, and the most important article stated that the countries agreed: "To permit the free importation of their respective products [of domestic origin], at the same time attempting to conduct similar customs policies with respect to other states, aiming at an eventual customs union (Zollverein)."

The "Treaty of Alliance," the other treaty signed on April 12th, consisted of a preamble and eight articles. The preamble gave the usual peaceful assurances, and contained guarantees of the territorial *status quo* in the Balkans. Article I approved the Mürzsteg program of reforms,[7] and promised the united coöperation and support of the two powers in carrying them out. Article II provided for reciprocal military aid against any attack no matter from whence it might come, be it in the interest of preserving their present territorial status and the independence

[7] For summary of the Mürzsteg agreement see Colonel Lamouche, *Quinze ans d'histoire balkanique 1904–1918* (Paris, 1928), pp. 40 ff.

of their respective countries, or for the safety and independence of the ruling hereditary houses. This clause was wide in scope, and the guarantee of dynasties must have been especially welcome to King Peter. Article III called for united action against any unfriendly action in Macedonia or Old Serbia, while the fourth article made mention of a special military convention which was to be drawn up to take care of the eventualities mentioned in the preceding articles. In the fifth article the allies, out of a desire to prepare the ground for an immediate agreement between Montenegro and Serbia, agreed to support a solution of the question of Albania favorable to the interests of Montenegro, whenever the occasion should arise. The last three articles dealt with the execution of the treaties. Article VI called for treatment and discussion of all questions which by letter or spirit arose from the treaty. However, in the next article the two allied states obliged themselves, in case they were unable to reach an agreement, to place all disputes before His Majesty, the Russian tsar, for final arbitration. In case the tsar refused to arbitrate the question referred to him, it was to be referred to the Permanent Court of Arbitration at The Hague. This principle of Russian arbitration was taken over directly by the treaty of 1912, although apparently at this later date it was thought unnecessary to provide for the Hague tribunal as a court of last extremity. According to the final article of the 1904 treaty, the pact was to be secret and could be communicated to a third state only after agreement between the allied countries. No definite time limit was set, although after five years the treaty was to be revised if the countries thought it necessary.

The Final Protocol drawn up the next day, April 13, 1904, was a covering document for the two treaties. It consisted of the usual preamble dealing with the exchange of credentials, and four articles. Various phrases of the treaties were more minutely defined in order to avoid future misinterpretation. As to the commercial treaty, it was noted that the proposed customs union was not to affect the condition of existing commercial treaties with other countries, and that efforts should be made to establish telegraphic relations with Russia in the cyrillic alphabet. As a supplement to Article I the two allied states promised to promote mutual tolerance between their fellow countrymen within the Ottoman Empire. Albania was understood to be within the boundaries of the vilayets of Scutari and Janina. The most important explanatory note specifically stated that the Sanjak of Novibazar was considered part of the Kossovo vilayet. This meant that Bulgaria pledged herself to oppose an Austrian annexation of a region which at that time was occupied by the forces of the Dual Monarchy. A final provision dealt with ratification and stated that the treaties should be kept in the personal archives of King Peter and Prince Ferdinand, it being permissible to place in the archives of the ministry of foreign affairs a copy of the treaty of friendship only.

With the foundation laid by these two treaties the governments started to negotiate the other agreements foreseen in the documents. By July, 1905, a tariff agreement had been reached which was to go into effect the following March, and was to continue up to March 1, 1917, at which time it was to be replaced by a common tariff rate for both countries.[8] It was hoped that by March 1, 1906 both countries would have concluded their separate agreements with Austria-Hungary, on which the treaty was more or less contingent.

Both countries were negotiating with Vienna when suddenly and without consulting Serbia, the Bulgarian government decided to lay the Serbian tariff agreement before the sobranje. The Serbian government was unpleasantly surprised by this, for knowledge of this Serbian-Bulgarian treaty would not simplify the Austrian-Serbian negotiations. An explanation from Sofia, that the Bulgarian government wanted only to have the new agreement ratified before the old Serbian treaty expired on January 1, 1906, did nothing to lighten the consequences of this precipitate action.

The publication of the tariff treaty did cause alarm at Vienna,

[8] Lončarević, pp. 98–9. For the text of the agreement see *Neue Freie Presse*, Jan. 7, 8, 1906.

and the Ballhausplatz immediately called on Serbia for a copy. This was furnished, and on January 11, 1906 Aehrenthal demanded of Serbia that the "tariff union" be dropped.[9] The answer from Belgrade was tantamount to a refusal. Serbia was now informed that Austria would not consider further negotiations unless Serbia agreed not to ratify the Bulgarian agreement meanwhile. Furthermore, Austria demanded that in case an Austrian-Serbian treaty were successfully concluded, Serbia should undertake all such modifications of the Serbian-Bulgarian treaty as Austria-Hungary should designate as necessary.[10]

Serbia accepted the first condition laid down by Vienna, but wished to alter the second, so as to make only such changes as the Austrian-Serbian treaty required. This answer was unacceptable to Vienna. Belgrade reiterated its standpoint, whereupon the Ballhausplatz closed the frontier to the importation of Serbian livestock. The Austrians justified their action by the Veterinary Convention of 1893. That prevention of the spread of disease was, however, only a pretext is shown by the fact that slaughtered cattle and hogs were also excluded.[11]

The affair had reached an acute stage. The famous Pig War was on. In Belgrade a large meeting of Serbian merchants hailed the stand of the government and spoke favorably of the tariff union. On February 2, the question came up in the Serbian skupština and here the Progressives and Old Radicals stressed the wisdom of coming to an understanding with the other Balkan powers. Pašić, leader of the Radicals, was reported as saying that:

> The Austro-Hungarian government in demanding the dropping of the tariff union had apparently forgotten that Serbia was an independent state. This demand of Austria-Hungary simply could not be reconciled with Serbia's dignity. The Serbian government had therefore acted wisely in refusing this demand. Although Serbia was not bound to inform anyone, the former government had made no secret of

[9] Lončarević, p. 104.

[10] *Ibid.*, pp. 107–8, Dr. Josef Baernreither, "Unsere Handelsbeziehungen zu Serbien," *Österreichische Rundschau*, XXIX (1911), 6–7.

[11] Heinrich Friedjung, *Das Zeitalter des Imperialismus* (3 vols.; Berlin, 1919), II, 191.

the fact that it was trying to obtain a rapprochement with Bulgaria, by concluding various conventions. He hoped that the Serbian-Bulgarian tariff union would remain. Serbia desired the friendship of Austria-Hungary, but likewise that of the Balkan states, for only in this fashion could the slogan, 'The Balkans to the Balkan peoples' be brought about.[12]

Towards the middle of February a *modus vivendi* was discovered. In a carefully drawn note, Austria demanded that the term *Zollunion* as a designation for the Serbian-Bulgarian agreement should be eliminated, and that a whole series of changes should be made covering those points which conflicted with the most-favored-nation principle. The Serbian government replied that the Serbian-Bulgarian customs union agreement (*Zollunionsvertrag*) had only come into being under the pressure of the new agrarian protective policy, and that it would be ready, in case a trade agreement were signed with Austria-Hungary, to make those modifications in the Bulgarian treaty which Austria had demanded in her note.[13] With this the difficulty over the Serbian-Bulgarian tariff union was settled, and negotiations between Belgrade and Vienna could continue. Nevertheless, these soon came to a halt and were finally broken off entirely, owing to Austrian demands for preferential treatment for her industries in the matter of Serbian state contracts, especially in the purchase of artillery. Serbia meanwhile turned her attention to trade agreements with other nations. Among them was one with Bulgaria based on the most-favored-nation principle, which went

[12] Lončarević, p. 116.

[13] Baernreither, *loc. cit.* The state of Austrian-Serbian tariff negotiations can be summarised as follows: March 1, 1906, expiration of existing Austrian-Serbian treaty; March 1–17, 1906, no agreement of any kind in force; March 17–July 7, 1906, a provisional agreement on the basis of the most-favored-nation principle in operation; July 7, 1906–September 1, 1908, no agreement in force; September 1, 1908–April 1, 1909, the treaty concluded March 14, 1908 was provisionally in force; April 1, 1909–January 24, 1911, no agreement; January 24, 1911, the treaty concluded on July 14, 1910 went into effect and continued so up to the World War. In addition to Baernreither's article see Dionys Jánossy, "Der handelspolitische Konflikt zwischen der österreichisch-ungarischen Monarchie und Serbien in den Jahren 1904–1910," *Jahrbuch des Wiener ungarischen historischen Instituts* (Budapest, 1932), II, 285–312; Maurice Schultz, "La politique économique d'Aehrenthal envers la Serbie," *Revue d'histoire de la guerre mondiale*, XIII (1935), 325–47; XIV (1935), 23–42.

into effect on December 6, 1906, being ratified by the skupština in February of 1907. Bulgaria also gave favorable rates to Serbian imports and to transit trade, and it appears that there was a secret agreement according to which the commercial treaty of 1897 was to continue in effect until a definite commercial treaty was concluded.[14]

The treaties of 1904 had borne little fruit. The attempt to give effect to the Treaty of Friendship by drawing up a tariff agreement had failed. Relations between Serbia and Bulgaria shortly became so bad that the political alliance treaty, although formally valid, became a dead letter.[15] The state of Serbian-Bulgarian relations at this time is admirably summarised in a lengthy memorandum drawn up by the Serbian foreign office.

> . . . With the appointment of Stanchov to be foreign minister of Bulgaria and especially after his visit to Vienna and Berlin, the relations between the two countries lost all of their former intimacy. In the years 1907 and 1908 the tension became so marked that for some moments (May and June, 1907) the danger existed that Bulgaria might declare war on Serbia. . . . The Bulgarian dissatisfaction with Serbia is caused, no matter what reasons one might advance, solely and alone by the fact that they feel that Serbia is the chief obstacle to the realisation of their aspirations. They desire that the Macedonian question should be a purely Bulgarian matter. The more the Serbian element in Macedonia gives evidence of its power, the sharper the tension between Bulgaria and Serbia will become.[16]

In the same vein Stanchov, while discussing foreign relations in the Bulgarian sobranje on November 20, 1907, stated:

> He was sorry to say that the relations with Serbia were not permeated with that spirit of brotherhood which should prevail between

[14] S.D., I, no. 120. For the treaty of 1897 see Martens, *Recueil général de traités*, 2d ser., XXV, 298–312.

[15] Substantially the material presented thus far has appeared in the author's article: "Die serbisch-bulgarischen Verträge von 1904," *Berliner Monatshefte*, XI (1933), 772–80.

[16] S.D., I, no. 121, pp. 131–2; see also no. 120; *British Documents on the Origins of the War, 1898–1914*, ed. G. P. Gooch and H. Temperley (11 vols.; London, 1926– ; hereafter cited as B.D.), IX, i, no. 52. This memorandum was drawn up in July, 1909 and sent to the Serbian ministers in St. Petersburg, London, Paris, and Rome so that they might inform the respective foreign offices as to the state of Serbian-Bulgarian treaty negotiations.

two nations of the same race; the Macedonian problem was the question which separated the two countries.[17]

Several months later, the English minister in Belgrade reported:

> To sum up the whole situation as regards the relations between Serbia and Bulgaria, it is clear that they can never be cordial and stable until the competition between the two nationalities for an eventual acquisition of the Slav countries still under Turkish rule comes to an end. M. Pašić was in favor of coöperating with Bulgaria for common aims, and of deferring the discussion of the rights of the two nations to the expected inheritance until it should actually fall due, but his intentions were frustrated by the uncompromising claim of the Bulgarians to the whole of the territory awarded to them by the treaty of San Stefano.[18]

The unfriendly relations between Serbia and Bulgaria were further complicated in 1908 by the declaration of Bulgarian independence and by the Austro-Hungarian annexation of Bosnia-Herzegovina.[19] Writing in October 1912, Berchtold stated:

> We must face the fact that our own method of action in the annexation of Bosnia and of the Herzegovina not only gave the first impulse to the Balkan Federation, but also unavoidably aroused a mistrust in the chancelleries of all great powers against the monarchy, and thereby created a bond of secret understanding which had never existed before in regard to their stand on our eastern policy.[20]

The origin of the league he traced back to the Russian attempts to form a Balkan league after the annexation crisis.[21] In general this is true, although Russia no doubt had a league in

[17] Schulthess, *Europäischer Geschichtskalender 1907* (Munich; hereafter cited as Schulthess), p. 339. See also A. Viallate, *La vie politique dans les deux mondes (1906–07)* (Paris, 1907), p. 331.

[18] B.D., V, 118.

[19] No attempt of course is made here to deal with all the ramifications of this crisis. For the diplomatic history of the annexation see the excellent studies: Momtchilo Nintchitch, *La crise bosniaque 1908–1909 et les puissances européennes* (2 vols.; Paris, 1937); Bernadotte E. Schmitt, *The Annexation of Bosnia 1908–1909* (Cambridge University Press, 1937). In regard to the Bulgarian declaration of independence see especially ch. III of Schmitt's volume.

[20] *Österreich-Ungarns Aussenpolitik von der bosnischen Krise 1908 bis zum Kriegsausbruch 1914*, ed. Ludwig Bittner and Hans Uebersberger (9 vols.; Vienna, 1930; hereafter cited as Ö-U.A.), IV, no. 3928.

[21] *Ibid.*, IV, no. 3787.

mind before 1908. Nor can its formation be credited to her efforts alone. The following Serbian statement hits nearer the mark:

> The annexation of Bosnia-Herzegovina laid bare the crisis in which the European balance of power — the sole reliable guarantee of peace — finds itself. It stirred up the consciousness of the Serbian race to battle, to a battle which the Entente powers have to wage against Teutonic hegemony; and at the same time it showed the connection of the Serbian question with the complex of other Balkan questions and the independence of the Balkan states. This accounts for the great interest of those governments in seeing that the power of resistance of the Serbian race be strengthened by a Serbian-Bulgarian, and eventually even by a Serbian-Bulgarian-Turkish, agreement.[22]

But these governments, i.e. the Entente, referred to above, were not the only powers interested. The others, especially Austria-Hungary, also had their ideas of a Balkan alignment. They hoped for a concert of Austria-Hungary, Bulgaria, and Rumania with variations by Greece and Turkey. Serbia was distinctly omitted, although there were many voices which sincerely urged bringing her into the fold. Montenegro both sides thought they might win and hold if they paid enough money. The programs of the two alliance groups were thus diametrically opposed. In one thing, however, they were agreed, neither side wanted to jeopardise its position and influence in Constantinople.

The question of Serbian-Bulgarian relations thus took on a decidedly European aspect with the annexation crisis of 1908. The Triple Entente had just been completed and this was to be its first test. England, thus far the most important factor in the balance of power, had quite definitely chosen sides and the liquidation of the annexation was to cement the ties of the Entente. The scales were so evenly balanced that it became extremely important on which side the small powers would align themselves, especially if there was the possibility of uniting them. Their combined forces might well have a deciding effect on any trial of strength.

[22] Circular telegram from the foreign office, July 20, 1909, S.D., I, no. 121.

The Balkan states, however, were looking after their own interests and were not to be stampeded into action. Only when the interests of the great powers coincided with their own, or when they stood a chance to gain thereby, were they willing to listen to the advice and promises made to them. The contest for allies was on.

Bulgaria, with an affair of her own to straighten out, naturally raised no objections to the annexation. Serbia, on the other hand, immediately raised her voice to protest and to demand a *quid pro quo*.

The annexation of Bosnia-Herzegovina did not come as a bolt from the clear sky to Belgrade. While at Carlsbad on September 4, 1908, Izvolsky had discussed the matter with Milovanović, pointing out to him the great concession he had obtained from Austria-Hungary in her promise to evacuate the Sanjak. Compensations for Serbia were also discussed, for according to the story which the Serbian premier told to Mr. Steed, Izvolsky asked him to present some suggestions as to Serbian wishes.[23] Milovanović no doubt called for a rectification of frontier at Austrian expense. At Buchlau several days later, according to Aehrenthal's report, Izvolsky made "the remarkable suggestion that it might be well to grant to Serbia and to Montenegro some rectifications of frontier in order to win their favor in regard to the annexation."[24] This Aehrenthal rejected, though he was willing to indicate to Serbia that, in case of greater changes in the Balkan peninsula, Austria would not oppose her expansion to the south. Serbia might also have a representative on the Danube Commission. Izvolsky thanked him for these concessions, but the Austrian refusal did not cause him to drop the

[23] H. W. Steed was correspondent of the London *Times*. See his *Through Thirty Years 1892-1922* (2 vols.; New York, 1924), I, 291; S.D., I, no. 6; B.D. IX, i, pp. 13-4, 777; *Die grosse Politik der Europäischen Kabinette, 1871-1914*, ed. Johannes Lepsius, Albrecht Mendelssohn Bartholdy, and Friedrich Thimme (40 vols.; Berlin, 1922-27; hereafter cited as G.P.), XXVI, ii, no. 9480. As a matter of fact the evacuation of the Sanjak was no concession obtained by Russia, but was a step voluntarily decided upon by the Ballhausplatz (Ö-U.A., I, nos. 9, 32, 48).

[24] Ö-U.A., I, no. 79.

plan of securing compensations for Serbia. On October 5th, two days before the Serbian note demanding compensations was launched, he told the Serbian representative in Paris that at the future conference, where Austria was to be led as Russia had been in 1878, Serbia might advance her wishes.[25]

At Carlsbad Milovanović was evidently of the opinion that under the conditions outlined by Izvolsky the annexation would be acceptable. On his way back to Belgrade he stopped off in Vienna and had an exceptionally friendly conversation with Aehrenthal.[26] Although Bosnia-Herzegovina was not mentioned, this very evasion, taken together with the conversation with Izvolsky, led him to the conclusion that annexation was imminent. This action, he told the English minister at Belgrade, would probably take place on December 2nd, the sixtieth anniversary of Francis Joseph's accession to the throne. "The effect of this annexation in Serbia," he continued, "would be incalculable and might lead to a veritable catastrophe. Difficult as the position of Serbia now was, the national sentiment was sustained by the hope of eventual expansion. Serbia asked for nothing at present but that the *status quo* should be maintained, and that no final settlement in favor of another power should be permitted in regard to a heritage which she regarded as her own." [27]

Milovanović, like Izvolsky, was wrong in his calculation as to when the annexation would occur. On October 5th the news reached Belgrade that Bulgaria had proclaimed her independence and that Austria-Hungary would announce the annexation of the two neighboring provinces on the 7th. Belgrade was in an uproar at once. Protest meetings were held and the streets resounded with the cry, "Down with Austria." [28] There was little agitation against Bulgaria, the Dual Monarchy being the butt of all demonstrations. On the 7th the government addressed a note

[25] S.D., I, no. 6.
[26] Ö-U.A., I, no. 78.
[27] B.D., V, no. 273.
[28] Lončarević, pp. 236–7; Ö-U.A., I, nos. 134, 135, 147.

to all powers signatory to the Treaty of Berlin protesting against the annexation:

> The Serbian government [so runs the concluding paragraph] could in the present case obtain full satisfaction only by the complete reestablishment of the situation in Bosnia-Herzegovina as established by the Treaty of Berlin. If this solution is considered absolutely impossible the Royal Government, appealing to the sentiments of justice of the powers signatory to the Treaty of Berlin, demands for Serbia a corresponding compensation, in order to maintain the guarantees indispensable to her existence as an independent state, and to reëstablish for the Serbian nation the same general guarantees of existence as they had been assured by the Treaty of Berlin.[29]

On the 10th the skupština was called into extraordinary session and gave the government its unconditional support.

With this backing the Serbian cabinet laid plans for diplomatic action on a broad front. They realised that they could not base their demands on any rights of Serbia, since the powers considered the whole question merely as a violation of the Berlin Treaty and of the sovereignty of the Sultan. Nationality also would not be recognised by the great powers as a legitimate argument, for to do so would raise questions in regard to their own territory. The Serbian plan was, therefore, to present the annexation as an immediate danger to the continued political existence of Serbia. The Serbs meant to make the Austrian action a Serbian question, and as such to place it before the forum of Europe, endeavoring to have the Serbian claims taken up as part of the program of the Entente. Once included in the policy of a syndicate of powers the Serbian question could be expanded or changed as necessary.[30]

All this, however, could only be accomplished if the whole question were kept open. To accomplish this, the Serbian government proposed to negotiate a treaty with Turkey in order to

[29] G.P., XXVI, i, no. 9091 Anlage; Lončarević, pp. 240–1. In Vienna Sektionschef von Szentgyörgy refused to receive the note when it was presented by the Serbian minister, although the latter permitted him to read it (Ö-U.A., I, no. 180).

[30] This statement of program is based on Premier Milovanović's secret report to the skupština on December 25, 1908 (quoted by Lončarević, pp. 253–4).

keep her from coming to an agreement with Austria-Hungary, and secondly, to raise the question of compensations. The Serbian demand for boundary rectification was to be the step which was to turn the annexation into a Serbian question and place it before the eyes of Europe. Thanks to the failure of Izvolsky's Straits policy in St. Petersburg as well as in London and Paris, they were to have plenty of aid in carrying out their program.[31]

To help accomplish these aims special delegates were dispatched to all the capitals. Foreign Minister Milovanović left for a visit to Berlin, Paris, London, and Rome; Crown Prince George and Pašić started for St. Petersburg, and the head of the Progressive Party, Stojan Novaković, for Constantinople.[32] Montenegro's special mission was welcomed at Belgrade and within a few days a Serbian-Montenegrin alliance was signed.[33] Montenegro willingly fell in with the plan of negotiating an agreement with Turkey and sent a delegate to Constantinople to help matters along.

Things soon began to happen, and by October 26th reports from both Constantinople and Belgrade informed the British foreign office that negotiations for an offensive and defensive alliance between Serbia and Turkey were under way.[34] By the end of the month the draft convention had reached Belgrade. Spalaiković, then in charge at the Serbian foreign office, proposed three amendments, the most important one being:

[31] W. L. Langer, "Russia, the Straits Question and the European Powers, 1904-8," *The English Historical Review*, XLIV (1929), 59-85; Schmitt, *Annexation of Bosnia*, pp. 35-6, 44-5; Nintchitch, *La crise bosniaque*, II, pp. 5 ff.

[32] Reports on these missions were made to the skupština on December 25, 1908-January 1, 1909. Since it was a secret session, according to the rules of order no minutes were kept, and the only record we have of these important reports are the private notes made by Marinko Stanojević, at that time secretary of the skupština. After the World War he published them in the Belgrade journal *Wreme*, and Lončarević has now published them in German translation (Lončarević, pp. 252-261). Citations bearing on these missions in the different collections of documents can be found in Schmitt, *Annexation of Bosnia*, pp. 65-72.

[33] See below, pp. 82-3.

[34] B.D., V, nos. 404, 405; on these negotiations see Nintchitch, *La crise bosniaque*, II, 85-95; "Montenegrinische Dokumente zur Annexionskrise" (summarised from the Cetinje periodical *Zapisi*, April-May, 1937), *Berliner Monatshefte*, XV (1937), 702-706.

". . . Turkey and Serbia should engage that neither of them should accept any proposed solution of the question of Bosnia-Herzegovina without previous agreement with the other." [35] Milovanović, at that time in London, immediately telegraphed his approval of the amendments. The one quoted above he considered absolutely essential, especially since Hardinge had just told him that Turkey would very likely come to a separate agreement with Austria on the basis of a financial consideration. "If Turkey wanted money," he advised, "she should demand territory and Serbia would buy it from her. In any case it was essential to work rapidly since Germany and Austria-Hungary had started steps towards an Austro-Hungarian-Turkish agreement." [36]

The Serbian changes were accepted by the Turkish statesmen, but they in return countered with an ". . . amendment to the effect that in case of a victorious war against Bulgaria the conquered territory should be divided between Serbia and Turkey, the former taking the western, the latter the eastern portion, and that the war indemnity should be divided equally." [37] Although the original draft convention was undoubtedly directed against Bulgaria as well as Austria-Hungary, this version brought up a new point. Bulgaria was specifically mentioned, and this Serbia could not sanction. Objections were at once made to the Porte and at the same time soundings were taken in London. If it should become necessary the Serbians wanted the British government to ". . . support the Serbian objection to the proposed article [mentioning Bulgaria] and to use their influence at Constantinople to persuade Turkey to accept the convention without it." [38] In spite of the Serbian request that no reference should be made to the matter just then, Downing Street did so. Shortly thereafter the grand vizier explained that ". . . owing to indiscretions committed at Belgrade, which led to the intervention of His Majesty's Ambassador against the

[35] B.D., V, no. 440. [36] S.D., I, no. 27.

[37] Whitehead to Grey, Nov. 23, 1908, B.D., V, no. 443. This telegram was relayed to the British ambassador at Constantinople.

[38] *Ibid.*

Convention, the matter must be dropped for the present." [39] What form this intervention took is not known. Undoubtedly it was to the effect that England did not favor an offensive alliance which was specifically directed against any one country, be it Austria or Bulgaria. This would at least be in line with British policy at this time.

Since the Porte wanted the article against Bulgaria retained, and both England and Russia had made it clear to Belgrade that they would not support a convention directed against Bulgaria, the negotiations made little progress. The draft convention was again changed, a defensive clause with an easily interpreted offensive turn in it being inserted to cover the Bulgarian question. This time the Turks flatly refused to guarantee not to recognise the annexation unless Serbia were to receive compensations.[40] To have done so would have tied their hands in case of separate negotiations with Austria.

Spalaiković, the secretary-general of the Serbian foreign office, hurried off to Constantinople to make one last try for the alliance, and, in case the Porte refused, to offer two general statements of friendship as an alternative.[41] It seemed at first as if the negotiations would succeed, but the Turkish cabinet evaded giving its signature under the pretext that they considered themselves only a provisional government. They wished to leave the actual signature of the convention to their successors, who would come into office after the Turkish parliament had met.[42] However, this was never to be. On December 14th the grand vizier informed the Austrian ambassador that the Serbian offers for a military convention had been rejected, a statement which Aehrenthal believed to be entirely honest and which was indeed true.[43]

The Serbian-Montenegrin attempt to negotiate an alliance

[39] Whitehead to Grey, Nov. 25, 1908, reporting conversation between grand vizier and Vukotić, special Montenegrin envoy to Constantinople, B.D., V, no. 455; see also no. 462, p. 508.

[40] *Ibid.*, V, no. 462.

[41] *Ibid.*, V, no. 472; see also Ö-U.A., I, no. 727.

[42] B.D., V, no. 482.

[43] Ö-U.A., I, nos. 742, 757, 777, 783; Lončarević, p. 257.

with Turkey and thus to prevent the recognition of the annexation of Bosnia-Herzegovina had failed. This policy never had the whole-hearted support of even the Entente powers. None of them wanted a Serbian-Montenegrin-Turkish agreement which might be directed against Bulgaria, and yet this was the only reason why Turkey had ever entertained the idea of a Serbian agreement. England, whose position at Constantinople was stronger than that of any other power, was not averse to a direct Austrian-Turkish settlement. English influence thus ran directly counter to Serbia's wishes.

Nor was the Porte entirely free from suspicions of Serbia. Hardly had the Austrian troops left the Sanjak, than the Ballhausplatz received a Turkish request for some sort of a guarantee that Serbia and Montenegro should not receive any part of this territory.[44] This became a cardinal point in the negotiations between the two countries the following spring, but Aehrenthal refused repeatedly to go beyond a promise of diplomatic support.[45] He might increase the troops in Bosnia in order to overawe Serbia, but he would not actively intervene. Germany would have been glad to see Austria undertake a military guarantee of this territory and the Kaiser made a marginal note on Aehrenthal's refusal, "Das ist Blödsinn! er muss!"[46]

The Serbian-Montenegrin proposals for alliance at Constantinople were definitely side-tracked when Austria-Hungary and Turkey came to an agreement about the annexation.[47] This agreement had been prepared not only through regular diplomatic channels but also by separate negotiations carried on by Consul-General Rappaport with the Young Turk Committee in

[44] Ö-U.A., I, nos. 309, 333, 551, 921.

[45] *Ibid.*, I, no. 948; II, nos. 1070, 1217, 1250.

[46] G.P., XXVI, ii, no. 9273; see also nos. 9270, 9271 note.

[47] By the middle of December, 1908 the Turkish boycott of Austrian ships and goods had been regulated, and final settlement hinged on the question of a money payment. On December 13th Pallavicini consented to present the Turkish views to Vienna, and the next day in a private letter he advocated meeting the Turkish wishes. It was not until January 7, 1909 that Aehrenthal agreed to this procedure (Ö-U.A., I, nos. 738, 743, 855). The final agreement of April 15, 1909 is to be found *ibid.*, II, no. 1522. For a detailed study of the Austrian-Turkish settlement see Schmitt, *Annexation of Bosnia*, ch. VIII.

Salonica. The point at issue was the Austro-Hungarian refusal to take over part of the Turkish state debt. It is interesting to note that Pallavicini, the able Austro-Hungarian ambassador at Constantinople, first advocated some financial compensation to Turkey at the very time when Spalaiković was in Constantinople making a last effort to obtain a Serbian-Turkish alliance. Whether there was a connection between the two is uncertain.[48] Nevertheless, the turn in Austrian policy and the resulting agreement did lead the grand vizier to refuse even the general statement of friendship which Spalaiković had proposed as a last alternative. This consideration was of only secondary importance, however, in view of the Porte's interest in an anti-Bulgarian agreement, which was quite unacceptable to the Entente powers, and consequently to Serbia herself.

In spite of the failure to put anything in writing, good relations continued between Serbia and Turkey, although Serbian attention now focussed on Bulgaria. For months the Entente powers had been advising Serbia to come to an agreement with Sofia, and Izvolsky in his famous Christmas (1908) speech before the duma had openly proclaimed the idea of a Balkan league. "Bulgaria, Serbia and Montenegro," so ran his concluding remarks, "must become imbued with the consciousness of the necessity of moral and political union. Russia's aim is to bring these states together and to combine them with Turkey, through means of common interests for the defense of their national and economic independence." [49] Sir Edward Grey thought the idea excellent and telegraphed to Nicolson, "I am quite in favor of this and will encourage it, whenever I can." [50]

Bülow and Aehrenthal at once pricked up their ears, and the German chancellor suggested to his colleague how pleased he would be with an Austrian-Bulgarian entente.[51] Aehrenthal had

[48] Pallavicini denies any connection (Ö-U.A., I, no. 738).

[49] Schulthess, 1908, p. 405.

[50] B.D., V, no. 493.

[51] G.P., XXVI, ii, no. 9298; Ö-U.A., I, no. 817. Neither Bülow nor Aehrenthal thought much of the possibility of the formation of a Balkan league. Bülow referred to it as a "Fanfaronade" and a "krankhafte Phantasie" (G.P., XXVI, ii, no. 9302; Ö-U.A., I, no. 861).

already been thinking of opening discussions with Sofia and he now did so. He promised the Bulgarian government that Austria would not permit a Serbian attack on Bulgaria in the event of a Bulgarian-Turkish war, and suggested that the two governments should enter upon an exchange of ideas in regard to an eventual joint attack by Turkey and Serbia on either Bulgaria or Austria-Hungary.[52] Aehrenthal had hardly launched his proposals when they were stalemated by the Bulgarian acceptance on February 1, 1909, of Russia's financial plan for the settlement of the Turkish-Bulgarian dispute.[53] Russia had been willing to dig down in her pockets to prevent a possible Austrian-Bulgarian rapprochement. Russia continued to win favor at Sofia when King Ferdinand's shrewd request of February 19th to attend the funeral of Grand Duke Vladimir was granted. "This request," so Izvolsky told the British and French ambassadors, "could not possibly be refused and the Russian government could not receive him otherwise than as king and give him sovereign honors." [54] This meant virtual recognition of the new international status of the Bulgarian state, although formal recognition was postponed to a later time.[55]

Izvolsky had distinctly scored a point with his policy at Sofia. Not only were better Russian-Bulgarian relations assured, but it was hoped that an important step had been taken toward a future Balkan league. In proposing the terms of the financial settlement to Bulgaria, Izvolsky had again pointed out the desirability of good relations between Bulgaria and Serbia. At this

[52] Ö-U.A., I, nos. 828, 835.

[53] According to the Bulgarian war minister this plan was suggested to Russia by the Tsankovists, the extreme Russophile party in Sofia (Hranilović to Conrad, Feb. 18, 1909, Ö-U.A., I, no. 1012). Under the agreement Bulgaria was to take over part of the Turkish war indemnity of 1878, and under favorable conditions make payment of the same to Russia. Russia in return renounced all right to indemnity payments from Turkey for a period of forty years (B.D., V, nos. 542, 543, 550; Schulthess, 1909, p. 610; Schmitt, *Annexation of Bosnia*, ch. IX).

[54] B.D., V, no. 584. The British government was not at all pleased with Russia's action. See also Harold Nicolson, *Portrait of a Diplomatist* (New York, 1930), p. 215; G. P., XXVI, ii, nos. 9338, 9340.

[55] Russia accorded Bulgaria official recognition on April 21, 1909; Italy, Germany, and Austria-Hungary on April 27th; Great Britain on April 23rd (Schulthess, 1909, p. 608; B.D., V, no. 851).

time Bulgaria did make ". . . advances to Serbia asking that the latter should at once recognize Bulgarian independence and offering in return a general agreement for mutual defense." [56] Milovanović, fearing a trap of some sort and not wishing to arouse Turkish susceptibilities, maintained a cold reserve. While Serbia never opposed the proclamation of Bulgarian independence, no steps had as yet been taken to regularise this *fait accompli.* The energy and time of the Serbians were devoted to more pressing matters. But in March, 1909, Milovanović paid a very pleasant two-day visit to Sofia and returned with "the impression that both states had common political interests which point to the necessity of closer ties between them." [57] The military revolution that broke out in Constantinople at the beginning of April influenced the Serbian government to sound Sofia on forming some such ties of friendship. An agreement for the protection of common interests was sought. Not satisfied with her own initiative, Serbia also asked the Entente powers [58] (and probably also Rome) [59] to urge the Bulgarian government to accept her proposal. ". . . An Entente of this kind," it was maintained, "would be the first step towards the realisation of a Balkan coalition which would be the surest means of preventing a further Austrian-German advance into the peninsula." [60] Sir Edward Grey thought the idea very good, but suggested that Serbia enter into direct negotiations with Bulgaria without the mediation of outsiders. "He therefore," so he told the Serbian minister, "could not do as Serbia wished." [61] But his actions

[56] Whitehead to Grey, Feb. 3, 1909, B.D., V, no. 553.

[57] *Graf Benckendorffs diplomatischer Schriftwechsel*, ed. B. von Siebert (3 vols.; Berlin, 1928; hereafter cited as Benckendorff), I, no. 42.

[58] *Ibid.*, I, nos. 71, 72; S.D., I, no. 100; B.D., V, no. 858.

[59] By April 28th Aehrenthal had wind of the Serbian solicitations, and according to his information Rome had also been asked to support the step (Ö-U.A., II, no. 1577). Although direct references to Serbian action in Rome are lacking it probably occurred. That Italy favored such an agreement at this time is clear (S.D., I, nos. 29, 30, 32, 33, 34, 57, 64; Lončarević, p. 255; B.D., IX, i, nos. 8, 9). The Consulta, along with the Entente foreign offices, was also informed in July, 1909 why these Serbian-Bulgarian negotiations had failed (S.D., I, nos. 120, 121; B.D., IX, i, no. 52).

[60] B.D., V, no. 858.

[61] Gruić to Milovanović, April 16, 1909, S.D., I, no. 101; B.D., IX, i, no. 2.

were better than his words and he proceeded to encourage the rapprochement at Sofia.[62] Russia was only too glad to lend her hand in furthering the cause of Slavic union, but she, like England, advised against doing anything which might provoke Austria.[63] No direct reference to French or Italian steps is available, although we know both favored such an agreement.

Bulgaria met the Serbian proposal of April, 1909, by asking for a clear statement of what the Serbian government had in mind. To this demand Milovanović demurred on the ground, as he expressed it, ". . . that he wished to enter into conversations with Bulgaria but not to be called upon to recite a monologue."[64] Besides, the need for a Serbian-Bulgarian agreement seemed less pressing than a few weeks earlier. The troubles in Turkey had not proved to be very serious and the signing of the Bulgarian-Turkish protocols relieved the tension in the Balkans. Negotiations between Belgrade and Sofia were not, however, completely dropped. The conflict between Serbia and Austria, heightened by Austria's cancellation of the provisional Austrian-Serbian tariff treaty on March 31, 1909, brought Serbia to feel more and more that a rapprochement with Bulgaria was necessary. The negotiations soon took an economic turn. The Serbian government proposed that the tariff union of 1905 — which had never gone into effect — should be used as a starting point for further discussions.[65] The Bulgarian statesmen shied at the idea, and on the whole assumed a dilatory attitude. Conversations continued but led to no definite results.

At London these negotiations were followed with interest. In May, 1909, the Serbian chargé spoke of the good relations existing between Bulgaria and Serbia and added that Serbia was doing all within her power to encourage a definite agreement between the two states. This policy had the complete approval of the British foreign office. Although unable to undertake any official measures to encourage such a conciliation, the British

[62] S.D., I, nos. 101 note, 103; B.D., IX, i, no. 2 note.
[63] Benckendorff, I, nos. 71, 72.
[64] B.D., V, no. 858.
[65] Benckendorff, I, nos. 73, 77.

government was ". . . willing at the proper time and place '*par un mot ci — par un mot là*' to show that they favored such a direction of policy." [66] Instead of a definite treaty the conclusion of an entente such as existed between England and France was recommended. Since there was solidarity of interests between Serbia and Bulgaria there was nothing to hinder such an understanding.

Although one might talk in London of the solidarity of Serbian and Bulgarian interests, in reality this did not seem to exist. In the speech which the Serbian minister was to make in presenting his credentials to King Ferdinand, Milovanović had carefully inserted the following passage:

> The duties of Slav solidarity, the call of blood, the common sufferings and hopes of the past, and more than all that, unshakeable conviction of the identity of our future destiny, causes us to welcome, as a new token of our common future, the success which Bulgaria has just achieved." [67]

In Sofia this was found to be too pronounced and the Bulgarians requested that the passage be stricken out, an action which displeased both Serbia and Russia.[68]

Nor did Macedonia bear witness to any common interests. The Serbs would not renounce their aspirations to this territory and the Bulgarians, as the German minister put it, "did not want to divide the Macedonian cake with anyone, least of all with the Serbs." [69] Towards the end of July, 1909, Serbia decided, since Bulgaria had not shown the slightest positive inclination toward a Serbian-Bulgarian rapprochement on either a commercial, economic, or purely political basis, to stop pressing the matter, and instructed her minister at Sofia not to mention the proposed agreement unless the question were raised by the Bulgarians.

[66] Gruić to Milovanović, May 25, 1909, S.D., I, no. 115. In October, 1909 Grey instructed the British minister at Sofia that ". . . while he should neglect no opportunity of furthering good relations between Bulgaria and Balkan states [it] is not desired to press this policy to a point which would create opposition in Bulgaria or elsewhere" (B.D., IX, i, no. 59 minute).

[67] S.D., I, no. 121, p. 133.

[68] *Ibid.*; Benckendorff, I, no. 94.

[69] Von Romberg to Bülow, June 3, 1909, G.P., XXVII, i, no. 9728.

Further insistence on their part they felt might do more harm than good to a possible future understanding, for which they still had hopes.[70]

The scene now shifted to Constantinople, where Charykov, the newly appointed ambassador of Russia to the Porte, made it part of his program to bring about a Balkan league which was to include Turkey.[71] He made little effort to conceal his desires, and his plan was not without the backing of the Russian government. St. Petersburg always advocated an understanding between the Balkan states and the Porte, as one of the best means of stopping the spread of German influence in the Near East. This policy had the further advantage that it would also meet with the approval of England and France, who still maintained a benevolent attitude towards the Ottoman state. Besides, such a policy of friendship towards Turkey might produce a second treaty of Unkiar Skelessi and the opening of the Straits.

From the autumn of 1909 until September, 1911, this combination, i.e., one which included Turkey, was the one most often referred to. Yet it was never taken seriously by any one except Charykov. It was distinctly a policy based on the *status quo* in which Russia was much interested at this time.[72] In 1908–1909 Russia was unable to go to war and had to back down. A second humiliation of this kind she wanted to avoid at all costs and consequently she desired time to make preparations.

For the same reason the Balkan States flirted with the idea. "An alliance with Turkey," as the Russian minister at Belgrade

[70] Serbia's conclusions were greatly influenced by Bulgaria's attitude towards Austria-Hungary (S.D., I, no. 121; B.D., V, no. 870). There were many rumors of an Austrian-Bulgarian and a Bulgarian-Turkish rapprochement at this time (B.D., IX, i, nos. 25, 27, 29, 31, 44).

[71] On the whole question of Charykov's policy see William L. Langer, "Russia, the Straits Question and the Origins of the Balkan League 1908–1912," *Political Science Quarterly*, XLIII (1928), 321–63. For further bibliographical references see B.D., IX, i, p. 320.

[72] In the autumn of 1909 Russia further insured herself in regard to the preservation of the *status quo* by concluding an agreement with Italy at Racconigi. "It was frankly directed against Austria . . . and in case the existing situation could not be maintained the Habsburg monarchy was to be excluded from any share in the spoils." (W. L. Langer, "Straits Question" *Political Science Quarterly*, XLIII (1928), 300.

put it, "would bring them no great advantage, but only a moment's pause in the chronic unrest on the peninsula, which they might use to gather their forces for the final reckoning with their arch enemy." [73] The Young Turks also toyed with the plan with the same purpose in mind.[74] It was a means of preserving peace, and would give them time to consolidate their power. At Constantinople it was also felt that such an agreement might forestall a Balkan combination which would exclude Turkey. Even Aehrenthal was not opposed to such *pourparlers*, for he was convinced that a Balkan league was a Utopian dream, since Bulgaria and Serbia would never be able to reconcile their aspirations to Macedonia. In his opinion such an agreement would give Turkey time to order her internal affairs, and would serve as a guarantee for the maintenance of the *status quo*, which he also desired.[75]

But even a Balkan league including Turkey necessitated a Serbian-Bulgarian understanding, and efforts were continually being made towards this end. On his visit to Paris and London in the autumn of 1909 Milovanović appealed to these friendly governments ". . . to use their influence at Sofia to bring about a better understanding between Serbia and Bulgaria." [76] On October 25, 1909, when King Ferdinand made a scientific excursion to the Kapaonik Monastery, Crown Prince Alexander of Serbia met him at the frontier station of Kruševać and amiabilities were exchanged.[77] Although he knew that his visit would be very welcome to the Serbian government, Ferdinand

[73] *Krasny Arkhiv*, VIII, no. 44 in German translation in *Berliner Monatshefte*, VIII, 464–5. (Hereafter *Krasny Arkhiv* will be cited as K.A. and the *Berliner Monatshefte* as *Berl. Mon.*)

[74] Ö-U.A., II, nos. 2042, 2043; see also G.P., XXVII, i, no. 9739.

[75] Ö-U.A., II, no. 2045.

[76] B.D., IX, i, no. 66; see also no. 81.

[77] Schulthess, 1909, p. 620. Reichenau, the German minister at Belgrade, thought King Ferdinand's visit was the result of Austrian refusal to support Bulgarian Macedonian claims (G.P., XXVII, i, no. 9735). Aehrenthal on the other hand held that there was a close connection between the visit and King Ferdinand's displeasure at not receiving the Golden Fleece. Until Francis Joseph granted Ferdinand this order in April, 1911 the Bulgarian sovereign had little friendship for the Austrian government (Ö-U.A., II, nos. 1679, 1843; III, no. 2502).

had always refused to visit Belgrade. Finally, towards the end of November while on his way back to Sofia from Hungary, he paid a four-hour visit to King Peter. He was received at the station by the king, crown prince, ministers Milovanović and Pašić, and by the members of the Russian legation. Amid shouts of "Hail the Balkan League! Hail the Serbian-Bulgarian friendship!" the two kings drove to the palace.[78]

From the communication made to the English government, it appears that the conversations held with Ferdinand were favorable to a rapprochement.[79] The Serbian minister was again assured of the good wishes of the English government, although it was pointed out that a written agreement or military convention might arouse suspicion in Turkey and cause her to join Austria-Hungary. As before the virtues of an entente as compared with an alliance were stressed. Similar advice was given to the Bulgarian minister at London.

Serbia had for some time hitched her political aspirations to the Russian bear. With the arrival of Hartwig, the new Russian minister, on September 14, 1909, the relationship between the two countries became even more cordial.[80] Whether Hartwig, after three years of isolation in Persia, had a detailed Balkan program may perhaps be questioned. Certainly Serbian policy was not changed by his advent. It continued on the lines already marked out. The broad outlines (anti-Austrian) were undoubtedly in Hartwig's mind, but Pašić must have greatly influenced his ideas as to Serbian needs. How far Hartwig followed the ideas of Pašić or Pašić those of Hartwig would be interesting to know. It was no doubt a case of diamond cut diamond, for when two such capable and strong-willed men work together there must be give and take. The main point is that there soon came to be complete harmony between the two, and three months

[78] Schulthess, 1909, p. 620; See also G.P., XXVII, i, no. 9735; B.D., IX, i, nos. 82, 84 enclosure.

[79] S.D., I, no. 130.

[80] Marco, "Nikolaus Hartwig. Serbiens Aussenpolitik vor dem Weltkrieg," *Die Kriegsschuldfrage*, VI (1928), 746. On Hartwig's influence see also below, pp. 156–7.

after Hartwig's arrival in Belgrade the Belgian representative at that capital reported, "He [Hartwig] has become the constant adviser of the Serbian government which undertakes no measure, makes no decision of any importance, without asking the decision of the representative of the tsar at Belgrade." [81]

Could Bulgaria be won as Serbia had been, Russia would have solved the question of a Balkan league. In spite of all suggestions and encouragement on the part of Russia and her Entente friends, Bulgaria could not be brought to make the decision for a Serbian alliance. She feared such an alliance would be more of a hindrance than a help to her national aspirations in Macedonia. Furthermore, King Ferdinand desired to remain a free lance until the opportune moment came for choosing sides. In order to tighten the bonds between Sofia and St. Petersburg, Russia now proposed to conclude a military convention which would have a broader basis than that of 1902. Rumors of such a step had more than once disturbed the cabinet in Vienna. Finally, in December, 1909, a draft agreement was worked out which was to serve as a basis for further negotiations.[82] It was distinctly a one-sided affair, and it is not surprising that King Ferdinand turned a deaf ear to the proposals when they were discussed with him on his visit to St. Petersburg in February, 1910.

On this occasion the whole problem of Balkan politics was gone over in detail, and Izvolsky gave Malinov, the Bulgarian premier, a clear and long exposé of Russian views on a Serbian-Bulgarian rapprochement. The desirability of maintaining friendly relations with Turkey was stressed and Ferdinand was bid Godspeed on his visit to Constantinople. On his heels

[81] *Amtliche Aktenstücke zur Geschichte der europäischen Politik 1885–1914. Die belgischen Dokumente zur Vorgeschichte des Weltkrieges*, ed. Bernhard Schwertfeger, Alfred Doren, and Wilhelm Köhler (5 vols.; Berlin, 1925; hereafter cited as *Die belgischen Dokumente*), IV, no. 85.

[82] *Sbornik sekretnikh dokumentov*, no. 2, pp. 44–50; S.D., II, no. 511. In regard to these Russian-Bulgarian negotiations see E. C. Helmreich and C. E. Black, "The Russo-Bulgarian Military Convention of 1902," *The Journal of Modern History*, IX (1937), 471–82.

came King Peter who had been invited to make a similar tour.[83] Such visits could not help but arouse comment, and diplomatic circles were agog with all sorts of rumors about a big Balkan confederation.

Turkey was willing to flirt with Bulgaria and Serbia, but she felt it unwise to have all her eggs in one basket. On the eve of the visits of the Balkan kings she renewed her offers to Rumania for a defensive alliance.[84] Conditions in Turkey seemed scarcely stable enough to King Carol to warrant making a definite treaty and so the proposition was not accepted. Nevertheless in May, 1910 the Rumanian war minister visited Constantinople and was favorably received. In August the grand vizier visited King Carol in Sinaia. The conversations during these visits never went beyond assurances of friendship and some trade negotiations.[85]

Rumors, however, soon appeared in the press and caused a stir among the cabinets. Sazonov, who now directed Russian foreign policy, at once drew the attention of Bulgaria to the conclusion of "this convention" and the consequent necessity of a rapprochement with Serbia.[86] The British chargé at St. Petersburg reported:

> Monsieur Sazonov, though he has only been a few weeks in charge of Russia's foreign affairs, has already given me to understand that he has definitely adopted the policy of promoting a combination between Serbia, Bulgaria, Greece and Montenegro, which in the event of a breakdown of the existing Turkish régime or of any other eventuality

[83] King Ferdinand was in St. Petersburg Feb. 23–March 3; King Peter, March 22–26, 1910. King Ferdinand reached Constantinople March 20th, King Peter the 4th of April (G.P., XXVII, i, 183–4). The sojourn of the Balkan kings in St. Petersburg played no small part in undermining the Austrian-Russian rapprochement negotiations of the spring of 1910. (B.D., IX, i, nos. 135, 136, 149, 154, 206).

[84] G.P., XXVII, i, no. 9774; Ö-U.A., II, no. 2089. Turkey had previously made a similar offer to Rumania in July, 1909 (G.P., XXVII, i, no. 9756; Ö-U.A., II, no. 1718).

[85] Ö-U.A., II, nos. 2229, 2230; G.P., XXVII, i, nos. 9775, 9776.

[86] Benckendorff, I, no. 290. The Bulgarian minister at Bucharest made extensive inquiries and decided that if there was any agreement at all between Rumania and Turkey it was only an oral understanding (Dr. G. Kalinkov, *Romŭniya i neĭnata politika spremo Bŭlgariya* [Rumania and her Bulgarian Policy] (Sofia, 1917), p. 76.

bringing about a general conflict in the Balkans would offer a substantial obstacle from a military point of view to an advance of Austria southwards.[87]

Spurred on by Sazonov's suggestions and by the harsh Turkish policy towards Bulgarian nationals in Macedonia, Malinov opened informal conversations not only with Belgrade but also with Athens.[88] They were to be no more successful than any of the others initiated during the past years.

Nor were the Russian-Bulgarian negotiations for a military convention more successful. These continued half-heartedly throughout 1910. All points were settled except questions concerning the Bulgarian occupation of Adrianople and the supreme command of a possible Bulgarian-Russian army. However, with the sudden death of the Russian minister at Sofia and the fall of the Malinov cabinet on March 29, 1911, these negotiations were dropped for the time being.[89]

The fall of the Malinov ministry over a minor matter relating to the election of the great sobranje was of importance for the development of a Serbian-Bulgarian understanding. Somewhat earlier, in discussing with the Austrian attaché Russia's suggestion that Bulgaria should better her relations with Serbia, General Nikolaev, the Bulgarian chief of staff, had stated:

> Certain as he was that the Malinov cabinet would not follow this suggestion very intensively, he could make no such assurance for a future Tsankovist or any other Russophile government. Such a government would even be willing to enter into an alliance with Serbia if Russia should ask it. The democrats on the contrary, would not shy at a war between Serbia and Bulgaria, if the protection of vital interests — for example in Macedonia — demanded it.[90]

Of the same tenor was the opinion of the Russian minister in Sofia. He felt that Malinov was not the proper personality to carry out the difficult negotiations with Serbia.

[87] O'Beirne to Grey, Oct. 20, 1910, B.D., IX, i, no. 194.

[88] Bouchier in London *Times* June 5, 1913; B.D., IX, i, nos. 155, 175, 189, 202.

[89] Dr. Al. Girginov, *Narodnata katastrofa voĭnite* 1912/13g. [The National Catastrophe. The Wars of 1912/13] (Sofia, 1926), p. 14.

[90] Ö-U.A., I, no. 1012; see also Benckendorff, I, no. 306.

The new Cabinet, headed by Gueshov and Danev, was distinctly pro-Russian. Its formation was well received in St. Petersburg and hopes were entertained that Bulgaria had finally realised where her interests lay. Nor was the move without the support of the Bulgarian people. In the elections held in June, 1911, the opposition suffered an overwhelming defeat, the governmental parties receiving 363 out of 426 mandates. It was an easy matter for them to put through the constitutional changes made necessary by the Bulgarian declaration of independence, and also to alter the constitution so that the king might enter upon political treaties without being forced to lay them before the sobranje.[91] The Russian government favored the latter proposal since they thought the object of the new law was to permit the conclusion of the Russian-Bulgarian treaty, which had hung fire since the new ministry came to power.[92]

The relations between St. Petersburg and Sofia now became very cordial. General Fitchev, the Bulgarian chief-of-staff, was invited to the grand maneuvers at Krasnoe-Selo and returned flattered with all the attention that had been shown him.[93] Crown Prince Boris, then a lad of seventeen, spent some weeks in southern Russia visiting his godfather, the tsar of all the Russias. Towards the end of the summer of 1911, the visit of the Russian fleet to Varna provided an occasion for a general expression of Bulgarian-Russian friendship. Nor was the ostentatious Turcophile policy, which was a conspicuous part of Gueshov's program, unwelcome to the Russian statesmen. It was what Russia had preached for some years and what she still continued to advise.

Yet the Bulgarian negotiations with Turkey made little progress. They dragged on through the summer but hardly got beyond the stage of conversations with the Turkish minister in Sofia. When H. W. Steed visited Sofia in August, 1911, Gueshov discussed Turkish affairs with him at great length, and received

[91] Schulthess, 1911, p. 526; B.D., IX, i, no. 509.

[92] A. Nekludoff, *Diplomatic Reminiscences 1911–17* (London, 1920), p. 28.

[93] *Ibid.*, pp. 29 ff. There were also some discussions at this time in regard to a Russian-Bulgarian military convention (B.D., IX, i, nos. 518, 534).

the advice not to hurry an understanding.[94] At about the same time the British minister reported that he had told Gueshov that: ". . . as his Excellency had at length taken decided views concerning Austrian designs, the first and most essential point was to establish an 'Entente' with Serbia. The latter would, I felt sure, seize the hand of friendship if held out by Bulgaria." [95] Gueshov states that he was surprised to hear such statements from Steed; this friendly advice from English sources may well have encouraged him to drop the sham of Turkish negotiations and turn in another direction. At any rate, early in September, almost a month before the outbreak of the Tripolitan War, he came to the conclusion that in order to keep the Bulgarians from being exterminated in Macedonia it would be necessary to come to an understanding, "not with Turkey, who had rejected our advances, but with our other neighbors." [96] He finally decided to act upon the feelers which Serbia had been making ever since his coming to power, and which had been carefully referred to at various times by the Russian minister.

Rizov, Bulgarian minister to Rome and a prominent leader of the Macedonian cause, happened to be on leave in Sofia at that time. From him Gueshov obtained the promise to assume the responsibility before the Macedonian Revolutionary Organisation for entering into an alliance with Serbia.[97] Rizov was on a footing of personal intimacy with the Serbian premier and knew many of the other Serbian statesmen. He had also been one of the negotiators of the treaty of 1904, and since this was to be used as a basis for the new negotiations he was particularly well qualified to go to Belgrade and open discussions.

Before the negotiations could really get under way the Tripolitan War broke out.[98] Things immediately took on a new tempo. On September 29th Nekludov, Russian minister to Sofia, ad-

[94] Gueshoff, p. 4.
[95] Bax-Ironside to Grey, Aug. 28, 1911, B.D., IX, i, no. 517.
[96] Gueshoff, p. 10.
[97] *Ibid.*, pp. 10, 19, 31; K.A., VIII, no. 7 (*Berl. Mon.*, VII, 708).
[98] War was declared on September 29, 1911 (Schulthess, 1911, p. 464).

vised that Bulgaria should first of all come to an agreement with Serbia and then, in accordance with Charykov's proposal, make an agreement with Greece and Montenegro.[99] Three days later he was informed that Bulgaria had decided to accept his advice and was even prepared to settle the Macedonian question with Serbia.[100] With the start of the Italian War, and apparently before receiving word as to the Bulgarian government's desire to begin negotiations, Milovanović broached the topic to the Bulgarian minister at Belgrade. As in April, 1909, he immediately asked the Entente powers for their good offices at Sofia in order to help the rapprochement along.[101] There are no records of such steps being taken at this time by either France or England, and in fact the secrecy of the negotiations precluded much help from them. They had, however, on previous occasions encouraged such a policy and that the English minister at least lent his sympathetic assistance is indicated by the fact that he was kept *au courant* of the main steps of the negotiations. At any rate, with Bulgaria willing to negotiate, Russian patronage alone was equal to the occasion.

Things finally appeared to be breaking as Russia wished. Nekludov, however, scenting probable danger, sounded a warning and telegraphed:

> . . . The union of Bulgaria and Serbia contains one dangerous element — the temptation to use it for offensive purposes. On the other hand, it must be kept in mind that such a favorable opportunity for settling the regrettable Serbian-Bulgarian enmity may not occur again. We must decide what is the more advantageous, to avoid the possible danger referred to above, or have a Serbian-Bulgarian agreement, which of course would be under our protection. If we decide for the latter, then it is necessary that I be informed of the conditions under which Russia is ready to sanction the agreement, and under what conditions our support might be counted on.[102]

[99] K.A., VIII, nos. 1, 2 (*Berl. Mon.*, VII, 699 ff.); S.D., I, no. 148.

[100] K.A., VIII, no. 4 (*Berl. Mon.*, VII, 703). The Bulgarian government thus apparently did not inform Russia of its plan to come to an agreement with Serbia until about three weeks after the decision had been made.

[101] S.D., I, no. 151.

[102] K.A., VIII, no. 4 (*Berl. Mon.*, VII, 704).

To this the Russian foreign office replied:

> In view of the complicated state of external affairs, we greet heartily the efforts of Bulgaria and Serbia to regulate and conform their interests. At the same time we approve the restrictions you made in reference to the immediate aim of the union, namely regulation of common interests within the limits of the maintenance of the *status quo*. Indeed an independent action on the part of the Slav states would not only not meet with our approval but would, according to our opinion, be a misfortune, as it would arouse and justify action on the part of Austria. The situation would of course be different if it should be the result of a provocative action on the part of Turkey. We hope that in this case both states will ask us for advice, and we would be ready to discuss the situation with them. For your personal orientation, I might add that our action will depend on the steps taken by Austria.[103]

There was thus no hesitation as to the desirability of the alliance, although the possibility of aggressive action was seen. To curb these offensive plans the specter of justifiable Austrian action was raised, in which case Russia would presumably leave the Balkan States to their fate. The next lines, however, took away all the sting of this threat, for not even a Diogenes or a Conan Doyle would be able to find a Balkan diplomat who could not discover a provocative action on the part of Turkey. In such an eventuality Russia's action would depend on future conversations. But if no direct guarantee of aid was to be given, the alliance was at least to be concluded in an atmosphere which would lead the Balkan statesmen to expect Russian aid, should Austria move. A "personal orientation" like the above could mean nothing else.

Although Russia was willing to help the negotiations along as much as possible, she nevertheless assumed the attitude that it was up to the two contracting parties themselves to formulate and draft the agreement. Hartwig had suggested this procedure

[103] K.A., VIII, no. 5 (*Berl. Mon.*, VII, 705). Sazonov, who was at that time at Davos recuperating from an illness, was very enthusiastic about the league. He exclaimed, "Well, but this is perfect! If only it could come off! Bulgaria closely allied to Serbia in the political and economic sphere, five hundred thousand bayonets to guard the Balkans — but this would bar the road forever to German penetration, Austrian invasion." He felt that Russian diplomacy was equal to preventing an attack on Turkey (Nekludoff, *Reminiscences*, pp. 45–6).

and on the whole it was followed, although on some occasions the Russian foreign office voiced its disapproval of the wording and suggested other changes.[104]

Finally Bulgaria and Serbia were ready to attempt anew what they had failed to accomplish in the agreements of 1904. The almost constant negotiations which had been nurtured by Russia and her Entente friends ever since the annexation crisis were at last to bear fruit.

[104] K.A., VIII, nos. 7, 36 (*Berl. Mon.*, VII, 708, 903); no. 42 (*Berl. Mon.*, VIII, 462); K.A., IX, nos. 46, 71 (*Berl. Mon.*, VIII, 469, 568). See also Otto Bickel, *Russland und die Entstehung des Balkanbundes 1912* (Berlin, 1933), pp. 95–120.

CHAPTER II

THE SERBIAN–BULGARIAN ALLIANCE, MARCH, 1912

BEFORE taking up the diplomatic skirmishing which preceded the signing of the Serbian-Bulgarian alliance treaty of March 1912, it will be necessary to consider briefly important forces which had come to the fore in Bulgaria and Serbia. In the former there was the Internal Macedonian Revolutionary Organisation; in the latter there was the Black Hand. These two organisations came to have great influence on the respective governments at Sofia and Belgrade, and were important factors in shaping the national policy of these states. As such they well merit separate attention.

The Internal Macedonian Revolutionary Organisation (I.M.R.O.) was established in 1893, and at that time its program was announced as, "Macedonia for the Macedonians." [1] Autonomy was the watchword and the question of joining Bulgaria was not openly raised. Yet the whole movement was distinctly a Bulgarian one, and everyone felt that if the Macedonians once obtained an independent administration they would unite with Bulgaria, just as Eastern Rumelia had done in 1885. It was for this reason that Serbia so strenuously opposed all movements tending toward autonomy, and refused to give that principle any real recognition in negotiating the alliance treaty with Bulgaria.

The Macedonian organisation grew rapidly and attempted a revolt in 1903 which ended in disaster and brought nothing better than the Mürzsteg program of reforms. Another period of guerilla warfare followed, and this time the I.M.R.O. directed

[1] The history of the organisation is conveniently summarised by Colonel Lamouche in his *Histoire balkanique*, pp. 24 ff. The central committee which directed the organisation was located most of the time at Salonica. See also Karl Strupp, *La situation juridique des macédoniens en Yougoslavie* (Paris, 1929), pp. 69 ff.

its efforts as much against the newly formed Greek and Serbian bands as against the Turks. The Young Turk revolution with its golden promises for the future brought about a brief lull in activity. The following account by Colonel Lamouche summarises admirably and briefly the ensuing course of events.

The Christians soon found themselves threatened with the loss of the tolerance they had enjoyed under Abdul-Hamid. After the disarmament, they met with the establishment of Muslim emigrés from Bosnia-Herzegovina and the enforcement of a law (not voted but applied) against the Bands which permitted all forms of arbitrary arrest; they saw the government restrain the rights of the Patriarchs and other religious chiefs, and attempt to interfere in the schools. The different Christian nationalities therefore felt the necessity of uniting before the common peril. The policy of the Young Turks had brought about the incredible result of reconciling the Greeks and the Bulgarians. The Macedonian Revolutionary Organisation renewed its activity and if the Greeks did not coöperate with it, they at least observed a benevolent neutrality. Dynamite again came into use. On December 11, 1911, a bomb exploded in a mosque at Shtip (Sanjak of Usküb) wounding several people. The Muslim population attacked the Bulgarians, killing 25, and wounding 169. On August 1, 1912, bombs were also set off in the bazaar of Kotchana, an important trading center in the same Sanjak, mostly Bulgarian in population. Two Bulgarians and only two Turks were victims to the explosion, but in the resulting general massacre 150 persons were killed and more than 250 wounded. In the interval 80 Bulgarians had been killed at Kyrchevo (Sanjak of Monastir) without any provocation, but on suspicion. These events as always led to the flight of many people to Bulgaria.[2]

The immigration to Bulgaria referred to by Colonel Lamouche had been characteristic of Macedonian history for some time. Macedonians by the thousands had flocked to Bulgaria, where they soon became an important part of the population and exercised great influence in Bulgarian life.[3] The I.M.R.O., know-

[2] Lamouche, *Histoire balkanique*, p. 109.

[3] Colonel Peter Dŭrvingov, *Istoriya na Makedono-Odrinskoto opŭlchenie* [History of the Macedonian-Adrianople Legion] (2 vols.; Sofia, 1919–1925), I, viii. Some interesting statistics in this connection are given in *The Bulgarian Question and the Balkan States*, ed. by the Bulgarian Ministry of Foreign Affairs (Sofia, 1919), pp. 209–23, 232–46.

ing no boundary lines, provided leadership among these expatriates as well as in Macedonia itself. It thus became impossible to separate the work and influence of the I.M.R.O. as such from the influence of the Macedonians in Bulgaria. There were no direct official relations between the Revolutionary Organisation and the Bulgarian government, although contacts were maintained through the Macedonians, who sat in practically every Bulgarian cabinet. The society was tolerated in Bulgaria, but seldom, especially in the later years, did the government actively support it. In fact it more often took steps against the organisation. The latter was of its own accord active enough, and exercised so strong an influence on Bulgarian public opinion that the government was if anything placed on the defensive.

The Revolutionary Organisation contributed substantially to the sequence of events which brought about the Balkan War. In the first place it was instrumental in bringing about the Balkan League. "Deeply convinced," so writes Minister Gueshov, "that the Macedonian question ought to be taken out of the hands of the Macedonian Revolutionary Committee as Cavour took the question of Italian unity out of the hands of the Italian revolutionists, I hastened to open negotiations."[4] It is also important that one of the first persons with whom he discussed the question was Rizov, one of the leaders of the Macedonians. To the latter Hartwig gave most of the credit for the Bulgarian initiative and telegraphed to St. Petersburg:

> King Ferdinand in order to please Austria has always opposed [a treaty with Serbia], and the Bulgarian government out of fear of the revenge of the Macedonian Committee could never reach the decision to make tangible concessions to Serbia in Macedonia. Rizov has now agreed to undertake the responsibility before the committee and to bring his influence to bear on them.[5]

[4] Gueshoff, p. 19. Dr. K. Stanishev, a prominent Macedonian, in an interview told the writer in May, 1930 that it was part of the policy of the I.M.R.O. to force the Bulgarian government to make an agreement with Serbia. The latter, however, was against an autonomous Macedonia and the two governments divided the territory without asking the Macedonians.

[5] K.A., VIII, no. 7 (*Berl. Mon.*, VII, 707).

But if Rizov was willing to shoulder ". . . the entire responsibility before the Macedonian public opinion for the territorial concessions . . ." made to Serbia, he also insisted on a clause covering autonomy. "I need hardly tell you," so he warned Milovanović in October 1912, "that no Bulgarian government will venture, even if it felt so disposed, to conclude with Serbia an understanding which does not provide for Macedonian autonomy." [6] Neither Serbs nor Greeks wanted to accept this, but Gueshov insisted and succeeded in getting clauses inserted which covered the principle of autonomy, if indeed only in vague form. He was paying lip service to the demands of the Macedonians, and diplomatically speaking the latter might be assured that they were provided for.[7]

Secondly, the I.M.R.O. effectively aroused public opinion, and brought pressure on the Bulgarian government to favor an active solution of the Macedonian problem.[8] This they did in many ways. The most effective method was their terroristic activity in Macedonia. These measures were undertaken in order to provoke the Turks to retaliation and by the resulting massacres draw attention to the state of affairs in Macedonia. Protest meetings were always organised after such events. The bombings at Kotchana in 1912 were but the climax of such deeds, and resulted in meetings throughout Bulgaria which called upon Bulgaria to declare war against the Turks.[9] The Revolutionary Organisation was the backbone of the war party in Bulgaria and did everything in its power to force the opening of hostilities.

Not only did the society facilitate the formation of the alli-

[6] Rizov to Gueshov, November 20, 1911, Gueshoff, pp. 30–1; D. Rizoff, *Die Bulgaren in ihren historischen, ethnographischen und politischen Grenzen* [*Atlas mit 40 Landkarten*] (Berlin, 1917), p. 67.

[7] See Harold Temperley's interesting remarks on diplomatic jargon in *Foreign Affairs*, IX (1931), pp. 318 ff.

[8] *Nationalism and War in the Near East*, by a Diplomatist, ed. Lord Courtney of Penwith (Oxford, 1915; hereafter cited as Diplomatist), p. 179; conversations in May, 1930 with Dr. K. Stanishev and Colonel Dŭrvingov.

[9] Schulthess, 1912, p. 466; G. P., XXXIII, no. 12122. Gueshov was disturbed by these events since they threatened to precipitate matters before he was ready (S.D., I, no. 180).

ances and press for war, but it also took an active part in the fighting once the die was cast. Up to the day of mobilisation the Bulgarian government had furnished the organisation with no money or supplies, nor had the war department made any plans for mobilising the many recent Macedonian immigrants resident in Bulgaria, although the Revolutionary Organisation had often requested it.[10] It was only after the decree of mobilisation had been signed on September 30, 1912, that coöperation between the government and the society took place. Colonels Protoguerov and Dŭrvingov, Bulgarian officers but Macedonians by birth, were furnished with money and guns, and asked to organise small groups. New bands were formed and proceeded to coöperate with the thirty-five bands already in Macedonia, hindering Turkish concentration and mobilisation, and acting as spies for the Bulgarian army. In fact a whole volunteer corps, a veritable legion, was formed.[11] They took an oath to King Ferdinand, were subject to military courts, and practically became part of the Bulgarian army. They fought bravely and took their full share of the burden and responsibility in the war which their propaganda had done so much to bring about. Later these Macedonians also had an important part in causing the interallied war of July, 1913.[12]

Although the Serbian revolutionary societies were also actively engaged in anti-Turk agitation in Macedonia, there was no connection between them and the Macedonian Revolutionary Organisation. The Serbian societies were of much more recent origin, and had a quite different history.

During the agitation over the annexation of Bosnia-Herzegovina in 1908–09 the *Narodna Odbrana* [National Defense] so-

[10] Dŭrvingov, *Istoriya na Makedono-Odrinskoto opŭlchenie*, I, 3.

[11] *Ibid.*, I, 9–14; *The Bulgarian Question*, pp. 23–4, 223. There were 30,000 Macedonians incorporated directly into the Bulgarian army. The volunteer corps numbered 14,670 and was divided into twelve batallions. The Serbian or Greek armies had no counterpart to these forces, which is significant as evidence of the national sentiment of the Macedonians. See also A. Rappaport, "Mazedonien und die Komitadschis," *Berliner Monatshefte*, VIII (1930), 731–47.

[12] See below, pp. 361–62, 365.

ciety was formed.[13] Its purpose was to protect and promote Serbian interests in the annexed provinces. While supposedly a cultural society working openly and above ground, it did not hesitate to include training in marksmanship, manufacture of bombs, and leadership of komitaji groups among its activities. It became a first-class revolutionary organisation and had its centers not only in Austrian territory but in Macedonia as well. However, it soon lost its driving force and the failure to keep up ardent nationalistic propaganda dissatisfied certain members. Under the leadership of men who had been "pioneers" in Macedonia and who felt that this region had been neglected, a new secret patriotic organisation was formed in May, 1911. The first article of the constitution of this organisation stated: "This organisation has been created with the object of realising the national ideal: The Union of all Serbs. . . ."[14] It was to be called *Uyedinyenye ili Smrt* [Union or Death] but soon became known as The Black Hand. Since the members preferred "terroristic action to intellectual propaganda" the organisation was to be kept secret, and, "to accomplish its tasks," so states Article 4, "the organisation

1) Brings influence to bear on government circles, on the various social classes and on the whole social life of the Kingdom of Serbia, regarded as Piedmont.

[13] No attempt is being made to give a detailed description or history of the Serbian secret societies. In addition to references in subsequent foot-notes attention might be called to the following: "Die Narodna Odbrana," *Die Kriegsschuldfrage*, V (1927), 192–225; Dr. M. Boghitschewitch, "Mord und Justizmord. Aus der Vorgeschichte des Mordes von Sarajewo und des Königreichs Jugoslawien," *Süddeutsche Monatshefte*, XXV (1929), 331–70; Ö-U.A., III, nos. 2911, 2921, 2928, 2929, 2966, 3041, IV, 3590, 3673, 3680; S.D., I, nos. 54, 55, 63; S. B. Fay, *The Origins of the World War* (2 vols.; New York, 1929), II, 53–92; B. E. Schmitt, *The Coming of the War 1914* (2 vols.; New York, 1930), I, 175–208; Roderich Gooss, *Das österreichisch-serbische Problem bis zur Kriegserklärung Österreich-Ungarns an Serbien, 28 Juli, 1914* [Gutachten vor dem Untersuchungsausschuss, Reihe 1, vol. 10] (Berlin, 1930), pp. 174–180. The provisional constitution of the *Slovenski Jug*, the predecessor of the *Narodna Odbrana* and the *Uyedinyenye ili Smrt*, is to be found in the *Berliner Monatshefte*, VIII (1930), 1142–56.

[14] For an English translation of the constitution see Dr. M. Boghitschewitsch, "The Serbian Society 'Union or Death' alias 'The Black Hand,'" *Die Kriegsschuldfrage*, IV (1926), 681–7.

2) Organises revolutionary action in all the territories inhabited by Serbs.
3) Outside the frontiers of Serbia uses every means available to fight the adversaries of this idea.
4) Maintains amicable relations with all states, peoples, organisations, and individuals who entertain feelings of friendship towards Serbia and the Serbian element.
5) Lends help and support in every way possible to all peoples and all organisations struggling for their national liberation and for their union.

This was a thorough plan of action; how successful it would be depended of course on the members themselves. Great numbers were not essential. The connections and influence of the members were what counted, and shortly they were in close touch with the most important men of the government, even with Crown Prince Alexander.[15] The organisation grew and became vigorous. The Serbian government, conscious that its membership centered in the army and harked back to the revolution of 1903, kept an eye on its development. Even the papers began to take notice of it,[16] and the Austrian minister sent several long reports to Vienna dealing with the subject. The British minister reported:

> Although I have tried several well-informed sources, it is impossible to obtain satisfactory information as to the actual scope of the movements [Black Hand; Serbian Union]. But one thing is certain and that is, that at least one powerful organisation headed by the Military does exist, and that its influence will have to be reckoned with as an important factor in the attitude of Serbia in case of complications arising in the Balkans. The Government will not be allowed to remain passive.[17]

Constantinople was perhaps even better informed than the other capitals, for when the Serbian army reached Usküb in 1912, a

[15] *Ibid.*; Schmitt, *Coming of the War*, I, 195 ff.; Ö-U.A., IV, nos. 3552, 3590.

[16] For a discussion of press clippings made in the press department of the Austrian foreign office see Ludwig Bittner, "Die Schwarze Hand," *Berliner Monatshefte*, X (1932), 55–64; also his article "Österreich-Ungarn und Serbien," *Historische Zeitschrift*, CXLIV (1931), 88–93.

[17] Barclay to Grey, Feb. 1, 1912, B.D., IX, i, no. 545.

large and very comprehensive Turkish dossier dedicated to the Black Hand was found.[18]

Many members of this new terroristic organisation had been and continued to be members of the older *Narodna Odbrana*, which was supposedly devoted to cultural and educational purposes. Thus it becomes a question, as impossible as it is unimportant, to decide when and where cultural activity ended and terroristic activity began. To distinguish between the two groups would be to maintain a distinction without a difference, especially after the Black Hand virtually took over the leadership of the *Narodna Odbrana*. Milan Vasić, a member of the central committee of the former, became the secretary of the *Narodna Odbrana*, and from that time on until the Balkan War, the work of the revolutionary organisations outside of Serbia was made one.[19]

Not only were the two great revolutionary societies virtually united, but they came in close touch with the Serbian foreign office. Towards the end of 1911 Colonel Dimitriević Apis, a member of the general staff and leader of the Black Hand, went to Milovanović and told him of the existence of the organisations and explained their work. He let it be known that the group he represented was in favor of common action with Bulgaria and urged the formation of an alliance. The foreign secretary was impressed and addressed Apis in the following works: "My young friend, put your Black Hand at my disposal and you will soon see what Milovanović will do for Serbdom." Popović, who reports this incident, continues:

> After the conversation . . . the *Uyedinyenye ili Smrt* organisation became, as far as South Serbia [Macedonia] was concerned, practically the executive organ of the ministry of foreign affairs. The proposals which the organisation made to Milovanović were adopted and he endeavored to carry them out. There existed the closest cooperation in work and the greatest activity in its execution. Dragutin

[18] Chedo A. Popović, "The Work of Union or Death in Preparing for the Balkan War," *Nova Europa*, XVI (1927), nos. 10, 11. A translation of these articles was kindly put at my disposal by Miss M. Edith Durham.

[19] *Ibid.*

Dimitriević Apis . . . plunged fully into it with absolute enthusiasm and élan, sparing neither strength nor time. In this work he found himself in his element.[20]

Professor Bernadotte Schmitt comments on this as follows:

The activity of the society in Bosnia is another story, but it is clear that originally the *Uyedinyenye ili Smrt* was on excellent terms with the Serbian Government which used it as a secret instrument for the promotion of the national ambitions.[21]

What then were some of the specific services which the Black Hand rendered? In the first place, as we have seen, it strengthened the Serbian government in its negotiations with Bulgaria. Instead of forming an opposition which would create difficulty over any possible concessions to Bulgaria in Macedonia, it lent its support to the cause of compromise. Secondly, it provided a means through which the government kept in contact with affairs in Macedonia and could influence them to its advantage. For this purpose, a komitaji school was opened towards the end of 1911, at Prokuplje, an out-of-the-way spot where it would attract as little attention as possible. Here Voja Tankosić as chief instructor taught youths from Serbia as well as from nearly all "unredeemed lands" how to handle weapons, use bombs, work with explosives, etc. The recruits were largely gathered by the frontier officers, who, Popović says, "went to the frontier in a twofold character, as officers sent by the general staff for military duties, and as private individuals who, as members of the Black Hand, might spread the national-revolutionary organisation through the zones arranged for work near the frontier." [22]

In the spring of 1912 the Serbian government worked actively with bands in Albania so that it would be possible to create difficulties there when it should prove necessary. Accord-

[20] *Ibid.*; Schmitt, *Coming of the War*, I, 197–8. That Milovanović and Apis came to an agreement at this time is also disclosed by Professor Slobodan Jovanović in his biographical articles on Milovanović in the Belgrade journal *Politika* in July, 1937 (summarised in *Berliner Monatshefte*, XV [1937], 912–13).

[21] Schmitt, *Coming of the War*, I, 198.

[22] Popović, *loc. cit.*

ing to Toshev, Bulgarian minister to Belgrade, Pasić and Hartwig were of the opinion that it was advisable to create as much unrest in Albania as possible, in order to feel the pulse of Austria and Italy.[23] In this work the Black Hand rendered valuable assistance. It undertook the difficult task of getting into touch with leaders of the Albanian revolt, conferring especially with Isa Boletin, one of the most important of the Albanian chieftains.[24] With the apparent success of the Albanian movement, the march to Usküb, and the settlement of August 1912,[25] this agitation took on new importance. It would be distinctly disadvantageous to Serbia if peace were established between Turkey and the Albanians, and several missions to Albania were undertaken by leaders of the Black Hand to see how matters stood. "Overcoming many difficulties the officers carried out their task successfully," [26] writes Popović, and it is a fact that Isa Boletin and many of the Albanians observed a "pro-ally" policy at the start of hostilities.

Furthermore the Black Hand aroused an intense patriotic spirit in the population and especially in the army. It pressed for an active solution of the problem, and when in the beginning of September, 1912, it appeared that the Serbian government was vacillating and might accept some half-way solution Dimitriević Apis called his colleagues to his office. He assured them that he was in constant contact with General Putnik, at

[23] Toshev, I, 336.

[24] Popović, *loc. cit.*; Marco, "Before the Battle of Kumanova," *Nova Europa*, XVI (1927), translations furnished to the author by Miss M. E. Durham. Isa Boletin turned against the Young Turks in part because they took away from him the quarry from which practically all Albania was supplied with millstones. It provided a lucrative revenue and had been given to Boletin by Abdul Hamid. The Young Turks also stopped the monthly subvention of fifty pounds which had been regularly paid the Albanian chieftain by the old régime (A. Kutschbach, *Der Brandherd Europas, 50 Jahre Balkan-Erinnerungen* [Leipzig, 1929], p. 249).

[25] Schulthess, 1912, p. 453; see below, p. 98.

[26] Popović, *loc. cit.* Austria was well informed on Serbian activity in Albania (Ö-U. A., IV, nos. 3675, 3679; Pomiankowski to war office, October 10, 1912, Österreichisch-Ungarisches Kriegsarchiv [Vienna; hereafter cited as Ö-U.K.A.], Ad. Res., no. 441 ex 1912; District authorities at Bijeljina, Sept. 10, 1912, no. 512, K. & K. Armeeinspektor in Sarajevo Res., no. 3831; Gellinek from Belgrade, Nov. 26, 1912, Evidenz Bureau B, no. 1600 res., Dec. 1, 1912).

that time chief of staff, and that the general was "sound." But this could not be said for the politicians and some other soldiers. Hartwig was also against the war since he did not think the allies could beat the Turks.[27] Apis was doing all he could to stir things up and advised the others to do the same, saying, "I beg you to get into relations with every kind of person you know and inject into them as big a dose of determination as you can. . . ." [28] This activity could not always have been to the liking of the Serbian government. Yet on the whole the society and the government worked together. In the work of preparing the Balkan War there was agreement and closest coöperation with the minister of foreign affairs, writes Popović in his article, significantly entitled "The Work of Union or Death in Preparing the Balkan War," and Bogičević states: "An historical examination of the events which led to the First Balkan War will establish that credit for the fact that Serbia went into this war belongs to the Officers' Corps." [29]

How far the last statement is true it is impossible to say and probably always will be. It is a question of how great was the influence of the Officers' Corps and more especially of that faction controlled by the Black Hand. Certainly the Black Hand had grown popular among the people, and the government continually appeared to show it more favor.[30] In fact, it became necessary to favor the society in order to avoid its opposition. Stanojević, who was extremely well informed on the organisation, states, "In the time of the First Balkan War in 1912, the

[27] On Hartwig's attitude towards the war see below, pp. 156–7. The former Bulgarian minister at Belgrade also states that early in the summer of 1912 Hartwig was against the opening of hostilities, since Russia had not yet obtained guarantees from England in regard to the Straits (Toshev, I, 326).

[28] Popović, *loc. cit.* For the influence of the organisation in 1912 see also Cedomir A. Popović, "Das Sarajewoer Attentat und die Organisation 'Vereinigung oder Tod,'" *Berliner Monatshefte*, X (1932), 1102–3; Jovanović's articles on Milovanović in *Politika* of July, 1912 as reported in *Berliner Monatshefte*, XV (1937), 912–13.

[29] M. Boghitchevitch, *Causes of the War* (London, 1919), p. 63; see also his *Le procès de Salonique, Juin 1917* (Paris, 1927), p. 6.

[30] Toshev, I, p. 329; see also the very thorough "Denkschrift des serbischen Sektionschefs d. R. Th. Stefanović-Vilovsky," June 27, 1912, Ö-U.A., IV, no. 3590.

organisation *Uyedinyenye ili Smrt* played a fairly large rôle." [31] It was, however, during the First Balkan War that the prestige of the army and its officers grew and their influence on the government became great.[32] In fact the organisation became so powerful by the spring of 1914 that an open conflict broke out between it and the central government in regard to the government of Macedonia.[33] Certainly in 1912 the Black Hand exercised no such influence as it did in 1914. Important as its activities were in bringing things to a head, Pašić was clearly in control and determined what direction events should take. But even Pašić had his ear to the ground and preferred to work with and not against the patriotic organisation.

As has been pointed out above, the Bulgarian decision to make an alliance with Serbia was reached in the first weeks of September, 1911, well before the outbreak of the Tripolitan War.[34] Rizov was to be sent to Belgrade to sound out the terrain and arrange an interview for Gueshov on the latter's return from a rest cure at Vichy. There was therefore no hurry for Rizov to leave Sofia, since the Bulgarian premier did not expect to start his vacation until after the elections, which were to be held on the 17th. Meanwhile the Turkish-Italian dispute was reaching a climax, and on September 25th an Italian expedition was dispatched to Tripoli, to be followed four days later by an official declaration of war. With this event both Serbia and Russia started to renew their agitation for a Serbian-Bulgarian alliance, and this time their suggestions were favorably received, as they fell in with the decision already reached by the Bulgarian government.

In the first days of October Rizov undertook his mission in Belgrade, and here the broad outlines of an understanding including a territorial settlement were discussed. It was agreed

[31] Stanoje Stanojević, *Die Ermordung des Erzherzogs Franz Ferdinand* (Frankfurt, 1923), p. 53.

[32] Conversation with Professor S. Stanojević in May, 1930.

[33] This centered on the question of the priority of civil over military officers (Stanojević, *op. cit.*, p. 54; Schmitt, *Coming of the War*, I, 198–201; Paul Herre, *Die kleinen Staaten Europas und die Entstehung des Weltkrieges*, pp. 436–7).

[34] See above, p. 32.

that any attack by a third party would constitute a *casus foederis*.[35]

From Belgrade Rizov went on to Vienna where he met Gueshov, who had cut short his stay at Vichy. They were joined by Stanchov, Bulgarian minister to Paris, and here the three statesmen worked out the principles which should regulate their understanding with Serbia. The treaty of 1904 was to be the basis. If they were unable to obtain autonomy for Macedonia they would agree to divide it. The treaty was to be defensive against all states, but the Bulgarian statesmen decided that they would even propose that the *casus foederis* should arise if either Austria-Hungary or Turkey attempted to occupy any territory on the Balkan peninsula, or even if the interests of Bulgaria and Serbia demanded that the Turkish question should be settled. The participation of Montenegro was to be provided for, and the agreement of Russia was to be a *conditio sine qua non* for the conclusion of the treaty.

In an interview with King Ferdinand on a train between Oderberg and Vienna, Gueshov obtained the approval of His Majesty to the above scheme, with the admonition to be *extremely careful* in carrying on the negotiations.[36] In order to lull suspicion Gueshov sent someone on ahead to travel under his name and pass directly through Belgrade, arriving himself incognito on a later train. There a Serbian coach was attached and for the next three hours, while the train sped on to Lipovo, Gueshov discussed the basis for an alliance with Milovanović, the Serbian premier. The division of spoils was of course the most difficult problem. Milovanović made the general suggestion that Serbia should receive all land north of the Shar Mountains, while Bulgaria should have Adrianople and the bulk of Macedonia. He was of the opinion that for the present it would be better not to try to draw a definite boundary line, but to reserve this partition to the arbitration of the Russian emperor.

[35] Gueshoff, pp. 13–4, 28.

[36] *Ibid.*, p. 14; "S. M. der König bestand besonders darauf sehr vorsichtig zu sein" (letter to the author from Stanchov May 30, 1930).

In doing this he was but reviving a clause of the treaty of 1904 which provided that all questions which could not be settled between them should be referred to the tsar. Gueshov was of course favorable to Russian participation and apparently raised no objection to this plan. The conversations went off very well and both premiers were satisfied with the result. Milovanović, who had entered upon the interview fearing that behind this unexpected readiness of King Ferdinand to negotiate there might be some sort of a trap hatched in Vienna, emerged with his suspicions entirely removed.[37]

On reaching Sofia, Gueshov found war feeling running high and the situation more critical than he anticipated. The council of ministers and the king sanctioned the general agreement he had reached with Milovanović, and he was empowered to open official negotiations at once. These were to be carried on in Sofia, Spalaiković, the Serbian minister, acting as intermediary with Belgrade. Besides Gueshov, whose private residence constituted the headquarters for negotiations, only Danev, president of the sobranje, Teodorov, the finance minister, and General Nikiforov, minister of war, were to be informed of the discussions.[38] In the meantime a Serbian-Bulgarian committee for the establishment of an economic rapprochement between the two countries met at Sofia. This aroused much critical comment in the Bulgarian press, which seemed to indicate that the old feeling of hostility to Serbia still prevailed.[39]

On November 3, 1911, Spalaiković returned to Sofia with the first Serbian draft of the proposed alliance. This did not meet with approval, since "the Serbians were reserving for themselves the right to declare war without [Bulgarian] consent, and article four not only said nothing of Macedonian autonomy but actually proposed that the two vilayets of Salonica and Monastir should

[37] For reports on this interview see: Gueshoff, pp. 15 ff.; K.A., VIII, nos. 16, 32, 34 (*Berl. Mon.*, VII, 782, 901–2); Bax-Ironside to Nicolson, Oct. 23, 1911, B.D., IX, i, no. 525.

[38] Gueshoff, pp. 17–19; K.A., IX, no. 47 (*Berl. Mon.*, VIII, 469); B.D., IX, i, no. 555.

[39] Bax-Ironside to Grey, Nov. 3, 14, 1911, B.D., IX, i, nos. 526, 527.

be reserved for the arbitration of the Russian Emperor." Several days later the Serbians modified the proposal, and this time suggested that three zones, "an uncontested Serbian zone, a contested zone to be reserved for the arbitration of the Russian Emperor, and an uncontested Bulgarian zone" be established.[40]

Neither did this draft meet with full approval in Bulgaria, since there was no mention of Macedonian autonomy, and the Bulgarian government always had the Macedonian Revolutionary Organisation to consider. Nor did Russia like the bellicose wording of the Serbian draft. For, as Neratov pointed out to Hartwig, these territorial divisions might preferably be referred to as "cultural spheres of influence" which would not interfere with the formal *status quo* principle.[41]

The scene of the negotiations now shifted temporarily to Paris, where King Peter, accompanied by Milovanović, was paying an official visit. At the gala performance of the opera Stanchov, the Bulgarian minister at Paris, impressed upon Milovanović the great dissatisfaction at Sofia over the last Serbian proposal. Passing the two men, de Selves, the French foreign minister, exclaimed, "Je passe à côté de vous non pour vous désunir," which brought forth the immediate rejoinder from Stanchov, "mais pour nous unir et bénir." The next day, Milovanović paid a visit to the Bulgarian legation where he went over the problem in detail with Stanchov and Rizov, who had left his post at Rome especially for this interview. Rizov pointed out that Serbia was now demanding much more than she had in the first conversations, and that such demands could never be accepted by the Bulgarians. The result was that Milovanović promised to call a conference of the Serbian leaders on his return to Belgrade, after which he would provide Spalaiković with new instructions.[42]

Towards the end of November, King Ferdinand paid a visit to Vienna, letting it be known that he would not be averse to

[40] Both quotations from Gueshoff, p. 23.

[41] K.A., IX, no. 46 (*Berl. Mon.*, VIII, 469).

[42] For reports on these meetings in Paris, see: Gueshoff, pp. 24–33; K.A., IX, no. 51 (*Berl. Mon.*, VIII, 473).

being received by Francis Joseph. The audience was arranged and took place on November 27th. The Austrian documents contain no direct record of this meeting, nor of the conversations between Aehrenthal and King Ferdinand.[43] Apparently they dealt only in generalities, King Ferdinand speaking distrustfully of the Serbs and hoping undoubtedly thereby to receive Aehrenthal's favor. He probably received the assurance, as he had in the past, that the Dual Monarchy would have no objection to Bulgarian expansion to the south.

Aehrenthal told the French ambassador that the king seemed pacifically inclined, although he had said that the "situation in the Balkans would become dangerous if [the Tripolitan] War dragged on until spring, or if Turkey emerged from the war seriously weakened. In that case agitation would begin again in Macedonia, and the party of action in Bulgaria would likewise agitate, organise demonstrations, and make use of bombs." [44] There is no evidence that there was any thought at this time of pushing a Bulgarian-Turkish-Rumanian agreement, as Russia feared.[45] Nevertheless the visit caused uneasiness in St. Petersburg, and this probably had its share in delaying the next Serbian proposal. Nekludov even suggested that all negotiations be halted for a time, since rumors in regard to them had begun to spread.

Negotiations thus far had also been disturbed by rumors of a Russian-Turkish agreement in regard to the Straits, something the Balkan states did not wish to see realised. With the beginning of the Tripolitan War Charykov had redoubled his efforts to bring about a great Balkan confederation. He coupled this with his designs for opening the Straits by agreement with Turkey. His plans, however, went askew and received an official

[43] Indirect accounts are to be found: Ö-U.A., III, nos. 3126, 3132, 3133, see also nos. 3000, 3001 for the arranging of the interview; B.D., IX, i, nos. 334, 342, 528; *Documents diplomatiques français (1871–1914)*, ed. by the Ministry of Foreign Affairs (Paris, 1929 — ; hereafter cited as D.D.F.), 3d. ser., I, nos. 247, 294.

[44] Cartwright to Grey, Dec. 1, 1911, B.D., IX, i, no. 334; see also D.D.F., 3d. ser., I, no. 261.

[45] K.A., IX, nos. 54, 58 (*Berl. Mon.*, VIII, 474, 477). Rumors of such an agreement also troubled Bucharest (Ö-U.A., III, nos. 3117, 3130, 3134).

disavowal from the Russian foreign office. With this the efforts for a Balkan confederation inclusive of Turkey ceased.[46]

By the end of December 1911, all points of the Serbian-Bulgarian treaty were settled except the question of boundaries. Bulgaria communicated her maximum concessions to Serbia, and Nekludov urged the Russian foreign office to bring pressure upon Belgrade to accept them. Belgrade countered by announcing her maximum concessions, and Hartwig in turn recommended pressure on Sofia.[47] Thus at the turn of the year things were at a standstill, and the next two months had to be spent in bridging the gap between the two points of view. To ease matters both countries agreed to detach these "stipulations affecting Macedonia" and also the clauses dealing with the "offensive alliance against Turkey" from the treaty proper and incorporate them in a secret annex.[48] Hartwig, Nekludov, and especially Romanovsky, the Russian military attaché in Sofia, never wearied in their rôle of mediators. The tsar even intervened personally, sending for the Bulgarian military attaché and requesting him to inform the Bulgarian minister of war "that he would view with favor a successful termination of the Serbian-Bulgarian negotiations." [49]

By January 30th, Nekludov was of the opinion that unless Serbia changed her attitude the negotiations would end in failure. Bulgaria had gone the limit in the matter of concessions. The boundary near Struga on Lake Ochrida was the last disputed point. Arguments flew back and forth. The celebration in Sofia of the majority of Crown Prince Boris gave a splendid opportunity for the manifestation of Balkan feeling.[50] A cab-

[46] On these negotiations see Langer, *Pol. Sci. Quart.*, XLIII (1928), 337–63; E. Adamov, *Die europäischen Mächte und die Türkei während des Weltkrieges* (2 vols.; Dresden, 1930), I, 16 ff.; Bickel, *Entstehung des Balkanbundes*, pp. 73–95.

[47] K.A., IX, nos. 62, 63, 65 (*Berl. Mon.*, VIII, 563–5); Nekludoff, *Reminiscences*, pp. 33–5.

[48] Gueshoff, p. 35; K.A., IX, no. 65 (*Berl. Mon.*, VIII, 565).

[49] Bax-Ironside to Nicolson, March 14, 1912, B.D., IX, i, no. 559; see also no. 566.

[50] Schulthess, 1912, p. 465; Anna Stancioff, *Recollections of a Bulgarian Diplomat's Wife* (London, 1930), p. 255; B.D., IX, i, no. 554.

inet crisis in Serbia, however, troubled Milovanović and it was not until February 13th, that Spalaiković was sent to Sofia with various conciliatory formulas and the instruction, in case Bulgaria refused these, to accept the Bulgarian offer.[51] Finally on March 7th the preliminary protocol was signed, and six days later, on the anniversary of the death of the Tsar Liberator, the treaty with its secret annex received validity. In presenting the document to King Ferdinand for his approval Gueshov is said to have remarked, "Sire, today is the 13th of March according to the new calendar." "Then I shall not sign this treaty as a Catholic," replied the king theatrically, "but as I am a Slav at this moment I shall sign it in accordance with the Orthodox calendar."[52]

The treaty provided that military conventions, which should be considered as integral parts of the agreement, should be drawn up. On April 16/29, 1912, the general military convention was concluded. This was supplemented on June 18/July 1 by a military agreement between the two chiefs of staff in regard to war with (a) Austria, and (b) Rumania, and on the next day (June 19/July 2) by a similar — if not quite so detailed — agreement against Turkey. This latter agreement was further modified on August 23/September 4 and September 15/28, 1912.[53]

[51] K.A., IX, no. 75 (*Berl. Mon.*, VIII, 571–2). On February 26th Bax-Ironside reported to Grey that the Bulgarian-Serbian boundary negotiations had been proceeding nicely but that a deadlock had occurred the previous day(B.D., IX, i, no. 555).

[52] Yovan Yovanovitch, "How Austria Willed War," *Balkan Review*, I, 76. Bax-Ironside reported that King Peter and Milovanović signed the treaty on March 11th, King Ferdinand on March 14th, the latter refusing to sign on the previous day since it was the 13th of the month (B.D., IX, i, no. 559).

[53] The treaty, annex, military convention and agreements, with the exceptions mentioned later, are to be found in: Gueshoff, pp. 112–127; Balkanicus, pp. 96–109 (military convention misdated here); Diplomatist, pp. 387–396; B.D., IX, ii, appendix II; *Doklad na parlamentarnata izpitatelna komisiya* [Report of the parliamentary commission of inquiry] (4 vols. and 3 supplements; Sofia, 1918–19; hereafter cited as *Doklad*), I, 159–173; B. D. Kesyakov, *Prinos kŭm diplomaticheskata istoriya na Bŭlgariya* [Contribution to the diplomatic history of *Bulgaria*] (4 vols.; Sofia, 1925–35), I, 36–48. The agreement between the two chiefs of staff of June 18/July 1 in regard to a possible war with Austria is to be found only in *Doklad*, I, 163–5, and Kesyakov, I, 42–3; see also E. C. Helmreich,

What did these instruments — treaty, secret annex, military convention, and additional agreements between the chiefs of staff — provide? Outside of the usual formulas of friendship, duration (to last until January 13, 1921), secrecy, etc., the treaty itself had only two important clauses. These were considered to be defensive, although that word as ever must undergo an extremely elastic interpretation to cover not only a guarantee of the respective states, but also of their territorial ambitions in the Turkish Empire. The contracting parties promised: "to come to each other's assistance with all their forces in the event of any Great Power attempting to annex, occupy, or even temporarily to invade with its armies any parts of the Balkan territories which are today under Turkish rule, if one of the parties considered this as contrary to its vital interests and a *casus belli*."[54] They also bound "themselves absolutely and without reservation to succor each other with their entire forces, in the event of one of them being attacked by one or more states."[55]

These articles should, however, be read in connection with articles two and three of the military convention where countries are specifically named. There it was agreed that an attack by Rumania or Turkey on either country, an attack by Austria-Hungary on Serbia, or even the sending of troops into the Sanjak of Novibazar, "on whatever pretext with or without the consent of Turkey," would at once bring the alliance into play. It is interesting to note that nothing is said in these clauses of a possible Italian invasion of the Balkan peninsula, nor in any other of the agreements.

The secret annex contained the offensive clauses directed against Turkey, with provisions making Russia the arbiter of all disputes. It also adjusted the territorial settlement. According to the annex, if conditions became so bad in Turkey that

---

"Ein Nachtrag zu dem serbisch-bulgarischen Abkommen von 1912," *Berliner Monatshefte*, XIII (1935), 1073–6. The agreement of June 18/July 1 dealing with the allocation of troops in case of war with Rumania is to be found only in Kesyakov, I, 43–5.

[54] Article II. Texts used are those published by Gueshoff, pp. 112–127.

[55] Article III.

one of the contracting parties thought military action indispensable, that party was at once to make a reasoned proposal to the other party. Should an agreement favorable to action be reached, Russia was to be notified at once, and if she did not disapprove, hostilities were to be opened. If no agreement was reached, Russia should also be informed and her opinion was to be binding on both parties. In case Russia should fail to express an opinion, and no agreement could be reached between the two parties, and one party nevertheless declared war, the other bound itself to maintain benevolent neutrality, and indeed to come to the aid of the former, should a third party take the side of Turkey.

As to the division of spoils, there were, so to speak, four allotments of territory. (1) Serbia was to receive outright all territory north and west of the Shar Mountains, (2) Bulgaria all east of the Rhodope Mountains and the river Struma. Should the contracting powers become convinced that it would be impossible to organise the remaining territory into an autonomous province the following division was proposed: (3) Bulgaria was to receive undisputed possession of all land up to a definitely demarcated line running from Mt. Golem on the Bulgarian frontier to Lake Ochrida. (4) The territory between this line and the boundary of the territory definitely granted to Serbia (Shar Mts.) was to constitute a contested zone, it being agreed that the Russian emperor, as arbiter, should draw the future boundary line somewhere within this region.[55a] No mention whatever was made of Albania or of the territory towards Salonica. In case of the division of Macedonia, Bulgaria was definitely assured a part, whereas the Serbians had no definite guarantee as to what they should receive. That the Russian tsar would give them most of the contested zone was quite cer-

[55a] The contested zone as drawn on the following map is based on: *Report of the International Commission to Inquire into the Causes and Conduct of the Balkan Wars*, published by the Carnegie Endowment for International Peace (Washington, 1914; hereafter cited as *Carnegie Report*), p. 45; Rizoff, *Die Bulgaren*, p. 67. For a discussion of the Serbian-Greek proposed boundaries of June, 1913 also shown on this map see below, pp. 347–49.

tain. It was only when Serbia came to demand more than this that trouble with Bulgaria arose, leading to the Second Balkan War.

The military convention, beyond the points already mentioned, dealt with purely military questions such as who was to command, how many troops each was to furnish, and in which regions they were to be concentrated.

The treaty was thus directed not only against Turkey but against Austria-Hungary as well. To Bulgaria the first was important, to Serbia and Russia — and for that matter, England and France — the latter. To stop the supposed *Drang nach Osten* was the real reason why Russia had sponsored the alliance.[56] The treaty would not only accomplish this, but would also stop the quarrelling among the small Slavic states and bring them directly into the Russian orbit, which in case of a general war meant on the side of the Triple Entente. It would establish Russian hegemony in the Balkans, and ensure that the tsar's word would have weight when the clearly impending dissolution of Turkey came about. For the present, however, Russia desired peace. Not that she was particularly interested in protecting Turkey, but simply because she herself was not ready for the liquidation. Unlike Poincaré, who thought that "this alliance, in the form in which it was drawn up, would inevitably lead to a war in the Balkans, with all the possible further consequences," Sazonov was of the opinion that although there was this possibility, there was less danger in the conclusion of an alliance, even of an aggressive character, than in doing without one.[57] Through the consultation and arbitration clauses he believed he could hold the Balkan states in check. As

[56] In an interview which the writer had with Baron Maurice Schilling in October, 1929, the former secretary of the Russian foreign office stressed the fact that the purpose of the league was to halt Austria-Hungary. See also Nekludoff, *Reminiscences*, p. 55; A. Zaionchkovskii, *Podgotovka rossii k mirovoi voine v mezhdunarodnom otnoshenii* [Russia's Preparation for the World War: International Relations] (Moscow, 1926), p. 261; B.D., IX, i, nos. 559, 572 enclosure.

[57] Quotation from Serge Sazonov, *Fateful Years, 1909–1916* (New York,

BOSNIA
Save R.
Belgrade
Island of Ada-Kaleh
R
Kragujevać
SERBIA
HERZEGOVINA
Plevlje
SANJAK OF NOVIBAZAR
Nish
Novibazar
KOSSOVO
Mitrovitza
B U
MONTENEGRO
Ragusa
Ipek
Plava
Gusinje
Podgoritza
Cetinje
Bocche di Cattaro
Sofia
Djakova
KOSSOVO POLJE
Prizren
Drin R.
Kustendil
Antivari
Scutari
MT. TARABOSH
SHAR MTS.
Kumanovo
Rujen
Uskub
Kotchana
Boyana R.
Veles
Bregalnitza R.
Shtip
ADRIATIC SEA
Strumitza
TUR
Durazzo
Tirana
Prilep
Struga
Ochrida
Ghevheli
L. Doiran
L. Ochrida
Monastir
L. Prespa
Struma R.
Kilkich
Vardar R.
Semeni R.
Devoli R.
Greek-Serbian division of Albania into spheres of influence according to annex to treaty of alliance.
Valona
Salonica
G. of Salonica
CHALCIDICE
C. Kephali
C. Stylos
Corfu
CORFU
Janina
AE
Paxos
Antipaxos
GREECE

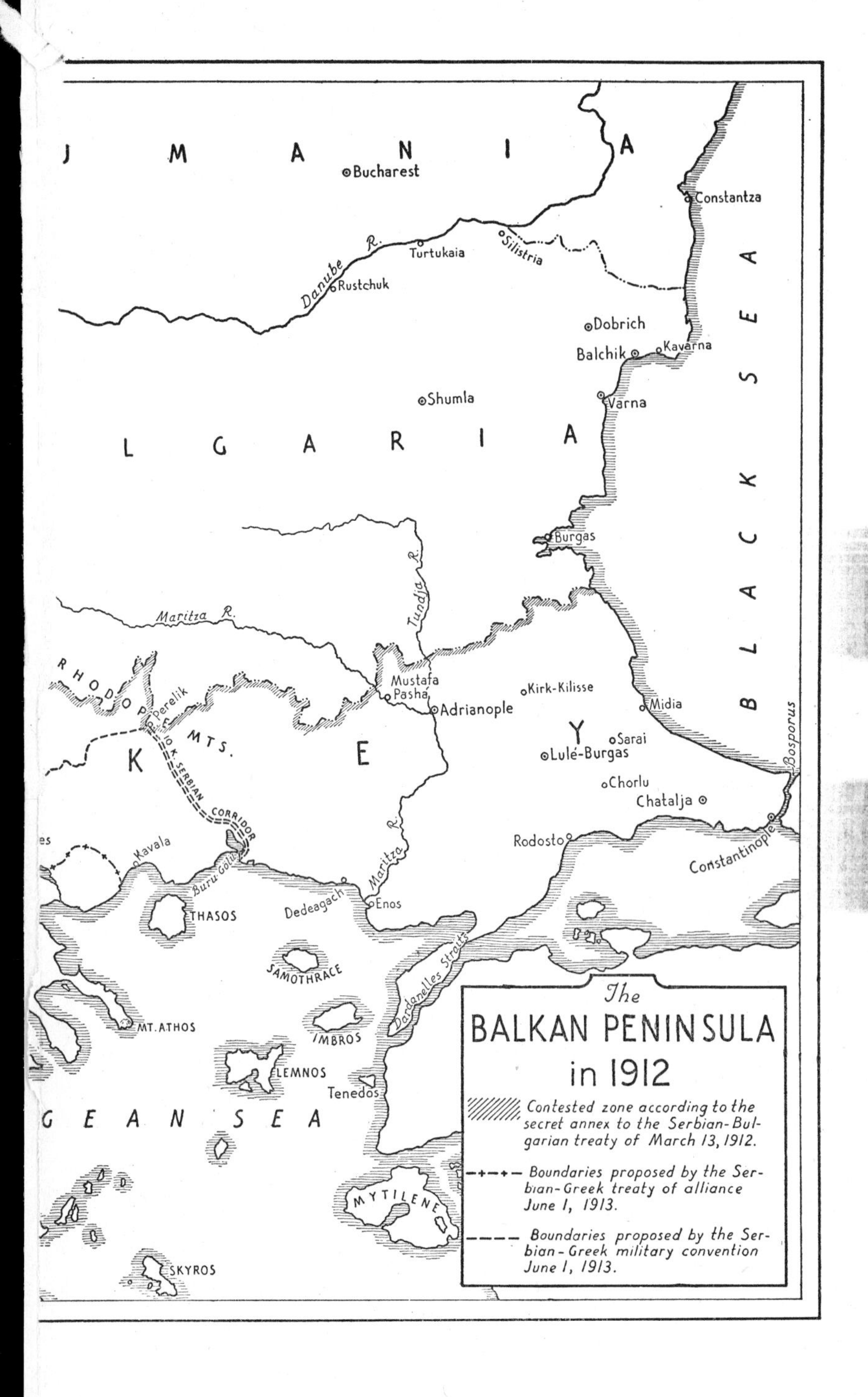

J M A N I A
Bucharest
Constantza
Danube R.
Turtukaia
Silistria
Rustchuk
Dobrich
Balchik
Kavarna
Shumla
Varna
L G A R I A
Burgas
Tundja R.
Maritza R.
RHODOPE MTS.
Perelik
Mustafa Pasha
Adrianople
Kirk-Kilisse
Midia
K E Y
Sarai
Lulé-Burgas
Chorlu
Chatalja
SERBIAN CORRIDOR
Kavala
Buru Gölü
Rodosto
Constantinople
Bosporus
Maritza R.
Dedeagach
Enos
THASOS
SAMOTHRACE
Dardanelles Straits
MT. ATHOS
IMBROS
LEMNOS
Tenedos
G E A N S E A
MYTILENE
SKYROS
B L A C K S E A
The BALKAN PENINSULA in 1912
Contested zone according to the secret annex to the Serbian-Bulgarian treaty of March 13, 1912.
Boundaries proposed by the Serbian-Greek treaty of alliance June 1, 1913.
Boundaries proposed by the Serbian-Greek military convention June 1, 1913.

Kokovtsov put it, "Bulgaria . . . would never move without Russia's permission and the Emperor Nicholas was far too prudent a sovereign to allow her to embark on a policy of adventure." [58]

Ever since 1903, Serbia had been actively seeking a Bulgarian alliance which might aid her in opposing the Dual Monarchy. Protection against Vienna was still a cardinal point in the final negotiations.[59] In some Serbian circles there was a fear of the conversion of the Dual Monarchy into a trialistic state, which might absorb an independent Serbia. Spalaiković, one of the negotiators of the accord, pointed out to his French colleague at Sofia the great protection which the Bulgarian agreement afforded against this contingency. In his opinion, it was necessary to increase Serbian territory at once, to prevent absorption into a reorganised Habsburg dominion.[60] But the protection which Serbia had obtained against Austria could serve as a safeguard while she realised her imperialistic ambitions towards the south. In 1912 Serbian aspirations were centered far more on the Sanjak and Macedonia than on Bosnia and Herzegovina. In view of Bulgaria's greater military strength and her long-touted claims to all of Macedonia, it seemed only wise to assure to Serbia her due share by agreement, rather than run the risk of being left out entirely. Besides, the treaty opened up the possibility of obtaining Albanian territory and the long desired outlet to the Adriatic.[61] The division of Macedonia and the offensive clauses against Turkey played such a predominant part in the negotiations that

---

1928), pp. 54–5. For further statements of Poincaré's views see D.D.F., 3d. ser., III, no. 340; IV, no. 184; Raymond Poincaré, *Au service de la France* (10 vols.; Paris, 1926–33; hereafter cited as Poincaré), II, ch. II, IV.

[58] Buchanan to Grey, July 18, 1912, B.D., IX, i, no. 594, also no. 595.

[59] M. Boghitchévitch, *Les causes de la guerre* (Paris, 1925), p. 54; Stanojević, *Die Ermordung des Erzherzogs Franz Ferdinand*, p. 26; Slobodan Jovanović, "Nicholas Pašić: After Ten Years," *Slavonic Review*, XV (1937), 374.

[60] Panafieu to Poincaré, May 28, 1912, D.D.F., 3d. ser., III, no. 48, also no. 155.

[61] Pašić obtained from both Sazonov and Kokovtsov in June 1912 a promise that Russia would never permit Austria to create a large Albania (S.D., I, no. 271; see also B.D., IX, i, no. 580).

one must assume that it was not merely protection against Austria that Serbia wanted. Only to Serbia was the treaty really the two-edged sword it has often been considered. She was ready to use it against either Austria or Turkey, whereas Russia always had Vienna rather than Constantinople in mind.

To Bulgaria the alliance from the very beginning was directed solely against Turkey, the Austrian provisions being only a necessary evil. To her friends she made no pretext of concealing her intention to bring about the solution of the Macedonian question. Nekludov continually reported this,[62] and Danev on his visit to Russia did not hide the Bulgarian plans under a bushel.[63] If Austria had invaded the Sanjak, would Bulgaria have fulfilled her alliance obligations? That of course is impossible to say, although a military agreement was drawn up to take care of that eventuality. Pašić, however, did not think so, and there were plenty of Serbs of the same opinion. The following episode is of interest in this respect.

Milovanović on the eve of signing the treaty called a conference of the party leaders and laid the treaty before them. In explaining the document he pointed out that, although he realised that he had made great concessions in Macedonia, it was the best that could be obtained, and that in return he had received Bulgaria's aid against Austria. He then asked each man in the conference if he was for the agreement, and whether he should sign. All said yes, except Pašić, who said neither yes nor no, telling Milovanović that he was foreign minister and must decide what was best. Later, when asked why he had answered thus, Pašić explained that far too many concessions had been made in return for very problematical help on the part of Bulgaria. Tsar Ferdinand would never go against Austria, and besides it would be hard to arouse feeling in Bulgaria favorable to such action. Then too, he had little faith in Ferdinand,

[62] Nekludoff, *Reminiscences*, pp. 55, 96.

[63] Conversation with Baron Schilling in Oct. 1929; S.D., I, no. 174; *Doklad*, I, 226; B.D., IX, i, nos. 585, 590.

and believed that he would inform Vienna at once of the whole agreement.[64]

For Europe as a whole the conclusion of the alliance had tremendous significance. The impossible had happened; a Balkan League was founded. Such a League, engineered by Russia, meant a decided swing in the balance of power to the Entente. Something would have to be done to rectify that balance — if indeed there was any truth in the theory that the best way to insure the peace of Europe was to maintain an equilibrium among the powers. Led by Vienna the powers of the Triple Alliance — or better Germany and Austria — attempted to accomplish this through peaceful diplomatic means during the following months. In this they were unsuccessful, and the tipping scales finally plunged all Europe into war.

But it was some time before the powers knew exactly what had happened. Pašić was wrong in his supposition; King Ferdinand did not inform Vienna of the treaty. In fact, the Ballhausplatz learned of it from Germany, and, if we are to judge from the Austrian documents and other printed material, it was many months before they knew the full contents of the agreement. The question of when the different countries found out about the treaty, and how much of it they knew, is not only interesting in itself, but is of importance in judging the policy each pursued.

The treaty had been negotiated with the greatest secrecy possible. Only a few people were informed on each side, and there were surprisingly few leaks. Austria-Hungary, Germany, and Rumania do not appear to have had an idea that serious negotiations were going on. The few rumors that did circulate usually centered on Charykov's plan for a large Balkan confederation, which no one took seriously and was consequently disregarded.[65] On January 5, 1912, we have the first and only report

[64] Dr. Milan Gavrilović who informed the writer of this incident has in his possession the memorandum of the treaty given to Pašić at the conference and upon which the latter noted his objections to the treaty. Dr. Gavrilović was employed in the Serbian foreign office in 1912, and for years was Pašić's secretary.

[65] Ö-U.A., III, nos. 3104, 3109, 3151. In December 1911 Turkey advanced

to reach Vienna on the possibility of Serbian-Bulgarian negotiations.[66] Ugron, the Austrian minister at Belgrade, had become alarmed over Spalaiković's frequent visits to Belgrade and his long conversations with Milovanović, Hartwig, and King Peter. He hunted up Toshev, his Bulgarian colleague, and sought an explanation from him. Although Toshev probably did not know the details of the agreement, he certainly knew what was in the air. Anyway he blandly proceeded to pull the wool over Ugron's eyes, and the Austrian minister became convinced that there was no truth in the rumors of an alliance. About the same time Danev told Tarnowski, the Austrian minister in Sofia, that an agreement with Serbia was impossible, and apparently was believed.[67] Germany and Rumania were no better informed.

The Entente powers knew more. Russia of course received copies of the treaty at once, Nekludov having them in his bag when he left Sofia for St. Petersburg two days after the treaty was signed. Officially they were to be presented to the tsar in May when Danev headed a mission to Livadia and in June when Pašić visited Moscow.[68]

Next to Russia, England more than any other power knew what was going on. By means of private letters to Sir Arthur Nicolson — which were "not even allowed to go into the department" — Sir H. Bax-Ironside, the British minister at Sofia, was able to keep his superiors informed.[69] In October, Bax-Ironside

---

feelers for a Balkan league under Austrian auspices. Aehrenthal thought this as much a Utopia as a league under Russian leadership, a view which Pallavicini heartily endorsed (*ibid.*, III, nos. 3151, 3172).

[66] Ugron from Belgrade, Ö-U.A., III, no. 3194. For the first definite information of the negotiation of the alliance from the Austrian legation at Belgrade see: Ugron to Berchtold, Oct. 6, 1912, *ibid.*, IV, no. 3969.

[67] *Ibid.*, III, no. 3280.

[68] K.A., IX, no. 78 (*Berl. Mon.*, VIII, 572); Gueshoff, pp. 43–4; B.D., IX, ii, no. 461 (p. 366); IX, i, nos. 580, 581; D.D.F., 3d. ser., III, nos. 151, 155; S.D., I, no. 271.

[69] B.D., IX, i, no. 560. The letters were apparently shown by Nicolson only to Grey and to the king (*ibid.*, IX, ii, no. 184). On the general question as to the knowledge England had of the treaties see, *ibid.*, IX, ii, 1006–1011 (appendix II).

was able to give a rather detailed account of the famous railway interview between Gueshov and Milovanović.[70] On January 18, 1912, he reported that pressure was being brought to bear on King Ferdinand to sign the treaty.[71] Other reports followed and on March 14th, 1912, the day after the conclusion of the negotiations, Bax-Ironside transmitted a summary of the treaty to London.[72] He had seen the original versions of the document, the one written in Bulgarian in longhand by Gueshov, the other in Serbian by Spalaiković. Gueshov was particularly anxious that this information be kept very secret — only Nicolson and Grey were to know — until the Russian government had made arrangements to disclose the contents of the treaty.[73] Significantly, the British minister made no mention of the secret annex to the treaty, although he stated that he would submit a map later showing how the future boundaries should be drawn in case of the break-up of European Turkey.[74] When, and if ever, this map was submitted to the foreign office is not clear. Although the Russian ambassador informed the foreign office of the treaty on April 6th,[75] the editors of the British documents state that it was not until Benckendorff communicated the secret annex on November 5, 1912, that the Government had definite information on the future partition of territory.[76] That a partition of spoils had been arranged was known at the foreign office long before this.[77] In reading the documents it must be

[70] *Ibid.*, IX, i, no. 525; see also, IX, ii, nos. 461, 572.

[71] *Ibid.*, IX, i, no. 543; Nicolson, *Portrait of a Diplomatist*, p. 274. The British documents show that Nicolson has not misdated this telegram in his biography as is assumed by Kurt Holdegel, *Frankreichs Politik im Nahen Orient und im Mittelmeer in der Zeit vom Ausbruch des italienisch-türkischen Krieges bis zum Zusammentritt der Londoner Botschafterkonferenz Oktober 1911–Dezember 1912* (Dresden, 1934), p. 56.

[72] B.D., IX, i, nos. 544, 555, 558, 559 enclosure.

[73] *Ibid.*, IX, i, nos. 558, 566, 572.

[74] *Ibid.*, IX, i, no. 559.

[75] *Ibid.*, IX, ii, 1007; see below, p. 62.

[76] *Ibid.*, IX, ii, 1008; see also no. 85. It was only on Poincaré's insistence that Sazonov made this November communication to Grey (D.D.F., 3d. ser., IV, no. 273).

[77] See especially, B.D., IX, i, nos. 555, 559, 569; Nicolson's minute on a conversation with Paul Cambon, *ibid.*, IX, ii, 1008.

remembered that while Nicolson and Grey knew all about the treaty, the rest of the men in the department who saw the general run of documents did not. Nicolson, to say the least, must have had his tongue in his cheek when in May 1912, in answer to a report on the territorial provisions of the treaty from the English chargé at St. Petersburg, he stated:

> You certainly have given me most important news with respect to Bulgaria and Serbia, and it shows me that the arrangement which has recently been concluded is of a more serious and far-reaching character than we originally supposed, and it is evident that the distribution of the spoils in Macedonia has been decided upon.[78]

As early as June, 1912, the conclusion of the military convention between Serbia and Bulgaria was reported from Sofia.[79] The foreign office, however, apparently knew very little of the content of this agreement.

On March 30, 1912, Sazonov decided to inform both Paris and London of the treaty and telegraphed as follows:

> With our consent an alliance has been concluded between Serbia and Bulgaria for mutual defense and protection of common interests in case the *status quo* on the Balkan peninsula is violated, or a third party attacks either of the contracting parties. Gueshov and the Serbian minister in Sofia, Spalaiković, have informed the English minister in Bulgaria of the conclusion of this treaty. Please inform Poincaré, at an opportune moment, orally, and for his personal information, of the above, stressing very earnestly the necessity of keeping the treaty absolutely secret. You can add, that inasmuch as a special secret clause pledges both parties to seek the opinion of Russia before they undertake active measures, we are of the opinion that we, in this fashion, have a means to influence both sides, and that at the same time we have erected a protective barrier against the expansion of influence of a certain Greater Power in the Balkans.[80]

The above telegram has been quoted in full for it contains all the information that any of the powers (Italy and England ex-

[78] *Ibid.*, IX, i, no. 570.

[79] *Ibid.*, IX, ii, 1009.

[80] F. Stieve (ed.), *Der diplomatische Schriftwechsel Iswolskis 1911–1914* (4 vols.; Berlin, 1925; hereafter cited as Izvolsky), II, no. 243; B.D., IX, ii, 1007; D.D.F., 3d. ser., II, no. 284.

cepted) had of the treaty for some time. It was among those documents turned over regularly to the German foreign office by a secretary of the Russian legation in London, and it is almost certain that it was from this source that Germany learned of the treaty.[81] At least the information conveyed to King Carol by Kiderlen-Waechter is practically identical with the above telegram. Kiderlen even excelled Sazonov in peaceful commentary, and wrote, "I take it, that Russia considers this agreement also, only as a means of keeping the Balkan states in hand, and to prevent their independent action." [82] Had Kiderlen known of the annex to the treaty with its offensive clauses and its division of Macedonia, he probably would have commented differently. But even with the scant information which the Germans possessed, it is not surprising that the Kaiser should have noted, "Lüge," on that portion of Pourtalès' report of April 26, 1913, where the latter relates that Sazonov had just told him that, "the treaties of alliance between the Balkan states had been concluded without Russian aid, and Russia had not been informed of them." [83]

It was not until more than a month later that King Carol passed on the information which he had received from Kiderlen to the Austrian minister.[84] Prince Fürstenberg reported it at once, but his report reached Vienna too late to catch Berchtold before the latter left for Berlin on his first official visit as foreign minister. Here Kiderlen informed him of the treaty and again put the document in a peaceful light.

[81] G.P., XXVIII, i, no. 9755 note. In a conversation in July, 1931 with Jagow, secretary of foreign affairs at Berlin 1913–1916, the writer asked him if Germany learned of the Serbian-Bulgarian treaty from the De Siebert documents. As he was not in the foreign office in the spring of 1912, he could not say definitely, although he thought this might well have been the case. The foreign office received these Russian documents from a secretary at the Russian embassy in London sometimes after only a few days and sometimes after weeks. He added that some Russian telegrams came via Berlin and these the German foreign office deciphered. Berchtold refers to the German knowledge of the treaty as coming from an "interzeptiertes Geheimdokument" (Ö-U.A., IV, no. 3540).

[82] Ernst Jäckh, *Kiderlen-Wächter — Der Staatsmann und Mensch* (2 vols.; Berlin, 1924), II, 185–6.

[83] G.P., XXXIV, ii, no. 13220 marginal note.

[84] Fürstenberg to Berchtold, May 21, 1912, Ö-U.A., IV, no. 3530.

> The agreement, [so Berchtold noted in his report] is purely defensive, and in a secret clause the Balkan states have pledged themselves to Russia not to take any offensive measures. From this it follows, that at present it would not suit Russia to aid these powers; that the St. Petersburg cabinet would not like to see an independent action on the part of the states themselves, since an eventual success would not be accredited to Russia, while a defeat would certainly harm Russian influence in the Balkans.[85]

From such incomplete knowledge of the treaty, it might appear as an instrument for the preservation of the *status quo*, something the Central Powers were as interested in maintaining as any one else. Neither Berchtold nor Kiderlen appear to have been unduly concerned about it. Berchtold naturally attempted to obtain corroboration of the agreement. Tarnowski, recently appointed to Sofia, continued to believe that no treaty existed, and when on October 12, 1912, he finally gave in, he still was of the opinion that it had only recently been signed.[86] Nor was better information forthcoming from Belgrade.[87] In June King Ferdinand and Queen Eleanor visited Vienna and Potsdam. The Serbs at once feared that Ferdinand had disclosed the treaty. This was not the case. Berchtold was unable to draw out his royal visitor, and received more information from the queen as to the existence of good relations with Greece and Serbia, than from the king.[88] Ferdinand, however, spoke warmly of the Albanians and the need for an independent Albanian government, and recommended that country to the special attention and care of Austria. To Berchtold this sounded like a proposal for the division of interests on the Balkan peninsula in which Serbia was not mentioned, and he refused to be drawn from his reserve.

Bit by bit the Austrians were to find out about the treaty. Detailed knowledge came very slowly, if we are to judge by the Austrian documents,[89] and even after the outbreak of the First

[85] *Ibid.*, IV, no. 3540.
[86] *Ibid.*, IV, no. 4065, see also nos. 3571, 3601, 3607, 3764.
[87] *Ibid.*, IV, nos. 3603, 3689, 3873, 3969. [88] *Ibid.*, IV, no. 3549.
[89] Berchtold informed the writer in June, 1930, that he found out some points

Balkan War the Austrians were anxious as to the duration of the alliance. In January 1913, Conrad asked the military attaché in Sofia if the obligations of the treaty extended beyond the war, and received the answer that they did not.[90] With the cooling of interallied relations and the growing possibility of a Bulgarian-Austrian rapprochement, news began to sift through more liberally, and on May 23, 1913, via Athens, the Ballhausplatz was informed that Bulgaria was pledged to back Serbia with arms against the Dual Monarchy.[91] In June 1913 Berchtold was still uneasy on this subject and wanted to know if Bulgaria were obligated to Serbia after the conclusion of peace, before he would consent to enter upon any *pourparlers*. Danev assured him that she was not, which of course was a diplomatic inaccuracy.[92] Berchtold was not satisfied with the assurances, for Danev later mixed his statements and up to the outbreak of the Second Balkan War the duration of the alliance apparently remained an uncleared point to the Austrian statesmen.

Italy, knowing of the treaty earlier than either of her allies, breathed no word to either of them. Baroli, the Italian minister in Belgrade, appears to have secured the information and he privately told Toshev that military coöperation with Italy was possible.[93] He also had conversations with Pašić and Milovanović on this subject. Gueshov was interested in Baroli's suggestions and on March 28, 1912, requested that the Italian minister come to Sofia before he went to Rome.[94] The Italian

of the treaties from intercepted dispatches. Only he, his cabinet chief, His Majesty, and Forgach knew about these and the deciphered messages were always immediately destroyed. Hence they would of course not appear in the Austrian documents. Yet in this way they could obtain information of only those points in the agreements which were telegraphed and the texts of the treaties were never communicated in this fashion. The first definite news of the Serbian-Bulgarian treaty apparently reached Vienna via Berlin as indicated above.

[90] Feldmarschall Conrad [Franz, Count Conrad von Hötzendorff], *Aus meiner Dientzeit 1906–1918* (5 vols.; Vienna, 1921–5; hereafter cited as Conrad), III, 31.

[91] Ö-U.A., VI, nos. 7123, 7411.

[92] *Ibid.*, VI, nos. 7433, 7448, 7449.

[93] Toshev, I, 334. On March 28, 1912 Baroli told the English minister at Belgrade that an "understanding had been arrived at" between Serbia and Bulgaria (B.D., IX, i, no. 565).

[94] Toshev, I, 335.

government, however, held itself in reserve and nothing came of the whole plan. Just how much Baroli knew of the Serbian-Bulgarian alliance, it is impossible to say. Bosdari, the Italian minister at Sofia, was not so well informed as his military attaché, who, thanks to his friendship with the Russian attaché, found out most of the points of the treaty.[95] It was from this source that the Consulta received most of its information.

It is surprising that France knew so little of the treaty. To judge by the documents, she knew virtually nothing of the negotiations,[96] and the first information she had of the treaty was furnished by Sazonov when on March 30, 1912, he sent the telegram quoted above.[97] This news, coming on the heels of the famous Russian questionnaire of February 14th,[98] in which Russia proposed a discussion of Near Eastern policy, caused alarm at the Quai d'Orsay. Poincaré was not as satisfied with Sazonov's peaceful assurances as Kiderlen had been, and feared that there might be a subsidiary clause which would involve Russia in case the *status quo* were disturbed. He immediately telegraphed the French representatives at the different capitals to check his information and to try to find out more about the agreements.

Panafieu in Sofia immediately returned a long report on a conversation with the Russian chargé d'affaires which added some details as to the treaties.[99] He reported that Prince Urussov was of the opinion that although Bulgaria and Serbia were bound to consult Russia if serious measures were contemplated, Russia in reality would not be "consulté préablement mais simplement avisé." Although the French minister at Belgrade had seen fit to report earlier a growing intimacy between

[95] Alessandro de Bosdari, *Delle guerre balcanische, della grande guerra e di alcuni fatti precedenti ad esse* (Milan, 1928), pp. 51–2; Nekludoff, *Reminiscences*, p. 83. It also appears that the Italian military attaché at St. Petersburg was very well informed about the treaty (Ö-U.A., IV, no. 4346).

[96] On January 18, 1912 Bax-Ironside reported: "The whole matter [i.e. treaty negotiations] is being kept very secret and is not even known at the French legation" (B.D., IX, i, no. 543; see also, IX, ii, no. 461, p. 364).

[97] See above, p. 62.

[98] D.D.F., 3d. ser., II, nos. 37, 43.

[99] *Ibid.*, II, nos. 297, 359.

Bulgaria and Serbia, he now could add little information.[100] Milovanović continued to deny the existence of a written agreement but admitted a rapprochement between the two countries. Nor was there any information to be had at Athens, or Constantinople.[101] From London, Poincaré had definite confirmation of the existence of the treaty and Nicolson added a few details which were unknown at Paris.[102] At St. Petersburg Sazonov assured Louis that the treaty was strictly defensive, that the powers from which aggression might come were not named, that Russia had not engaged herself, and that the treaty was based on the maintenance of the *status quo*. In fact he did not even "exclude the future adhesion of Turkey to the alliance." [103] If, however, the *status quo* were disturbed, Russia would never permit the great questions in the Orient to be settled without her.

Sazonov had been — to say the least — inexact. By a most liberal interpretation his statement might represent the terms of the treaty itself, but not of the secret annex nor of the military convention which were, however, considered integral parts of the agreement. Louis' telegram did not inspire confidence at the Quai d'Orsay. Poincaré continued to press for a discussion of the Russian questionnaire of February 14, 1912, dealing with Near Eastern affairs, but met with little response.[104] To straighten out this question was one of the objects which led Poincaré to make his visit to St. Petersburg in the first days of August, 1912. Here Sazonov translated to him from a Russian text the treaty and no doubt also the secret annex, for without that Poincaré would not have been informed of the Russian arbitration clauses, about which he would surely have asked.[105] That he was informed of the military convention with its specific

[100] *Ibid.*, II, nos. 225, 288, 336.

[101] *Ibid.*, II, nos. 315, 354; III, no. 226.

[102] *Ibid.*, II, no. 346; B.D., IX, ii, 1008.

[103] *Ibid.*, II, no. 302.

[104] *Ibid.*, II, nos. 43, 310, 312, 317, 370, 372, 402; III, nos. 5, 37; Poincaré, II, 34–5.

[105] D.D.F., 3d. ser., III, no. 264. For Sazonov's account of the interview see, Izvolsky, II, no. 401.

offensive features is unlikely. At least none of the accounts refer to it. Nevertheless he had enough information to call the agreement "une convention de guerre,"[106] and to pursue an active policy for the localisation of the conflict which he knew was bound to come.

On June 7, 1912, just at the time of King Ferdinand's visit to Vienna and Berlin, *Le Temps* had carried a notice of an agreement for the division of Macedonia. On November 24, 1913, just before King Ferdinand's second visit to Vienna of that autumn, the full text of the treaty and the military convention was published by *Le Matin*. Whether there was a connection between the newspaper article and the visit in 1912 it is impossible to say. In 1913, however, there can be little doubt that the treaties were published in order to embarrass Ferdinand and hinder his obtaining a rapprochement with Austria-Hungary. He at least considered this to be the case.[107] From whom *Le Matin* obtained the texts is not known. The fact of the treaties was by this time no great revelation to any government. Yet to judge by published sources there were even then many interesting details which were learned for the first time.

The power most concerned was Turkey. Her information at first seems to have been vague indeed. In June, 1912, her ambassadors had been vainly inquiring about Europe as to a rumored Serbian-Bulgarian alliance. In Paris, at last, they were informed that their suspicions were correct.[108] Certainly by September Turkey realised full well that the Balkan states were allied against her and meant to have war. This was one of the reasons why she started to mobilise her troops and prepare for war, an action which in turn caused the other states to come out in the open with similar military measures.

[106] D.D.F., 3d. ser., IV, no. 170.
[107] Ö-U.A., VII, nos. 9040, 9080.
[108] Lowther to Grey, June 17, 1912, B.D., IX, ii, 1009.

CHAPTER III

THE GREEK–BULGARIAN ALLIANCE, MAY, 1912

WHEREAS the Serbian-Bulgarian treaty of 1912 was the result of almost unbroken negotiations from 1904 on, the Greek-Bulgarian treaty had no such long and continued conversations as a background. There had, of course, often been talk of an alliance, especially in the early 'nineties when Tricoupis was playing a dominant rôle in Greek politics.[1] The disastrous war of 1897 and the failure of Ferdinand to respond to the overtures from Athens at that time did little to further friendship. In fact Greek policy took a decidedly anti-Bulgarian turn. In 1900 a Greek-Rumanian commercial treaty based on the most favored nation principle was signed. The next year King Carol and King George met at Abbazia, the visit being arranged by the Austrian foreign office. No treaty was signed, although there was talk of it in the newspapers; but an entente was reached, owing largely to the fear of Bulgaria which was felt in both countries.[2] For the same reason, Turkey showed a more friendly spirit and there were many feelers for a Greek-Turkish agreement.

The activity of the Bulgarian bands in Macedonia, which brought about the premature uprising of 1903, led to a conflict with the Greek element living in this territory.[3] In Athens they spoke no longer of isolated *attentats*, but of violent pressure against all the Greek inhabitants and the desire of the Bulgars to exterminate the entire Greek population of Macedonia. Clearly something had to be done about this. One way was to beat the Bulgarians at their own game. On September 9, 1903

[1] Edouard Driault et Michel Lhéritier, *Histoire diplomatique de la Grèce, de 1821 à nos jours* (5 vols.; Paris, 1925–6; hereafter cited as Driault and Lhéritier), IV, 178 ff.

[2] *Ibid.*, IV, 485–6.

[3] Alfred Rappaport, "Mazedonien und die Komitadschis," *Berliner Monatshefte*, VIII (1930), 740–3.

the Greek government informed its legations of the formation of the first Greek band. During the next years an intense propaganda was carried on which aimed at everyone and everything opposed to Greek nationality in Macedonia. "From the autumn of 1904 on," so M. Lhéritier summarises, "one hears more of Greek than of Bulgarian bands. The Hellenic counter-offensive was in full swing." [4]

Such activity naturally led to conflict with other komitaji groups, and to protests from the other Balkan governments as well as from the great powers. Bulgarian public opinion became excited, while the zeal used by the Greeks in converting the Vlach population led to a rupture of Greek-Rumanian relations. While these Greek-Rumanian difficulties were at their height, there was a vague gesture on the part of Sofia for a rapprochement with Greece. The Greek cabinet, however, maintained a cold reserve and nothing came of this.[5] Instead relations grew worse, for the Bulgarian bands, relying on the support of the Rumanian elements in Macedonia, increased their efforts and attacks against the Greeks. On the other hand, Greek-Turkish and Greek-Serbian relations improved.

The proclamation of Bulgarian independence created a great stir in Athens. How was one ever to stop the Bulgarians on the Macedonian front? Turkey also was alarmed and nothing seemed more natural than a Greek-Turkish agreement. In return for Greek support, Athens hoped that the Porte would permit a union of Crete with the mother country. The negotiations were fruitless. The Young Turks, who realised that they would have to accept the loss of Bulgaria and of Bosnia-Herzegovina, were determined not to give up Crete.

It was clear that neither Turkey nor the powers would ever permit Crete to join with Greece until forced to do so. But Greek finances were weak, the army and navy in poor shape, and conditions in general little better than in 1897. No one was anxious to have the lesson of that year repeated, and yet the

[4] Driault and Lhéritier, IV, 518.
[5] *Ibid.*, IV, 555.

Cretans and the people of Athens clamored for a settlement. Former leaders of bands in Macedonia who had lost their jobs because of the Young Turk Revolution and the end of the "Hamidian tyranny," flocked to Crete to bolster up the anti-Turkish spirit in that island.[6] The Cretans were hardly in need of this aid and their governmental assembly continued to vote annexation to Greece. They even decreed that all officials should take an oath to King George. Finally Turkey began to threaten coercive measures, but after many trials and much tribulation the powers brought about a temporary settlement which precluded military action.[7]

The government was in a bad hole and the dissatisfaction of the people with the spineless policy of the cabinet increased by leaps and bounds. In August, 1909, what virtually amounted to a revolution took place, and the military league came to dominate affairs.[8] Its régime was no better than the preceding ones. What was needed was a leader, and here Crete came to the rescue.

When the powers had again temporarily ended the revolutionary uprising in Crete, Venizelos, the acknowledged leader of the movement, decided that he could accomplish more if he transferred his activity to Athens. The people on the mainland received him with open arms and he was immediately elected to the Greek chamber. The Porte protested against a Cretan sitting in the Greek parliament, but as Venizelos had dual nationality he resigned his mandate to the Cretan assembly and proceeded to take his seat.[9] Without bowing to the military league under whose banner he had been elected, he soon organised a supporting faction in the chamber and on October 18, 1911, he became premier. A dissolution of parliament and new elections placed him firmly in the saddle.

[6] *Ibid.*, V, 38.

[7] Herbert Adams Gibbons, *Venizelos* (London, 1921), pp. 74–5. The Turkish boycott of Greek goods, however, continued (Driault and Lhéritier, V, 53–9).

[8] Driault and Lhéritier, V, 33.

[9] *Ibid.*, V, 49. Although Venizelos was born in Crete under Turkish rule his father was a born Greek and this entitled him to Greek citizenship.

With the advent of Venizelos to power, relations took a new turn between Athens and Sofia. The pressure put on Macedonia by the Young Turks from 1909 onward had brought about some reconciliation between the Christian races living there. Starting among the peasants this gradually spread to the clergy and to the upper classes, and warfare between the races practically ceased. The people began to unite against the rejuvenated Turkey and the way was smoothed for a reconciliation between the Balkan governments.[10] In any case Venizelos looked more to Crete than to Macedonia, and he had long ago reached the conviction that in order to strike Turkey a telling blow there must be sincere coöperation by all the Balkan states.[11] A strong Greece was essential but not enough. There must be an alliance with Bulgaria. For years he had been on friendly terms with J. D. Bourchier, the able *Times* correspondent in the Near East, and had often exchanged views with him on Balkan questions. As early as February 26, 1910 we have a definite record that the Bulgarian alliance was specifically mentioned, there being this note in Bourchier's diary: "Athens. Venizelos came to see me at 11 p.m., and stayed till 1 a.m.; unfolded all his views — even Bulgarian Alliance; evidently means to take the helm by-and-by here." [12]

Seven months later Bourchier's forecast was verified. Venizelos was at the head of the Greek government and the Bulgarian alliance became a definite plank in the Greek platform. Venizelos did not wish to precipitate matters while unprepared, and he consequently undertook a temporary Turcophile policy in order to gain time. The measures for the reform of the armed forces were continued, state finances and administration were

[10] Bourchier in London *Times*, June 4, 1913; Reginald Rankin, *The Inner History of the Balkan War* (New York, n.d.), pp. 12–3; K.A., VIII, no. 2 (*Berl. Mon.*, VII, 700–2); Ö-U.A., III, nos. 2254, 2341, 2347; Lamouche, *Histoire balkanique*, p. 109.

[11] Lady Grogan, *The Life of J. D. Bourchier* (London, n.d.), p. 216; Diplomatist, p. 148; Dem. J. D. Drossos, *La fondation de l'alliance balkanique* (Athens, 1929), p. 122.

[12] Grogan, *Bourchier*, p. 136.

given an overhauling, a regeneration of Greece was under way.[13] But in foreign affairs Crete was no longer to be sacrificed to Macedonian antagonisms; an alliance with Bulgaria was viewed with favor.

During the winter of 1910 and spring of 1911 many conversations took place between Venizelos and Bourchier. They saw each other almost daily. Encouraged and urged by the latter, the Greek premier decided to propose an alliance to Sofia.[14] Obtaining the consent of King George, Venizelos with the aid of Bourchier worked out an alliance proposal. It called for an entente with a view to common action for the defense of the privileges of the Christians in Turkey, and an eventual defensive alliance against a Turkish attack on either of the contracting parties.[15] This proposal along with letters to Gueshov and to King Ferdinand were given by Bourchier in a sealed package to a Mr. Butler, who was instructed to deliver them to H. W. Steed, Bourchier's fellow correspondent in Vienna.[16] Without divulging the contents of the package Steed was able to persuade the Bulgarian minister to dispatch a special courier to Sofia, and at the end of April, 1911, the proposal was in Gueshov's hands.

No immediate response was forthcoming. King Ferdinand was not indisposed to the suggestions, but naturally had no desire to be drawn into a war over Crete. Finally in September events took a step forward. Bourchier, who was then in Sofia, induced Ferdinand and Gueshov to entrust him with a verbal request for the negotiations to be put on a diplomatic basis, if he found the situation favorable at Athens. This decision was

[13] Gibbons, *Venizelos*, p. 102; D. J. Casavetti, *Hellas and the Balkan Wars* (London, 1914), p. 143.

[14] Grogan, *Bourchier*, p. 135; Rankin, *Inner History*, p. 143.

[15] Bourchier in London *Times*, June 5, 1913.

[16] Steed, *Through Thirty Years*, I, 360. Bourchier, in his note given to Lady Grogan, does not mention Steed but says Butler took the note personally to the Bulgarian legation (Grogan, *Bourchier*, p. 135). In his account in the London *Times* in June 1913 he, however, says that it was sent via Corfu to an Englishman in Vienna who delivered it to the Bulgarian legation. This latter account thus jibes with Steed's version. Mr. Butler had formerly acted as Bourchier's aid in Montenegro.

taken before the outbreak of the Tripolitan War and must have almost coincided with the decisions of the Bulgarian leaders to enter into *pourparlers* with Serbia. King George and Venizelos at once agreed, and Panas, the able Greek minister at Sofia, was put in charge of the negotiations.[17] Just as in the case of the Serbian treaty, Sofia was to be the center of things.

Panas at once became very active. Through the remaining weeks of September and the first weeks of October he had discussions first with Gueshov and then with Teodorov, who was in charge while the minister of foreign affairs was on his vacation. On October 16th, three days after Gueshov's return to Sofia, Panas made a definite proposition to him. "If [Gueshov] could assure him," so Panas concluded, "of Bulgaria's willingness to intervene in the event of a Turkish aggression on Greece, he was authorised to declare . . . that Greece in her turn will fight should Bulgaria be attacked by Turkey." [18] Gueshov promised to communicate the proposal to the king and the ministerial council. Both Urussov, the Russian chargé, and later Nekludov advised extreme caution in dealing with Athens, since ". . . Greece had in Crete a perpetual apple of discord with Turkey, and the Greeks once certain of Bulgarian help would permit themselves to be swept into an active, and consequently dangerous and egotistical policy." [19] The Bulgarian cabinet and especially King Ferdinand were, nevertheless, favorably inclined towards the proposal. To refuse their advances, as Gueshov told the Russian minister, might drive Greece into an Austrian-Rumanian-Albanian combination.[20]

The Russian foreign office itself kept discreetly silent in regard to the Greek-Bulgarian negotiations, and it was not until Gueshov insisted on knowing the view of the Russian government that Neratov, then in charge at St. Petersburg, made a

[17] Grogan, *Bourchier*, p. 136. Drossos starts his discussion of the Greek-Bulgarian negotiations at this point (*L'alliance balkanique*, pp. 23–4).

[18] Gueshoff, pp. 37–8; Drossos, *L'alliance balkanique*, p. 24.

[19] K.A., VIII, nos. 29, 33 (*Berl. Mon.*, VII, 900, 902).

[20] *Ibid.*, VIII, no. 33 (*Berl. Mon.*, VII, 902).

statement.[21] He referred the Russian minister at Sofia to a rather indefinite telegram, where he had laid down the principle that the Serbian-Bulgarian treaty should be based on the *status quo*, and should be drawn up in such a fashion that the other Balkan states and even Turkey might join. In other words the formula, *status quo*, should apply to Greece as well as to the others. Backed by these instructions Nekludov persuaded the Bulgarian cabinet of the necessity first of all for concluding a close defensive alliance with Serbia, which Greece might later join.

With Russia thus putting a cold douche on direct Bulgarian-Greek negotiations, it is no wonder that Gueshov told Bourchier when he saw him on November 3rd, that he did not know what to reply to his letters proposing a Balkan alliance. Panas was stalled off by the promise ". . . that Bulgaria . . . [was willing] to assist Greece in a war with Turkey on conditions which must be specified in a defensive treaty." [22]

No steps appear to have been taken towards this treaty during the following months. Sofia was too much taken up with the Serbian negotiations. When that agreement was practically under cover, Gueshov turned his attention to Greece. On February 6, 1912 he intrusted Bourchier with a verbal communication to Venizelos in which he expressed his satisfaction at the proposals already made, and invited Greece to renew discussions.[23] Bourchier delivered his message on February 19th and negotiations were promptly under way. By April 27, 1912, they had advanced so far that Panas was able to present a draft treaty. "In this preliminary project," according to Gueshov, "not only was nothing said about autonomy for Macedonia and Thrace, but even those privileges which had been granted to the Christian provinces of European Turkey by various international acts, particularly Article XXIII of the Treaty of Berlin, were passed over in silence." [24] Gueshov objected to this and sug-

[21] *Ibid.*, VIII, no. 41; see also, nos. 34, 36 (*Berl. Mon.*, VIII, 462; VII, 902–3).
[22] Grogan, *Bourchier*, p. 137; Gueshoff, p. 38.
[23] Grogan, *Bourchier*, p. 137; London *Times*, June 6, 1913.
[24] Gueshoff, p. 38.

gested a formula covering autonomy, which, however, was not adopted. Neither did the Greeks want to accede to his proposal for a clause recognising the right of Bulgaria to go to war for the rights of Christians in Turkey as based on treaties, for they thought this was getting autonomy inserted by falling back on Article XXIII of the Berlin Treaty. At this point the English government was discreetly approached by the Bulgarian statesmen and asked to put in a favorable word at Athens.[25] There is, however, no record of the foreign office having done this. Finally, the Greek cabinet did accept the Bulgarian formula, and on May 17/30th the treaty was signed. However, since it happened to be Tuesday, an unlucky day according to Orthodox superstition, Gueshov insisted that the document bear the date of May 16/29, 1912.[26] It happened that both the Serbian-Bulgarian and the Greek-Bulgarian treaties were signed on days which presaged an unlucky termination for Bulgaria.

In brief the treaty provided for:

> . . . A defensive alliance to remain in force for three years and to be kept secret, on the following terms: If one of the two states is attacked by Turkey, the other will declare war against Turkey; both states are to act jointly in relations with Turkey and the great powers and agree to make joint representations to the Sublime Porte for the protection and defense of Greek and Bulgarian Ottoman subjects. In an annex, however, the alliance was declared not to be operative in case of a war arising between Greece and Turkey over the admission of Cretans to the Greek Chamber of Deputies.[27]

Carefully drawn and strictly defensive in form, the treaty was really an offensive alliance. "Diplomatist," the anonymous but extremely well-informed student of the Near East, writes:

> Thus, in the Greek-Bulgarian treaty the obligation really is to take the field together on any systematic violation by Turkey of the treaty rights of either signatory, or of the law of nations, nominally it is only

[25] Bax-Ironside to Grey, April 29, 1912, B.D., IX, i, no. 568.

[26] Drossos, *L'alliance balkanique*, p. 26.

[27] As summarised by Gibbons, *Venizelos*, pp. 113–4. The text of the treaty and of the later military convention of October 5, 1912 can be found, Gueshoff, pp. 127–33; Balkanicus, pp. 110–15; Diplomatist, pp. 396–400; B.D., IX, ii, 1015–18.

to make joint representation to Turkey as to violation. The whole existence of the Empire in Europe being at this time a systematic violation of treaty rights and any joint representation being in the then temper of the Young Turks tantamount to a challenge, the elaborately "defensive" drafting could not conceal the offensive object of the agreement.[28]

The military convention foreseen by the treaty was not concluded until October 5th, five days after general mobilisation had been ordered in each country. Beyond the purely military provisions which were to be effective if either country were attacked by Turkey, the convention extended the letter of the alliance to include an attack on Turkey if this should be agreed upon by the two countries. In case one of the contracting parties attacked a third state other than Turkey the other was bound to friendly neutrality. Article VI also modified the restriction of the alliance as to Crete when it stated:

> If after Bulgaria and Greece have mobilised or commenced a joint war, the latter country should find itself obliged to settle the Cretan question in accordance with the wishes of the inhabitants of Crete, and, in consequence of that action is attacked by Turkey, Bulgaria undertakes to assist Greece. . . .

The way was thus prepared to precipitate the war with Turkey by the admission of Cretan representatives to the Greek parliament. This, according to a well laid plan, was to follow Montenegro's opening of hostilities.

In contrast to the Serbian-Bulgarian agreement, the Greek-Bulgarian treaty contained no territorial provisions. Greece attempted to remedy this in the first days of October, 1912, but Bulgaria was not willing to enter upon a settlement of this problem. More than a promise of Crete and the other islands in the Aegean, Bulgaria refused to give.[29]

Although Russia had been kept informed of the negotiations, she had not been instrumental in bringing them to a conclusion. If anything she had delayed them by her continual admonitions

[28] Diplomatist, p. 184.
[29] Driault and Lhéritier, V, 80.

in Sofia against the evil designs of the Greeks.[30] On the very eve of the signature of the treaty she raised some objections to the formulation of the treaty, but Gueshov did not see fit to prolong the negotiations. Both he and King Ferdinand wished to have the treaty under cover before they left for Vienna on the first official visit of the king and queen to the court of Francis Joseph.

The text of the treaty apparently was not shown to Serbia,[31] nor was it transmitted to St. Petersburg, although the Russian statesmen certainly knew all its provisions.[32] Sazonov evaded telling Poincaré any of the details of the treaty, and it was necessary for him to find out about it from other sources. In fact he was already informed of its conclusion and of its general contents from the reports of the French minister at Sofia.[33]

The British government knew that Greece and Bulgaria were negotiating and even before the treaty was actually signed Sazonov informed the British chargé of the conclusion of the agreement.[34] Bax-Ironside no doubt was fairly well informed when in the first days of June, 1912, he left Sofia for his vacation.[35] Mr. Barclay, who acted as chargé in his absence, was not the recipient of as many confidences as his superior had been. Nevertheless, as early as August 14th he was able to submit the gist of the treaty to London.[36]

The Ballhausplatz had wind of the Greek-Bulgarian treaty quite early. In a report on the visit of King Ferdinand on June 1–3rd, Berchtold noted:

> . . . Through secret channels we have received information about the existence of a Greek-Bulgarian agreement. In addition, according

[30] K.A., VIII, nos. 29, 33 (*Berl. Mon.*, VII, 900, 902); Benckendorff, II, no. 635.

[31] Balkanicus, p. 87.

[32] At least Sazonov maintained that he did not have the text at the time of Poincaré's visit in August (D.D.F., 3d. ser., III, no. 264). See also, K.A., XV, no. 1 (*Berl. Mon.*, VIII, 964); Benckendorff, II, no. 635.

[33] D.D.F., 3d. ser., III, nos. 10, 150, 235, 254; see also, nos. 226, 238, 257.

[34] O'Beirne to Grey, May 16, 1912, B.D., IX, i, no. 569; see also, no. 568; IX, ii, 1013–4.

[35] *Ibid.*, IX, i, no. 572 enclosure.

[36] *Ibid.*, IX, ii, 1015.

to information of the German cabinet, a defensive convention has been concluded between Serbia and Bulgaria. The Bulgarian-Greek treaty up to now appears not to have been communicated to the Russian government, whereas the Bulgarian-Serbian agreement was formed under Russian patronage.[37]

The news of the treaty caused no great alarm. To Berchtold it indicated "that at the given moment when the conditions in Turkey become unbearable the Balkan states desired to make a united advance." In view of the fact that a Balkan League had been formed and Serbia had ordered twenty-one million francs worth of ammunition with short-term delivery, Auffenberg, the Austrian minister of war, demanded additional funds in the budget discussions of July, 1912. But no more money was appropriated, and the additional batteries which he did order were purchased at his own risk and without authorisation.[38]

The service Russia had performed in the Serbian-Bulgarian negotiations was ably and efficiently fulfilled by Bourchier for the Greek-Bulgarian agreement. A warm friend of all Balkan nations, he had striven heart and soul for an understanding which he considered necessary for the settlement of conditions in the Near East. To him must go much of the credit not only for the settlement of differences between Sofia and Athens, but also for the rapprochement between Belgrade and Sofia. Although he had no direct part in these latter negotiations he helped them along by timely advice and prudent counsel.[39]

Few of the details are known about the negotiations of the summer of 1912 between Greece and Montenegro [40] or between Greece and Serbia. No formal alliances were drawn up, although informal and oral agreements were reached. In the negotiations with Serbia, the Greek foreign office went so far as to submit on October 22, 1912 the complete text of a proposed treaty of

[37] Ö-U.A., IV, no. 3549.

[38] Baron M. Auffenberg-Komarow, "Indirekte Kriegsschuld," *Berliner Monatshefte*, VI (1928), 551.

[39] Grogan, *Bourchier*, p. 136. See the appreciations of Bourchier written by Gueshov and Venizelos and printed as appendices, *ibid.*, pp. 209–17.

[40] See below, p. 89.

alliance to the Greek legation at Belgrade.[41] The war with Turkey had, however, begun by this time and further negotiations for an alliance were postponed until the spring of 1913.[42]

[41] Portions of this draft treaty quoted from the Greek archives are to be found in Driault and Lhéritier, V, 80–1. In October, 1912 the British minister at Sofia reported that an alliance between Greece and Serbia had been signed at Athens on October 6, 1912. Later he referred to this agreement as an entente (B.D., IX, ii, 1018–9). Hartwig on September 24, 1912 reported to St. Petersburg a Greek offer of an alliance to Serbia (S.D., II, 593). In November, 1912 the Greek minister at Vienna spoke of the defensive alliance between Greece and Serbia against Turkey (Ö-U.A., IV, no. 4572). In April, 1913 Venizelos told the British minister he was bound by the alliance with Serbia and Montenegro (B.D., IX, ii, no. 810). The French minister at Belgrade reported negotiations for a Greek-Serbian agreement and the signing of a military convention several days after the opening of hostilities (D.D.F., 3d. ser., IV, no. 347). On the other hand the French minister at Athens reported the existence of only an oral agreement between Serbia and Greece (*ibid.*, IV, no. 360) Mr. Gibbons states that Greece had no agreements with Serbia (*Venizelos*, p. 115). In answer to an inquiry at the Greek foreign office the editors of the British documents received the assurance that ". . . no treaty defensive or military was signed between Greece and Serbia before the first Balkan War. . . ." (B.D., IX, ii, 1018; see also Demetrius Caclamanos, "Reminiscences of the Balkan Wars," *Slavonic Review*, XVI (1937), 120). All told these references justify the conclusion made in the text that no formal alliance existed between Serbia and Greece during the war with Turkey.

[42] See below, pp. 346–49.

CHAPTER IV

MONTENEGRIN AGREEMENTS

WITH the accession of Peter Karageorgević to the Serbian throne in 1903, the efforts of Prince Nikita of Montenegro to swing the leadership of the Serbian race to Cetinje received a severe setback.[1] Inspired by the changes in the neighboring state and no less by the October Manifesto of the Russian tsar, Prince Nikita on December 19, 1905 proclaimed a democratic constitution for Montenegro. Things, however, did not run along smoothly. While Nikita did not object strenuously to the existence of a skupština, he did not like political parties, especially the opposition. In 1907 the constitution was suspended.[2] Political persecution at once set in, and many of the fugitives from Montenegro found their way to Belgrade, where they did little to further good relations between the two countries. Many of them joined the secret society *Slovenske Jug* and became active propagandists, directing much of their effort against the Montenegrin government.

In October, 1907 a plot to murder Prince Nikita came to light. Three men with bombs, presumably from the Serbian arsenal at Kragujevać, were apprehended and the incident became a signal for many other political arrests. Everything pointed to propaganda centering in Belgrade, and Nikita was exasperated with the Serbian government since it did nothing to put an end to the organisations.[3]

[1] This chapter has appeared in substantially the same form under the title, "Montenegro and the Formation of the Balkan League," *Slavonic Review*, XV (1937), 426–34.

[2] Wendel, *Der Kampf der Südslawen*, p. 524. "A parliament," so King Nikita confided to the Austrian military attaché, "is much too loose a rein for such an unschooled horse" (Gustav Hubka, "König Nikolaus von Montenegro," *Deutsche Revue*, XLVI, ii [1921], 31).

[3] The history of this plot is a complicated one and centers on the revelations of Nastić in his pamphlets *Finale* (Sarajevo, 1908) and *Wo ist die Wahrheit*

The relations between the two governments continued to be very strained. To Russia it seemed scandalous that such a state of affairs should exist between two Slavic states. In April, 1908, when Nikita visited St. Petersburg, he was emphatically advised to come to an understanding with Serbia. On the eve of the annexation crisis, Izvolsky told the Serbian minister in Paris the same thing,[4] and on every available occasion Russia let her dissatisfaction over this fraternal quarrel be known.

The annexation crisis did bring at least a temporary understanding between the countries. Both at once protested against the Austrian action, and on October 16, 1908 General Janko Vukotić left Cetinje for Belgrade with the intention of negotiating an agreement. On the way he was held up by the Austrian police and military officials in Agram, in spite of the letter he carried from the Austrian minister.[5] He protested, and Aehrenthal sent an apology to Cetinje, but this could not wipe out the anti-Austrian irritation with which Vukotić took up his task. The negotiations proceeded rapidly and in a few days the Austrian minister reported that, according to his information, Serbia and Montenegro had come to complete agreement on all matters.[6] At the gala dinner given to the Montenegrin special delegate, King Peter, lifting his glass to Prince Nikita and to Montenegro, mentioned "with enthusiasm the real unity and agreement which exist between the two independent Serbian states, not only in regard to the present difficult situation but also in regard to their future common policy." [7] In fact, a treaty of alliance was signed on October 24th. It expressed the unity of interests of the two countries, and pledged their close cooperation for the protection of common aims. A general military accord was to be drawn up in case it should be necessary to have

(Sarajevo, 1908). Recent investigations show there was more truth in Nastić's accounts than was formerly supposed. An interesting sidelight on the affair is to be had in the report of the Serbian minister at Cetinje of February 13, 1910 (S.D., I, no. 133). See also Gooss, *Das österreichisch-serbische Problem*, p. 174.

[4] Vesnić to Milovanović, October 5, 1908, S.D., I, no. 6.

[5] Ö-U.A., I, nos. 283, 342, 347b.

[6] *Ibid.*, I, no. 380.

[7] *Ibid.*, I, no. 389.

recourse to arms. This accord was to continue in effect as long as it was not replaced and completed by another accord.[8]

Montenegro now turned her attention to Turkey and attempted to further the Turkish-Serbian-Montenegrin entente which was under contemplation at that time. On November 16, 1908, General Vukotić arrived at Constantinople as a special envoy to negotiate an agreement. Here he was not to meet with the same success as in Belgrade, and the whole scheme fell through. Nevertheless it does show that Montenegro was at this time perfectly willing to enter into an agreement, primarily directed against Austria-Hungary to be sure, but also with a distinctly anti-Bulgarian tinge.[9]

The close coöperation called forth by the Balkan crisis soon disappeared. In the spring of 1910 evidence of another "Serbian Plot" on the life of Prince Nikita aroused an anti-Serbian outburst on the part of the members of the house of Petrović-Njegres in Cetinje.[10] There never had been any love lost between the rival houses and Prince Nikita's assumption of the royal title in October, 1910, did little to allay this feeling. Crown Prince Alexander represented Serbia at the festivities whereas King Ferdinand himself represented Bulgaria. The occasion was a fine opportunity for the manifestation of Balkan spirit, and rumors of a rapprochement circulated. Dr. Nikolaides, who is usually well informed, asserts that an agreement between the two newly created kings took place, to the effect that if Turkey of her own will or under duress should cede the Sanjak of Novibazar, Montenegro was to receive the western third of this territory.[11] Such a proposal might well have been agreed to by King Ferdinand. It was no more than what was later

[8] The text of the treaty from the Serbian archives is to be found in Nintchitch, *La crise bosniaque*, II, 83–4. It does not correspond to the text which was secretly delivered to Vienna (Ö-U.A., I, nos. 541, 599). Definite information about the military accord is lacking.

[9] See above, pp. 16–19; also, B.D., V, nos. 449, 462; "Montenegrinische Dokumente zur Annexionskrise," *Berliner Monatshefte*, XV (1937), 702–6.

[10] Ö-U.A., II, nos. 2009, 2025, 2123; S.D., I, no. 133.

[11] Cleanthes Nicolaides, *Griechenlands Anteil an den Balkankriegen 1912–13* (Vienna, 1914), p. 260.

promised to Montenegro in the summer of 1912. That it was written is very unlikely. In any case, less than a year later King Nikita appears to have thought it necessary to renew the discussions. Thus it was that at about the same time that Venizelos took his initiative for a Greek-Bulgarian entente through the *Times* correspondent, Bourchier, Nikita made proposals for a Montenegrin-Bulgarian entente through a Dutch correspondent, Baron de Gruyff.[12] De Gruyff not only delivered the letter to King Ferdinand, but also had a long interview in which he was asked to convey a reply to the Montenegrin king. Not wishing to arouse suspicion by his return to Cetinje, De Gruyff arranged to meet a special envoy in Trieste and there delivered the message for King Nikita. Nothing is known of the outcome of this episode. The friendship of Bulgaria, very obvious ever since King Ferdinand's visit to Cetinje, stimulated greatly the hopes and ambitions of the Montenegrins during the Albanian uprisings and Turkish border conflicts of these years.[13]

At about the same time King Nikita also made some attempts to enter into negotiations with the Serbian government for joint action in Macedonia. These advances were skilfully parried by the Serbian government. Serbia did not wish to become involved in the Turkish-Montenegrin border conflicts, nor to give King Nikita the "opportunity to proclaim that whilst he was prepared to champion Serb interests King Peter had been reluctant to join him." [14] For various reasons the Serbian government "did not think the moment opportune" and further negotiations were apparently not undertaken at this time. This is another example of the latent jealousy between the two dynasties.

On the outbreak of the Tripolitan War, Montenegro not only offered her aid to Italy, but proposed joint action to the other

[12] M. Edith Durham, *Twenty Years of Balkan Tangle* (London, 1920), pp. 222–3; Kutschbach, *Brandherd Europas*, p. 340. Miss Durham, who has the most complete account, says this occurred in June, 1911, while Kutschbach places it after the start of the Tripolitan War.

[13] Durham, *Balkan Tangle*, pp. 218, 220.

[14] Paget to Grey, April 11, 1911, B.D., IX, i, no. 470; see also, nos. 469, 470 enclosure, 514.

Balkan states.[15] Italy rejected the proffered assistance as she did the offers of other Balkan states. She wished to have the war localised and was as anxious as any of the other powers to keep the Balkan peninsula quiet. With Serbian-Bulgarian negotiations (of which Montenegro was to know little) just getting under way at Sofia, the proposal for joint action was somewhat premature and was not taken up. Meanwhile Nikita decided to blow the bellows a bit on another iron. On November 1st, wishing to assure himself the possession of Northern Albania, if "entirely against his or Austria's will the liquidation of Turkey should begin," he made a direct bid to Vienna for offensive and defensive alliance.[16] He was full of admiration for Francis Joseph and of expressions of his own loyalty. The Austrian minister, realising why the offers were made and the disturbing effects such an agreement would have, showed great reserve toward the proposal, a policy which Aehrenthal fully endorsed.[17]

The relations between Montenegro and Serbia were still very bad. In fact when Danev, in May, 1912, discussed with Sazonov the possibility of permitting Montenegro to join the Serbian-Bulgarian alliance, the latter advised against it, since open enmity existed between Montenegro and Serbia, and every political treaty between them would be insincere.[18] Moreover, an alliance of this kind would immediately become known to Austria. Although the Russian foreign office had continually expressed the view that it wanted the Serbian-Bulgarian treaty drawn so that the other Balkan states might join, and as late as April, 1912, informed France that it did not even exclude the possibility of Turkey's joining the League,[19] Sazonov now executed a *volte face*. Not only did he veto the adherence of Montenegro to the treaty, but he also expressed his approval

[15] K.A., VIII, nos. 6, 17 (*Berl. Mon.*, VII, 707, 784); Bourchier in London *Times*, June 13, 1913.

[16] Ö-U.A., III, no. 2857; Baron Wladimir Giesl, *Zwei Jahrzehnte im Nahen Orient* (Berlin, 1927), p. 224.

[17] Ö-U.A., III, no. 2903; Giesl, *Zwei Jahrzehnte*, p. 225.

[18] Benckendorff, II, no. 618.

[19] D.D.F., 3d. ser., II, no. 304.

when Danev told him that, although Bulgaria was negotiating with Greece, Greece had not been informed of the alliance between Sofia and Belgrade.[20]

Thus, when Bulgaria and Montenegro did enter upon negotiations, Montenegro was not asked to join the Serbian-Bulgarian alliance as such. The first exchange of ideas took place in Vienna, where the Bulgarian cabinet had temporarily established its headquarters. Gueshov had arrived with King Ferdinand for an official visit, Teodorov was just returning from financial negotiations in Paris, Danev from his mission to Russia, and Rizov was especially summoned from Rome.[21] Ferdinand and Gueshov soon left for Berlin. Immediately afterwards, King Nikita and his prime minister arrived at Vienna and moved into the guest apartments at the Hofburg.[22] Rizov, who had spent many years in Montenegro and was married to a Montenegrin, utilised his acquaintance with the Montenegrin prime minister to arrange a meeting. Danev was drawn into the meeting and here in the Hofburg under the very eyes of the officials of the Ballhausplatz, Montenegro pledged her willingness to act with Bulgaria.[23] Gregović, the Montenegrin minister, knew of the existence of the Serbian-Bulgarian treaty and was not only willing to keep step, but was ready to start the war some days earlier. He did insist that Montenegro must have financial aid and this was the main topic of conversation. The settlement of this point was not reached until the following August. As to territorial settlement, Bulgaria promised Monte-

[20] Benckendorff, II, no. 618.

[21] The discussions of the Bulgarian statesmen centered on making advances to Italy relative to the participation of the Balkan states in the Italian-Turkish war and for the conclusion of a common peace. Italy, however, did not wish to enter upon negotiations and nothing came of the Bulgarian plan (Conversation with Dr. Danev in May, 1930).

[22] For a description of this visit which took place on June 9-10, 1912, see Giesl, *Zwei Jahrzehnte*, pp. 227-9. On this occasion King Nikita was greatly flattered and pleased by being made commandant of the 55th infantry regiment of the Austro-Hungarian army.

[23] Gueshoff, p. 41. On these negotiations see also the well informed article, "The Balkan League, History of its Formation," by M. in *The Fortnightly Review*, XCIX (March, 1913), 430-40.

negro that she should have all the land that she might be able to conquer.[24]

Some weeks later King Nikita ratified the agreement and sent a proposal for common action to Sofia.[25] Gueshov, still wishing to avoid all suspicion, had planned to talk the matter over with Kolushev, the Bulgarian minister to Montenegro, in Munich, but events were moving with such rapidity that the latter was summoned to Sofia instead.[26] Kolushev brought with him Nikita's offer to take immediate action, and in a crown council held at Cham Kourya on August 26, 1912, the Bulgarian government decided to accept Nikita's proposal. The financial support which Montenegro was to receive was also agreed on.[27] On September 16, the Russian military agent in Montenegro sent to the general staff in St. Petersburg, the following telegram which sums up the results of the negotiations.

The military convention which has been concluded between Montenegro and Bulgaria in the form of an exchange of opinions is at present in Sofia awaiting confirmation. Its content is in brief as follows: Both sides pledge themselves to begin the war with all their forces, Montenegro not later than September 15/28th, Bulgaria not later than one month after the Montenegrin action; Montenegro is pledged to involve as great a number of Turkish troops as possible, Bulgaria pledging to pay 70,000 during every month of the war; in consideration of the fact that Bulgarian preparations are not yet complete, a postponement of the beginning of war operations is possible.

[24] Whether this promise was made in June or later in the summer was not clear from my conversation with Danev in May, 1930. He simply stated; "In the summer Bulgaria promised. . . ." On being asked if Serbia had also given these assurances Danev answered that at that time they were not discussing such matters much, since first of all there was the problem of how decisively Turkey would be defeated, and besides there was plenty of land in the Sanjak and neighbouring regions.

[25] Gueshoff, p. 41; *Doklad*, I, 193, 197.

[26] Gueshoff, p. 42. That Gueshov's precaution was in order is shown by the interest Kolushev's departure from Cetinje aroused in Germany, Austria-Hungary, Turkey, and Italy (Ö-U.A., III, nos. 3727, 3730, 3733, 3745; G.P., XXXIII, no. 12107).

[27] Gueshoff, p. 50. The exact amount of the subsidy is not clear. Toshev states (I, 361) that Bulgaria promised to pay 35,000 leva daily to Montenegro. In other words about one leva per day for each soldier in the Montenegrin army. Montenegro received similar subsidies from the other allies. Kesyakov states that the Bulgarian government was to pay 750,000 leva monthly and that this sum was paid for four months (*Diplomaticheskata istoriya*, I, 45 note).

It has been agreed to confront Serbia with the alliance with Bulgaria and the beginning of hostilities as a *fait accompli*; our foreign minister must be informed of the above, as well as of the fact that they have begun to transport war material to the frontier.[28]

The verbal agreement was thus distinctly an offensive instrument and it was definitely planned that Montenegro should start the ball rolling by her independent declaration of war.[29]

It would be interesting to determine how far the policy toward Serbia, outlined in the last paragraph of the above telegram, was followed. When Kolushev left for Sofia, the Serbian minister at Cetinje told his German colleague that Montenegro was probably sounding for common action. She had made a similar move in Belgrade but had been refused. Bogičević told Kiderlen the same.[30] Whatever was the reception of these early Montenegrin advances, Serbia willingly accepted King Nikita's offer for an alliance, made on September 21, 1912.[31] In order to avoid suspicion it was decided to conclude the negotiations in Switzerland, and on September 23/October 6, 1912 a formal treaty of alliance was signed.[32]

The treaty, consisting of a political section and a military convention, was to last for three years and was ratified on October 2/15, 1912. According to Bourchier the treaty had among its provisions a stipulation for separate military action, joint occupation of any Turkish town or village by Serbian and Montenegrin troops being forbidden.[33] The complete treaty has never been published, but indications are that it resembled to a great extent the Serbian-Bulgarian treaty. Not only was it

[28] K.A., XV, no. 12 (*Berl. Mon.*, VIII, 973–4); see also Benckendorff, II, no. 683.

[29] *Doklad*, I, 193; Toshev, I, 400; conversation with Danev, May, 1930.

[30] G.P., XXXIII, no. 12107. Montenegrin advances to Serbia were reported by the Russian minister at Belgrade on July 30th and August 13, 1912 (S.D., II, 592).

[31] Toshev, I, 383.

[32] Bourchier in London *Times*, June 13, 1913. The writer was able to verify the existence of the treaty in the treaty register at the Serbian archives in Belgrade. He was, however, unsuccessful in his attempts to obtain a copy of the document or any summary of its content. It is to be included in the forthcoming publication of the Serbian documents.

[33] London *Times*, June 13, 1913.

directed against Turkey, but also against Austria. The first article of the military convention stated, "In case of war with Austria-Hungary, Serbia and Montenegro will adopt a system of defensive tactics which does not exclude in certain directions and at favorable moments strategical offensive measures." [34] There appears to have been a territorial arrangement in regard to the partition of the Sanjak, certain regions being declared disputable and their allotment being reserved for the arbitration of one of the other Balkan rulers.[35] Whether there was a provision that Montenegro should start the war first, which would correspond to that portion of the Montenegrin-Bulgarian agreement, it is impossible to say. In any case, by the time the treaty was signed, the Montenegrin chargé at Constantinople had already in his hands the declaration of war.[36]

With the Montenegrin agreements the Balkan bloc was completed. Formal alliances existed between Bulgaria and Serbia, Bulgaria and Greece, Serbia and Montenegro, and a verbal agreement equal to alliance between Bulgaria and Montenegro. Greece also probably had some oral agreements with Montenegro [37] and Serbia, but her only definite alliance was with Bulgaria. The hub of the whole was Sofia, and as the hub turns, so turns the wheel. Sofia pressed for a war with Turkey.

[34] Lettre de M. Pierre Plamenatz, ancien Ministre des Affaires étrangères du Montenegro à M.M. . . , Londres, 23 mai, 1917, S.D., II, no. 977. Plamenatz was one of the men who negotiated the agreement (*Doklad*, I, 202). The amount of subsidy Serbia was to pay Montenegro was probably also a part of the military convention.

[35] "The Balkan League," *The Fortnightly Review*, XCIX (1913), 438.

[36] See below, p. 140.

[37] The Bulgarian minister at Cetinje reported that Montenegro had no agreements with Greece (Kolushev to Gueshov, Sept. 19, 1912, *Doklad*, I, 201 [no. 18]). On October 10, 1912 the British minister at Sofia reported to Grey: "Neither Bulgaria, Serbia, or Greece has yet signed any treaty with Montenegro, but it is understood that they will support Montenegrin claims, either to territorial aggrandisement or to monetary indemnity, at the conclusion of the war" (B.D., IX, ii, 1018). The French minister at Athens reported the existence of oral agreements only between Greece and Montenegro (Deville to Poincaré, Nov. 5, 1912, D.D.F., 3d. ser., IV, no. 360). Mr. Gibbons states that a defensive arrangement without a written treaty was made between Montenegro and Greece in June, 1912 (*Venizelos*, p. 115). No other evidence of importance has been found on the Greek-Montenegrin agreements.

CHAPTER V

THE SITUATION IN TURKEY

WHILE anti-Turkish movements were developing in the Christian Balkan states, affairs were not running smoothly in Turkey. The Young Turks had clearly not lived up to the promises which heralded their advent to power in July, 1908. The Committee of Union and Progress [1] was only definitely in control after the suppression of a counter-revolutionary coup and the deposition of Abdul Hamid in April, 1909. It was not without opposition and even within the Committee itself there were divisions and factions.[2] The failure of the new government to carry out any adequate reforms, its insistence on an ultra-nationalistic Turkish policy at the expense of non-Turkish elements, and above all its refusal to institute any form of decentralised administration, led to revolt and insurrection in all parts of the Empire. Albania, Yemen, Syria, Armenia, Macedonia, and even Constantinople and Turkey proper seethed with unrest and agitation. But in no section of the Empire was the situation more acute than in Albania.

Turkey's whole Albanian policy was impeded and complicated by the perpetual boundary disputes with Montenegro.

> The frontiers drawn by the Treaty of Berlin were so impossible that in many places they could not be defined, much less enforced. As the borderers themselves described it, "The frontier floated in blood." . . . Solid Albanian districts, which hated all things Slav, were handed over

[1] The Young Turks were the liberals, the party of reform, who were opposed to the policy of the conservatives or Old Turks. Many of them were driven into exile during the despotism of Abdul Hamid (1876–1909). Apparently it was in 1891 that a group of these exiles in Geneva formed themselves into a committee known as Union and Progress. They later moved their headquarters to Paris, and finally in 1906 to Salonica (Sir Harry Luke, *The Making of Modern Turkey* [London, 1936], pp. 145–6; see also, E. G. Mears, *Modern Turkey*, [New York, 1924], ch. XXI; Lamouche, *Histoire balkanique*, pp. 65–6).

[2] André Mandelstam, *Le sort de l'empire ottoman* (Paris, 1912), pp. 34 ff.; Izzet Pascha, *Denkwürdigkeiten* (Leipzig, 1927), p. 119.

to Montenegro, and solid Slav districts, which asked nothing better than to be Montenegrin or Serb, were handed over to the Turkish Empire. Worse, if possible, tribes and groups of tribes were divided and this, in a tribal land, should be avoided at almost any price. Debatable tracts were strewn all along the Montenegrin frontier.[3]

One of the chief centers of discontent was the territory of Rjanitza. This had been granted to Montenegro by the Treaty of Berlin, but the Albanians had opposed its cession so strenuously that it was traded for the territory of Dulcigno in 1880.[4] Now Montenegro was ready to cede small bits of territory centering in Yezero and Djamia in order to gain back Rjanitza. In fact a settlement to this effect had been agreed upon by a mixed commission in 1908, but Turkey had failed to take steps to ratify it.[5] In 1911 another commission met, but the results were nil.[6]

By this time the tribes of Northern Albania had become thoroughly disgusted with the Young Turk régime, and were ready for insurrection. For years the Albanians had been one of the chief props of the Turkish rule in Europe. "The Albanians kept the Ottoman Empire going until the revolution of 1908, because to the Albanians the unregenerate régime of Abdul Hamid meant license to plunder in Macedonia, liberal pay in Constantinople, and a *laisser faire* policy in Albania." [7] But all this changed with Abdul Hamid's abdication. The policy of disarming all Albanians, which the Young Turks had inaugurated in 1910, and the failure to pay the promised indemnity, aroused the opposition of the Albanians. Non-recognition of Albanian nationality, spending of money raised by Albanian taxes outside of Albania, failure to build roads, bridges, hospitals, schools, etc., employment of non-Albanians as officials in Albania, sending Albanian troops to serve in Asia Minor, un-

[3] M. E. Durham, *The Struggle for Scutari* (London, 1914), pp. 159–60; see also an interesting corroboration of Miss Durham's statement in Giesl's report to Berchtold, Oct. 1, 1912, Ö-U.A., III, no. 3895.

[4] Ö-U.K.A., Evidenzbureau, Montenegro 1912 B. no. 520; Sir Edward Hertslet, *The Map of Europe by Treaty* (4 vols.; London, 1875, 1891), IV, 2952–61; 2997–3034.

[5] Ö-U.A., IV, no. 3677 Beilage.

[6] *Ibid.*

[7] Diplomatist, p. 95.

just political imprisonment, punishment by flogging, were only some of the grievances which the Albanians nursed against the government at Constantinople.[8] It was a fertile field for propaganda and Montenegro did what she could to help the discontent along. She supplied the Albanians with guns, money, and promises of aid.[9] It was hoped that when the proper moment came, the revolting tribes out of a sense of gratitude would favor annexation to the realm of King Nikita. In 1910 Nikita had become king; what he needed next was a kingdom, and so he resorted to the policy of fishing in troubled waters.

Even before the Albanian revolt of 1911 got under way many Malissori fled across the Montenegrin frontier and soon the problem of Albanian refugees became an embarrassing one to Montenegro. It became even more so when Turkish successes caused the remaining tribesmen to call upon Montenegro for promised aid. Having said "A" would King Nikita say "B"? Using the pressure of emigrants as a pretext, he attempted to obtain some sort of a mandate from Europe to act as pacifier.[10] The powers, however, would not have this and continually warned him against an active policy.[11] They definitely refused Nikita's request that Montenegro be guaranteed against an attack by Turkey. On the other hand, Russia and Austria especially let the Porte know that they thought the Albanian question needed more real attention.[12]

Finally, in the first days of July, 1911, the Turkish govern-

[8] J. Swire, *Albania, The Rise of a Kingdom* (London, 1929), pp. 105–6; Schulthess, 1912, p. 454.

[9] Durham, *Struggle for Scutari*, pp. 41–136; Durham, *Balkan Tangle*, pp. 217 ff.; Giesl, *Zwei Jahrzehnte*, p. 223. For Montenegro's relation to the Albanian tribes in 1910 see, Ö-U.A., II, nos. 2197, 2209, 2210.

[10] Giesl, *Zwei Jahrzehnte*, p. 223.

[11] *Ibid.*; notes of the powers of April 6th and June 17, 1911, Schulthess, 1911, pp. 531–2; Ö-U.A., III, no. 2568. Russia particularly took a very pronounced stand and even forced the resignation of the bellicose Montenegrin war minister, Martinović (Schulthess, 1911, p. 532). In regard to the tension between Montenegro and Russia at this period see Giesl's reports (Ö-U.A., III, nos. 2569, 2580, 2592).

[12] See Russian note of May 23rd, Schulthess, 1911, p. 509; B.D., IX, i, nos. 473, 474. For Austrian warnings see Ö-U.A., II, nos. 2209, 2219, 2479; B.D., IX, i, nos. 476, 477.

ment took a definite stand and threatened Cetinje because of the help that was coming to the recalcitrant Albanians from across the borders. Montenegrin support of the uprising was no secret, and King Nikita boasted that he could bring the revolt to an end within twenty-four hours.[13] With the powers unwilling to support him and with no allies, King Nikita, however, could do nothing but give in to Turkey. After obtaining some minor concessions in behalf of the revolting Albanians he advised the latter to return to their homes. The cost of housing the refugees had become very burdensome and "this financial strain was apparently accentuated by the refusal of Russia to pay, pending the crisis, her usual subsidy to Montenegro."[14] Left to their fate, since the great powers even refused to guarantee the Turkish amnesty, the tribes reluctantly accepted the settlement offered them by the emissaries of the Porte.[15]

They were far from being satisfied. A host of grievances remained and Montenegro was not slow to take advantage of this discontent.

> Her policy was now to consolidate her position as the friend of the Malissori whose districts she hoped to annex, but not to precipitate war until the political situation was such that her troops could follow them to Skutari: in other words, until she was sure of the support of the Balkan States or of Russia, who had failed her in the previous year. She therefore carried on vigorous propaganda against the Turks, denounced the devastation they had wrought, although she subsequently excelled them in barbarity, and even succeeded in creating a dispute over the terms by which the Malissori had been induced to cease hostilities, by producing a faked copy of the agreement.[16]

With the outbreak of the Tripolitan War, the internal political situation in Turkey was not improved. The cabinet of Said

[13] Akers-Douglas to Grey, July 8, 1911, B.D., IX, i, no. 506.

[14] Lowther's annual report on Turkey for the year 1911, B.D., IX, i, no. 524.

[15] The Turkish offer of amnesty to the Albanians and the demands of the Albanians are to be found in B.D., IX, i, 475, 482–3. Miss M. E. Durham, the great friend of the Albanians, played an important part in bringing the Malissori to accept the offered terms and return to their homes (*Struggle for Scutari*, pp. 72 ff.). For Austrian and Italian influence at this time on the Albanians see, Giesl, *Zwei Jahrzehnte*, p. 223.

[16] Swire, *Albania*, pp. 111–2.

Pasha replaced that of Hakki Pasha,[17] and then on January 18, 1912, the sultan, with the consent of the Senate, dissolved the Chamber since it refused to sanction a proposed change in the constitution. This change would have given the Porte the unrestricted right to dissolve parliament in time of war.[18] A new election was held, in which, thanks to the coercion of the government, the Committee of Union and Progress obtained 215 out of 222 seats. "The only really representative institution now left was the army, and the army had been alienated by the failure to prepare against the Italian raid, and by the wasting on civil war with Arab and Albanian Moslems the resources that might have been kept to quell the Christian Balkan states." [19]

The arbitrary measures employed during the election caused hard feeling throughout Macedonia and Albania.[20] They added a few more straws to the already heavy load of grievances which were driving the Albanians to revolt. In spite of the Reform Commission which Constantinople sent out to investigate matters,[21] a general uprising took place during the summer, the Moslems of Kossovo leading off. As usual the government ordered the military to the fore. But this time insurrection broke out among the troops sent to restore peace. The garrisons at Monastir led the way and were soon followed by others.[22] The mutinies, which were a definite protest against the government of the Committee and were organised by the opposition, resulted in a law which provided for the dismissal and imprisonment for from two to four months of any army officer who should take part in a political meeting; should he be a member of a political party the prison term was increased two months.[23] In spite of this the officers formed a military league, modestly named "Saviors of the Nation," and demanded among other

[17] October 4, 1911 (Schulthess, 1911, p. 514).

[18] Schulthess, 1912, p. 441.

[19] Diplomatist, pp. 174–5.

[20] Izzet Pascha, *Denkwürdigkeiten*, p. 141; Général M. Moukhtar Pacha, *La Turquie, l'Allemagne et l'Europe, depuis le traité de Berlin jusqu'à la guerre mondiale* (Paris, 1924), p. 159.

[21] Constituted Feb. 13, 1912 (Schulthess, 1912, p. 442).

[22] *Ibid.*, p. 449; G. P., XXXIII, nos. 12060, 12061, 12064.

[23] Schulthess, 1912, p. 449.

things the resignation of the government.[24] The packed chamber resulting from the recent elections did Said Pasha little good in the face of such unconstitutional yet powerful opposition, and he was forced to give way.

On July 23rd, the new ministry under the leadership of the venerable Ghasi Ahmed Muktar Pasha came to power.[25] Most of the ministers were opponents of the Committee, although several were neutral and one or two were supporters of the displaced régime. One might be tempted to call it a coalition government, but in reality it was not, and the leaders of the Committee entered upon the rôle of opposition. Their very active and bitter agitation against the party in power, coupled with the influence which they were able to exercise upon it through their friends in the cabinet, without assuming any responsibility themselves, contributed much to the impotence of the government.

The new cabinet had come to power with the definite tasks of making peace with the Albanians as well as with Italy, purging the army of sedition, recouping finances, and also taking steps to meet possible aggression by the Balkan states.[26] It was clear from the outset that there could be no coöperation with the chamber which had been backed by the Committee, and so new elections were ordered.[27] The fight between the Committee of Union and Progress and the ministry for the control of the new assembly was on. Everything the cabinet did was severely criticised by the opposition. The Turkish government became completely subject to inner political strife and bickering at a time when trouble threatened in all parts of the Empire.[28] The

[24] *Ibid.*, p. 451; Mandelstam, *L'empire ottoman*, pp. 41 ff.

[25] The former senator Gabriel Effendi Noradounghian became minister of foreign affairs. For a list of the members of the cabinet see Schulthess, 1912, p. 451.

[26] Moukhtar Pacha, *La Turquie*, p. 159; D.D.F., 3d. ser., III, no. 225; Schulthess, 1912, p. 453. By this time the Turkish officials certainly knew of the existence of the Balkan alliances (S.D., I, 173; Ö-U.A., IV, no. 3852).

[27] The dissolution took place on August 5th, and the new elections were set for October 14, 1912 (Schulthess, 1912, p. 454).

[28] D. Iancovici, *Essai sur la crise balkanique 1912–13* (Paris, 1916), p. 92; Ahmed Emin, *The Development of Modern Turkey as Measured by its Press*

powers, especially England, felt they could not bring any pressure at Constantinople since "such a representation would weaken the present Turkish government by giving a weapon to the Committee and reactionaries which is just what we want to avoid." [29]

To surrender Tripoli, which was the only way to obtain peace from Italy, would have discredited the new ministry to begin with. Consequently, although they continued the peace negotiations which had been started, they permitted the war to drag on.[30] The Albanian trouble, which had really brought them to power, they were obliged to face at once. Montenegro had supported the Albanian revolt in 1912, just as she had done in 1911.[31] Montenegrin-Turkish border conflicts had started anew in the spring of 1912. Largely owing to the initiative of Russia, the third boundary commission in a period of four years was called together to settle matters.[32] Without even visiting the territory itself, but confining its labors to a study of maps in Cetinje, the commission came to an agreement.[33] Turkey again refused to ratify the results, since this might arouse all Albanians

---

(New York, 1914), p. 107; André Mary-Rousselière, *La Turquie constitutionnelle* (Rennes, 1925), pp. 113–116; G.P., XXXIII, nos. 12076, 12142; Mandelstam, *L'empire ottoman*, p. 144; see also the many changes in the cabinet which can be followed in Schulthess and in *Politische Chronik der Österreichisch-Ungarischen Monarchie*, ed. Karl Neisser (Vienna, 1910– ; hereafter cited as *Politische Chronik*), 1912, p. 339.

[29] Minute by H. Norman, Sept. 19, 1912, B.D., IX, i, 693.

[30] See G.P., XXX, ii, ch. CCXXXIX.

[31] The Turks thought Austria was behind the Albanian revolt (G.P., XXXIII, no. 12142; Izzet Pascha, *Denkwürdigkeiten*, p. 110). The Austrian documents show this not to have been the case (see especially Ö-U.A., V, no. 5701). The Austrians on the other hand thought Italy was probably aiding the Albanians (Ö-U.K.A. Evidenzbureau, Türkei T. no. 314, May 15, 1912; Ö-U.A., V, no. 5725; Leopold Freiherrn von Chlumecky, *Die Agonie des Dreibundes* (Vienna, 1915), p. 293). Italy's participation also appears unlikely, although little reliable material is at hand in regard to her actions. Most outside encouragement for the revolt came from Serbia and Montenegro (Benckendorff, II, nos. 607, 669; Ö-U.A., IV, nos. 3673 Beilage, 3680). The Bulgarian government, inasmuch as it encouraged Montenegro, must also be considered as being involved (S.D., II, no. 610).

[32] Ö-U.K.A., Evidenzbureau, Montenegro 1912 B. no. 520; Schulthess, 1912, p. 444.

[33] Durham, *Struggle for Scutari*, p. 160.

to revolt, as it would surrender some Albanian tribes which until then had remained loyal.[34] There was some truth in the statement, for the Albanian tribesmen did not wish to be placed under Montenegrin rule. Yet even when the Albanians were in full revolt in July, 1912, Turkey failed to ratify the agreement.[35] As was so often the case, the Turkish statesmen were long on promises but short on action.

In the beginning of August a virtual Montenegrin-Turkish battle took place at Mojkovać.[36] On the fifth of that month the Turkish minister presented a protest at Cetinje threatening to depart if no favorable answer was obtained.[37] His threat of the rupture of diplomatic relations was apparently made on his own initiative, for the government at Constantinople later disavowed him and ordered him to remain even after Montenegro had given what was admittedly an unsatisfactory reply. The minister, nevertheless, handed in his resignation and departed, leaving the legation in other hands.[38] Yielding to the pressure of the powers to moderate her action, Montenegro, on August 10, 1912, addressed a note to the signatories of the Treaty of Berlin requesting that they undertake the settlement of the boundary difficulty. The note ended in what practically constituted an ultimatum, stating:

> In the rather unlikely event, that the natural desire of Montenegro to see the powers effectively intervene in this affair, should not succeed in being immediately realised, Montenegro would find herself

[34] Mutius from Constantinople, July 10, 1912, G.P., XXXIII, no. 12067.

[35] It was not until the end of September, 1912 that Turkey promised Montenegro that she would ratify the boundary protocol. But even then she failed to say when she would do this, and with this omission Giesl thought Montenegro was fully justified in not placing any confidence in the Turkish promise (Ö-U.A., IV, no. 3895).

[36] G.P., XXXIII, no. 12079; B.D., IX, i, no. 604. The battle is well described by Miss Durham, *Struggle for Scutari*, pp. 161–2.

[37] G.P., XXXIII, no. 12080; D.D.F., 3d. ser., III, no. 245. Previously the Turkish government had attempted through the "requested" purchase of the summer residence of the Montenegrin legation on the Bosporus to win over King Nikita. The king having mislaid the deeds, the Turkish government stated that it by no means insisted on the transfer of these and made a large down payment. Such bribery had little effect (Ö-U.A., IV, no. 3666).

[38] G.P., XXXIII, no. 12081.

necessitated by the force of circumstances to defend her cause, whatever sacrifices it might cost.[39]

The powers as ever extolled the virtues of peace, but none took the occasion to answer the note sent by Montenegro.[40] They were all ready to advise, but none was ready to undertake any real steps towards solving the problem. Indeed, prudence seemed to warn, "Hands off! — or you will burn your fingers." That there was just cause for the hesitancy of the powers is shown by the following summary by the German ambassador to the Porte:

> As long as the Committee as successor of Abdul Hamid ruled autocratically and without opposition, a common warning of the powers might have been given some consideration. Today two parties of almost equal strength stand opposed, carefully and suspiciously watching each other. Any kind of a concession of the government in regard to an attempt of the powers to intervene would become a weapon in the hands of the opposition, for the army, i.e. the officers corps, which, as the supreme power, controls the political life, would immediately forsake the government and join the opposition.[41]

The descent of the Albanians, led by Isa Boletin, on Usküb, in August, 1912 brought the climax, if it did not completely end the revolt. The Turkish government now made concessions to the Albanians which seemed to indicate a future policy of decentralisation. The settlement virtually established autonomy for the Albanian vilayets of Scutari, Kossovo, Janina, and Monastir and was generally accepted among the Albanian tribes.[42] But some demands remained unfulfilled, and the old alliance between Turks and Albanians, which had been so valuable in all former wars, was not restored.

Such decentralisation was the antithesis of the political philosophy of the Young Turks who were strong advocates of a

[39] Ö-U.A., IV, no. 3677 Beilage.

[40] Nikita was probably not sorry for this omission, although he did voice his disapproval of this neglect and in justifying his declaration of war it played an important rôle (Ö-U.A., IV, nos. 3798, 3895, 3998; G.P., XXXIII, no. 12145).

[41] Wangenheim to Bethmann Hollweg, Sept. 8, 1912, G.P., XXXIII, no. 12142.

[42] Swire, *Albania*, pp. 123–4, 132.

centralised state. It provided one more issue for the political wrangle which was going on at Constantinople. Internal political strife increased. The opposition concentrated its efforts on winning over the army.[43] Nazim Pasha, the new war minister, on the other hand started at once to purge the Turkish forces of unreliable elements. Various changes in the personnel of the most important commands were made.[44] In the Macedonian garrisons those troops which had completed their last year of active service and the reserves that had been called to the colors were dismissed.[45] It is true that unrest and sedition were widespread among them, but even so, such a weakening of personnel was hardly advisable. Discipline was not restored by these measures, and the new recruits as they were slowly called in, joined thoroughly disorganised units. The result was that when mobilisation took place, there were around 50,000 quite untrained recruits and reservists in the army.[46] That the plan of campaign worked out by the chief of staff, Izzet Pasha, and approved by von der Goltz, was not followed when hostilities broke out, was also largely the result of the new appointments in the officers' corps which had been brought about by the political strife.[47]

The total unpreparedness of the army was evident and the Turkish leaders were aware of it. Even after mobilisation for the Balkan War had begun, according to the reports of the

[43] "Two leaders of the Committee have recently journeyed to Adrianople with 140,000 Turkish pounds . . . in order to bring that garrison to oppose the government" (Wangenheim to the foreign office, Aug. 1, 1912, G.P., XXXIII, no. 12076).

[44] Bericht K. & K. Majors Felix Wagner über Eindrücke von der Cataldja Armee, Ö-U.K.A., Evidenzbureau, Res. no. 3428 ex 1912.

[45] *Ibid.*; Izzet Pascha, *Denkwürdigkeiten*, p. 142; Ö-U.A., V, no. 4754.

[46] Report of Pomiankowski on, "Innerer Wert der türkischen Armee," Ö-U.K.A., ad Res. no. 454 ex 1912, Oct. 20, 1912. Pomiankowski stresses the fact that from 1908–1912 there had not been enough time for the German instruction to have any effect. The older and higher grades of officers are roundly condemned. (See also G.P., XXXIII, no. 12364; Ö-U.A., V, no. 4754.

[47] Izzet Pascha, *Denkwürdigkeiten*, pp. 172, 187, 219; Ö-U.A., V, no. 4574. The Balkan statesmen were of course long fully aware of this total disorganisation of the Turkish army and of the jealousies within the officer corps (B.D., IX, i, no. 516).

Austrian military attaché, the officers were far from optimistic in regard to victory.[48] "At the Sublime Porte," according to Muktar Pasha, "one was persuaded, with the exception perhaps of minister of war Nazim Pasha, that an armed conflict with the Balkan states could have only disastrous results for Turkey." [49] Izzet Pasha, who since February, 1911 had been kept out of the way by being dispatched to subdue the insurrection in Yemen, was absolutely opposed to undertaking a war. In his memoirs he writes:

> How does it come that the competent, well-meaning, and upright men who were members of the cabinet did not take steps relative to the approaching danger? Until this day I have not been able to explain this omission. In any case it is an indisputable fact that they rejected all really decisive efforts which might have avoided war.[50]

The answer to his question is to be found in the bitter political dissension in Turkey. It checkmated any real policy, and many officials were foolish enough to believe that the problem might be solved by undertaking a war.[51] The German ambassador, who was exerting himself to the utmost to bring about peace between Italy and Turkey, described the political situation in Turkey as follows:

> The inclination of the cabinet, influenced by Kiamil Pasha, to bow to the Balkan states and to the wishes of the great powers in the question of Macedonian reform, resulted in a counter-thrust by the army

[48] "Die Armeeleitung jedoch scheint die Lage nicht sehr optimistisch zu beurteilen und wenigstens für den Anfang des Krieges eine sehr schwierige Lage der ottomanischen Armeen vorauszusehen" (Ö-U.K.A., Res. no. 414, ex 1912, October 8, 1912). "Speziell in der Armee sind nicht alle Mannschaft und Offizierkorps siegesgewiss. . . ." (Ö-U.K.A., Res. no. 446, ex. 1912, October 19, 1912).

[49] Mouktar Pacha, *La Turquie*, pp. 169, 175. Moukhtar was the son of the grand vizier and was minister of marine.

[50] Izzet Pascha, *Denkwürdigkeiten*, p. 145; see also pp. 184–5.

[51] "In Beamtenkreisen erwartet man von Krieg Klärung der verworrenen äusseren und inneren Lage" (Wangenheim to foreign office, Sept. 27, 1912, G.P., XXXIII, no. 12171). On strife within the cabinet see, B.D., IX, i, nos. 696, 785; for the effect of this political strife on the army see, Lieutenant-Colonel Tyrrell to Sir G. Lowther, Jan. 28, 1913, B.D., IX, ii, no. 571 enclosure. In regard to the bellicose spirit of the Young Turks see also, Izzet Pascha, *Denkwürdigkeiten*, pp. 146–7, 219; Moukhtar Pacha, *La Turquie*, pp. 170 ff; G.P., XXX, ii, no. 11191, XXXIII, nos. 12241, 12242.

and the Unionists. They charged the government with cowardliness and treason to the fatherland. Cowed by street demonstrations, the grand vizier promised that he would not draw back from the war with the Balkan states. The first consequence of the victory of the nationalistic movement was the fear of the cabinet that the conditions of peace with Italy, which they had agreed to, might be turned into a noose for themselves. While the excited mob in the streets called for war, the ministerial council revised the peace formula which had been agreed upon with Nogara [the Italian peace delegate].[52]

That the Committee of Union and Progress pursued a bellicose policy, continually forcing the hand of the government, is clear. "A Diplomatist," writing in 1914, sharply but on the whole justly summarised the situation, when he wrote:

Moreover, although unable, or unwilling, to turn the government out and take their place, the Committee kept it disorganised and distracted by constant ministerial changes due to their intrigues. The situation might be summed up by saying that the peace party in control at the capital was completely checkmated and counteracted by the war party in control in Salonica. As exponents of the belligerent policy of the Macedo-Moslem minority, and fully exploiting the advantage of being the only organised political party, the Committee could pursue their policy of action with greater effect out of office than when hampered by the responsibilities of the Imperial Government, and they used their power relentlessly and unremittingly for forcing the country into war. The Empire, as a whole, did not want to fight the Balkan states for the privileged supremacy of the Macedo-Moslem over the Albanian and the Macedonian. But the Macedo-Moslem intended to fight for that supremacy and to use the whole forces of the Empire in that fight.[53]

If there was a war party in Turkey the same was true for the Balkan states. As has been pointed out there was the Macedonian Revolutionary Organisation with its aim of Macedonian autonomy and its pro-Bulgarian policy; there was the Black Hand with its desire to acquire territory for Serbia; there was the Cretan movement which complicated Greek-Turkish relations in Macedonia and pushed Greece into the alliance with

[52] Wangenheim to Bethmann Hollweg, Oct. 21, 1912, G.P., XXX, ii, no. 11215.
[53] Diplomatist, p. 178.

Bulgaria; there was also the Albanian nationalistic policy; and last, but not least, there were the ambitions of the Montenegrins to expand the territory of their newly-created kingdom. In each case the governments were closely in touch with these movements, and to a great extent identified with them. By the formation of the Balkan League they had taken a most important step towards the liquidation of Turkish possessions in Europe. But much remained to be done before they could actually go about seizing this territory, and they quietly set about to prepare for that eventful day.

CHAPTER VI

THE PREFACE TO MOBILISATION

THE summer of 1912 was a period of preparation. While keeping close watch on events in Turkey, the governments of the Balkan states undertook measures to strengthen their armed forces and to obtain a war chest.[1] But if they prepared for war, they acted as if they desired peace. The policy which they pursued is well illustrated by the following report from Spalaiković, the Serbian minister at Sofia:

Yesterday Gueshov explained to me in detail his views of the present situation, and the most advantageous policy for Serbia and Bulgaria to follow. According to his opinion one cannot think of any kind of action until autumn. Nothing must be done which might involve Serbia and Bulgaria in a premature action, or cause Turkey to conclude peace with Italy before we are ready. King Ferdinand and the Bulgarian government are determined not to undertake any action until autumn, on account of the internal situation in Russia, which, at the present moment, is extremely unfavorable for an action of the Balkan states against Turkey. Russia is on the eve of the duma elections which are to be held in September of this year, and until they are over with, nothing must happen which might call forth external complications. Danev, Gueshov, King Ferdinand have all been so informed, and Guchkov on his recent visit gave the same advice.

It will therefore be very welcome to Gueshov if the open conflict between the Young Turks and the present ministry should not break out at this time, if the situation in Albania should remain latent, and if the Turkish-Montenegrin conflicts should have no serious conse-

[1] Special mention should be made of the loan which Bulgaria negotiated in Paris through the good offices of Russia (Izvolsky, II, nos. 280, 283, 317, 346; D.D.F., 3d. ser., II, nos. 318, 320). In July a more or less private loan was made by the Russian ministry of the imperial household to King Ferdinand, this loan having been requested several months earlier by the Bulgarian sovereign (S.D., II, nos. 549, 591, 659). Towards the end of August, 1912 the French government, on account of the bellicose attitude of Sofia, stopped the floating of the Bulgarian loan on the French market. However, it was like locking the barn after the horse is stolen; it came too late (D.D.F., 3d. ser., II, nos. 338, 368, 471; Izvolsky, II, no. 429).

quences. The recent bomb affair at Kotchana was a very unpleasant surprise to him.[2] First, because the Bulgarian element had suffered, secondly, and most important, because this event might have unwelcome effects on his plans. Consequently he restricted himself to a single protest and influenced the newspapers to temper their anti-Turkish tirades. Desiring to mask the intentions of Bulgaria as long as possible he was afraid the eyes of the Turks would be opened and the true aims of Bulgaria be disclosed to them.

Nekludov's alarm telegram [3] which the Russian foreign office communicated to Germany, and also the declaration of Bogičević in Berlin,[4] were very unwelcome to him. The Germans immediately used these communications to influence Turkey to conclude peace with Italy, pointing out to the Turkish government the danger which threatened from the Balkan states if the war lasted any longer.[5]

In order to allay Turkey's fears, King Ferdinand has been living abroad and he will leave again immediately after the jubilee.[6] This shows how anxious the present Bulgarian government is to lull the suspicions of Turkey.

Neratov [assistant to Sazonov] has already twice drawn the attention of the Bulgarian statesmen to the necessity of maintaining a peaceful attitude at the present moment. Gueshov hopes that by autumn Italy will decide on some kind of common combination, something he is continually trying to bring about.[7]

[2] On July 31, 1912 Macedonian bands set off two bombs in the market place at Kotchana, provoking the Turkish officials to reprisals. This led to protests by the Bulgarian government (D.D.F., 3d. ser., III, nos. 246, 250, 255).

[3] Nekludov states in his memoirs: ". . . I concluded the telegram by expressing my deep rooted conviction that both on the Bulgarian and the Serbian side they were preparing for war and that they even intended to hasten events. 'Have you read Nekludoff's hysterical telegram?' the heads of departments and young secretaries of Sazonoff's set were continually asking each other. Alas! This telegram proved to be historical not hysterical" (*Reminiscences*, p. 96). The French and English representatives at Sofia thought Nekludov's estimate of the situation wrong (D.D.F., 3d. Ser., III, nos. 180, 198; Barclay to Grey, July 11, 1912, B.D., IX, i, no. 589). Nekludov himself later thought he had characterised the situation too pessimistically (G.P., XXXIII, no. 12069; D.D.F., 3d. ser., III, no. 198).

[4] Boghitchévitch, *Les causes de la guerre*, pp. 61–2; S.D., II, nos. 588, 589, 590.

[5] There is no evidence in the German documents that much was made of this argument in Constantinople at this time, although Germany was indeed trying to bring about the conclusion of peace between Turkey and Italy (G.P., XXX, ii, ch. ccxxxix).

[6] There were press attacks in Bulgaria at this time against the extended foreign vacations of the King (Ö-U.A., IV, no. 3706).

[7] The quotation is a paraphrase of S.D., I, no. 180. The report is dated July 17/30, 1912, but internal evidence shows that it should no doubt be July 30/August 12, 1912.

This interesting document shows clearly that Bulgaria was planning on war for the autumn. The reason for waiting is unique and is referred to in no other documents. If this counsel was really given by Russia and should be considered along with Russia's advice to maintain peace "in the present moment," the many warnings and protestations which Russia made in the Balkan capitals appear in a new light. The French minister at Sofia reported that Russia, after the conclusion of the Serbian-Bulgarian alliance, had given the two partners to understand that "peace and tranquillity ought to be maintained until the month of November." [8] With the lack of further substantiation however it seems unwise to pin too much on this phase of the document. The general description of Bulgarian policy is, nevertheless, sound. The German and Austrian ministers noted the careful stand taken by the Bulgarian government at the time of the Kotchana bomb outrages, and their general view was that the government was bent on a policy of peace.[9] The leaders in Sofia, however, knew full well in what direction they were steering, and they must be commended for their cleverness if they were able to convince the chancelleries of Europe that they were being reluctantly pushed on by agitated public opinion.

The importance of public opinion is of course not to be minimised, but the official Bulgarian government had a program, and that program was war. From the very start of the alliance negotiations, Sofia had never withheld this from Russia, and Nekludov reported continually that the Bulgarians were seeking

[8] Panafieu to Poincaré, Oct. 3, 1912, D.D.F., 3d. ser., IV, no. 39. Nelidov also told the Serbian chargé at St. Petersburg: "Aber der gegenwärtige Augenblick sei noch für keinerlei Aktionen geeignet. Dies habe er auch Herrn Daneff klar und offen zum Ausdrucke gebracht" (Tadić to foreign office, June 2, 1912, S.D., I, no. 174).

[9] Ö-U.A., IV, nos. 3746, 3747, see also nos. 3687, 3744; G.P., XXXIII, nos. 12110 note, 12185, 12225. This was also the attitude of the representative of the other powers (Ö-U.A., IV, nos. 3754, 3765, 3797, 3948; D.D.F., 3d. ser., III, nos. 180, 232, 321, 328, 349; B.D., IX, i, nos. 614, 615. On Aug. 18, 1912, John B. Jackson, the American minister to Bucharest and Sofia, reported: "The King and the present Bulgarian government are strongly in favor of maintaining peace. The Bulgarian public opinion . . . is in favor of an immediate war and there is talk of deposing the king if he 'does not do his duty'" (U. S. Embassy archives at Constantinople, Bulg. Series 106).

an active solution.[10] Kokovtsov, Russian minister-president, on September 25th honestly stated to the Austrian chargé that he thought the war would break out, that the allies would win, but that he did not believe in the forced position of the Bulgarian king or government. "The Bulgarians were very wise and very careful and appeared to be using this excuse as a pretext in order to seize the most opportune moment for the conquest of Macedonia." [11]

The programs of the other Balkan states were no different. Montenegro had of course long ago inscribed war on its banner. Serbia and Greece were perhaps more reticent in expressing their views but the very fact that they entered upon the treaties shows that they expected and anticipated a war with Turkey. Nor do their efforts to bring the Tripolitan War to Europe by offering their coöperation and service to Italy bespeak a pacifistic program.[12] In reality it became a question of determining when they were ready, and if Bulgaria forced the pace the others were not slow to follow. Serbia with her fear of Austria-Hungary, Greece with her uncompleted alliance negotiations might have desired to postpone events a bit more, but they did nothing to restrain Bulgaria which, as the most important and powerful state in the Balkans, took the lead.

One other item in Spalaiković's report deserves special notice. In July, 1912, Alexander Guchkov, former president of the Russian duma and leader of the Octobrists and at that time reporter of the military budget, made a circular tour of Constantinople, Sofia, Belgrade, Vienna. Ostensibly he was to assist at the inauguration of branch offices of one of the large Russian insurance companies; in reality he was out to sound the political

[10] Nekludoff, *Reminiscences*, pp. 55, 96; Gueshoff, p. 45.

[11] Ö-U.A., IV, no. 3847.

[12] Not very much is known about this aspect of Italian-Balkan relations. Giovanni Giolitti reports Venizelos' offer to join Italy (*Memoirs of My Life* [London, 1923], p. 356; see also, G.P., XXXIII, no. 12218 note). Montenegro had early proffered her aid (London *Times*, June 13, 1913, K.A., VIII, nos. 6, 7 [*Berl. Mon.*, VII, 705, 784]). Early in the spring the Serbians had taken diplomatic soundings at Rome (Toshev, I, 334). Gueshov worked on the plan throughout the summer (S.D., I, nos. 180, 182; also see above, p. 86, note no. 21).

terrain.[13] In Sofia as in Belgrade he was fêted by all the officials and held long conversations with them. The true state of affairs was not masked from him. He was informed straightway that Bulgaria expected to make war at the end of September, even if Russia would promise no aid and although Rumania might seize the Dobrudja. He was asked to convey this information to Sazonov and Kokovtsov, which he did. He then lost no time in spreading the tidings in various circles in St. Petersburg. In spite of the peaceful protestations of Paprikov, the Bulgarian minister, to whom he related the whole, Guchkov adhered to the certainty of the information which he had received in Sofia — war for the end of September.[14] Although Guchkov had stated in Sofia and Belgrade that no help might be expected from Russia, it appears that he was far from throwing cold water on any forward policy of the Balkan governments, and in fact encouraged them to proceed.[15]

Though Bulgaria did plan on war, Gueshov intended temporarily to adopt a policy of watchful waiting. The confidence inspired by him is illustrated by a minute written in August, 1912 at the British foreign office: "Gueshov's attitude is all that can be desired. So long as he remains at the helm peace will be preserved, but if he finds his position untenable and resigns, probably nothing can stop a Bulgarian attack on Turkey."[16] Gueshov's program received a rude shock when on August 13th Count Berchtold addressed a note to the powers.[17] Berchtold asked for an exchange of ideas as to encouraging the Turkish

[13] Nekludoff, *Reminiscences*, pp. 99–100.

[14] *Doklad*, I, 130. Eugene de Schelking, at that time special correspondent for a St. Petersburg daily, after visits in Belgrade and Sofia on July 24, 1912 sent a telegram to his paper predicting the opening of hostilities about the end of September (*Recollections of a Russian Diplomat* [New York, 1918], p. 188).

[15] This was confirmed to the writer in May 1930 by several Balkan statesmen who preferred not to be quoted. See also Nekludoff, *Reminiscences*, pp. 98 ff. On September 16, 1912 Szilassy protested to Sazonov over the extreme anti-Austrian article of *Glos Mosky*, the official organ of the Octobrists (Ö-U.A., IV, no. 3797). Kokovtsov himself later complained about the agitation of Guchkov (Ö-U.A., IV, no. 3867; G.P., XXXIII, no. 12258). Since the Balkan leaders relied so much on "unofficial Russia" (see below, pp. 154–6) the policy of Guchkov is important.

[16] B.D., IX, i, no. 597 minute.

[17] Ö-U.A., IV, no. 3687.

government in its newly adopted policy of decentralisation. He further suggested that the Balkan states might well be reminded that it would be in the interests of their co-nationals to grant the cabinet of Muktar Pasha time to work out administrative reforms. The recent administrative privileges which had been granted the Albanians, and the opposition which these measures had aroused in the Balkan states appeared to make such action advisable.

Berchtold's proposal at once caused alarm at Sofia as well as at the other Balkan capitals.[18] It was felt that the policy advocated in the note could only strengthen Turkey. The Balkan newspapers started a hue-and-cry against the Austrian project. Fearful that the autonomy which the Albanians had gained would only be detrimental to the other nationalities, the Balkan governments resolved to push ahead. King Nikita, still involved in his boundary disputes, took the initiative and renewed his invitation to King Ferdinand for active coöperation, expressing his willingness to set the ball rolling.[19] On August 26th, a Bulgarian crown council was held at Cham Kourya, and here the decision of the ministerial council to accept the offer of Montenegro was confirmed.[20] Empowered to conclude the agreement with Montenegro, Kolushev, the Bulgarian minister at Cetinje, returned at once to his post. It now remained to get in touch with the other allies and to make the final arrangements for the war. Greece had already on August 26th suggested a common protest to Turkey, under threat of war.[21] Now the governments at Athens and Belgrade accepted the decision of the Bulgarian crown council. War was under way.

The Bulgarian and Serbian chiefs of staff reconsidered their military convention. This time there was a clear difference of opinion as to where the principal theatre of war should be. The Bulgarians said the valley of the Maritza, the Serbians the val-

[18] *Ibid.*, IV, nos. 3712, 3728; G.P., XXXIII, no. 12110; Gueshoff, p. 49; Benckendorff, II, no. 670.

[19] *Doklad*, I, 193; Gueshoff, p. 50.

[20] Gueshoff, p. 50; B.D., IX, ii, no. 570 quoting from the *Mir* (Sofia) of Dec. 28, 1912.

[21] S.D., I, no. 183; D.D.F., 3d. ser., IV, nos. 347, 360.

ley of the Vardar.[22] It was an important point of difference so far as concentration of forces was concerned and led to further discussions. These culminated in an agreement of September 15/28, 1912, concluded at the very time when the decrees of mobilisation were being decided upon.[23] It embodied a compromise, the Bulgarians and Serbians agreeing each to concentrate a division in the region of Kyustendil-Dupnitza. At the same time the Bulgarians were negotiating their first military convention with Greece, which was not signed until September 22/October 5, 1912.[24]

The Serbian-Bulgarian treaty of alliance provided that when an agreement favorable to war had been reached it was to be communicated to Russia, and if the latter power was not opposed to it, military operations should begin as previously arranged.[25] This was the celebrated veto clause with which Sazonov hoped to control the destinies of the Balkan peninsula. He was now given an opportunity to see how much it was worth. About September 15th or 16th, he received very straightforward communications both from Nekludov at Sofia and from the Bulgarian minister at St. Petersburg.[26] Bulgaria desired to undertake a war with Turkey unless the powers could bring the Sultan to fulfill the Bulgarian demands in regard to the application of reforms under Article XXIII of the Treaty of Berlin. Sazonov became alarmed. He had always previously spoken of the Bulgarian government as being forced into a war and in general this continued to be his song. But this time he lapsed curiously and told the Austrian chargé that the Bulgarian minister had been pleading for war; that he had warned him as follows:

[22] Opinions of the representatives of the general staff drawn up at Belgrade September 5, 1912 (Gueshoff, p. 124).

[23] *Ibid.*, pp. 126–7. Should the Serbian army throw the Turks beyond the line of Usküb-Veles-Shtip, the Bulgarians might then move their divisions to the Maritza valley. This shows that the rapid sweeping victories which crowned the successes of the Balkan armies were not anticipated on the eve of mobilisation.

[24] See above, p. 77.

[25] Second paragraph of the secret annex to the Serbian-Bulgarian treaty of alliance (Gueshoff, p. 114).

[26] Izvolsky, II, no. 432; S.D., I, no. 197; Ö-U.A., IV, no. 3797.

"Oui, mais le jour après que vous aurez traversé la frontière turque, la paix sera faite entre la Porte et l'Italie et alors que ferez vous?" [27] At the same time he assured the German chargé that he had told Paprikov, "Je vous dis pour la 25ième fois que vous n'aurez pas à compter sur nous." [28]

Under the influence of the Bulgarian statement Sazonov again emphatically admonished each of the Balkan states to keep the peace, and sent out an appeal to the great powers for their co-operation in urging Turkey to undertake reforms.[29] To all of the Balkan governments he declared clearly that he declined all responsibility if war broke out, and in no case could they rely on support from Russia.[30] Montenegro was threatened with the cessation of subsidies should she continue in her agitation for war.[31] Bulgaria was warned of the conclusion of peace between Turkey and Italy, of the danger of a Rumanian attack, and of the likelihood of being deserted by her allies.[32]

[27] Szilassy to foreign office, Sept. 16, 1912, Ö-U.A., IV, no. 3797.

[28] Lucius to foreign office, Sept. 19, 1912, G.P., XXXIII, no. 12149.

[29] See below, pp. 120–22.

[30] Izvolsky, II, no. 432; S.D., I, no. 186; K.A., XV, no. 14 (*Berl. Mon.*, VIII, 1071–2); G.P., XXXIII, no. 12148; Ö-U.A., IV, nos. 3797, 3802, 3836.

[31] The subsidy granted by Russia to Montenegro was set at 600,000 rubles by the military agreement of 1910 between the two countries. These payments were stopped in the fall of 1912 because, "Montenegro declared war on Turkey and so had not fulfilled the chief obligation which Montenegro had assumed and which was the foundation of the military agreement between Russia and Montenegro" (*Die Internationalen Beziehungen im Zeitalter des Imperialismus. Dokumente aus den Archiven der Zarischen und Provisorischen Regierung*, published under the direction of the commission of the Central Executive Committee of the Soviet government; German ed. by Otto Hoetzch [Berlin, 1931–; hereafter cited as R.D.], 1 Reihe, I, no. 165; see also S.D., I, no. 249, II, no. 977; Ö-U.A., IV, no. 3836; D.D.F., 3d. ser., VIII, no. 109). In February and April, 1914 ministerial councils at St. Petersburg discussed resuming the payment of the subsidy (R.D., 1 Reihe, I, nos. 165, 180; II, no. 209). It was agreed to do so and the Montenegrin government was so informed. The whole question, however, became involved with the international loan to Montenegro and also with the projected plan (1914) of uniting Serbia and Montenegro (see below, p. 417). At the outbreak of the World War the subsidy payments, stopped in 1912, had not yet been resumed, and aid to Montenegro became a Triple Entente problem (R.D., 1 Reihe, II, nos. 69, 111, 118, 160, 195, 223, 329; III, nos. 65, 66, 73, 120, 397; IV, no. 36; V, nos. 150, 264; 2 Reihe, VII, i, no. 135).

[32] According to Venizelos' later statement he was on the point of proposing to the Porte "that in return for its nominal right of suzerainty and the payment of a small tribute it should recognise the right of Cretan deputies to take

The possibility of Rumanian intervention was something which faced both Bulgaria and Serbia. Gueshov during the summer had instructed the Bulgarian chargé to sound out Maiorescu as to the possibility of an agreement in case a Turkish catastrophe should occur. Maiorescu had declined to enter upon an exchange of views, ". . . contenting himself with a vague assurance that if matters reached a climax Bulgaria and Rumania could easily come to an agreement." [33]

Toward the end of August and during September, Bulgaria, without uncovering her future plans or making definite proposals, again broached the question; but Maiorescu's answer was the same.[34] He would make no promises one way or the other. Neither he nor Gueshov would commit themselves. That Rumania would insist on compensations should the *status quo* in Macedonia be broken was clear. But Bulgaria had a specific military understanding with Serbia as to Rumania [35] and could probably count on Russian support. Gueshov felt no need to expose his hand and guarantee to Rumania in advance a gift of Bulgarian territory. Turkey, it is interesting to note, also made advances to Rumania at this time, but likewise received a refusal.[36]

For Bulgaria, Russian aid had meant primarily holding Rumania in check; and now Russia declined her support. But this was not so bad after all, for it was only military aid which Russia withheld. In the spring of 1912, when Danev visited Russia, the Russian statesmen let it be known that they were opposed to war, but at the same time they promised diplomatic

---

their seats in the house." He was trying to avoid war since he "thought Greece had not been adequately prepared in the interval of two years since her regeneration. . . ." But the other states decided on war and "it was not permissible for us to remain passive spectators" (E. Venizelos, *The Vindication of Greek National Policy 1912–17* [London, 1918], p. 66).

[33] Gueshoff, p. 48; *Doklad*, I, 206; Kalinkov, *Romŭniya*, p. 94.

[34] *Doklad*, I, 212, 215; Kalinkov, *Romŭniya*, pp. 94 ff.; *Documents diplomatiques. Les événements de la péninsule balkanique; l'action de la Roumanie, septembre 1912–août 1913*, ed. by the ministry of foreign affairs (Bucharest, 1913; hereafter cited as *Rumanian Green Book*), no. 52.

[35] See above, p. 53.

[36] *Rumanian Green Book*, no. 1.

support, especially in regard to Rumania.[37] Then too there was the old Russian-Bulgarian convention of 1902, about the validity of which there might be some question, but which nevertheless was appealed to by both sides during the war.[38] There was always the possibility of a strong popular appeal to Russian public opinion, and the Balkan statesmen were counting on unofficial Russia, if events took a bad turn for the Slav cause. It might be noted here as a matter of fact that Russia did put herself out to prevent Rumania's participation in the first war. Not only was King Carol honored by being made field marshal at the very time of Balkan mobilisation, but Russia in other ways did all she could to keep Rumania quiet.[39]

Having received a declaration from Bulgaria to the effect that she would not undertake anything alone,[40] Sazonov now attempted to influence Serbia to withhold action. He used the same arguments which he had employed in Sofia, and in addition warned "that in case Serbia should attempt to coöperate with Bulgaria, Austria-Hungary would not lose the opportunity of occupying Serbian territory and Belgrade." [41] In such an eventuality Russia would leave Serbia to her fate. This was plain language and could hardly leave any doubt as to Russia's wishes. Hartwig in furthering the Serbian-Bulgarian alliance had always maintained that the Serbians would do as he said.[42] Would they do so this time? Or did Hartwig's view perhaps differ from that of the Russian foreign office? That he was not always a loyal interpreter of the wishes of St. Petersburg is hardly open to question. Whether this is one of the occasions when he misrepresented Russian policy to the Serbs, it is impos-

[37] Conversation with Danev, May, 1930; Gueshoff, p. 44.

[38] Helmreich and Black, *Journal of Modern History*, IX (1937), 471–83.

[39] Conversations in May, 1930 with Danev and in October, 1929 with Schebeko, Russian minister at Bucharest in 1912. In regard to the awarding of the field marshal staff see, K.A., XVI, no. 45 (*Berl. Mon.*, IX, 68); Ö-U.A., IV, nos. 4083, 4120. General Averescu interpreted it more as a warning than a bribe (Ö-U.K.A., Res. 98, Report of the military attaché at Bucharest, October 2, 1912).

[40] S.D., I, nos. 185, 197.

[41] *Ibid.*, I, nos. 185, 186; B.D., IX, i, nos. 732, 736, 737, 743.

[42] K.A., IX, no. 75 (*Berl. Mon.*, VIII, 571); Marco, "Hartwig" *Berliner Monatshefte*, VI (1928), 757; Nekludoff, *Reminiscences*, pp. 46, 107.

sible to say. In any case Serbia was too anxious to assure herself a portion in the liquidation of Turkey, to consider seriously any such desertion of the Balkan cause as Russia recommended. Yet the ever-present fear of an Austrian attack, heightened by this categorical declaration from St. Petersburg, urged a policy of caution. Clearly, more guarantees from Sofia were necessary.

In order to iron out all their difficulties Danev on September 21st had a secret meeting with Pašić on a railroad train between Lapovo and Nish.[43] Pašić expressed his fear of an Austrian invasion of the Sanjak and asked if they should really push it to war. Having gone thus far it seemed to Danev that they must go on. Besides he did not share Pašić's fear of an aggressive action on the part of Vienna.[44] He might well have been influenced by the assurances which Tarnowski, the Austrian minister at Sofia, had given him. The latter had stated that Austria-Hungary, although desiring the *status quo*, would hardly undertake to retard the evolution of a historical process, if the hour of fate again struck for Turkey.[45] Then too, Danev pointed out, the international political situation was such that the Dual Monarchy could hardly intervene. Should she do so with Italy still at war with Turkey, the Triple Alliance would be torn asunder. Surely the statesmen at Vienna would be careful to avoid such a step. Danev, however, did promise that if Austria moved, Bulgaria would send a definite number of troops to aid Serbia. Pašić returned to Belgrade satisfied that mobilisation might proceed.[46] His action in these days exemplifies a later characterisation of his political policy: ". . . He never brought about the events himself. He constantly awaited them, did

[43] Gueshoff, p. 51; Toshev, I, 381. Milovanović had died suddenly on July 1, 1912. (Rumors as to poison, Ö-U.A., IV, no. 3603). His cabinet was rearranged with Trifković as premier, who, however, was soon forced to resign. On September 12, 1912, Pašić became premier and minister of foreign affairs (*Politische Chronik, 1912*, pp. 312, 395). Although the meeting was supposedly secret, Russia knew of it immediately and Austria by September 30th (Marco, "Hartwig," *Berliner Monatshefte*, VI [1928], 756; Ö-U.A., IV, no. 3873).

[44] Conversation with Danev, May, 1930; see also Gueshoff, p. 51.

[45] Berchtold to Tarnowski, August 10, 1912, Ö-U.A., IV, no. 3678.

[46] Toshev, I, 381.

nothing either to slow them up or to hasten them, always waited and permitted time to carry out a part of his plan of action." [47]

On September 19th, Sazonov had issued his imperative warning to Belgrade. Three days later Popović, the Serbian minister at St. Petersburg, was assured by Neratov (then in charge of the foreign office) that although Serbia could not expect military aid, "she could again count [as in 1908] on Russia's diplomatic support, and that Russia was already negotiating with Austria-Hungary in order to keep her from undertaking an independent action." [48] Popović replied that no government in Serbia could withstand the popular demand for participation if Bulgaria declared war. "Besides," so Popović concluded, "it was a big question if in reality Russia would remain inactive and could quietly witness a South Slav catastrophe." On the same day Kokovtsov advised that the Balkan states should await the result of Sazonov's mission to England, France, and Germany; and that Russia under no circumstances would go to war. Rather would he resign as minister-president than sanction such a policy.[49] No comment is necessary to point out the discrepancies between the language of the two statesmen. With Russia negotiating to keep Austria out, how much did the threat of September 19th amount to?

We have no way of knowing just when this reassuring statement of Neratov reached Belgrade. For a few days Pašić still haggled over drawing up a mobilisation decree.[50] He maintained that if Austria-Hungary mobilised, all of Serbia's troops would have to be directed against her and none against Turkey. Bulgaria never accepted this arrangement. Finally Pašić agreed to

[47] Heinz Sasse, "Nicola Pašić," *Berliner Monatshefte*, XIV (1936), 41. See also, Jovanović, "Pašić," *Slavonic Review*, XV (1937), 370.

[48] Popović to foreign office, Sept. 22, 1913, S.D., I, no. 187; see also no. 189. In regard to Russia's refusal to grant military aid to Serbia if it were necessary, Popović reported: "Er [Neratov] sagte, dass er mit dem österreichisch-ungarischen Botschafter nicht so spreche, sondern nur mit mir."

[49] Popović to foreign office, Sept. 22, 1913, S.D., I, no. 188.

[50] This was probably due to Hartwig's advice not to rush matters (Benckendorff, II, no. 684).

mobilise, but stated that the future ultimatum would have to be couched in such terms that a conflict with Austria-Hungary or Rumania could be avoided, in case mobilisation brought about a threat of attack from these powers.[51] In the end the ultimatum presented at Constantinople was drawn up at Belgrade and was slightly amended by the Greek government.[52]

Montenegro had been prepared to start for some time. On September 17th she had been advised by Sofia to wait, since it would be "better for all concerned." [53] Montenegro then opened the negotiations noted above [54] for an alliance with Serbia, in the meantime assuring Bulgaria that she would wait for Bulgaria to set the day for the opening of hostilities.[55] On September 22nd, Turkey, in view of the alarming situation and the great inefficiency of her army due to the dismissal of reservists and active soldiers, prepared to call in 100,000 Redifs for maneuvers in Thrace.[56] The same day she issued a program of reforms for Macedonia.[57] On the 24th, several shipments of war materials which were being sent via Salonica to Serbia were stopped at Usküb. This of course brought a protest from Belgrade, and part of the shipments were freed.[58] The allies now started to prepare for large "maneuvers." Finally, on September 28th, it was definitely decided that public mobilisation should be ordered. After still more haggling as to the publication of the mobilisation decrees, the four powers simultaneously announced their mobilisation on September 30th–October 1st. What had secretly been going on for some time now became a legitimate above-board action.

While the Balkan states were thus so deliberately preparing for the opening of hostilities, Austria, Russia and France in-

[51] Toshev, I, 381–3.
[52] B.D., IX, ii, no. 6.
[53] *Doklad*, I, 202; B.D., IX, i, nos. 758, 763; D.D.F., 3d. ser., III, nos. 479, 481, IV, no. 1.
[54] See above, pp. 88–9.
[55] Kolushev from Cetinje, Sept. 21 and 28, 1912; *Doklad*, I, 202.
[56] G.P., XXXIII, nos. 12159, 12164, 12165; D.D.F., 3d. ser., III, no. 460.
[57] These were similar to the reforms extended earlier to Albania (D.D.F., 3d. ser., III, nos. 325, 326, 454).
[58] Schulthess, 1912, p. 456; G.P., XXXIII, no. 12171; B.D., IX, i, no. 740.

itiated various diplomatic steps for the purpose of pacifying the Balkans by the united action of Europe. These steps were all so closely interrelated that it seems best to treat them somewhat apart from the direct interallied negotiations. This is all the more justifiable since they did not alter the policy of the Balkan governments, who deliberately pursued a policy which they themselves charted. These efforts all centered in Constantinople, since all the powers recognised that reforms were necessary, if war was to be avoided. Here they had no more success than in the Balkan capitals. The chief significance of these diplomatic maneuvers, then, lies in the way they affected the great powers themselves.

Throughout the summer the powers individually had been urging Montenegro not to press the border conflicts to a declaration of war.[59] Then on August 13th, Berchtold sent to the powers his note suggesting joint representation at Constantinople in favor of decentralisation.[60] Why did he do this? Was it merely a gesture to emphasise his own importance?[61] On a copy of the telegram which was laid before Francis Joseph, Berchtold noted the following six reasons for his proposed action.

1. In view of the disturbed state in the Balkans . . . as most interested power to take the initiative in determining the guiding principles for common steps in respect to the Balkan governments.

2. To strengthen Turkey in its endeavors to bring about peace and order by inaugurating a decentralised régime.

3. To strengthen the Balkan states in their stand against the elements [bands, revolutionary societies] which through self-help want to bring about the realisation of their aspirations.

4. To document the unity of the great powers in their efforts to maintain the *status quo* in the Balkans and the integrity of Turkey.

5. To weaken the ostensible accord which has been concluded between the Entente Powers in regard to eastern affairs.

6. To dispel in a striking fashion the mistrust which is nourished

[59] See above, pp. 97–8.

[60] This note is summarised above, pp. 107–8.

[61] Fay, *Origins of the World War*, I, 436.

in many places of our Balkan policy; at the same time to take over the leading rôle in Near Eastern politics.[62]

Add to the above, the desire to forestall action by another power and to give an impression of activity at a moment when the press was buzzing with rumors about the Near East in connection with Poincaré's visit to St. Petersburg, and there seems to be no lack of motives to account for the action.[63] Points one and six, of course, indicate this desire to get ahead of any other power. This reason was only admitted after Kiderlen had suggested that he should be informed beforehand, when such wide-sweeping proposals were being considered.[64] There were also other reasons for not consulting Berlin first. At this time Berchtold had little faith in Germany's interest in upholding the *status quo* and did not bank much on her support. In fact this feeling had led him to take soundings in England a short time before, for an arrangement in regard to the preservation of existing territorial conditions in the Near East.[65] It undoubtedly was also a move to demonstrate to Europe that Austrian policy was not being made at Berlin.[66]

Although the powers all accepted the proposal it was earmarked for failure from the beginning, because the whole thing hinged on supporting a policy of decentralisation. While willing perhaps to listen to remarks on administrative decentralisation, the Turkish cabinet would not countenance any talk of political decentralisation.[67] To have done so would have strengthened their political opponents, and would no doubt have resulted in the return of the Committee of Union and Progress to power. Berchtold's proposal therefore met with a cold reception at

[62] Ö-U.A., IV, no. 3687 note.

[63] G.P., XXXIII, nos. 12101, 12087.

[64] Ö-U.A., IV, nos. 3714, 3771; G.P., XXXIII, no. 12101.

[65] Berchtold to Mensdorff, July 20, 1912; Ö-U.A., IV, no. 3633. Francis Joseph characterised this five-page communication as "ausgezeichnet." Grey was ready to discuss, but not enthusiastic (*ibid.*, nos. 3645, 3674; B.D., IX, i, no. 598).

[66] Ö-U.A., IV, no. 3674. The German foreign office was not pleased with the Austrian step, although it lent it support (D.D.F., 3d. ser., III, no. 288; G.P., XXXIII, nos. 12087, 12089 note, 12100.

[67] Minutes, August 21–2, 1912, B.D., IX, i, 628, 630.

Constantinople. Nor did the influence of the powers counteract party politics. Fearful of jeopardising their privileges in the Ottoman Empire the powers were reluctant to exercise anything like real pressure at Constantinople.[68]

Berchtold had hoped to strengthen his credit at the Porte; the result was just the opposite, and the others hoped to profit by it. Russia thought that before steps were taken at the Balkan capitals it would be well to have some positive assurance from Constantinople that the measures granted to the Albanians would also be extended to Macedonia.[69] The Russian statesmen, like those of the other cabinets, were opposed to any collective action at Constantinople. Berchtold accepted this restriction as quite in accord with his ideas, but pointed out that consequently one could not very well take collective steps at the Balkan capitals either.[70] No collective *démarches*, and yet the whole project was launched in order to document the unity of the great powers!

The invitation had been one to discuss, but while all expressed a willingness to do so, no one made any concrete proposals. On August 22nd, Sir Louis Mallet, assistant under-secretary for foreign affairs, remarked, in a conversation with the French chargé, that Grey thought the next move should come from Vienna. "If these overtures were not made Grey would no longer preoccupy himself with this affair, which would collapse of itself." [71] Berchtold on August 29th did address a second note to the powers.[72] He pointed out that he had not meant to intervene in Turkish politics, but had only hoped to give the new cabinet moral support by a declaration of faith from united Europe. Specifically, he suggested that the powers might gently encourage the cabinet to carry out the coming elections in such a way that all ethnic elements in Turkey might be represented.

[68] As a British foreign office official noted somewhat later: "Moreover, if we join in pressing Turkey to agree to a conference our negotiations regarding the Persian Gulf will be jeopardised" (Minute, Aug. 30, 1912, B.D., IX, i, 654).

[69] Ö-U.A., IV, no. 3710; B.D., IX, i, nos. 655, 660.

[70] Ö-U.A., IV, no. 3744.

[71] Fleuriau to Poincaré, Aug. 22, 1912, D.D.F., 3d. ser., III, no. 315.

[72] Ö-U.A., IV, no. 3744; B.D., IX, i, no. 672.

As to the Balkan states, since things had quieted down as a result of the first note (the calm before the storm), the powers would only be called upon to make individual representations as time and occasion required. The reception of this note was more whole-hearted, and it appears to have lulled the wholly unwarranted, yet natural suspicions, which the first note aroused.[73] But the results were no better. Berchtold had hinted at a possible step to be taken in Turkey, but all the others held back. Like Canute the powers sat, forbade the tide to rise and did nothing.

When Berchtold's second note arrived in Paris, Poincaré stated that he must discuss it with England and Russia before giving an answer.[74] While Berchtold had been attempting to unite all Europe, Poincaré and Sazonov were more concerned with establishing Entente solidarity. They were alarmed over the possibility that Vienna might issue a call for a conference.[75] If there was to be a conference (only Poincaré really wanted one) it should be summoned by the three Entente powers. Their aim at present was the one stated earlier by Russia, to obtain a public declaration from the Porte that the reforms granted to Albania would be extended to Macedonia.[76] Poincaré suggested that in accordance with the spirit of the secret accord of June 25th between France, Russia and England for the purpose of ending the Tripolitan War the agreement of the three powers was necessary for any collective action.[77] The British foreign office was willing to discuss *à trois* and even to advise the Turkish ambassador in London in accordance with the wishes of Poincaré and Sazonov, but noted that this was not at all the same

[73] Ö-U.A., IV, nos. 3756, 3758, 3760, 3765, 3769, 3776, 3778; Izvolsky, II, no. 429.

[74] D.D.F., 3d. ser., III, no. 357; B.D., IX, i, no. 706.

[75] D.D.F., 3d. ser., III, nos. 338, 348, 350; B.D., IX, i, nos. 671, 683, 695.

[76] D.D.F., 3d. ser., III, nos. 299, 306, 313, 336, 346; B.D., IX, i, nos. 680, 689 enclosure; Izvolsky, II, no. 408; Ö-U.A., IV, nos. 3756, 3762.

[77] D.D.F., 3d. ser., III, no. 348. Poincaré overemphasised this accord of June 25th, in which the three powers agreed that any intervention on behalf of the conclusion of peace in the Italian-Turkish conflict must be restricted to the issues which produced the conflict, and that such intervention should be made only after previous agreement among the five powers (*ibid.*, no. 140).

question as that of peace between Italy and Turkey.[78] Indeed Britain flatly refused to countenance separate Entente action at Constantinople, as Poincaré and Sazonov suggested. Nor was there any enthusiasm in London for a conference.

Vacations in the country and an extreme Turcophile policy did not lend themselves to immediate answers, and so it was not until September 10–11th that the English response reached Vienna. England looked forward to further conversations, so the answer read, and asked if other proposals might be expected from Austria. One can hardly blame Berchtold for not wanting to do all the talking himself, and he countered by saying that for the present he was content with "having again picked up the thread of general discussion. Should conditions in Turkey make common action by the powers necessary then further conversations might easily be resumed." [79] Grey was not displeased with this arrangement. Even before he had despatched his answer, he had told the French chargé that he thought his response would conclude the discussions started on August 14th.[80]

A week after England's answer had reached Berchtold, Sazonov, alarmed over the proposals of the Bulgarian government for the initiation of hostilities, became convinced that Bulgaria meant business. On September 17th he dispatched a circular note asking the powers to instruct their ambassadors at Constantinople to request that reforms guaranteeing the protection of persons and property, equality before the law, and participation in local administration along ethnic lines, be instituted.[81] He himself at once took this step, gave one final warning to the Balkan states [82] (something the others were not invited to do), and then departed on his long planned visit to London, Paris and Berlin. "The situation in the Near East," so he writes in his memoirs, "was such that a personal exchange of views with

[78] *Ibid.*, III, nos. 347, 353, 363; B.D., IX, i, nos. 690, 691, 694, 709, 710.

[79] Ö-U.A., IV, nos. 3778, 3776; B.D., IX, i, nos. 707, 713.

[80] D.D.F., 3d. ser., III, no. 375; B.D., IX, i, no. 715.

[81] G.P., XXXIII, no. 12150; D.D.F., 3d. ser., III, no. 428; Ö-U.A., IV, no. 3813; B.D., IX, i, nos. 719, 722; K.A., XV, no. 13 (*Berl. Mon.*, VIII, 1070).

[82] See above, p. 110.

those who controlled the foreign policy of our ally France, and of Great Britain which was friendly to us, appeared to me very desirable." [83]

The Russian proposal thus differed from the Austrian in that it called for pressure only on Turkey, and made no mention of united action at the Balkan capitals. If it succeeded, would not Russia be hailed as the liberator of Macedonia? This was the view which Kiderlen held, and he thought such action would increase the spirit and demands of the Balkan peoples rather than quiet them. In view of the recent Entente solidarity he took the position that he could give Russia a definite answer only after consultation with Austria.[84] Berchtold received the Russian move more sympathetically, although he pointed out that the concrete steps proposed were just what every power had objected to a few weeks earlier, and he had little hope of Turkey's accepting the suggestions. Nevertheless he took steps at Constantinople to support the Russian program.[85] Overly anxious to keep in the running he did not wait to find out the attitude of Berlin, but went ahead on his own hook. Later he apologised to Kiderlen for his precipitate action, but Kiderlen remained convinced that this was approaching matters the wrong way and refused to support the Russian proposal.[86] France and England were likewise not enthusiastic, although, on Sazonov's personal plea, Grey agreed to give "friendly advice" to the Porte. This he did through the Turkish ambassador at London, but was careful to add that he ". . . was opposed to making any formal representations at Constantinople as [he] thought that such steps would embarrass the Turkish Government." [87] The sum total of the Russian initiative was that the Turkish foreign office published a declaration extending the concessions made to Al-

[83] Sazonov, *Fateful Years*, p. 57.

[84] G.P., XXXIII, nos. 12151, 12153, 12155.

[85] Ö-U.A., IV, nos. 3812, 3821.

[86] *Ibid.*, IV, nos. 3838, 3850; G.P., XXXIII, nos. 12162, 12163, 12167, 12169.

[87] Grey to Marlin, Sept. 25, 1912, B.D., IX, i, no. 744; see also, Izvolsky, II, no. 437. Cambon reported that Grey was very concerned lest he stir up Mohammedan feeling within the British Empire (D.D.F., 3d. ser., III, nos. 430, 438).

bania to other regions.[88] Russia had done little to quiet the feeling in Turkey or to influence that government to change its policy. Later both the German and Austrian ambassadors at Constantinople were of the opinion that the first steps of Turkish mobilisation were directly due to the measure proposed by Sazonov.[89]

The scene now shifted to England where Sazonov paid a two weeks' visit. The conferences at Balmoral had no startling results as to Near Eastern affairs.[90] Sazonov returned with the firm conviction that England would take no steps which might resemble pressure on Turkey. Grey feared to jeopardise the present Turkish government, which would mean a return of the Young Turks with their Germanophile policy. As a matter of fact Grey was astonished that Sazonov said so little about Turkey.

> I was afraid, [Grey reports], that he might want us to take a very strong pro-Balkan and anti-Turk line. Instead of that, however, he was very emphatic about putting strong pressure on the Balkan states to keep the peace, and he did not ask for any peremptory language in Constantinople. So all was easy enough, and I agreed readily to the diplomatic steps that he advocated.[91]

Accordingly, Sazonov and Grey, on September 29th, addressed notes to the Russian and English representatives in the Near East.[92] If the representatives of the other powers received similar instructions Turkey was to be urged not to concentrate her troops near the frontier, and the Balkan states were to be persuaded to refrain from actual mobilisation. France, Germany and Austria were invited to send similar instructions,

[88] D.D.F., 3d. ser., III, no. 454, see also nos. 325, 326; Ö-U.A., IV, no. 3832 note.

[89] Ö-U.A., IV, no. 3916; G.P., XXXIII, no. 12187.

[90] Persia was the main topic of conversation (B.D., IX, i, 750–769; IX, ii, no. 57). Sazonov, as he might well have been, was quite satisfied with English assurances in regard to a possible Russian-German war (Izvolsky, II, no. 508; B.D., IX, i, no. 805).

[91] B.D., IX, i, no. 810; see also nos. 812, 813.

[92] Izvolsky, II, no. 450; B.D., IX, i, nos. 750, 751, 754, 755, 767; D.D.F., 3d. ser., III, no. 475.

which they immediately did. By the time the messages reached Constantinople official mobilisation had been ordered in the Balkan capitals and the ambassadors felt they could not give such advice to the Porte. Representations, although made in the Balkan capitals, naturally came too late to do any good.

In the meantime Poincaré had followed in the footsteps of Berchtold and Sazonov and brought forward a proposal. On September 22nd he drew up a *projet d'accord* which was first to be agreed upon by the Entente, and then to be presented to the Triple Alliance.[93] At this time the French premier was filled with concern for Entente solidarity. Izvolsky pointed out at once that he thought neither Grey nor Sazonov would accept such a plan since it would accentuate the division of Europe into two camps.[94] As a matter of fact they were willing to accept only two of the four points, objecting to those which envisaged a possible naval or military demonstration.[95] After further consultation with his "allied" colleagues and a sounding of Kiderlen, the original project was reduced to calling for the joint intervention of Austria and Russia, who as most interested powers were to speak in the name of Europe. But by the time this diplomatic fencing had taken place the Balkan states had called their men to arms.

Such are the broad outlines of the feeble joint attempts of Europe to pacify the Balkans up to mobilisation on September 30, 1912. The next day, after a conversation with Jules Cambon, Kiderlen noted: "We were agreed that for future measures it would be more to the point to figure with war as an established fact." [96] Even earlier he had told the British chargé:

> . . . It would be far more useful, if instead of repeating our good advice which is getting stale, all the powers could tell the Balkan states

[93] D.D.F., 3d. ser., III, no. 451; B.D., IX, i, no. 734 enclosure.

[94] Izvolsky, II, nos. 438, 439, 440; D.D.F., 3d. ser., III, nos. 453, 455; Poincaré, II, 214.

[95] B.D., IX, i, nos. 741, 745; Poincaré, II, 218–9; D.D.F., 3d. ser., III, no. 459. Sazonov later told Poincaré that he would have accepted the note, but Grey objected to two of the four points (*ibid.*, IV, no. 37 note).

[96] G.P., XXXIII, no. 12191; see also, D.D.F., 3d. ser., IV, no. 9.

definitely that all arrangements are made for localisation and that if they choose to fight they will have to fight it out and take the consequences.[97]

The powers, nevertheless, were going to make one last despairing bid for peace, although in fact the measures were now more concerned with localisation than with the prevention of war.

[97] Granville to Grey, Sept. 17, 1912, B.D., IX, i, no. 717.

CHAPTER VII

THE OPENING OF HOSTILITIES

WITH official mobilisation announced the Balkan states were well on the way towards the realisation of their ambitions. Although they were fully prepared to face the consequences which mobilisation presaged, they were at the same time anxious to put their case in as good a public light as possible. They all realised that the powers would expect to have some say in any settlement that might be made in the Balkans. Clearly it seemed best to advance carefully and try to convince Europe that it was only Turkey's refusal to undertake reforms which would lead to a rupture. Then too, mobilisation and concentration of troops could not be accomplished overnight, in spite of all the measures preparatory to war which had been taken. And besides, they needed time for interallied negotiation. When mobilisation was decreed on September 30, 1912, neither the Serbian-Montenegrin treaty nor the Bulgarian-Greek military convention were yet concluded, and the allies also had to discuss the ultimatum which was to be presented to Turkey.

At the beginning of September Serbia had advocated sending an ultimatum demanding reforms, which, being refused, would result in mobilisation and immediate declaration of war.[1] Sofia had long entertained the plan of having Montenegro open hostilities, which Nikita could do without much danger to himself.[2] It would serve to sound out Europe, and at the same time it would pave the way for the later participation of the other Balkan states. In addition Greece was to admit the Cretan deputies to her parliament. Then an ultimatum as to reforms was to be dispatched to Turkey, the rejection of which — and they had no doubt that it would be unacceptable — would mean war. In general this Bulgarian plan was followed, although

[1] S.D., I, no. 184. [2] *Doklad*, I, 193; Toshev, I, 400; also see above, pp. 87–8.

Greece had no desire to bring about the *casus foederis*, and admitted the deputies only after the ultimatum had been presented.[3] It likewise appears that Montenegro picked the moment to open hostilities (October 8, 1912) on her own initiative.[4]

Thus, for a few days, while the Balkan states made quiet haste, the powers continued their half-hearted efforts to prevent the opening of hostilities. Berchtold, who thought the pretext for war would be furnished either by Greek claims or by Bulgarian insistence on Article XXIII of the Berlin Treaty, on September 26th asked Germany for an exchange of opinion as to a policy to be followed.[5] To him it seemed that there were two possible courses to pursue: either the powers could declare to the Balkan states that they would permit no territorial changes, or Austria might declare that there were certain changes which she could not permit. The first he thought Russia would hardly agree to, while the second would have the opposite effect from that intended and would encourage the states to believe in the possibility of territorial expansion. In suggesting a declaration in favor of *status quo*, he was but pursuing the policy which Aehrenthal had followed in July, 1911 at the time of the Montenegrin-Albanian-Turkish difficulties.[6] The proposal at that time was limited to diplomatic action, for no power desired to support the declaration with arms. Berchtold undoubtedly favored the same restrictions now, for on September 14th a ministerial council had agreed that any action which might involve Austria in a war was to be avoided.[7]

[3] October 14, 1912 (Schulthess, 1912, p. 481); see also, Drossos, *L'alliance balkanique*, pp. 111–14; Constantine I, *A King's Private Letters. Letters of Constantine to Paola, Princess of Saxe Weimar 1912–1913* (London, 1925), p. 31.

[4] See below, pp. 138–45.

[5] G.P., XXXIII, no. 12168; Ö-U.A., IV, no. 3850. In the interview with Bethmann Hollweg in Buchlau on September 7–8th, Berchtold had already suggested issuing a declaration of *status quo* in case war threatened in the Balkans (*ibid.*, no. 3771).

[6] The documents in regard to the 1911 negotiations were not published, "da sie durch Einigung zwischen der Türkei und Montenegro in der Malissorenfrage gegenstandlos wurden" (Ö-U.A., III, no. 2574 note). In regard to negotiations for a declaration of *status quo* in 1910 see, *ibid.*, II, nos. 1995, 2001, 2015, 2036 Beilage; Izvolsky, II, no. 404; Benckendorff, II, no. 671.

[7] Ö-U.A., IV, no. 3787.

Grey and Sazonov were also in favor of a *status quo* declaration. They had willingly accepted that portion of Poincaré's *projet d'accord* of September 22nd, which provided for a declaration to the Balkan states that they "could not hope in case of an eventual victory to receive any territorial profit." [8] But neither Grey nor Sazonov relished Poincaré's proposal for a joint intervention of the powers. Poincaré was faced with the necessity of finding a way out. On September 26th, he had Paléologue, political director of the foreign office, engage the German chargé in a personal academic conversation on the means of providing some substantial force to the pacific admonitions which were being given to the Balkan states. He mentioned a possible naval demonstration but did not say anything about the *status quo*, merely raising the question "mais à qui de prendre l'initiative?" [9] Two days later Kiderlen took up the lead thrown out by Poincaré and asked Jules Cambon, the French ambassador, to come and talk over the Balkan situation. Armed with Berchtold's recent communication favoring a declaration of *status quo,* Kiderlen was in a good position to enter upon conversations. He suggested that "in his opinion this initiative [of which Paléologue had spoken] could only be taken by one of the two neighboring powers, Russia or Austria." [10] Kiderlen's further suggestions Cambon reported as follows:

> In case Russia took the initiative in making it known to the different Balkan states that the powers would not admit any territorial changes in the Balkans at the end of the war, one would be disposed here [Berlin] to urge Austria to associate herself with this *démarche.* Kiderlen thinks that he could tell me right at this moment that Austria would accept such a proposition.
>
> It seems to him that the presence of Sazonov at Paris furnishes Your Excellency the occasion to discuss this subject and, as he believes in the pacific intentions of Russia, he sees there a means of escape for Europe from the difficulties which face her. The declaration in ques-

[8] See above, p. 123.

[9] G.P., XXXIII, no. 12188.

[10] D.D.F., 3d. ser., III, no. 468, IV, no. 9. Kiderlen expressed much the same views to the Russian chargé on Oct. 1, 1912 (K.A., XV, no. 20 [*Berl. Mon.*, VIII, 1073]).

tion could not be taken adversely by the Balkan powers, for if it frustrated certain of their hopes, it would at the same time be a guarantee for them in case of reverses. It is true, added Kiderlen, that in case of the success of the Balkan powers it would be difficult to clear the troops from the territories occupied by them, but it is important to parry the immediate danger. The observation of Kiderlen appears sound. A *démarche* which would associate the action of Austria to that of Russia would also be of advantage in localising a conflict in case it broke out in the Balkans.

This was certainly a warm response to a mere unofficial feeler, and Poincaré acted upon it immediately. Since Kiderlen suggested that Austria would coöperate, Poincaré now went a bit further and asked Izvolsky to ascertain, in case a joint intervention of the powers should prove impossible, whether Sazonov would accept a dual initiative on the part of Russia and Austria.[11] The "ou," Russia *or* Austria, used by Kiderlen had become an "et," Russia *and* Austria, and thus, although it might be technically correct to speak of Poincaré's project of joint mediation,[12] the idea certainly goes back to the German secretary of foreign affairs.

Sazonov immediately accepted the new proposal as he thought it was the best way to prevent Austria from undertaking separate action.[13] It would bind her up to a certain point and prevent a reoccupation of the Sanjak. At the same time Berchtold was sounded on the plan, but it was not until October 5th that he received definite notification.[14] Confidentially Kiderlen had assured Cambon as early as October 2nd that Austria would agree to act with Russia.[15]

Sazonov was now in Paris, where he and Poincaré decided that they could collaborate on a note to be presented to the Near Eastern powers. A general sketch of the topics to be dealt with

[11] Izvolsky, II, no. 451; Poincaré, II, 221; D.D.F., 3d. ser., IV, nos. 8, 11.

[12] The editors of the German documents refer to it as Poincaré's idea (G.P., XXXIII, nos. 12188 note, 12189 note). Sazonov does the same (Izvolsky, II, no. 508, p. 297).

[13] D.D.F., 3d. ser., IV, nos. 8, 21, 25, 37; K.A., XVI, no. 45 (*Berl. Mon.*, IX, 67).

[14] Ö-U.A., IV, nos. 3922 note, 3949, 3964; D.D.F., 3d. ser., IV, no. 54.

[15] D.D.F., 3d. ser., IV, no. 18.

was dispatched to Berlin on October 3rd. Kiderlen willingly accepted the proposals, and made several suggestions as to the formulation of the note.[16] He got in touch with Berchtold, who promised to take the plan under advisement, although from the objections which he raised, it is clear that he was irritated by the procedure.[17] He found the German negotiations with France officious. On October 4th, Poincaré submitted the formally drafted note, having taken care to incorporate Kiderlen's suggestions as much as possible.[18] The French ambassadors at the capitals of the great powers were asked to ascertain whether the respective cabinets preferred a collective *démarche*, or joint action by Austria and Russia in the name of Europe.

Kiderlen was especially pleased with Poincaré's wording of the difficult problem of reform.[19] For the powers to declare "to take in hand the realisation of reforms" covered everything without promising anything. The procedure of presentation was immaterial to him, although he thought a dual initiative by Austria-Hungary and Russia best. Sir Edward Grey also favored the latter plan, but wanted it limited to the Balkan capitals.[20] At Constantinople, where every nation was equally interested, he wanted presentations by each of the powers individually. Berchtold was willing to join with Russia in a dual mandate at the Balkan capitals ". . . out of consideration for the influence such a method of procedure would have in the Balkan states." [21] He also felt, ". . . that it offered the possibility of smoothing the way for a more cordial relationship with Russia, whereas a refusal would have been interpreted to the contrary." But at Constantinople Berchtold preferred collective action. The Consulta, which was in a peculiar position since Italy was still at war with Turkey, was willing to sanction whatever the other powers might decide on.[22]

[16] *Ibid.*, IV, nos. 25, 28, 40; G.P., XXXIII, nos. 12213, 12214.
[17] Ö-U.A., IV, nos. 3943, 3991, 3996; G.P., XXXIII, no. 12229.
[18] D.D.F., 3d. ser., IV, no. 41.
[19] *Ibid.*, IV, nos. 40, 42, 45, 53.
[20] *Ibid.*, IV, nos. 31, 43, 57, 74; B.D., IX, i, no. 786.
[21] Ö-U.A., IV, 3987.
[22] D.D.F., 3d. ser., IV, nos. 52, 81, 108.

Various changes had to be made in the wording of the document to meet the wishes of the different cabinets. Grey proposed an entirely new formula for the step to be taken at Constantinople.[23] In fact Downing Street was the last to give its sanction to the whole procedure, and only at the last minute agreed that the presentation should be made collectively at the Porte instead of individually by each power.[24] The final wording of the note to the Balkan states was as follows:

The Russian and Austro-Hungarian governments declare to the Balkan states:

1. That the great powers strongly deprecate all measures that are likely to cause a disturbance of peace;

2. That basing themselves on article 23 of the Treaty of Berlin and acting in the interest of the populations, they take in their hands the execution of the reforms in the government of European Turkey, it being understood that the reforms do not infringe the sovereignty of H. M. the Sultan nor the integrity of the Turkish Empire. The declaration reserves for the powers the liberty of examining in common these reforms;

3. That if, notwithstanding all this, war should break out between the Balkan states and the Ottoman Empire, they will tolerate at the end of the conflict no modifications of the present territorial *status quo* in European Turkey.

The great powers will collectively make to the Sublime Porte the representations entailed by the present declaration.[25]

The note handed in at Constantinople was couched in different terms and had the following wording:

The undersigned ambassadors of Austria-Hungary, Great Britain, France, Russia, and Germany have been instructed by their governments to inform the Sublime Porte that the five powers take note of the intentions which the Turkish government has publicly announced of introducing reforms, and will immediately examine with the Sublime Porte, in the spirit of article 23 of the Treaty of Berlin and the Act of 1880, the reforms which the situation in European Turkey

[23] There were three main drafts of the proposal which are conveniently grouped, G.P., XXXIII, no. 12244; also given, D.D.F., 3d. ser., IV, nos. 41, 49, 63, 82.

[24] B.D., IX, i, no. 800 note; D.D.F., 3d. ser., IV, nos. 74, 80, 89.

[25] As quoted in Gueshoff, p. 52.

necessitates and the measures for guaranteeing their execution in the interest of the populations. It is understood that these reforms will not infringe the territorial integrity of the Empire.[26]

There were thus two main points to the whole diplomatic action: (1) reforms, (2) *status quo*. The declaration as to reform was vague and hinged on the good-will of Turkey. No one really thought it would be effective in hindering the outbreak of the war. The Kaiser's marginal comment was indeed fitting:

> These [reforms] will satisfy neither the Turks nor the Balkan states, above all not the Macedonians. Then the powers instead of Turkey will have the responsibility for all that happens. Likewise they will have the whole odium if the matter goes askew and the dissatisfaction of Turkey thrown in. An entirely hopeless arrangement, which is a *testimonium paupertatis* for Europe.[27]

A declaration for the *status quo* was as much a guarantee as a threat to the Balkan governments. If Turkey won, the Balkan states would lose no territory, while on the other hand, everyone was aware of the unwritten principle that Christian land once freed from Turkey should not be returned to Ottoman domination. France, Germany, England and Russia saw in the declaration of *status quo* chiefly a means of keeping Austria from advancing. Berchtold realised this, but favored the declaration since it bound Russia as well. At the same time it offered him a convenient star to which he might gracefully hitch his peaceful policy of non-intervention. It left the future open, and if later it should be found that territorial changes were unavoidable he would have a valuable bargaining lever in advancing any claims he might then wish to make. With a guarantee of *status quo* by the great powers, all territorial additions or advantages the Balkan states might obtain immediately would become concessions, and might justify a demand for compensations, or at least a full recognition of Austria's legitimate interests. What these interests would be, neither he nor anybody else at the Ballhausplatz was able or willing to state at

[26] *Ibid.*; B.D., IX, i, no. 752.
[27] G.P., XXXIII, no. 12235.

that moment.[28] Berchtold, it is true, was not overly pleased with the whole matter and told Tschirschky that he joined in only to avoid being singled out as a marpeace.[29] Above all Vienna was displeased with the way Germany had acted and did not like her close coöperation with the Entente.[30] Germany had spoken of localisation too soon and of avoiding the war not long enough.

In reality the whole purpose of the diplomatic step was to avoid a European war, not to avoid a Balkan war. Of course it was hoped that the declaration of *status quo* might restrain the Balkan states, but no one expected that it would. In fact the wind had been taken out of the sails of the powers, for the Balkan governments themselves declared that they desired no territorial annexations.[31] The declaration of reforms added little to former promises, and promises through their many repetitions and failures had lost all effectiveness. As a restraining action this touted *concert européen* meant little. Szápáry, then at the Vienna foreign office, thought it would have just the opposite effect for it would remove the threat of Austria's separate action, and serve as a "*carte blanche* for aggression against Turkey." [32] Indeed it does appear that Montenegro's declaration of war was hastened by the desire to get ahead of the anticipated action by the European Concert.

It was not until October 8th that the Austrian and Russian ministers were able to take the proposed step at the various Balkan capitals. In Athens Caromilas, the minister of foreign affairs, received the note and assured the ministers that since the project applied to all of the four Balkan states he would have to consult them before giving an answer.[33] In making the

[28] Ö-U.A., IV, no. 3928. Count Szápáry suggested to the writer in June, 1930, that it would have been hard to come out with a program of vital interests and then find that through the course of events they could not be maintained.

[29] G.P., XXXIII, no. 12235.

[30] Denkschrift des Grafen Szápáry, Oct. 7, 1912, Ö-U.A., IV, no. 3991; see also nos. 3996, 4022.

[31] On October 1, 1912 Neratov had suggested to Sofia that localisation would be easier if the Balkan states took their stand on the *status quo* (*Doklad*, I, 225–6). The Balkan states soon came forward with such declarations (Ö-U.A., IV, nos. 3948, 3967, 3969).

[32] Ö-U.A., IV, no. 3991.

[33] *Ibid.*, IV, no. 3992.

presentation in Sofia neither Tarnowski nor Nekludov thought it would have any effect,[34] and they were not disappointed. Gueshov, "full of desire" to follow the counsels of the great powers, assured them that this would have been possible ten days earlier but hardly at this time. He would, however, present it to the king and the council of ministers and would reserve his answer until he knew their decision. His personal opinion was that the references to reform were too vague and would hardly be acceptable.[35] At Belgrade Pašić answered that he would have to discuss the note with his colleagues and also with Sofia, but in the meantime he would do all he could to prevent the opening of hostilities. This, however, would not be easy as Montenegro had already declared war.[36]

The instructions for the Austrian and Russian ministers in Cetinje arrived on the morning of October 8th. Knowing that King Nikita expected to join his army at Podgoritza the ministers asked to be received as soon as they could decipher the messages. The king very obligingly delayed his departure until the afternoon, and at eleven o'clock Giesl and Giers solemnly gave utterance to the will of Europe.[37] Already at the highest instance, there was no need for further discussion and the king, who was well prepared, answered at once. He pointed out that the powers had ignored his request for intervention made more than two months before,[38] and after enumerating the many wrongs Montenegro had suffered at the hands of Turkey he concluded:

> Finally and above all the massacre of our brother Christians on the borders of Montenegro has not stopped and it has touched my heart strings. In this moment the situation of the kingdom is such that even if her allies free themselves of their engagements to her — which I do not suppose for an instant — the state of spirit of my people will oblige

[34] *Ibid.*, IV, no. 4010; Nekludov, *Reminiscences*, p. 109; K.A., XVI, no. 27 (*Berl. Mon.*, VIII, 1185).

[35] Ö-U.A., IV, no. 4009; B.D., IX, ii, no. 3.

[36] Ö-U.A., IV, no. 3993; B.D., IX, ii, no. 4.

[37] Gustav von Hubka, "Kritische Tage in Montenegro," *Berliner Monatshefte*, IX (1931), 30–1.

[38] See above, pp. 97–8.

me to enter into action. You understand me. I am deeply grieved that I cannot follow the counsels of the two friendly and protecting empires and especially of their gracious sovereigns who have always been so good to me.[39]

With that the king left for Podogoritza where he was ceremoniously to open hostilities the next morning at the stroke of eight, for at noon of the very day that the European Concert became audible (October 8, 1912) the Montenegrin chargé at Constantinople had presented the declaration of war.

The Montenegrin declaration of war had no apparent effect on the actions of the powers. They accepted the *fait accompli.* Nor did they accelerate their common action in Constantinople on which all reforms — the crux of the problem — depended. Although the *démarche* by the Austro-Hungarian and Russian ministers had been undertaken in all the Balkan capitals on October 8th, it was not until two days later that all ambassadors in Constantinople had obtained their instructions.[40] The note was of course taken under advisement and the Turkish officials were to ponder and temporise four days before venturing an answer.

While waiting for the answers of the Near Eastern powers to the note presented by the Austrian and Russian ministers, Poincaré took steps to prepare the powers for all eventualities. On October 10th, true to Entente solidarity, he first asked England and Russia about calling a conference to study reforms called for in the Ottoman law of 1880, to which Turkey had just been asked to agree.[41] England received the move favorably, but wanted to wait for the answer from the Porte. Sazonov was of the opinion that henceforth one should talk of terminating

[39] Ö-U.A., IV, no. 3998.

[40] This delay was no doubt in part due to England's holding out against collective action at Constantinople (D.D.F., 3d. ser., IV, nos. 74, 80, 89). According to the French documents the Austrian ambassador was the last to receive instructions, while the Austrian ambassador reported that the French minister was the one who held up matters (*ibid.*, no. 110; Ö-U.A., IV, nos. 4024, 4025).

[41] D.D.F., 3d. ser., IV, no. 112; for the English reply see, nos. 119, 127, 131; B.D., IX, ii, no. 38; for the Russian reply see, D.D.F., 3d. ser., IV, nos. 126, 140, 145.

the war rather than of preventing it. He suggested that a proposal for mediation after the first battle was more in order. Following the suggestions advanced from London, Poincaré worked out a program of four points.[42] If Turkey accepted the reforms then a conference was to be called immediately to study their application; if they were refused and war broke out then the powers should come together and work out a plan of mediation. Should the mediation succeed then reforms were to be discussed; should it fail, the methods of preserving the general peace and the common interests of Europe at the close of hostilities should be the program of the conference. There was thus to be a conference whichever way events turned. Austria-Hungary, Italy and Germany were not favorable to this procedure.[43] Russia also shared their view [44] and Poincaré's plan of a conference made little headway.

Meanwhile in the Balkans things began to move at a faster tempo. On October 13th Bulgaria, Serbia and Greece expressed appreciation to the powers for their interest in reforms as shown by the recent note, but pointed out:

> . . . after so many former promises, solemnly made by Turkey and confirmed by international treaties, it would be inhuman on their part not to attempt to obtain more radical and better defined reforms which, if fully and conscientiously applied, would not fail to improve their [i.e. the peoples' of European Turkey] present miserable lot. For this reason they [felt] constrained to address themselves directly to H. M. the Sultan, and to indicate the principles on which those reforms must be based, as well as the guarantees which must be given for their sincere execution.[45]

To this was appended a memorandum of their demands upon the Porte with an explanatory note. These demands were at the same time communicated to Constantinople.

[42] D.D.F., 3d. ser., IV, no. 138; B.D., IX, ii, no. 28.

[43] D.D.F., 3d. ser., IV, nos. 143, 153, 166, 182; G.P., XXXIII, nos. 12265, 12266; B.D., IX, ii, no. 29.

[44] D.D.F., 3d. ser., IV, no. 164.

[45] Gueshoff, pp. 54-5; Ö-U.A., IV, nos. 4066, 4078; B.D., IX, ii, no. 22, see also, no. 12.

. . . The Sublime Porte [was invited] to take, in concert with the great powers and the Balkan states, immediate measures for the elaboration and introduction in European Turkey of the reforms laid down in article 23 of the Treaty of Berlin, adopting as a basis the principle of ethnic nationalities (administrative autonomy of the provinces, Belgian and Swiss governors, elective local assemblies, gendarmerie, educational liberty and local militia), and entrusting their application to a superior council which will consist of an equal number of Mohammedans and Christians and will act under the control of the ambassadors of the great powers and the ministers of the four Balkan states.[46]

The Porte was asked to carry out these reforms, which were carefully defined in the accompanying explanatory note, within a period of six months. Meanwhile as evidence of acquiescence and good faith the Turkish army should be demobilised.

At Constantinople there were now two answers to deliberate upon, the one to the powers, the other to the Balkan states. The former were assured that Turkey had decided to undertake reforms, but that she was determined to carry them out herself.[47] The law of 1880 would be laid before parliament at once, and the new government would see that it was promptly and justly applied. Thus the powers received the cold shoulder when it came to "taking in hand" any reforms. In regard to the Balkan states the procedure was much simpler. They received no answer at all and the Turkish ministers were instructed to ask for their passports.[48]

With the allied and Turkish answers giving a polite but firm refusal to the powers it became useless to continue the sham of preventing war and Poincaré altered his plans for the Concert of Europe. It now became definitely a question of discussing mediation "en temps opportun" and a new point was added to the program, namely, that the powers would undertake nothing which was contrary to the sovereignty of the sultan and the integrity of the Ottoman Empire.[49] The idea of the conference was still a central part of the proposal and it met with the same

[46] Gueshoff, pp. 55–6; B.D., IX, ii, no. 24.
[47] Ö-U.A., IV, no. 4085.
[48] October 15, 1912 (Schulthess, 1912, p. 458; G.P., XXXIII, no. 12274).
[49] D.D.F., 3d. ser., IV, no. 164.

unenthusiastic reception. With hostilities beginning, even Poincaré realised the impracticability of a conference at that moment. He worked out a new draft which made no mention of a conference but only expressed the willingness of the powers to discuss together certain contingencies which might arise.[50] This formula was accepted by all with only slight emendations.

Through Poincaré's efforts contact had been maintained among the powers, and all had expressed their willingness to discuss matters further at the opportune moment. When that would be depended upon the course events took in the war. Just as at the time of mobilisation the action of the powers centered on localisation and not prevention of the Balkan War, so now at the outbreak of hostilities they no longer spoke of localisation but of terminating the conflict.

With all the armies mobilised, with negotiations ended, the declaration of war was the next step.[51] On October 17th the allied governments instructed their representatives at Constantinople to present the declaration of war the next day. Failure of Turkey to answer their note of October 13th, arbitrary detention of Serbian munitions, an embargo on Greek steamers, unlawful attacks on Serbian and Bulgarian posts by Turkish troops, and the rupture of diplomatic relations by the recall of the Ottoman ministers were some of the reasons advanced for the resort to arms. The Porte, however, forestalled the presentation of the note by the Serbian and Bulgarian ministers by handing them their passports on the morning of the seventeenth. At the same time they were informed that the intervention of Bulgaria and Serbia in the internal affairs of Turkey made it impossible to maintain peace any longer;[52] a state of war existed between Bulgaria, Serbia, and Turkey. The Greek minister being still accredited, presented the declaration of war on behalf of his government at noon on October 18,

[50] *Ibid.*, IV, no. 192; B.D., IX, ii, no. 46.

[51] Turkey meanwhile signed a preliminary peace treaty with Italy on October 15, and the final treaty at Lausanne on October 18, 1912 (Martens, *Traités*, 3d. ser., VII, 1–10).

[52] *Politische Chronik, 1912*, pp. 438–9; Gueshoff, pp. 57–8; B.D., IX, ii, no. 42.

1912.[53] The plan which had been adopted by the Balkan states during the summer had succeeded; Montenegro obtained allies, the powers an explanatory note.

Thus the action of the powers had come too late. As a matter of fact the powers had probably hastened the opening of hostilities. The Montenegrin chargé told the French ambassador to the Porte that the Balkan allies had been disquieted by rumors of the *démarche*, which was eventually made by the powers on October 8th.[54] In order to nullify this diplomatic action they desired to confront the powers with a *casus foederis* through the opening of hostilities by one of the allies against Turkey. Montenegro had been chosen since her grievances and her demands, touching questions of frontier, were of a different nature than those of the other Balkan states. "And this explanation," so Poincaré comments, "was neither absurd nor improbable, but it was not impossible either that the truth was very different. Le roi Nicolas était, comme la Montagne Noire, riche d'imprevu et plein de précipices." [55]

What is the truth about this independent declaration of war on the part of King Nikita? Pašić at once asserted that the declaration had been made without any ally being previously consulted.[56] Observers in Cetinje all seem to confirm this.[57] On the other hand we know for certain that the Montenegrin-Bulgarian understanding provided that Montenegro should open hostilities,[58] and with all the discussion that went on, Greece and Serbia undoubtedly also heard of this plan of starting the ball rolling. On September 8/21st and 15/28th, the Montenegrin government had informed Sofia that it was only waiting

[53] *Politische Chronik, 1912*, p. 440; B.D., IX, ii, no. 45.

[54] Bompard to Poincaré, Oct. 8, 1912, D.D.F., 3d. ser., IV, no. 88.

[55] Poincaré, II, 248.

[56] D.D.F., 3d. ser., IV, no. 98.

[57] Aynard from Cetinje to Poincaré, Oct. 8, 1912, D.D.F., 3d. ser., IV, no. 99; Eckardt from Cetinje to Bethmann Hollweg, Oct. 9, 1912, G.P., XXXIII, no. 12247; conversations with representatives of two other great powers then stationed in Cetinje who prefer not to be quoted directly; Durham, *Struggle for Scutari*, p. 183.

[58] *Doklad*, I, 193; Toshev, I, 400; K.A., XV, no. 12 (*Berl. Mon.*, VIII, 973–4); conversation with Danev, May, 1930.

for Bulgaria to set the day for attack.[59] However, with mobilisation going on in all countries, it appears that King Nikita took the initiative himself, and decided to declare war on October 8th. On October 4th Kolushev reported to Sofia, "The Montenegrin minister of foreign affairs sent me a message saying Montenegro had decided to open the war this coming Wednesday, October 9th." [60] A similar message must also have been sent to Greece, for on October 5th Crown Prince Constantine stated in a letter to Paola, Princess of Weimar, "It seems that Montenegro wants to begin hostilities next Wednesday. If that be the case she will probably drag us all in after her, and we are not ready." [61] We have no direct knowledge if Serbia was informed or not, although her representative in Cetinje must certainly have got wind of the matter. The Austrian and Russian ministers were informed of Montenegro's intentions at about this same time. On October 3rd Hubka, Austrian attaché in Cetinje, telegraphed to Vienna, "Minister of war figures on the complete readiness of the army at latest on Monday, October 7th, whereupon in every case offensive, even if the king of Bulgaria, etc., do not declare war." [62] On the same day, Giesl sent a similar telegram to the foreign office.[63] Giers, the Russian minister in Cetinje, likewise informed St. Petersburg, that war would start on the seventh or eighth.[64] He, however, said nothing of Montenegro's undertaking independent action, but reported as if King Nikita would be joining Bulgaria. The Russian attaché at Cetinje knew of Montenegrin plans by the middle of September.[65] As Paul Cambon reasoned, it would have been impossible for Montenegrin preparations to go forward in an army which was administered by a Russian mission, equipped and subsidised by Russia, without Russia's knowledge.[66] After the declaration

[59] *Doklad*, I, 202.
[60] *Ibid.*, I, 227 (no. 8).
[61] Constantine, *Letters*, p. 44.
[62] Ö-U.K.A., Evidenzbureau D. no. 771. Situation am Balkan, Oct. 4, 1912.
[63] Giesl to foreign office, Oct. 3, 1912, Ö-U.A., IV, no. 3934; see also, no. 3915.
[64] Izvolsky, II, no. 466.
[65] See above, pp. 87–8.
[66] Cambon to Poincaré, Oct. 9, 1912, D.D.F., 3d. ser., IV, no. 107.

of war the French chargé at St. Petersburg reported that Sazonov was not surprised since he knew fifteen days ago that Bulgaria planned to join in the hostilities which Montenegro was to initiate.[67]

As the above telegrams indicate, the decision to open hostilities on the eighth was probably reached on October 2nd or 3rd. By the sixth the Montenegrin chargé in Constantinople had been supplied with the declaration of war and instructions for presenting it at midday on Tuesday, October 8th.[68] Everything was prepared and the whole attitude in Cetinje was that war was at hand.[69]

Bound by an agreement to begin the war first and with his army ready for the offensive, are there perhaps other reasons that urged King Nikita to declare war? Count de Salis, the British representative in Cetinje, wrote in 1914,

> Briefly, danger of disturbances in this country may be caused by the desire of the ruling authorities to outdo Serbia in any demonstration of Serb patriotism, by the same spirit, in short, with which the King hastened to begin the Balkan War before his allies were ready.[70]

In other words, it was a matter of stealing a march on the Serbs, and this view of Montenegrin policy is shared by Miss Durham and Alfred Rappaport, two of the ablest Balkan scholars of today.[71] It was not simply a desire to get there first in the scramble for territory. Such initiative would at the same time increase the prestige of the dynasty and enhance its position in the struggle for the leadership of the Serbian race. In spite of the fact that Serbia and Montenegro were on the point of concluding an alliance at the outbreak of war,[72] the Montenegrins had few good words for the Serbs. Miss Durham writes: "Of

[67] Doulcet to Poincaré, Oct. 12, 1912, *ibid.*, IV, no. 126; see also, no. 199, III, no. 445.

[68] K.A., XVI, no. 26 (*Berl. Mon.*, VIII, 1184); D.D.F., 3d. ser., IV, no. 84; Poincaré, II, 247.

[69] Durham, *Struggle for Scutari*, pp. 181 ff.

[70] De Salis to Grey, July 23, 1914, B.D., XI, no. 651.

[71] Durham, *Struggle for Scutari*, p. 183; A. Rappaport, "Montenegros Eintritt in den Weltkrieg," *Berliner Monatshefte*, VII (1929), 948–9. Both of these scholars reiterated this view in conversations with the writer in 1929–30.

[72] See above, pp. 88–9.

the Serbs they had no opinion at all. When I asked, 'What is the Serbian army worth?' 'They are a lot of Swineherds,' was the invariable reply." [73] Hubka also reported that Prince Mirko spoke very disrespectfully of the Serbian officers, using the terms, "Mörderbande, Schweinerei." [74] Such feeling and ambition might well explain why Montenegro planned to inform Serbia of her Bulgarian agreement with its provision that Montenegro should begin the war, as a definitely settled matter.[75] How Serbia received the news, for she was probably informed during the negotiations, it is impossible to say. In any case she could hardly have done anything about such a *fait accompli*. If we had the complete text of the Serbian-Montenegrin alliance, which, according to all indications, had territorial provisions, we should be able to come to more definite conclusions on this episode of Serbian-Montenegrin relations.

There is, however, still one other point that needs to be considered in regard to Montenegro's decision to open hostilities. It was early charged, and the idea has persisted ever since, that King Nikita declared war earlier than the others in order to make a fortune on the bourse.[76] Such a charge is easily made, is hard to prove, and all references to it are always based on rumor or hearsay.

[73] Durham, *Struggle for Scutari*, p. 183.

[74] Attaché report of Sept. 24, 1912, Ö-U.K.A., Res. no. 58.

[75] K.A., XV, no. 12 (*Berl. Mon.*, VIII, 973–4).

[76] S.D., I, no. 304; B.D., IX, ii, no. 968; D.D.F., 3d. ser., VI, no. 503; above all Ö-U.A., IV, nos. 4058, 4340. The version published here is apparently given full credence by Boghitschewitsch, *Serbien und der Weltkrieg*, p. 142; O. H. Wedel in his review of the Austrian documents in *The Journal of Modern History*, III (1931), 99; Herre, *Die Kleinen Staaten*, p. 379. See also, Steed, *Through Thirty Years*, I, 362; Joseph M. Baernreither, *Fragmente eines politischen Tagebuches* (Berlin, 1929), p. 234; Frhr. v. Taube, *Der Grossen Katastrophe entgegen, Erinnerungen* (Berlin, 1929), p. 264; Ö-U.A., VI, no. 7257. Most of the above references refer to speculation in October, 1912, but some also refer to speculation on the part of King Nikita in May, 1913 at the time of the crisis over the evacuation of Scutari (see below, ch. XIV). The question of King Nikita's speculation was discussed with many statesmen who were in power in 1912–13. Their answers might perhaps best be summed up as a shrug of the shoulders; neither *yes* nor *no*. Baron Giesl and Jovan M. Jovanović, Serbian minister at Vienna, were the most inclined of any to give credence to the charges of speculation.

From what has been pointed out above there are sufficient motives to account for his action, and it appears unlikely that speculation on the bourse played a leading part in determining his policy. But even if it did not determine his policy, might he not have used the occasion to recoup a bit? It is well known that King Nikita was at times a heavy speculator. Whether the speculation took place or not, it is worth while to mention at least the most plausible, and about the only account available of how the affair was supposedly carried out. When Szécsen, the Austrian ambassador at Paris, asked Izvolsky what had determined Montenegro to declare war, the latter replied that he really did not know. The next day, seeing Szécsen again, Izvolsky told him that meanwhile he had heard from a very well-informed source the following about the opening of hostilities:

When Grand Duke Nikolas Nikolaievich was in attendance at the French maneuvers this summer [77] the king of Montenegro sent Prince Mirko to Paris.[78] The grand duke at that time, through the agency of the embassy, had received instructions from St. Petersburg to advise emphatically against every warlike adventure. This was done.[79] The visit of the prince, however, had a different purpose. He wanted to raise a loan of ten million francs in Paris, which of course, he was unable to do. Thereupon the prince went to the bank in question — the name of which Izvolsky alleged he did not know — with a different proposition. He said the war was unavoidable, the moment of beginning, however, depended pretty much on the Montenegrin government. He pledged himself to inform the said bank confidentially three days in advance. The bank could in this fashion make a huge coup on the bourse, but one must guarantee him one-half of the clear profit. The bank took up this proposition and being timely informed had played "à decouvert à la baisse" with large sums and in the last break of the

[77] His ceremonious inspection of the frontier forts, and the anti-German demonstrations of his wife called forth a protest from Germany (G.P., XXXI, no. 11599, XXXIII, no. 12256; see also Izvolsky, II, nos. 419, 443).

[78] According to other references it was Crown Prince Danilo and not Prince Mirko (Izvolsky, II, 442; Ö-U.A., IV, no. 3798; G.P., XXXIII, no. 12156).

[79] Izvolsky, II, nos. 441, 442. This probably formed the basis of the rumored, or in all probability actual meeting of the Paris representatives of the Balkan states under the chairmanship of the grand duke. News of this meeting seemed especially to interest the Kaiser (G.P., XXXIII, nos. 12160, 12216, 12237). Kiderlen called it pointedly to Sazonov's attention on his visit to Berlin on October 8, 1912 (*ibid.*, no. 12256 note).

market had made enormous profits. I told Izvolsky that the affair seemed very unlikely to me, whereupon he responded "Je ne sais naturellement pas si ce que l'on m'a raconté est vrai, mais ces gens sont capables de tout." True or not the most remarkable thing about the whole story is that Izvolsky tells it.[80]

About a month later Szécsen sent in a clipping from the *Libre Parole* which carried practically the same story as the above. At this time he commented, "In bourse circles the talk is that the support of Montenegro was made possible by the Viennese bank firm of Reitzes, who let their branch, O. Rosenberg, in Paris pay out an advance of ten millions to King Nikita." [81] These firms apparently have no record of accounts in King Nikita's name, which, of course, proves nothing either way.[82]

What can be said of this story? Poincaré's words, quoted above, seem equally appropriate here, that is, it "is neither absurd, nor improbable, but it is not impossible either that the truth is very different." [83] But even this account does not say that speculation was a cause for the declaration of war, but that Prince Mirko was only going to take advantage of something which was pretty well determined. The facts of the story hinge together quite well. It is the only reference that we have to Prince Mirko's activity in Paris. That he made attempts to obtain a loan is very probable, although neither Poincaré in his memoirs nor the French documents make any reference to them. Such efforts on his part were no doubt frowned upon by the French government, which at this time would not even sanction a Bulgarian loan.

As has been shown above the Montenegrin declaration of war

[80] Szécsen to Berchtold, Oct. 12, 1912, Ö-U.A., IV, no. 4058.

[81] *Ibid.*, IV, no. 4340.

[82] Personal inquiry by the author was made at Rosenbergs in Paris in October, 1929 and later at Reitzes in Vienna. On request Reitzes submitted the following statement: "Wien, den 19 März, 1930. Wir besitzen Ihr geehrtes Schreiben vom 18d. und können wir unsere mündliche Erklärungen nur wiederholen, wonach die von Ihnen erwähnten Gerüchte in Bezug auf eine Verbindung unserseits bezw. der Firma O. H. Rosenberg & Cie., Paris, mit dem montenegrinischen Königshause vollkommen aus der Luft gegriffen sind. Hochachtungsvoll, Das Sekretäriat."

[83] Poincaré, II, 248; see above, p. 138.

was not a matter of great secrecy and quite definite information could have been obtained in Cetinje by any competent observer two or three days before the opening of hostilities. The Russian and French foreign offices were even definitely informed on the 6th that the declaration of war would be made at noon on October 8th.[84] Information such as Prince Mirko supposedly pledged himself to give might well have leaked out from any number of sources.

It is true that there were breaks in the market which would have enabled someone to make a handsome profit both at this time and in May, 1913, when the Montenegrin royal house was also supposed to have made a coup.[85] The market started to break on Monday, October 7th and except for a slight rally the next day — probably closely related to the heralded display made on that day by the powers — continued to decline all that week. On Monday, October 14th, there was a rally which was not noticeably affected by the declaration of war by the other allied states on the 18th, a rather sharp drop taking place on the 21st which, however, did not carry over. The break occurred chiefly in industrials, stocks which were steady throughout September, the news of mobilisation bringing the first abrupt decline.[86]

After this rather lengthy discussion it seems that the following conclusions are in order. First, that the desire to enrich himself on the bourse played no deciding rôle in determining King Nikita to take the lead in declaring war. Secondly, that the break in the market was pronounced enough to enable a skillful speculator to make considerable gains. Thirdly, that if the Montenegrin royal house played the market no huge profits were made. There is some proof of having the pudding in eating

[84] See above, pp. 139–40.

[85] As will be shown later there were far weightier reasons to account for King Nikita's entrance into Scutari and his sudden decision to withdraw than a desire to make a coup on the bourse (see below, ch. XIV).

[86] Observations based on a study of the *Amtliches Kursblatt der Wiener Börse*, XXXVII (1912), XXXVIII (1913); see also tables in *Volkswirtschaftliche Chronik der Österreichisch-Ungarischen Monarchie* ed. Karl Neisser (Vienna, 1910–; hereafter cited as *Volkwirtschaftliche Chronik*), 1912, *passim*.

it, and there never were any evidences of superfluous wealth in Cetinje. Moreover money for the war was obtained by King Nikita from his allies and there was still enough money left for mobilisation from the recent Austrian loan.[87] There are also reports that Montenegro was negotiating other loans with likelihood of success which had no connection with the above rumors of stock speculation.[88] Fourthly, that Montenegro declared war at least in full agreement with Bulgaria and with the knowledge of Greece and Serbia. Further that such declaration was hastened by the anticipated note of the great powers, along with the desire to enhance the moral and material prestige of Montenegro as leader of the Serbian race.

[87] Ö-U.A., IV, no. 3798; conversation with a well informed personage who was in Cetinje at that time.

[88] Ö-U.A., IV, nos. 3798, 3915.

CHAPTER VIII

RUSSIA AND THE BALKAN STATES[1]

THE temptation always presents itself to group into three or four sentences the causes for this or that event. Nor is it a practice entirely to be condemned, for only through some such formulation can the trees become a wood. Should this be attempted in relation to the First Balkan War, the following three "causes," might be set up. First, the failure of Turkey to work out an adequate system of government for its subject nationalities, either before or after the revolution of 1908, together with the bitter internal political strife which in the eleventh hour prevented such reforms and concessions as might have forestalled the conflict. Second, the desire of the Balkan states — confident in their strength as a result of the formation of the Balkan League and urged on by certain groups and organisations — to liberate their co-nationals from the "Turkish yoke," and thus to realise in part their nationalistic and imperialistic ambitions. Third, the relation of the great powers to each other and to the Porte, which not only at all times prevented them from insisting at Constantinople on adequate reforms, but also led the Balkan states to conclude that, so far as Europe was concerned, the time was opportune for solving the Balkan problem as they themselves wished.

Were one, however, to pick out a single event which more than any other led to the outbreak of the war — one might almost call it the immediate cause — the formation of the Balkan League should undoubtedly be selected. It was only then that the Balkan states felt themselves in a position to take the matter of reform out of the hands of the powers and to settle things to their own liking. The statesmen of Europe all saw the League

[1] Various changes have been made in this chapter since it appeared under the title, "Russlands Einfluss auf den Balkanbund im Oktober 1912," *Berliner Monatshefte*, XI (1933), 217–45.

in this light. Poincaré, as soon as he knew the contents of the Serbian-Bulgarian treaty, realised what was in store for Europe, and on the eve of the war he stated:

> But nevertheless it is certain that she [Russia] knew all, and that far from protesting against it, she saw in this diplomatic document the means of assuring her hegemony in the Balkans. She perceives to-day that it is too late to stop the movement which she provoked, and as I told Sazonov and Izvolsky, she tries to apply the brake, but it was she who started the motor.[2]

Nicolson, the British permanent under-secretary of state had the same opinion as may be seen from the following letter:

> To my mind the primary cause of all that has happened is the secret alliance which Russia encouraged the four states to conclude. I imagine that Sazonov had in his mind in the first instance merely to gain a diplomatic success over Austria and to reëstablish Russian prestige in the Balkan peninsula. He should, however, have foreseen that by encouraging and promoting the close understanding between the four Balkan powers he was practically raising hopes and aspirations which they had some grounds for thinking Russia would enable them to realise. Moreover, unless our information is quite erroneous Bulgaria and Serbia even went so far as to peg out between themselves districts in Macedonia which would fall to each other when the Turkish Empire broke up.[3]

When Sazonov visited Berlin, Kiderlen pointed out to him that it had been a dangerous game "de patroniser l'alliance des États balkaniques," something the Russian foreign minister did not dispute, although he observed that Russia had insisted that the alliance should have no aggressive tendencies.[4] It is remarkable

[2] Poincaré to Paul Cambon, Oct. 15, 1912, D.D.F., 3d. ser., IV, no. 170; see also, III, no. 264; Izvolsky, II, no. 429; Poincaré, II, 214 ff.

[3] Nicolson to Hardinge, Oct. 9, 1912, B.D., IX, ii, no. 10. Buchanan, the British ambassador at St. Petersburg wrote in a similar vein: "Now that the fat is in the fire one is inclined to ask oneself who placed it there; and as without the Serbo-Bulgarian alliance there would probably have been no Balkan war, Russia as the prompter if not the actual creator of that alliance naturally incurs considerable responsibility" (Buchanan to Nicolson, Oct. 17, 1912, *ibid.*, no. 43). Bertie, the British ambassador at Paris, was apparently of the same opinion (Ö-U.A., IV, no. 4178).

[4] Aufzeichnung des Staatssekretärs von Kiderlen, Oct. 9, 1912, G.P., XXXIII, no. 12256. In regard to this remark the Kaiser made the marginal note, "Das diese sowas nicht ernst nehmen würden war Russland klar."

that Kiderlen apparently gave full credence to Sazonov's statement, though he added that it was no surprise that the Balkan states had broken the bounds of the Russian veto. Berchtold also saw clearly the danger of the Russian-patronised League and its relation to the war.[5] Indeed Russia herself realised full well what she had been responsible for. On October 2nd, Neratov, who was making preparations for the coming conflict, telegraphed to Sazonov about taking over the legation of the Balkan states in case war was declared and naïvely added: "In order not to arouse the suspicion that we have encouraged the alliance of the four states it would be desirable if Greece would turn to some other power, for example, France." [6]

The precaution of Neratov was useless for by that time all governments knew that Russia had acted as godfather to the League. The League itself had already awakened suspicions at all the foreign offices. Particularly was this true at the Quai d'Orsay. The Serbian-Bulgarian alliance sounded ominous to Poincaré, especially when considered in connection with the Russian questionnaire on Balkan affairs of February, 1912.[7] He immediately entered upon negotiations with Sazonov, but due largely to the reserve shown by Russia, no definite results were reached.[8] One of the chief aims of Poincaré on his visit to St. Petersburg in August, 1912, was to clear up the question of Russia's Balkan policy. At that time, in order to make clear what France's position would be in case of complications in the Near East, Poincaré thought it necessary to point out that:

> Public opinion in France would not permit the French government to decide on a military action in a purely Balkan matter unless Germany became involved and through its initiative brought about a *casus foederis*. In this latter case [Russia] could count on the exact and complete fulfillment by France of her obligations.[9]

[5] Ö-U.A., IV, nos. 3771, 3787.

[6] Izvolsky, II, no. 461; see also, Benckendorff, II, no. 674; Sazonov, *Fateful Years*, p. 57.

[7] D.D.F., 3d. ser., II, nos. 43, 289, 294.

[8] *Ibid.*, II, nos. 312, 317, 370, 402; III, no. 5.

[9] Izvolsky, II, no. 401; Poincaré, II, 117–8.

Poincaré considered the Serbian-Bulgarian alliance as "une convention de guerre."[10] It was his knowledge of this treaty which influenced him to receive favorably Berchtold's and Sazonov's proposals relative to the Balkans, and prompted him to initiate and carry through his projects for the prevention and localisation of the war. Having opened the Paris money markets to Bulgaria only on the intercession of Russia, on the eve of the war he closed them as a final means of restraining Sofia. But while this action was taken in Paris, the French minister at Sofia appears to have used other language. He did not hide his sympathy for the Balkan cause and sanctioned the steps which the Bulgarians were taking in regard to the war.[11]

While doing his best to avoid a general European conflagration, Poincaré worked ardently for the diplomatic success of Russia and for the success of the Balkan states. Throughout the crisis he was extremely solicitous for Entente solidarity. He worked unceasingly for this, and gave Russia his full support. Entente solidarity, success of the Balkan states for the sake of Russia and the Entente, prevention of a European war were the keynotes of French policy in October, 1912. Luckily this program was to be achieved without going beyond diplomatic measures. Had Germany, or Austria backed by Germany, chosen to dispute any of these points, then, according to the declaration made in St. Petersburg, France would have been willing to honor her military pledges. France had virtually given Russia a blank check on which she might inscribe whatever she wished. Aid was not guaranteed if Russia became involved in a war with Austria-Hungary alone, but both Poincaré and Sazonov knew that Germany would not stand aside in an Austrian-Russian conflict.

As to England Sazonov felt that the British statesmen could never be brought to exert real pressure on Turkey in the matter

[10] D.D.F., 3d. ser., III, no. 264.
[11] S.D., I, no. 195.

of reforms.[12] In this he was right, for as Arthur Nicolson put it:

> . . . we [i.e. the foreign office] were desirous of not using language at Constantinople which would merely incense the Turks and do more harm than good. We succeeded, I think, to a certain extent in modifying the representations which were to be made at Stamboul. I need not say that we have always kept most carefully in view the necessity of us doing as little as possible to arouse Moslem feelings, as we know very well the effect which would be produced amongst our Mussulmans in India.[13]

The policy of Downing Street, like that of the Wilhelmstrasse, was one of reserve, a policy of watchful waiting. But without reforms there was sure to be a Balkan war. When the situation became serious England, nevertheless, was willing to join the other powers in attempting to prevent and localise the war. Although willing to maintain Entente solidarity, and to discuss matters *à trois*, Sir Edward Grey stressed more than either Poincaré or Sazonov the necessity of drawing in Austria and Germany so as not to present them with a *fait accompli.* He took the stand that Austria-Hungary and Russia, as most interested powers, should come to some decision as to European policy. England would then direct her path accordingly.[14]

Sazonov's visit to London towards the end of September, 1912 had gone off very well. The conversations had shown that there were no serious English-Russian differences, and Sazonov had good reason to believe that England did not look askance at his general policy. Sir Edward Grey had even informed him that:

> An agreement exists between France and England, in accordance with which in case of a war with Germany, England has entered upon

[12] Izvolsky, II, no. 508; Sazonov, *Fateful Years*, pp. 62–3; B.D., IX, i, nos. 811, 812, 813. [13] Nicolson to Hardinge, Oct. 9, 1912, B.D., IX, ii, no. 10.

[14] Benckendorff, II, nos. 676, 691; G.P., XXXIII, nos. 12253, 12284. The Kaiser also believed in the necessity of Russia and Austria coming to an agreement among themselves, and thought this afforded a common ground on which an Anglo-German rapprochement might be built (G.P., XXXIII, no. 12253 marginal note). There were some advances for a more intimate exchange of ideas between Berlin and London at this time, but the rapidity with which events developed in the Near East put a stop to such conversations (*ibid.*, nos. 12240, 12284, 12287, 12295).

the obligation not only to help France by sea, but also by landing troops on the continent.[15]

King George likewise assured him, "We shall sink every single German merchant ship we shall get hold of." [16]

What significance can be attached to these declarations has often been debated in regard to the origins of the World War. Since France had promised her aid as soon as Germany entered the lists, the English statements must have been rather reassuring to Sazonov at a time when there was a real possibility of becoming involved in a general European conflict.

Russia had brought about the Balkan League, the Balkan League had brought the war. Of this there can be no doubt. But was this in line with Russia's wishes?

First of all it must be considered that the Balkan League, so far as St. Petersburg was concerned, was a weapon to be used against Austria-Hungary. When Pašić was in St. Petersburg in June, 1912 he discussed with both Sazonov and Kokovtsov the danger which confronted the League, "if Austria's designs for a large Albania were not dissipated." [17] Both of the Russian statesmen agreed that Austria's plans could not be permitted to materialise. It is sometimes stated that Russia hoped that the League would enable the Balkan states to take care of themselves without her aid.[18] This latter motivation cannot be considered seriously, for certainly no Russian official in the spring of 1912 would have held the opinion that the Balkan states with a population of ten million could alone withstand the Austrian Empire. Against Turkey the League was a horse of another color. And a self-sufficient Balkan League could only have Turkey in mind. In fact the Russian government was not opposed to a war between the Balkan states and Turkey. They

[15] Izvolsky, II, no. 508, p. 291. Grey's version is not as definite as this but does indicate that the general topic was discussed (B.D., IX, i, no. 805). On English plans for landing troops on the continent see, Carl Hosse, *Die englisch-belgischen Aufmarschpläne gegen Deutschland vor dem Weltkriege* (Vienna, 1930).

[16] Izvolsky, II, no. 508, p. 291.

[17] S.D., I, no. 271; B.D., IX, i, no. 580.

[18] Sazonov, *Fateful Years*, p. 55. This view was also expressed to the author in 1929–30 by several diplomats who had been in the Russian service in 1912.

could not have sponsored the treaties, nor sanctioned such division of spoils if they were interested in preserving the Ottoman Empire. Sazonov says in his memoirs that the alliance was encouraged since he was convinced that war would come and that Russia ". . . hoped that by showing a united front they [the Balkan states] might reduce the risks attendant on their inevitable and impending struggle with the Young Turks over the Balkan problem and perhaps with Austria-Hungary also, in the event, always to be reckoned with, that the latter should attempt a hostile move." [19] After mentioning the victories of the Balkan states he notes later, "The Balkan alliance, constituted with the good wishes of Russia, had brilliantly justified the hopes reposed in it." [20] While the Russian statesmen foresaw the coming struggle and in principle were not opposed to it — they would not have been worthy of the name of "Big Slav Brother" if they had been opposed — this does not necessarily mean that they favored the outbreak of the war in 1912. The anti-Turkish provisions of the treaty were necessary because the Balkan states were interested in them, and without them Russia could not have brought about the League with its anti-Austrian point. They had to take the one to get the other, and they were willing to make the bargain.

By the famous veto-clause which had been inserted in the Serbian-Bulgarian treaty, Russia thought that her leadership of the League and consequently her position as arbiter of peace and war had been guaranteed. Strangely enough, it was this clause which calmed both Kiderlen and Berchtold. They thought that Russia was militarily unprepared and desirous of general peace, and that the Balkan states would not budge without Russian consent. Officially and formally the Russian government certainly warned the Balkan states against the opening of hostilities. The question then presents itself, why did the latter disregard this veto?

The real truth was that the Balkan states had decided and de-

[19] Sazonov, *Fateful Years*, p. 55.
[20] *Ibid.*, p. 72.

termined on their own policy and were not to be stopped by Russia or by the powers in general. They had come to the conclusion that the time was opportune and conditions favorable to their cause; Russia apparently was of the other opinion. And this was primarily what lay behind the whole Russian veto, that is, the moment had not come. Sazonov himself told the French chargé, in September, 1912, "if it was a question of starting things, it is Russia and not Bulgaria which ought to determine the moment, and that moment is not yet come." [21] Russia had certainly advised Danev in favor of peace on his visit to St. Petersburg and many times since, but behind every warning stood the question of opportuneness. The ending of the Tripolitan War, the threat of Austrian intervention, the inability of Russia to help out, all these arguments hinged on the time element.[22] Later the threat that Europe might maintain the *status quo* even if the Balkan allies won, was added. Yet Russia's support of the *status quo* was more a means of restraining Austria than a proposal for stopping the war.

The whole question in reality simmers down to this point: that Russia thought she would become involved in the war if it broke out and felt that she was not sufficiently prepared to undertake a conflict. In the minutes of the meeting of the French and Russian chiefs of staff of August 31, 1911, in view of Russian unpreparedness, it was stated: "Under these circumstances it seems that Russia will not be in a position for two years to wage a war with Germany with the slightest chance of success." [23] In the meeting of July, 1912, the situation was not much better.[24] The Russian officers at this time pointed out that, for reasons of morale, Russia could not stand a defeat by

[21] Doulcet to Poincaré, Sept. 14, 1912, D.D.F., 3d. ser., III, no. 402; see also, no. 460.

[22] S.D., I, nos. 185, 187, 188; *Doklad*, I, 226; also see above, pp. 104, 110.

[23] W. A. Suchomlinow, *Erinnerungen* (Berlin, 1924), p. 257; for a slightly different version, Izvolsky, I, no. 117. For Russia's desire to see serious complications avoided for a year or so see, *Les Carnets de Georges Louis* (2 vols.; Paris, 1925), I, 241; Ernest Judet, *Georges Louis* (Paris, 1925), p. 144.

[24] Suchomlinov, *Erinnerungen*, p. 261; Izvolsky, II, no. 367; D.D.F., 3d. ser., III, no. 200.

Austria. Intervention of Sweden was also feared, and then significantly it was stated that new railroads made it possible for Turkey to mobilise more quickly.

It was a matter of difference of interests and opinions, and the Balkan states acted according to their own dictates. They thought it was time to strike, and had no intention to let the iron cool. Yet behind the whole attitude of the Balkan states towards the official Russian veto and Russian threats, was the idea that this was not the real feeling of Russia and perhaps not even of the Russian government. It certainly did not correspond to the encouragement which Russia had recently given to the Balkan states. Public opinion in Russia was clearly out of sympathy with the policy of the Sängerbrücke and the Balkan statesmen knew that similar opinion had driven the government to action in 1827 and 1877.[25] The Balkan governments always counted on "unofficial Russia." [26] Mention has been made of Guchkov and his circle.[27] On the eve of the war Serbia sent a special delegate to St. Petersburg. He despatched home encouraging reports on Russian opinion in which he maintained that the government did not want war, but society was of a different opinion; conditions were not as in 1908, and Russia would march if need be.[28] Pašić told the English minister that the "idea is ineradicable [in Serbia and Bulgaria that] . . . notwithstanding Russia's official declarations, public opinion in Russia will not permit Balkan states to be abandoned. . . ." [29] In the opinion of the French minister, shared fully by his Austrian colleague, Serbia always relied ". . . sur du concours eventuel de la Russie 'non officielle.' . . ." [30] "It has of course been im-

[25] Doulcet to Poincaré, October 11, 1912, D.D.F., 3d. ser., IV, no. 123. For a telling indictment of the inconsistency of Russian policy at this time see, Panafieu to Poincaré, Oct. 3, 1912, *ibid.*, no. 39.

[26] For a good description of Russian opinion see, Pourtalès to Bethmann Hollweg, Oct. 12, 1912, G.P., XXXIII, no. 12270.

[27] See above, pp. 106–7.

[28] This was Professor Radovan Košutić who had also been sent to Russia at the time of the annexation crisis. For his reports in 1908 see, S.D., I, nos. 70, 75, 82, 135; for those in 1912, *ibid.*, nos. 200, 201, 204, 289.

[29] Barclay to Grey, Sept. 23, 1913, B.D., IX, i, no. 737; see also, IX, ii, 367.

[30] D.D.F., 3d. ser., IV, no. 577; Ö-U.A., IV, nos. 4020, 4035.

possible," so ran the opinion at the foreign office in London, "for Russia to make the Balkan states believe that in all eventualities she would leave them to their fate; and, as a matter of the fact, the Balkan states are quite right in not believing this." [31]

Even in the inner circle in St. Petersburg every one does not appear to have used the same language. Sazonov and Kokovtsov seem to have been consistent and united in their admonitions and in their policy.[32] Neratov, on the other hand, who had charge of the foreign office when Sazonov was absent, does not appear to have been so firm in his language.[33] Nelidov, the director of the press, even declared to the correspondents, "that the intervention of Russia in the war would be unavoidable, and mentioned that public opinion would force the government to intervene; it was unthinkable that Russia would not help the Balkan states to obtain an expansion of territory." [34] A few days later when Thurn mentioned this to Kokovtsov and Sazonov, the latter called the press chief to task. Nelidov denied having made incriminating statements, but nevertheless he was given an opportunity to depart with a Red Cross unit for Greece. Whereupon Thurn telegraphed to Vienna; "This remedy leads to the conclusion that the former press chief could not have been entirely guiltless; it shows on the other hand the good-will of Sazonov [35] to maintain at least order and discipline in his own household." The military circles with their advice and their preparation also spoke a different language from that emanating from the foreign office.[36]

With this division of opinions in Russia, it is not surprising

[31] Minute, Oct. 1, 1912, B.D., IX, i, 706.

[32] This is borne out in general by all the documents on this period. In a conversation with Count Kokovtsov in October, 1929, the latter assured the writer that Sazonov took all major steps only after consultation with him.

[33] S.D., I, nos. 187, 198; Izvolsky, II, no. 470. Kiderlen had confidence in Sazonov, but not in Neratov (Ö-U.A., IV, no. 3914).

[34] Pourtalès to Bethmann Hollweg, Oct. 12, 1912, G.P., XXXIII, no. 12270.

[35] Thurn to foreign office, Oct. 18, 1912, Ö-U.A., IV, no. 4135.

[36] Paul Cambon in an excellent statement on Russian policy felt certain that there was divided council in St. Petersburg (D.D.F., 3d. ser., IV, no. 107). See also the views of Jules Cambon (*ibid.*, no. 199).

that the imperial ministers in the various Balkan capitals followed a somewhat independent interpretation of their instructions. Russian foreign representatives were rather notorious for this under the old régime, and in 1912, well aware of the determination of the Balkan states, it was hard for them to jeopardise by a direct negation the ambitions which they had done so much to arouse. The military attaché in Sofia, Romanovsky, apparently was especially active in urging Bulgaria to go on.[37] Although Hartwig delivered the warnings of Sazonov, he did little to restrain the Serbs. He was always consulted on the most secret questions and there is not one shred of evidence that he ever disapproved of Serbian action. Toshev, former Bulgarian minister to Serbia, specifically states that Hartwig told him and also the Serbian leaders not to worry about the advice of "foolish Sazonov," and assured them that they might rely on Russian public opinion and material support.[38] Both Hartwig and Nekludov were jubilant — the latter even wept with joy — when mobilisation was really under way.[39] Hartwig's position at Belgrade is worthy of special notice. On October 10th the English minister at Belgrade reported:

> I regret that there are many reasons to suspect Russian minister is not acting straightforwardly. He promoted Serbo-Bulgarian entente and has always encouraged Serbia to rely on Russian support. His position in present crisis is consequently awkward and he seems to overcome the difficulty by carrying out his instructions officially while privately encouraging Serbia to count upon Russian sympathy and to think in spite of declaration of the powers concerning maintenance of *status quo* if the Balkan states acquire territory they cannot be turned out.[40]

Hartwig soon threw "off the mask" and "expressed himself as disgusted with Monsieur Sazonov's policy" to the Rumanian minister.[41] In the eyes of the British and French ministers

[37] G.P., XXXIII, no. 12219; Ö-U.A., IV, no. 4145. [38] Toshev, I, 413.

[39] *Ibid.*; S.D., I, no. 195. [40] Paget to Grey, Oct. 10, 1912, B.D., IX, ii, no. 11.

[41] Paget to Grey, Oct. 19, 1912, *ibid.*, IX, ii, no. 48. Jules Cambon reported to Poincaré that Hartwig was assuring Pašić that Sazonov's policy was not that of the Russian people and if the Turks won the people of Russia would come to the aid of the Balkan states (D.D.F., 3d. ser., IV, no. 199).

Hartwig was the real power in Belgrade. Later in connection with the conflict over a Serbian Adriatic port, Paget reported to London:

> Hartwig manipulates the Serbians as he pleases and if he wanted could induce them to come to some reasonable arrangement but he pursues his own and not Monsieur Sazonov's policy, he is more Serbian than the Serbians themselves and more Austro-phobe than the Serbians and one consequently never knows what he may be doing.[42]

On October 23rd, Descos reported to Paris that Serbian policy was so dominated by Hartwig that Serbia "had ceased to be a simple *Zweigniederlassung* of the Grand Empire, as one was wont to say at Vienna, but had become Russia herself." [43] His further reports have constant reference to Hartwig's influence and in 1914 Descos stated that ". . . during the whole period of the Balkan crisis Hartwig could justly pass as the director of Serbian policy." [44]

With foreign representatives of this type the official peace policy of the Russian government must have had little effect in Sofia or Belgrade. Nor may it be forgotten that even the formal warnings were interrupted by assurances of diplomatic support, by the information that negotiations were going on to restrain Austria, and by measures such as the trial mobilisation and the awarding of the Russian field marshal's staff to King Carol.

A word must here be said of the Russian trial mobilisation which took place exactly at the time of the mobilisation of the armies of the Balkan states. Russia at once gave assurances that this measure had no connection whatever with the Balkan crisis; it had been planned for some time.[45] Both the German and the Austrian foreign offices accepted these explanations and raised no difficulty. Berchtold assured the Austrian Delega-

[42] Paget to Grey, Nov. 22, 1912, B.D., IX, ii, no. 257.

[43] D.D.F., 3d. ser., IV, no. 228.

[44] Descos to Viviani, June 17, 1914, D.D.F., 3d. ser., X, no. 394; see also, IV, no. 577; V, nos. 126, 220, 554; VI, nos. 142, 368; X, nos. 499, 511.

[45] G.P., XXXIII, no. 12193; Ö-U.A., IV, no. 3901. In regard to Russian mobilisation measures see, Rudolf Kiszling, "Russlands Kriegsvorbereitungen im Herbst 1912 und ihre Rückwirkungen auf Österreich-Ungarn," *Berliner Monatshefte*, XIII (1935), 181–92.

tions that there was no cause for alarm and the papers carried reassuring statements.[46] On the 29th of September news of the trial mobilisation likewise reached Paris from Warsaw and created a stir in the papers.[47]

But if the German and Austrian foreign offices were not exactly alarmed, they followed events closely. The matter was mentioned to Sazonov on his visit to Berlin and it later became the subject of an exchange of various dispatches, in which Germany asked that she be notified in the future of all trial mobilisations. Sazonov recognized the correctness of Germany's wish, but gave no definite promises.[48]

In Vienna Berchtold asked the chief of staff to watch Russian preparations with increased attention.[49] There are many reports in the Austrian *Kriegsarchiv* dealing with this matter. If mere reports ever justify counter-measures, then the Austrian chief of staff would certainly have been justified in taking far-reaching steps. This however was not done. The Austrians scrutinised all reports carefully, and the summaries made by the *Evidenzbureau* were very moderate in tone.[50] Up to October 7th the reports showed that Russia — "without doubt in connection with the Balkan crisis" — had undertaken the following measures:

1) Wide calling in of reservists in all circles of Russian Poland for training which is to be ended October 20th (all arms of the years 1905, 1907; parts of the levy of 1904, 1906).
2) Retention of the third year's levy [*dritter Präsenzjahrgang*] in the same region.
3) Preparedness for a trial mobilisation in certain circles of Russian Poland, the carrying out of which, however, is to be ordered later (16–19th Oct.).

[46] *Die Zeit* (Vienna), October 2, 7, 8, 1912.

[47] Izvolsky, II, no. 452.

[48] G.P., XXXIII, nos. 12256, 12180 note.

[49] Ö-U.K.A., Res. Gestb., no. 3980 (1912).

[50] For example, Ö-U.K.A., Berichte des Evidenz Bureau, Ev. Br., no. 2327, Oct. 7, 1912; Ev. Br., no. 2327, I, Oct. 11, 1912; Ev. Br., no. 2327, II, Oct. 30, 1912; Ev. Br., no. 2327, III, Nov. 8, 1912; also the report of Oct. 4, 1912.

4) Completion of the peace time strength, partial increase of "erhöhte Friedenstände" in the region of Warsaw.
5) Contemplation of certain troop movements.[51]

No measures, however, were taken in the provinces bordering on the monarchy.

On October 13th, Schemua in a note to Auffenberg stated:

> Military measures taken by Russia cannot be determined as having connection with Balkan crisis, but it can be suspected. The reservists were called in September 30th, and trial mobilisation was also ordered. When Austria did not intervene this was postponed until October 20th when first battles might take place. This "Rückendeckung" has enabled the Balkan states to place all troops against Turkey and leave none against Austria and Rumania.[52]

The suspicion of the Austrian officials that there was a connection between the Russian mobilisation and the events in the Balkans was justified. Taube holds there was a direct relation.[53] He is of the opinion that the military, who did not recognize the authority of Sazonov, thought that peace could no longer be maintained in the Balkans, and had taken advantage of the foreign minister's absence to obtain the consent of the tsar for a trial mobilisation. On October 3rd, Popović sent a telegram to Belgrade in which he went out of his way to state: "The Russian government has assured Austria-Hungary and Germany that the mobilisation in Poland had no connection whatever with the situation in the Balkans and is not directed against the central powers." [54] In a conversation with the writer on May 23, 1930, Popović expressed the opinion that there was a direct connection between the events in the Balkans and the mobilisation. Another order, having to do with a general, not trial, mobilisation, indicates that Russia at least contemplated the

[51] Ö-U.K.A., Ev. Br., no. 2327.

[52] Ö-U.K.A., K. & K. Chef des Gestb., Zur Res. Gestb., no. 4302, Oct. 13, 1912.

[53] Taube was formerly professor of international law at the University in St. Petersburg, a member of the Russian upper chamber, and at times acted as adviser to the government. See his, *Erinnerungen*, p. 256–7. Thurn also reported that Sazonov stated that he had not been consulted about carrying out the maneuvers (Ö-U.A., IV, no. 4091).

[54] S.D., I, no. 196.

possibility of war from the time when the Serbian-Bulgarian treaty was signed. On February 28/March 12, 1912, the day before that alliance was concluded, the tsar had approved a measure providing:

> On the announcement of general mobilisation in the districts of European Russia as a result of political developments on the western borders, the telegram in regard to mobilisation will serve at the same time as the All Highest order in regard to the opening of hostilities against Austria or Germany.[55]
>
> As concerns Rumania, out of consideration that this power might not join our enemies at once, the opening of hostilities against her can follow only upon the receipt of a special telegram.[56]

This order was of course circulated to the Russian commanders, and in view of the disturbed situation received renewed attention in the autumn of 1912. On September 30th, the day of Balkan mobilisation and of trial mobilisation in Russia, the chief of staff of the Warsaw military district communicated this order to the commander of the VI Army Corps.[57] This latter notice was captured by the German army during the World War. In order to set the document in its proper light, Count Montgelas wrote to General Dobrovsky, who was director of the Russian mobilisation department in 1914 and after the war resided in Belgrade. The general replied: "The order contains instructions which were to be operative in case of a war which

[55] In December, 1912 this was changed so as to require a special telegram for the opening of hostilities (Gunther Frantz, *Russlands Eintritt in den Weltkrieg* [Berlin, 1924], p. 237).

[56] Ö-U.K.A., Ev. Br., no. 6055, Oct. 10, 1912; Frantz, *Russlands Eintritt in den Weltkrieg*, p. 234.

[57] Count Max Montgelas, *The Case for the Central Powers* (London, 1925), pp. 56, 235–6. A copy of this order dated August 1, 1912 had come into the hands of the Austrians by October. The *Evidenzbureau* characterised it as an "anscheinend glaubwürdigen Kopie," and added this comment: "Falls diese Mobilisierungsweisung tatsächlich besteht so wäre dies ein Zeichen, dass Unternehmungen der Kavallerie, Grenzwache, Raids, und dgl. möglichst bald nach dem wahrscheinlich geheim erlassenen Mobilisierungsbefehle beginnen werden und man daher auf Ueberraschungen gefasst sein muss." (Ö-U.K.A., Ev. Br., no. 6055, Oct. 11, 1912). With this document in their possession it is surprising that the Vienna chief of staff took Russian military measures so calmly. The significance of this document as cited by Montegelas is stressed by E. Adamov, *Die Europäischen Mächte und die Türkei während des Weltkrieges*, I, 37; Taube, *Erinnerungen*, pp. 257–8.

was expected in 1912, in connection with the declaration of war on Turkey made at that time by Serbia and Bulgaria." [58] War had of course not yet been declared on September 30th, but this hardly detracts from the significance of this statement. Sukhomlinov in discussing the above order states that it "shows the close inner connection between the offensive of the army and the political situation, as well as the logical consequence with which the war minister or better the general staff worked." [59]

It is hard to judge the real significance of the trial mobilisation. It probably was a broad gesture signifying that Russia meant to have her say in the coming events and would not suffer a humiliation such as that of 1908–9.[60] She did not desire war, but such military measures as those which were to follow later can only be interpreted as methods of keeping Austria in check. They were decided upon at a time when no one was certain as to what attitude Austria would take and the invasion of the Sanjak seemed almost a certainty to the Russian statesmen. Had Austria moved, what would have followed is problematical. Sazonov at least continually threatened that under certain circumstances he could give no guarantee as to what public opinion would force him to do.[61] Russia would in all likelihood have actually come to the aid of the Balkan states, for such an advance by Austria would have led — under the terms of the Balkan alliance — to a war between the Dual Monarchy and the Balkan League. Neither unofficial nor official Russia would have permitted a victory of Austria-Hungary over the small Slavic states.

Just how far the military measures had the support of the foreign office is hard to say.[62] Most of the documents we have, showing Sazonov's disapproval, were meant for foreign con-

[58] Montgelas, *Case for the Central Powers*, p. 228.

[59] As quoted by Taube, *Erinnerungen*, p. 258.

[60] This was Berchtold's opinion (Note an den Chef des Generalstabs, Oct. 26, 1912, Ö-U.A., IV, no. 4183).

[61] *Ibid.*, IV, nos. 4077, 4091; D.D.F., 3d. ser., II, no. 304.

[62] Sazonov on Oct. 14, 1912 told the Austrian ambassador that he would have disapproved of the trial mobilisation had he been consulted, but that it was ended and normal conditions restored (Ö-U.A., IV, no. 4091). That this was not the case is clear from Neratov's letter to Kokovtsov (Benckendorff, II, no. 696).

sumption, and until more internal documents are available this phase of the problem will remain somewhat obscure. We do have one report of October 23rd, in which Neratov, Sazonov's assistant, definitely approves of the military measures then being taken.[63] As to the effects of the Russian military measures, there is no evidence that Austrian or German foreign policy was noticeably affected by the news of the trial mobilisation on October 1st. Neither country at that time desired to pursue an active policy and their decisions were made quite independent of these measures in Russian Poland. In the Balkan states it no doubt took much of the sting out of Russia's warnings and led the allies to believe in material support from Russia.

Trial mobilisation and negotiations in Vienna and Bucharest were the most important, but not the only steps which Russia undertook in behalf of the Balkan states. Outwardly in opposition to the war, she nevertheless took action to ensure their victory. On October 3rd Neratov suggested that Sazonov advise Italy not to be too generous in her terms to Turkey at the close of the Tripolitan War, especially in the matter of indemnity, since Turkey would surely agree to Italy's figure.[64] Neratov indicated that the less money Turkey had, the better would be the outlook, if not for preventing war in the Balkans, at least for shortening it. And this was at a time when Russia was using the conclusion of the Tripolitan War as an argument to dissuade Bulgaria from attacking Turkey! Instead of desiring the conclusion of peace between Italy and Turkey, as she had in the spring, Russia now wanted the Tripolitan War protracted in the interests of the Balkan powers. She also aided Bulgaria to obtain permission from the Ballhausplatz for the transportation of war material through Austria-Hungary.[65]

Plans were also discussed for landing Russian troops in Bulgarian ports, and the Russian Black Sea fleet was distinctly on the alert for all possible events.[66] Representations were made in

[63] Benckendorff, II, no. 696. Zaionchkovski quoting from Russian archives ascribes this report to Sazonov (*Podgotovka rossii*, p. 272).

[64] Izvolsky, II, nos. 462, 481. [65] *Ibid.*, II, no. 489; Ö-U.A., IV, no. 3977.

[66] K.A., XV, no. 21 (*Berl. Mon.*, VIII, 1073).

Constantinople to keep Turkey from extending naval operations to the Black Sea.[67] Neratov was willing to go even so far as to buy off possible Austrian opposition to this exclusion of the Black Sea from the theater of war, by permitting Austria to declare that the northern part of the Sanjak should not be the scene of any military operations.[68] Definite decision on this matter was postponed until Sazonov's return from his visit to western Europe, and by that time things had clearly advanced beyond the stage where such a declaration could be made.

Fearing that a long drawn-out war would be unfavorable to the allies, the Russian government as early as October 11th — seven days before the opening of hostilities by Bulgaria — started to discuss plans for mediation and bringing the war to a safe conclusion.[69] Clearly Russia had no premonition of how successful the Balkan states were to be.

Taking everything into consideration it seems that the Balkan states were justified in not taking the Russian warnings seriously. In their eyes there were two groups in Russia; the foreign office and unofficial Russia, the latter having many people of rank, position, and official station under its banners. The one urged them to stop, the other to go on. They chose to pin their hopes on the latter for their voices had the more sincere ring. In fact, after the great victories, when Sazonov was trying to regain his prestige in the Balkan capitals, he scouted the idea that there was any difference between "his policy and that of unofficial Russia." [70] Such charges did not even merit an answer, and the reason he had permitted this "apparent difference" to exist was that it would help him in his negotiations with the other

[67] K.A., XV, no. 25 (*Berl. Mon.*, VIII, 1075). Russia's declaration that she would not permit Turkey to carry the war into the Black Sea goes back to suggestions in telegrams of Nekludov of September 6 and 20, 1912 (Benckendorff, II, no. 682).

[68] K.A., XV, no. 25 (*Berl. Mon.*, VIII, 1075–6).

[69] K.A., XV, no. 28 (*Berl. Mon.*, VIII, 1185–6); D.D.F., 3d. ser., IV, nos. 126, 135.

[70] K.A., XVI, no. 45 (*Berl. Mon.*, IX, 66 ff.). This section of the document was omitted when it was published in 1914 (*Zeitschrift für Internationales Recht*, ed. Th. Niemeyer [Leipzig, 1915], XXV, 136, trans. from *Russian Orange Book on the Balkan War, August 1912–July 1913*).

cabinets if he could point to his difficult position at home. *Status quo* had only been agreed upon to hinder a separate action by Austria-Hungary, and he forthwith assured the Balkan states that it could no longer be maintained since the whole situation had been changed by the Turkish refusal to accept reforms. A most curious process of reasoning, to be sure.

Sazonov thus united himself with unofficial Russia which had urged war. His warnings appear as mere steps to lull the suspicions of Europe. The Russian veto never existed. This document wipes away the many assurances to the powers and the whole impression which was prevalent in all the European capitals. The document, however, was meant to restore prestige and position in the Balkans and also to advise kindly against taking Adrianople. It is worth while speculating what he would have written had Turkey won the first great battles. Yet even if the document is not taken at face value it does show that the Russian foreign office was in principle not opposed to the initiative of the Balkan states.[71] Sazonov wanted to be on the safe side whichever way the war went. While willing to do all in his power to help the Balkan governments he desired to avoid all responsibility. He could hardly have followed any other policy if he did not want to appear before Europe as a marpeace or, on the other hand, to sacrifice entirely the position Russia had but recently won as leader and protector of the small Balkan states. The Russian statesmen had patronised the Balkan League in order to lead it; they ended by having the leadership taken from their hands although the partnership remained intact. Pressed by the independent and determined action of the Balkan governments they trimmed their sails accordingly and handled the diplomatic situation adroitly.

[71] The following comment in regard to excerpts from *Le livre noire,* ed. René Marchand (3 vols.; Paris, 1922–34) describes fairly accurately the situation: "Hinter den Kulissen sympathisierte sie [Russia] durchaus mit dem Vorhaben der Balkanstaaten, da sich deren Ziele mit den grossslawischen Interessen deckten. Vor den Kulissen, auf der Bühne des diplomatischen Schauspiels, stimmte sie willig und wohlklingend in den Chor des europäischen Konzertes ein, der die Erhaltung des Friedens verlangte" (Anonymus, "Das diplomatische Doppelspiel Russlands beim Ausbruch des ersten Balkankrieges," *Archiv für Politik und Geschichte,* II [1924], 416).

CHAPTER IX

THE BALKAN POLICY OF AUSTRIA-HUNGARY

THE policy of no country caused so much anxiety at the outbreak of the Balkan War as that of Austria-Hungary.[1] No one felt sure what the Ballhausplatz was going to do. In fact the Viennese officials themselves had to face that problem. They had to choose between the policy of non-intervention, of no further territorial expansion, which had been their platform since at least 1908, and the policy which was often "shoved into their shoes" of reoccupation of the Sanjak and expansion *au delà de Mitrovica* to Salonica. There were some scattered voices which advocated the latter, but it never was near to becoming the official policy. To decide for the former when an aggressive action was expected was not an easy decision to make. Yet that was what the foreign office did.

This decision has often been criticised. Then and afterwards many have thought that a more active policy should have been followed. Whether that was advisable belongs of course to the *ifs* of history. Yet considering the situation at that time it was the only reasonable policy that Berchtold could have followed. Especially was this so since both the emperor and the heir apparent, as well as the heads of the dual governments and even the common minister of war, were against anything which might involve the Dual Monarchy in a conflict.[2] Nor did the attitude of Germany or the whole international situation encourage a different policy.

[1] Portions of this chapter appeared under the title, "Die tieferen Ursachen der Politik Berchtolds im Oktober 1912," *Berliner Monatshefte*, X (1932), 218–44.

[2] Ö-U.A., IV, no. 3787; Nintchitch, "Les repugnances de François Ferdinand à une guerre contre la Serbie," in his *La crise bosniaque*, II, 213–22; Leopold von Chlumecky, *Erzherzog Franz Ferdinands Wirken und Wollen* (Berlin, 1929), p. 139; Theodor von Sosnosky, *Franz Ferdinand, Der Erzherzog-Thronfolger* (Berlin, 1929), pp. 146–54; Conrad, III, 127, 155, 160: Joseph Redlich, *Emperor Francis Joseph of Austria* (London, 1929), p. 521.

It is also stated frequently that Austrian action was motivated by the idea that the Balkan states would be defeated in the coming war.[3] This myth belongs in the limbo to which the charge that Austria desired territorial expansion to Salonica has been relegated. The Ballhausplatz did not shape its policy in expectation of a Turkish victory. But neither the Austrians nor anyone else, including the Balkan statesmen themselves, expected the overwhelming and rapid collapse of Turkey. Vienna thought the war would be a long drawn-out affair and that there would be plenty of time and occasion to insure Austrian "vital interests." In other words it was a policy *à la Napoleon III* in 1866. What the monarchy's vital interests were neither Berchtold nor anyone else could state at the beginning of October.[4] Clearly these would depend on the course events took in the war.

The above generalisations are so broad and sweeping that they require somewhat more detailed analysis. This may be conveniently arranged about the following fundamental thesis: the policy followed in 1912 was the direct result and continuation of the policy of Austria-Hungary in the past, and especially that laid down by Aehrenthal subsequent to the annexation of Bosnia-Herzegovina in 1908. A consideration of this thesis will refute in great part the charge that the Ballhausplatz based its policy on the idea that Turkey would be victorious. Other specific documents from the eve of the war can also be drawn in to support this refutation.

In 1897 when the break-up of Turkey seemed imminent the question of the future arrangement of the Balkan peninsula was the subject of various discussions in Vienna, especially preparatory to the visit of Francis Joseph to St. Petersburg which was to take place that spring. The Austrian ministers had little confidence in Muraviev, the Russian foreign minister, and did not expect to make any definitive agreements. Nevertheless it was thought well to be prepared. On April 2, 1897 the chief of staff,

[3] For example, Sazonoff, *Fateful Years*, p. 70; Redlich, *Francis Joseph*, pp. 521–2; Steed, *Through Thirty Years*, I, 362; Boghitschewitsch, *Serbien und der Weltkrieg*, p. 158; Schmitt, *Coming of the War*, I, 104, 132.

[4] Denkschrift, Oct. 2, 1912, Ö-U.A., IV, no. 3928.

Count Beck, drew up a memorandum dealing with the possibilities of a change of *status quo* in the Balkans, in which he pointed out that the eastern shore of the Adriatic must either go to Austria-Hungary or to a small new state which would be subject to the monarchy. As to the Sanjak (Tara Thar territory) he concluded:

> We can absolutely not do without the immediate possession of these territories. This is in no way on account of the region itself, for in itself it certainly is not worth coveting. Also we do not need the Tara Thar territory on account of the connection to Salonica, for the natural way to Salonica leads — as it appears one cannot often enough reiterate — through the Morava valley, that is through Serbia. But Serbia and Montenegro must remain isolated from one another, and this is only to be accomplished by our taking the strip of territory which lies between them directly into our own hands.[5]

He was willing to give to Serbia the Kossovo Polje, Montenegro the territory of Plava-Gusinje and, if it could not be avoided, Scutari, but in this case the Montenegrin territory must not reach the Drin valley. Albania was to reach to the watershed between the Adriatic and the Aegean and the rest of the territory was to be made into an independent Macedonia, which was to become the real prop for Austrian power in the Balkans.

On April 19, 1897 the whole question of the future of Turkey was the subject of a conference attended by foreign minister Goluchowski, finance minister Kallay, chief of staff Beck and Sektionschef Merey.[6] The memoir of Count Beck served as a basis for discussion. Kallay, Goluchowski and apparently Merey were against an independent Macedonia, but they were all agreed on the necessity of keeping any great power from establishing itself on the eastern shores of the Adriatic. Likewise they were all in favor of annexing the Sanjak, although the foreign minis-

[5] Beiträge zur Klarstellung der bei einer etwäigen Änderung des *status quo* auf der Balkan Halbinsel in Betracht zu ziehenden Verhältnis, 2 Beilagen, April 2, 1897, Ö-U.K.A., Operations Bureau Fasz. 46.

[6] Notizen über die Besprechungen des Chef des Generalstabs mit dem Minister des Äussern Goluchowski am 19/4/97, Ö-U.K.A., Operations Bureau Fasz. 46. The document consulted has Merey's report on one side in red ink, Beck's report on the other side in black ink.

ter thought the city of Novibazar ought to go to Serbia. After each had expressed his opinion they took a map, and with this before them discussed and traced the future boundaries in the Balkans. Their division, tentative as it was, is not only interesting in showing the views of the Ballhausplatz at this period, but also comes remarkably close to the division which would have resulted in 1912–3 had the second Balkan War not occurred. Bulgaria was cut shorter in 1897 than she would have been in 1912, while Greece was the most favored child of all. The following summarises their territorial allotments. Austria would obtain Bosnia-Herzegovina, the Sanjak minus Novibazar, and the occupation of the ports of Durazzo and Valona was designated as desirable. Serbia was to obtain the Kossovo Polje and territory including Usküb; Montenegro, Ipek and Djakova, thus bringing the countries into direct contact. An attempt which they thought would probably not succeed was to be made to obtain the boundary line Rustchuk-Shumla-Varna for Rumania. Bulgaria was to receive the territory between the Maritza and the Struma and up to the watershed between the Ionian and the Aegean seas. Greece was to obtain Crete, the territory up to the Struma, thus including Salonica, with the northern boundary at Seres, running westward to include Janina. Serbia and Greece were thus not to have a common frontier. Albania was to be made into an independent state with Scutari and the lake of Ochrida entirely within its boundaries.

The chief of staff was not at all satisfied with the way the conference went and severely criticised the whole plan.[7] Above all he was absolutely opposed to permitting Serbia and Montenegro to have a common frontier, and did not share the opinion of the conference that this juxtaposition was unimportant. The conference on the other hand had considered that "the common border would be overawed and dominated by our position in the Sanjak of Novibazar."[8] Subsequently in St. Petersburg,

[7] Reflexionen mit Bezug auf die am 19 April 1897 stattgefundenen Besprechungen, Ö-U.K.A., Operations Bureau Fasz. 46.

[8] Notizen über die Besprechungen des Chefs des Generalstabs mit dem Minister des Äussern Goluchowski am 19/4/97, Ö-U.K.A., Operations Bureau Fasz. 46.

Austria-Hungary and Russia agreed that, if it should be impossible to maintain the *status quo* in the Balkans, neither country would attempt to make any conquests, nor would they permit any other great power to do so.[9] As to the more definite provisions in regard to partition of territory or the establishment of Albania, Russia reserved these questions for the future. Goluchowski's feeler for a definite arrangement was not taken up by Russia.[10]

Thus neither in the agreement with Russia, nor in the ministerial discussions preparatory to this meeting, was there any hint of active intervention on the break-up of Turkey. Of course Austria-Hungary would have to be heard in the final settlement, which was exactly what Berchtold said in 1912. In 1897 it was but natural that the monarchy should demand the annexation of Bosnia-Herzegovina. But even then the Ballhausplatz had departed a long way from the principles set up by Andrássy in 1879 in regard to the Sanjak.[11] The ministers were now for the annexation of only a part of this territory and were not opposed to a common frontier for Montenegro and Serbia, which had been the main argument for occupying the Sanjak.

With the agreement of 1897 the Balkan question was to be "put on ice," for the next decade.[12] Nevertheless it was often discussed and Austria-Hungary and Russia entered upon the Mürzsteg agreement, the declaration of neutrality of 1904,[13] and the whole tortuous reform plan of the next year. Yet during the entire period the fundamental policy remained the same. Goluchowski remained convinced of the impossibility of maintaining Turkey in Europe and his ideas now as before were based on dividing the territory between the different Balkan

[9] A. F. Pribram, *The Secret Treaties of Austria-Hungary 1879–1914* (2 vols.; Cambridge, Mass., 1920), I, 185–95.

[10] "Das Petersburger Kabinet ist auf dieses Ansinnen, wie seinerzeit auf die Vorschläge Grafen Goluchowski von Jahre 1897 nicht eingegangen" (Denkschrift [Hietzing], Aug. 15, 1909, Ö-U.A., II, no. 1720, p. 441).

[11] Denkschrift (Semmering), Aug. 9, 1908, *ibid.*, I, no. 32.

[12] Fay, *Origins of the World War*, I, 364–5.

[13] Pribram, *Secret Treaties*, I, 236–9.

states and the creation of an independent Albania.[14] No further specific plans for the division of territory are at hand — if ever there were any made in this period [15] — although with the general swing in politics Austria would undoubtedly have shown a somewhat more favorable attitude toward Bulgaria than in 1897.

The Young Turk Revolution in July 1908 opened a new chapter in Near Eastern history. Although favorably inclined toward this Turkish awakening, Aehrenthal looked forward to trouble in the Balkans. He envisaged "either a period of general anarchy or in the near future a war of Turkey with Bulgaria and Serbia, or even with other powers." [16] The question thus presented itself anew as to what position Austria-Hungary should take in the face of these eventualities.

> I think [so he wrote to the Austrian minister-president von Beck] that in regard to this there can be no important difference of opinion. It is a lesson of experience, that the monarchy at the outbreak of a new crisis in the Orient guards its interests best by remaining as long as possible a quiet but watchful observer. This I have already discussed with the cabinet. The strict carrying out of this non-intervention principle is however endangered as long as our garrisons are in the Sanjak of Novibazar. These find themselves somewhat in the air; the Lim line is no advantageous defensive position. Any sort of incident, the outburst of an anarchistic movement, or a massacre of Christians in these territories would involve us in an intervention with considerable military forces against our will and contrary to our interests. If we do not want to become involved in Turkish troubles (Händel) we must at once make up our mind to withdraw our garrison from Plevlje which no longer serves any military or political purpose. I am convinced, out of consideration for the prestige of the monarchy and the just pride of the army, that such a step could only be de-

[14] Erich Brandenburg, *Von Bismarck zum Weltkriege* (Berlin, 1925), p. 173; Herre, *Die Kleinen Staaten*, p. 328.

[15] "Die Frage auf welche Weise der Balkan unter die Balkanvölker aufgeteilt werden könnte ist am Ballplatz niemals aktuel gewesen, weil das ganze Bestreben der massgebenden Faktoren auf die Erhaltung der Türkei gerichtet war" (Graf A. Hoyos, *Der deutsch-englische Gegensatz und sein Einfluss auf die Balkanpolitik Österreich-Ungarns* [Berlin, 1922], p. 36; see also E. R. Steinitz, *Rings um Sasonow* [Berlin, 1928], p. 68).

[16] Private letter, Aehrenthal to Beck, Aug. 7, 1908, Ö-U.A., I, no. 29.

termined upon in connection with another measure, and this would be: The Annexation of Bosnia and the Herzegovina.[17]

There were other reasons which need not be gone into here for undertaking the annexation at that time, just as there were other reasons for evacuating the Sanjak.[18] The important point is that the Ballhausplatz surrendered of its own free will that joint occupation of the Sanjak which Andrássy in 1879 said epitomised Austro-Hungarian Near Eastern policy. This policy Andrássy had characterised as "maintenance of Turkey so long and so far as there is nothing better to replace it, and the prevention of the formation of great Slavic entities where Turkish rule succumbs to decay." [19]

Aehrenthal wrote in his famous *Semmering Denkschrift* of August 9, 1908, that "from these principles [those advanced by Andrássy] it would be possible to draw the conclusion that the monarchy absolutely would have to lay hands on the Sanjak when Turkish rule collapsed in these regions." [20] Aehrenthal then examined at great length whether such action would be wise from a military, political or financial view-point. In each case his conclusion was "no." [21] As to maintaining Turkey he pointed out that the occupation was irksome to the Porte and that better relations might be obtained by clearing out. As to the second fundamental principle of Andrássy's policy, the prevention of the formation of a great Slav state, the occupation of the Sanjak would hardly prevent that. Besides, even if Monte-

[17] *Ibid.*

[18] For example see, *ibid.*, I, nos. 32, 40.

[19] As quoted by Aehrenthal, *ibid.*, I, no. 32.

[20] *Ibid.*

[21] Austria was limited by treaty to a garrison of four to five thousand and these were scattered in three garrisons at Plevlje, Pyepolje, Proboj (Conrad, I, 99). From the military side the argument for the evacuation was that the Sanjak was too narrow and geographically unfavorable for the advance of an army in a war. Besides, the garrisons might easily be cut off in case of war with Montenegro, Serbia, or Turkey. Politically it seemed best to evacuate. It did not look as if Serbia and Montenegro would be apt to agree on the division of the Sanjak. If Austria stayed in the territory it would unite them and increase the Pan-Slav agitation. Further it would also bring about the opposition of the Albanians whose friendship Austria coveted. Financially the cost of garrisoning and fortifying the Sanjak would be ruinous (Ö-U.A., I, no. 32).

negro and Serbia were kept apart Austria still would not have "those safe boundaries which are necessary for any far-seeing eastern policy." Such safe boundaries could not be obtained "if we do not decide to seize the evil at the roots and make an end to the Great-Serbian dreams of the future." [22] He then stressed the Bulgarian-Serb antagonism and sketched the future as follows:

> If we favor the Bulgarian side in this quarrel and further the creation of a great Bulgaria at the cost of Serbia, the necessary preparations have been made to lay our hands on the rest of Serbia at some moment when the situation in Europe is favorable.
>
> Then we would have the safe boundaries which I referred to: an independent Albania under our leadership, a Montenegro with which we have friendly relations, and a great Bulgaria which out of thanks is obligated to us.
>
> I conclude therefore that the annexation of the Sanjak would bring us no real advantages, and that we can reach the goal of our Balkan policy, not by way of Novibazar, but only via Belgrade.

It was the suggestion contained in this statement which had led Conrad to consent to the evacuation, which, in itself, he questioned on grounds of prestige, especially among the Balkan peoples.[23] If the important question of the annexation of Bosnia-Herzegovina could be accomplished only with this sacrifice, well and good; the small corridor of the Sanjak was no military asset anyway and the whole Austrian-Serbian problem would have to be settled at some time by war. Relative to these ideas Conrad later wrote, "I remained true to the same, Baron Aehrenthal later changed them." [24]

One might question whether Aehrenthal even in 1908 really planned to carry out the program he had outlined. At least he certainly did not expect to intervene on the collapse of Turkey and prevent the division of the Sanjak between Serbia and Montenegro. In the same memoir, after mentioning that Austria did not want Salonica, he speaks specifically of Serbia and Montenegro as the new lords of the Sanjak and the legal suc-

[22] Ö-U.A., I, no. 32, p. 32; see also, Conrad, I, 108.

[23] Conrad, I, 98, 593–6.

[24] *Ibid.*, I, 108.

cessors of Turkey. That his policy was directed toward non-intervention is shown clearly also from the letter sent to Beck which is quoted in part above.[25] That the garrisons in the Sanjak hindered a policy of non-intervention was likewise stressed by Aehrenthal in the ministerial conference of August 19, 1908, when the whole problem of the contemplated annexation of Bosnia-Herzegovina and evacuation of the Sanjak was discussed. In a conversation with Hardinge at Ischl that same August, Aehrenthal again maintained that Austria would not lift a finger to stop the natural collapse of Turkey.[26]

At the ministerial conference of August 19th, only the Hungarian minister-president, Dr. Wekerle, questioned the advisability of abandoning the Sanjak. He wanted to know if it would not be possible to surrender the right of occupation in such a way that Austria-Hungary might again enter if Turkey were unable to hold this territory. Aehrenthal thought not, for once the Berlin Treaty had been torn up through the annexation one could not fall back on a clause of that treaty.[27]

The wisdom of evacuating the Sanjak has often been questioned.[28] Yet it was not much farther than Goluchowski would have gone in 1897 when he was willing to permit Serbia and Montenegro to have a common frontier. In 1912 when the question of the Sanjak was again up for discussion, it was once more decided that this territory was of no value to Austria.[29] And now having once decided to give up the position, Aehrenthal guarded against being drawn back into this "mouse-trap" as he characterised it.[30] One argument advanced for withdrawal was that it would be a friendly gesture to Turkey. Yet the Porte was not overjoyed by this turn of events and as early as October 17, 1908, made advances to obtain an Austro-Hungarian guar-

[25] See above, p. 170. [26] Ö-U.A., I, no. 36. [27] *Ibid.*, I, no. 40.

[28] Denkschrift betreffend die Sandschakfrage, Oct. 25(?), 1912, *ibid.*, IV, no. 4171; *Die Zeit*, Nov. 16, 1912; Nintchitch, *La crise bosniaque*, II, 276–7; Hans Uebersberger in his review of Nintchitch's volumes in *Berliner Monatshefte*, XV (1937), 719; Chlumecky, *Franz Ferdinands Wirken und Wollen*, p. 100; Herre, *Die Kleinen Staaten*, p. 353.

[29] Ö-U.A., IV, nos. 4118, 4171.

[30] G.P., XXVI, ii, no. 9273.

antee that this territory should never go to Serbia or Montenegro.[31] These were repeated at various times, especially during the first months of 1909. Aehrenthal was finally willing to discuss the matter, since he hoped by a declaration of diplomatic support to influence Turkey to fortify this region and above all to build the proposed Sanjak railroad.[32] Later, he also pointed out that Turkey could hardly ask for protection against these Slav states and still permit Serbian war material to be transported through Turkish territory. The restriction of shipments of military supplies henceforth became a cardinal point in the discussion. Various drafts and counterdrafts of proposed declarations were made.[33] Although Aehrenthal went so far as to promise "tout son appui et son concours efficace" in regard to the Sanjak, he nevertheless always made it clear that Austria-Hungary could not and would not guarantee military aid. A strengthening of troops in Bosnia-Herzegovina which might intimidate Serbia was as far as he would go.[34] What Turkey wanted, and what Germany thought Austria ought to give, was just this guarantee of military support.[35] When Aehrenthal refused this in spite of German suggestions, Turkey no longer desired to carry on the *pour-parlers* and the matter was dropped.[36]

In his negotiations with Turkey Aehrenthal thus held firm to his decision for a policy of "non-intervention." In July, 1909, he expressed the same view to Bratianu and, much to the surprise of the Rumanian statesman, assured him that he would absolutely not intervene to stop a Balkan war. He recommended that Rumania should endeavor to obtain an agreement with Bulgaria before the outbreak of such a future war.[37]

[31] Ö-U.A., I, nos. 309, 333; see also, nos. 907, 921, II, no. 1070.

[32] *Ibid.*, I, no. 948, II, no. 1105.

[33] *Ibid.*, I, no. 948, II, nos. 1104, 1217, 1250, 1311, 1320.

[34] *Ibid.*, II, no. 1433; G.P., XXVI, ii, no. 9273.

[35] Ö-U.A., II, nos. 1181, 1199, 1233, 1601; G.P., XXVI, ii, nos. 9271 note, 9273 marginal note. Germany was of the opinion that Austria-Hungary would have to take back the Sanjak, something the Kaiser favored in July, 1914 (*Die deutschen Dokumente zum Kriegsausbruch 1914*, ed. Max Montgelas and Walter Schücking [4 vols.; Berlin, 1927], I, no. 29).

[36] Ö-U.A., II, nos. 1521, 1601.

[37] *Ibid.*, II, no. 1689.

About the same time he entered into discussions with Italy as to the future status of the Balkans.[38] These culminated in the agreement with Italy of December, 1909, in which it was explicitly stated that Article VII of the Treaty of the Triple Alliance applied to the Sanjak as well as to the other parts of the Ottoman Empire. This meant that there were now three Italian-Austrian Balkan agreements: (1) Article VII of the treaty of alliance which provided for compensations should either Italy or Austria-Hungary temporarily or permanently occupy any part of the Balkans, the Ottoman coasts, or islands in the Adriatic and in the Aegean.[39] (2) The Goluchowski-Visconti-Venosta exchange of notes of 1900–1901, which formulated the decision reached in 1897 at the time of Goluchowski's visit at Monza, and provided for the creation of an autonomous Albania, should it be impossible to maintain any longer the *status quo* in the Balkans.[40] (3) The agreement of 1909 in which Austria-Hungary recognised Italy's claims to compensation should the Dual Monarchy ever be forced "to proceed to a temporary or permanent occupation of the Sanjak." [41] By these agreements Austria had definitely bound herself to Italian coöperation or compensation in Balkan affairs. The agreement of 1909 was supposed to be an assurance that Austria-Hungary had definitely given up the Sanjak, and also a sort of renewal of the declaration made in 1907 at Desio. Here Aehrenthal had told Tittoni that he thought that both Austria and Italy should follow a policy of non-intervention if the *status quo* were threatened.[42]

Thus Aehrenthal's decision was to remain aloof and let affairs run their course when the expected break-up of Turkey should occur. In the final rearrangement, Austria-Hungary was of course to have her say, and Aehrenthal's aims might be sum-

[38] *Ibid.*, II, nos. 1659, 1664, 1734, 1849.

[39] First inserted as Article I of the separate treaty between Austria-Hungary and Italy of Feb. 20, 1887; later incorporated as Article VII of the third treaty of the Triple Alliance of 1891 and carried over as such into the later treaties (Pribram, *Secret Treaties*, I, 109, 155).

[40] *Ibid.*, I, 196–201.

[41] *Ibid.*, I, 241; Ö-U.A., II, no. 1848.

[42] Ö-U.A., II, nos. 1664, 1720.

marised as follows: (1) compensation for Rumania; (2) as large a Bulgaria as possible in order to maintain her rivalry with Serbia; (3) an autonomous Albania, but no Austrian protectorate or civilising mission *à la* Bosnia-Herzegovina for this region; (4) no incorporation of Serbia with the monarchy as Conrad wished. Aehrenthal hoped by a more rational Serb policy in Agram and Sarajevo to win the Serbs and Montenegrins for economic and later military agreements with the monarchy. He himself epitomised this future policy as, "In Europe to uphold the balance of power among the great powers, in the Near East not to oppose the natural development of the Balkan states, but also to favor the balance of power according to expediency, whereby, naturally Rumania and Bulgaria are to receive special consideration." [43] To this political course Aehrenthal remained true up to his death. His negotiations with Russia as to Balkan policy in 1910,[44] his attitude towards the Albanian troubles in 1911,[45] his conduct during the Tripolitan War [46] all show this to be the case. And it was this policy which Berchtold took over and continued in February of 1912.

But there is another side of Aehrenthal's policy which must be mentioned, for this was also taken over in 1912. Aehrenthal did not convince Europe and especially the Balkan states, that Austria had no further aspirations on Turkish territory. The legend of the *Drang nach Salonica*, and the rumors of a reoccupation of the Sanjak remained. Nor did Aehrenthal try very hard to dispel this conception.[47] When Milovanović in August

[43] Denkschrift (Hietzing), Aug. 15, 1909, Ö-U.A., II, no. 1720.

[44] See above, p. 126, note 6.

[45] Ö-U.A., III, nos. 2492, 2495, 2567, 2568, 2571, 2574.

[46] *Ibid.*, III, no. 2809. During the Tripolitan War he definitely told Turkey that although he might increase the number of troops in Bosnia-Herzegovina he would not think of occupying the Sanjak again if Turkish territory were threatened, even if requested to do so by Turkey (Aehrenthal to Pallavicini, Nov. 25, 1911, *ibid.*, no. 2986).

[47] As Count Hoyos states: "Der Eingeweihte weiss aber das der Fall kein so einfacher war, dass vielmehr in gewissem Sinne die Legende [march to Salonica] nicht absterben durfte, bei der eigentümlicher Veranlagung der Balkanvölker unter der Asche lebendig erhalten werden musste, wollten wir uns nicht der Gefahr aussetzen den ganzen Balkan unter russische Autorität zu bringen. . . ." (Hoyos' article in Steinitz, *Rings um Sasonow*, pp. 65–6).

of 1909 inquired as to what position Austria would take if Serbia found it necessary to increase her territory in the Sanjak, Aehrenthal evaded answering him.[48] He had treated Pašić the same way two years earlier. Nor did Milovanović receive more information when he visited Vienna in 1910.[49] Aehrenthal also refused his consent to publishing the exchange of notes with Russia in the spring of 1910, because he did not want to declare publicly for a policy of *status quo*. He was afraid the Entente was scheming to bind his hands.[50] When Cartwright, the English ambassador, asked what Austria would do in case of a Turkish-Bulgarian war, Aehrenthal treated him as he had treated Milovanović, evading a direct reply.[51] Nor was Aehrenthal pleased when Bethmann assured Sazonov at Potsdam, that Austria-Hungary had no plans of expansion in the Balkans.[52] And this was all at a time when the Friedjung and Vasić trials had aroused general suspicion of Austrian policy at all the European capitals.[53]

Rumors of a reoccupation of the Sanjak spread and certainly did much to arouse anti-Austrian sentiment in Belgrade.[54] Would it have been wise to dispel this idea and make a friendly gesture toward Serbia? Aehrenthal thought not and in fact welcomed the spread of this misconceived notion of Austrian policy. A telegram to Cetinje dated October 25, 1911 so well characterises and explains this whole side of the Austrian policy that it must be quoted at length.

Very confidential. From Your Honor's report of the 17th I note with great interest that rumors are circulating in political circles, to

[48] Ö-U.A., II, nos. 1727, 1778; J. Baernreither, "Aehrenthal und Milovanovitch," *Deutsche Revue*, XLVII (1922), 84–9.

[49] Ö-U.A., II, nos. 1988, 2226.

[50] *Ibid.*, II, nos. 2001, 2015, 2019 marginal note, 2036; III, no. 2347.

[51] *Ibid.*, II, no. 2006. Cartwright received the same treatment in September 1912 at the hands of Berchtold (*ibid.*, IV, no. 3778).

[52] Ö-U.A., III, nos. 2313, 2554; IV, no. 3991.

[53] See the excellent article by Alfred Rappaport von Arbengau, "Rund um den Friedjungprozess," *Berliner Monatshefte*, IX (1931), 339–57.

[54] "Das Märchen von der Wiederbesetzung des Sandschaks wurde hier so oft wiedererzählt dass man es nunmehr glaubt" (Attaché Gellinek from Belgrade, Jan. 12, 1912, Ö-U.K.A., Res., no. 4; see also his report of Oct. 30, 1911, Ö-U.A., III, no. 2849; K.A., VIII, no. 8 [*Berl. Mon.*, VII, 709]).

the effect that an agreement has been reached between M. Gregović and myself, in accordance with which a reoccupation of the Sanjak is envisaged, in which case Montenegro is to receive the territories of Scutari, Berane, etc. That Your Honor took no position in regard to these rumors — in which it goes without saying there is no word of truth — meets my full approval. It in no way meets my disapproval if similar versions which charge us with an aggressive policy in the Balkans are spread in Montenegro and find a sympathetic reception by the populace, at the same time arousing a certain unrest and uncertainty at the Slavic legations, specifically at the Russian. Especially Serbia and Russia, but also Italy, have a great interest, that peace be maintained in the Balkans at the present moment. The more these states believe in the possibility of our troops marching into the Sanjak, and the greater their fears that we might use a disturbance in the Balkans for an advance, the more they will endeavour to prevent the disturbance of peace in the Balkans, and thus not give us — according to their opinion — a welcome opportunity for such an action. Thus in this fashion indirectly we will again further the attainment of our one goal, the maintenance of the *status quo* in the Balkans.[55]

No other document shows so clearly the dual phases of Aehrenthal's policy in regard to the liquidation of Turkey. In reality it was based on non-intervention; in public opinion in Austria-Hungary as well as elsewhere, it was based on intervention. Most of the charges of vacillation, or weakness, made against the real policy when it was applied in 1912 were due to this difference between what was and what was thought to be the platform of the Ballhausplatz. No power entirely unmasks its political aims and so the action of Aehrenthal is understandable. Yet the wisdom of this action is certainly open to question.[56] It was a policy of bluff. He had no intention of backing it up, for he was determined on non-intervention. A bluff is dangerous at all times, for when it is called, prestige suffers. This is what happened in 1912; the penalty was paid in 1918.

In February, 1912, Berchtold became the heir of this policy. Industrious and capable as he was, although certainly in the be-

[55] Ö-U.A., III, no. 2823.

[56] Berchtold himself questioned it in October 1912 (Denkschrift betreffend die Sandschakfrage, Oct. 25(?), 1912, Ö-U.A., IV, no. 4171).

ginning none too well-informed as to the intricacies of the Balkan and Pan-Serb problems, he could not evolve a new Balkan program overnight. Nor was there reason to do so, for the fundamental Austrian aims remained the same. A new element had been added to the problem, it is true, but this prevented rather than encouraged a change of policy. Aehrenthal had died with the conviction that a Balkan League was a utopia; Berchtold within three months was presented with it as a *fait accompli.*

Berchtold during the summer had no definite idea of the distinct anti-Austrian points of the Balkan League,[57] although he knew it boded no good for the monarchy. Clearly the coalition ought to be broken up, but to accomplish this it seemed best not to depart from the old policy of non-intervention. To have acted otherwise would have not only increased the Serbian hatred of Austria-Hungary, but would definitely have antagonised Bulgaria, on whom Austria now as formerly pinned her hopes.[58] Besides it would have undoubtedly involved Austria in a war with the League and also Russia. Had Austria marched into the Sanjak we know from the military conventions and guarantees exchanged between Bulgaria and Serbia, Serbia would have attacked Austria-Hungary. Even in the light of later events, it seems as if it would have been unwise to settle matters then when the Balkan League was intact. Far wiser was it to wait until the expected internal squabbles should disrupt the League, and so it appeared to the Austrian statesmen, with the possible exception of one or two military men.

Nor did the international situation favor a more active policy. The surviving tension of the Morocco crisis, the German-English rivalry, just brought home by the failure of the Haldane mission,[59] the French-Russian naval convention, and the Russian patronage of the League were all sufficiently discouraging.

[57] See above, pp. 63–5.

[58] See Cemal Tukin, *Die politischen Beziehungen zwischen Österreich-Ungarn und Bulgarien von 1908 bis zum Bukarester Frieden* (Hamburg, 1936), *passim*, especially p. 234.

[59] E. C. Helmreich, "Die Haldane Mission," *Berliner Monatshefte*, XII (1934), 112–143; see also Ö-U.A., IV, no. 3612.

In addition there was the very possible lack of support from Italy and Germany.

The Tripolitan War had not led to better Austrian-Italian relations. The Ballhausplatz had taken a very definite stand against the extension of hostilities to European and Asiatic Turkey.[60] It was hardly to be expected that Italy would now assume a more benevolent attitude towards Austrian intervention in a quarrel over European Turkey than Austria had previously accorded her. As long as the Italian army and navy were tied up in Tripoli, the Consulta eyed Austrian policy with redoubled suspicion.

Nor did the Austrian statesmen feel confident of the position Germany would take. The shining armor, which Germany had put on rather late in the annexation crisis for the protection and help of Austria-Hungary, was tarnished to Austrian eyes, at the Potsdam conference of 1910. No less than the French and English ministers, the diplomats in Vienna were disturbed by this meeting. Especially were they displeased with the direct assurance that Bethmann had given Sazonov that, "Germany had never obligated herself to support Austro-Hungarian plans in the Balkans." [61] In other words Germany took her stand on a very strict interpretation of the alliance treaty. Although the Ballhausplatz really had no definite plans for expansion, such a declaration, nevertheless, hampered future diplomatic sparring. In retaliation Austria-Hungary had maintained a decidedly reserved attitude during the 1911 Morocco crisis, and displayed no intention of bringing down upon herself the displeasure of various other European governments for the sake of Morocco, especially since trouble loomed ahead in the Balkans.[62]

[60] Brandenburg, *Von Bismarck zum Weltkriege*, pp. 348 ff.; Friedrich Stieve, *Die Tragödie der Bundesgenossen. Deutschland und Österreich-Ungarn 1908–1914* (Munich, 1930), pp. 79 ff.

[61] Ö-U.A., III, no. 2554. In general on Austrian-German relations of this period see Stieve, *Die Tragödie der Bundesgenossen*, ch. III; O. H. Wedel, *Austro-German Diplomatic Relations 1908–1914* (Stamford, 1932); E. C. Helmreich, "The Conflict between Germany and Austria over Balkan Policy, 1913–1914," *Essays in the History of Modern Europe*, ed. Donald C. McKay (New York, 1936), pp. 130–148.

[62] Ö-U.A., III, no. 2554.

As was the case with Italy so it was with Germany; the Tripolitan War did not bring Austria closer to her ally. The Austrian statesmen came to the conclusion that Germany no longer had the same interest in maintaining Turkey that she had manifested before 1910. They felt that they could not rely on Germany's support in an attempt to maintain the existence of the Ottoman Empire in Europe.[63] In addition, on the eve of the Balkan crisis there were a whole series of misunderstandings between Berlin and Vienna. In the first place, the Austrians were not exactly pleased or satisfied with the fraternising of Tsar and Kaiser at Baltischport in 1912.[64] Then Berchtold issued his note of August 13, 1912 without previously consulting Kiderlen, which led the latter to protest.[65] Hardly had the affair been smoothed over than a new difference arose in regard to the proposal of Sazonov for intervention at Constantinople.[66] Kiderlen wanted to discuss with Vienna what their joint stand should be, but Berchtold had no thought of this procedure and went ahead on his own hook. Again there was dissatisfaction in Berlin, again apologies came from Vienna. Then Kiderlen cooperated heartily with France in getting the declaration of *status quo* under way for the European Concert. This German-Entente collaboration aroused displeasure and condemnation from Vienna and a call was made for more alliance solidarity as against the Entente.[67] Kiderlen protested against what he thought were the unjust charges of Vienna and asked for a statement of Austrian policy. A short time later Berchtold showed Tschirschky, the German ambassador at Vienna, the report of Kiderlen's interview with Sazonov, which had been sent him from Berlin. This brought forth a sharp rebuke from Kiderlen, for papers confidentially sent to Berchtold should not be shown to others. Again Berchtold had to make apology.[68]

[63] *Ibid.*, IV, no. 3633.

[64] *Ibid.*, IV, nos. 3633, 3991.

[65] Jäckh, *Kiderlen-Wächter*, II, 187–8; Ö-U.A., IV, nos. 3714, 3771; also see above, pp. 107–8; 116–7.

[66] See above, p. 121.

[67] Ö-U.A., IV, nos. 3991, 3996, 4022; also see above, pp. 127–32.

[68] G.P., XXXIII, no. 12272 note; Ö-U.A., IV, no. 4131.

These incidents, all of no supreme importance, show the pin-pricks and irritation between the allies. In Berlin they were afraid the Ballhausplatz would confront them with a *fait accompli*, and were dissatisfied with the apparent lack of any definite policy in Vienna.[69] Vienna was not sure of German support and thought Berlin had little sympathy for the vital Balkan interests of Austria. The whole situation from the Austrian standpoint is well summed up in Berchtold's report of the conversation which he had with Bethmann-Hollweg in Buchlau on September 7–8th. Here, after mentioning that the meeting had brought the old assurances for coöperation, he significantly added: "The ever-present doubts of the adequacy of the German Alliance as regards the monarchy's Mediterranean, and especially her Adriatic problems could, it is true, not be wiped off the map." [70]

This lack of harmony between Berlin and Vienna undoubtedly played a part in determining Austrian policy. Yet it would be going too far to credit Berlin with keeping Vienna from armed intervention in October, 1912, for all indications are that Vienna itself did not wish to pursue such a course. On the other hand the supporters, and also critics, of the Austrian policy should not blame Germany too much for lack of sufficient support for a policy of expansion. Germany could not be expected to be more Austrian than the Austrians themselves. In fact Germany in 1909 — out of consideration for German-Turkish interests — had urged Austria to undertake obligations which would have led her back into the Sanjak.[71] The Kaiser apparently would have been willing to back this step by extending the alliance to cover it. There are also some indications that, had the Ballhausplatz come out with a clear-cut demand in October, 1912 for the Sanjak, Kiderlen would have supported it.[72] But the Viennese

[69] Jäckh, *Kiderlen-Wächter*, II, 187–8; Ö-U.A., IV, no. 4131.

[70] Ö-U.A., IV, no. 3771.

[71] G.P., XXVI, ii, nos. 9271, 9273; Ö-U.A., II, nos. 1181, 1199, 1233.

[72] Ö-U.A., IV, no. 4022; G.P., XXXIII, no. 12257; Chlumecky, *Franz Ferdinands Wirken und Wollen*, pp. 145 ff.; Moltke to Conrad, Feb. 2, 1913, Conrad, III, 145. Bogitschewitsch states Kiderlen told him that he had urgently warned

statesmen did not want this territory and were quite content to watch, wait, and listen. In general, however, throughout the crisis and the years immediately preceding, Germany, instead of moving Austria-Hungary to a more active policy and pushing her toward Salonica, urged the Dual Monarchy in one way or another to continue the conservative policy on which it had launched.

The stand Germany took on the eve of the Balkan crisis can be briefly summarised. She was eager to have Turkey conclude peace with Italy and lent her good offices to this cause. The fact that Turkey haggled so long and did not follow the advice of Germany was one of the things which made the Kaiser very anti-Turkish at the start of the war.[73] The Wilhelmstrasse along with the other cabinets advocated peace at the various Balkan capitals, but from the first days of mobilisation Germany was against doing anything to hinder the outbreak of the war. She supported the diplomatic action of Europe of October 8th because she regarded it expressly as a means of localising the conflict and not as a means of restricting the Balkan states.[74]

The Kaiser was at his hunting-lodge at Rominten during the last part of September, 1912, and was not kept informed of the developing crisis in the Balkans. When the news of mobilisation reached him, he called the foreign office to task, whereupon the most important documents were forwarded to him. With a keen realisation of how far matters had gone, the Kaiser cut himself clear of all diplomatic bickering and on October 4th wrote a

---

Berchtold not to occupy the Sanjak (*Serbien und der Weltkrieg*, p. 162). Neither the German nor Austrian documents contain such a warning. It would have been inconsistent with the general reserve Germany maintained at this time and also with Kiderlen's words to Szögyény (Oct. 10, 1912, Ö-U.A., IV, no. 4022). That the whole attitude of Germany, especially towards localisation, did not encourage Austria to go on, and that the passive policy followed at Vienna met the full support of Berlin is, of course, true. But there is a vast difference between encouraging a step and supporting it after it once has been taken. Yet Austria herself did not want to take that step.

[73] G.P., XXXIII, no. 12202 note. The failure of the Turks to come to an agreement with Greece in regard to Crete also entered in (*ibid.*, no. 12288 marginal note; see also Giolitti, *Memoirs*, p. 375).

[74] G.P., XXXIII, no. 12244.

straightforward and clear-cut outline of the policy to be followed. To prevent the opening of hostilities would mean a collapse of the Balkan dynasties, which would make it harder to keep order in that troubled region than ever before. As matters stood there would be a war sooner or later, and it would be better to have it at this time when it did not suit Russia and France than later, since the two Entente allies were not yet ready to face a conflict with Germany.

> The Balkan states [he continued] have the conception and the urge, that they must expand; this can be done only at the expense of Turkey; as this cannot be done peacefully, they will fight for it; and they unite *ad hoc* in order to make possible this expansion. This the great powers simply want to hinder without any further ado.??! With what right? For whose benefit? I won't go along with them. Just as we did not permit anyone to dictate to us in '64, '66, '70, just as little can I and do I wish to hinder or to interfere with others.
>
> Just let the war come. Then the Balkan states will demonstrate what they are capable of doing, and if they have a right to existence. If they defeat Turkey, then they were right, and they are entitled to certain compensation. If they are defeated, then they will become less important, and will remain quiet and peaceful for a long time, and the territorial question will disappear. The great powers must form a ring about the scene of battle, where the conflict must remain and run its course. The powers must maintain a quiet reserve and not undertake a hasty action. This implies, according to my opinion, above all no interference now for the sake of that so-called "beloved peace"; it would be full of unhealthy and evil consequences. Just let those people go ahead; they will either receive a trouncing or give one, afterwards there is always time to talk. The Eastern Question must be solved with Blood and Iron. But at a time favorable to us! That is now! [75]

The last portion of the Kaiser's memorandum has been quoted in full, for it states clearly the policy followed by Germany. Of course the foreign office had to dress it up in language and action to make it presentable in the Concert of Powers. But the above remained the guiding principle.

Thus in harmony with the policy of Aehrenthal and also with the policy of Italy and Germany, Berchtold, on August 10th,

[75] G.P., XXXIII, no. 12225.

informed Bulgaria that Austria wished the *status quo* maintained, but would not hinder "with her own body" the evolution of historical processes in Turkey.[76] Following the same Aehrenthalian tradition he promulgated his famous notes of August 13th and 29th, supported Sazonov's proposal, and lent his ready coöperation to the action by the European Concert.[77] In like fashion he refused the invitation of the Turks to reoccupy the Sanjak.[78] But the other element of Aehrenthal's policy he also maintained. That is, in public the uncertainty as to Austrian action in the Sanjak remained. The Austrian diplomats were told to avoid this issue.[79] Berchtold likewise used indefinite language to the German chargé,[80] and Russia was not definitely assured until the eve of the opening of hostilities that Austria would not invade this territory.[81] In fact it was not until after the war had started that the foreign office reached a decision like that of 1908, as to the definite abandonment of this territory.[82]

With the storm clouds casting their shadows over all Europe, the Austrian officials carefully considered whether they should adopt a more active policy, or adhere to the traditional one. In a ministerial conference on September 14th, Berchtold raised the question, and the consensus of opinion was that a policy which might involve Austria in a war should be avoided.[83] Auffenberg, the minister of war, thought that in view of the lack of guns and equipment it would be best to avoid anything that might lead to a general action. Later he took this question up with the chief of staff, Schemua, and asked him to draw up a study on the Russian army and the chances Austria would have in a possible conflict.[84] After pointing out that only in artillery

[76] Ö-U.A., IV, no. 3678.

[77] See above, pp. 107–8, 116–22.

[78] Ö-U.A., IV, nos. 3935, 4139, 4152, 4164.

[79] *Ibid.*, IV, nos. 4036, 4054, 4071.

[80] *Ibid.*, IV, no. 3850. The same attitude was maintained toward San Giuliano in the interviews at Pisa and Florence on Oct. 22–3, 1912 (*ibid.*, no. 4181).

[81] *Ibid.*, IV, nos. 4032, 4050, 4063; Izvolsky, II, no. 510.

[82] Ö-U.A., IV, nos. 4118, 4171.

[83] *Ibid.*, IV, no. 3787.

[84] Ö-U.K.A., Zu Res. Gestb., no. 4302 (1912), Kriegsministerium Präs., no. 9887, Oct. 9, 1912.

was Russia superior, Schemua's report stated: "In general according to my opinion one can conclude that even in a war in which we would have to fight it out with Russia alone, the chances of an ultimate victory are in no way unfavorable." [85]

In fact Schemua had pleaded for a more active policy from the start. In an able memoir of the 28th of September he presented his views, and demanded the occupation of the Kossovo Polje in order to prevent the union of Serbia and Montenegro and to obtain a connection with Albania.[86] He was above all for Austria's declaring her aims publicly and then sticking to them. Naturally he called for an increase in the military establishment and wanted complete "B" [87] mobilisation for the moment Serbia declared war. Such a policy was of course absolutely opposed to the wishes of either the war [88] or foreign offices, and in a succinct memoir Berchtold pointed out to him the advantages of a policy of non-intervention.

> Today it would not even be possible [so Berchtold answered Schemua's demand for a public proclamation of Austrian aims] to formulate concrete "desiderata," inasmuch as only the development of events in the theater of war can bring clarification as to how far our specific interests in the Balkans are affected by the success or failure of the one or the other parties.[89]

On the 5th of October Schemua again sent a note to Berchtold asking what position Austria was going to take if Serbia invaded the Sanjak.[90] This was followed by a statement on the 7th of the military measures Russia was taking,[91] and on the

[85] Ö-U.K.A., Zu Res. Gestb., no. 4302, Oct. 13, 1912.

[86] Denkschrift des Chefs des Generalstabs an den Kaiser, Sept. 28, 1912, Ö-U.A., IV, no. 3869. Schemua's demands were very similar to those put forward by Chief of Staff Beck in 1897 (see above, p. 167).

[87] That is, for war in the Balkans in contrast with "R" mobilisation in case of war with Russia.

[88] Auffenberg-Komarow, *Aus Österreichs Höhe und Niedergang* (Munich, 1921), pp. 207–8; Ö-U.A., IV, no. 3787.

[89] Denkschrift, Oct. 2, 1912, Ö-U.A., IV, no. 3928.

[90] Ö-U.K.A., Res. Gestb., no. 3946; read to His Majesty in audience Oct. 8, 1912.

[91] Ö-U.K.A., Res. Gestb., no. 3980; read to His Majesty in audience Oct. 8, 1912.

18th with a long memoir calling attention to the fact that he had not received an answer to his note of the 5th.[92] This time he mentioned the difficulty of getting the Serbs to give up the Sanjak once they had occupied it. Real military successes on the part of Turkey he held to be unlikely. Again the Russian military measures were reviewed, and he pointed out that the chances for Austria in single-handed combat with Russia, so long as Serbia and Montenegro were engaged in the war with Turkey, were "durchaus nicht ungünstig," if Russia were not permitted to get too great a jump in preparatory measures. Here as in the notes of September 28th and October 5th, he decidedly urged an active policy and there is no mention of unpreparedness. Evidently Archduke Francis Ferdinand was mistaken when he said that Schemua and Auffenberg had stated in ministerial council, "The army is not ready for war; it is in worse shape than in 1866." [93] Auffenberg, it is true, spoke of unpreparedness in the ministerial conference of September 14th, and his opposition to an active policy is stated in his memoirs.[94] But neither in the documents nor in the Kriegsarchiv are there any traces of Schemua's attendance at a ministerial conference in this period, nor of any such statements as Francis Ferdinand attributed to him. It undoubtedly was a slip of the tongue on the part of the archduke, or in Conrad's recording of the conversation. Schemua's memoir of October 18th was at least presented to Francis Ferdinand, and probably the others were also. Schemua read them all to the emperor in audience.

It was not until October 26th that Berchtold formulated a written answer to Schemua, which was a recapitulation and explanation of previous conversations.[95] The Sanjak, which Schemua thought ought to be reoccupied, is here definitely abandoned and instead attention is concentrated on Albania.

[92] Ö-U.K.A., Res. Gestb., no. 4221; read to His Majesty in audience Oct. 22, 1912.

[93] As reported by Conrad, III, 76.

[94] Ö-U.A., IV, no. 3787; Auffenberg, *Aus Österreichs Höhe und Niedergang*, pp. 208, 210, 219.

[95] Ö-U.A., IV, no. 4183.

The definite statement is also made that Austria is not going to intervene during the war although in the peace settlement there would be certain things which Austria would not permit under any circumstances. What these things were is not mentioned, for the Ballhausplatz had not yet definitely formulated its program.[96] What Austria's demands would be still depended on the events of the war.

Schemua, backed by Potiorek, commandant in Bosnia-Herzegovina, and some other military personages, was the sole voice in the inner circle in Vienna calling for action. Although the troops stationed in Bosnia-Herzegovina and near the Serbian frontier assumed a state of increased watchfulness and men on leave were recalled,[97] no wide-sweeping measures which could be compared to the trial mobilisation and calling in of recruits in Russia were undertaken in the Dual Monarchy at this time. Schemua's requests for an increase in troops, largely based on demands of Potiorek for "Kriegstand," were all refused, Francis Joseph agreeing only, on October 4th, to "Preparations for increase in strength of troops on the basis of the law of 1888" (Vorsorgen zur Standeserhöhung nach den 88er Gesetzen).[98] His Majesty however continued to be against actually putting the law into operation. The Russian ambassador protested on October 9th about the military measures that were being taken. Berchtold assured him that he had no intention to undertake an active policy, but if a conflagration were burning in his neighbor's house, a man would hardly consult another how to stop the fire from spreading to his own property.[99] Sazonov apparently accepted the explanation with good grace.[100] The first real military measures were taken when Francis Joseph on October 31st sanctioned the retention of the third year levy of troops for

[96] The traditional general aims such as a guarantee for a commercial route to Salonica, prevention of a great power getting a foothold on the eastern shores of the Adriatic, an Albanian state, a small Serbia, of course, remained (Ö-U.A., IV, no. 3961).

[97] *Die Zeit* (Abendblatt), Oct. 1, 1912.

[98] Ö-U.K.A., Beilage Res. Gestb., no. 4819 (1912).

[99] Ö-U.A., IV, no. 4017.

[100] G.P., XXXIII, no. 12269.

Bosnia-Herzegovina at the same time that new recruits were called in.[101] On the same day 7000 reserve troops were sent to Bosnia and henceforward other military measures were to be taken.[102]

In the foreign office there never was the slightest intention of following an active policy. The old program of "*status quo* and non-intervention" carried off the honors.[103] From the outbreak of the war it became a question of what changes would be permitted. To study this question conferences were held by the various heads and officials of the foreign office. In the first one, on October 16th — eight days after the opening of hostilities by Montenegro — the policy of non-intervention was reaffirmed and it was unanimously decided that there was but one thing which could necessitate Austria-Hungary's going beyond diplomatic steps. That was "the establishment of a great power on the eastern shore of the Adriatic, or the Ionian Sea."[104] Certainly the foreign office was keeping an open mind to all possible changes. The further question whether any possible territorial addition in the Balkans was of vital interest to the monarchy, was unanimously decided in the negative, although the opportuneness of several rectifications of frontier (Lovčen, the Sanjak border, Ada-Kaleh) was pointed out. Some changes naturally appeared more desirable than others, but only in regard to Albania was there anything approaching a definite decision. Albania was to solve everything. It was to save the prestige of the monarchy and atone for abandoning the Sanjak, while at

[101] Francis Joseph's approvals of October 4th and 31st were the only favorable actions Schemua had on eleven distinct demands for various military measures made between Sept. 28th and Nov. 15, 1912 (Ö-U.K.A., Beilage Res. Gestb., no. 4819 [1912]). This bears out the statement made by Auffenberg in his memoirs that for six weeks he withstood the demands of Schemua and Potiorek for mobilisation measures (*Aus Österreichs Höhe und Niedergang*, p. 208).

[102] Darstellung der anlässlich der Balkankrise 1912/13 getroffenen militärischen Massnahmen, Ö-U.K.A., Zu Abt. 10, no. 400 res. von 1914, p. 12; also, Beilage I, Uebersicht über die wichtigsten anlässlich der Balkankrise 1912/13 getroffenen militärischen Massnahmen (reprinted as Appendix I, see below, pp. 461–62).

[103] It should be emphasised that Austrian policy was not *status quo* alone, but also non-intervention when the *status quo* was threatened.

[104] Ö-U.A., IV, no. 4118.

the same time preventing any other great power from setting foot on the eastern side of the Adriatic. But even in regard to Albania the Austrians had no clear vision of the future. It is of great interest that even the possibility of a united Serb-Bulgar-Montenegrin state created no great alarm. In such an eventuality it was expected that closer coöperation on the part of Italy would offset this new danger. On a later occasion it was added that such a state would finally put an end to the vacillation as to whether the Dual Monarchy were a western or an eastern power, a matter which had "brought so much uncertainty into Austrian policy." [105] This was certainly not very energetic support of that old principle of Austrian policy — prevention of a great Slav state on the borders of the monarchy. But these were only speculations and by no means constituted a policy; the establishment of a future program, the determination of Austria's vital interests depended on just how the war went.

After what has been said to show that Berchtold's policy in 1912 was but a continuation of that laid down by his predecessor, it is unnecessary to say much more to prove that it was not based on the idea that Turkey would win. Both Goluchowski and Aehrenthal had figured on the collapse of Turkish power in Europe and shaped their policy accordingly. Berchtold did the same. Field Marshal Goltz in his *Denkwürdigkeiten* goes a long way to explain why there was an exaggerated opinion of Turkish strength in some circles. He states that he conducted "false" publicity about the strength of the Turkish army in order to keep the Balkan states from attacking, thus giving Turkey time to reorganise.[106] His confidential reports to Berlin however always stated the true facts. The victory of the Balkan troops, however, would in all likelihood not have been so easily obtained if the new Turkish leaders had not cast aside the original plan of campaign which had been prepared for this very

[105] Ö-U.A., IV, no. 4140.

[106] Generalfeldmarschall Goltz, *Denkwürdigkeiten* (Berlin, 1929), pp. 316, 321. The Belgian minister at Berlin thought Kiderlen and the other officials were unpleasantly surprised by the Bulgarian victories (Baron Beyens, *Deux années à Berlin 1912–1914* [2 vols.; Paris, 1931], I, 82–7).

emergency.[107] Political strife at Constantinople was largely responsible for this; Izzet Pasha told the British attaché, "we have a good army, but it is impossible to do anything with it on account of these miserable politics." [108] The possibility of a Turkish victory was always there,[109] and was taken into consideration, but it never was taken as a basis for Austrian policy. What Berchtold did figure on was that however the war went, it would be a somewhat drawn-out affair, a matter at least of weeks instead of days as it turned out to be.[110] Neither Pallavicini nor Pomiankowski, the very able Austrian attaché at Constantinople, gave him cause for optimism in regard to the Turks.[111] Schemua also pointed out directly in his memoranda that a Turkish victory was very unlikely.[112] Nor do any of the many documents in the great Austrian collection, the memoranda and protocols of ministerial conferences, etc., mention that any policy was based on the supposition of a Turkish victory.

[107] Izzet Pascha, *Denkwürdigkeiten*, pp. 171 ff., 186 ff.; Goltz, *Denkwürdigkeiten*, p. 321; Attaché Pomiankowski from Constantinople, Nov. 25, 1912, Ö-U.K.A., Res., no. 499/2 mal.; B.D., IX, ii, no. 571 enclosure.

[108] Lieutenant-Colonel Tyrell to Lowther, Jan. 28, 1913, B.D., IX, ii, no. 571 enclosure.

[109] Even the Bulgarian statesmen took this into consideration as is shown by their discussions with St. Petersburg for intervention in regard to the conclusion of peace. After the first great victories the Bulgarian government no longer had any interest in carrying forward these negotiations (*Doklad*, I, 220, 234 [no. 29], 235 [nos. 31, 33], 237 [no. 37]).

[110] In an interview in 1930 Count Berchtold assured the writer that he did not expect an overwhelming victory of either side, especially in view of the length of the Tripolitan War. Similarly Count Szápáry stated that Austrian policy was in no way based on the supposition that Turkey would win, and Austria did not abstain from intervention on that account. He added that opinion differed in the foreign office, indeed several men, especially Pogatscher, an expert on Turkish affairs, held from the start that the Balkan states would win.

[111] Ö-U.A., IV, nos. 3959, 3961, 4132. An examination of the attaché reports in the Vienna Kriegsarchiv shows that these reports did not give the Austrian officials cause to believe in a Turkish victory. This was especially true of Pomiankowski's reports: Ö-U.K.A., Res., no. 411, Oct. 5, 1912; Res., no. 414, Oct. 8, 1912; Res., no. 436, Oct. 14, 1912; Res., no. 446, Oct. 19, 1912; Res., no. 454, Oct. 20, 1912; the report of about Oct. 14, 1912 on the spirit of the Turkish troops was slightly more favorable (Ev. Br. T., no. 23/124, Oct. 31, 1912). See also, Joseph Pomiankowski, *Der Zusammenbruch des ottomanischen Reiches* (Vienna, 1928), pp. 34, 48. Pomiankowski's statements in his reports and in his book do not coincide with the statements which Auffenberg says he made in the summer of 1912 (*Aus Österreichs Höhe und Niedergang*, p. 203).

[112] Ö-U.K.A., Res. Gestb., no. 4221 (1912); Ö-U.A., IV, no. 3869.

The "why" of Austrian policy is of course a complicated question to answer, if it can be answered at all, and cannot be dealt with here. However, the one fundamental reason for Austrian policy was that Austria-Hungary had no desire for additional territory, because under the complicated structure of the monarchy the ministers feared that the state could not assimilate an increase of Slavic population.[113] Dualism and internal difficulties forced the monarchy to a conservative foreign policy.

[113] Statements by Berchtold and Hoyos in Steinitz, *Rings um Sasonow*, pp. 46, 68; conversation with Berchtold, June, 1930. Tisza, minister-president of Hungary in July, 1914 absolutely refused to sanction any designs for the annexation of Serbian territory (Ö-U.A., VIII, nos. 10118, 10272). For Archduke Francis Ferdinand's attitude towards incorporation of Serbian territory in the monarchy, see Sosnosky, *Franz Ferdinand*, pp. 146 ff.; Leopold Freiherr von Chlumecky, "Franz Ferdinands Aussenpolitik, aus persönlichen Erinnerungen," *Berliner Monatshefte*, XII (1934), 459–60.

CHAPTER X

THE WAR UP TO THE DECEMBER ARMISTICE

THE eighteen days which intervened between general mobilisation on October 1st and the declaration of war on October 18th gave the Balkan states ample time to concentrate their troops and prepare for a vigorous offensive. According to the agreement between the Bulgarian and Serbian general staffs, the Serbian army was to push forward into Macedonia, while the Bulgarian army was to concentrate its efforts on the valley of the Maritza.[1] Geography determined that Greece should attack to the northward. Her efforts were also to be directed towards securing naval supremacy in the Aegean in order to intercept maritime communication between Asia Minor and European Turkey. For the first part of the war, at least, none of the allies with the exception of Montenegro were to employ any considerable forces in Albania.

The Turkish general staff, after the events of 1908, had worked out campaign plans for a possible war with any of the Balkan states separately or in alliance.[2] For the event of a conflict with the four states as allies, the chief of staff had planned that the Turkish forces in the Maritza valley should retire to the line Sarai-Chorlu-Rodosto. Here they were to remain on the defensive and await reinforcements from Asiatic Turkey. Then only was an offensive to be undertaken. In Macedonia they were to rely upon guerilla warfare. Rather than risk defeat they were to retreat into the Albanian hills where they would be able to reorganise and build up an army.

The political disturbances existing in Constantinople during the summer of 1912 had led to a reorganisation of the general staff.[3] Although Izzet Pasha remained titular chief, new officers

[1] Agreement between the Bulgarian and Serbian general staffs of Sept. 28, 1912 (Gueshoff, pp. 126–7).

[2] Izzet Pascha, *Denkwürdigkeiten*, pp. 172–80.

[3] See above, pp. 93–101.

were appointed who were little inclined to follow the old plans. Izzet himself was removed from all influence since he had been sent off to subdue the revolt in Yemen, and was not even recalled at the outbreak of the Tripolitan War. The change in officers and the dismissal of many trained troops in August and September, 1912, brought it about that the Turkish army when mobilised was thoroughly disorganised, and largely made up of raw recruits. Supplies, transport facilities, sanitary and hospital equipment were entirely inadequate as later events showed. The Austrian attaché reported on November 25th that the Turkish forces were worse off for means of communication than they had been one hundred years ago.[4] It took from seven to eight hours for the generals to agree on a command and get it to the troops. No telegraphic system existed partly because of lack of material and partly because of indolence. Consequently the Turkish generals had to rely on couriers. The old system of relays in use in former campaigns had apparently been forgotten.

The Turkish officers must have realised their unpreparedness, for they were not at all confident of victory. Yet on October 17th they decided to throw overboard the plan which Izzet Pasha had worked out and which had received the approval of von der Goltz. Instead of remaining on the defensive, the Turkish army was ordered to undertake an offensive action. The Turks were moved to take this step by the fact that the Balkan states had not attacked so rapidly as everyone had expected. Because of this delay sufficient concentration of Turkish forces had taken place to warrant an offensive. According to the information at Turkish headquarters the Bulgarians had only about 75,000 men to the east of the Tundja, while the Turks could muster around 140,000.[5] If the Bulgarians could be defeated the Constantinople-Salonica railway would be safe and Turkey's control of the harbor of Burgas assured. This would be important for later transport of troops. The Austrian attaché thought the plan sound and courageous, but

[4] Ö-U.K.A., Res., no. 499/2 mal., Nov. 25, 1912.

[5] *Ibid.*

was doubtful whether the Turkish army was well enough prepared for such an offensive action.[6]

Pomiankowski's doubts were fully justified. On October 22–23 the Bulgarians were overwhelmingly victorious at Kirk-Kilisse. The next day the Serbs, overcoming less opposition, won a striking victory at Kumanovo. Both Bulgarian and Serbian armies pushed forward. On October 29–31 the Bulgarians won the battle of Lulé-Burgas, and soon the Turks were driven to the Chatalja line of fortifications. On November 15–18th the Serbs captured Monastir. Meanwhile the Greek army, meeting no great opposition, advanced rapidly. On November 8th, King Constantine was able to enter Salonica at the head of his victorious army, only to be forced several days later to share the occupation with the Bulgarians. The Greeks had won in the race for Salonica, but Bulgaria was not disposed to surrender her Aegean aspirations so easily.

In the north, in the meantime, Montenegro had continued the operations against Turkey which she had begun on October 8th. At the beginning the Montenegrin army was divided into three groups.[7] One group invaded the Kossovo vilayet, while the other two advanced on Scutari from opposite sides of the lake, via Podgoritza and the Tarabosh, respectively. Having received warnings from Italy and Russia, and having made promises to Austria not to invade the Sanjak, Montenegro did not direct her efforts in this direction during the first days of hostilities. However, after the Serbs and other allies joined in the conflict, King Nikita did his best to occupy his share of that territory.

Even the Serbians did not enter the Sanjak until three or four days after the declaration of war.[8] Since the Turks had

[6] Ö-U.K.A., Ad. Res., no. 446 ex 1912, Oct. 19, 1912.

[7] Durham, *Struggle for Scutari*, p. 183.

[8] The Belgian minister at Belgrade thought Serbia had delayed entering the Sanjak because of Austria (*Die belgischen Dokumente*, V, 123). Professor Stanojević of the University of Belgrade assured the writer that he knew for certain that the slight delay in entering the Sanjak was due to the desire of the Serbian commander to wait until his supply train was fully mobilised and in perfect order. The question of what Austria would do did not enter into consideration.

withdrawn most of their troops [9] the occupation of this territory was no great military feat, and by October 30th the whole district was in the possession of Serbia and Montenegro. Made secure by the great allied victories in the south, the third Serbian army under General Yanković pushed on toward the Adriatic. On November 30th the Serbs occupied Durazzo, at the very time when Albanian independence was being proclaimed at Valona.

The Montenegrins had expected little opposition in capturing Scutari.[10] Yet their advance was relatively slow. It was not until the end of October that they were able to surround the city. Everyone expected that the fortress would be captured at any moment,[11] and its impending fall convinced even the Austrian statesmen that the city would have to be given to Montenegro in the future peace settlement.[12] Contrary to all expectations the Montenegrins were unable to capture the city. This was in part due to improvement in the fortifications made in the summer of 1912,[13] but especially to the intrepid defense inspired by the able Turkish general, Hussein Pasha. This surprising resistance had its share in changing the Austrian views as to the allocation of Scutari when the question of Albanian boundaries arose.

The overwhelming and rapid victories of the Balkan states took all Europe by surprise. With the outbreak of hostilities the

[9] Attaché report from Constantinople, Oct. 16, 1912, Ö-U.K.A., Ad. Res., no. 441.

[10] Attaché report from Cetinje, Nov. 13, 1912, Ö-U.K.A., Res., no. 198; Swire, *Albania*, p. 139.

[11] *Die Zeit*, Oct. 11, Nov. 2, 1912; London *Times*, Oct. 28, 1912; *Fremdenblatt*, Nov. 15, 1912; Schemua, the Austrian chief of staff, in his memoir of Nov. 9, 1912 speaks of the coming fall of Scutari (Ö-U.K.A., Res. Gestb., no. 4611; see also Evidenz Bureau, B., nos. 1171, 1181).

[12] Conversation in 1930 with A. Rappaport, who in 1912 was the Albanian expert at the Ballhausplatz. See also, Ö-U.A., IV, nos. 4170, 4469.

[13] Durham, *Struggle for Scutari*, pp. 129–30, 148. On Oct. 16, 1912 Pomiankowski reported: "Nach dem Projekte des türkishen Generalstabes soll die Festung Skutari im Stande sein, sich gegen einen doppelt überlegenen Gegner mindestens drei Monate lang zu halten. Der Umfang der ganzen Festung beträgt ungefähr 25 km., die Defensivbesatzung 15,000 Mann" (Ö-U.K.A., Ad. Res., no. 440 ex 1912).

powers had concluded their mutual efforts for the prevention and localisation of the war with an agreement to discuss "en temps opportun" the problem of mediation between the belligerents.[14] It was a nice general phrase and really bound no one. Russia wanted the intervention to take place after the first decisive victory, for she feared that a long-drawn-out war would be disadvantageous to the Balkan states.[15] Bulgaria even entered upon negotiations with St. Petersburg with the aim of securing Russia's initiative in a mediatory action. But the first victories over the Turkish armies caused Bulgaria to drop all such discussions.

On October 25th Kiderlen in conversations with Jules Cambon and Sir E. Goschen advanced the opinion that mediation could only be undertaken when it was certain how the war would end.[16] Earlier he had suggested to England and now he repeated the suggestion to Cambon, that England, France, and Germany should discuss what concessions might be made to the Balkan states in case Turkey were defeated. He would then try to win over Austria to these concessions, and Russia might be advised of them since she would hardly be opposed to concessions favorable to the Balkan states. Poincaré misunderstood Kiderlen's intentions[17] and thought this was a step to isolate Russia. He immediately informed St. Petersburg of this attempted coup by Kiderlen, and suggested that Russia parry the whole German proposal by calling for immediate mediation of the powers.[18] Poincaré's chief concern, as a matter of fact, was that any conversations with England should center in Paris, not in Berlin.

Sazonov was not disturbed by Kiderlen's activities, which he considered to be merely an effort to bring about an English-

[14] See above, pp. 136–37.
[15] D.D.F., 3d. ser., IV, no. 135; B.D., IX, ii, nos. 53, 54.
[16] D.D.F., 3d. ser., IV, no. 240; G.P., XXXIII, no. 12302; B.D., IX, ii, no. 61; see also nos. 62, 66, 70.
[17] See the views of J. Cambon and Goschen, D.D.F., 3d. ser., IV, nos. 253, 270, 294; see also G.P., XXXIII, no. 12302 note.
[18] D.D.F., 3d. ser., IV, no. 247.

German rapprochement.[19] But news of friendly relations between Bulgaria and Austria caused him on October 29th to request Poincaré to act.[20] The latter was to ask the powers to join in a statement declaring their disinterestedness, so far as compensations for themselves were concerned. This was to serve as a basis for mediation by the powers. Stressing the fact that England and Russia had already agreed to the proposition, Poincaré now asked Rome, Berlin and Vienna to accept the following formula:

> The powers, recognising that the time is approaching when they may exercise their mediation between the belligerents of the Balkan Peninsula, and continuing to retain as their chief concern the maintenance of European peace, declare that they will apply themselves to their common task in a spirit of absolute disinterestedness.[21]

When France had proposed that Russia adhere to a similar declaration during the Tripolitan War, the Russian statesmen had refused, on the score that it would appear to the Russian public and especially to the small Slavic states as if Russia were forsaking her century-old Balkan policy.[22] With the Balkan states victorious the question appeared in a new light. Russia was now primarily interested in tying Austria's hands and in getting the latter to unmask her aims. England and France supported the declaration for the same reason. Berchtold, of course, could not accept the declaration, and for much the same reasons as those Russia herself had advanced when she refused to adhere to the earlier French proposal in June, 1912. Austria as a neighboring power did have interests in the Balkan peninsula and no statesmen could declare uprightly that this was not true. To the French ambassador Berchtold remonstrated that if, as Austrian foreign minister, he should sign such a declara-

[19] D.D.F., 3d. ser., IV, no. 258; Izvolsky, II, no. 533; see also G.P., XXXIII, no. 12439.

[20] D.D.F., 3d. ser., IV, no. 274; Izvolsky, II, no. 534; K.A., XVI, no. 44 (*Berl. Mon.*, IX, 64); Minute, Oct. 29, 1912, B.D., IX, ii, 61.

[21] Oct. 30, 1912, D.D.F., 3d. ser., IV, no. 284.

[22] Poincaré, II, 289; Izvolsky, II, nos. 325, 337, 347; Nicolson, *Portrait of a Diplomatist*, p. 275.

tion, he would deserve to be shot. Out of considerations of sheer honesty he could not accept Poincaré's proposal.[23]

Since Poincaré had mentioned that England and Russia had agreed to his proposal, it was but natural that the official answers of the central powers should be identical. Berlin was responsible for drafting the answer of November 4th, in which the desire to help in any mediatory action was stressed. No mention was made of the declaration of disinterestedness. Instead they were of the opinion that "mediation could be undertaken only at the moment when it should be asked for by one of the belligerents, and when the situation should be more closely defined."[24] This response caused Poincaré to drop further plans for a conference for which he had already submitted proposals to London and St. Petersburg.

On the same day that the Triple Alliance replied to Poincaré's feeler, Turkey asked the various powers to intervene in favor of an armistice. The communication made by the grand vizier to the ambassadors in Constantinople differed somewhat from the communication made by the Turkish ambassadors in the various capitals. The former spoke of intervention for the imposition of an armistice while the latter spoke of mediation in favor of peace.[25] Poincaré refused to act upon the first formulation since it was inconsistent with neutrality, but as soon as the word mediation was used he took up the request. The German emperor also was absolutely opposed to anything that might be interpreted as an attempt to restrain the Balkan states in their victorious march, although he thought that with the proper explanations, the Turkish request could be passed on to the Balkan governments.[26] The government in Constantinople repeated its request for mediation, and finally after various exchanges of notes, it was decided that all the powers

[23] Ö-U.A., IV, no. 4216; D.D.F., 3d. ser., IV, nos. 297, 304; B.D., IX, ii, no. 83; G.P., XXXIII, no. 12310; Poincaré, II, 291.

[24] D.D.F., 3d. ser., IV, nos. 338, 339, 341; G.P., XXXIII, nos. 12307, 12311, 12312.

[25] D.D.F., 3d. ser., IV, nos. 328, 334, 337, 348, 353, 362; G.P., XXXIII, nos. 12324, 12325, 12334; B.D., IX, ii, nos. 110, 113 ed. note, 114.

[26] G.P., XXXIII, nos. 12319, 12321; B.D., IX, ii, no. 116.

should simultaneously pass on the request to the Balkan capitals. This was finally done on November 14th, but since Turkey had already addressed herself directly to the Balkan governments, the good offices of the powers came too late.[27] The Balkan states proceeded to negotiate directly with the Porte without the aid of the powers.

The movement for the cessation of hostilities was especially welcome to Russia. Immediately after the first Bulgarian victories, Sazonov became alarmed over the unexpected Balkan success. His original standpoint was that all the territory up to and including Adrianople must remain in Turkish possession.[28] France, realising what it would cost to veto Bulgarian aspirations so abruptly, hinted that it would be well not to oppose the capture of Adrianople.[29] The Russian military leaders before long also came to the conclusion that Adrianople was not a question of vital Russian interest. The Bulgarians might have that city if they captured it, but under no circumstances were they to be permitted to rule in Constantinople.[30] Should the Bulgarians enter the latter city, Russia would immediately send her Black Sea fleet through the Bosporus and anchor before the Golden Horn. France and England were called upon to help restrain the Bulgarians [31] and they accordingly supported the steps for mediation warmly. Austria-Hungary and Germany, on the other hand, were non-committal

[27] The British embassy at Constantinople without authorisation from the foreign office was instrumental in initiating the direct negotiations between Turkey and the allies (B.D., IX, ii, no. 287). On Nov. 11th Turkey had asked Mr. Rockhill, the American ambassador at Constantinople, if the United States might not act as mediator if the powers failed to do so. Rockhill advised urging direct negotiations between Turkey and the Balkan allies (Rockhill to State Department, Nov. 11, 1912, Constantinople Embassy Archive).

[28] K.A., XVI, no. 45 (*Berl. Mon.*, IX, 66–7); Izvolsky, II, nos. 541, 544.

[29] K.A., XVI, no. 49 (*Berl. Mon.*, IX, 70–1); Izvolsky, II, nos. 556, 559; D.D.F., 3d. ser., IV, no. 313; B.D., IX, ii, no. 123.

[30] Izvolsky, II, nos. 547, 557; *Doklad*, I, 661; D.D.F., 3d. ser., IV, no. 343; B.D., IX, ii, no. 119; G.P., XXXIII, no. 12427; Ö-U.A., IV, no. 4283. Russia later agreed not to oppose a temporary occupation of Constantinople (Izvolsky, II, no. 552; B.D., IX, ii, no. 215 enclosure; D.D.F., 3d. ser., IV, no. 389).

[31] Izvolsky, II, nos. 542, 547, 556; B.D., IX, ii, nos. 85, 88, 97, 102, 109, 122; D.D.F., 3d. ser., IV, nos. 307, 358.

as to Constantinople and would not have opposed Ferdinand's entering that city.[32]

The fall of Constantinople really seemed imminent.[33] Nothing apparently could stop the advance of the victorious Bulgarians. Concern was widespread over probable riots and Christian massacres in Constantinople when the retreating Turkish troops reached the city. All the powers dispatched warships to the Dardanelles for the protection of their respective nationals.[34] Guards were placed around the various embassies and plans were drawn up for the evacuation of the foreign population in case of need.

The Bulgarian cabinet was disposed to listen to the warnings and advice from the Entente countries.[35] They were not in favor of entering the city. King Ferdinand and most of the army, on the other hand, approved such an advance, and the Bulgarian sovereign was aflame with the desire to have a *Te Deum* sung in St. Sophia.[36] Had it been possible the Bulgarian army would undoubtedly have advanced and dictated the peace on the shores of the Bosporus. But their victorious onrush was halted at the Chatalja fortifications. The armies had moved so rapidly that it was imperative that they should stop to reorganise and gather their strength. Supplies had to be brought up, and with no railways in their control this was a long labori-

[32] Ö-U.A., IV, no. 4282; G.P., XXXIII, nos. 12297 marginal note, 12320.

[33] "Bulgarian occupation of Constantinople may now become a *fait accompli* any day" (Grey to Buchanan, Nov. 1, 1912, B.D., IX, ii, no. 88); Ö-U.A., IV, no. 4422; Gerhard von Mutius, "Die Türkei 1911–1914. Aus unveröffentlichen Lebenserinnerungen," *Preussische Jahrbücher*, CCXXXVI (1934), 216. On Nov. 4, 1912 the American ambassador at Constantinople reported: "Foreigners here, as well as the Christian population, are very panicky" (Rockhill to State Dept., Const. Emb. Archive).

[34] Turkey granted permission for the ships to enter the Dardanelles on Nov. 3, 1912 (Rockhill to State Dept., Nov. 4, 1912, Const. Emb. Archive). The United States joined the other powers in sending warships to Turkish waters.

[35] Conversation with Danev in May, 1930; Iv. Ev. Gueshov, *Prestŭpnoto bezumie i anketata po nego. Fakti i dokumenti.* [The Criminal Folly and the Investigation concerning it. Facts and Documents] (Sofia, 1914), p. 36; *Doklad*, I, 662; B.D., IX, ii, no. 109; D.D.F., 3d. ser., IV, no. 495; Ö-U.A., IV, no. 4378.

[36] Conversation with Danev in May, 1930; Ö-U.A., IV, no. 4362; Hans Roger Madol, *Ferdinand von Bulgarien. Der Traum von Byzanz* (Berlin, 1931), pp. 141–8.

ous task. The roads were well-nigh impassable as a result of the unusually heavy rains. Ox-drawn carts making five or ten miles a day are not a rapid means of transportation over a long line of communication. And yet every cartridge, every ounce of flour, every wounded soldier had to be transported in this fashion.[37] It is a remarkable tribute to Bulgarian courage and tenacity that the troops even reached the Chatalja lines. Then too, Turkish troops when guarding a relatively short defensive position were quite different opponents than when they were engaged in offensive operations, which none of their officers knew how to direct properly. The result was that the attack on the Chatalja lines on November 17–18th was unsuccessful. It cost Bulgaria ten to fifteen thousand men and for some time no more serious attempts were made to force these fortifications.

While the Bulgarians were bearing the brunt of the attack in Thrace, the other allies were occupying territory in Macedonia and Albania. The statesmen in Sofia feared that at the coming peace settlement the argument would be advanced that "possession is nine points of the law." Consequently they were anxious to turn their activities to those regions where they hoped to make their future gains.

The Turks had been defeated on all fronts. With the exception of the three fortresses of Scutari, Janina, and Adrianople, all the territory which the Balkan states had really hoped to capture was in their possession. Therefore there was no great objection to concluding an armistice.

Montenegro and Serbia commissioned the Bulgarians to act as their representatives in carrying on the negotiations with Turkey. Greece sent her own delegates.[38] Having already exchanged various memoranda on the conditions of armistice, active *pourparlers* were started just outside the Chatalja lines on November 25th. On December 3rd an armistice was signed,

[37] Diplomatist, pp. 204–5.

[38] D.D.F., 3d. ser., IV, no. 536; Lt. Colonel breveté Boucabeille, *La guerre turco-balkanique* (Paris, 1914), p. 221.

of which the most important provisions were as follows:

1. The armistice was to last until the conclusion of peace or the rupture of peace negotiations.
2. Peace negotiations were to begin in London on December 13th.
3. Four days notification was to be necessary before reopening hostilities in case peace negotiations failed.
4. The belligerent armies were to remain in their respective positions, a neutral zone being established between them.
5. The besieged Turkish fortresses were not to be reprovisioned.
6. The Turkish government obligated itself to raise the blockade of the Black Sea ports and permit the provisioning of the Bulgarian troops, by means of the Black Sea routes as well as by means of the Adrianople railroad.[39]

Greece refused to adhere to the armistice terms as Turkey would not cede the fortress of Janina.[40] In spite of the state of war which continued to exist between Turkey and Greece, Greece was permitted to join the peace negotiations in London, and active fighting ceased. Conversely, while Montenegro was officially at peace, the skirmishes and bombardments at Scutari continued.[41]

The armistice bore witness to the total defeat of the Turkish army. Everywhere attempts were made to explain this overwhelming victory on the part of the allies. France hailed the allied victories as evidence of the superiority of Creusot over Krupp artillery,[42] although the French papers were silent when the Bulgarians were halted at the Chatalja lines. That gave the German papers a chance to combat the French assertions.[43] The reputation of the Prussian military drill, which was supposedly prevalent in the Turkish army, was sullied, and

[39] *Ibid.*, pp. 221–223; B.D., IX, ii, no. 332.

[40] Boucabeille, *La guerre turco-balkanique*, p. 224; Ö-U.A., V, no. 4806.

[41] Hortense Zambaur, *Die Belagerung von Skutari* (Berlin, 1914), pp. 39–43.

[42] G.P., XXXI, no. 11529; XXXIII, nos. 12303, 12331.

[43] For example, *Münchener Allgemeine Zeitung*, Nov. 30, 1912; *Neue Freie Presse*, Nov. 24, 1912; article by Imhof Pasha, *Fremdenblatt*, Feb. 1, 1913.

the prestige of the French military system was correspondingly increased. Certainly the defeat of Turkey did little to bring about a more conciliatory tone in the French and German press.

The "why" of Turkish defeat can be answered in part by recalling the efficient military forces which the Balkan states placed in the field. But equally important was the great unpreparedness of the Turkish army. All accounts bear witness to this.[44] The German system of drill had never really been instituted. It did the Turks no good to have modern Krupp guns if they did not know how to use them. Aside from the lack of supplies, means of transportation, etc., the greatest factor in reducing the strength of the Turkish forces was the lack of an efficient officer corps.[45] The changes in government on the eve of the war, which were reflected in the army's high command, did not aid matters. Then too, the wholesale dismissal of mutinous, but trained soldiers in the months preceding the war, was bound to make an inefficient force of raw recruits. In this regard the German ambassador reported:

> Among the Turkish troops there were many who had never had a gun in their hands. One sees many wounded soldiers with broken noses, the result of having held their guns improperly while firing. Many reserve battalions had only two officers.[46]

[44] Goltz, *Denkwürdigkeiten*, p. 317; Bernhard Schmiterlow, *Aus dem Leben des Generalfeldmarschalls Freiherr von der Goltz* (Berlin, 1926), p. 109; Pomiankowski, *Zusammenbruch des ottomanischen Reiches*, p. 32; M. Mouktar Pacha, *La Turquie*, p. 144; M. Mouktar Pacha, *Mon commandant au cours de la campagne des Balkans* (Paris, 1913), pp. 6–7, 184–5; Izzet Fuad Pacha, *Paroles de Vaincu* (Paris, 1913), pp. 35–8; Izzet Pascha, *Denkwürdigkeiten*, p. 144; Lancelot Lawton, "A German View of Turkish Defeat," *The Fortnightly Review*, XCIX (March, 1913); *Neue Freie Presse*, Nov. 24, 1912; Bericht des K. & K. Major Felix Wagner über Eindrucke von der Cataldja Armee. Ursachen der Türkischen Niederlagen, Ö-U.K.A., Evidenz Bureau Res., no. 3428 ex 1912.

[45] Pomiankowski characterised the generals as the weakest part of the Turkish army and reported further: Unter dem hamidischen Regime ausschliesslich durch Protektion hinaufgekommen, entsprechen die türkischen Generäle zum allergrössten Teile in keiner Richtung den an hohe Truppenführer zu stellenden Anforderungen. Militärisch meist gänzlich unwissend, sind viele von ihnen auch physisch nicht im Stande, die Anstrengungen eines Feldzuges zu ertragen. Die meisten reiten gar nie, besitzen auch keine Pferde und spielen, wenn sie einmal zufällig zu Pferde steigen müssen, die traurigste Figur. Der Prozentsatz jener Generäle welche ihre Divisionen und Korps von der Kanzlei aus kommandieren, ist in der Türkei hoch . . ." (Ö-U.K.A., Ad. Res., no. 454, Oct. 20, 1912).

[46] Wangenheim to Kiderlen-Wächter, Nov. 7, 1912, G.P., XXXIII, no. 12364.

The following conclusion made by Wangenheim is sound and summarises the situation well:

> The reason for the collapse of Turkey is not to be sought in the lack of military qualities of the Turkish people, but in the culpable carelessness and the moral degeneracy of those who are responsible for the leadership of these unfortunate people. For years the German reform officers pointed out that flour was as necessary in a war as powder, and that the army would be short of everything if the transport system were neglected. With this in view huge sums were thrown away in the effort to obtain supply and ammunition transports, ambulances, etc. This material, however, was never obtained, because the factories that were to deliver the goods refused to pay the "bakshish" which the responsible authorities demanded.[47]

In proposing a declaration of disinterestedness, the Entente statesmen had hoped to obtain a statement of policy from the Ballhausplatz. Everyone realised that Austria had certain aims and desires which she would insist upon in the coming peace settlement. Now, the Entente powers wanted to know what these aims were. The six great powers had united in declaring to the Balkan governments that, whatever the outcome of the war, no changes in territory would be permitted. With the overwhelming defeat of the Turks everyone realised that the *status quo* was gone. The question then arose as to just what changes Austria would permit and whether she would demand compensations in return.

Germany was as interested as the Entente powers in finding out the plans of the Austrian statesmen. In October, 1912, Kiderlen noted:

> Berchtold is causing me great vexation because he absolutely does not know what he really wants! The point is that he isn't anything more than a "Cavalier." We must do everything possible to avoid the political leadership being transferred from Berlin to Vienna, as Aehrenthal was able to do in respect to Bülow. That would cost us dearly some day.[48]

Kiderlen was exaggerating, and his official language does not maintain this tenor. On October 26th he made the same sug-

[47] *Ibid.*; see also XXXIII, no. 12331; Ö-U.A., V, no. 4754; above, pp. 193–94.
[48] Jäckh, *Kiderlen-Wächter*, II, 188.

gestion to Austria which he had made earlier to France and England, regarding discussions of the changes in territory which a breach of the *status quo* would necessitate.[49] Berchtold accepted the German suggestion at once, and promised that he would shortly submit a memorandum of the Austrian view of the problem.

During October several ministerial conferences were held at the Ballhausplatz in which various questions touching Austrian interests were discussed.[50] Out of these discussions a program was eventually shaped, which was communicated to Berlin on October 30th, the same day on which Poincaré advanced the Entente proposal for disinterestedness. In submitting the program Berchtold stated that although it was evident that the *status quo* could no longer be maintained, it was still impossible to set up an absolutely final program. Much depended on future developments. Was all of European Turkey to be divided? Was an autonomous region to be set up? Would the Balkan states be satisfied with small territorial gains? Whatever the final decision would be, Berchtold felt that the following points were necessary to protect Austria's vital interests:

1. The consent of Austria-Hungary to an increase in territory of a neighboring state must be contingent on guarantees that the neighboring state will not pursue a hostile policy towards the monarchy in the future. In this respect Serbia is primarily meant. . . . Through a close economic union (*Anschluss*), which will also contain many advantages to Serbia, a common sphere of interests can be created which may insure friendly neighborly relations for a long time. The closer the tie, the more Serbia can count on Austria's kindly disposition toward Serbian expansion. The same holds for Montenegro.
2. The desire of Serbia for territorial expansion to the Adriatic must absolutely be refused. Such ambition can be taken as a sure sign that Serbia does not hope to live

[49] See above, p. 197; Ö-U.A., IV, nos. 4172, 4174, 4185.
[50] Ö-U.A., IV, nos. 4118, 4128, 4140, 4170.

in friendship with the monarchy for any length of time and does not wish to make use of a Bosnian port. A Serbian corridor to the Adriatic through Albania would be, of course, incompatible with the creation of a Serbian nationalistic state, such as Serbia claims to desire.

3. The unrestricted development of Albania stands in close connection with the interests of the monarchy. Austria-Hungary can not tolerate any other great power in this section of the Adriatic; therefore an Albania capable of an independent existence must be created.
4. The rightful claims of Rumania to compensations must be met.
5. Austria-Hungary must demand minor boundary rectifications. This applies chiefly to the island of Ada Kaleh in the Danube which at present is occupied by Austrian troops but belongs to Turkey.
6. Austria-Hungary must have guarantees for the freedom of trade in the territory which formerly belonged to Turkey.
7. Austria-Hungary must insist upon safeguarding her various other economic interests in the Balkan peninsula. The building of a railway to Salonica and the conversion of that city into a free port is asked.[51]

In asking Emperor William for permission to express to Count Berchtold Germany's support of the above program, Kiderlen characterised the Austrian proposals as "moderate and very reasonable."[52] According to Szögyény, the Kaiser found Berchtold's views entirely correct, and was determined to support Austria's aims.[53]

With slight changes in wording, the above points were submitted to Rome and Bucharest on November 3, 1912, and on

[51] Translated and paraphrased from Ö-U.A., IV, no. 4205; see also G.P., XXXIII, no. 12320.

[52] G.P., XXXIII, no. 12320.

[53] Ö-U.A., IV, no. 4275. Szögyény based his telegram on a conversation with Kiderlen. That the Kaiser did not agree so blandly with all of the program is clear from his marginal comments (G.P., XXXIII, no. 12320).

the following day to London, Paris, and St. Petersburg.[54] In each case it was emphasised that this was not a definitely fixed program but only the general principles which would have to be adapted to the course of events. A day later, November 5th, before the Austrian Delegation assembled in Budapest, Berchtold declared: "We are ready to take into consideration the new situation created by the victories of the Balkan states and so establish a basis for permanent friendly relations with these states."[55] The declaration had the full approval of the Delegations, and Berchtold must be given credit for being the first statesman to declare publicly that the *status quo* was ended and the Balkan states were to obtain territorial aggrandisement.

With these declarations the statesmen in the different capitals of the great powers knew where Austria stood. Considering what everyone had expected the Dual Monarchy to demand, the present program was very moderate. Two points raised serious difficulty. There were the question of a Serbian port on the Adriatic and the creation of a viable Albania. To grant the first was to destroy the latter, and for the time being the problem facing Europe was whether Serbia was to be permitted to have territorial access to the sea. The statesmen in Belgrade of course declared it a *conditio sine qua non.* On the other hand the statesmen in Vienna were just as determined that Serbian territory should not reach the Adriatic. Just as the Serbian claim for compensations became a general European question in 1908, so now this new Serbian problem became the center of European diplomacy.

Russia naturally attempted to persuade Austria to modify her stand on this question. Vienna was assured that Russia did not hope to convert a possible Serbian port into a Russian naval base. If Russia wanted to do this, she might just as well make use of the Montenegrin port of Antivari which might be

[54] Ö-U.A., IV, nos. 4256, 4266.

[55] *Parlamentarische Chronik. Beilage zur Politischen und Volkwirtschaftlichen Chronik der österreichisch-ungarischen Monarchie*, ed. Karl Neisser (Vienna, 1911– ; hereafter cited as *Parlamentarische Chronik*), 1912, p. 876.

had for a *pourboire*.[56] In Russian eyes it was bad policy for Austria to antagonise Serbia in this fashion, for it would but increase Serbian hatred for the Dual Monarchy and turn her into a standing enemy.[57] In Austria there were a few scattered voices which echoed this opinion. Liberals such as Masaryk, Kramař and Baernreither were heart and soul for granting Serbia a port.[58] Thurn and Szilassy of the embassy at St. Petersburg and even Auffenberg, the minister of war, found it the best plan.[59] At the Ballhausplatz, however, there was never the slightest inclination to give in on this question. Goluchowski in 1897 would have been willing to permit Serbia and Montenegro to become neighboring states. Aehrenthal in 1908 went a bit farther, and was willing to abandon the Sanjak entirely. Yet both of these statesmen were absolutely opposed to Serbia's reaching the sea. In 1912 Berchtold remained true to this inherited policy.[60]

The reasons Austria advanced were as follows. Serbian expansion would jeopardise the existence of an Albanian state which both Austria and Italy wished to see established. It was entirely contrary to the principle of nationality and the slogan "The Balkans for the Balkan peoples" which Serbia was herself so loudly proclaiming. A small corridor leading to a purely Serbian port was also vetoed, since it would be only a cause for continual disturbance and a temptation for Serbia to increase her territory at the expense of the Albanians. Economically the port was not necessary since Serbia might be assured a com-

[56] Ö-U.A., IV, nos. 4449, 4550.

[57] *Ibid.*, IV, nos. 4284, 4361, 4620. The Kaiser also favored a Serbian port on the Adriatic, but under the influence of Bethmann Hollweg and Kiderlen he modified his views and agreed to support the Austrian position (G.P., XXXIII, nos. 12339, 12349 note). Rumania would have also liked to see Serbia get a seaport (Ö-U.A., IV, no. 4385).

[58] *Die Zeit*, Dec. 12, 1912; *Neue Freie Presse*, Dec. 18, 1912; Baernreither, *Fragmente*, pp. 171–84; Thomas G. Masaryk, *The Making of a State* (New York, 1927), pp. 2–3; *Parlamentarische Chronik*, 1912, pp. 171 ff.

[59] Ö-U.A., IV, no. 4165; G.P., XXXIII, no. 12317; Baron J. von Szilassy, *Der Untergang der Donau Monarchie. Diplomatische Erinnerungen* (Berlin, 1921), pp. 217, 220; Auffenberg, *Aus Österreichs Höhe und Niedergang*, p. 213.

[60] See above, ch. IX.

mercial *débouché* under international guarantees on both the Aegean and the Adriatic. Austria, whose economic interests were certainly as great as Serbia's, was asking for no more in regard to Salonica.[61]

Such were the reasons which were publicly advanced. Behind them of course was the desire to lessen Serbia's economic independence. Politically, a Serbia reaching the Adriatic would also be undesirable, since it would enhance the prestige of Serbia and consequently increase the irredentist agitation among the Slavs of the monarchy.[62] Nicolson in a minute drawn up at the foreign office formulated exactly the Austrian position when he wrote:

> After the revival of the "Great Serb" idea now become an active and living force, Serbia's establishment on the Adriatic and with a band of territory running thereto would soon develop into a large Serb Kingdom including Croatia, Slavonia, Dalmatia and the Banat. This would be disastrous to the Dual Monarchy, and to me it is clear that Austria cannot, and from her point of view should not, permit Serbia to establish herself in any shape or form on the Adriatic.[63]

Most important of all was the fact that the monarchy did not wish to see the equilibrium of the Adriatic changed. She was determined not to have a shift of power in this section, and for this reason the Austrian statesmen had entered into the agreements with Italy which provided for the establishment of an Albanian state, when the Turkish Empire in Europe should disappear. A Serb port would mean a Russian port in the Adriatic and this could not be permitted. Even in such a case, to be sure, Austria could only be shut off if Italy joined with Russia or Serbia. But this was exactly what was feared in some circles. Tschirschky reported Berchtold as saying:

> Naturally he could not tell the Russian ambassador that Austria saw in a Serbian port — which could easily be changed into a naval

[61] Arguments advanced, Ö-U.A., IV, nos. 4205, 4326, 4359; V, no. 4843.

[62] Ö-U.K.A., Res. Gestb., no. 4611, Nov. 9, 1912. This memoir by Schemua is in answer to Berchtold's communication of Oct. 26, 1912 (Ö-U.A., IV, no. 4183).

[63] B.D., IX, ii, 136. Grey initialed this minute without comment.

base — only a Russian forepost, with the help of which Russia in a given moment could encircle the monarchy from the south and whence with Italian help the Adriatic could be entirely closed.[64]

In his memoir of November 9th Schemua also declared:

> A Serbian state on the Adriatic could at any time extend its hand to Italy, be it to show a preference to her in economic matters, or for the pursuance of common political steps against the monarchy.[65]

Francis Ferdinand was known to be no lover of Italy, and there is evidence that his opposition to a Serbian port and insistence on an independent Albania was based on his fear of possible future Serbian-Italian coöperation.[66] In 1908, when it was a question of abolishing the servitudes placed on Montenegrin ports by the Treaty of Berlin, the Archduke wrote:

> . . . Likewise I am absolutely opposed to the abrogation of that paragraph (I believe it is XIX) of the treaty of Berlin in respect to Montenegro, as these infamous false rascals can not be given a naval base which would become a highly dangerous strategic and tactical base for the Italian fleet. That would be an enormous danger and unacceptable to us, no matter how much Tittoni might wish it. One must remain adamant there.[67]

What was true for a Montenegrin port in 1908 would undoubtedly be true for a Serbian port in 1912.

Despite their conflicting interests in the Adriatic, Vienna and Rome coöperated in keeping Serbia from the sea. Fear and suspicion of Italy was general in Austria-Hungary, and the possibility of Serbian-Italian coöperation was no doubt a factor in influencing certain Austrians, notably Francis Ferdinand, to oppose Serbian territorial expansion to the Adriatic.[68] The French ambassador at Rome reported that Italians feared a Serbian port might eventually become an Austrian one, after

[64] G.P., XXXIII, no. 12317.

[65] Ö-U.K.A., Res. Gestb., no. 4611, Nov. 9, 1912.

[66] Chlumecky, *Franz Ferdinands Wirken und Wollen*, pp. 127, 130–1, 134, 160.

[67] Privatschreiben, Oct. 20, 1908, Ö-U.A., I, no. 347a.

[68] In conversations in 1930 Count Berchtold and Count Szápáry assured the author that the fear of Serbian-Italian coöperation did not enter into the considerations of the Austrian government when they opposed a Serbian port. This is borne out by the various memoirs and protocols published in the Austrian documents.

an Austrian-Serbian war.[69] Hence Italy was ready to oppose the accomplishment of this Serbian ambition. Austrian and Italian desire for a self-sufficient Albania — which a Serbian port would jeopardise — was in part, then, the result of mutual distrust. This coöperation was important for it meant a united front on the part of the Triple Alliance. Italy, however, did not exert herself as Austria did on behalf of their common policy. The Consulta would probably have agreed to a Serbian corridor, had Austria been at all inclined to do so.[70] Throughout the affair the onus for the negation of Serbian wishes was placed on the shoulders of Austria.

How serious the Serbian port question would become depended on the support which Russia and the other Entente powers gave to Belgrade. On November 7th, on the express instructions of his government, the Serbian chargé at Berlin made an energetic protest against Austria's position in regard to Serbian expansion to the Adriatic.[71] He pointed out that according to the plan of partition agreed upon by the Balkan states and sanctioned by Russia, all Albania was apportioned among the different allies. If Austria opposed this division of Albania, Serbia would be assured the support not only of Bulgaria but also of Russia. Should it reach this point the Serbian government would like to know if Germany would support Austria against Russia. This was indeed rather bold and impolite language for a small state to use in addressing a great power. None of the powers approved and Kiderlen made it perfectly clear not only to Serbia but to England, France and Russia as well, that in the eventualities referred to, Austria-Hungary, Italy, and Germany would present a united front, for they could not permit Serbian expansion to the Adriatic.[72]

[69] Poincaré, II, 314; see also, B.D., IX, ii, no. 172.

[70] Ö-U.A., IV, nos. 4586, 4638, 4788.

[71] G.P., XXXIII, no. 12338. In general on this topic see, Richard Giesche, *Der serbische Zugang zum Meer und die europäische Krise 1912* (Stuttgart, 1932).

[72] G.P., XXXIII, no. 12338 note; Benckendorff, II, no. 717; K.A., XVI, no. 54 (*Berl. Mon.*, XI, 73); B.D., IX, ii, nos. 150, 151; D.D.F., 3d. ser., IV, nos. 379, 380, 390.

The interview between Kiderlen and Dr. Bogičević was only part of a daring program which Belgrade had set in motion. Serbian armies were in full swing to the Adriatic coast, although the Ballhausplatz let it be known that such action was not only undesirable but utterly useless. Meanwhile all Europe was nervous as to whether Austria would take up arms to force Serbia to withdraw from the sea. Just like their colleague in Berlin the Serbian representatives in London and Paris firmly set forth Serbia's claims.[73] Yet the most energetic action of all was reserved for Vienna.

On November 8th the Serbian minister appeared at the Ballhausplatz, and presented a complaint in regard to the actions of the Austrian consul Prochaska, when the Serbians captured Prizren.[74] The charges were that Prochaska had summoned the Turks and Albanians to battle against the Serbians, and had encouraged them not to surrender but to fight on. In addition the Serbian troops had been shot at from the roof of the consulate. In order to avoid future troubles, the Serbian government requested that the consul be recalled.

Berchtold replied that he doubted the charges, since an Austrian official would hardly act in this fashion. The Serbian government had, however, stopped all means of communication so that he had been unable to get in touch with his representatives in the theater of war. Nevertheless he would investigate the matter at once, and requested the Serbian government to aid him in communicating with the different Austrian consulates. The reopening of courier and code telegram service seemed essential before he could give a definite answer to the Serbian charges. On November 12th Berchtold went a step farther, and requested permission to send a special delegate to investigate the matter on the spot.[75] In spite of repeated requests from the Austrian minister at Belgrade, it was not until November 19th that the Serbian government granted the Austrian requests.

[73] Benckendorff, II, no. 711; B.D., IX, ii, no. 142; Poincaré, II, 313; D.D.F., 3d. ser., IV, no. 390.

[74] Ö-U.A., IV, no. 4316.

[75] *Ibid.*, IV, nos. 4316, 4380.

Code or courier service were not actually restored until November 25th.[76]

On this date Consul Edl, who was sent immediately to investigate matters, reached Usküb.[77] Here he met Prochaska who had come there from Prizren. This was only the beginning of the investigation, which was essential in order to answer the serious charges which the Serbian government had laid in Vienna. It was also necessary for Edl to go to Mitrovitza, for on November 17th Consul Tahy, who was stationed there, had turned up in Budapest, having forsaken his post because of the strictures placed on his actions by the Serbian officers.[78] The Austrian emissary also wished to look into this matter.

News of the "Consular Affair" had of course spread and caused great uneasiness. Tales circulated that all kinds of things had happened to Prochaska, even emasculation.[79] These tales were not confined to Austria-Hungary but were told with great glee in the Montenegrin army.[80] They were cited as evidence of what the Serbs would do to the Austrians after they had finished with the Turks. But in reality there was no cause for this alarm over the personal safety of Prochaska. On November 8th, the day the Serbian government raised its protest in Vienna, the Ballhausplatz published in the papers the news that an inquiry had been made in Belgrade about Prochaska, adding the following comment: "The Serbian government has kindly informed us that the consul is well, and that sufficient care will be taken for his protection." [81]

On November 17th the *Neue Freie Presse* published, under favorable commentary, a telegram from the Serbian government stating that no harm had come to Prochaska. This was

[76] *Ibid.*, IV, nos. 4492, 4493; *Politische Chronik*, 1912, p. 489; *Neue Freie Presse*, Nov. 27, 1912.

[77] Ö-U.A., IV, no. 4625.

[78] *Ibid.*, IV, no. 4461; *Die Zeit*, Nov. 17, 1912.

[79] For example see the interpellation brought in the Hungarian Delegation on November 20, 1912 (*Parlamentarische Chronik*, 1912, p. 911); also the summary in the London *Times*, Dec. 16, 1912.

[80] Durham, *Struggle for Scutari*, pp. 234, 253–4; Durham, *Balkan Tangle*, p. 234; conversation with Miss Durham in August 1929.

[81] *Die Zeit*, Nov. 8, 1912.

followed by a telegram from the consul himself, in answer to a telegram directed to him by the editor.[82] Two postcards also arrived from Prochaska.[83] And yet during all this time the government had not been able to get in touch with him and no official communication from Prochaska had arrived at the foreign office. It was the withholding of official communication which aroused feeling and brought forth anti-Serbian comments in the Austrian press. Finally on November 26th word came from the Austrian consul at Usküb of Prochaska's safe arrival there,[84] and this news was passed on at once to the press. *Die Zeit* commented: "With this one of the most dangerous points in the conflict which has arisen between the monarchy and Serbia has been settled." [85]

There was no official denial of the continued reports of violence done to Prochaska. The fact that the newspaper accounts heralding his personal safety were not denied was considered enough evidence to dispel the rumors.[86] The point in which the Austrian statesmen were interested was the charge brought by the Serbian government, and in regard to this they had no material on which to base a statement. The first report from Prochaska himself reached the foreign office on November 27th,[87] but it was not until two weeks later that Edl arrived at Vienna to deliver his report.

During the whole month of November and the beginning of December the main question of whether Serbia should receive a port on the Adriatic was befogged by the consular affair. The situation was further complicated by Russia's retention of her third year levy of troops, who were usually dismissed in Octo-

[82] *Neue Freie Presse*, Nov. 21, 1912 Abendblatt. Prochaska answered the telegram of the editor of Nov. 15th on Nov. 17th, but the answer was not received until Nov. 21st. (*Ibid.*, Nov. 22, 1912). It was not until Nov. 27th that the first official telegram from Prochaska reached Vienna (Ö-U.A., IV, no. 4646).

[83] *Die Zeit*, Nov. 20, 1912.

[84] Consul Maryan von Heimroth to Berchtold, Nov. 25, 1912, Ö-U.A., IV, no. 4625.

[85] *Die Zeit*, Nov. 26, 1912; see also, *Neue Freie Presse*, Nov. 26, 1912; London *Times*, Nov. 27, 1912; *Fremdenblatt*, Nov. 28, 1912.

[86] *Fremdenblatt*, Dec. 12, 1912.

[87] Ö-U.A., IV, no. 4646; see also nos. 4647, 4664, 4730.

ber when the new recruits were called in.[88] The result was an increase of about 400,000 in the standing army. Other minor military measures were also taken. The Russians were prompted by fear of what Austria might do, but there can be no doubt that their military measures preceded those taken by the Dual Monarchy. Gradually step by step the Austrian generals were able to wring from Francis Joseph the consent for some additional measures.[89] It would be difficult to say whether Austria-Hungary or Russia took more far-reaching measures at this time. It appears, however, that greater preparedness existed in Russia. The important fact for the consideration at hand is that both Austria and Russia were arming, and the diplomatic negotiations had to be carried out in this atmosphere.

The tension prevalent at that time may be gauged by the desire of the Viennese authorities to send Prince Hohenlohe as special envoy from Francis Joseph to the tsar, with an appeal to settle the Serbian question amicably. Kiderlen advised against this procedure, since he feared the mission might fail, and thus complicate matters enormously.[90] On November 28–29th, when the smoke had not yet cleared, the Austrian representatives in Belgrade, Cetinje, Durazzo, and St. Petersburg received instructions as to what they should do in case war broke out.[91] The most important archives were to be packed immediately so that they might be taken along at a minute's notice. In 1914 the Austrian representatives were referred to this order when the time came for them to leave the various capitals.[92] One might wonder if the archives rested in packing cases throughout the intervening period.

On November 4–5th Austria had set forth her policy. On November 6–8th the Serbian representatives in London, Paris, and Berlin had energetically argued for Serbian expansion to the Adriatic, and in Vienna the consular affair had been

[88] G.P., XXXIII, nos. 12360, 12370, 12375, 12394; Frantz, *Russlands Eintritt in den Weltkrieg*, pp. 20–1; Gunther Frantz, *Russland auf dem Wege zur Katastrophe* (Berlin, 1926), p. 19.

[89] See below, Appendix I, pp. 461–62.

[90] G.P., XXXIII, nos. 12391, 12403; Ö-U.A., IV, nos. 4477, 4509.

[91] Ö-U.A., IV, no. 4710.

[92] *Ibid.*, VIII, nos. 10229, 10396.

launched. Up to this point Russia had been furthering Serbian policy. The language which the Serbian minister used to Kiderlen, and especially the statement that Russia would support Serbia with arms, alarmed and irritated Sazonov. In addition Poincaré had cold-shouldered the Russian request that the Quai d'Orsay "should take the initiative in suggesting to the powers a mediation on the basis of the Russian programme" for territorial settlement.[93] This would have meant not only taking steps to prevent the Bulgarians from entering Constantinople, but also openly supporting a Serbian port on the Adriatic. Poincaré knew Austria was dead-set against this Serbian advance to the sea and was disinclined to burn his fingers by putting forward Russian proposals. Grey and Kiderlen also let it be known at St. Petersburg that the Serbian representatives were going rather far in their pronouncements. Sazonov now called Belgrade to account and asked Paris and London to join in advising Serbia to moderate her demands.[94] The German, Austrian, and British ambassadors all noted a distinctly less Serbophile atmosphere at the Russian foreign office.[95]

Nevertheless in a few days the old feeling seemed to return, and the ambassadors were at a loss to account for this change. Some thought that it was perhaps the influence of Hartwig at Belgrade or the less peaceful attitude of the tsar, who was at that time in Spala surrounded by a military entourage. The influence of Rasputin who had just been recalled to favor because of the illness of the tsarevitch was also eyed with distrust.[96] It was feared that Rasputin had been bribed to advocate an anti-Austrian policy by the two Montenegrin grand duchesses.

[93] B.D., IX, ii, nos. 139, 143; D.D.F., 3d. ser., IV, nos. 358, 361.

[94] Izvolsky, II, nos. 558, 562, 563; B.D., IX, ii, nos. 171, 177, 228 enclosure, 229 enclosure; D.D.F., 3d. ser., IV, nos. 411 annotation, 431, 432, 452, 460.

[95] G.P., XXXIII, nos. 12383, 12387, 12415; Ö-U.A., IV, nos. 4361, 4483, 4510, 4550, 4588; B.D., IX, ii, nos. 195, 205, 291.

[96] Ö-U.A., IV, nos. 4550, 4588; G.P., XXXIII, no. 12415; B.D., IX, ii, nos. 219, 291. Rasputin was reputed to have the ability to cure the tsarevitch's attacks of haemophilia. That the tsar was quite militarily minded at Spala is clear from Kokovtsov's account (*Out of My Past. The Memoirs of Count Kokovtsov*, ed. H. H. Fisher [Stanford University Press, 1935], pp. 339–40).

It is of course impossible definitely to account for this change of attitude in St. Petersburg. Villiers at the British foreign office said, "M. Sazonov is a sad wobbler," [97] and Buchanan, the British ambassador to Russia, complained: "Sazonov is so continually changing his ground that it is difficult to follow the successive phases of pessimism and optimism through which he passes." [98] True to this characterisation, already on November 22nd the German ambassador thought he could note a return to a more moderate attitude on the part of Sazonov.[99] Three days later the Russian foreign minister told the Italian chargé that Serbia should only try to get a commercial outlet to the Adriatic and that he had told Belgrade this. The Italian envoy reported this to his Austrian colleague who telegraphed to Vienna: "The Italian chargé was so surprised over this unexpected change of front on the part of Sazonov that he could not believe his own ears, and asked Sazonov to repeat the statement about the advice he had given to Serbia." [100] Sazonov later gave similar assurances to the Austrian ambassador personally, and even stated in regard to Hartwig, "Je vous assure, je le tiendrai en main." "It is only to be hoped," so Thurn concluded his report, "that after the position assumed here during the past week, this entirely unbelievable, mild and conciliatory attitude will last longer than the favorable period of about two weeks ago." [101] The British ambassador also noted the change in front and reported, ". . . it is an undoubted fact that, since the Emperor has returned to Tsarskoe Selo, where His Majesty is in immediate touch with his ministers, Monsieur Sazonov has once more lowered his tone and taken a calmer view of the international situation." [102]

[97] Minute, Nov. 28, 1912, B.D., IX, ii, 215.

[98] Buchanan to Nicolson, Nov. 28, 1912, *ibid.*, IX, ii, no. 303.

[99] Ö-U.A., IV, no. 4566; see also G.P., XXXIII, nos. 12417, 12440, 12467.

[100] Ö-U.A., IV, no. 4640.

[101] *Ibid.*, IV, no. 4641. For protests of the German, Italian, Austrian, and British ambassadors on Hartwig's actions see G.P., XXXIII, nos. 12417, 12467; B.D. IX, ii, nos. 225, 237, 238.

[102] Buchanan to Grey, Nov. 27, 1912, B.D., IX, ii, no. 291; see also nos. 303, 371.

This time the Russian attitude did last and with that the question of a Serbian port in reality ended. Not only did Sazonov remain steadfast but he lived up to his promise and brought Hartwig into line. The Russian minister counseled the Serbians to give way. Descos, the French minister at Belgrade, later noted that Hartwig was a changed man since his "more decisive than usual" admonition from St. Petersburg.[103] The Serbians of course did not accept their defeat at once, but with Austria and Italy willing to grant Serbia an economic outlet and Russia backing this policy, the outcome was certain, despite continued tension.

What determined Russia to this last change in front? From the time Sazonov definitely knew the Austrian aims, he had not held out many hopes to Serbia. The question had been, did Austria really mean to stand by her guns? The Bogičević-Kiderlen conversation had led him to warn Serbia to assume a more temperate attitude, but St. Petersburg was not then certain that Austria meant all she said. On November 21st Poincaré telegraphed to St. Petersburg that Tittoni had told him that in spite of the Racconigi accord Italy would stand by Austria on the question of a Serbian port.[104] Preparatory military measures were being taken in the Dual Monarchy (as well as in Russia) and the joint visit of Francis Ferdinand and Chief of Staff Schemua to Berlin on November 22, 1912 led Russia to believe that matters were becoming serious. The visit caused great excitement on the banks of the Neva, and from that time on, in the words of the Serbian minister, there was no more talk of Serbian territorial expansion to the sea.[105]

At the very time the archduke and Schemua visited Berlin, important decisions were being made at St. Petersburg. At a conference of the commanders of the Warsaw and Kiev military districts which was presided over by the tsar, it was decided to mobilise the entire Kiev district and part of the Warsaw dis-

[103] Descos to Poincaré, Jan. 15, 1913, D.D.F., 3d. ser., V, no. 220.

[104] *Ibid.*, IV, no. 507.

[105] Conversation in 1930 with D. Popović, Serbian minister at St. Petersburg in 1912.

trict and to prepare to mobilise the Odessa district.[106] Before issuing the orders, however, it was thought best to inform Sazonov, Kokovtsov and several of the other ministers. On the morning of November 23rd a council was held in the tsar's study at Tsarskoe Selo. Here the tsar informed them of the forthcoming mobilisation, adding naïvely, "I wish to stress particularly the fact that this refers exclusively to our Austrian frontier and that we have no intention whatever of taking any steps against Germany. Our mutual relations leave nothing to be desired and I have every reason to hope for the support of Emperor William." [107]

Kokovtsov was aghast at this news of the machinations of Sukhomlinov, the minister of war. Ever a pillar of moderation and common sense, Kokovtsov pointed out the practical certainty of war if these orders were carried through. As a compromise, he suggested issuing a special ukase, again extending the term for the third year levy, this time for six months. This would increase tremendously the effectiveness of the army, but avoid the dangers inherent in mobilisation. Sazonov also opposed the mobilisation measures, pointing out that ". . . even if we were ready for a war, which was by no means the case, we had no right to undertake such steps without first coming to an understanding with our allies." [108] Although there is no record that Sazonov made use of this information at the council, his recent inquiries as to what France and England would do in case of an Austrian attack on Serbia had brought at best evasive replies and a query as to what Russia's action would be.[109] One thing, however, was certain. England did not think a Serbian port was worth a European war.[110] The result of the council was that the mobilisation measures were not initiated. Instead of inaugurating an aggressive military policy which

[106] Kokovtsov, *Memoirs*, p. 345; Zaionchkovski, *Podgotovka rossii*, p. 281.

[107] Kokovtsov, *Memoirs*, p. 345.

[108] *Ibid.*, p. 347.

[109] B.D., IX, ii, nos. 202, 209, 216, 238, 303; D.D.F., 3d. ser., IV, nos. 443, 469, 507.

[110] B.D., IX, ii, nos. 280, 283, 321. The moderating influence of Grey on Sazonov is stressed by Giesche, *Der serbische Zugang zum Meer*, pp. 27–40, 53, 59.

could only have encouraged Serbian expansionist designs, Russia fell in line with the other powers of Europe.

On November 18th Kiderlen had renewed general discussions by suggesting to England and France that the powers ought to decide just what changes they would permit in the coming peace settlement. According to his view, there were five points which the powers ought to reserve for their own decision: 1) Albania, 2) Adrianople and Constantinople, 3) Mount Athos, 4) the rectification of the Rumanian frontier, 5) the disposition of the Aegean Islands.[111] Toward the end of October he had suggested a similar discussion *à trois*,[112] but now he thought Russia, Italy, and Austria-Hungary might well be drawn in.

This suggestion was favorably received in London and Paris. With General Schemua and Francis Ferdinand visiting Berlin, Poincaré feared the central powers might take the initiative in calling a conference. He did not relish this prospect, and telegraphed Paul Cambon that he thought England and France ought to decide about a conference, before it was too late.[113]

To the suggestion of Kiderlen and Poincaré, Sir Edward Grey added one of his own. In order to avoid the delay and misunderstandings which inevitably arose when negotiations were carried on by telegraph between the capitals, he thought it would be well to concentrate them in one place. This meant a conference. But since, according to Kiderlen's proposal, it was only a matter of preliminary discussions, Grey suggested that it would be proper to delegate the task to the ambassadors of the great powers at some one capital. He thought Paris ought to be the city.[114]

Although Kiderlen later claimed that he had suggested the ambassadorial conference [115] the documents indicate that it was Grey who hit upon this happy solution. The first mention of it

[111] G.P., XXXIV, i, no. 12500; D.D.F., 3d. ser., IV, no. 483. Kiderlen did not suggest as many points for discussion to London as he did to Paris (B.D., IX, ii, no. 243, 247; Benckendorff, II, no. 727).

[112] See above, p. 197.

[113] Poincaré to P. Cambon, Nov. 22, 1912, D.D.F., 3d. ser., IV, no. 520.

[114] Cambon to Poincaré, Nov. 22, 1912, *ibid.*, IV, no. 524; B.D., IX, ii, no. 249.

[115] G.P., XXXIII, no. 12447 marginal note; XXXIV, i, no. 12503 note.

was in a conversation between Grey and Cambon on November 22nd. Benckendorff, the Russian ambassador at London, was led to believe that Poincaré had proposed this solution and he passed this information on to St. Petersburg.[116] This was of course not the case since Poincaré wanted a grand general conference attended by the Balkan states as well as the great powers.[117] He had issued a call for such a conference on October 15th, but the project was still-born. Cambon now made it out as if Grey's proposal was no new initiative but simply the application of Poincaré's project to Kiderlen's suggestion.[118] After some further attempts to win support for his original plan Poincaré accepted the "modified version" and concentrated his efforts on bringing the ambassadorial conference to Paris. Being the first statesman to have proposed a conference, he thought well established precedent should be followed "in having the conference on the territory of that power which provoked it."

Sazonov now took a hand and he too felt that he had a direct part in proposing the final solution. He suggested that all questions should be discussed by the ambassadors at the French capital.[119] Grey and Poincaré of course agreed and told Sazonov what a good plan he had proposed. Finally on Poincaré's advice Sazonov asked Grey to take the initiative in forming a conference of ambassadors.[120]

Having already suggested the idea to the German ambassador at a luncheon at the foreign office, Grey now officially made a formal inquiry at Berlin. How would the German government "view a proposal that instructions should be sent to the six ambassadors at one of the capitals . . . to consult together and submit to their Governments propositions on three points:

1. To what extent are the allies free to change the map of Europe without any stipulations being made by the great powers?

[116] Benckendorff, II, no. 727.
[117] D.D.F., 3d. ser., IV, nos. 499, 569, 570; G.P., XXXIV, i, no. 12503 note.
[118] D.D.F., 3d. ser., IV, no. 556.
[119] *Ibid.*, IV, no. 573; B.D., IX, ii, no. 270.
[120] B.D., IX, ii, no. 296; D.D.F., 3d. ser., IV, no. 587.

2. On what points must the great powers reserve their right to have some say in the settlement? Albania, the access of Serbia to the Adriatic, and the Aegean Islands are the points of greatest importance that occur to . . . [the British Government] assuming that the allies do not attempt to claim the Constantinople Straits.
3. What settlement on each of these points would secure the assent and support of the six powers? [121]

Sir Edward Grey suggested Paris as a possible meeting place and asked that Kiderlen sound Austria on the plan. The German foreign secretary did this at once, stressing his inclination to accept the proposal, although he recommended London as the seat of the conference.[122] News of Sir Edward's suggestion had got into the press, and so the British government did not await the result of Kiderlen's inquiry at Vienna, but sounded the Ballhausplatz directly.

Berchtold viewed the suggestion with favor, since "such academic conversations would perhaps lead to practical results, without involving the dangers that would be associated with a conference." [123] But he felt bound to make a reservation to the effect that, since Austria-Hungary and Italy had warned Belgrade and Cetinje that they must not expect territorial expansion along the Albanian coast, the Austrian ambassador could not discuss this question. Serbia, on the other hand, might be granted a commercial outlet to the Adriatic, and the conditions involved here might be discussed. After obtaining the assent of Italy and Germany to this restriction, Austria informed Sir Edward Grey of her willingness to enter upon an ambassadorial conference, under the above condition. Like Kiderlen, Berchtold favored London as the meeting place. The half-hearted attempt of the Triple Alliance to obtain the participation of the Rumanian minister in the conference came to nothing.[124]

[121] G.P., XXXIV, i, no. 12504; B.D., IX, ii, no. 297; Ö-U.A., IV, no. 4708.
[122] G.P., XXXIV, i, no. 12505, B.D., IX, ii, no. 339; Ö-U.A., IV, no. 4701.
[123] Ö-U.A., V, no. 4735; B.D., IX, ii, nos. 311, 345.
[124] B.D., IX, ii, nos. 353 enclosure, 356, 357, 364, 373, 382 ed. note.

Grey was not especially pleased with this qualified approval, but since the discussions were not to be binding, any country might restrict its ambassador as it saw fit. Not wishing to injure the susceptibilities of Poincaré, he pleaded for Paris as a meeting place, but Kiderlen, with the full approval of the Kaiser, would not listen to this. Rather no conference at all than a conference in Paris, where Izvolsky would be given free rein to carry on his intrigues.[125] Finally it was agreed to by all, that the preliminary ambassadorial conference was to be held in London. Although Poincaré still spoke of the "Final Conference," the other powers had given up that idea entirely.

In proposing the discussions Grey argued, "Without some such consultation, the views of Austria-Hungary and Russia cannot be reconciled, or even definitely ascertained, and there is danger that they may drift through mobilisation into an irreconcilable attitude."[126] About November 22nd Russia informed the Triple Alliance that Serbia would have to be satisfied with a commercial outlet.[127] Although reports came in that Belgrade had accepted this decision, there was no official declaration to this effect. In fact quite the contrary was the case. On November 25th Pašić stated in the London *Times*:

> It is essential that Serbia should possess about fifty kilometers from Alessio to Durazzo. This coastline would be joined to what was formerly Old Serbia, approximately by the territory between a line from Durazzo to Ochrida Lake in the south, and one from Alessio to Djakova in the north.
>
> For this minimum Serbia is prepared to make every sacrifice, since not to do so would be false to her national duty. No Serbian statesman or government dare betray the future welfare of the country by considering for a moment even the abandonment of this minimum.[128]

[125] G.P., XXXIV, i, nos. 12503, 12508, 12525. Russia also preferred London to Paris as the seat of a conference (B.D., IX, ii, no. 339).

[126] G.P., XXXIV, i, no. 12504.

[127] See above, p. 218.

[128] Pašić, greatly annoyed, claimed that Steed to whom he had given the interview had without authorisation attached his name to the article (B.D., IX, ii, nos. 330, 347). The interview created a very unfavorable impression at all the Entente capitals and Pašić was advised against making any further similar statements (S.D., II, nos. 221, 222, 225; Benckendorff, II, nos. 736, 737; B.D., IX, ii, nos. 220 note, 272, 309).

Austria had in the meantime not changed her views. In fact in some matters she had even become less generous to the Balkan states. Montenegro had failed to capture Scutari. King Nikita had refused abruptly the suggestion that cession of territory on the Lovčen might win Austria's consent to the incorporation of Scutari with Montenegro.[129] From now on the Ballhausplatz set up as a cardinal point in its program the awarding of Scutari to the future Albanian state. The fate of Scutari was to become the nightmare of the ambassadorial conference.

In the question of Serbian territorial expansion to the Adriatic, the Ballhausplatz remained adamant. In November, 1912, with the cognisance and sanction of Count Berchtold, Professor Redlich journeyed to Belgrade and discussed with Pašić possible economic agreements between Austria and Serbia. He was followed by others, above all by Professor Masaryk, who made the journey at the instigation of the editor of the *Neue Freie Presse* and of various German deputies of the Austrian chamber.[130] This time Pašić asked his visitor to inform Berchtold unofficially of the Serbian views. Serbia was eager to have better commercial relations with Austria, and from 1917 on, when her present commercial treaties would expire, Serbia

[129] Baron Giesl, when he was instructed to sound King Nikita on this exchange, asked permission to make the proposal on his own initiative. The failure to negotiate the exchange thus did not compromise the Ballhausplatz (Ö-U.A., IV, nos. 4467, 4482, 4537, 4576, 4577, 4609; B.D., IX, ii, no. 269). The Italians, however, obtained wind of the affair and asked embarrassing questions (*ibid.*, V, nos. 5156, 5383; Giesl, *Zwei Jahrzehnte*, p. 246). Giesl writing without access to the documents and from undated notes has erroneously put this incident in May instead of November (*ibid.*, p. 246). In an interview in June, 1930 he assured the writer that this must be a mistake on his part as he made the advance for an exchange of territory only once and the documents were of course right. The exchange, however, was later again considered in some circles in Austria (Conrad, II, 402 ff.; III, 128, 163; Hubka, "Kritische Tage in Montenegro," *Berliner Monatshefte*, IX [1931], 38).

[130] Redlich, *Francis Joseph*, p. 522; Baernreither, *Fragmente*, p. 183; Ö-U.A., V, no. 4893; B.D., IX, ii, nos. 125, 263, 366, 383, 385, 417; summary of the activity of the various emissaries in D.D.F., 3d. ser., V, no. 126. Yovanovitch states that Redlich proposed to Pašić a customs union "in order that the monarchy might recognise the acquisitions made by Serbia in the war against Turkey" ("How Austria Willed the War," *Balkan Review*, I, 78).

would be willing to grant Austria and Germany special privileges. Up to that time no special concessions were possible, although Serbia would be glad to make state contracts with Austrian firms. But in return, Serbia must have a port on the Adriatic with a corridor under her full sovereignty. Should Austria veto a Serbian port, then there would be nothing else for Serbia to do but conclude a tariff union with Bulgaria. Professor Masaryk pointed out that Austria could hardly make such advances for an agreement, whereupon Pašić expressed his willingness to come to Vienna in order to plead his own case to Berchtold.[131]

Berchtold found it impossible to enter into such discussions at this time since Austria had agreed to discuss the various questions raised by Pašić at the ambassadorial conference in London. Austria could not separate herself from these powers, and the results of the London discussions would have to be awaited. Later attempts to persuade Berchtold to invite Pašić to Vienna met with the same answer: that matters rested in the hands of the London conference.[132]

Berchtold's refusal to receive Pašić has often been criticised. Taking into consideration the policy proclaimed by the Ballhausplatz, he could not have acted differently. To have received Pašić would have meant permitting Serbian territorial expansion to the sea, for this was the condition which Pašić set up. Both Austria and Italy had declared that this very exclusion of Serbia from the Adriatic must be a condition *sine qua non* of the peace settlement. It was too late to back out, even had Berchtold been disposed to do so. Italy most certainly would have objected to such an Austrian-Serbian pact. Besides, promises for agreements in 1917 were not a very substantial basis on which to base a policy of the present. The Serbian-Austrian tariff negotiations, 1906–1912, had taught that lesson.

[131] Masaryk, *Making of a State*, pp. 2–3; Baernreither, *Fragmente*, p. 183; H. Kanner, *Kaiserliche Katastrophen-politik* (Leipzig, 1922), pp. 110 ff.; Ö-U.A., V, no. 4893; D.D.F., 3d. ser., V, no. 71; Comte Sforza, *Pachitch* (Paris, 1938), p. 111.

[132] Ö-U.A., V, no. 4893; Baernreither, *Fragmente*, pp. 181, 185.

While the decision to discuss all questions at an ambassadorial conference did much to ease the relations between the various governments, plenty of tension remained. Russia still retained her third year levy of troops under colors, and Austria also took defensive measures. The return of Serbian troops from the theater of war brought with it the possibility of an attack which might be aided by South Slav disturbances within the monarchy itself. The military pleaded for additional safeguards both on account of external and internal conditions, and these were reluctantly granted by Berchtold.[133] The Austrian preparations took on new importance when Conrad became chief of staff on December 12, 1912.[134] At the same time Krobatin relieved Auffenberg at the war office. Such changes aroused attention in all the capitals. Rumors reached Belgrade that Austria was about to present an ultimatum to Serbia, and the latter at once sought advice at the Entente capitals as to an answer.[135]

Sazonov was alarmed. Naturally enough, he thought that the ultimatum could only be the result of the consular affair, which had not yet been settled. Wishing to be prepared for any questions which might arise at a coming ministerial conference,

[133] "Er [Berchtold] anerkännt die militärischen Forderungen und würdige Potioreks innerpolitische Argumente; er fügte bei dass S. K. & K. Hoheit, der durchlauchister Herr, Erzherzog Franz Ferdinand, den Zeitpunkt als den gebietenden bezeichnet haben in dem sich serbische Divisionen gegen unsere Grenzen bewegen. Als Graf Berchtold erfuhr dass es sich nur um 2700 Mann handle, fielen alle seine nebensächlichen Bedenken weg" (Ausprechen des G. Berchtold laut Meldung Oberst v. Boogs, Dec. 5, 1912, Ö-U.K.A., Zu. Abt. 10, no. 400 Res.). For Berchtold's opposition to later military measures see, Ö-U.A., V, nos. 5059, 5204; Cartwright to Nicolson, Jan. 3, 1913, B.D., IX, ii, no. 447.

[134] Schemua considered resigning as chief of staff early in November. He objected to Conrad's handing in long political memoranda, and to his being consulted by the minister of foreign affairs. The mission of Conrad to Bucharest about which Schemua had not been consulted also aroused his ire (Ö-U.K.A., Akten aus dem Nachlass Schemuas. This document is numbered Gestb., no. 4819 von 1912, but apparently never was registered. It bears two dates, Nov. 8 and Nov. 18th, and was drafted by Schemua in long hand). It was not until Dec. 8, 1912 that Schemua asked to be relieved of his office "on account of his health" (K. & k. Chef des Generalstabes $\frac{50\text{-}1 \text{ de } 1912}{16}$). Conrad was told on Dec. 7th that he was to resume his old office of chief of staff, but did not receive his formal appointment until Dec. 12, 1912 (Conrad, II, 373 ff.).

[135] D.D.F., 3d. ser., V, nos. 23, 24, 42.

he asked Berchtold for a reassuring statement about the various rumors, and also as to the appointment of Conrad. Admitting that the consular incident was a purely Austrian-Serbian affair, he asked if the settlement of this difficulty might not be postponed for a time. He did not want relations to become acute, on the very eve of the ambassadorial conference.[136]

Berchtold furnished the statement at once. In view of the agitated state of public opinion, he thought it unwise to postpone the settlement of the consular affair any longer. Sazonov, however, might rest assured that there was no cause for worry. The Viennese government had never even considered an ultimatum.

On December 13th, Consul Edl returned to Vienna after conducting his official investigation at Usküb.[137] The papers clamored for an official statement, which was given on December 17th. First and foremost the consul was safe, and there was absolutely no foundation for the reports in regard to his personal maltreatment. Delay in making the report had been due to the great distances and war conditions. On the other hand the charges of the Serbian government were unfounded. According to international law, Serbia had committed an error, and the monarchy would demand some satisfaction. Since Serbia had already consented to an investigation, she would no doubt meet the demands which the Austrian government would make.[138]

The communiqué was criticised by many of the newspapers.[139] They were of the opinion that the declaration should have been made much earlier. Such delay had only disrupted business and created a war scare. This criticism called forth an official commentary on December 21st, in which it was pointed out that the public had been informed that Prochaska

[136] Ö-U.A., V, no. 4872; for Berchtold's answer see, no. 4888.
[137] *Ibid.*, V, no. 5806; *Neue Freie Presse*, Dec. 13, 1912.
[138] *Fremdenblatt*, Dec. 17, 1912.
[139] For example: *Die Zeit*, Dec. 17, 1912; *Neue Freie Presse*, Dec. 17, 1912; *Frankfurter Zeitung*, Dec. 17, 18, 1912; London *Times*, Dec. 18, 1912 (quoting Vienna papers); Ö-U.A., V, no. 4961 (quoting French papers).

was safe, as soon as he had been heard from.[140] Only the final report was held until Edl had concluded his investigations. This was correct enough, but the foreign office had devoted most of the communiqué on December 17th to assuring the people that the consul was in good health. Such drafting was unfortunate. Were an official statement on the health of the consul necessary, the foreign office should have issued one at the end of November, when Prochaska's written reports arrived in Vienna.

The documents contain no record of the oral report of Edl when he reached Vienna. Yet there can be no doubt that the Serbian military authorities were in the wrong.[141] Had Berchtold wished, the report of Prochaska furnished him with enough material to levy serious charges. The Austrian official mail pouches were intercepted;[142] the Catholics over whom Austria claimed a protectorate were maltreated; the consul had received discourteous treatment; false charges had been levied by the Serbian government.[143] In addition the Serbian government had severed abruptly all communication between the Austrian foreign office and its consulates, and had been slow to restore it, despite the need for investigation of the Serbian complaints.

Ugron, on the other hand, after talking with Edl, had the impression that, although the Serbian military authorities had acted incorrectly, the consuls might have got along with them, had they "manifested more calm coolness and employed a more tactful approach."[144] He also pleaded as a mitigating circum-

[140] *Fremdenblatt*, Dec. 21, 1912; see also, Ö-U.A., V, nos. 4981, 4987.

[141] Pašić himself admitted: "In der Prochaska-Affäre haben wir, da wirklich von seiten der Militärorgane kleine Unregelmässigkeiten vorlagen. . . ." (Pašić to Gabrilović at Cetinje, Jan. 5, 1913, S.D., I, no. 259). See also Ö-U.A., IV, nos. 4646, 4647, 4664, 4730; V, nos. 4968, 4987.

[142] Prochaska's letters taken from the courier had been transmitted to the Russian foreign office and then returned to Belgrade (S.D., I, nos. 227, 228, 229, 232, 233, 234). This might account for some of the delays on the Serbian side.

[143] See Prochaska's complaint on this score, Ö-U.A., IV, no. 4664; also excerpts from General Janković's diary published by Ludwig Schargl, "Die Affäre des österreichisch-ungarischen Konsuls Prochaska im ersten Balkankriege, 1912" *Berliner Monatshefte*, VII (1929), 350.

[144] Ugron to foreign office, Dec. 13, 1912, Ö-U.A., V, no. 4896.

stance lack of education and the spirit of victory. He thought an apology and ceremonious hoisting of the flag over the Austrian consulates ought to be all Austria should demand. This position was, as a matter of fact, the one taken by Austria.[145]

On December 21, 1912, Pašić of his own accord visited the Austrian legation in Belgrade, and apologised for the missteps of the Serbian military authorities. He inquired what further satisfaction Austria demanded, and was told that in addition to the apology, it was of importance to Austria that her flag should be ceremoniously raised over the consulates in Mitrovitza and Prizren. The Austrian consuls were to be in attendance, in full uniform, and a detachment of Serbian troops was to pay full military honors. Pašić agreed to these demands but reserved his final answer until he had consulted with the military authorities.[146] He also told the Austrian minister that the Serbian ministerial council had just decided to resign all claims for Serbian territorial expansion to the sea.

On January 16, 1913, the Austrian flag was hoisted over the consulate in Prizren, and on the following day in Mitrovitza.[147] This ended the consular incident, which dated back to November 8th, when the Serbians brought their charges against Prochaska.

The Austrian foreign office had issued the statement on the Prochaska incident on December 17th. It was clear that there would be no further serious complications. The same day the ambassadors held their first session in London. Things looked brighter in all Europe.

[145] *Ibid.*, V, no. 4968.

[146] *Ibid.*, V, nos. 5004, 5005. On Dec. 28th Berchtold protested against the delay on Serbia's part, which brought an excuse from Pašić on the 30th and final acceptance of the Austrian conditions on Jan. 1, 1913 (*ibid.*, nos. 5090, 5118, 5148).

[147] *Fremdenblatt*, Jan. 16, 17, 1913.

CHAPTER XI

THE LINE-UP OF EUROPE

THE period just discussed, ending with the armistice and the calling of an ambassadorial conference in London, was one of considerable stress and strain in Europe. The month of November, 1912 was an uneasy one. The Balkan War was still going on; the fall of Constantinople was threatening; a Serbian army was marching to the sea, while Austria announced her opposition to Serbian territorial expansion to the Adriatic; Serbian charges had been levelled against an Austrian consul and an Austrian investigation was under way; Russia had seemed to back Serbia and both Russia and Austria were arming. Under these conditions it is not surprising that the various powers began to ask each other what they should do in case things came to a showdown. Alliance obligations were gone over and tested.

On November 4th a letter from Poincaré to Izvolsky stressed the advisability of entering upon conversations with regard to a common policy, should Austria attempt territorial aggrandisement. "I desire to know," Poincaré concluded, "if the Imperial government is, like us, strictly hostile to all annexation of Ottoman territory by a great power, and if it will be disposed to examine with France, as well as with England, how this danger should be met." [1]

In forwarding this letter to Sazonov, Izvolsky commented as follows:

> This proposal was made after a discussion in the ministerial council. It contains an entirely new standpoint for France in the question of Austrian territorial expansion on the Balkan peninsula. Up to now France has always declared that local, to some extent purely Balkan, questions could only call for diplomatic steps and no kind of active intervention. Now, however, she appears to realise

[1] D.D.F., 3d. ser., IV, no. 346; Izvolsky, II, no. 554.

that territorial conquests of Austria would disturb the balance of power and therefore jeopardise France's own interests.[2]

As Izvolsky carefully pointed out this was a new interpretation of the alliance by France. Before the Balkan victories the French had been far more strict in interpreting their Balkan interests and alliance obligations. At about this time Poincaré made a widely-noted address at Nantes. In this he stressed French and Russian solidarity and Izvolsky reported:

> Today all the Paris papers without exception warmly support Poincaré's speech. On the whole one notices that under the impression of the recent events, and in accordance with the well-known saying that nothing is as successful as success, an important change in attitude in favor of the Balkan states and the Russian viewpoint has taken place here.[3]

The Russian ambassador thought it well to help this change in French attitude along, and requested funds from his government with which to manipulate the French press.[4]

Sazonov naturally was willing to enter into discussions, and inquired not only of the French but also of the English government what their attitude would be if an Austrian-Serbian conflict developed.[5] Poincaré felt he could give a definite answer only when he knew what action Russia proposed to take in such an eventuality.[6] He complained to Izvolsky that Russia seemed disposed to justify her restrictive measures at Belgrade by saying that France and England under no circumstances would permit themselves to be embroiled in a war with the Triple Alliance. He was afraid that, as in 1908, France was being made the scapegoat at Belgrade on behalf of Russian diplomacy. While insisting always that it was up to Russia to inform

[2] Izvolsky, II, no. 554; see also Izvolsky's comments in K.A., XVI, no. 53 (*Berl. Mon.*, IX, 72).

[3] Schulthess, 1912, pp. 383–4 (October 27, 1912); Izvolsky, II, no. 532.

[4] Izvolsky, II, nos. 539, 561, 564, 625, 628, 633, 647, 648, 649.

[5] *Ibid.*, II, nos. 563, 566 Anlage; D.D.F., 3d. ser., IV, no. 432; B.D., IX, ii, no. 202.

[6] D.D.F., 3d. ser., IV, nos. 443, 468, 469; Poincaré, II, 328, 334, 337 ff.; B.D., IX, ii, nos. 209, 213.

France first as to her proposed action in an Austrian-Serbian conflict, Poincaré never hesitated to promise that France would live up to her alliance obligations. If Germany supported Austria, France would march.[7]

At the same time Poincaré reviewed the French-Italian accord anew with the Italian ambassador at Paris. Tittoni used rather discouraging language at times and pointed out that Italy had previous obligations to Austria in regard to the Balkans.[8] On the other hand the French ambassador at Rome received clear-cut expressions of loyalty to the accord from San Giuliano, the Italian foreign minister.[9] Russia apparently had never been fully informed of this French-Italian accord of 1902, but now it was revealed to her.[10] In return France was informed of the Racconigi agreements between Italy and Russia.[11] England had long known of the French-Italian accord and was kept informed in regard to the new discussions. On their own initiative the British statesmen made some effort at this time to obtain a similar agreement with Italy. Specifically each country was to guarantee the territorial *status quo* of Northern Africa. In this fashion Downing Street aimed to prevent a possible Italian expedition to Egypt. In spite of many mutual assurances of friendship no definite agreement was reached between Rome and London.[11a]

Interested as he was in the attitude of France, Sazonov no doubt was more concerned over the position England would take if Austria should attack Serbia.[12] Throughout the past months Downing Street had been very much concerned about

[7] Izvolsky, II, nos. 567, 569; D.D.F., 3d. ser., IV, no. 494; Poincaré, II, 399–40; B.D., IX, ii, no. 328.

[8] D.D.F., 3d. ser., IV, nos. 502, 507, 517; Poincaré, 341–2.

[9] D.D.F., 3d. ser., IV, no. 560; B.D., X, ii, nos. 424, 425, 426.

[10] Izvolsky, II, nos. 574, 575, 592, 606.

[11] D.D.F., 3d. ser., IV, no. 625; for summary of the agreement see above, p. 25, note 72.

[11a] B.D., X, ii, ch. XCVI, part II.

[12] On English-Russian relations in this period see the section, "Die Balkankrisen 1912–13" in Amalie Dengler, *Der englische Botschafter Sir George Buchanan und seine Stellung zu Deutschland* (Berlin, 1937), pp. 54–80; Giesche, *Der serbische Zugang zum Meer*, pp. 37–40 and passim.

maintaining the Entente with Russia. Special care was taken not to injure Russian feelings and every effort was made to support Russia when it was at all possible. The sad state of Persian affairs was a constant reminder of the necessity of good relations with St. Petersburg. Grey now parried Sazonov's definite inquiry, and replied that in case of a Serbian-Austrian conflict, England's attitude would depend on the origin of the contingency and on the attitude of the other powers.[13] As has been already pointed out he did indicate that a Serbian port was not a satisfactory "contingency." Ever fearful of the rupture of the Entente, Nicolson apparently was more helpful. He thought, so he told the Russian and French ambassadors, that if a war broke out between the Triple Alliance and the Dual Alliance, England would aid the latter.[14]

This discussion of alliance and entente relationships also had its London-Paris episode. Intermittent conversations which for some time in the past had touched on their mutual obligations, now culminated in an exchange of letters between Sir Edward Grey and Paul Cambon, in which the moral, if not formal, obligations between France and England were put on paper.[15] A definite inquiry, however, by Poincaré on December 5, 1912 as to what action Grey proposed to take if France in accordance with her alliance obligations had to go to the aid of Russia, brought only the evasive reply that this would depend on the attitude of parliament, which in turn was contingent on how the crisis arose. Nicolson replied more encouragingly when

[13] B.D., IX, ii, nos. 202, 209, 216, 238, 303. The Russian ambassador at London thought that two conditions would be necessary if England were to intervene. First, that France should join and in this fashion the war should be turned into a general conflict; secondly, that the onus for the attack should fall on Austria and Germany (Benckendorff, II, nos. 720, 724). Paul Cambon reported that Grey spoke of diplomatic support at Vienna and Berlin, but did not repulse *a priori* more effective coöperation (Cambon to Poincaré, Nov. 13, 1912, D.D.F., 3d. ser., IV, no. 445).

[14] Benckendorff, II, no. 721; B.D., IX, ii, no. 322; D.D.F., 3d. ser., IV, no. 622.

[15] For the agreements see B.D., X, ii, nos. 413–17; Viscount Grey of Fallodon, *Twenty-five Years, 1892–1916* (2 vols.; New York, 1925), I, 93 ff.; D.D.F., 3d. ser., IV, no. 534 annexe; see also, Richard Dietrich, "Die Bemühungen Frankreichs zur Festigung der Entente Cordiale 1911–12," *Berliner Monatshefte*, XII (1934), 767–784.

Cambon discussed this problem with him.[16] Both Paris and St. Petersburg were, however, informed of the definite pronouncement which the British government had made at Berlin, that in case of a conflict England's neutrality was not to be figured on.[17] The French and English naval and military experts also went over their agreement. General Wilson, the English chief of staff, with the approval of Grey made a secret visit to France on the 26th of November in order to study "what measures were to be taken in case of a Franco-German conflict and Belgium should be clearly hostile."[18] Both France and England paid especially close attention at this time to the attitude of the government at Brussels.

How far the French military men were inclined to support Russia can be seen from the following report of a conversation which Nicolson had with General Wilson on the latter's return from Switzerland, via France, in February, 1913.

> He tells me that the soldiers are of the opinion that it would be far better for France if a conflict were not too long postponed. Their reasons are that if it would come now, it would be in consequence of the Balkan difficulties, and therefore they would be able to secure the whole-hearted support of Russia. Were a conflict to be postponed and eventually to arise over some difficulty between Germany and France alone, they had some doubts — treaty notwithstanding — whether Russia would go whole-heartedly on their side. They impressed upon Wilson that Russia was exceedingly strong, both in her military organisations and also in her financial condition, and was therefore far less dependent on French support, either in a mili-

[16] D.D.F., 3d. ser., IV, nos. 612, 622; B.D., IX, ii, no. 328.

[17] August Bach, "Die November- und Dezemberkrise 1912," *Berliner Monatshefte*, XIII (1935), 112–115; B.D., X, ii, nos. 452, 453, 470; D.D.F., 3d. ser., V, no. 248.

[18] D.D.F., 3d. ser., V, no. 53; *The Personal Memoirs of Joffre*, trans. T. Bentley Mott (2 vols.; New York, 1932), I, 54; on this general topic see also, Ernst Kabisch, "Die Militär- und Marinekonventionen der Triple-Entente vor dem Ausbruch des Weltkrieges," *Die Kriegsschuldfrage*, V (1927), 282–309; Bernard Schwertfeger, "Die militärpolitischen Beziehungen Frankreichs und Englands zu Belgien im Jahre 1912," *Berliner Monatshefte*, XI (1933), 541–64; B. Schwertfeger, "Die militärpolitischen Beziehungen Frankreichs und Englands zu Belgien nach 1912," *Berliner Monatshefte*, XII (1934), 594–614; George Ashton, "The Entente Cordiale and the Military Conversations," *Quarterly Review*, CCLVIII (1932), 363–83.

tary or a financial sense. In short, that Russia was now well able to look after herself, and might be inclined to take a line of her own. (This I gather is not quite the view of the French government who are nervous lest they should be dragged into a war over Balkan affairs in which the French public have no great interest.)[19]

On the above report Grey quite correctly placed the following minute: "The French government clearly do not want to be dragged into war over the Balkans, and are working to prevent Russia precipitating a conflict over that. We on our side can be no party to France precipitating a conflict for the revanche." [20]

Germany, Italy and Austria, no less busily than the Entente, were also going over their alliance ties. During the month of November, 1912, the negotiations for the renewal of the Triple Alliance treaties, which had been hanging fire, were brought to a successful conclusion. Austria-Hungary had much less confidence in Italy than did Germany, but nevertheless was anxious to present a united front with her southern neighbor on the Serbian and Albanian questions. This apparent solidarity of the Triple Alliance influenced greatly the action of the Entente in the fall of 1912. If they could not divide the Alliance they preferred not to come to a showdown with it.

The visit of Archduke Francis Ferdinand and Chief of Staff Schemua to Berlin on November 22–23, 1912, coming at the very time when the Serbian port question was approaching a crisis,[21] was an impressive manifestation of German and Austrian friendship. Francis Ferdinand was only too glad to accept the invitation of the Kaiser to attend the hunt which was to be held at Springe. Already on November 13th Tschirschky re-

[19] B.D., IX, ii, no. 656; Nicolson, *Portrait of a Diplomatist*, p. 288. The Russian military attaché also reported a desire for active intervention in Paris circles (Rudolf Kiszling, "Russlands Kriegsvorbereitung im Herbst 1912 und ihre Rückwirkung auf Österreich-Ungarn," *Berliner Monatshefte*, XIII [1935], 187). In this connection see also the expressions on the part of the French government that Russia was not taking sufficient military steps in the fall of 1912 (D.D.F., 3d. ser., V, nos. 22, 48, 103; Izvolsky, II, nos. 614, 620, 630, 639, 640). Benckendorff in February, 1913, thought that among the great powers France was the least opposed to war (Benckendorff, III, no. 896). See also, Giesche, *Der serbische Zugang zum Meer*, pp. 70–4; Zaionchkovski, *Podgotovka rossii*, p. 280.

[20] B.D., IX, ii, 533.

[21] See above, p. 219.

ported that the archduke had expressed his intentions of "talking over the whole complex of current political questions with His Majesty on this occasion." [22] And so from the start the meeting was to have a political importance.

Some of the more moderate political personages led by Professor Redlich urged that Francis Ferdinand be accompanied by Conrad or by Potiorek, the Landeschef of Bosnia-Herzegovina. In this way a real Balkan expert might make it clear to Kiderlen that the position Austria was assuming had to do not merely with a Serbian port or Albania, but rather with the whole future policy and position of the monarchy.[23] But Conrad was not available, since he was already scheduled for a mission to Bucharest, and Potiorek could hardly leave Serajevo at that critical moment. Finally it was decided that Schemua should go to Berlin on the same day as the archduke to discuss matters with von Moltke, the German chief of staff. Officially it was not to be a joint visit, but according to the *Neue Freie Presse* it was the archduke himself who wanted his visit and Schemua's visit to Berlin to coincide.[24]

On November 18th, Kiderlen was informed that in view of Russian military measures and the disorganised state of Austrian troops in Galicia — the result of the transition from three-year to two-year term of service — Austria was contemplating an increase in the numerical strength of her eastern army corps.[25] These measures would be carried out as quietly as possible, but were necessary as a defense against a possible surprise attack of Russia, should Serbia provoke a war. In

[22] G.P., XXXIII, no. 12369. Chlumecky states: "Inzwischen sollte sich der Thronfolger nach Berlin begeben um sich der Unterstützung Deutschlands zu versichern" (*Franz Ferdinands Willen und Wollen*, p. 135). The papers throughout stressed the political importance of the visit (see especially, *Neue Freie Presse*, Nov. 10, 22, 23, 1912; *Fremdenblatt*, Nov. 23, 1912; *Frankfurter Zeitung*, Nov. 23, 24, 1912; *Norddeutsche Allgemeine Zeitung*, Nov. 22, 1912; London *Times*, Nov. 23, 1912.

[23] Chlumecky, *Franz Ferdinands Willen und Wollen*, p. 135.

[24] *Neue Freie Presse*, Nov. 23, 1912.

[25] G.P., XXXIII, no. 12395; Ö-U.A., IV, no. 4476; for Kiderlen's answer see no. 4495. On Nov. 20, 1912 Kiderlen promised that Germany would live up to its alliance obligations as it had done in 1908 (*ibid.*, no. 4511).

answer, Kiderlen attempted to minimise the importance of Russia's military measures, but agreed on the advisability of Austria's strengthening her forces. On November 19th, probably before Kiderlen's approval arrived, the decision to strengthen the Galician corps was made at a crown council. In informing Tschirschky of this decision, the Austrian war minister, General Auffenberg, stated:

> We shall see how Russia reacts to our border measures. If she accepts them quietly, then we shall have free hand against Serbia. We need at least fifty years of peace in the monarchy in order to bring our South Slavs to order, and this peace can only be obtained if the hope of the South Slavs for Russian support is definitely set aside. Otherwise the monarchy will go to pieces.[26]

The news of this military measure was of extreme importance and enhanced the significance of the coming visit of the archduke. After reading Tschirschky's telegram the Kaiser wrote the following note to Kiderlen.

> Have just read the report of the ambassador at Vienna. According to an announcement of Herr von Bienertts [Austrian attaché], tomorrow morning, November 22nd, General Schemua, chief of staff of the Austrian army arrives in Berlin, on the order of his Majesty the Emperor, in order to discuss with Moltke eventual military operations. Both gentlemen are coming to see me after their discussion. According to the European press, especially the English, it appears that in general Austria is considered as being the provoked party. With this, the situation that I wish is attained. Should Russian counter measures follow, which might force Francis Joseph to declare war, then he has the right on his side and I am ready, as I told the chancellor recently in Letzlingen, to carry through the *casus foederis* in its fullest meaning and with all its consequences. . . .[27]

The Kaiser was well aware of the critical state of affairs, and what his decision to support Austria meant. On the telegram announcing Francis Joseph's decision to strengthen his eastern

[26] Tschirschky to the foreign office, Nov. 21, 1912; G.P., XXXIII, no. 12404. Francis Joseph in assenting to the measure characterised the situation as more difficult than in 1866. See also, Auffenberg, *Aus Österreichs Höhe und Niedergang*, p. 218.

[27] William II to Kiderlen, Nov. 21, 1912, G. P., XXXIII, no. 12405.

army corps he noted: "This can develop into the European war and for us a battle for existence with three great powers; it depends upon our quickly obtaining a clear picture of affairs in London and Paris." [28] The German chief of staff followed closely all military steps that were being taken in France and Russia, and was well posted for conversations with his Austrian colleague.[29]

On arriving in Berlin at 7:35 A. M. on November 22nd, Schemua, attired in civilian garb, went to see Moltke.

> Our conversation, [so Schemua wrote in his report of his journey] brought the confirmation of the agreements of May of this year, and also resulted in complete agreement in the judgment of the general situation. Moltke showed complete understanding in judging our situation in respect to Russia and Serbia, and thought he might also ask for certain measures on the German-Russian border, possibly even calling in reservists. He emphasised again and again that we could absolutely count on their support if we were threatened from Russia, and that it was also important for Germany's interests that we should not be weakened. He grasps fully the earnestness of the situation. The mobilisation of Germany results automatically in mobilisation in France, and two mobilised armies side by side create an untenable situation which will surely result in a conflict.
>
> Moltke hopes to finish with France in four to five weeks, and then turn to the East. The German chief of staff wanted to know if Austria would retain any troops against Italy, and was satisfied when he was told she would not.
>
> Emperor William, clad in the uniform of an Austrian field marshal, then appeared. He spoke of certain recent reports which had come to him. A big industrialist had just returned from France, and he had seen no evidence of mobilisation. Russia also was not ready for war. This would only be in two years. The emperor attempted to allay suspicions in regard to Italy. King Victor Emmanuel had told the German crown prince, on his visit to Italy two years ago, that Italy would be true to her obligations. San Giuliano, on his recent visit to Berlin, had also spoken out clearly against a Serbian port. His Majesty then told Moltke it might be well to talk matters over with the Italian staff so that there might be a public expression of the alliance.

[28] *Ibid.*, XXXIII, no. 12404 marginal note; see also, no. 12395.
[29] *Ibid.*, XXXIII, nos. 12407, 12412.

His Majesty then turned again towards me and emphatically emphasised that we could rely fully on his support under all circumstances. Conditions in Russia were unclear because of the domestic differences; beyond a doubt the Russian minister in Belgrade and Ambassador Izvolsky in Paris were the chief instigators. The fear of political and revolutionary manifestations in Russia was also a cause of their military measures. The emperor then left for the railway station to welcome the archduke.[30]

The report as sketched above is taken from a draft written by Schemua himself in long hand. It shows clearly that Germany was not urging Austria onward. Rather the contrary was true. On the other hand there is no criticism of Austria's policy, nor of the military steps she had taken. Both the Kaiser and Moltke expressed repeatedly Germany's readiness to lend Austria her full support. Likewise it is quite clear that Schemua was not pleading for an especially active policy. Certainly he was not urging an attack on either Serbia or Russia. It was a question of standing by the declaration of Austrian aims that had been advanced by the Ballhausplatz.

On arriving in Berlin, Francis Ferdinand was received at the station with full ceremony by the Kaiser.[31] They were soon closeted in political discussion, after which the archduke telegraphed to Vienna:

Conversation with Emperor William came out extraordinarily well. Emperor was especially gracious, and declared he wanted to support us in everything. Full security in regard to this support. Absolutely against conference of the powers. Have definitely stated our standpoint. Emperor William says that as soon as our prestige demands it we should take energetic action against Serbia, and we could be certain of his support. According to his, and also Kiderlen's opinion it would be necessary to state definitely our standpoint to the powers, especially to England, that we could not permit a port and corridor.

[30] Bericht über meinen Aufenthalt in Berlin, Nov. 22, 1912, Ö-U.K.A., Akten aus dem Nachlass Schemuas, Fasz. 161. For the complete German text see, E. C. Helmreich, "An Unpublished Report on Austro-German Military Conversations of November, 1912," *The Journal of Modern History*, V (1933), 205–7; reprinted with an additional letter of Schemua to Moltke of May 25, 1912, in *Berliner Monatshefte*, XI (1933), 893–97.

[31] *Neue Freie Presse*, Nov. 22, 1912 Abendblatt; *Frankfurter Zeitung*, Nov. 22, 1912 Abendblatt; *Politische Chronik*, 1912, 474.

Met with great sympathy and agreement here; in respect to Russia rather an irritated attitude. More details Sunday verbally.[32]

On the same day the archduke had commissioned the Austrian ambassador to send a telegram to Vienna which stressed even more the promise of full German support. According to Szögyény's version, "Emperor William had assured him [Francis Ferdinand] that if it became a question of prestige for Austria-Hungary, he would not even fear a world war, and that he would be ready to enter into a war with the three Entente powers. In regard to the position Serbia was taking the German Emperor expressed himself caustically."[33]

In the afternoon the emperor and Francis Ferdinand, accompanied by the other members of the hunting party, left for Springe. Bethmann Hollweg, Szögyény, and Moltke were among the guests, and so the hunting expedition retained a distinct political flavor.[34] According to press reports the emperor, Francis Ferdinand, and Bethmann conversed throughout the dinner hour. Afterwards a "Bierabend" was inaugurated, and it was not until 1:30 A. M. that the party broke up. The following day, after a hunt in the morning and in the afternoon, the party left for Berlin. Arriving at the station of Wildpark at nine o'clock, the party spent some minutes in the royal waiting room until the archduke's train departed at 9:25.[35] The archduke accompanied by Szögyény went on to Berlin, where the private car was switched to the regular night train for Vienna.

Szögyény telegraphed the next morning to the Ballhausplatz that Francis Ferdinand was extraordinarily pleased with the visit, and would report verbally to Berchtold and the emperor

[32] Franz Ferdinand to Vienna, Nov. 22, 1912, Ö-U.A., IV, no. 4571.

[33] *Ibid.*, IV, no. 4559.

[34] According to the published lists the guests at the hunt were: Obersthofmeister Freiherr von Rumerskirch, Botschafter Graf Szögyény, Militärattaché von Bienerth, Fürst zu Schaumburg-Lippe, Prinz Adolf zu Schaumburg-Lippe, Reichskanzler von Bethmann Hollweg, Minister Freiherr von Schorlemer, and Staatssekretär von Tirpitz (*Neue Freie Presse*, Nov. 23, 1912). That Moltke was also present is clear from his report to Jagow (Feb. 6, 1913, G.P., XXXIV, i, no. 12793).

[35] *Neue Freie Presse*, Nov. 23, 1912 Abendblatt, Nov. 24, 1912 Morgenblatt; *Frankfurter Zeitung*, Nov. 24, 1912.

the next day.[36] On November 25th, he reported further that Kiderlen, Bethmann, and the Kaiser were very pleased with the visit. "The Kaiser also was in full accord with the archduke's views and judgment of the present situation." [37]

Of the oral report made by Francis Ferdinand no record has ever been published. In fact the four exceptionally short telegrams in the Austrian collection and a report by Moltke are the only direct accounts we have of the conversations.[38] Recent biographers of the archduke have glided over the visit with scarcely a reference to it.[39] In commenting on the interview, the editors of *Die Grosse Politik* state:

> During the visit of the archduke-heir apparent in Berlin and Springe on November 22–23rd, and the presence at the same time of General Schemua in Berlin, the Kaiser stood up against the demands of the archduke, who had been influenced by Conrad, and maintained his old position that he did not want to be drawn into a war over a Serbian port.[40]

The evidence the editors draw on to support this statement is scanty, and rests chiefly on the report of the Belgian minister to Berlin, who stated:

> The archduke told the Berlin statesmen that the monarchy had arrived at the limit of the concessions that it could make to its neighbor. The emperor — and his advisers were no less profuse in their counsels of moderation — in accompanying his host to the railway station stated in his familiar, but expressive language, "Surtout pas de bêtises!" I can, on the faith of the ambassadors who repeated it to me, guarantee the authenticity of this counsel which has escaped the indiscretions of the newspapers. . . . There is no

[36] Szögyény to foreign office, Nov. 24, 1912, Ö-U.A., IV, no. 4594.

[37] *Ibid.*, IV, no. 4606. Chlumecky, drawing on information from people who saw Francis Ferdinand after his return, writes: "Er [Francis Ferdinand] habe das Empfinden dass der Deutsche Kaiser ihm voll vertraue, ebenso aber auch dass Oesterreich-Ungarn auf Deutschland unter allen Umständen rechnen könne" (*Franz Ferdinands Wirken und Wollen*, p. 91).

[38] Ö-U.A., IV, nos. 4571, 4559, 4594, 4606; G.P., XXXIV, i, no. 12793.

[39] Chlumecky, *Franz Ferdinands Wirken und Wollen*, pp. 91, 135; Sosnosky, *Franz Ferdinand*, pp. 150–1; Maurice Muret, *L'archiduc François Ferdinand* (Paris, 1932), pp. 238–9.

[40] G.P., XXXIII, no. 12405 note.

doubt that the emperor, the chancellor, and the secretary of foreign affairs are passionately pacifist.[41]

The words put into the mouth of the emperor are so unlike the language that he used either to Francis Ferdinand or to Schemua, as reported above, that one need hardly say more to question the truth of the Belgian minister's story. As has been pointed out, "accompanying his host to the station," was but a matter of waiting while the archduke changed trains at the small station of Wildpark on his return from Springe. No ambassadors outside of Szögyény were in the hunting party, and so the ambassadors to whom the Belgian minister refers must have obtained the statement at least at second hand. The report sent to Brussels was written November 30th, and most of the conclusions are based on the article in the *Norddeutsche Allgemeine Zeitung* of November 25th, and resulting press comments. It is also significant that the Belgian government deleted this part of the telegram when they sent it to the other Belgian embassies.[42]

The editors of *Die Grosse Politik*, in making the statement quoted above, apparently overshot the mark. Francis Ferdinand did not come as an advocate of a bellicose policy. In fact Moltke had the impression that he was positively opposed to energetic action, and thought he would always join the peace party in Austria. "He is not a man of action," was Moltke's complaint.[43] Certainly this hardly bespeaks a sabre-rattling attitude. Both Schemua and Francis Ferdinand were perfectly satisfied with their interviews. They received complete appro-

[41] *Belgische Aktenstücke 1905–1914*, ed. German foreign office (Berlin, 1915), pp. 112–3; *Die belgischen Dokumente, Erster Ergänzungsband*, pp. 262–3.

[42] It is therefore not to be found in the volumes which give only the circular telegrams sent by the Belgian foreign office to their various legations at the different capitals in Europe as, for instance, Bernard Schwertfeger, *Zur europäischen Politik 1897–1914, Unveröffentlichen Dokumente* (5 vols.; Berlin, 1919); nor in the fifth volume of *Die belgischen Dokumente*, but only in the first supplementary volume of the latter.

[43] G.P., XXXIV, i, no. 12793. Kiderlen told J. Cambon that "the Archduke Francis Ferdinand was very calm and very pacific, although he let it be clearly understood that Austria would not go beyond the concessions already granted to Serbia" (D.D.F., 3d. ser., IV, no. 551).

bation for Austria's policy and promises of full support in carrying it out. The Kaiser's promise to support Austria-Hungary even if she should march against Belgrade for prestige reasons was certainly not language calculated to restrain an archduke bent on war.

These interviews apparently gave Austria an unusual sense of security, which was rudely shattered when Kiderlen, on November 25th, published a statement in the semi-official *Norddeutsche Allgemeine Zeitung*.[44] In this article he sharply denied exaggerated press dispatches of a Viennese journal which were tending to increase the tension of the political situation. Ostensibly this was to quiet the bourse, but in reality Kiderlen wanted it to act as a cold douche in Vienna and St. Petersburg. In the statement Kiderlen stressed the fact that all questions would have to be settled by the powers jointly and not by any power alone. The German foreign office had found it advisable to put a damper on the exuberant utterances of the Kaiser to Francis Ferdinand.

With the exception of the *Neue Freie Presse*, the Vienna papers carried only the concluding paragraph of Kiderlen's article supplied them by the Ballhausplatz. This led Kiderlen to note on November 29th:

> To be allied! — and still nothing but mistrust and misunderstandings and independent policy. When we explain something in the *Norddeutsche Allgemeine Zeitung*, then in Vienna they are so stupid as to suppress and conceal our notice. No wonder if the rumor of a split between Berlin and Vienna develops. And in addition this "Pedagogue" Tschirschky as ambassador.[45]

The Austrian statesmen did not hide their dissatisfaction with Kiderlen's article and asked for a dementi or an additional explanation.[46] The archduke was especially put out about the fact that this article differed so much from the spirit and language

[44] Reprinted, Ö-U.A., IV, no. 4658 note; G.P., XXXIII, no. 12453 note.

[45] Jäckh, *Kiderlen-Wächter*, II, 192; see also Kiderlen to Tschirschky, Nov. 30, 1912, G.P., XXXIII, no. 12457.

[46] Ö-U.A., IV, nos. 4671, 4675, 4702; G.P., XXXIII, nos. 12456, 12453. Kiderlen refused to make a further statement (*ibid.*, no. 12457).

which he had met with in Berlin only a few days earlier.[47] The marginalia of the Kaiser to some press reports show that he did not wholly approve of this new check on Vienna.[48]

It was not the interviews in Berlin and Springe, but rather the "Kalter Wasserstrahl" of the *Norddeutscher Allgemeine Zeitung* that caused Vienna uneasiness about the German attitude toward the Near Eastern situation. But the statesmen in Vienna were not planning on a solution through war, and it is going too far to say that Germany was responsible for holding Austria back. In fact, instead of Austrian general policy becoming more peaceful after Springe, it became more aggressive. At the beginning of December more military measures were taken in Austria, and the military party felt as if things were going to be solved by the sword. This feeling was enhanced when General Conrad was reappointed as chief of staff, for he was known to be a staunch advocate of a military solution of Austria's Near Eastern problems.

But whatever jubilation there was in the other states of Europe or dissatisfaction in Austria-Hungary over the article in the *Norddeutsche Allgemeine Zeitung*, these feelings were reversed when Bethmann Hollweg on December 2nd declared in the Reichstag:

> Should there be — which we do not hope — insoluble differences (when it comes to settling the affairs in the Near East) it will be a matter for those powers which are directly interested in that specific case to see that their interests are recognised. That holds also for our allies. If, however, in making good their interests they are unexpectedly attacked by a third party, and thereby their existence is threatened, then we would, true to our alliance obligations, have to step resolutely to the side of our ally.[49]

It was a clear public statement of Germany's position. Vienna could not and did not expect more. Berchtold indicated to

[47] G.P., XXXIII, no. 12456; *Die belgischen Dokumente,* V, 126–7.

[48] G.P., XXXIII, no. 12405 note, p. 375.

[49] Schulthess, 1912, p. 244. Kiderlen told the British ambassador that personally he thought Bethmann's speech "a little sharp" (B.D., IX, ii, no. 327).

Tschirschky his deep appreciation for this expression of German support.[50] On the other hand the speech was not well received in the Entente capitals.[51] The English government apparently was especially excited about it and Poincaré again took this occasion to try to pin Sir Edward Grey down to a definite pledge of support.[52]

It was not enough for the great powers to test their various alliance ties among themselves. It was equally important to take the smaller states into consideration. The Entente of course desired to keep the Balkan League intact; the Triple Alliance wished to see it disrupted. Austria was especially interested in finding out whether she would have to deal with a united Balkan League or only with Serbia and Montenegro on the Albanian and Serbian port questions. She was also interested in bringing about a Bulgarian-Rumanian settlement, which would bring both these countries into the Austrian orbit.

In Sofia, too, the politicians thought it was high time to start playing for Austrian friendship. This was very welcome to Berchtold, and he gladly granted Danev an audience at Budapest on November 9, 1912.[53] Not only that, but he arranged that the Bulgarian statesman should be received by both the emperor and the heir apparent.

Danev endeavored to enlist Austrian support in bringing about a rapid conclusion of peace. He supported the Serbian demands for an Adriatic port, but only half-heartedly, or so the Austrians thought. They believed that if it came to a test Bulgaria would not support Serbia in a conflict over a Serbian port.[54] Danev, on the other hand, received the impression that the question of a Serbian port would not be made a cause of war by the Dual Monarchy, and later intimated as much to

[50] Tschirschky to Bethmann Hollweg, Dec. 3, 1912, G. P., XXXIII, no. 12474.

[51] Ö-U.A., V, nos. 4756, 4823; G.P., XXXIII, nos. 12475, 12481, 12490; D.D.F., 3d. ser., IV, nos. 605, 612, 615, 622; B.D., IX, ii, nos. 321, 322, 335, 352, 363; Benckendorff, II, no. 747.

[52] See above, pp. 234–35.

[53] Ö-U.A., IV, nos. 4301, 4302, 4312.

[54] *Ibid.*, IV, nos. 4362, 4363, 4378.

Belgrade.[55] Bulgarian-Rumanian difficulties were discussed but here results were practically nil. Danev protested against the cession of any Bulgarian territory, and denied that Rumania's neutrality alone entitled her to compensations. King Carol had been invited to coöperate in the war against the Turks, but had refused to do so.[56] If Carol even now, for example, would threaten intervention, thus forcing the Turks to make an unconditional peace, the Bulgarian government might be able to make some territorial concessions.[57]

No sooner had Danev left Budapest than Berchtold decided to send General Conrad on a special mission to Bucharest, to inform King Carol of this conversation, and in general to tighten the bonds between Austria-Hungary and Rumania. At the request of Rumania the mission was postponed for several weeks since a visit from Danev was expected in the coming days. This suited Berchtold, since his aim was to further a Bulgarian-Rumanian agreement. Danev, however, was by this time busy negotiating the armistice, and so after all Conrad preceded him to Bucharest.

Ostensibly the visit was to express the condolences of Francis Joseph on the death of the Countess of Flanders, the sister of King Carol. In reality Conrad was to inform the Rumanian king on various matters.[58] Above all the king was to be assured of Austrian support in his desires for compensations. Conrad was also to attempt to put into writing some sort of military agreement for a possible campaign against Russia. He was able to draw up a short written agreement with the Rumanian chief of staff as to the concentration of Rumanian troops, and felt

[55] B.D., IX, ii, no. 186; Ö-U.A., IV, no. 4430. Berchtold protested against this assumption on the part of Danev (*ibid.*, nos. 4460, 4472, 4527; B.D., IX, ii, no. 240).

[56] King Carol told Conrad that this was absolutely not the case (Conrad, II, 357). According to the Rumanian and Bulgarian documents it appears that Bulgaria made general advances for an agreement which Rumania refused to take up. There is no evidence of a direct request for Rumanian support on the part of Bulgaria (see above, p. 111).

[57] Ö-U.A., IV, no. 4362. Berchtold passed this information on to Bucharest (*ibid.*, nos. 4368, 4621).

[58] For Conrad's instructions see, *ibid.*, IV, nos. 4670, 4698; Conrad, II, 352–3.

that Austria-Hungary could rely on the support of Rumania in such a war. On the other hand he thought it essential that the monarchy should see that Rumania's wish for compensations were satisfied. The mission went off extraordinarily well and Conrad was very much pleased with the results.[59]

But Russia was not to be outdone in Bucharest, nor were the Rumanians anxious to flout her. An inquiry from St. Petersburg as to whether Russia should in the future consider Rumania as a friend or enemy met with a friendly response and the French minister at Bucharest was very optimistic over the establishment of a Russian-Rumanian entente.[60] Hartwig felt called upon to confide to the Rumanian minister at Belgrade, that Rumania had best join hands with Russia in order to obtain Transylvania when the Hapsburg monarchy went to pieces.[61] On December 10th the tsar sent Grand Duke Nikolas Mikhailovich to present the field marshal's staff to King Carol the award of which had been announced on the day the Balkan states mobilised.[62] Russia also promised her aid and influence in persuading Bulgaria to make "compensation" to Rumania.[63]

Neither Austria nor Russia succeeded in bringing about an agreement between these two states. Bulgaria remained in the Russian sphere of influence; Rumania continued to be attached to the Triple Alliance. When the change in line-up did come with the World War it was merely an exchange of partners.

[59] For the report on the visit see, Conrad, II, 354–63. The Austrian documents contain no information on the mission of Sektionschef Riedl who accompanied Conrad, and who was to further a Rumanian-Austro-Hungarian tariff union (Conrad, II, 369).

[60] D.D.F., 3d. ser., IV, no. 608; V, no. 79.

[61] Ö-U.A., IV, nos. 4381, 4417, 4448.

[62] For the report of the grand duke to the tsar see, Frantz, *Russland auf dem Wege zur Katastrophe*, p. 316. King Carol is recorded as having said that although he might remain neutral in a Russian-German war, he could never draw his sword against Germany. Rumanian-Russian relations were decidedly on the mend. See also, Benckendorff, II, no. 761; D.D.F., 3d. ser., V, nos. 58, 67; Russian Orange Book on the Balkan Wars, as quoted in *Zeitschrift für Internationales Recht*, XXV, 165.

[63] Benckendorff, II, no. 761; *Rumanian Green Book*, no. 25; D.D.F., 3d. ser., V, no. 4.

CHAPTER XII

UNSUCCESSFUL NEGOTIATIONS, DECEMBER, 1912–FEBRUARY, 1913

ON DECEMBER 17th, Mensdorff, Lichnowsky, Imperiali, Benckendorff, and Paul Cambon, as representatives of the great powers of the continent,[1] answered the invitation of Sir Edward Grey to assemble at the foreign office and inaugurate the ambassadorial conferences. These men were, however, representatives of the Triple Entente and Triple Alliance as well, and this fact was to dominate their actions. There had already been some exchange of ideas among the powers of each group.[2] In short, Lichnowsky and Imperiali were to support the views which Mensdorff advanced, Cambon on the other hand was to coöperate with Sir Edward Grey in supporting the propositions of Count Benckendorff.

Sir Edward Grey quite naturally was chosen chairman of the conference. In presiding he used English, but the ambassadors carried on the discussions in French. No minutes were kept, although it became an established practice that Cambon should summarise the various discussions. This was essential, for in this fashion the main points of each discussion were dispatched in identical versions to the different capitals. Lichnowsky was a newcomer, having been but recently appointed to his London post. Yet he was not unacquainted with his colleagues. In fact, Benckendorff, Mensdorff, and Lichnowsky were cousins,

[1] Respectively ambassadors of Austria-Hungary, Germany, Italy, Russia, and France.

[2] For the general instructions to the ambassadors see, Ö-U.A., V, nos. 4924, 4925; G.P., XXXIV, i, no. 12540; D.D.F., 3d. ser., V, nos. 70, 75; Benckendorff, II, nos. 756, 761. The work of the conference can now be fully described from the reports in the various collections of documents. For an interesting summary of newspaper reports, etc., which show what the public knew of the work of the conference while it was meeting see, Theodor Niemeyer, "Die Londoner Botschaftervereinigung," *Jahrbuch des Völkerrechts*, II (1914), 487–523.

a relationship which brought criticism in their respective countries, where it was charged that family friendship jeopardised national interests.[3]

The conference was to be extremely informal. Grey writes that the members usually met about four o'clock and after an adjournment for tea, continued their discussions until six or seven.[4] There were no regular days set for meetings. They got together whenever they were ready to discuss a certain point. If matters reached a deadlock, they adjourned, and referred the question to the respective foreign offices.

Usually the sessions turned out to be extremely verbose affairs. Imperiali, true to his Neapolitan blood, was the most fluent of all the ambassadors. Mensdorff estimated that his Italian colleague used more words than all the others combined.[5] But all the talking was not done in the meetings. Most of what was accomplished was the result of preliminary personal discussions among the individual ambassadors. Sir Edward Grey as chairman of the conference took the lead in furthering these, and when things reached a critical stage, he established the agenda for the next meeting by private consultation with the different ambassadors. Mensdorff, Lichnowsky and Imperiali, especially the first two, went over the measures together. Yet theirs was not always a united front. Mensdorff complained to Vienna of this, and Lichnowsky was reprimanded by the German foreign office.[6] The Russian ambassador also noted the lack of full harmony in the opposing camp.[7] The Entente rep-

[3] Ö-U.A., V, no. 5430; G.P., XXXIII, no. 12438 note; Fürst K. M. Lichnowsky, *Auf dem Wege zum Abgrund* (2 vols.; Dresden, 1927), I, 105. For an interesting biographical article on Benckendorff see, Wladimir v. Korostovetz, "Graf Alexander Konstantinowitsch Benckendorff," *Berliner Monatshefte*, XIV (1936), 887–901.

[4] Grey, *Twenty-five Years*, I, 256.

[5] Ö-U.A., V, no. 5630; see also, Grey, *Twenty-five Years*, I, 265.

[6] Ö-U.A., V, nos. 4988; 5012; G.P., XXXIV, i, nos. 12556, 12763; Lichnowsky, *Auf dem Wege zum Abgrund*, I, 99, 104. Kiderlen had a very low opinion of Lichnowsky's ability (see J. Cambon's remarks in the preface of: N. Schebeko, *Souvenirs. Essai historique sur les origines de la guerre de 1914* [Paris, 1936], p. 21).

[7] Benckendorff, III, no. 796.

resentatives likewise had their intimate *tête à têtes*. Throughout there was the closest coöperation between Cambon and Benckendorff. Grey, although in general siding with Russia, as was expected, still maintained a neutrality which received full recognition. He won the confidence of all.[8] Like the speaker of the house of commons, although he might belong to one party, in his leadership of the conference Sir Edward Grey was impartial.

In summoning the conference, Grey had proposed that three questions seemed especially suited for such an informal discussion.[9] These were: (1) Serbian access to the sea, (2) Albania, (3) the disposition of the Aegean Islands. While willing to discuss a Serbian commercial outlet, Austria had refused to recognise the possibility of Serbian territorial expansion to the Adriatic as a legitimate subject for the conference. The Austrian view on this phase of Serbian expansion had been accepted by the other powers, and so this point offered no difficulty to the ambassadors. At the first meeting, after very little discussion, the following formula was adopted.

> A commercial outlet will be reserved to Serbia in a free and neutral Albanian port, which will be served by an international railway under European control, and under the protection of a special international force. Serbia is to have freedom of transit for all merchandise including munitions of war.[10]

At this meeting the Conference also agreed that, "Albanian autonomy should be guaranteed and controlled by the six powers under the sovereignty of the Sultan." Since Austria-Hungary and Italy had taken the lead in proposing the establishment of

[8] "Sir E. Grey hingegen ist eminent unparteiisch" (Mensdorff to foreign office, June 6, 1913, Ö-U. A., VI, no. 7292). Th. A. Ippen, Austrian expert assigned to aid Mensdorff, spoke very highly to the writer of Grey's conduct of the conference. Lichnowsky writes in the same vein (*Auf dem Wege zum Abgrund*, I, 103–4). Germany on the whole was satisfied with Grey's leadership, but his hesitancy in sanctioning measures for clearing the Montenegrins out of Scutari brought forth criticism (G.P., XXXIV, ii, nos. 13252, marginal note, 13254; for a general criticism see, XXXIV, i, no. 12561 note).

[9] G. P., XXXIV, i, no. 12504.

[10] *Ibid.*, XXXIV, i, no. 12545; Ö-U.A., V, no. 4944; B.D., IX, ii, no. 391; D.D.F., 3d. ser., V, nos. 78, 85; Benckendorff, II, nos. 765, 766, 767.

an Albanian state, they were invited to draw up a general plan of its future government.

Benckendorff, much to the relief of the Austrian ambassador, now advanced the proposition that the future Albania should border on Montenegro and Greece. This definitely ended the question of Serbian territorial expansion to the Adriatic, and brought up the problem of the boundaries of Albania. A long discussion ensued, in which Mensdorff took the stand that all territory inhabited by Albanians must be reserved to the new state. This meant that cities like Ipek and Scutari could not be granted to Montenegro. Benckendorff and Cambon protested against this; Lichnowsky weakly supported Mensdorff; Imperiali pleaded lack of instructions on this point.

The first day foretold the future of the conference. Austria was to be the champion of Albania, Russia the opponent. The one wanted Albania as large as possible; the other desired to assure to the allied states the maximum of territorial gains. The one wanted Scutari to go to Albania; the other wanted it to go to Montenegro.

Representing a state which was the very negation of nationalism, the Austrian statesmen stepped forward and inscribed upon their banner, "Albania for the Albanians." In this, they were but carrying on an old policy of the monarchy. Whatever the attitude towards nationalism may have been at home, the Ballhausplatz was always in favor of nationalism among the Albanians. For years the monarchy had been carrying on nationalistic propaganda in this region. Clergy and schools were subsidised.[11] Although originally this instruction sub-

[11] The Austrian schools were mostly ecclesiastical and not wholly dependent on the foreign office. The schools subsidised by Italy, on the other hand, were mostly state schools. In 1912 the budget of the Austrian foreign office was charged with 148,000 Kronen for Albanian schools. For example, in 1916 the school in Djakova received 1100.20 Kr., while the Frères d'école Chrétien received 4450 Kr. every three months. (I am indebted for these figures to Alfred Rappaport who was the Albanian expert at the Austrian foreign office for many years. He assured me that it would be impossible to make a general statement on the amount of money spent, since even after special investigation he could only give me the above figures. No figures are available on money paid to the clergy. This was sometimes paid through the Vatican, and at other times directly.)

sidised by Austria was carried on in Italian, in the years just before the Balkan War a shift to German was undertaken. With the lack of a generally recognised alphabet, little instruction could be carried on in Albanian itself. The Austrian consuls sent to Albania were directed to stir up national feeling, so that when the break-up of Turkey came, the Albanians would be capable of setting up a separate state. With this in view, Austria also subsidised a newspaper, which was at first printed in Brussels and later in England. The paper was distributed in various ways, especially through the different Austrian posts located in Albania.[12]

In addition the Austrian religious protectorate over the Catholic Albanians gave her a special interest in this area. This protectorate dated back to the treaty of Vienna of 1615, when the Holy Roman Emperor was given rights similar to those granted to France in various earlier capitulations. The protectorate was recognised and renewed in later treaties between the emperor and the sultan, and was further expanded by various decrees and laws guaranteeing religious rights to the Catholics. Whenever any of these rights were violated, be it the case of an alien Catholic or native Turkish Catholic, the emperor could intervene. In theory his right extended to the Holy Places in Jerusalem, although these were generally taken to be under the French protectorate. In practice Austria confined her claim of protection to Turkey in Europe.[13]

Austria's Albanian policy, then, was not of recent origin. Behind it first and foremost lay the desire to keep any great power from obtaining direct or indirect control of the eastern shores of the Adriatic. The possibility of economic exploita-

[12] There were similar papers published in Sofia, but Th. A. Ippen, who was sent to Albania in 1897 as an Austrian consul, informed the writer that these were not subsidised by Austria. In regard to Austrian propaganda in Albania see also, Freiherr von Musulin, *Das Haus am Ballplatz* (Munich, 1924), pp. 148 ff.

[13] In regard to Austria's religious protectorate in Turkey see, Th. A. Ippen, "Das religiöse Protectorat Oesterreich-Ungarns in der Turkei," *Die Kultur*, III (1902), 298–316; "Das Kultusprotektorat Oesterreich-Ungarns in der Türkei," *Fremdenblatt*, Feb. 2, 1913; Dr. Graf von Mülinen, *Die lateinische Kirche im Türkischen Reiche* (Berlin, 1901).

tion of Albania was an argument that found favor among the Austrian public,[14] but played scarcely any part in determining the actions of the Ballhausplatz.[15] The military advantages of an Albanian state in case of war, were a more serious consideration, as the essays by Conrad show.[16] Reluctance to surrender the Catholic Malissores to an Orthodox Serbia or Montenegro undoubtedly was also a factor in some circles. It is true that some thought Austria should saturate Montenegro with Albanian territory, thus tearing that country away from the Slavic influences of Serbia and Russia.[17] That this policy would have been successful is very doubtful. It surely would have lost Austria the sympathy of the Albanians, and would have led inevitably to Italian predominance in Southern Albania. The chances were ten to one that any additional Adriatic territory given to Montenegro would become a Serbian outlet. Austria desired to forestall both Serbian and Italian Adriatic aspirations.

Whether it would be possible to establish an Albania which would be able to survive seemed dubious to most of the statesmen of Europe. Certainly it could not be done, if much of the territory inhabited by Albanians were annexed to Serbia and Montenegro. The Austrian statesmen, who staked their policy on Albania, were therefore determined that the state should be made as "lebensfähig" as possible. On the other hand they realised full well that consideration would have to be shown to the events of the war. The victors would demand their spoils. Just how short they could be cut in the Albanian field was the question which interested Austria at the London conference.

"During today's session the conference made no substantial progress," was the way Benckendorff began his report of the

[14] For example, *Was will das Österreichische-Albanien Komitee?* ed. Österreichisches Albanien Komitee (Vienna, 1914).

[15] Conversations in 1930 with Berchtold, Szápáry, and Rappaport.

[16] Conrad, II, 322 ff.

[17] Alfred Rappaport, "Montenegros Eintritt in den Weltkrieg," *Berliner Monatshefte*, VII (1929), 949–50.

second meeting of the ambassadors.[18] Mensdorff, basing his arguments on an ethnographic map,[19] argued for his view on the Albanian frontier. All the ambassadors protested that ethnographic considerations were an insufficient basis. Finally Mensdorff agreed to bring a map to the next session with the proposed Austrian boundary-line carefully traced. This was exactly what Sazonov wished, for it would then be only a matter of rectifying the Austrian proposal.[20]

At the same session the ambassadors dealt briefly with two other subjects. Serbia had informed the conference of her willingness to accept its decisions even if this meant giving up direct access to the Adriatic. The ambassadors now asked their governments to approve a public statement of their decision in this matter. The fate of the Aegean Islands was also briefly discussed; the consensus of opinion was that they should be neutralised. Benckendorff was the only one who was in a position to make a definite statement. He proposed that the islands should go to Greece, except for the four located near the Dardanelles. These would have to go to Turkey.

On December 10th there had been an informal meeting at the Ballhausplatz, at which the future boundary of Albania was traced.[21] The map thus drawn excluded the three important cities of Ipek, Prizren, and Ochrida from Albania, as it was thought that these three cities would have to be ceded to Serbia. This map was supplied to Mensdorff along with instructions to use the three cities as compensations in bargain-

[18] Dec. 18, 1912, Benckendorff, II, no. 768, see also no. 769; Ö-U. A., V, nos. 4957, 4958, 4960; G.P., XXXIV, i, no. 12549; D.D.F., 3d. ser., V, no. 85; B.D., IX, ii, no. 394.

[19] Mr. Ippen informed the writer that this map had been prepared by Baron Giesl while he was attaché at Constantinople.

[20] Benckendorff, II, no. 756.

[21] This was largely the work of Ippen and Rappaport (Conversation with Ippen; A. Rappaport, "Albaniens Werdegang" *Die Kriegsschuldfrage*, V [1927], 831; see also Ö-U.A., V, nos. 4957, 4974). The three proposed boundaries on the following map of Albania are based on photostats obtained at the Archives in Vienna. The boundary as drawn in 1914 is based on Stieler's *Handatlas*; Swire, *Albania*, p. 280; S. Saucerman, *International Transfers of Territory in Europe with Names of the Affected Political Subdivisions as of 1910–1914 and the Present* (Washington, 1937), p. 197.

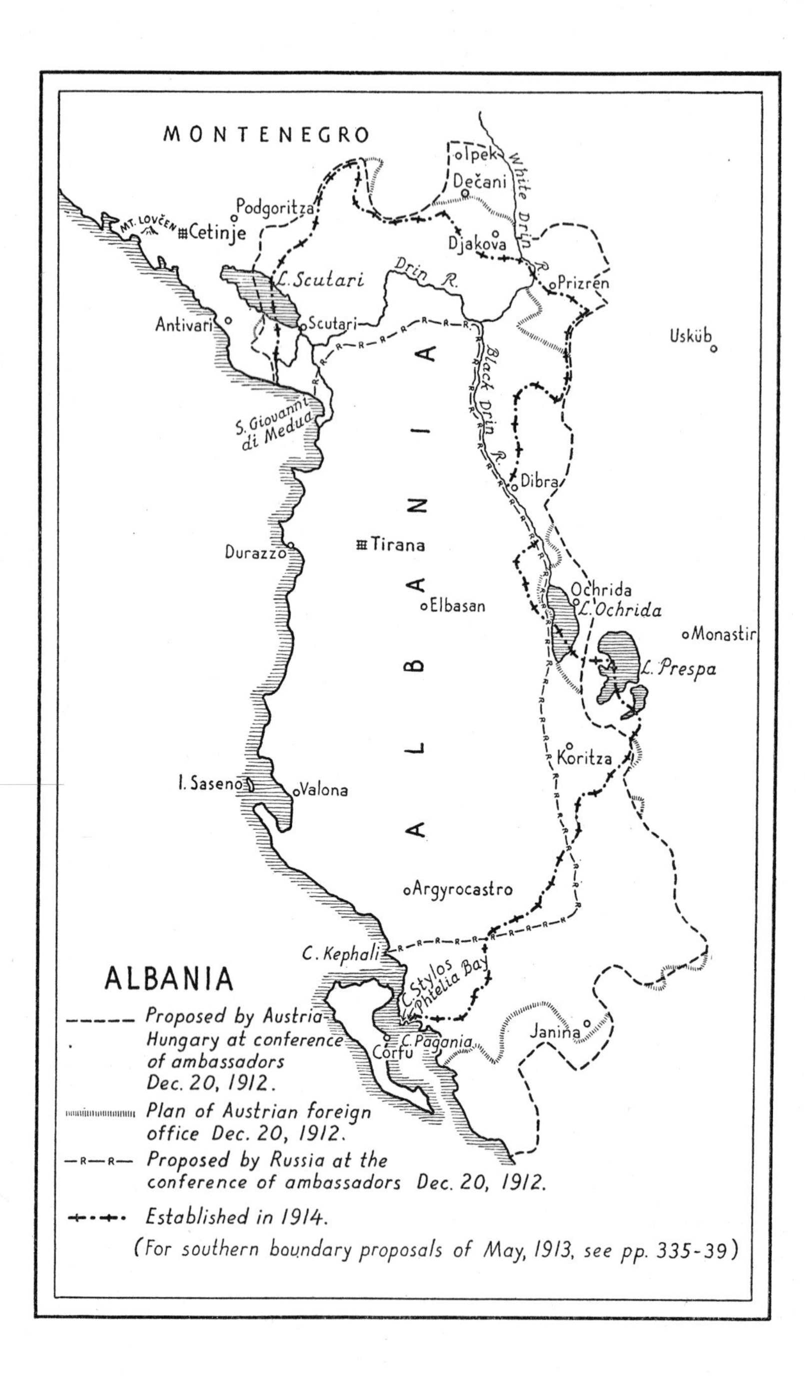
MONTENEGRO
MT. LOVČEN
Cetinje
Podgoritza
Ipek
Dečani
White Drin
Djakova
Prizren
Usküb
Drin R.
L. Scutari
Scutari
Antivari
S. Giovanni di Medua
Black Drin R.
A L B A N I A
Dibra
Tirana
Durazzo
Elbasan
Ochrida
L. Ochrida
Monastir
L. Prespa
Koritza
I. Saseno
Valona
Argyrocastro
C. Kephali
C. Stylos
Phtelia Bay
C. Pagania
Corfu
Janina
ALBANIA
Proposed by Austria-Hungary at conference of ambassadors Dec. 20, 1912.
Plan of Austrian foreign office Dec. 20, 1912.
Proposed by Russia at the conference of ambassadors Dec. 20, 1912.
Established in 1914.
(For southern boundary proposals of May, 1913, see pp. 335-39)

ing over the border. Obviously Mensdorff could not present this map to the conference, and so he drew up a new one, including the three cities in Albania.

Mensdorffs' map was not favorably received by the conference. Imperiali said he had no instructions as to Scutari. Lichnowsky was hesitant and urged Mensdorff to give in on this point, since he knew Sir Edward Grey was going to support the Russian view. Having accepted the Austrian demand with regard to a Serbian port, Sir Edward Grey felt that Russia should have her way on Scutari. Benckendorff protested against the Austrian proposal, and consented to furnish a map at the next meeting, with Russia's proposal for a boundary line.[22]

The conference held three meetings, December 17, 18, 20th, and then adjourned until January 2nd. The ambassadors hoped that by that time the question of Scutari would be settled through direct negotiations between St. Petersburg and Vienna. Until that was accomplished little could be done.

But direct negotiations between St. Petersburg and Vienna were complicated by a more pressing question. The Austrian military measures inaugurated at the end of November and the beginning of December were completed. The troops in Bosnia-Herzegovina and Dalmatia were on war footing, and the garrisons centering in Agram, Temesvar, Budapest, Krakau, Przemysl, and Lemberg had been materially strengthened. In all the Austrians called about 224,000 men to the colors, although the Russians estimated the number to be 300,000.[23] On the other side Russia had spent eighty millions of rubles completing the supplies for the army and still retained her third year levy under colors. This meant that the Russian army had been increased by approximately 350,000, of which about 150,000 were kept on the eastern frontier.[24] But unless the tsar issued a special ukas these troops would have to be dismissed

[22] Lichnowsky to foreign office, Dec. 20, 1912, G.P., XXXIV, i, no. 12557; Ö-U.A., V, no. 4995; Benckendorff, II, nos. 778, 779; D.D.F., 3d. ser., V, no. 100; B.D., IX, ii, nos. 395, 399, 403.

[23] Louis to Poincaré, Jan. 2, 1913, D.D.F., 3d. ser., V, no. 154; see also below, Appendix I, pp. 461–62.

[24] D.D.F., 3d. ser., V, no. 154.

on January 1st.[25] It thus became an urgent matter to bring about a decrease in Austrian forces, so that Russia might permit the third year levy to return to their homes. Sazonov asked directly in Vienna and also through Berlin about a common reduction of troops.[26] Sir Edward Grey, Poincaré, and even King George V urged Austria to demobilise.[27] Berchtold refused to do so. Until the Serbian army withdrew from Albania, the increase in Austrian troops was necessary. In this fashion Serbia would be kept from undertaking any foolish steps against the monarchy. Besides, to demobilise would only increase the demands of the Balkan states.[28] The latter statement shows that Austria intended her military measures as a means of backing up her claims at the London conference. Szápáry later termed the efforts of the Entente to get Austria to demobilise as "Demobilisierungsrummel," and credited the success which seemed to be coming to Austrian diplomacy in the first weeks of January, to Austria's polite but firm refusal to let anyone else decide as to her "right to self-determination in regard to the army." [29] In the declaration guaranteeing Serbia a commercial outlet on the Adriatic, Serbia had been given the right to import arms. Austria-Hungary now raised the question whether this right existed also in time of war. Since the port was to be located in a neutralised country it could not be blockaded.[30] Sazonov thought the question had no practical importance, for the ships could always be stopped and searched for contraband

[25] For Kokovtsov's advice to follow this procedure see above, p. 220. It was later discovered that no special ukas was necessary and that the troops could be held under colors by virtue of an old law (Report of Kokovtsov to tsar, reprinted in *Berliner Monatshefte*, VI [1928], 1070–1; see also Benckendorff, III, no. 804; B.D., IX, ii, no. 455; Ö-U.A., V, no. 5213).

[26] Ö-U.A., V, nos. 5035, 5075, 5200; see also nos. 5065, 5150, 5167; G.P., XXXIV, i, nos. 12570, 12572, 12558 note.

[27] Ö-U.A., V, nos. 4979, 5028, 5109; D.D.F., 3d. ser., V, nos. 96, 145; B.D., IX, ii, no. 398; Benckendorff, II, no. 773; G.P., XXXIV, i, nos, 12563, 12629.

[28] Ö-U.A., V, nos. 5085, 5088, 5146; G.P., XXXIV, i, no. 12585; B.D., IX, ii, nos. 406, 416, 425, 447.

[29] Private letter to Szécsen, Jan. 9, 1913, Ö-U.A., V, no. 5296.

[30] *Ibid.*, V, nos. 5015, 5087. Poincaré and the Austrian ambassador at Paris were apparently the first to discuss this question (*ibid.*, IV, no. 4613; D.D.F., 3d. ser., V, no. 141).

on the high seas. Yet there was the possibility of traffic in coastwise vessels which would never be on the high seas. The question was debated back and forth, but the cabinets never came to a common decision. It only took time which might have been better devoted to settling the question of Scutari.

On January 2nd the ambassadorial conference met again. As the cabinets had not reached any settlement about the Albanian frontier, the ambassadors postponed this topic and turned their attention to the question of the islands.[31] In the last session before the Christmas holidays, Benckendorff had stated that the four islands near the Dardanelles ought to be retained by Turkey. He now reversed his position, and proposed that these four islands, under special guarantee, should go to Greece.[32] France and England favored this settlement, whereas the ambassadors of the Triple Alliance pleaded lack of instructions. Nothing remained but to wait until these arrived. The conference was at a standstill.

While the ambassadors of the great powers had been attempting to solve their difficulties before the fireplace in Downing Street, the plenipotentiaries of the belligerent states were discussing peace terms in St. James' Palace. On December 16th the "Conference of St. James" had been formally opened by Sir Edward Grey.[33] A delay occurred the very next day. The Turkish representatives felt that they could not negotiate with the Greek delegates, since Greece had not signed the armistice. New instructions soon set aside this difficulty, but the negotiations made little progress. The Turkish representatives were none too conciliatory, nor were they disposed to hasten the conclusion of peace. They had to keep their eyes on political conditions in Constantinople. Every concession they made had to be weighed with reference to the effect it would have on the op-

[31] Sazonov did not want the Albanian frontiers discussed until he was assured that Austria-Hungary was disarming and asked Grey to devise some method of postponing that discussion (B.D., IX, ii, nos. 438, 443).

[32] Ö-U.A., V, nos. 5162, 5174; B.D., IX, ii, no. 437; D.D.F., 3d. ser., V, no. 160; G.P., XXXIV, i, no. 12600; Benckendorff, III, no. 793.

[33] B.D., IX, ii, 292 ed. note. For the names of the delegates and the protocols of this "Conference of St. James" see, *ibid.*, Appendix III, pp. 1026–63.

position party headed by the Committee of Union and Progress. Friendly advice by the powers at Constantinople produced no results.

The allied representatives continued to demand the cession of the islands and Adrianople. Finally a note was presented to the Turks, covering these points. The Turkish government refused to accept the terms, and on January 6th the negotiations were suspended.[34] The allies originally had the intention of denouncing the armistice, but on the advice of the powers they did not cut off the possibility of future discussions. Consequently they decided only to "suspend the work of the conference."

Already the powers had at various times individually advised the Porte against a resumption of hostilities at all costs. The action of Russia had been the most energetic. On December 23rd she had declared that if war were resumed, she could not guarantee to remain neutral.[35] This declaration caused more furor in the other capitals than in Constantinople. France and England were especially put out by this unilateral statement of policy by the Russian foreign office. On January 4th the ambassadorial conference met and devoted the whole session to deciding what should be done if the allied-Turkish peace negotiations ended in failure. This seemed very likely at that moment, and Sir Edward Grey proposed collective action at Constantinople. Turkey was to be reminded that she apparently did not realise who had won the war, and that according to the opinion of the powers, Adrianople and the islands would have to be ceded. Certain of the latter could be neutralised so that they would not constitute a menace to Turkey. Cambon, without authorisation from Paris, suggested that it might be well to consider a means of levying pressure on Turkey in order to influence her to accept these conditions. He proposed a naval demonstration.[36]

[34] D.D.F., 3d. ser., V, no. 182 Annexe I and II; see also B.D., IX, ii, no. 478.

[35] Izvolsky, II, no. 645; D.D.F., 3d. ser., V, nos. 111, 113, 117; B.D., IX, ii, nos. 411, 432.

[36] Ö-U.A., V, no. 5188; G.P., XXXIV, i, no. 12616; B.D., IX, ii, nos. 448, 451; D.D.F., 3d. ser., V, nos. 167, 168.

In submitting this proposal to Berlin, Lichnowsky added the confidential information that Grey was not very favorably disposed toward it. This information was welcome to the German statesmen, for although they wanted close coöperation with England, they did not wish to bring anything like armed pressure on the Porte. "It does not seem to me," so the Kaiser told Jules Cambon, "that the powers ought to intervene in a military way in order to assure Bulgaria the fruits of the war. We shall advise the Turks to abandon Adrianople. We shall not contest this city's going to Bulgaria, but if the Turks refuse to cede it, then the Bulgarians must take it themselves." [37] The Kaiser felt that a naval demonstration was not only incompatible with neutrality, but that it was entirely impractical. What would happen to the ships of the powers, which were at that time lying at anchor in Constantinople? How could these be turned into a demonstration over night? Certainly they could not remain inactive while other ships demonstrated at a different port. He quite rightly characterised it as "einfach militärischer Blödsinn" and "ungeheuerliche Dummheit." [38] Austria and Italy supported the German view, and so the idea of a naval demonstration was dropped. Instead it was proposed to send ships to Besika Bay so as to have them in readiness if internal conditions in Turkey required. The Wilhelmstrasse frowned upon this plan also, although it was more favorably received in Vienna and Rome.[39] The Italians even joined England in sending ships.

With the definite suspension of Allied-Turkish negotiations on January 6th, the time arrived for Grey's proposed collective action to which all the powers had agreed. At first the London conference decided to ask the ambassadors in Constantinople to formulate the terms of the note.[40] Then it occurred to Cambon

[37] Cambon to Poincaré, Jan. 12, 1913, D.D.F., 3d. ser., V, no. 210; Poincaré, III, 10.

[38] G.P., XXXIV, i, nos. 12650 notes, 12662; B.D., IX, ii, nos. 456, 500.

[39] G.P., XXXIV, i, no. 12682; Ö-U.A., V, nos. 5270, 5530; Benckendorff, III, no. 840.

[40] Ö-U.A., V, no. 5530; B.D., IX, ii, nos. 451 note, 462, 465; D.D.F., 3d. ser., V, no. 188. For the note drawn up at Constantinople see G.P., XXXIV, i, no. 12652.

that a note drawn up by the representatives at the Sublime Porte could not have the effect of one drawn up by the cabinets. Consequently he was instructed by the ambassadorial conference to phrase a note which was then dispatched to the different governments for their approval.[41] Various minor changes were of course necessary. Even with the London conference acting as a clearing house, it was not until January 17, 1913 that the note could be presented at the Porte. In it Turkey was reminded that a prolongation of the war would jeopardise her possession of Constantinople and perhaps even of the Asiatic provinces. In any case she would need the moral and material support of the powers to eradicate the ravages of war and consolidate her remaining territories. This support could only be guaranteed if the Porte accepted the advice of the powers to cede Adrianople and the islands. The powers on the other hand would safeguard the Mohammedan interests in Adrianople and would see that the islands did not constitute a threat against Turkey.[42]

In order to bring additional pressure on Turkey, Sazonov proposed a warning by the Triple Entente. France and England objected to this separation from the European concert.[43] Grey, however, in repeated conversations with the Turkish negotiators at London, urged them to meet the demands of the Balkan states as the powers would do nothing to save Adrianople for the sultan.[44] As a further means of influencing the Porte the Balkan states proposed to denounce the armistice on the day when the powers presented their note. This plan was later dropped. It had nevertheless angered the Kaiser, who noted:

> An indescribable impertinence! By that the great powers are degraded to accomplices of the Balkan states, and their note, which was meant as friendly advice, is changed into a Balkan ultimatum; through it we half-way join the side of the Balkan states. *Das ist*

[41] D.D.F., 3d. ser., V, no. 204 Annexe; Ö-U.A., V, no. 5319; B.D., IX, ii, no. 489.

[42] D.D.F., 3d. ser., V, no. 230.

[43] *Ibid.*, V, nos. 224, 226, 232; B.D., IX, ii, nos. 513 minute, 515, 518, 521 minutes, 531 minute.

[44] B.D., IX, ii, nos. 490, 495, 496, 515, 529.

eine ungeheuerliche Schweinerei, die ich unter gar keinen Umständen mitmache! I shall absolutely not participate in any further similar anti-Turkish steps of the powers.[45]

This statement is indicative of a change in Germany's attitude toward the Balkan question. With the death of Kiderlen on December 30, 1912, Bethmann-Hollweg was forced to take over the direction of foreign policy in more detail. The Kaiser also took a more direct hand in affairs. Kiderlen had accepted the Austrian plan of attempting to win Bulgarian friendship. He had suggested supporting the Bulgarian claim to Salonica, a proposal which was very welcome to the Ballhausplatz.[46] Although the Kaiser was definitely anti-Turk at the start of the war,[47] his pro-ally ardor started to cool, when it seemed to him that the Entente was trying to turn the collective note into an armed intervention on behalf of the allied states. He became indignant over the proposed naval demonstration. The likelihood of the war spreading to Asiatic Turkey — a possibility which was increased by Russia's declaration that she could not guarantee her neutrality if the war were continued — was perhaps even more important in changing his attitude. Turkey in Europe might disappear; Turkey in Asia was a different question. This change was so generally noticed that the Kaiser felt called upon to protest to Szögyény against allegations of his Turcophilism.[48]

But even more important was the change in German policy in regard to Rumania. Kiderlen had never felt called upon to go out of his way to support Rumania's claim for compensations in return for her neutrality during the war. Now Germany proposed that the powers should undertake a joint *démarche* at

[45] G.P., XXXIV, i, no. 12678 Schlussbemerkung.

[46] *Ibid.*, XXXIV, i, nos. 12546, 12565, 12587; Ö-U.A., V, no. 5023; see also nos. 4837, 6127; VI, nos. 6862, 7497, 7506; VII, no. 8157 for further evidence of Kiderlen's Bulgarophilism.

[47] G.P., XXXIII, nos. 12202 note, 12288 marginal note; Giolitti, *Memoirs*, p. 375; R. W. Seton-Watson, "William II's Balkan Policy," *The Slavonic Review*, VII (1928), 1–29.

[48] Szögyény to foreign office, Jan. 19, 1913, Ö-U.A., V, no. 5445, see also no. 6127; Izvolsky, III, no. 679; Benckendorff, III, no. 829; Cambon to Poincaré, Jan. 20, 1913, D.D.F., 3d. ser., V, no. 237.

Sofia in behalf of Rumania. This action was to be the complement of the collective note to the Porte. If the powers helped Bulgaria to obtain Adrianople they should at the same time help Rumania to obtain Silistria. Lichnowsky introduced this project several times at the ambassadorial conference where it found only the none too ardent support of Austria-Hungary and Italy.[49] Closely allied with the desire to obtain satisfaction for Rumania was the reappearance of distrust of Bulgaria. Kiderlen, as has been mentioned, had definitely desired to unite Bulgaria as closely as possible to the Triple Alliance. Zimmermann, who, as under-secretary, took over the foreign office, instructed Lichnowsky in the same vein on January 3rd.[50] Shortly thereafter the Bulgarian-Rumanian negotiations came to a standstill.[51] From then on an anti-Bulgarian attitude came to the fore. Later, indeed, the foreign office, on the specific instructions of the Kaiser, was to come out openly in support of Greek claims to Salonica. At the same time Austria was encouraged to seek her future salvation in an agreement with Serbia, rather than in an agreement with Bulgaria. "Now as formerly," the Kaiser wrote in March, 1913, "I am of the opinion that the combination of Serbia, Rumania, and Greece under the leadership of Austria is the most natural and the best, because Turkey would rather join such a union than a Bulgarian one." [52] At the same time Szögyény reported: "The enthusiasm of Emperor Wilhelm for the Bulgarian feats of arms has again disappeared, and his well known marked antipathy for King Ferdinand has again won the upper hand." [53] This

[49] G.P., XXXIV, i, nos. 12630, 12681; Benckendorff, III, nos. 811, 816, 819; B.D., IX, ii, no. 477; D.D.F., 3d. ser., V, no. 197; Poincaré, III, 6–7.

[50] G.P., XXXIV, i, no. 12601. Cambon reported that Zimmermann held the same opinions as Kiderlen had (Jan. 4, 1913, D.D.F., 3d. ser., V, no. 173). See also, B.D., IX, ii, no. 485.

[51] See below, pp. 269–78. The pro-Rumanian attitude of Germany was no doubt helped along by the fact that at this very time negotiations for the renewal of the Rumanian-Triple Alliance agreement were under way (Pribram, *Secret Treaties*, I, 260 ff.; G.P., XXX, ii, 581–593).

[52] G.P., XXXIV, ii, no. 12937 marginal note; see also nos. 12934 note, 12937, 12969; Ö-U.A., V, nos. 6126, 6127, 6128; VI, nos. 6862, 7076.

[53] Szögyény to foreign office, March 13, 1913, Ö-U.A., V, no. 6127.

change, as Szögyény rightly noted, appeared after the death of Kiderlen. It was first brought to light by the discussions concerning the collective *démarche* in Constantinople.

While awaiting the Turkish answer to the collective note of January 17th the ambassadorial conference had resumed discussions respecting the Albanian frontier. Since December 20th they had side-tracked this question. In the interval negotiations had been going on between the cabinets. Italy, which at the beginning would have been quite willing to see Scutari go to Montenegro,[54] now supported the Austrian view that this city would have to be incorporated into Albania. Rumors of a possible Austrian-Montenegrin exchange of the Lovčen for Scutari no doubt played a part in bringing about this coöperation between Rome and Vienna. If Scutari went to Albania the chances of this exchange of territory would be ended. Although Italy in the autumn raised no objections to "slight rectifications [never defined] of the frontier at Cattaro" in favor of Austria,[55] she now maintained that she would never permit Austria to obtain the Lovčen.[56] With that mountain in her possession Austria would dominate all of Montenegro. Incidentally of course, Austria would also have one of the finest naval bases in the world in the Bay of Cattaro.

Berchtold early suggested that Montenegro might be given territory in other regions as a sort of a compensation for Scutari.[57] He proposed further that the Boyana River might be regulated. This would lower materially the level of the Lake of Scutari, and give Montenegro a very substantial increase in arable land. The Italian minister accepted this idea, but thought that King Nikita would have to obtain some additional territory in the plain about Scutari, even if the city went to Albania.[58] He also suggested a financial payment to Monte-

[54] *Ibid.*, V, nos. 5056, 5071; G.P., XXXIV, i, no. 12574; Benckendorff, III, nos. 796, 797; B.D., IX, ii, no. 467.

[55] Ö-U.A., IV, nos. 4503, 4638.

[56] Ö-U.A., V, no. 5156; G.P., XXXIV, i, no. 12610; B.D., IX, ii, no. 452.

[57] Ö-U.A., V, nos. 5198, 5212; G.P., XXXIV, i, no. 12623; B.D., IX, ii, nos. 464, 467, 469, 526.

[58] Ö-U.A., V, no. 5272. One branch of the Drin flows into the sea below San Giovanni de Medua, the other into the Boyana a very short distance below the

negro. While opposed to the cession of territory about Scutari to Montenegro, Berchtold accepted the idea of compensations in general.[59] However, no agreement was reached as to what Montenegro was to receive, and the question of compensations remained open all spring.

Sazonov did not think much of the plan of regulating the Boyana, yet he agreed to accept any solution which would satisfy Montenegro.[60] In other words he was willing to concede Scutari if a sufficient *quid pro quo* were obtained. In fact rumors circulated that Russia would yield in this matter. Sazonov stoutly denied this, and Benckendorff was instructed to insist as firmly as ever that Montenegro must have Scutari.[61] He should, however, not assume a position which made further concessions impossible. Mensdorff likewise was to maintain that the city would have to go to Albania. Nevertheless, Grey was confidentially informed (January 7th) that if Scutari went to Albania Austria would accept a compromise on the eastern border.[62] Later the Ballhausplatz indicated that it would not insist on Ochrida, Ipek, or Prizren.[63]

In the ambassadorial conference, however, the discussions had so far been limited to the future of Scutari. With the Austrian and Russian ambassadors holding to their positions, it is not surprising that when the ambassadors met on January 22nd little progress was made.[64] Benckendorff stressed the danger of the deposition of the Montenegrin royal house if Scutari went to Albania. Mensdorff, energetically supported by Imperiali, pointed out that the city was entirely Albanian,

---

Lake of Scutari. In the spring the Boyana cannot take all the water of the Drin and it backs up into the lake, flooding large areas. The plan of regulating the flow of the rivers is practicable.

[59] Ö-U.A., V, nos. 5703, 5764.

[60] Benckendorff, III, nos. 817, 830; see also, Ö-U.A., V, no. 5212.

[61] Benckendorff, III, nos. 820, 822, 830; Izvolsky, III, no. 658; G.P., XXXIV, i, no. 12608.

[62] Ö-U.A., V, nos. 5244, 5269; B.D., IX, ii, no. 464.

[63] Berchtold to Mensdorff, Jan. 14, 20, 1913, Ö-U.A., V, nos. 5384, 5459; B.D., IX, ii, no. 520.

[64] Ö-U.A., V, nos. 5488, 5489; Benckendorff, III, no. 835; B.D., IX, ii, no. 543; D.D.F., 3d. ser., V, no. 243; G.P., XXXIV, i, no. 12719.

and the economic center of all the northern Albanian tribes. As a result of this meeting Benckendorff recommended to Sazonov that Russia give way. It would show Russia's conciliatory spirit and throw the blame of war on Austria-Hungary. Besides, Scutari was the single point on which the Triple Alliance was united, and it would be wise to break up this coöperation as soon as possible.[65]

Sazonov now connected the problem of Scutari with the definition of the rest of the Albanian frontier. If that were drawn in accordance with Russian wishes, he might agree that Scutari be awarded to Albania. He insisted that Djakova should go to Montenegro or Serbia. In the meeting of the ambassadors on January 25th Benckendorff advanced this new proposal.[66]

The Albanian boundary was now completely on the bargaining counter. Russia was willing to trade Scutari, and the price she demanded was Djakova. Although the Ballhausplatz was willing to make some concessions, it flatly refused to agree that Djakova should be excluded from Albania. It was a purely Albanian village, and as the center of the Mohammedan Malissores could not be ceded to another state. It was now proposed that Lichnowsky and Grey should work out a compromise.[67] The suggestion was favorably received, and while this was being done, the ambassadorial conference marked time on boundary discussion. The new German foreign secretary, von Jagow, suggested to Szögyény that some sort of concession ought to be made by Austria. "In view of the disparity between the issue at stake, and the possible results, if only out of consideration for her German ally [Austria] ought not to become intransigent on this question." [68]

The attention of the powers was momentarily diverted from their frontier difficulties by the events at Constantinople. The

[65] Benckendorff, III, no. 836.

[66] *Ibid.*, III, no. 841, see also no. 838; G.P., XXXIV, i, no. 12738; Ö-U.A., V, no. 5535; B.D., IX, ii, no. 559; D.D.F., 3d. ser., V, no. 262.

[67] B.D., IX, ii, no. 554; Ö-U.A., V, nos. 5534, 5561.

[68] Szögyény to foreign office, Jan. 26, 1913, Ö-U.A., V, no. 5540.

note of the powers advising Turkey to surrender Adrianople and the islands was handed to the Porte on January 17th.[69] The cabinet was disposed to accept it but called a council of the chief religious, civil, and military dignitaries to decide on the question. This body met on January 22nd and with a vote of sixty-nine to one decided to conclude peace.[70] Before the note to the powers could be drawn up, the Young Turks under the leadership of Enver Bey supported "by some forty men" engineered a coup d'état on January 23, 1913. They met with no resistance and the shooting of Nazim Pasha was hardly more than an assassination.[71] The Committee of Union and Progress, which had been intriguing ever since it was ousted from power in July, 1912, was back in the saddle.

The Committee immediately embarked on an extreme nationalistic program. The cabinet of Ghazi Muktar was charged with high treason for concluding the Peace of Lausanne with Italy. Word was given out that no such dishonorable peace would be concluded with the Balkan states. Yet the answer to the collective note of the powers submitted on January 30th, was not so intransigent as was generally expected.

The new cabinet was prepared to cede that part of Adrianople which was located on the right bank of the Maritza. The left bank with its mosques, graves of the sultans, and various historic shrines could not be separated from Turkey. The islands of the Aegean were necessary for the protection of the Dardanelles and Turkey's Asiatic possessions. To cede them to Greece would only cause continued unrest. Realising that the powers desired to avoid this, and that they were interested in preserving the integrity of the Straits, the Porte was sure that it could safely accept the decision of the powers in this matter. A request for the abolition of various capitulations was appended to the note.[72]

No sooner had the Turkish government submitted its answer,

[69] See above, p. 262.
[70] Schulthess, 1913, p. 628; B.D., IX, ii, no. 544; D.D.F., 3d. ser., V, no. 306.
[71] B.D., IX, ii, no. 545; Diplomatist, pp. 220–1.
[72] B.D., IX, ii, 461 ed. note, 468–70; Ö-U.A., V, nos. 5606, 5607.

than the Balkan states denounced the armistice. Hostilities were to be resumed on February 3rd.

In addition to the ambassadorial and peace conferences, direct Rumanian-Bulgarian negotiations were being carried on in London. These also reached a crisis at the end of January, 1913. The point at issue in this dispute was the cession of territory by Bulgaria to Rumania. Rumania claimed that she remained neutral at the beginning of the war because there had been a definite understanding that the *status quo* was to be maintained. Her action had enabled the allies to defeat Turkey. Now that territorial changes were to be made, she felt justified in demanding a rectification of her southwestern frontier.

In making this demand Rumania was not advancing a new policy. In 1897 the Ballhausplatz had recognised her claim to territory if European Turkey were to be divided.[73] In 1909 Bratianu, then premier of Rumania, tried to obtain from Berlin and Vienna a guarantee of compensations if Bulgaria annexed Macedonia. Such a declaration would have been a material extension of alliance obligations, and both Aehrenthal and Bethmann-Hollweg had refused to undertake this guarantee.[74] Bratianu was advised to assume such an attitude that Bulgaria, before undertaking any attack on Turkey, would be forced to seek an accord with Rumania. At the same time it was pointed out that it would be against Rumania's interests to ask for great territorial compensations. Any territory which Rumania might obtain would be inhabited largely by Bulgarians, and this could only lead to future hostility and *revanche* on the part of Sofia.

Nevertheless in the following years Rumania continued to insist on the necessity of obtaining compensations if Bulgaria increased her territory. It was a policy generally known throughout Europe. Yet Rumania had no definite assurances that she would obtain this *quid pro quo*. In spite of the plead-

[73] See above, p. 168.

[74] Ö-U.A., II, no. 1731, see also, nos. 1689, 1740; G.P., XXVII, i, nos. 9756, 9760, 9761, 9764, 9767.

ings of the Austrian representative at Bucharest, Vienna always refused to promise more than a benevolent attitude.[75] What Austria refused Russia might grant, and the Austrian representatives at the Rumanian capital feared this possibility. The Rumanian statesmen did refuse the Turkish advances for an alliance or military convention, which might have checked the Bulgarian plans.[76] But when the Bulgarians endeavored to enter upon negotiations for an agreement in the summer of 1912, Bucharest was not disposed to take them up either.[77] Bourchier, who visited Sinaia only a few days before the mobilisation of the Balkan allies, "found little response to his suggestion that Rumania should join the Balkan alliance." [78] Carol was optimistic and felt there would be no war; but even if the Turkish-Bulgarian conflict came, he apparently did not intend to intervene.[79] He thought that he would gain more by waiting and watching developments. This also was in line with the advice he received from the great powers. It appears that the Rumanian government was led to hope for the support of Russia in the matter of compensations if she abstained from intervention.[80] Austria and Germany were both against an active policy on the part of Rumania, and assured her that Rumanian interests would receive their full consideration and support.[81]

On October 2, 1912, the Bulgarian minister at Bucharest very discreetly touched on the rumored Rumanian-Turkish military convention, and asked what the attitude of Rumania would be, if a Bulgarian-Turkish war broke out. He was assured that Rumania had no obligations to Turkey, and that "Rumania

[75] Ö-U.A., III, nos. 2563, 3532, 3569; Hranilović to Vienna, Nov. 11, 1911, Ö-U.K.A., Res., no. 139; G.P., XXVII, i, nos. 9771, 9772, 9773.

[76] See above, pp. 29, 111. [77] See above, p. 111.

[78] Grogan, *Bourchier*, p. 142.

[79] See especially, Ö-U.A., IV, nos. 4120, 4122; G.P., XXXIII, no. 12215. This was no new policy in Rumanian circles, for it was the policy Take Jonescu had advocated in 1906 in a conversation with the British minister (B.D., V, 122–3).

[80] *Rumanian Green Book*, no. 25; Benckendorff, II, no. 761; *Zeitschrift für Internationales Recht*, XXV, 165.

[81] Ö-U.A., IV, nos. 4085, 4166, 4212, 4222, 4237; G.P., XXXIII, nos. 12293, 12301, 12314.

would remain neutral as long as there were no territorial changes."[82] Well might the Bulgarian government express its appreciation of this declaration, for it meant that as long as the *status quo* — which was being proclaimed by all Europe, including the Balkan states themselves — remained, the danger of a Rumanian attack in the rear was removed. The sudden calling off of the Rumanian maneuvers in the Dobrudja, "on account of the high waters of the Danube"[83] must also have been a welcome confirmation of this neutral attitude.

As soon as it became evident that the *status quo* was not to be maintained, Rumania let it be known that she would have to obtain compensations. On October 27, 1912 Russia was called upon to further this idea at Sofia.[84] Austria-Hungary likewise made it one of the points of policy which she communicated to the powers. None of the cabinets raised any serious objections, as it was generally recognised to be a question of politics and expediency. Even Germany and Austria-Hungary never maintained that Rumania had any legal right to compensation.

In the middle of November, the Rumanian government expected a visit from Danev, who was to inaugurate the negotiations for compensations. The conclusion of the armistice delayed matters, and it was not until December 8th that Danev went to Bucharest. He was en route to the peace conference at London, and from sheer lack of time the questions could only be touched upon. Danev promised that the Rumanian population in those sections of Macedonia which were to be incorporated into Bulgaria should have the free use of their native language in church and school. He saw no objection to the Rumanian government's continuing the practice of subsidising these schools, if it desired. While opposed to all territorial concessions and specifically to the cession of Silistria he did not

[82] *Rumanian Green Book*, nos. 1, 7.

[83] G.P., XXXIII, no. 12215; Gellinek to Vienna, Sept. 28, 1912, Ö-U.K.A., Res., no. 176 note; Paul Lindenberg, *König Karl von Rumänien* (2 vols.; Berlin, 1923), I, 117. See also, Nicolas Basilesco, *La Roumanie dans la guerre et dans la paix* (2 vols.; Paris, 1919), I, 82.

[84] Schebeko, *Souvenirs*, p. 141.

show himself recalcitrant, and the Rumanian statesmen apparently thought an agreement might be arranged without difficulty. Danev was opposed to entering upon discussions immediately. He thought they should be postponed until after the conclusion of peace with Turkey. Then the allies would be partitioning the territories among themselves and the Rumanian-Bulgarian negotiations would be properly a part of these discussions.[85]

But the Rumanian government had no intention of delaying matters. In their view Rumanian claims should become a part of the diplomatic settlement which was to be negotiated in London. Since Mişu, the Rumanian minister at Constantinople, was well acquainted with the Bulgarian delegates to the peace conference, he was transferred to London, and officially charged with concluding an agreement with Bulgaria. Take Jonescu, minister of the interior, was commissioned to be his special aid. The Bulgarian government in the end invested Danev with full powers to negotiate with the Rumanian statesmen.

In Rumania itself, the question of compensations quickly became a matter of internal politics.[86] The opposition shouted loudly about Rumania's neglected interests, and the government had to have something for the gallery. Opinion differed as to just how big a frontier rectification was necessary. Mişu was given a map with four proposed lines traced on it, and was instructed to obtain a boundary as far to the south as possible.[87] All of Rumania's demands centered on Silistria, a city the Bul-

[85] *Rumanian Green Book*, no. 13. For Jonescu's impression of Danev's visit see, Poincaré, III, 4. At Vienna Danev spoke favorably of the conversations at Bucharest and stated that he thought all Rumania wanted was a moral satisfaction (Ö-U.A., V, no. 5891). In Berlin Danev gave the impression that the dispute with Rumania would be easily settled (G.P., XXXIV, i, no. 12531). On the other hand Danev was surprised at the lack of interest Kiderlen showed in Rumanian affairs and at his desire not to interfere in the boundary disputes (Conversation with Danev in May, 1930; see also B.D., IX, ii, no. 446). To the writer Danev averred that he had made no definite promises at Bucharest; he had made only unofficial soundings. As the Rumanian-Bulgarian negotiations developed, the Rumanians thought Danev was going back on his word given on his visit to Bucharest (*Rumanian Green Book*, nos. 28, 34, 36; Ö-U.A., V, no. 5219).

[86] Ö-U.A., V, no. 5950; G.P., XXXIV, i, no. 12642.

[87] *Rumanian Green Book*, no. 18.

garian government steadfastly maintained it could never cede. The Silistrian regiment which had fought heroically for the Bulgarian fatherland could never be asked to return to a foreign country. The fortifications might be razed, Rumania might get slight boundary rectifications in other places, but a purely Bulgarian city could never be surrendered.

It was not until January 2nd that Danev and Mişu got down to discussions in London. The Rumanian statesman offered the diplomatic support of his country in bringing Turkey to surrender Adrianople, and extolled the economic advantages to Bulgaria of the proposed Rumanian bridge over the Danube. Danev had previously let it be known through Vienna that it would be easier for Bulgaria to cede territory if Rumania aided in some way or another against Turkey. Now the offer of Rumanian support was rejected as coming too late. Since the powers were all trying to bring Turkey to cede Adrianople, Rumanian aid might easily be dispensed with. "Conforming to his instructions Danev stated that the Bulgarian government could accord only a very slight rectification of the Rumanian frontier in the Dobrudja; instead of the present sinuosity, a direct line." [88] He, however, indicated that he had not spoken his last word.

The next day conversations were continued. Take Jonescu had just arrived in London, having stopped off in Paris to solicit Poincaré's support.[89] But his presence only complicated discussions. Personal altercations soon developed between him and Danev. He felt that Danev was going back on the promises he had made in Bucharest. Jonescu had apparently spoken to Poincaré of supposed Bulgarian engagements made by Danev and when Danev heard of this he considered it a personal insult to his integrity.[90] He refused to continue discussions and maintained that some one else would have to be charged to carry on the work.

[88] *Ibid.*, no. 23.

[89] Take Jonescu, *Some Personal Impressions* (New York, 1920), pp. 3–7; Poincaré, III, 3–4.

[90] *Rumanian Green Book*, nos. 28, 34, 36, 40; B.D., IX, ii, 1069.

On January 6th King Ferdinand, in order to win Russian favor, especially in regard to the dispute with Rumania, sent finance minister Teodorov to St. Petersburg. He entrusted him with a letter to the tsar stating:

> Teodorov will expound to Your Majesty the danger which the position taken by Rumania, full of consequences as it is, creates for Bulgaria. Rumania, not contented with a rectification of frontiers, wishes to force Bulgaria to important concessions in recognition of her neutrality during the recent campaign and demands the village of Silistria, which the Rumanian army is preparing at present to take.[91]

What Ferdinand wrote that Rumania was preparing to do, threatened to become an actuality on January 7th when Maiorescu informed the Rumanian minister at Sofia:

> Under these conditions the pretext given by Danev of awaiting new instructions seems just a way of shilly-shallying, which Rumania in her present state of mind will not allow. The situation thus becoming more serious, the government has decided to occupy with military force without mobilisation and without declaration of war the territory which it claims in the Dobrudja.[92]

This statement not only caused alarm at Sofia, but also at the capitals of the great powers where news of the contemplated action arrived on January 8th.[93] Counsels of moderation soon were pouring in on Bucharest. When the Austrian minister was notified of the Rumanian plan, he was asked to ascertain what position his government would take in case Russia became involved in a war. Faced with this direct question, Berchtold could hardly do other than say that Austria would be loyal to the alliance; but that the alliance was a purely defensive pact, and an invasion of Bulgaria hardly fell within its terms.[94] While warning Rumania against such an action, Berch-

[91] Quoted by Poincaré, III, 5.

[92] *Rumanian Green Book*, no. 29; Gueshov, *Prestŭpnoto bezume*, p. 60.

[93] *Rumanian Green Book*, no. 32; Ö-U.A., V, no. 5262; *Zeitschrift für Internationales Recht*, XXV, 165–6; G.P., XXXIV, i, nos. 12642, 12648, 12661, 12667; B.D., IX, ii, no. 469, also p. 1069; D.D.F., 3d. ser., V, nos. 196, 207.

[94] Ö-U.A., V, nos. 5279, 5334.

told nevertheless stated that if Rumania found herself in a conflict with both Bulgaria and Serbia, Austria would come to her aid. He stressed the view that so long as there were means of settling the dispute by negotiations, it would be extremely unwise to send Rumanian troops across the border. The Austrian answer met with the full approval of Germany, and the Wilhelmstrasse on January 10th also dispatched its word of warning to Bucharest.[95]

It was up to Bulgaria to make a move of some sort if she wanted diplomatic negotiations continued. For some time the Bulgarian statesmen had been considering a definite formulation of what Bulgaria would be willing to grant to Rumania. Danev had talked the matter over with Benckendorff and apparently hit on a four-point program.[96] Now with things reaching a crucial stage Gueshov asked the Russian government to present the proposals to Rumania. On January 8th Schebeko transmitted the following program to Maiorescu:

1. Ecclesiastical and school autonomy for the Kutso-Vlachs in Macedonia.

2. Dismantling of the fortifications at Silistria, and as a last resort a cession of the territory Medjidie-Tabia.

3. Rectification of the frontier and cession of approximately twenty villages to Rumania.

4. Guarantee to Rumania of her possession of the Dobrudja.[97]

The last point was especially distasteful to Maiorescu, for Rumania could not recognise that she was holding her own territory by the grace of Bulgaria. The fact that Bulgaria asked Russia to act as mediator and thus sought Russian protection also aroused resentment.[98]

These proposals were taken up in the discussions which

[95] *Ibid.*, V, no. 5367; G.P., XXXIV, i, no. 12674; *Rumanian Green Book*, nos. 35, 39.

[96] *Doklad*, I, 683–4 (no. 66), 684–5 (no. 69).

[97] Maiorescu to King Carol, Jan. 8, 1913, *Rumanian Green Book*, no. 32; see also, B.D., IX, ii, 1069; D.D.F., 3d. ser., V, no. 202.

[98] Ö-U.A., V, no. 5311; see also, G.P., XXXIV, i, no. 12648.

were resumed in London on January 9th between Mişu, Jonescu, and Danev. But the latter still pleaded lack of instructions and little progress was made. Bulgaria clearly wanted to rely on Russian mediation, while Rumania preferred direct negotiations. Danev finally offered a triangle of territory with a base of five or six kilometers on the Black Sea. This was refused as insufficient. On January 16th Jonescu returned to Bucharest and it looked as if negotiations would be halted again.

Bulgaria now pushed her cause at St. Petersburg. On January 17th Teodorov, who still remained at the Russian capital, appealed to Sazonov for aid against Rumania. He invoked historic tradition and also the Russian-Bulgarian military convention of 1902. But Sazonov, in spite of renewed efforts on the part of Gueshov, refused to recognise any obligation under the convention of 1902, holding that it was no longer valid.[99]

At a cabinet council at Bucharest on January 25th some of the Rumanian ministers favored immediate action. They were, however, overruled and it was decided for the present to insist only on a written statement of the two viewpoints.[100] The Turkish coup d'état of January 23rd presaged a resumption of hostilities and it was better to watch and wait a little longer. The Bulgarians also became slightly more amiable and on January 29th a *procès-verbal* was drawn up and signed by Mişu and Danev. Its main statements were:

1. Bulgaria concedes ecclesiastical and school autonomy to the Kutso-Vlachs in Macedonia. The right of Rumania to grant subsidies to these institutions is recognised.

2. Rumania demands the line of Turtukaia-Balchik.

3. Dr. Danev objects to the increase in Rumanian demands. Once M. Jonescu proposed the line Silistria-Balchik, and now the line Turtukaia-Balchik is demanded.

4. Bulgaria offers: a) Dismantling of Silistria, with permis-

[99] *Doklad*, I, 706–7 (no. 125); E. C. Helmreich and C. E. Black, "The Russo-Bulgarian Military Convention of 1902," *The Journal of Modern History*, IX (1937), 471–82.

[100] D.D.F., 3d. ser., V, no. 258; B.D., IX, ii, 1069; *Rumanian Green Book*, no. 54.

sion to Rumania to erect as many fortifications in the Dobrudja as she wishes; b) two small triangles of territory — irregularities in the present boundary — and an additional triangle basing on the Black Sea. In this way the Rumanian port of Mangalia will be protected.[101]

This protocol was referred to the two governments. The very next day the Turkish answer to the collective note of the powers arrived in London. Immediately the allies ended the armistice. Danev left for Sofia, and the possibility of continuing the London discussions between Rumania and Bulgaria was ended. The war was about to be renewed.

The powers were again faced with the problem of localising the conflict. In fact, ever since the coup d'état at Constantinople, they had been exchanging telegrams in regard to this matter. The possibility of Russian intervention caused the greatest concern. Both Grey and Jonnart, who had succeeded Poincaré at the foreign office, at once advised Sazonov against undertaking a military demonstration on the border of Armenia.[102] Such an action would jeopardise English-Russian relations and the whole Entente. Above all Russia should not take any step without first discussing it with her allies. Italy was especially alarmed, and feared that Russia was about to raise the Straits question.[103] Although Germany was not excited about the Straits, she shared Italy's fear that Russia might take some action which would endanger Turkey's Asiatic territories. In that case Germany could not stand aside.[104] Berchtold, in view of the coup d'état, proposed that the powers continue their policy of neutrality, and by further coöperation avoid an isolated intervention by any one state.[105]

While the powers all eyed each other with circumspection,

[101] Protocole de Londres du 16/29 janvier 1913, *Rumanian Green Book*, no. 61 bis.

[102] D.D.F., 3d. ser., V, nos. 251, 288, 291; B.D., IX, ii, nos. 561, 563, 564.

[103] Ö-U.A., V, no. 5547; G.P., XXXIV, i, no. 12769; B.D., IX, ii, no. 585.

[104] G.P., XXXIV, i, nos. 12725, 12737, 12744; Ö-U.A., V, nos. 5559, 5625; B.D., IX, ii, nos. 542, 546, 561, 564, 585.

[105] Ö-U.A., V, nos. 5528, 5550, 5553, 5594; G.P., XXXIV, i, no. 12739; B.D., IX, ii, no. 586.

they also paid attention to Rumania which might be tempted to send a few troops to seize Silistria. Then the applecart would be upset. On January 29th Sazonov issued a clear-cut warning to Bucharest that Russia would intervene if Rumanian troops crossed the Bulgarian border.[106] He also took occasion to inform England and France of the Russian-Bulgarian military convention of 1902, as if he considered it valid and urged them to support his warnings to Rumania.[107] This they did, for the news of the Russian-Bulgarian convention was more than disquieting since it increased the chances of a general war developing out of a Rumanian-Bulgarian conflict. Jonnart protested anew about not being consulted beforehand, and Sazonov promised that henceforth he would always get in touch with the Quai d'Orsay before issuing any such threats as he had made to Bucharest.[108]

Germany and Austria, who were renewing their alliance treaty with Rumania just at this time, also advised the latter against marching into Bulgaria and recommended further negotiations.[109] Quite aside from the wishes of the powers, King Carol was not really anxious to mix in the war. He was content to hold his army back and to propose to Sofia a resumption of diplomatic negotiations.

The armistice had been signed on December 3rd; war was resumed on February 3, 1913. What had been the results of two months of negotiations?

The peace conference had of course ended in failure. The new Turkish government was willing to cede only part of the city of Adrianople, and refused to make a clear-cut statement regarding the islands. The Balkan states, without seriously considering the proposals, proclaimed the terms unacceptable. In

[106] Sazonov to Schebeko, Jan. 29, 1913, *Zeitschrift für Internationales Recht*, XXV, 166–7; Izvolsky, III, no. 707; *Rumanian Green Book*, nos. 63, 64; D.D.F., 3d. ser., V, no. 294.

[107] Sazonov to Benckendorff, Jan. 29, 1913, Benckendorff, II, 121–2; Izvolsky, III, no. 706; see also, D.D.F., 3d. ser., V, no. 287; B.D., IX, ii, 1005, Appendix I.

[108] Izvolsky, III, no. 712; D.D.F., 3d. ser., V, nos. 288, 309, 420.

[109] Ö-U.A., V, nos. 5571, 5621, 5727; G.P., XXXIV, i, nos. 12751, 12778 note, 12781, 12782, 12783; XXX, ii, nos. 11298–11306.

fact it was a hopeless arrangement. The Kaiser rightly characterised the joint occupation of Adrianople as "Heller Unsinn," and compared it to a French-German condominium of Metz.[110]

The Bulgarian-Rumanian negotiations had also reached no definite settlement. A written statement of their respective views had, however, been signed on January 29th, and this could be used as a basis for further conversations, which were resumed in February.

The ambassadorial conference had produced no great outward results, although it had shown its value as a clearing house. The problem of a Serbian port had been definitely settled. The question of the islands showed a difference of opinion between the two alliance groups. The Triple Alliance, led by Italy, wanted the four large islands near the Asiatic coast to go to Turkey; the Triple Entente wanted them to go to Greece. There the matter rested. No decision had been reached on the Albanian frontier. Scutari was still an open question, although negotiations for a compromise settlement were under way. Germany and England were earnestly endeavoring to work out an agreement. France remained passive. Benckendorff himself reported on February 25th: "In any case, nothing has shown me yet that France has taken an active part in working toward compromise. Now a compromise is peace, beyond compromise lies war." [111] In fact when the rumor reached Paris that Sazonov had given in about Scutari, Poincaré told Izvolsky, "that he was somewhat astonished over the news, and that he feared the impression which further concessions to Austria would make, not only in France but elsewhere." [112]

The negotiations between Russia and Austria for a reduction of armed forces had led to no result. On the other hand, no increases had been made. Nor had the war party in either country received any support on the part of the civil government. Now, however, the problem of a reduction of armed

[110] G.P., XXXIV, i, no. 12754 marginal note.

[111] Benckendorff, III, no. 896; see also Grey's estimate of Cambon's part at the conference (*Twenty-five Years*, I, 264).

[112] Izvolsky to Benckendorff, Jan. 2, 1913, Izvolsky, III, no. 658.

forces appeared to be on the way toward solution. Just after the change of government at Constantinople, and at a time when Sir Edward Grey had adjourned the discussion on the Albanian frontier because it was "getting rather serious,"[113] the Austrian government, on the initiative of the emperor, decided to send Prince Hohenlohe on a special mission to St. Petersburg.[114] He was to convey a personal message from Francis Joseph to the tsar, and endeavor to dispel the mistrust which had arisen in Russia in regard to Austrian policy. Sazonov favored the mission, and hoped that it might lead to a reduction of forces.[115]

With compromise negotiations as to Albania and the islands going on, and with Prince Hohenlohe en route to St. Petersburg, the diplomatic situation at the moment when the allies resumed hostilities appeared to be taking a more favorable turn.

[113] Benckendorff, III, no. 841.

[114] Berchtold to Thurn, Jan. 27, 1913, Ö-U.A., V, no. 5564. The sending of Hohenlohe on a mission to St. Petersburg had been considered in December (see above, p. 216).

[115] Ö-U.A., V, nos. 5599, 5615.

CHAPTER XIII

BOUNDARY DISPUTES, FEBRUARY–APRIL, 1913

WITH the resumption of hostilities, February 3, 1913, the Bulgarians concentrated their efforts on capturing Adrianople. The city had been besieged since the early weeks of the war, and during the armistice had received no supplies of food or ammunition. The question now was whether the Turkish Chatalja army would be able to come to its relief. As a matter of fact the Bulgarian position at Chatalja was not very favorable. Before their lines stood a vastly improved Turkish army, while on the rear flank (Gallipoli) there was another strongly entrenched force. Besides, the two hundred mile line of ox-cart communication was open to an attack from the Sea of Marmora or from the Black Sea. The Bulgarian army, therefore, remained on the defensive at Chatalja, offensive operations being restricted to taking Adrianople.[1]

To the west the Greeks renewed their attack on Janina, and occupied further sections of Epirus.[2] Macedonia and Albania having been already conquered, the Serbians had no special objective. They supplied Bulgaria with some artillery and troops for the offensive at Adrianople. This aid, which went beyond the disposition of troops established in the military convention, was one of the main reasons which Serbia later advanced for the revision of the territorial settlement of the alliance. Serbia likewise lent her aid to Montenegro which was

[1] In regard to the siege of Adrianople which lasted until March 26, 1913, see Piarion de Mondesir, *Siège et prise d'Andrinople, novembre 1912–mars 1913* (Paris, 1914); R. P. Paul Christoff, *Journal du siège d'Andrinople. Notes quotidiennes d'un siège* (Paris, 1914); Diplomatist, pp. 237 ff.

[2] Greece although taking part in the Conference of St. James had never subscribed to the armistice. On January 18, 1913 a naval engagement between Greek and Turkish ships had taken place in which two Turkish cruisers were seriously damaged. Greek control of the Aegean was now assured (B.D., IX, ii, 430 ed. note).

again confronted with the old task of hammering away at Scutari.

While the allies were busy endeavoring to force the Turkish fortresses, the powers resumed their discussions about the Albanian frontier. Much hinged on the success of Prince Hohenlohe's mission to St. Petersburg. If this were successful the solution of all the pending problems would be made easier.

Sazonov hoped that Hohenlohe would bring at least some concession in respect to Albania or in regard to the demobilisation of the Austrian forces. This was not the intention of Berchtold. The mission was not to deal with anything so specific. According to his idea, Hohenlohe would have fulfilled his task if he made clear to the Russian government: (1) the importance to Austria of the problems created by the changes in the Balkans, (2) the absence of any Austrian tendencies hostile to Russia.[3]

On February 4th, the tsar received Hohenlohe in audience. The meeting went off very well. In regard to Serbia, the emperor pledged his word that the Serbian troops would be withdrawn from the Adriatic. On the other hand, he raised the question of Austrian armament. This Hohenlohe parried by saying that Austrian action was the result of Russian measures; these Russian measures had upset His Majesty Francis Joseph very much.[4]

That evening there was a gala dinner at the Austrian legation. The meal was a success, but the conversations were not. After dinner, when Sazonov initiated political discussion, he did it in such a manner and tone of voice, that Hohenlohe retorted that he preferred not to discuss matters, if it had to be done in that spirit.[5] That ended the conversations for the evening. The next day Sazonov was in a better mood, and everything went off smoothly. Prince Hohenlohe on his word of honor informed Sazonov just what military measures had been taken. The

[3] Ö-U.A., V, no. 5679; for Sazonov's views see no. 5615.
[4] *Ibid.*, V, no. 5675; see also, D.D.F., 3d. ser., V, no. 362.
[5] Ö-U.A., V, no. 5751.

fifteenth and sixteenth corps in Bosnia-Herzegovina were completely mobilised; the corps in Galicia and in Hungary had been strengthened. This declaration was accepted in full faith. Sazonov in return pointed out the desirability of a reduction of some sort. Prince Hohenlohe felt that this was impossible until the end of the war; had Austria-Hungary intentions of attacking either Russia or Serbia she would have done so much earlier. Yet the monarchy must be prepared against possible aggressive steps in Bosnia-Herzegovina. The question of Scutari was also reviewed, Sazonov stressing the great danger that confronted the Montenegrin royal house. Hohenlohe repeated the Austrian views and insisted on the importance of establishing a viable Albania.[6]

The conversations with Count Kokovtsov and General Sukhomlinov touched on much the same points as the one with the foreign minister. Again the anxiety about Austrian military measures, and the desire for a reduction of troops was emphasised. This was likewise the tenor of the final interview with the tsar, and of the letter which he asked the prince to deliver to Francis Joseph.[7]

Although Hohenlohe felt that the Russian officials were earnestly attempting to avoid any serious complication with the monarchy, he was greatly impressed by the anti-German and anti-Austrian feeling prevalent in St. Petersburg. He thought that Berchtold's last proposals in regard to Albania would lead to a settlement, but that some concession ought to be made in regard to the reduction of troops.

The Ballhausplatz issued a favorable commentary on the prince's return to Vienna. It was couched in general terms and ended in a paean of praise for the principle, "The Balkans for the Balkan peoples." [8] Not a word was said about reduction of troops. In fact, in view of the difficult state of the Albanian and Rumanian frontier negotiations, Berchtold was not disposed to

[6] *Ibid.*, V, nos. 5697, 5698, 5751; Benckendorff, III, no. 856; B.D., IX, ii, nos. 590, 592, 599; D.D.F., 3d. ser., V, no. 366.

[7] On these interviews see, Ö-U.A., V, nos. 5699, 5721, 5722.

[8] *Fremdenblatt*, Feb. 13, 1913.

lessen the forces.[9] The Russian statesmen on the other hand felt that they could not surrender Slavic claims under the threat of Austrian cannons. They wanted a tangible indication that Austria had no intention of intervening. The Austrians wanted concrete evidence that the settlement in the Balkans would be in line with their wishes. One said disarm and then negotiate; the other said negotiate and then disarm.

The sending of Prince Hohenlohe and the reception he received in St. Petersburg was a real gesture of friendliness on both sides. Yet it brought no immediate results. On February 6th, Lichnowsky advanced a compromise proposal for the Albanian frontier to the ambassadorial conference.[10] To have been a real compromise it should have contained concessions by both Austria and Russia. As it was, Lichnowsky consulted only Grey and Mensdorff, and his proposal was simply a matter of further Austrian concessions. Benckendorff had surrendered nothing and had not even given an indication that Russia would accept the compromise. Sir Edward Grey proposed solving the difficulties by sending a commission to determine the exact boundary line, on the basis of ethnography, geography, and customs of the locality.

In St. Petersburg, the Austrian offer as put forward by Lichnowsky was considered insufficient. Yet Sazonov, though he maintained a stiff front, was far from confident of success in the negotiations. On February 9th, when the Serbian minister threatened resistance to the decisions of the ambassadorial conference, if Djakova and Dibra went to Albania, Sazonov told him: "Then you will have to wage war all alone against Austria-Hungary. Austria will attack you, and we do not want a war about Djakova. With great effort we have won Prizren, Ipek, and Dečani for you, but Djakova and Dibra are purely Albanian towns." [11] This warning incensed Pašić, and he wrote to the Serbian minister at St. Petersburg, claiming that Sazonov

[9] Ö-U.A., V, no. 5711.
[10] G.P., XXXIV, i, no. 12799; Ö-U.A., V, no. 5693; B.D., IX, ii, no. 605.
[11] S.D., I, no. 270.

and Kokovtsov had promised him in the summer not to permit Austria to develop her Albanian plans. He continued:

> Here it is not a matter of Djakova, Dibra and Scutari, but the question is: Is Russia with its friends stronger or weaker than Austria and its friends? The whole Slavic world and everybody else will consider Russia defeated through the policy and threats of Austria. The belief and confidence in Russia will not only be weakened, but it will be annihilated, and the Austrian-German policy will triumph. Without a battle, nobody in Serbia will permit Djakova and Dibra to become Albanian. If Serbia is defeated on the battlefield, then it will at least not be scorned by the whole world, for the world will honor a nation which does not give itself alive into the slavery of Austria.[12]

This extreme language by Pašić brought forth only words of moderation and vague promises as to the future from Sazonov. He had no hope for Scutari, the chances in regard to Djakova were very bad, but the prospect of winning Dibra seemed quite good. England and France had advised Russia that they did not want the rupture of peace over this question. Russia did not want war. Sazonov then added these words of advice:

> If Pašić should resign and a non-conciliatory government assume the reins, this would just suit Austria. Therefore it would be best to be satisfied with the great achievements and organise the new Serbia, in order at a later moment, when the time has come, to open up the Austro-Hungarian sore, which today is not yet as ripe as the Turkish.[13]

At the same time the Serbian representatives at London and Paris threatened active intervention if Serbia's wishes were further neglected.[14] Benckendorff lectured Vesnić warmly, and expressed his astonishment that a Serbian representative should use such language at a time, "when the whole seriousness of the situation was caused by Russia's energetic support of Serbia."[15]

[12] *Ibid.*, I, no. 271.
[13] *Ibid.*, I, no. 276; see also, no. 277; D.D.F., V, nos. 504, 574.
[14] B.D., IX, ii, no. 603; D.D.F., 3d. ser., V, nos. 363, 379.
[15] Benckendorff to Sazonov, Feb. 10, 1913, Benckendorff, III, no. 861. Paul Cambon's personal opinion, so he told Vesnić, was that the Serbian note was "an act of folly" (D.D.F., 3d. ser., V, no. 379).

Grey, who felt that the Serbians took "no account of the nature and wishes or needs of the population," [16] informed Pašić that Serbia should be satisfied with the great gains she had made. While willing to continue diplomatic support of the Serbian cause he considered it madness to risk a war over Djakova and Dibra.

While threatening the Entente powers, Pašić attempted to win Vienna with gentler words. Serbia, he said, really desired good relations with Austria and would very much like to make an economic and commercial agreement with the monarchy. No Serbian government, however, could ask the parliament to ratify such a pact if Djakova and Dibra went to Albania. If these cities were guaranteed to Serbia he was willing to make a visit to Vienna and discuss arrangements.[17] Although Jovanović raised a protest at the Ballhausplatz, it appears that he did not mention a possible commercial treaty as Pašić instructed.[18] In any case, the Ballhausplatz would not have been cajoled in this fashion. Nor are there indications that Pašić was very sincere in proposing this commercial treaty. In fact at this very time he told Sazonov that as soon as a principle was supported by Austria, it was bad for Serbia.[19]

Montenegro of course trumpeted her claims even louder than Serbia. In spite of admonitions from St. Petersburg that Scutari was to go to Albania the attack on the city was pushed with renewed vigor. Serbia responded to King Nikita's solicitations, sending troops to aid in the siege.[20] Austria-Hungary had always advanced the argument that Montenegro, being unable to capture Scutari, had no claims on the city. On February 11th, in an official article in the *Fremdenblatt*, it was announced that

[16] B.D., IX, ii, no. 589 minute; see also nos. 610, 641; D.D.F., 3d. ser., V, no. 395.

[17] S.D., I, no. 269; Ö-U.A., V, nos. 5897, 5922.

[18] Tagesbericht über einen Besuch des serbischen Gesandten, Feb. 20, 1913 Ö-U.A., V, no. 5878.

[19] Pašić to Popović, Feb. 9, 1913, S.D., I, no. 271.

[20] Descos, the French minister at Belgrade, thought that Hartwig, contrary to Sazonov's policy, did not oppose the dispatch of Serbian troops to Scutari (D.D.F., 3d. ser., V, nos. 423, 574).

no matter what was the result of the Montenegrin siege, it would not alter the fate of the city. Nevertheless the idea was generally held that it would make a difference. For this very reason time seemed to be working in favor of the Russian view. Berchtold realised that if Montenegro captured Scutari before the ambassadorial conference reached a decision, it would complicate the whole question immensely. He therefore desired a settlement as soon as possible, and was willing to surrender various points in order to hurry matters along.

The Lichnowsky "compromise" called forth a Russian counter-proposal, which Grey privately communicated to the ambassadors of the Triple Alliance on February 14th.[21] Russia still insisted that the whole of Lake Scutari must go to Montenegro, even if Scutari itself went to Albania. Only the shore line from the mouth of the Boyana to the territory of the bay of Litcheni Hoti might go to Albania. Such a boundary would have been utterly absurd, considering the fact that the bazaar of Scutari is located on the shores of the lake, over which Albania was to have no rights. Besides, the Tarabosh, which dominates the whole city, was to go to King Nikita. Mensdorff had just cause to complain about the proposal.

Benckendorff called Sazonov's attention to the feeling prevalent in London, that Russia was intentionally delaying negotiations. Now with Sir Edward Grey as a go-between, both St. Petersburg and Vienna went a step farther. Russia conceded the Tarabosh, and the small Liuma territory;[22] Austria conceded Dibra.[23] But this still did not bring a settlement, although Sazonov had already authorised Benckendorff, as a last concession, to cede Djakova in return for Dibra.[24] Now that Berchtold had surrendered Dibra, instead of making an equally valuable concession Sazonov decided to try for Djakova also.

[21] B.D., IX, ii, nos. 608, 614, 619; Ö-U.A., V, nos. 5801, 5815; Benckendorff, III, nos. 872, 875.

[22] Benckendorff, III, nos. 874, 877; Ö-U.A., V, no. 5889.

[23] Ö-U.A., V, nos. 5855, 5879, 5904; B.D., IX, ii, nos. 633 minute, 634, 642 enclosure.

[24] Benckendorff, III, no. 868.

The boundary dispute continued. Grey, thinking that it was useless to continue discussions in London, suggested on February 21st an adjournment of the conference until the cabinets had settled the dispute. But the ambassadors objected, and for form's sake, if for nothing else, meetings were continued.[25]

In order to simplify further negotiations, Berchtold on February 22nd proposed to Russia a common reduction of troops.[26] This was a distinct concession to the Russian viewpoint and something for which Sazonov had been clamoring ever since December. It was decided to announce the joint reduction of troops by identical press communiqués. But a difficulty immediately presented itself. In addition to the statement that this action was the result of an exchange of letters between the two sovereigns, Sazonov wanted a declaration "that Austria-Hungary had no plans for aggression on her southern neighbor." [27] Berchtold very naturally objected to such a statement, since Austria had never had aggressive plans. He saw no need of headlining this as a new policy. Finally a common wording was agreed upon, and the communiqués were published on March 11th. On the same day Austria took steps towards a reduction of the Galician corps, it being understood that Austrian measures were to be limited to this area.[28] The Russian orders for the dismissal of the troops which had been retained after they had completed their three years of service, were issued on March 20th. Confidentially Sazonov informed the British ambassador that the "number of these reservists is 380,000 but as recruits summoned to the colours last October are now fit for service their loss will not be felt." [29]

In publishing the identical announcements of a reduction of forces, the St. Petersburg telegraph agency appended an explanatory commentary. This stated that the Vienna cabinet

[25] B.D., IX, ii, no. 647; Ö-U.A., V, no. 5888.

[26] Ö-U.A., V, no. 5910; G.P., XXXIV, i, no. 12914. In spite of Francis Ferdinand's request to support the measure, Conrad continued to oppose the reduction of troops (Conrad, III, 127–8).

[27] Ö-U.A., V, no. 5985; B.D., IX, ii, nos. 680, 685.

[28] Ö-U.A., V, nos. 5910, 6112; see also, no. 6224.

[29] Buchanan to Grey, March 2, 1913, B.D., IX, ii, no. 674.

had made the statement, "that the Austro-Hungarian monarchy had no aggressive designs against her southern neighbor." [30] This was exactly the passage which Berchtold had eliminated from Sazonov's first proposal. Now it appeared anyway, and he felt called upon to issue a counter-communiqué. This appeared in the *Fremdenblatt* on March 13th, and pointed out that the commentary of the Russian telegraphic agency was unnecessary, since Berchtold had declared before the Delegations in November that Austria had no aggressive designs against the Balkan states.[31] Austria had not abandoned any "designs" as a result of the recent discussions.

This statement and other comments in the Viennese press brought a protest from St. Petersburg and a request for an explanation. It appears that Sazonov had shown the commentary to the Austrian ambassador and asked his consent for publication. Since Thurn thought it did not vary materially in content from the indicated commentary which Berchtold proposed to make, he had raised no objections. Sazonov gave the two communications to the telegraphic agency at different times, and had they appeared separately, they would have aroused no great attention. Unfortunately the agency combined the two. Thurn absolved Sazonov of all disloyalty, and shouldered the blame for the incident.[32]

Berchtold, however, was not disposed to make the statement in the Austrian press which both Thurn and Sazonov requested. He informed the Russian ambassador in Vienna that he could scarcely revoke his communiqué, the content of which had never been contested by Sazonov, since it merely emphasised Austria's pacific policy in the Balkans. Other press comments were a direct result of the publication of the notice in St. Petersburg, for which Berchtold could not be responsible.[33] This did not satisfy Sazonov, who asked a second time for an additional

[30] Reprinted, Ö-U.A., V, no. 6120.

[31] Reprinted, *ibid.*, V, no. 6121.

[32] Thurn to Berchtold, March 13, 1913, *ibid.*, V, no. 6134; see also, B.D., IX, ii, nos. 714, 731; D.D.F., 3d. ser., V, nos. 585, 586.

[33] Ö-U.A., V, nos. 6154, 6155 b, Beilage; *Politische Chronik*, 1913, p. 80.

article in the *Fremdenblatt*.[34] Berchtold felt it best not to revive the discussion in this fashion. Besides it could only be cleared up entirely by publishing all the documents. He was willing to do this if Sazonov desired.[35] There the matter rested.

While Austria had met the wishes of Russia in regard to the reduction of troops, the latter made no concessions on the Albanian frontier in return. Dibra having been previously surrendered by Austria, the battle continued over Djakova, a town of about 6,000 people. Neither side apparently would give way. The dispatch of Serbian troops to aid in the siege of Scutari threatened to bring a victory to Montenegrin arms at any moment. Obviously it would be well for Austria if the northern boundary of Albania were settled before this happened. "Possession is nine points of the law," was a proverb well known at the Ballhausplatz.

Consequently on March 4th, Mensdorff indicated to Downing Street that Berchtold might agree that a commission should settle the future of Djakova as Grey had suggested, if Russia would accept Austria's proposed boundary in regard to the Boyana River and the Lake of Scutari. At the same time the powers were to notify Serbia and Montenegro that they would insist on carrying out their decisions, and that Serbian and Montenegrin troops would have to be withdrawn from Albanian territory.[36] Grey had already outlined a similar plan to Berlin, pointing out:

> It must be borne in mind that if Austria gives way about Djakova as well as Dibra, and Russia thereupon accepts the rest of the last Austrian line, Russia becomes a party to agreeing that Montenegro is to be prevented from obtaining or retaining Scutari and that Scutari ceases to become a danger to European peace. Russia must also become a party to seeing that Serbia withdraws from all places inside the agreed Albanian frontier.[37]

[34] Ö-U.A., V, no. 6207. Thurn likewise asked Berchtold to issue another explanatory article (*ibid.*, nos. 6134, 6187).

[35] *Ibid.*, V, no. 6206.

[36] *Ibid.*, V, no. 6012.

[37] B.D., IX, ii, no. 664; see also no. 678; G.P., XXXIV, i, no. 12915 Anlage, XXXIV, ii, 12936 Anlage.

Von Jagow passed this on to Berchtold who now definitely agreed to permit a commission to decide on Djakova on condition that Sazonov should make a formal declaration in line with Grey's statement.[38]

Grey now got in touch with St. Petersburg, where he had already unsuccessfully brought up the problem of Serbian evacuation of Albania once the boundaries were settled.[39] Sazonov was willing to accept settlement of the boundary by a commission, but only under the condition that Austria should declare in advance that Djakova was to go to Serbia. As he viewed it, the commission would always be useful for settling boundary details and various economic guarantees for local trading. In respect to Scutari, Sazonov "was prepared to join any diplomatic pressure but could not consent to use of force by Austria. He feared that it would be very difficult to make King Nicolas give it up if taken." [40] As Villiers noted at the British foreign office, the Russian reply, "really asks the Austrians to go the whole distance in regard to Djakova without going far enough itself according to Austrian ideas in regard to Scutari." [41] Although Sazonov's references to Scutari were not passed on to Vienna, his reply was considered "indiscutable." [42] Here it was held that the commission was to be free to decide who was to obtain Djakova, and if it should be given to Serbia, to work out economic, cultural and religious guarantees for the Albanian inhabitants. Unless the ambassadorial conference could give some guarantee that findings of the commission would be adhered to, Berchtold felt that the discussions in London might as well be discontinued.

This sounded a new note and Grey was not pleased with the prospects of the rupture of the London conference. He imme-

[38] G.P., XXXIV, ii, no. 12939; Ö-U.A., V, nos. 6024, 6069; B.D., IX, ii, nos. 691, 695.

[39] B.D., IX, ii, nos. 688, 690, 692, 702, D.D.F., 3d. ser., V, no. 556; Ö-U.A., V, no. 6091.

[40] B.D., IX, ii, no. 705.

[41] Minute, *ibid.*, IX, ii, 576.

[42] Ö-U.A., V, no. 6142; B.D., IX, ii, nos. 719, 721, 730.

diately got in touch with St. Petersburg.[43] Sazonov was week-ending and things were delayed a few days more. (At this same time, the recriminations over the press communiqués in regard to the demobilisation of the troops were at their height.)[43a] Finally indications arrived that Sazonov had not meant to give a final answer on the prospect of settling the question of Djakova by a commission. He would not demand a definite statement from Austria in regard to Djakova, if he were assured either from the make-up of the commission or from its instructions, that the city would not go to Albania. In that case he would be ready to make a declaration at once to Serbia and Montenegro that the boundaries established by the London Conference would have to be respected.[44]

Berchtold, ever anxious to see the question settled, at once proposed that Grey be left to appoint the commission.[45] Sazonov supposed that settlement in this fashion was merely a method Austria had adopted of saving her face. The Austrian ambassador had apparently even hinted that his government would not look askance at a commission packed in favor of Russia.[46] Grey, who had no objections to such a solution "as long as they do not ask me to pack it for them," informed both sides that he "could not be responsible for anything but the appointment of an impartial commission."[47] Luckily, Grey never had to appoint the commission. On March 21st the Austrian government announced its willingness to surrender Djakova outright on the understanding that there would be effective protection for Albanian and Catholic minorities in the territory which was being transferred to Serbia and Montenegro; and that the rest of the northern boundary of Albania would be drawn in accordance with the Austrian proposal. Also the six powers were to demand and secure "the immediate cessation

[43] D.D.F., 3d. ser., VI, no. 9; Ö-U.A., V, no. 6160.

[43a] See above, pp. 288–90.

[44] B.D., IX, ii, nos. 719, 724, 726; Ö-U.A., V, nos. 6180, 6188.

[45] Ö-U.A., V, no. 6201.

[46] B.D., IX, ii, nos. 724, 738, 743.

[47] Minute, *ibid.*, IX, ii, 593; see also nos. 736, 741.

of hostilities in and the evacuation of those territories allotted to Albania." [48] The Austrian leaders felt that the maltreatment of the Albanian tribes by the Montenegrin and Serbian forces made it advisable to avoid the delay which the sending of a commission would entail. It was a wise decision on their part, since there was practically no hope of saving Djakova for Albania.

Russia under the prodding of Grey and the other powers accepted these Austrian conditions. The long dispute over the northern boundary — the quarrel over Dibra and Djakova as the editors of the *Grosse Politik* term it — was ended. But why had Austria suddenly changed her position and surrendered Djakova? When the Kaiser heard the news he noted, "Na endlich! Das hätten wir schon längst haben können! He [Berchtold] takes an awfully long time to make up his mind." [49] But it was not as simple as all that. Berchtold had made up his mind to do his best to create an Albanian state, and all the cities could not be excluded from Albania without a struggle. He also had a very good case. As an official in the British foreign office noted, "The Austrians are right in this case [Djakova] and really very reasonable." [50] The town was almost one hundred per cent Albanian and was an old established market place for the neighboring Albanian tribes. Had Berchtold not held out so obstinately for Djakova, Russia would not have made the concessions she did make. He did not lack much of being successful. Sazonov was far from confident who would win out in the diplomatic duel. Benckendorff wrote:

> Austrian obstinacy was broken by Russian perseverance, and by the support of the cabinets of London and Paris, as well as those of Berlin and Rome. . . . Both Grey and Cambon were dubious at times whether it would be possible to save Djakova [from] Albania. A last effort has put over the saving of Djakova.[51]

[48] *Ibid.*, IX, ii, nos. 742, 746; Ö-U.A., V, no. 6230.

[49] G.P., XXXIV, ii, no. 13002 marginal note; see also no. 13007 marginal note.

[50] Minute, B.D., IX, ii, 513.

[51] Benckendorff, III, no. 921.

Berchtold was fighting the fight for Djakova single-handed. He never had one word of encouragement from either Germany or Italy, although they went through the formality of supporting the Austrian viewpoint.[52] Even the Austrian ambassadors in London and St. Petersburg advocated giving in to Russia. Mensdorff was so excited with the good news of the surrender of Djakova, that he upset a bowl of daffodils when he bustled into the room to tell Grey about it. After swabbing off the ambassador's frock coat with a towel the two diplomats fraternised over Djakova.[53]

In spite of the considerations already mentioned, Berchtold might have continued the battle for Djakova, had Francis Joseph not counselled a surrender.[54] The question had reached the point where a decision had to be made. Either it was necessary to give up the city, or Austria must take a firmer stand and incur the definite hostility of Russia. The emperor decided for the former course.

On March 22nd, the ambassadors in London set to work on the basis of the Austrian concession of Djakova. They agreed that Serbia and Montenegro should be notified at once of the decision in respect to the Albanian frontier. They further suggested:

> That the six powers could declare at the same time that it was indispensable to take some immediate steps in order to assure the effective protection of the Catholic, Mohammedan, and Albanian population in the territories ceded to Montenegro and to Serbia. The Albanian question not being affected by the continuation of the war by Serbia and Montenegro, the six powers could likewise instruct

[52] Von Jagow immediately sent Berchtold a telegram thanking him for surrendering Djakova (G.P., XXXIV, ii, no. 13003). Sazonov writes "I am bound in fairness to add that in this matter [cession of Ipek, Djakova, Prizren, and Dibra] Russian diplomacy received the support of the Berlin cabinet" (*Fateful Years*, p. 91).

[53] Grey, *Twenty-five Years*, I, 259.

[54] Count Berchtold in June, 1930 assured the writer that His Majesty played a direct part in the surrender of Djakova. See also, Alfred von Wegerer, "Graf Berchtolds Interview über den Kriegsausbruch," *Berliner Monatshefte*, XIII (1935), 520; Szilassy, *Untergang der Donau-Monarchie*, pp. 241–2. Alfred Rappaport writes that the decision to surrender Djakova surprised the officials at the Ballhausplatz ("Albaniens Werdegang," *Die Kriegsschuldfrage*, V [1927], 833).

their representatives at Cetinje and at Belgrade to invite the governments to which they were accredited to raise the siege of Scutari, to end the hostilities in the territory abandoned to Albania, and to proceed rapidly to the evacuation of this territory.[55]

This last declaration was what Berchtold had wanted the ambassadorial conference to adopt as early as March 6th.[56] But at that time the powers were not yet ready for such a collective step, as the northern boundary was not yet settled. Individually warnings had, however, been delivered in Cetinje and Belgrade.[57]

Now that Djakova had been conceded, the Austrian statesmen were determined that the boundary as agreed upon should be respected. As early as February 25th Russia had suggested at the ambassadorial conference that the powers should obtain permission for the civilian population to withdraw from the besieged cities, Adrianople, Janina and Scutari. Food was running short and it seemed the only humanitarian thing to do. On Berchtold's suggestion, the conference also agreed that the allies should be asked to place no obstacles in the way of organised measures to aid the inhabitants after they had left the besieged cities.[58] Such a *démarche* had been made in Cetinje on March 14th.

Although willing to permit the foreign inhabitants to depart from Scutari, the Montenegrin government felt that they could not grant similar permission to the native civilians. This concession did not satisfy the Austrian authorities, especially since constant reports indicated grave maltreatment of the Albanians on the part of the Montenegrins.[59] Catholics were being forced to join the Orthodox church *en masse*. Palić, a Franciscan friar, had been put to death while under the escort of Montenegrin troops.[60] Recalling her duty as protector of Christians in this

[55] Ö-U.A., V, no. 6261; B.D., IX, ii, no. 747; D.D.F., 3d. ser., VI, no. 49.

[56] Ö-U.A., V, no. 6053; B.D., IX, ii, no. 688.

[57] Ö-U.A., V, nos. 6009, 6103, 6141, 6205; D.D.F., 3d. ser., VI, nos. 32, 42.

[58] For Sazonov's and Berchtold's proposals see, Ö-U.A., V, nos. 5936, 5965; B.D. IX, ii, no. 659 and note.

[59] Ö-U.A., V, nos. 6175, 6197, 6213 note.

[60] See below, p. 316. Austrian-Montenegrin relations were further complicated

region, Austria protested to the Montenegrin government. "Now that it was a matter of religion one was ready for extreme measures," was the way Conrad summed up a special conference called to consider the question.[61] It was charged that shells were being aimed directly at the unfortified portions of the city.

On the evening of March 18th, after a meeting with Conrad and others, Berchtold had decided, "in view of the suggestion Russia had made at the London conference," to demand that Montenegro should stop all bombardment until the civilian population of Scutari withdrew.[62] In order to lend weight to this request an Austrian squadron was dispatched to the Bay of Cattaro. The next evening at a second conference it was agreed that, if Montenegro should refuse to stay the bombardment, there should be a naval demonstration and a peaceful blockade of the coast.[63] The Austrian-Montenegrin border should also be closed to all exports and imports. If this were not sufficient, and the situation became more serious, then mobilisation against Serbia and Montenegro was to follow. Conrad steadfastly held out against any small military expeditions which might easily run into difficulties and discredit the army. Italy was invited to join with Austria in the measures to be taken at Cetinje. San Giuliano, however, felt the proposal for the withdrawal of civilians very impractical. Where were they to go? One could hardly expect them to camp in the open.[64]

In view of the concession of Djakova on March 21st and the statement of the ambassadorial conference on March 22nd, Austria now considered that it was high time to put these reso-

---

at this time by the so called Skodra affair. The Turkish cruiser "Hamidie" bombarded San Giovanni de Medua, and a Greek transport filled with Serbian troops was set on fire. The Hungarian ship "Skodra" saved some of the troops, but the captain, unwilling to risk the fire of the Turkish man of war, refused to continue his efforts. Thereupon a Montenegrin lieutenant "insulted and threatened" the captain of the "Skodra" for which Austria now demanded an apology (Conrad, III, 171 ff.).

[61] Conrad, III, 177.

[62] *Ibid.*, III, 174; Ö-U.A., V, no. 6197. The powers were notified of the Austrian *démarche* on March 19–20, 1913 (*ibid.*, nos. 6205, 6219; D.D.F., 3d. ser., VI, no. 34).

[63] Conrad, III, 177.

[64] Ö-U.A., V, nos. 6205, 6221, 6277; D.D.F., 3d. ser., VI, no. 33.

lutions into effect. On March 23rd–24th, the powers were informed of Austria's intention to use peaceful coercive measures if Montenegro continued to neglect the decisions and advice of the powers.[65] Sazonov was much upset by the news and he confided to Thurn that March 25th was one of the most difficult days of his life; "the decision to take very serious steps hung by a hair." [66] Russia had just started to dismiss her third levy on March 20th. Now the question was weighed whether she would not have to call the troops back to the colors. Grey, who was fearful that King Nikita might provoke Austria to undertake some really decisive action counselled moderation at St. Petersburg.[67] Sazonov restrained himself to making a vigorous protest at Vienna. This had its effect in Vienna, and only Conrad and Krobatin, the minister of war, continued to demand energetic action.[68]

An unforeseen complication put another spoke in the wheel of any immediate Austrian action. King Nikita agreed to permit the civilians to withdraw from Scutari, but Essad Pasha, the Turkish commander, refused. At once pressure was brought to bear at Constantinople to change this situation. At the same time the Montenegrin government was informed by Vienna that all bombardment must be postponed until the question of civilians was regulated. The Turkish government dispatched via Austria the necessary instructions to the commander of Scutari.[69] But the departure of civilians never took place, for the Montenegrins renewed the bombardment. Attention was again concentrated on bringing King Nikita to terms.

The Austrian threat of separate action had also caused alarm in London. The ambassadorial conference immediately roused itself to action. On March 22nd it had recommended that the

[65] The telegrams left Vienna at midnight on March 22, 1913 (Ö-U.A., V, no. 6253).

[66] Thurn to foreign office, March 27, 1913, *ibid.*, V, no. 6338; see also, no. 6372; G.P., XXXIV, ii, no. 13017; D.D.F., 3d. ser., VI, no. 66.

[67] B.D., IX, ii, nos. 746, 752.

[68] "Dieser Schreckschuss Russlands genügte . . . " (Conrad, III, 186).

[69] In regard to these negotiations with Turkey see, Ö-U.A., V, nos. 6301, 6305, 6307, 6331; D.D.F., 3d. ser., VI, nos. 64, 76.

powers present a joint note at Cetinje and Belgrade in order to make clear that the siege of Scutari might just as well be abandoned. No one expected great results from this warning and expectations were to be fully justified.[70] Lichnowsky on March 26th suggested giving Austria and Italy a joint mandate to see that the will of the powers was respected.[71] This met with little favor, and Grey proposed a common naval demonstration. Berchtold welcomed this proposal. It was a happy way out, all the more so since Italy did not favor an Austrian-Italian mandate, and no one wanted Austria to act by herself.

Berchtold had informed Grey that if the Montenegrins renewed the bombardment, and the powers did not act, Austria would.[72] Therefore, when on March 30th the cannons on the Tarabosh sounded again, the signal was given for getting the naval demonstration under way. Grey immediately ordered English ships to Corfu, and the five ambassadors recommended to their governments that they should send ships to Adriatic waters.[73]

Since Russia could not participate in the demonstration, Germany felt that she should also refrain.[74] It would keep the sides even, so to speak. But on the request of both Berchtold and Grey, the Wilhelmstrasse agreed to send a ship. The Kaiser welcomed it as a special opportunity of coöperating with England and wrote: "England an der Seite des 3 Bundes im Mittelmeer gegen Slaventhum demonstrirend! Wer hätte vor Jahresfrist so was für möglich gehalten! Fast too good to be true. Das muss man erleben um es zu glauben!!! Oh Triple Entente!!!" [75] At that time there did seem to be a division of the

[70] The note was presented in Cetinje on March 28th and at Belgrade on March 29th; the Montenegrin reply was given on April 1st and the Serbian on April 6th (D.D.F., 3d. ser., VI, nos. 97, 110, 160; B.D., IX, ii, no. 773).

[71] Ö-U.A., V, nos. 6281, 6314; see also, D.D.F., 3d. ser., VI, no. 71.

[72] Ö-U.A., V, no. 6364.

[73] *Ibid.*, V, no. 6384; G.P., XXXIV, ii, no. 13058; B.D., IX, ii, no. 766.

[74] G.P., XXXIV, ii, nos. 13024 note, 13061.

[75] *Ibid.*, XXXIV, ii, no. 13060 marginal note; see also, B.D., X, ii, no. 475. The "Breslau" was sent as the "Goeben" was commanded by an admiral, and the Kaiser did not want to have a German in command of the blockade (G.P., XXXIV, ii, no. 13061).

Entente since France at first refused to take part in the naval demonstration. Not until Russia gave her a special commission was she willing to join in the demonstration.[76] For the sake of internal politics the French government did not wish to give the appearance of forsaking the Russian alliance and joining in an anti-Slav action without the consent of St. Petersburg. Grey, who was from the first willing to undertake an international obligation, nevertheless made English participation contingent on that of France, since to act without her would indicate a "rapprochement between England and the Triple Alliance, or at least a divergence of views among the powers of the Triple Entente."[77] He urged France to join, pointing out that if she did not, all that was left was a joint action by Italy and Austria, or an action by Austria alone. Grey also urged Russia to give France the authorisation desired. He even threatened to suspend the conference of ambassadors. As he noted himself, he told the Russian and French ambassadors at London:

> The Austrian, Italian and German governments had all given instructions for warships to be sent to Antivari. They were quite entitled to do so, knowing that every great power had acquiesced in a naval demonstration. . . . I could not send British ships without either French or Russian, as partner with the Triple Alliance. If, however, we did not participate in the naval demonstration, we must declare that we raised no objection to the action taken by others to make the Albanian agreement respected. Any powers that were a party to this agreement must either join in taking steps to make it respected or, if not prepared to do so, must not obstruct the steps taken by others. This was the only honourable course. I felt also that the British government ought not to be a party to further agreements unless it was clear that the agreement already come to was to

[76] Izvolsky, III, nos. 793, 796, 814; D.D.F., 3d. ser., VI, nos. 74, 88, 174; B.D., IX, ii, nos. 762, 771, 780, 794. Anti-German feeling was running very high in France at this time on account of the proposed German military law. This agitation was increased during the month of April, 1913, by the so-called Lunéville (Zeppelin on French soil) and Nancy (mistreatment of German travellers at Nancy) incidents (G.P., XXXIX, ch. CCXCIV; D.D.F., 3d. ser., VI, nos. 188, 193, 307, 310, 312, 313, 315, 342).

[77] D.D.F., 3d. ser., VI, no. 181; see also no. 148; B.D., IX, ii, nos. 772, 779, 781 note, 789, 790.

be respected; and, as far as we were concerned, the meetings of the ambassadors must be suspended till this was clear.[78]

Sazonov, however, had lost all patience with King Nikita. He sent a categorical admonition to Montenegro to quit the siege of Scutari,[79] and at the same time earnestly besought France and England to send ships.[80] In order to give France the desired public assurance that Russia supported the action of the powers, he issued an official communiqué to the Russian press. With that the naval demonstration came into being, and on April 6th ships of the five powers appeared before Antivari. In the opinion of Grey and Nicolson it was France rather than Russia which had delayed the demonstration.[81]

The battle between Montenegro and Europe had reached a new stage. United Europe was speaking in the loudest voice it could muster. But they spoke from the sea and the Montenegrins were on land. On the heights of the Tarabosh the soldiers faced the Adriatic and thumbed their noses.

While the powers were providing a sanction for their decision on the Albanian frontier they also turned their attention to settling the difficulties between Rumania and Bulgaria. The resumption of hostilities had interrupted the negotiations between these two countries which were being carried on in London.[82] On February 12th, however, discussions had been resumed at Sofia through regular diplomatic channels. Rumania still insisted on Silistria. In spite of strong pressure by Russia, supported by France and England,[83] the Bulgarian government would make only a small additional concession along the Black Sea beyond the terms suggested in the *procès-verbal* of Janu-

[78] Grey to Bertie, April 2, 1913, B.D., IX, ii, no. 795; see also, no. 790; D.D.F., 3d. ser., VI, no. 167.

[79] D.D.F., 3d. ser., VI, nos. 169, 172, 235, 246, 267.

[80] *Ibid.*, VI, no. 169; B.D., IX, ii, nos. 791, 793 minute; Sir George Buchanan, *My Mission to Russia and Other Diplomatic Memories* (2 vols.; Boston, 1923), I, 130.

[81] B.D., IX, ii, 643 minute.

[82] See above, p. 277.

[83] B.D., IX, ii, nos. 620, 625, 627, 631, 658 enclosure; D.D.F., 3d. ser., V, nos. 387, 394, 400, 402, 405, 410, 447.

ary 29th.[84] A new rupture of negotiations loomed ahead. Fear gripped the Entente capitals that Rumania would mobilise and send her troops to occupy the desired territory around Silistria. On February 14th the ambassadors at London discussed means of settling the dispute.[85] Grey had already advised both countries to resort to the mediation of the powers if they could not reach an agreement themselves; now it was recommended that the other powers should tender the same advice. All the governments did so at once, and on February 22nd Rumania asked the powers to mediate.[86] Two days later Sofia did likewise, expressing somewhat more clearly a willingness to accept any decision the powers might make.[87] Subsequently the Rumanian government gave the powers secret assurance that it accepted the mediation on the same terms as Bulgaria.[88] After some additional prodding both governments expressed a desire to see the negotiations carried on in St. Petersburg and so it was decided to entrust the task to the ambassadors accredited there.

This second conference of ambassadors did not get into action for some time. The more pressing questions of Albania outlined above occupied the attention of the powers. There had also been some difficulties about procedure at the conference.[89] Should a majority vote decide the issue? In case of a tie how should it be broken? A super-arbiter was suggested, but immediately the question arose as to how he was to be selected, since the vote would stand three against three. In despair von Jagow proposed solving the whole dispute by lot. Berchtold and San Giuliano objected to settling political questions in this fashion, the latter truly characterising it as the bankruptcy of diplomacy. Finally it was agreed to follow Berchtold's sensible

[84] *Rumanian Green Book*, nos. 81, 83; B.D., IX, ii, 1069; D.D.F., 3d. ser., V, nos. 410, 511 annexe.

[85] Ö-U.A., V, no. 5799; B.D., IX, ii, no. 617; G.P., XXXIV, i, no. 12845.

[86] *Rumanian Green Book*, nos. 90, 91; Ö-U.A., V, no. 5902; D.D.F., 3d. ser., V, no. 436.

[87] Ö-U.A., V, no. 5932; D.D.F., 3d. ser., V, nos. 441, 464.

[88] *Rumanian Green Book*, no. 99; B.D., IX, ii, no. 673; D.D.F., 3d. ser., V, nos. 495, 510; Ö-U.A., V, nos. 5935, 5963, 5978.

[89] G.P., XXXIV, ii, nos. 12942, 12949, 12951, 12976.

suggestion that unanimity was necessary. It was up to the powers to agree upon a decision among themselves.[90]

This was not to be so difficult as it appeared at the first glance. Much of the opposition to the cession of Silistria was sham. The claim of Rumania to some sort of compensation was generally recognised. Sazonov had long been urging Bulgaria to be more conciliatory and on the very eve of the conference attempted to persuade Sofia to ". . . cede Silistria together with two triangles on the Dobrudja frontier in return for the payment of a money indemnity by Rumania and the renunciation of her claims to accession of territory on the Black Sea littoral." [91] In fact all the powers, although for their own reasons, were anxious to follow the instructions given to Delcassé "de ménager les Roumains sans blesser les Bulgares." [92]

When the St. Petersburg conference did meet on March 31st the situation had changed in the theater of war. On March 26th the Bulgarians had captured Adrianople. The rejoicing in Bulgaria knew no bounds. It reëchoed throughout Russia. A *Te Deum* was celebrated in Catherine Hall by the priests who were members of the Duma. Rodzianko, president of the assembly, led the choir formed by the deputies. The Bulgarian minister, Bobchev, and Danev, who was in St. Petersburg in connection with the settlement of the Rumanian-Bulgarian difficulties, were summoned to the Duma by telephone and took part in the general celebration. The Bulgarian and Russian national anthems were sung. It was a day for the Pan-Slavs.[93] Such demonstrations, however, did nothing to simplify the cession of Bulgarian territory to Rumania.

The fall of Adrianople brought a wave of jubilation in France also. The old story of the superiority of French over German artillery was revived. National feeling, already aroused over

[90] G.P., XXXIV, ii, nos. 12961, 12968, 12992; Ö-U.A., V, nos. 6184, 6227, 6246.
[91] B.D., IX, ii, no. 769 note.
[92] Delcassé to Pichon, April 4, 1913, D.D.F., 3d. ser., VI, no. 191.
[93] M. V. Rodzianko, *The Reign of Rasputin* (London, 1927), p. 79; G.P., XXXIV, ii, no. 13036; *Die belgischen Dokumente*, V, no. 59; Ö-U.A., V, nos. 6596, 6597.

the new German military law, was increased. Nothing should be done which would weaken the alliance ties with Russia. Delcassé, the very "personification of the Franco-Russian Alliance," had only recently been named ambassador to Russia.[94] He was charged with a special mission of awaking Russia to the need of improving her railway communications to the East. Pan-Slavs received his appointment "with an outburst of joy as being an added sign that France would henceforth serve as a *point d'appui* for Slavism in its struggle against the Germanic Powers." [95] His appointment was also well received in England and it was generally believed "that his mission to Russia would consolidate the ties between all three of the Powers in the Triple Entente." [96]

England, as her conduct in regard to the naval demonstration shows, was as anxious as France to do nothing which might even question the solidarity of the Entente. The budget of the admiralty, which was introduced in the house of commons on March 26th, clearly indicated in which direction English policy was bent.[97] At the St. Petersburg conference there was at all times the closest coöperation between Sazonov, Delcassé and Buchanan.

The Triple Alliance, however, entered the St. Petersburg conference divided against itself. All three powers agreed that Rumania was to have compensations, preferably the line Silistria-Balchik. But here unity ended. Berchtold placed almost equal importance on his plan that Bulgaria should receive some additional territory elsewhere as compensation for Silistria. Only in this way could the ill-will which would accompany the surrender to Rumania be wiped out. This was essential if Bulgaria were to become a satellite of the Triple Alliance. He proposed giving Salonica to Bulgaria as Kiderlen had suggested earlier.[97a]

[94] Charles W. Porter, *The Career of Theophile Delcassé* (Philadelphia, 1936), p. 311.

[95] *Ibid.*, p. 313.

[96] *Ibid.*

[97] Schulthess, 1913, p. 502.

[97a] See above, p. 263.

This suggestion now received a flat refusal in Berlin.[98] The Kaiser was determined that Salonica should go to Greece. He would not see his brother-in-law, who had just ascended the Greek throne, receive this reversal at the very start of his reign. Besides, the Wilhelmstrasse had become very anti-Bulgarian. The Germans thought Berchtold's policy all wrong and liable to cost the friendship of Rumania. Austria might, therefore, advocate a Bulgarian Salonica at St. Petersburg, but Germany would not. Italy, having no desire to see Greece strengthened, adopted the Austrian viewpoint in this matter.[99]

At the first roundtable discussion, Sazonov as chairman suggested that the ambassadors should present their views according to seniority. It thus happened that the first statement fell to the lot of Pourtalès, representing Germany. He dwelt "especially on the fact that it was in consequence of the assurances given by the powers that there should be no change in the territorial *status quo*, that Rumania had maintained her attitude of reserve during the war, and that now that the Balkan states were to acquire a large accession of territory, Rumania was entitled to some compensation." [100] Since Delcassé had just replaced Louis, it was up to Buchanan, the English ambassador, to present the arguments on the other side. He did this in a very energetic and clear-cut fashion. Rumania had absolutely no legal right to compensations, for there "was no principle of international law [which] entitled a State to demand a cession of territory from one of its neighbors on the ground of the latter's aggrandisement in another direction." On the other hand he recognised Rumania's grievance and felt that certain lesser boundary rectifications might be granted to her. Thurn, representing Austria, continued the arguments for the alliance, and suggested that Salonica might be granted to Bulgaria. This was opposed by Delcassé, since it would only be solving one

[98] G.P., XXXIV, i, no. 12926; XXXIV, ii, no. 12964.

[99] G.P., XXXIV, ii, no. 12950; Ö-U.A., V, nos. 5984, 6025.

[100] Quotations in this paragraph from: Buchanan, *My Mission to Russia*, I, 134; for other reports on this session of the conference see, B.D., IX, ii, no. 769; D.D.F., 3d. ser., VI, no. 145; G.P., XXXIV, ii, no. 13074; Ö-U.A., V, no. 6396.

problem by creating a more serious Greek-Bulgarian one.[101] Carlotti, the recently appointed Italian ambassador, reiterated the arguments advanced by his alliance colleagues, and came out strongly in support of Salonica's going to Bulgaria. Sazonov ended the session with an attempt to harmonise the different viewpoints. The Rumanian claims could not be judged on a legal basis alone. Salonica would under all circumstances have to go to Greece, but compensations for Bulgaria might be found in other areas. He thought that since Turkey had already lost so much, she might as well cede a little additional land.

On April 4th at a second meeting the discussions were carried forward. The ambassadors of the Triple Alliance argued warmly for giving Silistria to Rumania, the English ambassador, who had once represented England at Sofia, taking the lead in opposing them. Finally Delcassé suggested a compromise, which was, of course, accepted by Sazonov and Buchanan. The others pressed for more, but the complete solidarity of the Entente led them to submit the following communication to their governments.

> The representatives of Russia, England, and France accept in principle the cession of Silistria to Rumania on the condition:
> 1. That all the other territorial demands of Rumania be dropped.
> 2. That the Rumanian government compensate the Bulgarian inhabitants of Silistria who wish to leave the city. . . .[102]

At the next session (April 7th) the representatives of the Alliance continued their argument that Silistria was not enough to satisfy Rumania.[103] The wind was, however, taken out of their sails, when Sazonov stated that King Carol had recently said he would be satisfied if he only obtained half of Silistria.

[101] "From a secret and sure source" the French government had early heard of the Austrian desire to compensate Bulgaria with Salonica. The Entente powers all opposed it because of their fear of Austrian dominance in that port (D.D.F., 3d. ser., V, nos. 506, 536, 577).

[102] Ö-U.A., VI, no. 6453; D.D.F., 3d. ser., VI, no. 191; B.D., IX, ii, no. 828 enclosure, I.

[103] Ö-U.A., VI, no. 6505, see also nos. 6425, 6594; B.D., IX, ii, no. 828 enclosure, II; D.D.F., 3d. ser., VI, no. 228.

Thurn again advanced his theory of compensations for Bulgaria, but this time it met with no response whatever.

The Entente statesmen finally proposed the following settlement:

1. Cession of Silistria to Rumania with a radius of three kilometers.
2. Compensations for the Bulgarians who leave the ceded territory.
3. No Bulgarian fortifications to be erected between Silistria and the Black Sea.
4. Safeguarding of Rumania's national and cultural demands on behalf of the Kutso-Vlachs.[104]

In reporting this proposition Thurn stated, "further concessions for Rumania or territorial compensations for Bulgaria are unobtainable due to the position of the powers of the Triple Entente." Nevertheless, Berchtold decided to make one more try. Rumania should obtain some territory on the Black Sea, and Bulgaria the islands of Thasos and Samothrace in the Aegean. But the arguments of Pourtalès, Thurn and Carlotti fell on deaf ears. No further cessions were to be obtained.[105] Sazonov had promised Greece his support on this question, and, besides, the fate of the islands could not be decided at this time.

Berchtold seeing that nothing was to be obtained in the way of territory proposed a declaration stating that Bulgaria would receive special consideration later. Von Jagow, ever fearful of the effect Berchtold's Bulgarophile policy would have on Rumania, reluctantly supported this demand.[106] At St. Petersburg it met with opposition, and in its stead the following statement of appreciation was adopted.

> Before breaking up, the conference desires to state that the known disposition of Bulgaria to consent to some sacrifices, in order to main-

[104] This summary was submitted to Vienna on April 7th (Ö-U.A., VI, no. 6506), but was not formulated into the protocols of the conference until April 15th (B.D., IX, ii, nos. 854 enclosure, 856).

[105] See, Ö-U.A., VI, nos. 6521, 6556, 6573; B.D., IX, ii, no. 853; D.D.F., 3d. ser., VI, no. 278.

[106] Ö-U.A., VI, nos. 6605, 6629.

tain and reaffirm the ties of friendship with Rumania, has singularly aided their task. They express the conviction that the cession of Silistria to Rumania will not fail to produce the result which was sought by all. His Majesty, King Ferdinand and his government deserve the appreciation of the powers.[107]

On April 17th all ambassadors adhered to the four points of the Entente proposition summarised above. Statements as to the appointment of local commissions were later added. It was only on May 8th that the ambassadors signed the final draft of the so-called St. Petersburg Protocol.[108]

Already steps had been taken to obtain the formal acceptance of the settlement by Bulgaria and Rumania. The Bulgarian statesmen, however, at once asked that the agreement be kept secret until the final peace with Turkey was concluded. Negotiations to this end were just getting under way. Almost simultaneously with the conclusion of the main task of the St. Petersburg conference the hostilities in the Balkans came to a halt.

After the capture of Adrianople, March 26, 1913, there had been some talk of attempting to force the Chatalja lines. It had caused a flurry of uneasiness in the Entente capitals, for Sazonov still maintained that a Bulgarian army in Constantinople would necessitate a Russian fleet in the Sea of Marmora.[109] Sazonov wanted the Triple Entente powers to act jointly at Sofia in favor of the immediate cessation of hostilities. There had also been rumors of sending an international fleet to Constantinople.[110]

But the Bulgarian government, now as in the autumn, had no desire to enter the Turkish capital. There was cholera in the Bulgarian army and it was indeed extremely questionable if

[107] Ö-U.A., VI, nos. 6643, 6650. At the request of Bulgaria the whole wording of the declaration was changed (*ibid.*, nos. 6829, 6884, 6916, 6918, 6940, 6946, 6963). The final wording is to be found: *ibid.*, no. 6964; B.D., IX, ii, no. 970 enclosure, D.D.F., 3d. ser., VI, no. 522 annexe.

[108] B.D., IX, ii, no. 970.

[109] Izvolsky, III, nos. 826, 828, 829; D.D.F., 3d. ser., VI, nos. 127, 130, 131; B.D., IX, ii, nos. 800, 807, 815; Zaionchkovski, *Podgotovka rossii*, p. 291.

[110] B.D., IX, ii, nos. 840, 843, 846, 849; D.D.F., 3d. ser., VI, nos. 217, 243, 293.

the Chatalja lines could be forced. Already armed clashes were taking place between the allied forces themselves. After the capture of Janina, March 6, 1913, and while the Bulgarians were still occupied before Adrianople, the weight of the Greek army had been shifted to Macedonia. This occupation of territory led to disputes and conflicts with the small Bulgarian garrisons stationed there. Bulgaria desired a rapid conclusion of an armistice so that it might transfer its army from Thrace to Macedonia. This was of course what the Greeks and Serbians, who were secretly negotiating an alliance against Bulgaria, did not want. Therefore, the latter undertook to delay as much as possible negotiations which would lead to the conclusion of peace.

All the powers were anxious to see an armistice concluded and formal peace negotiations begun. They freely offered this information at all the Balkan capitals. Finally direct negotiations between Bulgaria and Turkey led on April 15th to a suspension of hostilities for a ten day period.[111] The terms of the agreement as put into writing was but a summary of an oral understanding and never had the formality of an armistice. It was later extended from time to time. Serbia and Greece, but not Montenegro fell into line. With the exception of the fighting at Scutari the hostilities against Turkey were ended.

The war had been reopened on February 3rd; the first suspension of hostilities came on April 15th. During this period the powers had arranged most of the details of the settlement among themselves.[112] The mission of Prince Hohenlohe had ultimately led to a reduction of forces in Austria-Hungary and Russia. But this disarmament had done little to bring about better feeling between the two countries. It had practically no effect on the settlement of the northern Albanian frontier. In this question Russia, with the loyal support of England and France, had been able to force Austria to concede Dibra and

[111] D.D.F., 3d. ser., VI, nos. 306, 318; B.D., IX, ii, no. 857; G.P., XXXIV, ii, nos. 13164, 13169, 13170, 13184.

[112] For the discussions which were going on at this time preliminary to the peace negotiations see below, pp. 326–29.

Djakova, in order to obtain Scutari. The Austrian statesmen had been moved to make their final concessions, only in order to settle the boundary before the fall of Scutari would add new complications. The conference of ambassadors at St. Petersburg had come to a decision on the Rumanian-Bulgarian dispute. Whether this would be loyally accepted by the two states was uncertain. The powers all hoped that the cessation of hostilities would soon lead to a rapid conclusion of peace. Montenegro, however, continued to flout the advice of all the governments. King Nikita scoffed at the international naval demonstration and his "Struggle for Scutari" turned into a struggle versus Europe.

CHAPTER XIV

MONTENEGRO VERSUS EUROPE

On April 5th, Admiral Burney, as senior officer of the international fleet lying before Antivari, notified the Montenegrin government of the purpose of the naval demonstration. He demanded recognition of the wishes of the powers in regard to Scutari. Instead of being overawed, the Montenegrin minister of foreign affairs calmly expressed his regret at the presence of the fleet, and charged the powers with a breach of neutrality. The siege of Scutari would be continued.[1]

Berchtold had already raised the question at the various capitals as to what should be done if the demonstration were not effective. He suggested a blockade and the landing of some detachments at different points.[2] Although the cabinets opposed the latter proposal they did agree to a limited blockade. France was strongly against extending the closure of the coast as far as Durazzo, as this would inconvenience the Serbian and Greek troops occupying that part of Albania.[3] On April 10th, Admiral Burney, in the name of the powers, declared the coast between Antivari and the mouth of the Drin blockaded. Ships within this zone were granted forty-eight hours to depart.

"What do they want to do to us?" was the question King Nikita placed before the Austrian attaché. "For our part we still have several sheep and goats which will enable us to live; just so the provisions do not run too short for the diplomats at the Grand Hotel."[4] As a matter of fact the blockade could not injure Montenegro very much. The food supply was adequate, and only the week before a Russian ship had brought a cargo

[1] B.D., IX, ii, nos. 809 enclosure, 811; Ö-U.A., VI, nos. 6460, 6480.

[2] Ö-U.A., VI, no. 6418. For the various steps leading to the blockade see, B.D., IX, ii, 656 ed. note.

[3] D.D.F., 3d. ser., VI, nos. 204, 209, 213; Ö-U.A., VI, nos. 6482, 6484.

[4] Gustav von Hubka, "Kritische Tage in Montenegro," *Berliner Monatshefte*, IX (1931), 33.

of military supplies. According to Sazonov these were gifts which had been made in 1911, but could not be delivered up to this time on account of the Tripolitan War. More accurate than Sazonov's version was the statement of the French chargé at Cetinje, that this shipment of arms was the result of the special efforts of the two daughters of King Nikita, now grand duchesses at the imperial court.[5] The important thing was that these military supplies did come from Russia and the arrival of the gift at this particular moment seemed inopportune, to say the least, to Austria.

The blockade, however, did pave the way for the withdrawal of the Serbian forces before Scutari. About April 1st General Bojović, a Serb, had been given command of the operations. Some Serbian troops had been transported from Salonica and more were expected. As soon as they arrived a general assault on Scutari was to be undertaken. The blockade now placed such difficulties in the way that no further efforts were made to carry out this plan. There was little else for the Serbian statesmen to do but to follow the advice of the powers, and withdraw their forces. This was done on April 4th, but only after Sazonov, on Grey's suggestion, had taken Hartwig to task and had forced him to make Russia's position on the question of Scutari perfectly clear to the government at Belgrade.[6]

The siege continued as a purely Montenegrin operation. Each day the international fleet steamed back and forth between San Giovanni de Medua and Antivari, but did nothing to force King Nikita to respect the words of the lords of Europe. At London the conference continued to talk. The possibility of

[5] Tailhand to Jonnart, April 2, 1913, D.D.F., 3d. ser., VI, no. 172; see also, V, no. 477; Ö-U.A., VI, nos. 6416, 6576, 6580; B.D., IX, ii, no. 807. Kokovtsov reports that in January, 1913 Grand Duchess Militsa Nikolaeva asked him among other things for a shipment of military supplies. He fails to make clear how many of these requests were eventually met, but this shipment of arms to Montenegro is evidence that not all were turned down (Kokovtsov, *Memoirs*, pp. 357–59).

[6] B.D., IX, ii, nos. 819, 821, 834, 841; D.D.F., 3d. ser., VI, nos. 277, 322, 368. Austria also brought pressure upon Serbia to withdraw her troops from Scutari (Ö-U.A., VI, nos. 6560, 6576, 6580; S.D., I, nos. 291, 293).

bribing Nikita with financial compensations was discussed. Italy and Russia especially were behind this plan, and had obtained the reluctant consent of the other cabinets.[7] Grey maintained that while he raised no objections, ". . . the British government could not themselves give money to Montenegro, and that this was a matter to be dealt with by any powers that were prepared to compensate the King of Montenegro by dealing with him direct." [8] But to put the scheme into operation was not so simple. It was generally conceded that the compensation was to be in the form of a guaranteed loan on which Montenegro was to pay no interest. Berchtold unwillingly agreed to the plan, but insisted that the money should be used for the general economic good of Montenegro and not to enrich King Nikita.[9] Grey, even, after consultation with the cabinet, agreed that England would underwrite her share of the loan.[10] Finally, on April 17th, the ambassadors were in a position to propose to their respective governments that Montenegro should be granted a loan. In order to make it easier for Nikita to meet the demands of Europe, it was suggested that the Sublime Porte should surrender Scutari to the powers. The withdrawal could be more easily explained to the Montenegrin citizenry if this took place.[11]

In the meantime, King Nikita stole a march on the powers by declaring that he could not accept any financial compensations, except of course, an indemnity from Turkey. He must continue the siege. "Of course you will understand," reported Count de Salis to Grey, "that when the right moment comes (it does not seem to have quite come yet) the King will take the money." [12]

[7] Giolitti states that it was Austria who proposed giving Montenegro financial compensations (*Memoirs*, p. 367). The documents show that the contrary was the case (Ö-U.A., V, nos. 5703, 5764, 6395; VI, nos. 6466, 6486, 6519, 6520, 6538, 6566, 6571, 6729; G.P., XXXIV, ii, nos. 13055, 13068, 13123; B.D., IX, ii, nos. 770, 778, 806).

[8] B.D., IX, ii, nos. 805, 806.

[9] Ö-U.A., VI, nos. 6466, 6519.

[10] *Ibid.*, VI, no. 6658; B.D., IX, ii, no. 860.

[11] This plan was proposed by Jules Cambon (D.D.F., 3d. ser., VI, nos. 232, 356; see also, Ö-U.A., VI, no. 6695; B.D., IX, ii, no. 869).

[12] De Salis to Grey, April 20, 1913, B.D., IX, ii, no. 865.

A spell of bad weather had delayed military operations. On April 17th, just after the other allies had agreed upon a suspension of hostilities, the bombardment of Scutari was renewed. Within the city food was running short. Prices rose beyond the reach of the greater part of the populace. Bread was no longer obtainable even for the troops, and the soldiers began to grumble over their continuous diet of horse meat. Mutiny was in the air. On April 20th, Turkish emissaries were sent to the Montenegrin headquarters. The next day General Vukotić and Peter Plamenatz went to Scutari, and the terms of the capitulation were settled. Essad Pasha was to surrender the city, but was to be permitted to leave with full military honors. The soldiers were to retain their arms and such supplies as could be carried.[13]

Scutari had capitulated. At two o'clock on the morning of April 23rd a salute of twenty-one guns heralded the goods news to the citizens of Cetinje. The streets were at once filled with an excited populace. Dram shops started to do a rushing business, and by morning most of the male populace showed the effects of the repeated toasts to victory. Revolvers were discharged, and in the morning the Austrian attaché found evidences on the front of his house which indicated that all shots had not been fired into the air. As a final joke, a donkey dressed in black, and bearing a huge placard derogatory to Austrian policy was driven before the Austrian legation. Learning later that the donkey belonged to the stable of the king, Giesl remarked to one of the court functionaries, that only "due respect for a royal ass" had prevented him from confiscating the animal.[14]

Popular approval manifested itself in street demonstrations in all the Balkan capitals, and even in St. Petersburg. It was

[13] Zambaur, *Belagerung von Skutari*, p. 183; Durham, *Struggle for Scutari*, p. 277; Rankin, *Inner History*, p. 225; *Jahrbuch des Völkerrechts* (1914), ii, 44.

[14] Reports as to the inscription of the placard vary. Giesl cites it as being, "Oesterreichischer Minister des Auessern"; Hubka as, "Wiener Diplomatie"; Miss Durham as, "Neue Freie Presse" (Giesl, *Zwei Jahrzehnte*, p. 317; Hubka, "Kritische Tage in Montenegro," *Berliner Monatshefte*, IX (1931), 35; Durham, *Struggle for Scutari*, p. 277). All three of these witnesses were in Cetinje at that time.

a day of Slav rejoicing. Governmental sympathy was not in all cases so wholehearted. In Belgrade particularly, the Austrian minister noted that the Serbian officials were far from elated at Montenegro's single-handed victory.[15]

The brilliance of the Montenegrin victory has been questioned. Certain it is that Scutari did not capitulate before an assault, but after negotiations. Essad Pasha, apparently, made a bargain with Nikita (and Serbia?) to become king of the new Albania in return for surrendering Scutari to Montenegro.[16] On the other hand, it is true that the Turkish troops were faced with a shortage of ammunition.[17] All accounts testify to the lack of food within the city.[18] People were dying of starvation at the rate of thirty to forty a day. On April 22nd Essad called together a conference of notables of Scutari. They all agreed — Mohammedans and Christians — that he must surrender.[19] The step was more than justified, although Essad may well have taken advantage of Nikita's impatience to secure favorable terms for himself. To surrender to King Nikita brought compensations; to surrender to the powers brought nothing. Essad, who was every inch an adventurer, naturally chose the former.

The Montenegrin army entered Scutari on April 24th, and proceeded to take over the government of the city. In the late afternoon the Turkish troops marched off to Tirana. The powers now had the task of prying the Montenegrins out of Scutari.

Berchtold at once notified the other powers that they must make good their word, or Austria would see to it herself that

[15] Ö-U.A., VI, no. 6735.

[16] B.D., IX, ii, 734 ed. note, no. 1071; Izvolsky, III, nos. 847, 856; S.D., I, nos. 298, 299; Durham, *Struggle for Scutari*, p. 277; Giesl, *Zwei Jahrzehnte*, p. 243; D.D.F., 3d. ser., VI, nos. 377, 400, VII, no. 535. From a secret source the French foreign office heard that the secret transactions between Essad Pasha, the King of Montenegro, and the Serbian government had been conducted in clandestine fashion by the Russian consul at Scutari (*ibid.*, VI, no. 482).

[17] Karl Egli, *Drei Monate vor Skutari* (Bern, 1913), p. 131; Hubka, "Kritische Tage in Montenegro," *Berliner Monatshefte*, IX (1931), 34.

[18] Durham, *Struggle for Scutari*, p. 280; Zambaur, *Belagerung von Skutari*, pp. 176 ff.; Egli, *Drei Monate vor Skutari*, pp. 140 ff.

[19] Zambaur, *Belagerung von Skutari*, p. 187.

King Nikita respected the decisions of the powers in regard to Northern Albania. He suggested landing detachments or bombardment of several coastal cities.[20] Now that Scutari had fallen, he could not consider financial compensations to Nikita until all Montenegrin troops were definitely withdrawn.

At London the ambassadors did not wait for any prodding, but held an extra meeting. They agreed that a note should be sent to Cetinje, informing King Nikita that the capture of Scutari had not altered the situation. He should turn the city over to the commander of the international fleet. Berchtold at once agreed to this action, but pressed for a discussion as to what measures should be taken if the note brought no results. Only if the powers decided at once what they would do in that case, would Austria refrain from starting independent action.[21]

Sazonov, who had been slow to join in the first place, now thought the capture of Scutari altered conditions. He requested Pichon and Grey to take the initiative in demanding territorial, as well as financial, compensations for Montenegro.[22] This they refused to do, and in the end Sazonov agreed to join the other powers in making a collective *démarche* at Cetinje. Further coercive measures he would not agree to, nor did he feel able to give French statesmen public authorisation to join any disciplinary action, as he had done in the case of the naval demonstration. It would arouse public opinion too much. He recommended that France and England should go ahead with the central powers, while Russia must remain aloof.[23]

San Giuliano might easily have been won over to additional compensations, but Berchtold was immovable. This question, however, was not raised when the ambassadors met on April 25th, to consider what should be done if Montenegro failed

[20] Ö-U.A., VI, no. 6716; B.D., IX, ii, no. 877. Berchtold had suggested these measures also earlier, before the fall of Scutari (Ö-U.A., VI, no. 6704; B.D., IX, ii, no. 870).

[21] Ö-U.A., VI, no. 6741; see also, no. 6721.

[22] B.D., IX, ii, nos. 876, 886, 887, 892; D.D.F., 3d. ser., VI, nos. 373, 375. Pichon had replaced Jonnart at the French foreign office in March, 1913.

[23] Izvolsky, III, no. 855; B.D., IX, ii, nos. 895 minute, 911; D.D.F., 3d. ser., VI, no. 403 annexe II.

to give a satisfactory answer to the note. The Alliance favored landing some troops; the Entente opposed it. In the end the conference recommended a severer blockade and withdrawal of prospects for financial compensation.[24]

Finally by Sunday morning, April 27th, all the representatives of the powers at Cetinje had received instructions to join in presenting the note. Unable to find any one at the foreign office, they sent a copy to the home of the foreign minister. He received it, but as it happened to be Easter, tradition forbade carrying on any business. An answer could only be given after the holidays were over.[25]

In these same days Austria demanded special satisfaction and apology from the Montenegrin government in regard to two other incidents. One was the case of the Franciscan Palić, who had been arrested and shot while under the escort of Montenegrin troops.[26] The affair had been complicated by forced conversion of Catholics to Orthodoxy, and by anti-Albanian measures in general. Berchtold now made the following demands:

1. Montenegro should erect a memorial cross to Palić, and take steps to facilitate the erection of a memorial chapel which Austria was going to build. At the dedication of these, a Montenegrin officer of the rank of general or minister was to be present.
2. Montenegro should take the necessary steps to have the body removed to Zumbi. [Palić had not yet been buried according to Catholic ritual or in holy ground.] Montenegro should be officially represented at the funeral services.

[24] Ö-U.A., VI, no. 6760; B.D., IX, ii, no. 889; D.D.F., 3d. ser., VI, no. 388.

[25] De Salis to Grey, April 28, 1913, B.D., IX, ii, no. 896 enclosures; Ö-U.A., VI, no. 6788.

[26] The Montenegrin government claimed that Palić was a rebel and had been shot while trying to escape. Berchtold insisted on an investigation by the Austrian consul at Prizren and the Archbishop of Usküb. Although these men came to no definite decision, their investigation did show that the Montenegrins had not dealt according to rules of justice and had not treated the Franciscan with the special consideration due a cleric (Ö-U.A., VI, nos. 6092, 6198, 6311, 6617, 6786; Durham, *Struggle for Scutari*, p. 267).

3. Montenegro was to permit Catholics either to go to Albania or to Serbia. This was to be announced by public proclamation. [It was considered unsafe for Catholics to live in Montenegro.][27]

The other incident which led to special Austrian demands had occurred as a result of the interruption by Montenegro of all post and telegraph service between Cetinje and Cattaro on April 21st. In order to get his dispatches through, Giesl sent attaché Hubka to Cattaro in the legation automobile. Near the border a trench cut across the road made it impossible to proceed. Hubka set out on foot, but was detained by a border patrol. On the intervention of Giesl he was later permitted to complete the journey. Rocks had also been thrown at the automobile, which, if they found no other mark, at least hit the prestige of the monarchy. The Ballhausplatz now demanded an investigation and punishment of the offenders, and an official apology.[28]

These two separate moves by Austria were an added complication. In each case Montenegro delayed her answer, and then refused to meet the demands completely.[29] They became part and parcel of the Scutari question, and were not adjusted until the general settlement. On April 28th, King Nikita did make a diplomatic bid for Austrian friendship. He sounded the Austrian minister on an exchange of the Lovčen for the privilege of remaining in Scutari. These advances were sharply repulsed by Giesl, as he felt that they were but a ruse to gain time. Later the negotiations would be made known to the powers and Austrian policy pilloried.[30]

While awaiting the answer of King Nikita to their note, the

[27] Berchtold to Giesl, April 27, 1913, Ö-U.A., VI, no. 6786. Miss Durham writes: "Austria intervened sharply. Had she not done so, in the words of a Catholic refugee, 'There would not have been a Catholic left in the district'" (*Struggle for Scutari*, p. 269; see also D.D.F., 3d. ser., VI, no. 51).

[28] Ö-U.A., VI, no. 6798; D.D.F., 3d. ser., VI, no. 423.

[29] Ö-U.A., VI, nos. 6846, 6878.

[30] *Ibid.*, VI, no. 6799. For discussions in regard to a possible cession of the Lovčen in November–December, 1912 see above, p. 225.

powers continued to discuss what to do next. At the conference of ambassadors on April 28th, Mensdorff declared that unless the powers took some real measures to bring Montenegro to terms, Austria would be forced to act alone. The Triple Alliance pressed for the landing of troops, but the Entente thought this premature. Instead Grey tentatively — he lacked cabinet approval as yet — suggested informing King Nikita that the immediate evacuation of Scutari would bring him financial aid; otherwise he would be left to his fate. Fate, presumably, in this case, was Austria.[31]

In order to be prepared, Berchtold meanwhile invited Italy to undertake joint intervention in Albania if the necessity should arise. At Rome this invitation aroused little enthusiasm.[32] San Giuliano, and above all, Giolitti felt there was no need for active intervention. In view of their agreements, they however invited Berchtold to discuss with them before taking any definite action. Delay was their keynote. Finally they did agree to a parallel action if it should become necessary. Austria would operate against Scutari; Italy against Valona. Apparently the Consulta thought it best to be in possession of a forfeit in case Austria seized the Lovčen. This proposal of parallel action was not acceptable at the Ballhausplatz, although it had the backing of Germany.[33] The Entente powers were also much opposed to it, for obviously there was little reason for having armed intervention in southern Albania in order to get the Montenegrins out of Scutari.

Grey, as the go-between of the ambassadors, realised full well the seriousness of the situation. Much to Sazonov's dissatisfaction he had already announced publicly that if Montenegro did not surrender Scutari to the powers, "Great Britain would make no objection to any other power, as a last resort, taking reasonable and necessary measures to achieve the fulfillment of the agreement on Scutari to which the British government had been

[31] *Ibid.*, VI, nos. 6804, 6806.

[32] *Ibid.*, VI, nos. 6793, 6807, 6808; see also, B.D., IX, ii, nos. 897, 907; D.D.F., 3d. ser., VI, no. 427.

[33] G.P., XXXIV, ii, no. 13258; Ö-U.A., VI, no. 6915; Conrad, III, 298.

a part." [34] Sazonov was now called upon to define his line of action should Austria take the initiative.[35] He had been urging England and France to join Austria in a possible military expedition. This France refused to do without a specific public mandate from Russia, which Sazonov said he could not give. Grey refused to act without France for it might ". . . have the appearance of acting against the wishes of Russia and of separating ourselves from France. Such a position in this matter would be most repugnant to His Majesty's Government and to public opinion. . . ." [36] Sazonov, however, dallied and refused to define his policy. Grey's definite question he parried with another:

> For the present . . . Russia's attitude would be one of abstention, and they would wait on events. They were most anxious to avoid being dragged into war. They were not afraid of Austria, but Germany had also to be reckoned with, and though in such case France would support Russia it was not known what England would do, and England alone of all powers was in a position to strike a mortal . . . (blow) at Germany.[37]

By the time Grey had to answer this extremely important question, another proposal for further joint action at Cetinje had been launched. The Montenegrin minister at London had indicated that King Nikita might surrender Scutari if he were guaranteed additional "territorial compensation commensurate with his sacrifices as well as financial aid to reëstablish the economic situation of his country." [38] Seizing upon this as a means of gaining time, Grey on May 1st had persuaded the ambassadors to recommend to their government a further step at Cetinje.[39] Nikita was to be cajoled with the possibility of finan-

[34] B.D., IX, ii, no. 899, see also no. 894.

[35] *Ibid.*, IX, ii, nos. 911, 912.

[36] *Ibid.*, IX, ii, no. 920.

[37] *Ibid.*, IX, ii, no. 925.

[38] *Ibid.*, IX, ii, nos. 922, 927.

[39] B.D., IX, ii, no. 927; D.D.F., 3d. ser., VI, no. 458; Ö-U.A., VI, no. 6847. Berchtold felt that at this state of the negotiations he could not join in such action, although he would be glad if the other powers made such a proposal (*ibid.*, no. 6866; B.D., IX, ii, no. 900). The evident maneuvers for delay by the Entente powers irritated the Kaiser. He became very caustic in his utterances and felt that the only solution of the problem was in a rapid decisive action by Austria (G.P., XXXIV, ii, nos. 13252 notes, 13254).

cial aid if he surrendered at once. Failure to do so would forfeit all claims to compensations and eventually he would be forced to leave the city anyway. There was to be no mention of territorial compensation, something Russia continually proposed during these days.

This new proposal for united action made it somewhat easier for Grey to answer Sazonov's question as to what England would do if war broke out. After instructing the English ambassador to urge immediate action at Cetinje, Grey stated:

> If all this fails there is no alternative but some forcible measure to give effect to decision of powers. The British Government cannot go further in this direction without France, and France will not move without mandate from Russia, which minister of foreign affairs says he cannot give. All that we can work for therefore will be to secure that whatever action Austria takes should be as little provocative as possible to Russian opinion. I see no chance of Austria giving territorial compensation to Montenegro. Whenever Austria takes separate action I shall have to explain attitude of British Government in Parliament. . . . I shall endeavour to make any statement of mine not inconsistent with anything that Russian minister of foreign affairs may have to say, but I want him to realise the impossibility of taking objection to action of Austria if it be really taken only in last resort, and is limited to securing evacuation by measures as little harsh as possible.[40]

This was a polite but clear cut assurance that Montenegro's goose was cooked; that Great Britain would not oppose separate Austrian action, let alone considering it a possible *casus belli*.

The Montenegrin answer of April 30th to the collective note of the powers showed that the Lord of the Black Mountains had no intention of heeding their summons.[41] In Vienna things were slowly coming to a head. On April 29th "Volle Kriegsbereitschaft" for Bosnia-Herzegovina-Dalmatia was decreed.[42] Papers began to talk more and more of separate Austrian action.[43] On May 2nd, a ministerial council was held, attended

[40] Grey to Buchanan, May 2, 1913, B.D., IX, ii, no. 934.

[41] *Ibid.*, IX, ii, no. 914 enclosure; Ö-U.A., VI, no. 6825.

[42] Ö-U.K.A., Zu Abt. 10, no. 400 res. von 1914, Beilage I.

[43] *Die Zeit*, April 29, 30, May 1, 3, 4, 1913; *Fremdenblatt*, May 1, 3, 4, 1913; see also, B.D., IX, ii, no. 904.

by the three common ministers, and by the minister-presidents and finance ministers of Hungary and Austria. Berchtold gave a short résumé of foreign policy, pointing out that Scutari was the key of Austria's Balkan policy. It was essential to an Albanian state. Besides, it had become a question of prestige, and Austria's demands would have to be met in one way or another. Just what course events would take it was impossible to say, but the following were possibilities.

1. The ambassadorial conference might decide at the last moment on some effective international coercive measure.
2. Italy might coöperate in spite of the onerous restrictions it placed in regard to military matters.
3. Austria might take independent action against Montenegro.

Much also hinged upon the action of King Nikita, and upon whether complete occupation of Albania should prove necessary. "This much," Berchtold concluded, "is certain, we must figure with the possibility — not to say probability — of a conflict with Montenegro, in the course of which the intervention of its sister state, Serbia, must be considered." [44]

A general discussion followed. Krobatin, and especially Bilinski, advocated military measures against both Serbia and Montenegro. They felt nothing else was left for the monarchy but war. As supervisor of Bosnia, Bilinski felt the necessity of a manifestation of strength by the monarchy. The Austrian ministers — Stürgkh and Zaleski — both advocated independent action by the monarchy. The Hungarian ministers — Lukacs and Teleszky — on the other hand, were opposed to anything which might lead to war or separate Austro-Hungarian action. Berchtold expressed his regret that there was so little desire for joint action with Italy.

In view of the demands of Potiorek (governor of Bosnia-Herzegovina), and of the additional weight they would give to

[44] Ö-U.A., VI, no. 6870.

Austrian diplomatic steps the following measures were decided upon.

1. Calling in of the "Nichtaktiven" of the first, second, and third reserve.
2. Financial authorisation for the purchase of horses up to war footing (12.9 millions).
3. Authorisation of five millions for defense of Cattaro.
4. Financial authorisation for the upkeep of the purchased horses.

The calling in of the "Landsturm" in Dalmatia was postponed in view of the objections of the Austrian minister-president. He feared the general economic disruption which this measure would cause.[45] In regard to these decisions, the official survey of the military measures taken by the monarchy during the Balkan crisis states:

> With the calling in of all "Nichtaktiven" in Bosnia and Herzegovina on May 3rd, the last step was taken for the attainment of complete "Kriegsbereitschaft" in Bosnia-Herzegovina-Dalmatia. Mobilisation was in full swing, even if it was not so labelled.[46]

Giesl was instructed to make preparations for turning over the Austrian legation to the German minister.[47] In Cetinje the rumor spread that Austria was about to send troops across the border. A sudden panic hit the Montenegrin government and there were long conferences in the king's palace. There was no new collective *démarche*, but all the representatives of the powers, each in his own way, worked on the Montenegrin government to surrender before the Austrian government presented

[45] *Ibid.*; Conrad, III, 294. Potiorek as early as December wanted to call in all the "Nichtaktiven" in order to remove them from the influence of Pan-Serb agitators (Potiorek to Bilinski, Dec. 17, 1912, Ö-U.K.A., K. & K. Armeeinspektor in Sarajevo, Res. no. 7185).

[46] Darstellung der anlässlich der Balkankrise 1912/13 getroffenen militärischen Massnahmen, Ö-U.K.A., Zu Abt. 10, no. 400 res. von 1914, p. 86.

[47] Reference to such instructions are apparently lacking in either the German or Austrian documents or in Conrad's memoirs. However see, Giesl, *Zwei Jahrzehnte*, p. 247; Hubka, "Kritische Tage in Montenegro," *Berliner Monatshefte*, IX (1931), 35.

a summons.[48] Count de Salis, the English minister, spoke as clearly and no doubt as effectively as any of them, when he said:

> Austria is on the point of taking separate action. She may do so immediately unless Montenegro complies with the representation of the powers already made. . . . If Montenegro complies peaceably with the demand of the powers to evacuate Scutari she will obtain some economic assistance, which has already been favorably considered by the powers. If she continues to resist she will certainly be expelled from Scutari by force, she must abandon all hope of economic assistance afterwards and the consequences will be most disastrous. This is the real alternative.[49]

On May 3rd, Crown Prince Danilo asked the German representative to influence Giesl to have the Austrian military measures delayed for forty-eight hours. The ministry had resigned and the new ministry would agree to the demands of the powers the next day. Giesl submitted this request to Vienna, but at the same time asked that an ultimatum be presented to Montenegro at once.[50] It should demand satisfaction in regard to Scutari, and also in regard to the incidents of Palić and of the military attaché.

Whether this ultimatum should be sent or not was discussed in a ministerial council at Vienna on May 4th.[51] The news had arrived that King Nikita had agreed to evacuate Scutari. Therefore, Berchtold was against an ultimatum. Yet the consensus of opinion in the council was otherwise, and he was requested to ask His Majesty to sanction a summons to Montenegro. This Francis Joseph refused to do. Instead of the ultimatum Berchtold sent a warning telegram.[52] Montenegro might still escape a direct summons from Austria, if she acted quickly. At the same time he informed Giesl not to complicate the evacuation of Scutari by stressing the two other minor Austrian grievances.

[48] Giesl to foreign office, May 6, 1913, Ö-U.A., VI, no. 6932.

[49] Grey to De Salis, May 1, 1913, B.D., IX, ii, no. 923; see also no. 947.

[50] G.P., XXXIV, ii, no. 13266; Ö-U.A., VI, nos. 6873, 6932; Giesl, *Zwei Jahrzehnte*, p. 247.

[51] No report on this council is to be found in the Austrian documents, but see Conrad, III, 297–8.

[52] Berchtold to Giesl, May 4, 1913, Ö-U.A., VI, no. 6888; Conrad, III, 298.

In the early evening hours of May 4th King Nikita communicated his decision to evacuate Scutari to the English minister at Cetinje. The capitulation — largely the wording of Count de Salis — was as follows:

> My government has explained in its note of April 30th the reasons for its position in the question of Scutari. This position conforms to the established principles of justice. I affirm once more, with my people, our right consecrated by history and by conquest. My dignity, as well as that of my people not allowing me to submit to an isolated summons, I entrust the fate of the city to the hands of the powers.[53]

The news of the surrender was published in the papers on May 5th. At the same time the Montenegrin government notified Giesl that it would meet all the Austrian demands in regard to the Palić and military attaché incidents.[54]

The crisis was broken, and the bourse immediately took an upward trend.[55] In Vienna Berchtold breathed a sigh of relief, and rejoiced that events had taken a peaceful turn.[56] Conrad was not so happy. He regarded it as another lost opportunity for assuring the future of the monarchy.[57] The military measures which had been put into operation in Bosnia-Herzegovina were countermanded. On May 7th Potiorek was ordered to stop buying horses, requisitioning transport material, etc. The next day the reserves which had been called to the colors on May 3rd were dismissed.[58]

On May 14th detachments were landed from the international fleet, and the government of Scutari passed to the hands of the

[53] De Salis to Grey, May 4, 1913, B.D., IX, ii, no. 948.

[54] Ö-U.A., VI, nos. 6890, 6891.

[55] As had been the case in October, 1912 King Nikita was charged with having used the political crisis to recoup his fortune on the stock market (G.P., XXXIV, ii, nos. 13276, 13340; S.D., I, no. 304; see above, pp. 141–45).

[56] G.P., XXXIV, ii, no. 13272. At the British foreign office Nicolson, by no means an Austrophile, thought Berchtold had "throughout shown very great patience and forbearance" (Private letter Nicolson to Cartwright, May 13, 1913, B.D., IX, ii, no. 972).

[57] G.P., XXXIV, ii, no. 13276; Conrad, III, 298 ff.

[58] Darstellung der anlässlich der Balkankrise 1912/13 getroffenen militärischen Massnahmen, Ö-U.K.A., Zu Abt. 10, no. 400 res. von 1914, p. 86; also see below, Appendix, I, pp. 461–62.

powers.[59] The same day the Montenegrin troops trailed over the wooden Boyana bridge, and sought their homes beyond the Tarabosh.

Not only Austria-Hungary but Europe had been spared a war. Austrian military measures against Montenegro would almost inevitably have been extended to the Sanjak. In that case Serbia might well have lived up to her repeated threats to attack the Austrian forces. In view of the tension which had developed in Serbian-Bulgarian relations it is questionable if Bulgaria would have lived up to the terms of the alliance treaty. Bulgaria was busy enough garrisoning Macedonia. Sazonov had at times declared that he might countenance action against Montenegro alone, but never could sanction Austrian action against Serbia.[60] Germany, although doing everything to restrain the Austrians, had nevertheless promised to fulfill her alliance obligations. The Wilhelmstrasse had granted its sanction for Austrian action against Scutari and would no doubt have come to Austria's side had Russia intervened. Luckily events were not pushed to the extreme. There was no desire for war on the part of the supreme governing officials in Vienna. The Austrian government was manifestly only taking steps to enforce a decision agreed upon by all the powers. This Grey took every occasion to point out. While unwilling to join with Austria in forceful measures — chiefly out of a desire to maintain harmony within the Entente — Grey's unequivocal declarations that he would not oppose separate Austrian action were, through the weight they carried in Cetinje, Belgrade, and St. Petersburg, of the utmost importance in bringing about a peaceful settlement. In May, 1913 Grey felt himself standing on the firm ground of international coöperation. In July, 1914 there was no such well prepared foundation and Grey's voice did not ring so clearly, nor so effectively.

[59] The commanders of the international fleet had been authorised to negotiate the terms of surrender with King Nikita (B.D., IX, ii, nos. 952, 954, p. 786 ed. note). For the terms of the surrender see, *Zeitschrift für Internationales Recht*, XXV, 263–4. Miss Durham gives a vivid description of the Montenegrin occupation of Scutari (*Struggle for Scutari*, pp. 282–90).

[60] B.D., IX, ii, nos. 820, 928.

CHAPTER XV

THE LONDON SETTLEMENT

UNTIL the problem of Scutari was settled not much progress could be made with peace negotiations. Preparations for these had long been under way. As early as February 11th, eight days after the renewal of the war, the Turkish government had asked the powers to mediate for peace on the basis of the Turkish answer to the collective note of January 17th. Since the Balkan governments had already categorically declared the Turkish answer unacceptable, the London conference felt it was useless to base any action on it.[1] They felt, however, that a mediatory action might be undertaken on the basis of the note itself rather than the answer. In other words, this meant that Turkey must surrender the islands and Adrianople.

With the fortunes of war going against them, the cabinet dominated by the Committee of Union and Progress submitted the following declaration on February 28th to the London conference: "The Imperial Ottoman government accepts the mediation of the great powers for the purposes of establishing peace." [2] This was an unreserved acceptance of mediation by the powers. The allies were now asked if they would accept on the same terms. Flushed with the victories of October, the Balkan states were determined to repeat them. The disrupted peace negotiations had taught the lesson that it was well to conquer what one wanted to possess. Consequently on March 14th the allied states presented identical answers to the powers, in which they made numerous reservations in regard to future boundaries, the Aegean Islands, and the question of an indemnity.[3] Yet the principle of mediation was accepted, and on this the ambassadors started to build.

[1] Ö-U.A., V, no. 5761; B.D., IX, ii, nos. 602 minute, 609.

[2] Ö-U.A., V, no. 5981; B.D., IX, ii, no. 668; D.D.F., 3d. ser., V, no. 480.

[3] Ö-U.A., V, nos. 6157, 6158; B.D., IX, ii, nos. 713, 715; D.D.F., 3d. ser., V, no. 587.

The next step was to draw up a basis for negotiations, and the following formula was decided upon:

1. The frontier of European Turkey will start at Enos, follow the course of the Maritza to the Ergene, and hence to Midia. All territories to the west of this line will be ceded by Turkey to the allies, with the exception of Albania, the delimitation and government of which are reserved to the powers.
2. The question of the islands of the Aegean will be left to the decision of the powers.
3. Turkey will divest itself completely of any interest in Crete.
4. The powers can not favor a demand for indemnity, but they will admit the allies to take part at the discussions of the international commission at Paris, for the equitable regulation of their participation in the Ottoman debt, and the financial charges of the territories which will be attributed to them. Turkey will likewise be invited to take part at the deliberations of this commission.
5. From the acceptance of this basis of peace preliminaries the hostilities ought to end.[4]

After being approved by the various cabinets this statement of peace preliminaries was jointly presented at the Balkan capitals on March 22nd, and in Constantinople on March 31st. The French and Russian representatives, as was customary in joint *démarches* at this period, were always the last to obtain their instructions and delayed the presentation of the notes.[5]

While the Turkish government accepted the conditions for peace set forth by the ambassadors immediately,[6] it took the allies two weeks to negotiate a reply. Only on April 5th, the day

[4] D.D.F., 3d. ser., VI, nos. 2, 31; Ö-U.A., V, no. 6163; G.P., XXXIV, ii, no. 13014 Anlage; B.D., IX, ii, no. 749 enclosure.

[5] Ö-U.A., VI, no. 6462; G.P., XXXIV, ii, no. 13014; B.D., IX, ii, nos. 759, 764, 767; D.D.F., 3d. ser., VI, nos. 89, 138, 158.

[6] Bompard to Pichon, April 1, 1913, D.D.F., 3d. ser., VI, no. 147; see also, no. 141.

on which the combined fleet of the powers appeared off the shores of Montenegro, was the answer of the allies at hand. They wanted the islands to be ceded directly to themselves without intervention of the powers; to be informed beforehand what the boundaries of Albania were to be; and, above all, they laid claim to an indemnity.[7] Russia was willing to satisfy the last claim, at least in some measure, but it was opposed by the other powers, notably England and Germany. Since the ambassadors at London felt that these reservations could not be entirely accepted, a new note was necessary. There was the customary delay and it was not until April 13–16th that the second joint note was delivered at the various Balkan capitals. This stated that the disposition of the islands would have to be left to the decision of the powers; that the Albanian boundaries would be announced as soon as they were established; and that all financial questions must be reserved for the commission at Paris where the Balkan states would have representation.[8]

But the allies were not disposed to accept these terms without a protest. They replied on April 21st:

> . . . In their sincere desire to aid and bring to a successful conclusion the proffered mediation, the allied states, beseeching the powers anew to maintain a benevolent attitude towards the principle of a war indemnity, declare that they accept this mediation, reserving for themselves in the course of the negotiations the right to discuss with the great powers the questions pertaining to the islands and the definitive limitation of the frontiers of Thrace and of all Albania.[9]

The powers considered the answer an "acceptance of the bases of peace" formulated by the ambassadors at London, although they notified the allies that they could not admit any discussion of the islands or the Albanian frontier. Since Turkey had already accepted the terms without reservation the powers now collectively "invited the belligerents to cease hostilities im-

[7] Deville to Pichon, April 5, 1913, *ibid.*, VI, no. 200; see also, Ö-U.A., VI, no. 6472; B.D., IX, ii, no. 808.

[8] Ö-U.A., VI, no. 6514; D.D.F., 3d. ser., VI, no. 241; B.D., IX, ii, nos. 816, 846 note. A statement on the northern and northeastern boundary of Albania was submitted to the Balkan states on April 14–18th (*ibid.*, nos. 846 note, 847).

[9] B.D., IX, ii, no. 867; D.D.F., 3d. ser., VI, no. 348.

mediately and to designate their plenipotentiaries and the place where the peace conference was to be held." [10] The suspension of hostilities then in force for a ten day period was continued.[11] But the allies, quarrelling among themselves, were none too quick to respond to this invitation to a peace conference. It was not until the middle of May that the peace delegates reached London.

In order to facilitate the conclusion of peace, Grey at the request of the Bulgarian minister had a draft treaty worked out.[12] It incorporated the general principles of settlement which had been accepted by Turkey and the allies. The English draft was worked over by Cambon, and the French version was submitted to the conference on May 5th.[13] Berchtold would have preferred one or two slight changes, but did not insist when the ambassadors expressed a reluctance to tamper with the text. It had already been submitted to the Balkan states, and one change would surely call for another.

By this time the Scutari crisis had passed and the ambassadors took a well-earned holiday of twelve days. When they reassembled on May 20th various requests for a change in the wording of the draft treaty were made by the Balkan peace delegates. None of the changes were of fundamental importance, and the ambassadors agreed to the following resolution, proposed by Grey:

> The powers feel that a discussion on the modification of the treaty would inevitably lead to delays, and they express the hope that Turkey and the allies will arrive as soon as possible at an accord on the conclusion of peace.[14]

Despite the advice of all the great powers, the peace delegates continued to delay about coming to an agreement. Bulgaria and Turkey were ready to sign; the others were not.[15]

[10] Resolution of the London conference, April 23, 1913, Ö-U.A., VI, no. 6724.
[11] See above, p. 308. [12] B.D., IX, ii, nos. 899 note, 927 note, 967 note.
[13] D.D.F., 3d. ser., VI, nos. 479, 501; Ö-U.A., VI, no. 6936; G.P., XXXIV, ii, no. 13279.
[14] B.D., IX, ii, no. 985; Ö-U.A., VI, no. 7082; D.D.F., 3d. ser., VI, no. 569.
[15] Ö-U.A., VI, nos. 7037, 7063, 7128.

Meanwhile conditions in Macedonia were becoming more critical every hour. Rumors of fighting between Bulgarians and Serbians, and between Bulgarians and Greeks reached Europe. On May 23rd, an alarm telegram from Queen Sophie of Greece (sister of the Kaiser) reached Berlin. Bulgarian troops were encroaching on the neutral zone which had been established between the Greek and Bulgarian armies. The situation was very bad, and she feared an armed conflict would develop.[16] The Tsar of Russia and the King of England were in Berlin at that moment, as guests of honor at the marriage of Princess Victoria Luise to Duke Ernst August of Braunschweig and Lüneburg. William II discussed the telegram with his fellow sovereigns. The three rulers had little sympathy or liking for their colleague at Sofia. In agreement with William II and George V, Tsar Nicholas on May 24th dispatched a warning telegram to King Ferdinand. Should war result from the invasion of the neutral zone by Bulgarian troops, the responsibility would rest on Bulgaria. At the request of the tsar, the Kaiser sent a similar telegram the next day.[17]

In London the negotiations made little progress. Greece more than any other power delayed proceedings. Venizelos felt that he could not sign the treaty without some assurance that he would be able to discuss the question of Albania and the Aegean Islands with the powers.[18] On May 27th Grey, who was getting impatient over all the haggling, received all the chief delegates (except the Montenegrins) individually at the foreign office. In very plain words he told each one that the powers wanted the peace preliminaries signed. The delegates had been in London over a week now, and were no farther along than when they started. This could go on no longer. If they did not intend to sign, they might just as well leave London.[19]

The ultimatum, "sign or leave," had a salutary effect. The

[16] G.P., XXXIV, ii, no. 13331; D.D.F., 3d. ser., VI, nos. 616, 635.

[17] For the text of the tsar's and Kaiser's telegrams see, G.P., XXXIV, ii no. 13331 and note; see also, B.D., X, ii, no. 476.

[18] B.D., IX, ii, nos. 984, 1004; D.D.F., 3d. ser., VI, nos. 524, 548, 565.

[19] B.D., IX, ii, nos. 1003, 1006; Ö-U.A., VI, no. 7168.

delegates got in touch with their home governments at once, and on May 30, 1913 the preliminaries of peace were signed. The text was identical with the draft drawn up by Cambon and laid before the ambassadorial conference on May 5th. In summary the treaty provided:

I. After the formal ratification of the treaty there shall be perpetual peace and amity between the contracting parties.

II. Turkey shall cede to the allies all Turkish territory on the mainland of Europe situated west of a line drawn from Enos to Midia, and this boundary shall be delimited by an international commission.

III. The delimitation of Albania, and all other questions relating to Albania, shall be left to the powers.

IV. Turkey shall cede to the allies the island of Crete, and shall renounce in their favor all her sovereign and other rights in the island.

V. The contracting parties shall leave the powers to decide the fate of all the Turkish islands situated in the Aegean, with the exception of Crete and the peninsula of Mount Athos.

VI. The contracting parties shall leave to the international commission, which is to meet in Paris, the settlement of the financial questions arising out of the recent war and out of the consequent redistribution of territory.

VII. Questions relating to prisoners of war, jurisdiction, nationality, and commerce shall be settled by special conventions.

VIII. The treaty shall be ratified as soon as possible.[20]

Peace was at last restored between the allies and Turkey. The First Balkan War was at an end. It was now the task of the Balkan states to divide the spoils of victory.

[20] As summarised by the London *Times*, May 30, 1913 and reprinted in Rankin, *Inner History*, pp. 515–16; for full text of the treaty see B.D., IX, ii, 1049–51; D.D.F., 3d. ser., VI, no. 479, see also no. 648; *Jahrbuch des Völkerrechts* (1914), II, 46–7; Martens, *Traités*, 3d. ser., VIII, 16–19.

In announcing to the ambassadors' conference the signature of the Preliminaries of London, Grey stated that three questions remained which were in the competence of the ambassadors' conference. These were (1) the organisation of a government for Albania, (2) the delimitation of the southeastern and southern boundary of Albania, (3) the future status of the Aegean Islands.[21] When these problems were settled he proposed that the conference should be adjourned. In the past the ambassadors had not devoted much time to these matters. Now they prepared to tackle them in earnest.

The establishment of an independent Albania being due to the initiative of Austria and Italy, the ambassadorial conference at its first meeting (December 17, 1912) charged the representatives of these two powers with the task of drawing up a project of government for the future state.[22] In the intervening months, desultory negotiations on this subject had been carried on between Vienna and Rome. By the beginning of April a draft statute had been worked out. It provided for an independent neutralised state, a gendarmerie in charge of officers from one of the smaller states of Europe, and an international commission which should work out a judicial system for the state. The capitulations should continue in force for the time being. The prince, who was to head the state, was to be nominated by Austria and Italy, subject to the approval of the Albanians and of the great powers.[23]

On May 8th Mensdorff and Imperiali had submitted the proposed statute of Albania to the ambassadorial conference.[24] It was not discussed, but was submitted at once to the different cabinets. When the ambassadors reassembled on May 20th, Cambon subjected the Austrian-Italian project to a severe criticism. Albania was not ready for a definite government, above

[21] B.D., IX, ii, no. 1019; Ö-U.A., VI, no. 7207; G.P., XXXIV, ii, no. 13334; D.D.F., 3d. ser., VI, no. 653.

[22] Ö-U.A., V, no. 4944; see above, pp. 251–52.

[23] Ö-U.A., VI, no. 6554 Beilage II. The provisions providing for the nominal suzerainty of the sultan were later dropped (*ibid.*, nos. 6821, 6954).

[24] Ö-U.A., VI, no. 6954; D.D.F., 3d. ser., VI, no. 520.

all no prince should be appointed. No one really knew anything about conditions in the interior. He suggested a provisional government by a commission. Since Austria and Italy had decided for gendarme officers from the smaller, and more or less neutral, states of Europe, he argued for officers from the great powers as in Macedonia in 1903.[25]

Cambon's stand nettled Berchtold and San Giuliano. They felt that he was raising unnecessary difficulties, and only trying to delay matters. Besides, Cambon's ignorance of Albanian matters did not perforce extend to them. They wanted a definite settlement of the main features of the Albanian government and no provisional arrangements.

In order to hasten the solution and also relieve himself and the ambassadorial conference of an arduous task, Grey proposed submitting the whole question to a sub-commission. Until the main outlines were agreed to, Berchtold felt it was impossible to accept this solution.[26] The discussions dragged on, and it was not until July 29th that a project for the government of Albania was finally adopted.[27] This varied somewhat from the original Austrian-Italian proposal. Albania was to be an independent neutralised state with a sovereign prince designated by the powers. The gendarmerie was to be in command of Swedish officers,[28] and an international control commission (one representative of each of the great powers and one Albanian) was to be charged with the supervision of the civil and financial administration of the country. In addition this commission was to draw up detailed projects for the organisation of all the branches of administration.

The choice of a ruler caused much discussion. Should he be a Catholic, Protestant, or Mohammedan? The Consulta was opposed to the first, the Pope to the second, while the Ballhausplatz favored a Catholic prince. In an effort to solve the prob-

[25] D.D.F., 3d. ser., VI, nos. 552, 569; Ö-U.A., VI, nos. 7085, 7096, 7169, 7298.

[26] Ö-U.A., VI, no. 7079; see also, no. 7067.

[27] *Ibid.*, VI, no. 8147; B.D., IX, ii, no. 1186; Prinz Wilhelm zu Wied, Fürst von Albanien, *Denkschrift über Albanien* (Berlin, 1917), p. 65.

[28] Dutch officers were finally chosen.

lem and at the same time to enlist the support of the Kaiser, Berchtold inquired if the latter would not appoint the future ruler. The honor was gratefully declined.[29] Instead King Carol came forward and proposed Prince William of Wied, the nephew of Carmen Sylva.[30] The prince's wife, the beautiful and ambitious Sophie of Schoenburg-Waldenburg, was instrumental in forwarding his candidacy. This seemed a happy solution. No one had anything against him, for he had never done anything to attract attention. All of the great powers were anxious to be agreeable to Rumania and King Carol's sponsorship assured the prince of success.[31] The Kaiser thought him unfitted for the task. For one thing the future ruler of Albania ought to have an independent income of such proportions that he would be able to bolster the finances of the state. This the prince lacked.[32] But all the other suggested candidates — the Duke of Montpensier, Duke William von Urach, Prince William of Sweden, Prince Karl von Hohenzollern, to name but a few — were unacceptable for far weightier reasons. The final choice was to fall on the Prince of Wied.[33]

Having borne the brunt of the burden in regard to the northern boundary, the Ballhausplatz desired Italy to take the lead in the discussions of the southern frontier. Berchtold asked San Giuliano to make suggestions.[34] The Italian chief of staff was much alarmed over the possibility of a great Greek naval base,

[29] Ö-U.A., VI, no. 6998; see also, no. 6951; B.D., X, ii, no. 475.

[30] *Ibid.*, VI, no. 7076; G.P., XXXVI, i, no. 14073; Swire, *Albania*, pp. 194 ff.

[31] Desire to win Rumanian friendship played a great part in bringing Sazonov to approve the Prince of Wied (D.D.F., 3d. ser., VIII, no. 431; R.D., I Reihe, III, no. 185).

[32] William II, *Memoirs* (New York, 1922), pp. 165–6; G.P., XXXVI, i, nos. 14065, 14073, 14076 marginal notes.

[33] The prince was notified of his choice by the powers in December, 1913. After assuring himself of a loan guaranteed by Austria and Italy he accepted the throne on February 6, 1914 (G.P., XXXVI, ii, no. 14411). His "triumphal entry" into Durazzo took place March 7, 1914. From the start he was faced with serious insurrections and revolts. In June, 1914 the powers sent battleships to Durazzo to lend support. The outbreak of the World War caused the prince to leave Albania on September 3, 1914. At Paris in 1919 there was no "principle of legitimacy" and the prince, although willing, never occupied the Albanian throne again (see, Prinz Wilhelm zu Wied, *Denkschrift über Albanien*).

[34] Ö-U.A., VI, no. 6409.

if Greece obtained complete control of the Channel of Corfu. The Consulta consequently proposed that the Albanian boundary should start at the mouth of the Kalamas, which is well towards the south of the channel. Germany, on the other hand, following a policy favorable to King Constantine, wanted the boundary to start at Cape Kephali, well beyond the northern end of the channel. In order to bring about harmony within the alliance, the Ballhausplatz proposed a compromise line.[35] It was finally agreed to start off bargaining, by proposing a line which should start at Cape Pagania, and if this did not go through, to concede the shore line up to Phtelia, a point just below Cape Stylos. More than this Italy would not grant.[36]

To the east the boundary should start at Lake Ochrida, and include Koritza. There was some uncertainty as to how the boundary should be drawn between this point and the coast. Italy was willing to grant the land of the Pindus-Wallachians to Greece. To this Berchtold objected, especially since Rumania was asking that this territory should go to Albania.[37] The two cardinal points of the Austrian-Italian proposal, however, were Cape Stylos and Koritza. Imperiali spoke of them as the pillars of Hercules.[38]

Cambon undertook to carry the burden of the opposition. Greece submitted memoranda to the conference demanding most of what has now become Southern Albania. Above all Koritza, "a predominantly Greek city," must become part of Greece.[39]

Up to the end of May the ambassadors had hardly ever discussed the southern boundary in a regular session. Grey did his best to settle the problem outside of the conference. He suggested that the task be left to a local commission. This suggestion was acceptable to the Alliance only if the main points

[35] *Ibid.*, VI, no. 6569; see also nos. 6553, 6638.

[36] *Ibid.*, VI, no. 6747.

[37] *Ibid.*, VI, nos. 7210, 7288; see also, nos. 6853, 7211, 7233. Germany favored giving this territory to Greece (G.P., XXXV, no. 13625 note).

[38] Ö-U.A., VI, no. 7334.

[39] Edith Pierpont Stickney, *Southern Albania or Northern Epirus in European International Affairs, 1912–1923* (Stanford University Press, 1926), pp. 27 ff.

of the boundary were previously settled.[40] The discussions continued throughout June and July. The question of the future status of the Aegean Islands was drawn in. Since Greece was the chief claimant in both instances, the powers thought it well to discuss "islands and boundary" together. The possibilities for bargaining were greatly increased in this way.

The Entente, as has been pointed out, stood for all the islands going to Greece.[41] San Giuliano had originally led the Alliance in opposing this policy. He wavered and the leadership passed to von Jagow. Very Grecophile in all other fields, in this question the Wilhelmstrasse sided against Greece. In the interest of Germany's policy in Asia Minor, von Jagow was determined that the islands of Imbros and Tenedos must go to Turkey.[42] They were necessary for the protection of the Straits. The other larger islands along the Asiatic coast — Mitylene and Chios — might go to Greece under special restrictions. He felt that concessions in regard to the islands should be used to bring about a settlement of the Epirus boundary.

This was the idea of all the statesmen. Concessions in one field required a fitting compensation in the other.

The whole problem of a *quid pro quo* was complicated by the fact that Italy held some of the islands which Greece wanted. Under the terms of the Treaty of Lausanne, Italy had obligated herself to return these islands to Turkey as soon as all Turkish troops had been withdrawn from Tripoli. The Alliance powers maintained that these islands were beyond the jurisdiction of the powers in the settlement of the present dispute. At times Italy, however, indicated that she might consent to turn the islands over to Greece, if some way could be found to circumvent the formal obligations of the Lausanne Treaty.[43]

[40] Ö-U.A., VI, nos. 7067, 7079.

[41] See above, p. 259. For an excellent summary by Paul Cambon of the discussions of the ambassadors about the Aegean Islands, see Cambon to Pichon, Oct. 5, 1913, D.D.F., 3d. ser., VIII, no. 265 annexe.

[42] G.P., XXXIV, ii, nos. 13293, 13305; B.D., IX, ii, no. 988. None of the powers were seriously opposed to returning these islands to Turkey.

[43] Ö-U.A., VI, nos. 6589, 6984; G.P., XXXIV, ii, no. 13305; B.D., IX, ii, no. 1060.

The outbreak of the Second Balkan War in July made the task of the powers even more difficult. Finally, Grey, ever restless to get away from London, pressed for an adjournment of the ambassadorial conference. None of the powers, however, desired to see the conference end if these questions remained unsettled.

On August 1st, Grey after previous discussion with the ambassadors individually informed the conference that he thought an agreement could be arranged on the following basis.

I. An international commission will proceed to the delimitation of the southeastern and southern boundary of Albania with instruction to incorporate Koritza, Stylos, and Saseno in Albania.

II. The Channel of Corfu shall be neutralized.

III. Greece, under certain restrictions of neutrality, shall retain possession of the isles inhabited by a majority of Greeks, and which are actually occupied by the Greek forces, with the exception of Tenedos, Imbros, and Thasos.

IV. Italy is to declare, in conformity with Article II of the Treaty of Lausanne, that as soon as the Ottoman troops and artillery are withdrawn fom Cyrenaica she will restore the islands to Turkey.

V. At the moment of final settlement the powers will decide on the fate of these islands.[44]

The different powers had various objections to make to this formulation. Berchtold wanted the work of the proposed boundary commission precisely described and elaborated a project to this end.[45] The French government wanted it understood that since Koritza and Cape Stylos were both going to Albania, Italy should cede the islands it was occupying to Greece.[46] France was motivated, of course, not only by the desire to gain favor at Athens, but also to bring Italy to evacuate the

[44] B.D., IX, ii, no. 1195; Ö-U.A., VII, no. 8166. Saseno (mentioned in point one) is a small island in the Bay of Valona and at that time belonged to Greece.

[45] Ö-U.A., VII, no. 8264; B.D., IX, ii, no. 1226.

[46] D.D.F., 3d. ser., VII, nos. 547, 556, 558; B.D., IX, ii, no. 1202.

Dodecanese. The Consulta flatly refused to surrender the islands to Greece, but gave profuse assurances about eventual evacuation.

Grey now brought pressure to hasten a decision. If there was to be a settlement it must be at once, for the last possible date for a meeting of a conference was August 11th. The following day he would have to make a statement in the house of commons, for the summer holidays were at hand. The ambassadors got down to work. They met some of Berchtold's views in respect to the boundary commission. On other points he gave way. The southern boundary was finally settled on the principles of Point I above. The whole of the ancient Kaza of Koritza, Cape Stylos, and the island of Saseno were definitely to go to Albania; a commission was to be empowered to draw a line in respect to other points somewhere between the northern line originally suggested by Venizelos to the conference and the southern line advanced by the Austrian and Italian ambassadors. The commission was to start work September 1st, complete its task by November 30th, and within a month after that, all Greek troops were to be withdrawn from Albanian territory.[47]

While Grey was as much opposed as any French statesman to Italy's retention of the Dodecanese and was quite willing to see these islands go to Greece, he felt that this problem could not be settled at this time. He therefore proposed that France should relinquish her position that these islands must definitely be promised to Greece.[48] Eventually a compromise formula was worked out incorporating the principles of Points IV and V of Grey's project of August 1st.[49] As to the islands in Greek occupation, no serious objection was raised to Point III of the above program. Germany wanted the little island of Casteloritza lying between Rhodes and Cape Chelidonia to remain under Turkish sovereignty. There were also some reservations made in regard to Thasos since it was recognised that this was part of

[47] Ö-U.A., VII, no. 8353; B.D., IX, ii, no. 1226, also Appendix V, pp. 1065–8.
[48] D.D.F., 3d. ser., VII, no. 569.
[49] Ö-U.A., VII, nos. 8333, 8334, 8351; B.D., IX, ii, 1065–8.

the Kavalla question,[50] which still hung fire. All agreed that Imbros and Tenedos, lying at the very entrance of the Dardanelles, should be returned to the sultan. No attempt was made to state what was meant by "under certain restrictions of neutrality" nor were efforts made to determine what islands were "inhabited by a majority of Greeks." Neither fools nor angels, the ambassadors preferred to tread no further. Sir Arthur Nicolson correctly summarised the situation when he wrote to Hardinge in October, 1913: "No formal decision was come to by the powers with regard to those islands in Greek occupation, though there was perhaps an understanding that the majority of them were to remain in Greek hands." [51]

Disposition of the Aegean Islands and regulation of the southern boundary of Albania were always Siamese twins. Grey thought, ". . . the inclusion in Albania of Koritza and Stylos was only agreed to on an understanding between the powers that the islands, except Tenedos and Imbros, should go to Greece." [52] Time, however, changes understandings, and negotiations during the next months were to show all too clearly that the question of the islands was still in suspense. It had been partly solved, but not settled by the ambassadors.

At the final meeting of the conference of ambassadors the Austrian representative attempted to clarify the status of Mount Athos. He pointed out that so far, the conference had been unable to settle its international character. However, an accord had been reached on the following points:

1. That Mt. Athos should have an independent and neutral autonomy.
2. The governing council should be composed of one representative from each of the twenty monasteries among which the territory of the mountain is divided.
3. This council should control a police force for the maintenance of order and should have at its command no more

[50] See below, pp. 391–95, 398.

[51] Private letter, Nicolson to Hardinge, Oct. 29, 1913, B.D., X, i, no. 59; see also, G.P., XXXVI, ii, nos. 14218, 14219.

[52] Grey to Bertie, Dec. 12, 1913, B.D., X, i, no. 91.

than two armed vessels of less than 300 tons. These were not to be equipped with torpedo tubes or guns of more than 7 cm. caliber.

4. Orthodox religious communities of all the powers should have the right of leasing land for the purpose of establishing new foundations. Such foundations, however, would have to obtain the consent of one of the twenty proprietary monasteries and abide by the ancient usages.[53]

There were two points in regard to Mt. Athos on which the powers had been unable to agree. These were (1) the establishment of a protectorate of all the Orthodox powers and (2) the formulation of a statute for the administration of the community. The Austrian ambassador recommended that these two points be reserved for future decision by the powers. None of his colleagues objected and the conference hastened to conclude its deliberations. Vacations beckoned.

No better epitaph for the ambassadors' conference of London can be written than that penned by Sir Edward Grey:

> There was no formal finish; the ambassadors were not photographed in a group; there were no votes of thanks; no valedictory speeches; they just stopped meeting. The conference had not settled anything, not even the details of the Albanian boundaries; but it had served a useful purpose. It had been something to which point after point could be referred; it had been a means of keeping all the six powers in direct and friendly touch. The mere fact that it was in existence, and that it would have to be broken up before peace was broken, was in itself an appreciable barrier against war. It was a means of gaining time, and the longer it remained in being, the more reluctance there was for it to disperse. The governments concerned got used to it, and to the habit of making it useful. When the conference ceased to meet, the danger to the peace of Europe was over; the things that it did not settle were not threatening that peace; the things that had threatened the relations between the great powers in 1912–1913 it had deprived of their dangerous features.[54]

The ambassadors adjourned *sine die*, August 11, 1913.

[53] Account of the last meeting of the ambassadors, August 11, 1913, B.D., IX, ii, 1065–8.

[54] Passage paraphrased from Grey, *Twenty-five Years*, I, 262–3.

CHAPTER XVI

THE RUPTURE OF THE BALKAN LEAGUE

AFTER the signature of the preliminaries of peace, the Balkan delegates with the exception of Danev and Vesnić remained in London and continued their negotiations. The first question to be decided was whether "the treaty of peace should be considered as a definitive treaty or as a preliminary treaty." [1] After a great deal of discussion it was agreed that the treaty should be considered definitive and not merely preliminary. But once this decision was made it did not end matters. The treaty was patently not complete and efforts were made to draw up the special conventions envisaged by Article VII. The problems of nationality and religious cults in the ceded areas, the exchange of prisoners of war, the restoration of abrogated treaties, provision for friendly arbitration in the future, proved to be too much for the delegates to settle. On June 9, 1913, the peace conference was officially ended, the conclusion of the necessary complementary conventions being reserved for direct negotiation between the different cabinets and Turkey.[2]

This failure to come to an agreement is direct evidence of the great dissension which had arisen within the ranks of the allies. In considering the differences which finally led to the rupture of the League the positions taken by Austria-Hungary and Russia are of prime importance.

Although the Bulgarian-Rumanian boundary dispute had been technically settled at the St. Petersburg conference, it had not resulted in friendly relations between the two governments. The Ballhausplatz set itself to remedy this state of affairs. Berchtold now as formerly urged both Gueshov and Maiorescu to conclude a secret treaty by which Rumania would give Bul-

[1] Protocol, no. 13, June 6, 1913, B.D., IX, ii, 1053.

[2] See below, ch. XIX.

garia a guarantee of neutrality in return for acquisition of certain territory. King Carol had declared at various times, that if Bulgaria would cede Silistria he would be willing to enter upon such an agreement with King Ferdinand. Now that Silistria was to go to Rumania, Berchtold called these statements to the attention of the Rumanian government.[3] Maiorescu expressed his willingness to negotiate, but still felt that before Rumania could undertake any obligations, Bulgaria ought to show some further tangible signs of friendship. In short Bulgaria ought to cede more land to Rumania. He was willing to enter into discussions, and awaited an advance from Bulgaria.[4]

Knowing the demands of Rumania, the Bulgarian statesmen were not anxious to enter upon conversations. Nevertheless, Gueshov, as early as April 18, 1913, promised Tarnowski that he would instruct the Bulgarian minister at Bucharest to open negotiations.[5] Something went wrong with these advances, and word was passed to Vienna that Rumania had repulsed the bid for discussions. Inquiry was at once made at Bucharest, and Maiorescu repeated his assurances that he was ready to open discussions as soon as Bulgaria made definite advances.[6] A misunderstanding must have crept in somewhere.

Berchtold wished to assure Gueshov of Austria's friendship for Bulgaria. Tarnowski was to tell him "for his personal information only":

> Bulgaria can expect the fulfillment of her aspirations — be it by means of direct settlement with her allies, be it by means of mediation — only if she shows herself determined to put through her desiderata against her allies, and the powers are placed under the pressure of a threatening situation in the Balkans. . . . As it is, there is the possibility that the Sofia cabinet in the near future will be forced to take a stand against Serbian and Greek pretensions. For her position in this eventuality, her relationship to the Rumanian government will be a determining factor, wherefore we can not refrain from again stressing the vital interest Bulgaria has in establish-

[3] Ö-U.A., VI, no. 6630; see also V, nos. 6257, 6327, 6360, 6362, 6363.

[4] *Ibid.*, VI, nos. 6706, 6845, 6864, 6887.

[5] *Ibid.*, VI, no. 6677.

[6] *Ibid.*, VI, nos. 6732, 6740, 6770, 6864.

ing the most intimate relations possible with Rumania. . . . Bulgaria can depend upon it that should her aspirations come up for discussion either in direct negotiations with her allies or in the council of the great powers we would in every case give them our warmest support; in neither case would we agree to any definite settlement of the Balkan problems in which the interests of Bulgaria were not according to our views sufficiently considered.[7]

Berchtold regretted that Germany did not always take a favorable view toward Bulgarian aspirations. In order to overcome this opposition in Berlin he recommended that Bulgaria should pay the Kaiser some sort of military courtesy. William II had a special weakness for recognition of this kind, and it would no doubt have a good effect on Bulgarian-German relations.[8] Berchtold at this time and later did not fail to make it plain that material aid from Austria must depend on an understanding with Rumania.

Berchtold's communication had little effect on Gueshov.[9] He could not bring himself to open negotiations with Rumania. He thought that Bucharest was trying to extract a larger concession from Bulgaria by raising the specter of a Rumanian-Greek-Serbian combination. That Serbian-Greek negotiations were going on, and that these countries had even made advances to Rumania was known to Gueshov.[10] Yet he did nothing. Against Serbia and Greece alone, Bulgaria did not need the help of Austria-Hungary. If Berchtold really wanted to do something for Bulgaria he should keep Rumania from intervening in a war. He felt that if Bulgaria ever wanted to make the concessions which Rumania demanded, Rumanian neutrality could be obtained without the aid of Austria.

[7] Berchtold to Tarnowski, April 16, 1913, *ibid.*, VI, no. 6652. Later when instructing Tarnowski to call the attention of Gueshov again to this declaration Berchtold stated: "The prerequisite for our assuming such an attitude would of course be that Bulgaria pursued a purely Bulgarian policy, and also continued to take care to come to an understanding with Rumania" (May 16, 1913, *ibid.*, no. 7030).

[8] The Bulgarian statesmen were in a quandary over what act of courtesy they might show the Kaiser, but finally decided on placing a large order for military supplies in Germany (*ibid.*, VI, nos. 6713, 6949).

[9] *Ibid.*, VI, no. 6662; see also no. 6989.

[10] *Ibid.*, VI, no. 6662; B.D., IX, ii, no. 989; D.D.F., 3d. ser., VI, no. 577.

Ever since April 15th, when Bulgaria, on the urgent advice of Russia, had ended hostilities with Turkey, more cordial relations existed between St. Petersburg and Sofia. About the beginning of May, Tarnowski became thoroughly disgusted with Gueshov and his pro-Russian attitude. In a dispatch to Vienna he recommended more consideration for Rumania, since Bulgaria could absolutely not be depended upon. Gueshov would in fact try to settle the difficulties with Serbia in order to avoid making a treaty with Rumania. Only an intransigent attitude on Serbia's part might help the cause of the monarchy.[11]

Nevertheless, Berchtold did continue his Bulgarophile policy. Up to the Peace Preliminaries of London, as well as later, he repeatedly urged both cabinets to negotiate a treaty.[12] He warned Bucharest against entering an alliance with Serbia and Greece. He asked Berlin to do the same, whereupon von Jagow on May 29, 1913 sent the following telegram to the German minister at Bucharest:

> The Austro-Hungarian minister has been instructed to advise the Rumanian government against a common policy with Serbia, since by such action Rumania would perforce come into opposition with Austria-Hungary, and thereby with the policy of the Triple Alliance. The monarchy could not passively permit the formation of a great Serbia at the expense of Bulgaria. Please inform the Austro-Hungarian representative that you have similar instructions.
>
> When it happens to be convenient would you explain to the Rumanian government in a friendly way, without insisting, the above standpoint.[13]

This was weak support and well illustrates the difference of views on Balkan matters between the Ballhausplatz and the Wilhelmstrasse. Rumania in return declared that just as Austria could not tolerate a great Serbia, so Rumania could not

[11] Tarnowski to foreign office, May 4, 1913, Ö-U.A., VI, no. 6901; see also, nos. 6815, 7012, 7044.

[12] *Ibid.*, VI, nos. 6630, 6903, 6948, 6989, 7030, 7043, 7053, 7103, 7149, 7152, 7191; for a discussion of the Austro-Bulgarian negotiations after the Preliminaries of London see below, pp. 370–79.

[13] Jagow to Waldthausen, May 29, 1913, G.P., XXXIV, ii, no. 13343; see also, Ö-U.A., VI, nos. 7180, 7221, 7224.

tolerate a great Bulgaria.[14] This von Jagow thought logical. He felt that he could not ask King Carol to remain aloof at the moment when a Serbian-Bulgarian conflict would make it possible for Rumania to realise her aspirations. To do so would drive Rumania into the arms of Russia.

If Rumania [von Jagow concluded] is to remain neutral in an eventual Serbian-Bulgarian conflict, then, according to my opinion, Austria-Hungary must at least see to it that Bulgaria promises territorial compensations — possibly a surrender of territory up to Balchik — to Rumania. Otherwise Austria-Hungary can not possibly demand that Rumania sacrifice her vital interests.[15]

Berchtold continued to do his best to influence the cabinet at Sofia to make the necessary concessions to gain a Rumanian alliance. But the Russophile Gueshov-Danev cabinet were not to be influenced; they would not change the orientation of Bulgarian policy. They trusted to Russia to prevent an attack on Bulgaria by Serbia, and saw no need of buying Rumanian neutrality for the future.

While Austria was trying to break up the Balkan League, and to win Bulgaria for the Triple Alliance, Russia was doing her best to keep the League together. News of the interallied difficulties and squabbles caused great concern in St. Petersburg.[16] Serbia, towards the end of February, had formally demanded of Bulgaria a revision of the territorial provisions of the alliance.[17] This was of course refused. The dispute continued. In order to find a way out, Sazonov on April 30th, sent the following declaration to the Russian ministers at Belgrade and Sofia.

. . . Without entering into any discussion as regards the substance of their quarrel, on which we are anxious to preserve the most absolute impartiality towards either side, we deem it our duty to remind them of a stipulation in the Serbian-Bulgarian treaty which cannot

[14] Ö-U.A., VI, no. 7153; G.P., XXXIV, ii, nos. 13346, 13348.

[15] Jagow to Szögyény, May 30, 1914, G.P., XXXIV, ii, no. 13348.

[16] See the telegrams quoted in Gueshoff, pp. 75–80; Izvolsky, III, nos. 823, 824; *Zeitschrift für Internationales Recht*, XXV, 149–61.

[17] S.D., I, no. 278; *Doklad*, I, 405–8.

lose its force, whatever system of interpretation be adopted, viz., that every dispute concerning the interpretation or the application of the treaty and the military convention must be submitted to the arbitration of Russia, as soon as one of the sides declares that it is impossible to attain agreement by direct negotiations.

Without waiting for the request of either party, which would denote an extreme tension between them, Russia leaves it to the two allied governments to inform her in due time that all disagreements will be settled in the way indicated by the treaty and not by armed force.[18]

Pašić in his reply spoke of his friendship for Bulgaria and his desire to negotiate an understanding directly with her. To suggest that the treaty be reëxamined in view of changed circumstances did not mean it was being torn up. If negotiations were unsuccessful, nothing remained but to have Russian arbitration, which he accepted.[19] Gueshov was favorable to arbitration, and in answer to a direct inquiry Sazonov assured him that "at the first request of either party Russia was ready to accept the office of arbiter." [20]

This did not mean that the dispute was to be submitted forthwith to the arbitration of Russia. Yet it did encourage the Bulgarian statesmen to believe that Russia would see to it that a peaceful settlement was brought about. This seemed to justify the Rumanian policy of the Gueshov-Danev cabinet as the following statement from an official Bulgarian apology shows.

In the belief that the arbitration of the Russian Emperor would solve the Serbian-Bulgarian differences, and that a general arbitration of the Entente would in the same manner regulate the Bulgarian-Greek difference, the Sofia Cabinet concluded that the support of Rumania was unnecessary and refused all further concession.[21]

While Bulgaria's relations with Serbia and Greece grew constantly worse, day by day Serbia and Greece drew closer together. As early as January 1913 Crown Prince Alexander of Serbia and Prince Nicholas of Greece had entered upon some

[18] Gueshoff, p. 77; D.D.F., 3d. ser., VI, no. 449.
[19] Hartwig to Sazonov, *Zeitschrift für Internationales Recht*, XXV, 151.
[20] *Ibid.*, XXV, 152; Gueshoff, pp. 78–9.
[21] *The Bulgarian Question*, p. 88.

conversations in Salonica in regard to an alliance in case Bulgaria attacked either of her allies.[22] This was before the resumption of hostilities against Turkey, and Venizelos was still in London marking time at the peace conference. Informed of these conversations he advised maintaining great reserve, but agreed to stop off at Belgrade on his return and talk things over with Pašić. In a crown council on April 19/May 2nd the Greek authorities definitely decided to negotiate an alliance with Serbia. Under pressure of repeated reports of skirmishes with Bulgarian forces in Macedonia, Serbia and Greece on April 22/May 5th signed a protocol providing for a common policy in respect to Bulgaria.[23] Greece and Serbia were to divide all territory west of the Vardar and to have a common frontier. On May 1/17th as a supplement to the protocol a preliminary military convention was signed *ad referendum*.[24] These two agreements show how great the rift in the Balkan League had become at the time of the May peace negotiations in London. On June 1st, the day after the peace treaty with Turkey was signed, Greece and Serbia gave final form to their agreement by concluding an alliance treaty with a confidential annex and a military convention with secret additional declarations. In these agreements Serbia and Greece decided how the future boundaries in the Balkans were to be drawn. As it was recognised that the great powers were going to decide on the frontiers of Albania they limited themselves to dividing this future state into Greek and Serbian spheres of influence. In regard to Macedonia the "principle of effective occupation" was to be followed.[25]

[22] A. F. Frangulis, *La Grèce et la crise mondiale* (2 vols.; Paris, 1926), I, 97–101.

[23] For the text of this agreement see, B.D., IX, ii, 1019–20.

[24] *Ibid.*, IX, ii, 1022–3. This convention was never ratified but was replaced by the military convention of May 19/June 1, 1913 (*ibid.*, pp. 1023–26).

[25] The provisions in regard to Albania were incorporated into a "Declaration confidentielle annexe au traité d'alliance et d'amitié" (Driault and Lhéritier, V, 120; see also, B.D., X, i, no. 20; Ö-U.A., VII, 8908). This declaration is not among the Greek-Serbian agreements given in *The Greek White Book. Diplomatic Documents, 1913–1917*, trans., Theodore P. Ion (New York, n. d.; French ed. Paris, 1918), pp. 20–31; B.D., IX, ii, 1018–1026.

Two contingencies were provided for: (1) if the territory was partitioned peacefully; (2) if a war with Bulgaria should arise. In the treaty of alliance those boundaries were sketched which were to be insisted upon if the dispute were settled by negotiation or arbitration. There was to be a common Serbian-Greek frontier from Lake Ochrida extending a little south of Monastir to the Vardar at Ghevheli. From here, the Serbian-Bulgarian frontier was to extend up the left bank of the Vardar to the confluence of the Bojimia-Dere where it was to bend eastward to the old Bulgarian frontier. From Ghevheli the Greek-Bulgarian frontier was to extend to the southeast leaving the entire Chalcidicean peninsula to Greece. If Bulgaria refused to settle on these lines and arbitration became impossible then the allies bound "themselves solemnly to afford assistance to each other with all their armed forces and not to conclude peace subsequently except jointly and together" (Art. V of treaty). In this contingency the military convention provided the future boundary settlement. This naturally was mutually more generous. From the Vardar west the boundary was to be the same as foreseen in the treaty. To the eastward, however, they extended their shares by simply drawing a line from the Vardar to Perelik. Serbia was to have "the right to occupy definitively and to annex the country lying to the north and the northwest of the said line"; Greece all the territory to the south and east (Art. VII of the military convention). In addition Serbia was to have the right of occupying a ten-kilometer corridor to the sea to the north of Xanthi and on the left shore of the Nesto-Mesta. Greece, however, was guaranteed free passage through the corridor, and her right to be sole claimant to the territory to the east was recognised.[25a]

The boundaries as laid down by the military convention which the Greek minister of foreign affairs insisted "shall constitute the eventual frontier between Greece and Serbia" [26] left very little to Bulgaria. They did not presage a rapid conclusion

[25a] See map facing p. 56.
[26] *Greek White Book*, p. 41.

of peace in case of war. While each country had *carte blanche* to certain districts it would be up to each individually to occupy them. Later it did happen that Serbia was ready for peace, days before Greece had finished her conquests.

On Serbia's insistence, the final treaty of alliance of June 1st, unlike the preliminary agreement of May 5th, was phrased in general terms.[27] It was a mutual guarantee of protection against any unprovoked attack by a third party without reference solely to Bulgaria. Thus it would cover, for example, an attack on one of the allies by Austria or Turkey. The detailed provisions of the treaty and particularly of the military convention, however, show that its *raison d'être* was Bulgaria. The allies, for example, bound themselves "not to come to any special understanding with Bulgaria, to afford each other constant assistance, and to proceed always together, upholding mutually their territorial claims and the boundary lines . . . indicated" in the treaty.[28]

Not only did the Serbs and the Greeks negotiate an alliance between themselves but they sought also to recruit other allies. In the beginning of April both countries had put out feelers for a Rumanian alliance. But these advances were politely refused, since Maiorescu like Gueshov believed that Greece and Serbia were only using the bugaboo of Rumanian negotiations to bring pressure on Bulgaria.[29] After all there might be a compromise settlement of the Turkish booty and then the Balkan League would unite more firmly than ever against Rumania. Until war actually broke out between Greece, Serbia and Bulgaria, Maiorescu thought it advisable to keep his hands free. Advances from Athens and Belgrade were cordially received, but Rumania did not feel called upon to enter upon active negotiations. Maiorescu, however, did express his anti-Bulgarian attitude and his willingness to coöperate with Serbia and Greece. And yet up to the very end Greece and Serbia were not abso-

[27] Driault and Lhéritier, V, 118. That Greece was more the soliciting than the solicited power is clear from the documents printed in the *Greek White Book*.

[28] Article II of the treaty of June 1, 1913.

[29] *Rumanian Green Book*, no. 130; see also, nos. 134, 137.

lutely certain that Rumania would join with them against Bulgaria.[30]

There is little information available on the negotiations with Montenegro at this time. Here Serbia apparently took the lead and pointed out the obligations of Montenegro under the Serbian-Montenegrin alliance. As early as June 24th King Nikita informed the Austrian military attaché that he was answering Serbia's request for aid by mobilising 14,000 men.[31] The Bulgarian minister at Cetinje was not left in doubt as to Montenegro's choice if hostilities were opened. On June 27th the Montenegrin foreign minister announced that in case of war between Bulgaria and Serbia, Montenegro in accordance with alliance obligations entered upon the previous year would join Serbia.[32]

Animated by a sense of *Realpolitik*, the Serbians and Greeks each began separate negotiations with Turkey early in June, 1913.[33] Greece's first concern was to have Turkey retain a large army on the Chatalja line, as a means of bringing pressure on Bulgaria. Should Bulgaria attack its former allies, then Turkey was to be free to do what she wished in Thrace. Greece more than Serbia pushed for an alliance with Turkey.[34] Berlin, favorably inclined to the plan, was constantly kept informed of the progress of these negotiations. Various drafts of a treaty were drawn up. Among the articles, there were some promising each other mutual aid against Bulgaria. Although no definite treaty was signed at this time, the negotiations did establish a community of interest which made it easy for Turkey to intervene when the Second Balkan War broke out. In order to further

[30] On June 30, 1913 Venizelos asked the German foreign office to bring "all its authority" to bear at Bucharest in order to bring Rumania to attack Bulgaria (G.P., XXXV, no. 13438).

[31] Ö-U.A., VI, no. 7479; see also, D.D.F., 3d. ser., VII, no. 203.

[32] Kolushev to Danev, June 27, 1913, *Doklad*, I, 1137 (no. 12); see also, nos. 5, 9, 11, pp. 1135–6; Toshev, II, 320–1, 347–8; S.D., I, no. 314; B.D., IX, ii, nos. 1070, 1071; Ö-U.A., VI, no. 7478.

[33] G.P., XXXV, nos. 13374, 13379.

[34] On these negotiations see, *ibid.*, XXXV, nos. 13382, 13385, 13386, 13389, 13394, 13399, 13409, 13416, 13426, 13430, 13438.

this intervention Serbia in the opening days of that conflict sent a special delegate to Constantinople. Protests from Russia and France, together with the rapid victories over Bulgaria which lessened the value of Turkish support, stopped those negotiations short of an alliance.[35]

Besides negotiating for allies in the Balkans, Serbia and Greece did their best to ingratiate themselves with the great powers. They had always been friendly with the Entente. This policy they successfully continued. Serbia under the guidance of Pašić and Hartwig was able to keep on friendly terms with Russia in spite of her demands for additional Macedonian territory. Greece too rose more and more in favor at the court of St. Petersburg.

Greece also adroitly made advances for an agreement at Berlin. Ex-premier Theotokis, who officially notified the Kaiser of King Constantine's accession to the throne, was full of expressions of love for the Triple Alliance. If the Alliance powers would only protect Greece from Bulgaria, Greece would willingly sign a treaty with them.[36] Venizelos, however, was not prepared to tie himself by an alliance, and Theotokis's advances were not backed by the Greek foreign office.[37] Yet the Greek feelers in Berlin, Constantinople, and Bucharest pleased the German statesmen. To them it was an ideal combination, and these negotiations did much to deprive Berchtold of any effective German support in his effort to bring about a Bulgarian-Rumanian rapprochement. In Vienna, where Greece's pro-Serbian leanings were known, the advances from Athens, whether direct or via Berlin, awakened little enthusiasm.

Altogether, the Serbian and Greek statesmen were extremely clever and far-sighted. They prepared the ground well for their assault upon Bulgarian territorial aspirations. While busy with this task they assiduously carried on their diplomatic nego-

[35] On the Serbian-Turkish negotiations see, S.D., I, nos. 327–32; 337–42.

[36] G.P., XXXV, nos. 13450–52. Although King Constantine ascended the throne March 18, 1913 it was not until the middle of June that the official notification visits were made.

[37] *Ibid.*, XXXV, nos. 13455, 13466.

tiations with Bulgaria. With ends such as they had in mind (already manifested to Sofia by their policy of "de-Bulgarisation" of Macedonia) [38] these efforts could only end in failure. Meanwhile Bulgaria had been playing more or less a lone hand. Before the start of the First Balkan War she had failed to reach an agreement with Greece over a future territorial settlement.[39] On October 25, 1912 Greece had submitted a plan of partition to Bulgaria which would have reserved to Greece a population of 2,000,000 and left to Bulgaria territories inhabited by 1,300,000.[40] The statesmen at Sofia were indignant, those at Athens intractable. At the London negotiations in January, 1913 Venizelos made some advances which gave promise of conciliation. He, as well as Gueshov, was anxious to reach a settlement within the alliance. The latter was even willing to renounce Bulgaria's claim to Salonica in order to provide a basis for arbitration.[41] However, both in Athens and in Sofia other more powerful factions pressed nationalistic claims which made a friendly settlement impossible.

On May 2, 1913, through the London *Times* correspondent Bouchier, the Bulgarian government was informed that Venizelos was willing to accept as "the future Greek-Bulgarian frontier the line of lakes which form the base of the Chalcidicean peninsula, in exchange for Salonica." [42] This letter made a great impression upon the Bulgarian cabinet. They instructed the Bulgarian minister at Athens to open negotiations with Venizelos. By the time these got under way the Greek statesmen were bound by their signed agreements with Serbia. Although no longer a free agent, Venizelos nevertheless entered upon some shortlived conversations. Outwardly relations between the two countries seemed to be improved. While admitting the fact

[38] *Doklad*, I, 1193–1200.

[39] See above, p. 77. Until the alliance with Serbia of June, 1913 Greece had no formal written agreement which assured her of definite territorial annexations.

[40] Gueshoff, p. 67.

[41] *Ibid.*, p. 90; *Doklad*, I, 1149.

[42] Gueshoff, p. 108; Grogan, *Bourchier*, p. 147; see also reports of the Russian ministers at Sofia and Athens, *Zeitschrift für Internationales Recht*, XXV, 154, 156.

Prince Nicholas concluded: ". . . but it is evident alas that all measures calculated to ward off the fatal rupture could only be provisional. Indeed the antagonism between the troops had already reached such a pitch that the slightest incident would suffice to bring about a fatal collision." [43] Bad blood had existed between the two armies since the Greek troops, by a matter of a few hours, had beaten the Bulgarians to Salonica. Added to this was the fact that Greece continued to transfer as many troops as possible to Macedonia in order to garrison territories to which she laid claim. These were now coming into more and more contact with the Bulgarian forces, which were being shifted from the Chatalja lines.

Bulgarian relations with Serbia were even worse than those with Greece. Belgrade had very early shown her dissatisfaction with the settlement envisaged by the original treaty of alliance with Bulgaria. Even before the start of the war, Pašić in a circular to the Serbian representatives abroad stated that Serbia's new frontier must incorporate Prilep, Kitchevo, and Ochrida.[44] Under the terms of the alliance these towns were to go to Bulgaria.

As the Serbians arms met with one success after another, the demands for more Macedonian territory became louder and louder among the Serbian populace and especially in the army. In January, 1913, the Serbian government for the first time officially requested a redefinition of the frontier fixed by the treaty of alliance.[45] Throughout the following months the subject was discussed. Instead of nearing a settlement, relations between the allies became more bitter. Serbia based her claims largely on four points which were reiterated time after time.

1. Bulgaria by failing to send the agreed number of troops to the Vardar Valley had broken her treaty obligations and laid a heavier burden on Serbia than originally provided by their agreement.

2. Serbia had sent more troops than was provided by the

[43] Prince Nicholas of Greece, *My Fifty Years* (2nd. ed.; London, n. d.), p. 243.

[44] Gueshoff, p. 62; *Carnegie Report*, pp. 59–60.

[45] Gueshoff, p. 90.

treaty and had even sent guns and troops to help in the capture of Adrianople. Originally the boundaries had been drawn according to the supposed strength of the two countries, but the war had shown that Serbia was stronger than had been estimated.

3. At the time of the treaty it was held that Serbia would obtain territory extending to the Adriatic. The powers had now deprived Serbia of this westward expansion through the establishment of Albania, and Serbia must have fitting compensation in Macedonia. Not Serbia alone but Bulgaria as well should pay for this action of the powers.

4. Bulgaria was going to obtain far more territory in Thrace than had been anticipated. For these unexpected acquisitions — won only through the aid of Serbian arms — Bulgaria should be willing to cede some additional portions of Macedonia to Serbia.[46]

It was not difficult for the Bulgarian statesmen to refute the demands of the Serbians. Legally the Bulgarian position was strong. The arrangement between the military staffs of September 28, 1912 had relieved Bulgaria of its obligation to send 100,000 troops to the Vardar. After all, the war was to be fought jointly and Serbian aid at Adrianople like Serbian aid at Scutari was against the common enemy. When the powers forced Serbia to sacrifice her aspirations to an Adriatic port, this did not mean that they were imposing this sacrifice on Bulgaria. The powers had similarly forced Bulgaria to cede Silistria to Rumania, but Bulgaria did not ask her allies to bear this burden. As to Bulgarian acquisitions in Thrace the secret annex to the treaty of alliance definitely recognised "the right of Bulgaria to the territory east of the Rhodope Mts. and the River Struma." Danev maintained that this phrase had always been understood "as including all the region of Adrianople." [47]

[46] See the Serbian notes of Feb. 22 and May 25, 1913 (S.D., I, no. 278; *Doklad*, I, 405–8, 473–80). See also Danev's reply of June 18, 1913 (*Doklad*, I, 509–21; *The Bulgarian Question*, pp. 164–171).

[47] *The Bulgarian Question*, pp. 164–171; *Doklad*, I, 509–21; *Carnegie Report*, pp. 61–2.

Serbia's demands for more territory were not unreasonable considering the turn events had taken. Unwilling to accept the altered situation, certain Bulgarian statesmen backed by the Bulgarian populace demanded not only the territory guaranteed by the treaty to Bulgaria but all of Macedonia. Their cry, "Macedonian autonomy" which in practice meant a Macedonia united with Bulgaria, had nearly prevented the formation of the Balkan League in 1912. It now brought about its rupture.

Gueshov, unable to fulfill his policy of keeping the Balkan alliance intact by "having recourse to arbitration with Serbia and Greece," and believing war inevitable, resigned as premier on May 30, 1913.[48] Before leaving office, however, he met Pašić at Tsaribrod on June 1st, the interview having been suggested by Sazonov. At this meeting "nothing was said . . . about the revision of the treaty."[49] Gueshov advocated the publication of the alliance treaties so as to enlighten public opinion in Serbia as to their true content. Pašić naturally refused this proposal. Just before his departure for Tsaribrod he had made a public declaration to the skupština as to what the future Serbian boundaries had to be.[50] To publish the alliance treaties now would weaken his position. Much had been expected from this friendly exchange of views, but outside of deciding to hold a later meeting of all the Balkan premiers at Salonica the result was nil. In case this gathering at Salonica led to no results mention was made of resorting to arbitration by the tsar, although nothing definite was agreed upon in this respect. It is well to recall that on this very June day another Serbian official at Salonica was binding Serbia to a territorial program that was expressly directed against Bulgaria.[51]

Danev, who now became head of the government at Sofia, was obsessed by the legal rights of Bulgaria. The treaty was a treaty; its provisions were there to be fulfilled. It was patent to all that the Balkan states would never come to an agreement

[48] Gueshoff, p. 91; *Doklad*, I, 1183.
[49] Gueshoff, p. 74.
[50] B.D., IX, ii, no. 1015; D.D.F., 3d. ser., VII, no. 40; *Carnegie Report*, p. 63.
[51] See above, pp. 347–49.

among themselves without help. Russia, ever anxious to preserve intact the Balkan League, made renewed efforts to bring about a settlement. In April and again formally on May 19, 1913, Bulgaria had asked Russia to arbitrate the difference with Serbia.[52] The Russian government was willing to undertake this difficult task. Serbia, on the other hand, agreed to this arbitration only if it should prove impossible to reach an agreement with Bulgaria directly.[53] Events now had reached such a state that on June 8th the tsar risked his own prestige and sent a personal telegram to the sovereigns of Bulgaria and Serbia advising them to ask for the arbitration foreseen by the alliance treaty. He concluded his telegram with a threat that he would side against the recalcitrant party:

> Accepting the function of an arbitrator not as a prerogative but as a difficult obligation which I cannot avoid, I consider that I should remind Your Majesties that a war between the allies would not find me indifferent. In fact, I should like to make it clear that the state which commences that war will be held responsible before the Slav cause, and that I reserve to myself full liberty concerning the attitude which Russia will adopt at the end of such a criminal war.[54]

At Belgrade, Hartwig recognised the implications of the tsar's warning. He counselled caution; above all there should be no Serbian proclamation annexing Macedonia. If the war must come, Serbia must see that Bulgaria provoked it. He advised asking Russia to arbitrate, at the same time demanding revision of the treaty.[55] King Peter's reply to the tsar indeed was largely concerned with arguments for treaty revision.[56] The necessity for a common Serbian-Greek boundary was stressed. There were many expressions of admiration and loyalty to Russia. On the other hand, as the French ambassa-

[52] Gueshoff, p. 73; Balkanicus, p. 45; *Zeitschrift für Internationales Recht*, XXV, 151–4.

[53] Hartwig to Sazonov, May 4, 1913, Gueshoff, p. 79.

[54] D.D.F., 3d. ser., VII, no. 122 annexe; B.D., IX, ii, no. 1055 enclosure. For a good account of the circumstances attending the sending of these telegrams see, Sazonov, *Fateful Years*, pp. 94–5.

[55] Letter from Hartwig to Pašić as quoted in *The Bulgarian Question*, p. 42; Toshev, II, 320.

[56] King Peter to Tsar Nicholas II, June 11, 1913, S.D., I, no. 310.

dor at once noted, there was "not one word about arbitration." [57] King Ferdinand's reply was not very different. It was filled with honeyed words and arguments that Bulgaria must have all of Macedonia. He took care to point out that Bulgaria had already in April asked the tsar to arbitrate under the terms of the alliance treaty. He still stood by this position.[58]

While the replies of the Serbian and Bulgarian sovereigns were not entirely satisfactory they nevertheless indicated a desire to extricate themselves from a difficult position through the help of Russia. Sazonov considered that the first round had been won and now invited the minister-presidents of Bulgaria, Serbia, and Greece — and if it was desired by them a representative of Montenegro — to come to St. Petersburg where all pending questions could be settled. He would have welcomed a mutual demobilisation, but if this occasioned difficulties he promised that this problem would be the first one to be considered when the ministers arrived.[59]

Meanwhile direct negotiations between Serbia and Bulgaria over demobilisation and arbitration were reaching a climax. Danev accepted the Serbian proposal for reducing the effective troops by one-fourth, but conditioned it upon the inauguration of a joint occupation of the contested zone as defined in Article II of the secret annex to the treaty of alliance. After such an arrangement had been ironed out, he proposed that the two governments should "ask the Russian Emperor to exercise his right of arbitration on the basis of the alliance treaty and its annex as well as some memoranda which the two parties would present within a week's time." [60]

[57] Delcassé to Pichon, June 13, 1913; D.D.F., 3d. ser., VII, no. 109; see also, no. 111.

[58] *Ibid.*, VII, no. 122 annexe; B.D., IX, ii, no. 1049. Sazonov writes: "There is no doubt that . . . Ferdinand's answer expressed the King's consent to submit the Balkan quarrel to the Emperor's decision more categorically than . . . did King Peter's" (*Fateful Years*, p. 96).

[59] *Doklad*, I, 502; Izvolsky, III, no. 913; D.D.F., 3d. ser., VII, nos. 117, 124; *Zeitschrift für Internationales Recht*, XXV, 157.

[60] D.D.F., 3d. ser., VII, no. 196 annexe I; see also no. 145. The Serbian proposal had been made to Bulgaria on June 12th and had been followed two days later by a similar one from Athens (*ibid.*, nos. 96, 196).

It is clear that Danev felt that he could go to St. Petersburg only after having received from Serbia a guarantee both of demobilisation and of her willingness to arbitrate within the framework of the treaty.[61] Such guarantees Pašić always carefully avoided giving. Since his strictly legal position was weak, he always made it clear that while accepting arbitration it was not to be restricted to the so-called "disputed zone." The Serbian government wanted free arbitration and the simultaneous settlement of Greek claims.

The negotiations seemed to have reached an impasse. Sazonov became irritated over the dilatory fashion in which his invitation to "come to St. Petersburg" was received.[62] He gave Hartwig preemptory orders to get Pašić to make the minimum concessions necessary to bring Danev to St. Petersburg.[63] Finally on June 21st he thought he had sufficient assurances from Serbia to satisfy the Bulgarians. He thereupon asked the two governments to submit a memoir within four days which should give all arguments in support of their respective claims.[64] Sofia was assured that Serbia had accepted Russian arbitration without any reservations.[65] The Serbians in reality had not gone so far. Before the skupština on June 30, 1913, Pašić declared that he had accepted arbitration because he was convinced that it would go beyond the limits of the treaty and also because he was informed that the Greek-Bulgarian conflict would be settled at the same time.[66]

Although Venizelos was apparently ready to go to St. Petersburg if the others consented,[67] relations between Bulgaria and

[61] *Doklad*, I, 502 (no. 166); 157 (no. 173); 522 (no. 183); B.D., IX, ii, no. 1074; D.D.F., 3d. ser., VII, no. 166.

[62] Izvolsky, III, no. 927; B.D., IX, ii, no. 1086.

[63] Sazonov to Hartwig, June 18, 1913, *Zeitschrift für Internationales Recht*, XXV, 159.

[64] Izvolsky, III, no. 931; D.D.F., 3d. ser., VII, nos. 170, 178, 182.

[65] *Doklad*, I, 529 (no. 197); *Carnegie Report*, p. 67.

[66] *Carnegie Report*, p. 64; G.P., XXXV, no. 13408 note. For Sazonov's promises to Pašić in respect to the arbitration of Greek-Bulgarian difficulties see, Sazonov to Hartwig, June 6, 1913, *Zeitschrift für Internationales Recht*, XXV, 158–159.

[67] B.D., IX, ii, no. 1056.

Greece were hardly in a state for arbitration. Here matters had gone from bad to worse.[68] The general staffs of both countries concentrated their troops in Macedonia. General Savov, commander in chief of the Bulgarian army, aware of the Greek-Serbian partition treaty, pressed for occupation by the Bulgarian army of those territories definitely ceded by Serbia in the alliance treaty. If these territories remained unoccupied by Bulgarian forces any longer, Savov concluded, they ". . . will remain in the hands of the Greeks and Serbians, since it is difficult to suppose that they will be peacefully handed over to us." [69] Moreover the army was getting restless. Either action or demobilisation within ten days was the demand with which Savov confronted the Bulgarian government.[70]

On June 22, 1913 a ministerial council was held at Sofia. It was faced with two propositions: (1) Russia's request for submission within four days of arguments in support of Bulgaria's claims and for attendance at the conference in St. Petersburg; (2) General Savov's demands of either action or demobilisation within ten days. Danev had apparently reached the conclusion that war was inevitable and that it was better to fight it now than later.[71] Sponsored by Teodorov, the finance-minister, a policy of peace was however adopted. That same day Danev, General Savov, and Teodorov went to King Ferdinand's summer palace at Vranya to make a report. Here it was definitely decided to call upon Russia to make an arbitral award on the basis of the original alliance treaty. Fearful that this award might be delayed — a thing the military authorities felt necessary to forestall because of the temper of the army — it was decided to ask Russia to make the award within seven days. This fateful decision to ask Russia to act within a certain time limit was Gen-

[68] For example see the Bulgarian answer to the Greek government's proposal for demobilisation (D.D.F., 3d. ser., VII, no. 196 annexe II).

[69] General Savov to the commander of the fourth army, June 21, 1913, *Carnegie Report*, pp. 65–6; see also, B.D., IX, ii, no. 1080.

[70] Savov's testimony, *Doklad*, I, supplement, p. 261; *Carnegie Report*, p. 66.

[71] *Carnegie Report*, p. 66. Before the Bulgarian parliamentary committee of inquiry, General Savov testified: "Danev was for war because if we went to St. Petersburg we would lose" (*Doklad*, I, supplement, p. 261).

eral Savov's suggestion. He himself testified later, ". . . in a sense at this meeting at Vranya the question had been decided; if within seven days the arbiter does not award the decision Bulgaria must fight." [72]

Danev immediately expressed to Sazonov his willingness to go to St. Petersburg if the tsar should find it possible to make an arbitral award between Serbia and Bulgaria within the specified time. He felt that after the announcement of the Serbian-Bulgarian award other points such as the Greek claims could be settled.[73] At Sofia preparations were made for the departure of the mission. At St. Petersburg Sazonov received the Bulgarian note without excitement. As he had just asked both the Serbian and Bulgarian governments to submit a memoir stating their respective positions he felt he must await their arrival.[74] His failure to take cognisance of the request for an award within a limited time irritated Danev and caused him to telegraph to the Bulgarian minister:

> I authorise you to inform the Imperial Government that the formula of arbitration and the seven-day period for the awarding of the decision were our final proposals, made as an ultimate concession and permitting us to control the situation on the frontier which constitutes a great danger and does not permit of any delay. Sazonov's answer is a definite refusal because he does not fix a limited period for the awarding of the decision. Under such circumstances we are forced to stop any further negotiations. Tomorrow Toshev will be recalled.[75]

Sazonov, who was "suffering from a severe gastric attack complicated by kidney troubles," [76] was incensed by the sharp protest and threat almost in the form of an ultimatum. He washed his hands of Bulgaria and told the Bulgarian minister:

> Your announcement does not surprise me. I have been aware of the actions of your government for several days. You are acting

[72] *Doklad*, I, supplement, p. 262; see also, Balkanicus, p. 56.

[73] *Doklad*, I, 529 (no. 198); Nekludov to Sazonov, June 22, 1913, *Zeitschrift für Internationales Recht*, XXV, 159.

[74] *Doklad*, I, 531 (no. 200); Sazonov to Nekludov, June 23, 1913, *Zeitschrift für Internationales Recht*, XXV, 160.

[75] Danev to Bobchev, June 24, 1913, *Doklad*, I, 532 (no. 201).

[76] B.D., IX, ii, no. 1089.

on the advice of Austria. You are free. Thus the Serbs with their folly and you with your incorrect attitude have rejected Russia and Slavdom. The Russian emperor did not expect an ultimatum with a time limit in which to declare his decisions concerning the Serbian-Bulgarian difference. However, he would have fulfilled his difficult mission with expedition. Now, after your declaration I communicate ours to you! Do not expect anything from us, and forget the existence of any of our engagements from 1902 until today.[77]

Danev was greatly upset by this communication. Obviously he could not leave for St. Petersburg after receiving this "dressing-down." A telegram was immediately sent to Bobchev, the Bulgarian minister at St. Petersburg, branding Sazonov's charge of Austrian influence as an insult.[78] Danev again explained the necessity of having the arbitral award made within a limited time as the Bulgarian government had used the promise of immediate settlement as a bribe in restraining the army. He regretted that Sazonov sought other explanations, and pleaded that the Russian government should notify him as quickly as possible as to when he could expect the arbitral award. As a pledge of confidence he postponed the recall of the Bulgarian minister at Belgrade. While protesting his loyalty at St. Petersburg, Danev on the other hand did not in any way attempt to push negotiations with Serbia which might have gone a long way towards appeasing Russia.

At Sofia there was great tension. Macedonian elements brought pressure upon the government not to give in to the Serbian and Greek demands. On June 26th the *Macedonian-Adrianople Brotherhoods* issued a call to arms "to the citizens of United Bulgaria," stating: "It is with arms that we must defend our right and complete the great work — the freeing of

[77] Bobchev to Danev, June 25, 1913, *Doklad*, I, 532–3 (no. 205). This telegram is printed in slightly different wording by Balkanicus, p. 62; see also, B.D., IX, ii, nos. 1085, 1087, 1089; D.D.F., 3d. ser., VII, no. 209. In regard to this denunciation of the Russian-Bulgarian accord of 1902, see Helmreich and Black, "The Russo-Bulgarian Military Convention of 1902," *Journal of Modern History*, IX (1937), 470–82.

[78] Danev to Bobchev, June 26, 1913, *Doklad*, I, 533 (no. 206); see also, Nekludov, to Sazonov, June 27, 1913, *Zeitschrift für Internationales Recht*, XXV, 161; D.D.F., 3d. ser., VII, no. 218 annexe II.

Macedonia." [79] The next day the executive committee of the organisation "hailed the king as Tsar Liberator," and pointedly expressed their desire to see a United Bulgaria. "With faith in our undoubtedly just cause and in Bulgarian power," the king in turn expressed the hope that the cause for which their forefathers had struggled so long would finally receive "its only just solution." [80] The Macedonians were afraid that the Bulgarian government would accept an arbitral award which would divide Macedonia. They even threatened Danev and King Ferdinand with assassination if they resorted to arbitration at St. Petersburg.[81] But the Macedonians were not the only ones in Bulgaria favoring an active policy. "Public opinion with few exceptions was for war." [82] From the 26–29th of June the government "gathered information as to the spirit of the army" and established that it was "in full war competence." [83]

On June 28th General Savov sent out orders that the next day towards evening an attack should be made against the Serbian and Greek positions.[84] This order had been given him by the king with the knowledge and apparent approval of Danev. As this is one of the most disputed points in the history of the Balkan Wars some of the more pertinent evidence should be cited. King Ferdinand on July 18th told the Austrian minister that he ordered the attack against Serbia but that the attack against Greece had been made against his will and on the order of Danev. This was the first time that the Austrian minister had seen the king since August, 1912.[85] This fact alone, although it is also substantiated by much other evidence, should

[79] Toshev, II, 346.

[80] *Ibid.*, II, 349.

[81] *Ibid.*, II, 473; *Carnegie Report*, p. 67; Madol, *Ferdinand von Bulgarien*, p. 166.

[82] *Carnegie Report*, p. 67; Toshev, II, 479.

[83] *Doklad*, I, 1184; see also, 535–6.

[84] *Carnegie Report*, p. 67; Toshev, II, 362–3; see also, Cemal Tukin, *Die politischen Beziehungen zwischen Österreich-Ungarn und Bulgarien von 1908 bis zum Bukarester Frieden*, p. 213.

[85] Tarnowski to foreign office, July 18, 1913, Ö-U.A., VI, no. 7838. The French minister at Sofia saw fit to report that King Ferdinand saw practically none of the foreign ministers during the war (Panafieu to Jonnart, March 17, 1913, D.D.F., 3d. ser., VI, no. 15).

disprove Poincaré's charge that the king gave the order to attack only after a meeting with the Austrian minister.[86] Before the Bulgarian parliamentary commission General Savov testified that Danev did not ask him about the extent of the military activities (June 29–July 2) because he knew everything in detail; he kept himself informed in greatest detail by telephone.[87] This would indicate a close collaboration, as there might well be, between the minister-president and the chief-of-staff in time of crisis. Danev himself testified that although he knew there had been incidents on June 29/30th he did not realize their extent until he consulted General Savov on June 30th.[88] Everything indicates that Danev was opposed to any settlement outside of the terms of the Serbian treaty and generally favored a more aggressive policy than that pursued by Gueshov whom he had replaced.[89] The general conclusion of the Bulgarian commission therefore seems sound:

> The attack on the Serbian and Greek lines in Macedonia during the night of June 29–30th was made on the order given by the commander-in-chief H. M. the King, to his chief assistant (General Savov) and this order was given not without the knowledge of the minister-president, Dr. Danev, who approved of it as a coercive measure against the Russian imperial government, thus hastening the awarding of the decision on the controversy with Serbia.[90]

The position of the Bulgarian cabinet is another matter. Certainly the whole cabinet was aware that General Savov on June 21st had insisted either on demobilisation or attack within ten days. They also knew of the request to Russia on July 22nd that the arbitral award be made within seven days. When the attack was made on June 29/30th the cabinet, however, apparently knew nothing of it beforehand.[91] Certain it is that the cabinet as a body never authorised or even sanctioned General Savov's orders. Officially they learned of the advance of the armies first at a council meeting on July 1st. Here under threat

[86] Poincaré, III, 223.
[87] *Doklad*, I, 1150.
[88] *Doklad*, I, supplement, p. 83.
[89] *Doklad*, I, 1149, 1157.
[90] *Doklad*, I, 1202.
[91] *Doklad*, I, supplement, p. 211; Balkanicus, p. 72.

of resignation the cabinet forced through a decision to halt the attack.[92]

General Savov has stated that at 10 A. M. on July 1st Danev gave him written orders to stop the attack.[93] One hour later the personal confidant of the king, Dobrovich, came to him and transmitted an oral order from the king to continue the attack.[94] Bewildered by this apparent diversity of policy he refused to change the commands to stop the attack, which he had already given out on the basis of Danev's written order. That evening after it was apparent that the Serbians had not in similar fashion stopped their offensive he requested Danev to permit him to enter into action.[95] He assured the minister-president that he would force the Serbians to sue for peace by July 7th before the Rumanians had a chance to mobilise. Danev replied that the government could not permit him to cross the frontier. Savov was left with the impression that Danev would have liked to see him act on his own responsibility. This he refused to do. On July 3rd he was summoned by the king and relieved of his duties, "because you did not fulfill my command to continue the military attack." [96] The Russophile General Dimitriev was now placed in command.

The day after the attack an appeal had been dispatched to Sazonov requesting him to stop counter-action by Serbia and Greece, as Bulgaria had ordered her troops to halt. Sazonov attempted to do this but his advice went unheeded.[97] At Belgrade and Athens the governments had long before accepted the impossibility of settling peacefully with their former comrade in arms. Bulgaria was now the aggressor and had placed herself in the wrong. From their viewpoints the situation was perfect. Arbitration by the powers of the Entente as foreseen

[92] *Carnegie Report*, p. 68.

[93] *Doklad*, I, supplement, p. 262.

[94] *Doklad*, I, supplement, p. 272.

[95] *Doklad*, I, supplement, p. 281.

[96] *Doklad*, I, supplement, pp. 262, 272. Danev corroborates that this was the reason why Savov was dismissed (*ibid.*, p. 82).

[97] *Carnegie Report*, p. 69; Tukin, *Die politischen Beziehungen zwischen Österreich-Ungarn und Bulgarien*, p. 213.

by Article V of the alliance treaty of June 1st was entirely forgotten.[98] The Greek and Serbian troops, finally unleashed, sprang to attack. No effort was ever made to call them to a halt.[99]

While the Bulgarian attack precipitated the conflict it can not be gainsaid that Serbia and Greece had done much to provoke it. The attack was no surprise and there is plenty of evidence that the conflict would have been precipitated later — very likely from the Greek or Serbian side — even if General Savov had not issued his fatal order to advance.[100] In Bulgaria it was generally believed that their victorious heroes could easily defeat the Greeks and Serbs. The generals, flushed with the spirit of victory, were not averse to demonstrating this superiority. Even the moderate General R. Dimitriev was convinced that Salonica could be reached in three days and Belgrade in five.[101] General Fitchev, who felt that he knew the Serbian army better than anyone, confidentially told the French attaché that the Serbs could not last eight days before a Bulgarian attack.[102]

Specifically what caused King Ferdinand to sanction the order to advance is hard to say. Fear of assassination at the hands of the Macedonians might well have entered into the decision. Undoubtedly the Macedonians pushed the king onward and approved of the orders to attack.[103] More fundamental no

[98] Such arbitration, while favored by Russia, was unwelcome to England or France and it would no doubt have been useless for the Greek or Serbian governments to fall back upon it (B.D., IX, ii, no. 1024).

[99] S. D., I, no. 317; *Doklad*, I, 1155 (no. 8); Toshev, II, 364.

[100] In accordance with the terms of the Serbian-Montenegrin alliance and also in line with public opinion in Cetinje, Montenegrin troops left to join the Serbian forces for the war on Bulgaria even before the Bulgarian attack (Gavrilović to Pašić, June 28, 1913, S.D., I, no. 314; for further references to Montenegrin mobilisation and policy see, Ö-U.A., VI, nos. 7478, 7479; D.D.F., 3d. ser., VII, nos. 95, 203). See also the Serbian documents published by Gueshoff, pp. 102 ff.; D.D.F., 3d. ser., VII, nos. 251, 471; Sazonov, *Fateful Years*, p. 95.

[101] Toshev, II, 474.

[102] De Matharel to Étienne, Ministre de la Guerre, July 1, 1913, D.D.F., 3d. ser., VII, no. 251.

[103] Conversation in May, 1930 with Colonel Peter Dŭrvingov who commanded the Macedonian legions fighting with the Bulgarian forces during the Balkan Wars. In regard to the influence of the Macedonians see above, pp. 361–

doubt was the idea that through a threat of force Russia might be brought to show more favor to the Bulgarian cause.[103a] Sazonov's answer to Danev's request had been a cold one. Ferdinand was charged with pursuing an Austrian policy; he might well have decided to make a threat of this possibility. The government at Sofia knew how desirous Russia was to keep the Balkan League intact. Ferdinand might well have believed that Russia, or the other powers of Europe, would in the last moment stop a new conflagration in the Balkans, out of fear of a general European war. Sazonov, however, did not push his warnings at Belgrade or Athens. He lived up to his threat of June 25th and Bulgaria was left to her fate. The other powers were indisposed to interfere and concentrated their attention anew on a policy of localisation.

The Bulgarian attack of June 29/30 is explicable only as part of a policy of arbitration and not as one directly opposed to it. General Savov always considered this advance as a political demonstration rather than as a military measure. In his order to the commanding generals he stated the purpose of the attack to be:

1. To raise the morale of our troops and to show them that our ex-allies are our enemies.
2. To compel Russian diplomacy, by danger of a declaration of war, to make a speedy settlement.
3. To force our allies to take a more conciliatory attitude under pressure.
4. To occupy forcibly the territories claimed by us and held by them, until foreign intervention stops further military action, which action must therefore be prompt as intervention may come at any moment.[104]

62; also, Ö-U.A., VI, no. 7769; A. Gauvain, *L'Europe au jour le jour* (14 vols.; Paris, 1917–23), V, 310; *The Bulgarian Question*, p. 223; Kosta Todoroff, "The Macedonian Organisation Yesterday and Today," *Foreign Affairs*, VI (1928), 476; Stoyan Christowe, *Heroes and Assassins* (New York, 1935), p. 129.

[103a] *Doklad*, I, 1149.

[104] Diplomatist, p. 266.

Military action was thus intended as a means of strengthening Bulgaria's position in the settlement which was to come through the mediation of Russia. The policy of arbitration was never abandoned at Sofia in these days. On June 30th Danev handed to the Russian legation the requested memoir stating Bulgaria's position at length and announced his readiness to leave for St. Petersburg.[105] A Russian steamer lay at Varna ready to take him to Russian soil.[106] The immediate outbreak of war through the refusal of Serbia and Greece to countermand the orders to attack dashed these hopes of arbitration. Danev did not have to sail the Black Sea.

King Ferdinand as well as his advisers had greatly miscalculated to what extent Russia at this time was pursuing an anti-Bulgarian policy, especially at Bucharest. Had the Bulgarian leaders decided on a policy of war instead of arbitration on June 28/29th it seems likely they would first have reached an understanding with Austria and Rumania. This omission cost them dear when the Serbians and Greeks answered the Bulgarian "demonstration" with a declaration of war. Richard von Mach in his book reports General Savov as declaring: "He had not given the order [to attack], but only passed on the order, after the king had assured him that at the first exchange of shots between Bulgaria and Serbia an Austro-Hungarian corps would cross the Danube." [107] That Ferdinand ever had such a promise is unlikely. It is, however, important to consider at some length the positions taken by the powers and especially by Austria and Rumania at the outbreak of the Second Balkan War.

[105] *Doklad*, I, 537 (no. 222).

[106] As late as July 4, 1913 Tarnowski reported to Vienna: "Ich weiss dass bis heute sowohl Danew als Nekludow noch Hoffnung dieser Reise hätten" (Ö-U.A., VI, no. 7627).

[107] Richard von Mach, *Aus bewegter Balkanzeit, 1879–1918* (Berlin, 1928), p. 235.

CHAPTER XVII

THE POWERS AND THE OUTBREAK OF THE SECOND BALKAN WAR

WHILE the Balkan states were busily brewing their fratricidal war, the London ambassadors' conference had kept pegging away at Albanian problems. The danger of another war complicated matters. In order to help the cause of peace the conference, on the initiative of Russia, suggested on June 5th that the powers intervene jointly at the different Balkan capitals to urge immediate demobilisation.[1] All the powers agreed to this and again the slow process of getting concerted action at the Balkan capitals began. It was at this point that the tsar sent his special telegrams to King Peter and King Ferdinand asking them in the interest of Slavdom to arbitrate their differences. Serbia also proposed partial demobilisation to Sofia, hoping that this would lead to settlement of their differences by general arbitration, that is, arbitration not limited by the treaty.[2] Berchtold was nettled by the tsar's reference to Pan-Slav patronage in the Balkans, and was unwilling to do anything which might give the impression that Austria was supporting Russia. He also felt that he could no longer participate in the joint demobilisation *démarche*, since it would appear that the powers were directly supporting Serbian policy.[3] Through a misinterpretation of his instructions the Austrian minister took part in a joint *démarche* at Belgrade, but at the other capitals collective action of the powers did not take place.

Austria's action, uncriticised at Berlin and Rome, aroused resentment at the capitals of the other great powers. This was increased when Count Tisza, recently appointed minister-president of Hungary, in answer to the tsar's telegrams made a

[1] Ö-U.A., VI, no. 7282; G.P., XXXV, no. 13380 note.
[2] See above, pp. 357–58.
[3] Ö-U.A., VI, nos. 7368, 7369, 7430; G.P., XXXV, nos. 13395, 13396.

provocative statement on Austrian policy. Tisza stressed the independence of the Balkan states and maintained that they should be left to themselves to settle their own difficulties. No one state had the right to consider itself the Lord Protector and arbiter of the independent Balkan peoples.[4]

Unsuccessful in maintaining peace, the powers were again faced with the problem of localising the conflict.[5] Their respective positions were much the same as they had been when this question faced Europe in October, 1912. It was generally realised that Russia would neither intervene to stop the inter-allied conflict, nor to prevent Rumanian action. Grey proposed at the ambassadorial conference that the various governments be requested to state their positions.[6] Everything hinged on Vienna. Berchtold felt that a public declaration of non-intervention would only encourage the Balkan states in their bloody quarrels and might lead them to overthrow the decisions already made, notably in regard to Albania. Furthermore he did not want to bind his hands in advance, as no one could foresee the outcome of events.[7] Consequently no united declaration of localisation and non-intervention was made.

Behind the demand for united action which came from some of the powers was of course the desire to curb Austria. Now, as in October, 1912, active intervention on the part of the Dual Monarchy was feared. In reality, the Ballhausplatz was determined to continue its policy of watchful waiting.

Before the Preliminaries of London were signed most of the troops which had been mobilised in the monarchy had been dismissed. Only those in Bosnia-Herzegovina remained on a war footing. Public opinion in the monarchy demanded that even they be demobilised.[8] Bilinski, as supervisor of the prov-

[4] Karl Wipperman, *Deutscher Geschichtskalender*, 1913, part I, pp. 432–3; Ö-U.A., VI, nos. 7430, 7436, 7576; G.P., XXXV, nos. 13396, 13410.

[5] G.P., XXXV, no. 13481.

[6] Ö-U.A., VI, no. 7690; G.P., XXXV, no. 13494. Grey and Pichon had previously agreed on such a policy on the occasion of Poincaré's visit to England, June 24–7, 1913 (D.D.F., 3d. ser., VII, no. 233).

[7] Ö-U.A., VI, nos. 7670, 7699; G.P., XXXV, no. 13499.

[8] Conrad, III, 376; see also p. 371.

inces, wanted the special ordinances enacted during the recent crisis done away with and reforms instituted. As the conflict between the Balkan states neared, Berchtold decided to continue the peaceful policy which he had launched. At the outbreak of hostilities he would watch and wait and only if Serbia seemed likely to win might he intervene. Conrad saw little prospect of a war. Internal affairs within the monarchy were just quieting down after the recent mobilisation. Public opinion was definitely in favor of peace. Francis Joseph and Francis Ferdinand were alike opposed to any war-like policy.[9]

The past winter and spring had, to be sure, not led to better Austrian-Serbian relations. Dissatisfaction had grown among the subject Slav groups. More and more they began to regard Serbia as the Piedmont of a great South Slav state. Because of internal reasons the leaders of the monarchy had reached the conclusion that Serbia's prestige must be dimmed and her dreams of expansion shattered. Serbia must not be permitted to become too large. Austria hoped therefore that Bulgaria would obtain the greater share of the Turkish booty. A large and saturated Bulgaria would arouse the antagonism of Serbia. Thus Austria would have support in keeping Serbia in check. In addition it would mean the end of the Balkan League which was the aim of Austrian diplomacy at this time. Could this be accomplished peacefully, well and good. If not, Austria was not unwilling to see a war between the Balkan states. Should this war come, Austria hoped that Bulgaria would win. It was generally held that Bulgaria could deal with Greece and Serbia alone, but Rumanian intervention would certainly give the *coup de grâce* to Bulgaria. It was for this reason that Berchtold made such efforts to bring about a neutrality agreement between Sofia and Bucharest in the month after the Preliminaries of London.

For some time the Bulgarian statesmen had evaded giving Austria a clear-cut statement as to what their future relation

[9] E. C. Helmreich, "The Conflict between Germany and Austria over Balkan Policy, 1913–1914," *Essays in the History of Modern Europe*, pp. 137–9; Émile Laloy, "L'Autriche et la Serbie en juillet 1913," *Mercure de France*, CCL (1934), 153–68.

to the monarchy would be. In June, after peace had been concluded and it still looked as if the pro-Russian policy would be continued at Sofia, Berchtold felt it was high time to have a show down. It was time to convince the Bulgarians that Austria might follow a policy other than a Bulgarophile one. Gueshov had inquired on May 29th as to what Austria's policy would be in case of an inter-allied war.[10] Berchtold answered with a counter-question. He wanted to know: "If Bulgaria after the conclusion of peace with Turkey had any obligations in respect to any country, which, even if it were only under certain special conditions, obligated Bulgaria to undertake war against the monarchy." [11] Tarnowski was instructed to press for a definite answer to this question.

The Austrian minister had a difficult task. King Ferdinand did not express himself, although special care was taken to approach him through his personal confidant Dobrovich. Gueshov refused to give an answer, as he had just resigned as minister-president.[12] The Bulgarian cabinet crisis dragged on. It was not until June 18th that Tarnowski was able to discuss the general situation with Danev, who was now in charge. The latter could not deny that the Serbian-Bulgarian treaty was still in force, since Bulgaria was demanding that Serbia fulfill its provisions. Nevertheless if it came to war, the treaty would be abrogated and consequently there would be no more obligations. Danev felt that Austria would hardly care to intervene in such a war between small states. Nevertheless he would be interested to know just what Austria's attitude would be. What he really wanted was Austrian mediation between Rumania and Bulgaria.[13]

Such evasive answers brought no assurances from Vienna. Again Berchtold pointed out that Bulgaria could expect no promises from Austria so long as she was unwilling to guarantee a friendly policy in the future.[14] Finally on June 21st Danev,

[10] Ö-U.A., VI, no. 7202.
[11] Berchtold to Tarnowski, May 30, 1913, *ibid.*, VI, no. 7214; see also, no. 7265.
[12] *Ibid.*, VI, nos. 7276, 7300.
[13] *Ibid.*, VI, nos. 7408, 7409, 7422.
[14] Berchtold to Tarnowski, June 20, 1913, *ibid.*, VI, no. 7433.

totally misrepresenting the contents of the Serbian-Bulgarian treaty, stated categorically that Bulgaria was not bound any longer to join in an anti-Austrian war. Not only would the Serbian treaty expire when the present difficulties were settled, but Bulgaria would never enter into a combination directed against Austria. He promised Bulgarian friendship for the future.[15]

Well might the Bulgarian government decide to turn an attentive ear towards Austria. The situation between Serbia and Bulgaria was fast becoming critical. Danev's personal paper *Bŭlgariya* declared: "Diplomatic means between Serbia and Bulgaria are used up. Nothing is left for Bulgaria but to use other more effective measures." [16] Berchtold, ever patient, was gratified to have Danev's categorical declaration of friendship. He now in turn defined Austria's position.

> We are determined to follow the same (Bulgarophile) policy in the future as in the past, as long as Bulgarian policy follows the lines sketched by Danev and takes due consideration for our interests. As to what our policy would actually be under certain future conditions, the position we would take in case of a Bulgarian conflict with Serbia and Greece is of most import. In view of the open hostility of Serbia towards us a further material and moral strengthening of Serbia at the cost of Bulgaria would be absolutely contrary to our interests. Bulgaria can therefore in this case count not only on our sympathies but also our active aid, if circumstance should lead us to fear the above undesirable developments; the latter (active aid), however, only on the condition that Bulgaria shows consideration for Rumania's wishes and offers such compensations for Rumanian neutrality as will make it possible for us to advocate at Bucharest, with some justice and chance of success, an agreement on this basis. . . . In case of the second alternative — if it is possible for Bulgaria to settle her differences peacefully with Serbia — which of course we would only welcome, we would continue our Bulgarophile course. We do this of course on the supposition that Danev's promise is fulfilled and that also in this case the alliance relationship with Serbia is ended after the final definitive peace with Turkey is established.[17]

[15] *Ibid.*, VI, nos. 7448, 7449.

[16] As quoted, *ibid.*, VI, no. 7449.

[17] Berchtold to Tarnowski, June 24, 1913, *ibid.*, VI, no. 7486.

Now as before Berchtold conditioned his offer of help. Only if Bulgaria came to an agreement with Rumania would Austria come to her aid. This stand he had taken earlier and it remained his position before, during, and even after the Second Balkan War.

The insistence that Bulgaria make a settlement with Rumania nettled Danev. He could not understand why great powers like Austria and Germany could not get Rumania to do what they wanted. He even talked of how difficult it would be for Bulgaria not to renew the Serbian alliance and suggested that it might be well for future Austrian-Bulgarian relations if a friendly relationship developed between Russia and Austria.[18] His words were not those of a suppliant asking for Austrian aid. Nor were they words of gratitude for proffered assistance. They were more in the nature of a threat, holding up as the price of Bulgarian friendship greater pressure by Austria at Bucharest in order to smooth the way for a Rumanian-Bulgarian agreement.

Meanwhile Bulgarian-Rumanian relations were actually growing worse. Immediately after the Preliminaries of London, Gueshov had notified Rumania of Bulgaria's willingness to appoint the boundary commission provided for by the Protocol of St. Petersburg.[19] A special delegate, empowered to carry on "further negotiations," was to be sent to Bucharest within a few days. The June ministerial crisis at Sofia however delayed things. Finally Danev, instead of sending a delegate to Bucharest, inquired of the Rumanian minister at Sofia what his government would demand as compensation for neutrality in case of war.[20] Ghika, of course, had no instructions, but through

[18] *Ibid.*, VI, no. 7499; see also, nos. 7553, 7629.

[19] Fürstenberg to foreign office, June 3, 1913, *ibid.*, VI, no. 7263. This boundary commission was not constituted until June 21st. It immediately met with difficulties and had not completed its work when the Second Balkan War broke out (*Rumanian Green Book*, pp. 115–45).

[20] Ö-U.A., VI, nos. 7409, 7425, 7437. In speaking of these Bulgarian advances King Carol told the German minister: "In einer langen Unterredung mit dem rumänischen Gesandten habe er [Danev] nur Phrasen, lauter Quatsch gesagt, keine bestimmten Anträge gestellt" (Waldthausen to foreign office, June 20, 1913, G.P., XXXV, no. 13403).

Vienna the information came that Rumania would demand the line Turtukaia-Balchik as a guarantee for her neutrality.[21] Danev could not bring himself to make proposals for negotiations, even though Rumania declared on June 27th that in case of war she would mobilise against Bulgaria.[22]

Unfortunately party strife was very keen at Sofia, and Danev — like Gueshov before him — did not wish to burden his party with the onus of more territorial cessions to Rumania.[23] He temporised further. On June 29th Berchtold was asked to find out if Rumania would still be disposed to negotiate in case Bulgaria came forward with concrete proposals.[24] Berchtold urged Danev to make his proposals at once to Bucharest, and immediately advised the Rumanian leaders of the forthcoming Bulgarian offer, asking them to give it friendly consideration. He furthermore requested both Rome and Berlin to bring pressure at Bucharest in favor of an agreement with Bulgaria.[25] This Austria's allies refused to do.

But no Bulgarian offer materialised. Despite the outbreak of hostilities on June 29/30th Danev still could not bring himself to make a definite offer to Rumania. On July 2nd he tendered his resignation, which was considered by a crown council on July 3rd. At this meeting a long discussion took place as to whether there should be a radical change in the orientation of Bulgarian policy. Danev was called upon to state his views with regard to Austria and Rumania. The Austrian minister reported his statements, of course at second-hand, as follows:

> Danev insisted very decidedly that Bulgaria had no ground to spoil her relations to Russia and seek a rapprochement with the monarchy from which it had nothing to expect. Austria-Hungary

[21] Ö-U.A., VI, nos. 7437, 7453.

[22] *Ibid.*, VI, nos. 7520, 7525; G.P., XXXV, no. 13434; D.D.F., 3d. ser., VII, no. 231.

[23] Toshev, II, 477–8.

[24] Ö-U.A., VI, no. 7552; see also, nos. 7555, 7556, 7563.

[25] Berchtold had already taken such steps at Rome and Berlin on June 28th (Ö-U.A., VI, nos. 7506, 7512, 7528, 7538) and repeated them on July 4th (*ibid.*, no. 7612). Both requests were refused (*ibid.*, nos. 7512, 7566, 7584, 7645, 7676, 7747; G.P., XXXV, nos. 13428, 13490).

only aimed at bringing about an agreement with Rumania and to this end advised the cession of the Turtukaia-Balchik line. For this Bulgaria did not need Austria. At the price of such sacrifice Bulgaria could make an agreement with Rumania without the monarchy. In addition Austria-Hungary had only indicated possible intervention *à la* Khevenhüller, only vice versa, in case Serbia should be victorious. As a Serbian victory is excluded, this promise, as also the friendship of Austria-Hungary, had no practical worth to Bulgaria.[26]

After thinking the discussion over, King Ferdinand on July 4th refused to accept Danev's resignation, expressing his complete confidence in him.[27] Although the opposition leaders had expressed more friendly views to Tarnowski, the latter was nevertheless convinced that there was not one party leader who would shoulder the disgrace of ceding more territory to Rumania.[28] In Sofia the opinion was held that so long as a Russophile government continued in power Russia would never permit Rumania to damage Bulgaria too much.

This attitude of the Bulgarian leaders was too much even for Berchtold, who, in spite of much opposition, continually advocated a pro-Bulgarian policy. On July 5th he informed the archduke that in view of present tendencies at Sofia it would be necessary "to maintain greater reserve towards Bulgaria and to modify Austria's position in favor of Rumania." [29] In a conference with the emperor at Ischl this policy of reserve towards Bulgaria was sanctioned.[30] Nevertheless, when on July 5th Danev again requested Berchtold to find out — now that Rumania had mobilised — whether the Rumanian statesmen were still willing to negotiate and what their terms would be, Berchtold undertook the thankless task.[31] It was to be a final attempt at media-

[26] Tarnowski to Berchtold, July 4, 1913, Ö-U.A., VI, no. 7629. That Danev believed he could buy off Rumania at the last moment is confirmed by the English and French ministers at Sofia (B.D., IX, ii, no. 1097; D.D.F., 3d. ser., VII, no. 231).

[27] *Doklad*, I, 1157 (no. 13), supplement, p. 211; Toshev, II, 373.

[28] Ö-U.A., VI, nos. 7631, 7756.

[29] *Ibid.*, VI, no. 7644; see also, no. 7669 in which the archduke expresses his gratification in respect to this turn in Austrian policy.

[30] B.D., IX, ii, no. 1123.

[31] Ö-U.A., VI, nos. 7639, 7649, 7652.

tion, a policy which he had been striving single-handed to put through for so many months. He also requested Danev to communicate to Vienna what Bulgaria was willing to offer. Beyond an unofficial offer from King Ferdinand to cede the line Turtukaia-Dobrich-Kavarna — which was less than Rumania had demanded before her mobilisation, Berchtold received no offer from either capital.[32]

Meanwhile Bulgaria had turned again to Russia. On July 4th Danev appealed to Sazonov to stop Rumania.[33] This he refused to do since this would mean intervention on behalf of Bulgaria against Serbia and Greece.[34] But the Bulgarian cabinet still built its hopes on Russian rather than on Austrian aid. On July 7th they asked King Ferdinand to appeal anew to St. Petersburg, and on July 8th with the express sanction of the king, Danev made overtures through both the Bulgarian minister at St. Petersburg and the Russian minister at Sofia.[35] Sazonov was asked to bring about the cessation of hostilities. The latter, while willing to extend his good offices to Bulgaria, did not press her case at any of the capitals. Belgrade and Athens were not to be stopped at this point, and on July 11th the Rumanian forces advanced into Bulgarian territory.

There was no doubt in the mind of the British ambassador at St. Petersburg that Russia had even encouraged Rumania to attack Bulgaria.[36] Whereas Russia had taken steps to keep Rumania from active intervention in the fall of 1912, she now assured Rumania that she would not hinder her if steps were taken against Bulgaria. Fearful of Bulgaria's aspirations on Constantinople and suspicious of her future policy, Russia was now definitely playing an anti-Bulgarian game. Because of the high-handed independent action of the Bulgarian statesmen,

[32] Ö-U.A., VI, no. 7667. Even this offer of King Ferdinand was withdrawn later (*ibid.*, nos. 7704, 7715).

[33] *Doklad*, I, 788 (no. 327).

[34] *Ibid.*, I, 790 (no. 334).

[35] *Ibid.*, I, 1161–2 (nos. 28, 30); Ö-U.A., VI, no. 7705; B.D., IX, ii, nos. 1125, 1129, 1131, 1138.

[36] B.D., IX, ii, no. 1128; see also nos. 1127, 1089, 1093; S.D., I, no. 321; Ö-U.A., VII, no. 8731; G.P., XXXV, no. 13422; *Doklad*, I, 1193.

Russia left the Bulgarian people in the lurch. Nor did King Ferdinand personally strengthen the Bulgarian cause at St. Petersburg. Here as at the other royal courts of Europe he was distrusted and cordially disliked. At Bucharest the Russian minister was ably seconded by his French colleague, who was anxious to win Rumania for the Entente. Blondel urged the Rumanians to mobilise, although this action was later disavowed by the French foreign office.[37] At Bucharest French and Russian influences were bent on detaching Rumania from the Triple Alliance. There is much evidence showing how diligently and successfully they worked at this task. With the approval and encouragement of Russia and France, Rumania took steps at this time which were to lead her directly from the Triple Alliance into the Triple Entente.

The Triple Alliance, forced by the necessity of loyalty to an ally, were bound hand and foot by the demands of Rumania for aggrandisement. Germany, fearful of driving Rumania into the beckoning arms of Russia and France, counselled almost slavish fulfillment of Rumanian demands. Unwillingness on the part of Germany to further Berchtold's policy of Rumanian-Bulgarian rapprochement robbed it of what little chance of success it may have had. While Austria pressed for a Bulgarian-Rumanian rapprochement, Germany, for dynastic reasons primarily, was anxious to have a Greek-Rumanian treaty concluded. This played into the hands of the Entente, which aimed at a Greek-Rumanian-Serbian agreement. Thus the Serbian problem, complicated now by Rumanian-Serbian friendship, became much more acute for the Dual Monarchy. Rumania was indeed the focal point of the Second Balkan War.

Berchtold's policy at this time was a bold and difficult one. It was designed to curb Serbia and thus lessen its power of attraction to the Slavs of the monarchy, all without active Austrian intervention. Austrian action was to be avoided, if possible, since it would no doubt mean Russian counter-intervention and the long-feared European war. At various times

[37] D.D.F., 3d. ser., VII, nos. 253, 267, 284.

Berchtold did threaten that if Serbia was to be unduly increased in size, Austria would be forced into active intervention. But what constituted "undue expansion" was never defined.

The charge that Austria incited Bulgaria to attack lacks all substantiation.[38] Certainly there had been no definite promises of aid. The Bulgarian commission of inquiry found no evidence of Austrian influence in their careful study of the events leading to the outbreak of hostilities. The Danev government insisted then and in the following days on a Russian orientation of Bulgarian policy. Bulgarian claims and plans for territorial settlements, the pressure of the Macedonian party and the state of public opinion within Bulgaria are factors enough to account for the attitude of the government at Sofia.

Nor is it true that it was German or Italian influence which restrained Austria from attacking Serbia at this time. As late as July 4th, Berchtold vainly attempted to gain German and Italian aid in bringing about a Bulgarian-Rumanian rapprochement.[39] In doing so, he argued that this would do more than anything else to prevent a Bulgarian defeat. The Austrian ambassador at Rome interpreted his instructions as if Austria were requesting Italian aid, if Serbia were victorious. The Italian foreign office was alarmed and sent a sharp protest to Vienna. At Berlin, Berchtold's intimation that Austria might be forced to intervene to prevent the creation of a large Serbia caused no such consternation. But the German foreign office absolutely refused to bring the requested pressure at Bucharest for fear of driving Rumania into the arms of the Entente.[40] It was really the intervention of Rumania which upset Berchtold's plans. Bulgaria, attacked on all sides, could not do Austria's work for

[38] See above, p. 363. Ferdinand in 1914 denied to the Russian minister that Austria in any way instigated Bulgaria to attack Serbia (Sawinski to foreign office, Feb. 19, 1914, R.D., I Reihe, I, no. 291). It is also of significance that after the Second Balkan War, in their conversations with the Austrian statesmen, the Bulgarians never mention any possible instigation by the Austrian statesmen to attack Serbia (Ö-U.A., VII–VIII, *passim*).

[39] Ö-U.A., VI, no. 7612.

[40] See, E. C. Helmreich, "The Conflict between Germany and Austria over Balkan Policy, 1913–14," *Essays in the History of Modern Europe*, pp. 137–9.

her. Yet it was impossible, after Rumania declared war, for Austria to attack Serbia without going against her own ally of many years' standing. This no responsible Austrian statesman was willing to advocate. Neither the emperor nor the archduke would ever have consented to military action against Rumania. Although both Germany and Italy advised Austria against rushing in with arms it was not their counsels which were the determining factor.

Force of circumstances, in which Rumania played a leading rôle, made it impossible for Berchtold to step in and redress the balance between Bulgaria and Serbia. For the time being he was doomed to attempt to salvage as much as he could through diplomatic channels. He still bravely announced that Austria's vital interests would have to be considered in the final peace settlement, which he reserved the right to approve. Unrestrained by the great powers, the Christian Balkan states set about in bloody fashion to divide the booty torn from the hands of the Infidel.

CHAPTER XVIII

THE WAR AND THE TREATY OF BUCHAREST

THE efforts which the Bulgarian government made to stop hostilities immediately after General Savov's attack of June 29th–30th were of no avail. In fact they only disorganised the Bulgarian forces and made them more vulnerable to the Greek and Serbian counterattacks. On July 1st, the Greeks captured the small Bulgarian garrison at Salonica. On July 3rd the Rumanian government amid popular rejoicing issued general mobilisation orders; on July 5th and 6th Greece and Serbia made formal declaration of war. This latter step was not taken by Rumania until July 10th and was immediately followed by an advance across the frontier. To add to Bulgaria's burdens, Turkey, defying the admonitions of the great powers, on July 12th sent its armies into Thrace and by the 22nd had retaken Adrianople. The Serbs and Greeks pushed their advance, neither giving nor receiving much quarter. Peculiarly bitter vengeance characterised this fratricidal carnage. Beset on all sides and with no clear and unified leadership at Sofia, the over-confident Bulgarian armies were forced to retreat. The Rumanian forces, meeting no opposition, swept on toward Sofia.[1] Their advance was more like maneuvers on a large scale than a military campaign. It was evident that Bulgaria would have to accept peace at any price. All that was left to her was to hope that the powers might restrain the greed of the victorious coalition.

[1] Schebeko states that it was on the advice of Russia that the cabinet at Sofia ordered the Bulgarian army to offer no resistance to the Rumanian forces (*Souvenirs*, p. 159; see also D.D.F., 3d. ser., VII, no. 340). On the military aspects of the Second Balkan War see, Colonel de Dreyer, *La débâcle bulgare; deuxième guerre balkanique de 1913* (Paris, 1916); B. P. L. Boucabeille, *La guerre inter-balkanique; événements militaires et politiques survenus jusqu'en octobre 1913* (Paris, 1914); Alain de Penennrun, *40 jours de guerre dans les Balkans; la campagne serbo-bulgare en juillet, 1913* (Paris, 1914).

Since Bulgaria had placed her case in Russian hands as early as July 8th, Sazonov was the first to act. He proposed on July 9th at all the Balkan capitals:

(1) The immediate cessation of military operations and the conclusion of an armistice between the commanders-in-chief of the belligerents.

(2) The immediate arrival at St. Petersburg of responsible representatives of the belligerents in order to establish the bases of peace with equally benevolent aid to all by Russia in her rôle as mediatory power.[2]

Thus Sazonov, although calling attention to the fact that "events . . . had resulted in the effective abrogation of the treaty," still desired to act as arbiter. Furthermore he threatened that "non-acceptance of the above conditions — which guarantee the interests of all the Balkan states — would result in making solely those states responsible which did not accept them and would at the same time deny to them all hope of possible support coming from Russia."

Bulgaria at once accepted the Russian proposal without reservation and should therefore have merited Sazonov's good will in the future.[3] At Belgrade and even more at Athens, Sazonov's program met with opposition.[4] Both cabinets protested their willingness to stop hostilities but insisted on the necessity of signing the preliminaries of peace on the battlefield. Bulgarian perfidy was too well known to risk her reorganising her forces during an armistice. Pašić insisted that Bulgaria must take the first step and make her overtures by direct negotiation through an emissary.[5] Neither Greece nor Serbia felt that a definite answer could be given without consulting the other. It was announced that in order to unite on a common

[2] Communication from Count Benckendorff, July 10, 1913, B.D., IX, ii, no. 1131.

[3] *Doklad*, I, 1164 (no. 35); B.D., IX, ii, 903 minute.

[4] *Rumanian Green Book*, nos. 197, 198, 202; Izvolsky, III, no. 954; Driault and Lhéritier, V, 126; B.D., IX, ii, no. 1132.

[5] Paget to Grey, July 12, 1913, B.D., IX, ii, no. 1137; see also, *Rumanian Green Book*, no. 204; S.D., I, no. 345.

policy Pašić and Venizelos would meet at Nish on July 16th. The Serbian minister confidently informed St. Petersburg that he had hopes of curbing the excessive demands of Greece.

Rumania countered the Russian proposal by stating that if Bulgaria would cede the Turtukaia-Balchik line and "there was the certainty of a definitive accord among the Balkan states" she would gladly stop the advances of the Rumanian forces.[6] Immediately on July 12th Russia passed this information on to Sofia and also the main terms of the general territorial settlement as envisaged at St. Petersburg.[7] Bulgaria thereupon authorised Russia to offer Rumania the Turtukaia-Balchik line on the condition that Rumania should not occupy additional territory and that her troops should not cross the Danube at other points. Rumania was further to aid in establishing peace between Bulgaria and the other Balkan states.[8] Berchtold had long pleaded with Danev to offer Rumania this very strip of territory and ironically enough Sazonov now had the pleasure of handing it over to Rumania. Schebeko had promised that the cession of this territory would stop Rumanian hostilities within forty-eight hours.[9] He was a poor prophet. The Rumanian government sent troops deeper into Bulgarian territory and dispatched a note to all the powers insisting on the necessity of continuing the conflict until a stable peace could be established. Rumania did, however, give notice that although more territory would be occupied, she would limit further annexations to the Turtukaia-Dobrich-Balchik line, with a certain number of kilometers to the west and south according to the conformation of the terrain.[10] Although the last indefinite phrase

[6] Blondel to Pichon, July 11, 1913, D.D.F., 3d. ser., VII, no. 335.

[7] *Ibid.*, VII, nos. 351, 352, 360. According to Sazonov the future boundary between Bulgaria and Serbia should follow the watershed of the Vardar, Shtip going to Serbia; Greece would be joined with Serbia near Ghevheli and the Greek frontier would continue eastward to the valley of the Struma, Seres going to Greece. These proposals for a general settlement were also sent to the other Balkan capitals.

[8] *Doklad*, I, 1164 (no. 37); D.D.F., 3d. ser., VII, nos. 360, 362; B.D., IX, ii, no. 1144.

[9] D.D.F., 3d. ser., VII, no. 352.

[10] *Rumanian Green Book*, no. 206.

permitted the possibility of expansion like an accordion the Rumanian statement was well received by the powers.

The Russian attempts at mediation had produced no results. Repeated efforts had failed to stop the Rumanian advance. Serbia and Greece had not accepted the Russian proposal. Filled with despair, Danev made a last appeal to Russia on July 14th.[11] Embarrassed by Bulgaria's willingness to place her difficulties on Russia's shoulders, Sazonov had begun to fight shy of acting as arbiter. Instead, he advised Bulgaria to send delegates to Nish where Pašić and Venizelos were scheduled to hold their conference.[12] If Bulgaria would consent to do this, then he would continue his efforts at Belgrade and Athens. At the latter two capitals he suggested conducting general negotiations at Nish, using the Russian proposal for territorial partition of July 12, 1913, as a basis for discussion.

Helpless, the Bulgarians agreed to send delegates to Nish, but confidence in Russia was gone. Russia's inability to stop the Rumanian advance and the collapse of the prospects of Russian arbitration brought about the resignation of the Danev cabinet on July 15th.[13] The leaders of the opposition had already sounded Vienna as to what support they might expect from this quarter, and the new ministry, headed by Radoslavov, with Genadiev as foreign minister, was generally considered pro-Austrian.

Although it was recognised that there would have to be another conference of some sort to ratify any settlement which

[11] *Doklad*, I, 800 (no. 363).

[12] D.D.F., 3d. ser., VII, nos. 352, 365, 372; see also no. 366.

[13] The Danev cabinet had tendered its resignation once before on July 2nd, but it had been continued in office (see above, p. 374). On July 13th Danev submitted his resignation again and a crown council was held that evening, the fall of the cabinet being announced on July 15th. Malinov's efforts to form a coalition cabinet failed because the socialists and agrarians refused to coöperate. Finally on July 17th the Radoslavov cabinet was formed, composed of liberals (Radoslavov), national liberals (Stambulov), and young liberals (Tonchev). See Toshev, II, 399–403. A letter of July 6th in which Radoslavov, Tonchev, and Genadiev advised King Ferdinand to turn to Austria for help came into Russian hands in October, 1913 and aroused deep and lasting resentment at St. Petersburg against the Radoslavov government (R.D., I Reihe, I, nos. 291, 354; III, no. 43 note).

might be made at Nish, Sazonov's original plan for a conference at St. Petersburg rapidly dropped out of the picture. None of the Balkan allies had taken kindly to it, and Rumania had flatly refused to go to the Russian capital.[14] Maiorescu had at first favored a European conference, but he soon joined Serbia and Greece in advocating direct settlement by the belligerents themselves.[15] France, too, was not enthusiastic about Sazonov's desire to gather his protégés around his table. Pichon, the French foreign minister, recommended that for the present Russia should restrict her efforts to bringing about the cessation of hostilities. The actual territorial division should be left to future direct negotiations among the Balkan states, or to the great powers.[16]

At Berlin there was no opposition to a conference at St. Petersburg, since it was probable that Sazonov would reap a harvest of ingratitude. Jagow approached Vienna on the general question of a future conference. Berchtold had just learned that Maiorescu favored a meeting of Balkan and Rumanian delegates, at which the territorial settlement could be arranged subject to later ratification by the powers. The Rumanian statesman suggested that he would be able to act as the voice of the Ballhausplatz at such a meeting.[17] This arrangement gave alluring prospects of Austria's exerting direct influence on the negotiations. Consequently Berchtold vetoed the idea of a meeting at St. Petersburg and spoke in favor of a conference at Bucharest.[18] The German foreign office at once took up this idea and passed it on to Athens. Venizelos received it favorably and in turn communicated it to Belgrade and Bucharest. The Rumanian statesmen had for some time been considering such a conference.[19] King Ferdinand of Bulgaria

[14] D.D.F., 3d. ser., VII, no. 338; Ö-U.A., VI, no. 7726. King Constantine telegraphed to his foreign minister: "I do not want to go to St. Petersburg under any circumstances" (Driault and Lhéritier, V, 126).

[15] Ö-U.A., VI, no. 7752; see also, nos. 7726, 7738; G.P., XXXV, no. 13502.

[16] Pichon to Delcassé, July 12, 1913, D.D.F., 3d. ser., VII, no. 347.

[17] Fürstenberg to foreign office, July 13, 1913, Ö-U.A., VI, no. 7752.

[18] Tschirschky to foreign office, July 14, 1913, G.P., XXXV, no. 13514.

[19] *Rumanian Green Book*, no. 207; D.D.F., 3d. ser., VII, no. 354.

was very much in favor of it, for he thought that Austria would be more able to work on his behalf at Bucharest than at some other capital.[20] By July 18th it was generally agreed among the powers that there should be a conference at Bucharest.

The great problem was the cessation of hostilities. Russia had persuaded Bulgaria that this could be brought about by direct negotiations at Nish. Bulgarian delegates, accompanied by the Russian attaché, finally went to Nish on July 20th, hoping to meet there with the other belligerents.[21] The Greek and Serbian premiers by this time had already held a secret meeting at Usküb,[22] and although Rumanian, Serbian, and Montenegrin representatives held themselves in readiness at Belgrade to go to Nish, no Greek delegation appeared.

During these days the powers bombarded the different Balkan capitals with recommendations for the rapid cessation of hostilities. Russia was particularly insistent at Athens, where King Constantine seemed set on conquering most of Macedonia and the entire Aegean coastline.[23] News of threatened revolution and the possible overthrow of the dynasty at Sofia alarmed the powers. The steady advance of the Turkish forces beyond the Enos-Midia line and reports of Turkish massacres brought home to the capitals of Europe the necessity of a rapid conclusion of hostilities. Until fighting ceased among the Christian Balkan states the powers could not take action against Turkey without partisan intervention in the major conflict. But Greece, knowing what she was entitled to by the terms of her alliance with Serbia, and that possession would no doubt be the law at

[20] Ö-U.A., VI, no. 7837.

[21] D.D.F., 3d. ser., VII, nos. 428, 432. The Bulgarians had originally desired that a Russian delegation represent them, but this Sazonov refused (*Doklad*, I, 1166 [nos. 41, 42]). He did, however, authorise Hartwig to be prepared to act for the Bulgarians until their arrival (D.D.F., 3d. ser., VII, nos. 370, 402). In the end the Russian attaché was to act only as a liaison officer to get the Bulgarian delegation through the Serbian lines. For opposition to his presence at Nish see, G.P., XXXV, nos. 13564, 13566.

[22] D.D.F., 3d. ser., VII, no. 420.

[23] It should be pointed out that throughout these negotiations King Constantine was much less conciliatory than Venizelos (see, Driault and Lhéritier, V, 129 ff.).

the peace conference, was intent on further conquests. Followed by Serbia, Greece continued to insist that the preliminaries of peace and the armistice should be signed at one and the same time, and also on the field of battle. This contention Rumania rejected, being determined that, whether the armistice was signed at Nish or elsewhere, both the preliminaries and final peace settlement were to be negotiated at Bucharest. To show how this deadlock was broken it is necessary to consider the policies of the new Radoslavov government in Bulgaria.

Even before they had taken office, the new Bulgarian ministers had been informed that they could expect help from Austria only if in the future they did not join in an alliance with Serbia and if they reached an agreement with Rumania.[24] On July 15th King Ferdinand had made a personal appeal to Francis Joseph for aid.[25] Berchtold went to Ischl for a special consultation with the emperor, whereupon the Bulgarian sovereign was advised to make a direct personal appeal to King Carol and to offer him the Turtukaia-Balchik line. In addition he should call attention to the dangerous situation of the Bulgarian dynasty, imploring King Carol to stop the advance of his troops and to influence Greece and Serbia to conclude an armistice.[26] Austria immediately asked King Carol to give the forthcoming Bulgarian plea a favorable hearing and at the same time requested the cabinets of Berlin and Rome to further the plan.[27]

Rumanian affairs at Sofia at this time were in the hands of the Italian legation, while Bulgaria was represented at Bucharest through the Russian legation. To the irritation of the Russian minister at Bucharest, Genadiev chose to use the Italian channel of communication. On July 17, 1913 he again expressed the desire of the Bulgarian government to enter upon negotiations with Rumania and renewed the offer of the Turtukaia-Balchik line. This offer, apparently, was not as clear-cut as the one made earlier by Danev through the Russian minister, a fact which irritated the Rumanian statesmen.[28] They saw no cause

[24] Ö-U.A., VI, no. 7780. [25] *Ibid.*, VI, no. 7781. [26] *Ibid.*, VI, no. 7814.
[27] *Ibid.*, VI, no. 7797. [28] *Rumanian Green Book*, nos. 213, 222, 224.

to alter their policy of refusing to make a separate agreement. Maiorescu, as he told the French minister, feared Bulgaria would not keep its word, and besides, Rumania could not leave Serbia exposed to a new Bulgarian attack. Continued participation at the side of Serbia had the added advantage of preventing a possible Austrian ultimatum to Serbia.[29]

King Ferdinand now decided to follow the advice from Vienna and made a direct appeal to King Carol.[30] This time the Bulgarian efforts bore results. Rumania consented to halt, at least temporarily, the advance of troops, and agreed to bring pressure on the allies to end hostilities.[31] She then notified Greece that Rumania would consider entering upon separate negotiations with Bulgaria, if Greece did not agree to signing both the preliminaries of peace and the final treaty at Bucharest.[32] This notice, together with the rumors that the advance of the Rumanian troops had been halted, was no doubt more effective in Athens than the constant admonitions of the powers. In order to satisfy the Rumanians, the Greek statesmen proposed the conclusion of all negotiations at Bucharest.[33] But they still insisted on a simultaneous signature of the armistice and peace preliminaries. Pašić was quite willing to fall in with

[29] *Ibid.*, no. 215; D.D.F., 3d. ser., VII, no. 388.

[30] Ö-U.A., VI, no. 7891; D.D.F., 3d. ser., VII, no. 431; for an earlier appeal to King Carol see, *Doklad*, I, 800 (no. 365). Alexander Hoyos, who had been sent by the Austrian government on a special mission, was at the Rumanian capital when King Ferdinand's telegram arrived. His presence no doubt helped the Bulgarian cause. At least he was impressed by his friendly reception, and the Rumanian reply to the Bulgarian plea pleased the Viennese government (Ö-U.A., VI, no. 7892). Cholera in the Rumanian army and the desire to forestall a Serbian advance into Vidin were no doubt important factors in influencing the decision of the leaders at Bucharest (*ibid.*, no. 8142; G.P., XXXV, no. 13695; D.D.F., 3d. ser., VII, no. 459; N. Iorga, "Comment la Roumanie s'est détachée de la Triplice d'après les documents austro-hongrois et les souvenirs personnels," *Revue historique du sud-est européen*, IX [1932], 280).

[31] On July 21st the Bulgarian government was formally assured that the Rumanian troops would not enter Sofia (B.D., IX, ii, 1073; G.P., XXXV, no. 13572; *Rumanian Green Book*, no. 230). Russia also brought pressure upon the Rumanian government to halt the advance of its troops (Sazonov to Schebeko, *Zeitschrift für Internationales Recht*, XXV, 163; R.D., I Reihe, I, no. 291; Schebeko, *Souvenirs*, pp. 160–1).

[32] D.D.F., 3d. ser., VII, nos. 438, 442; Ö-U.A., VI, no. 7892.

[33] *Rumanian Green Book*, no. 240.

this plan, and, as he had said earlier, "the Montenegrins would of course follow Serbia." [34] On July 24th Maiorescu notified Sofia that "the other belligerents having already consented, the Rumanian government awaited the immediate arrival at Bucharest of Bulgarian delegates to discuss the armistice, the preliminaries of peace, and the conclusion of a definitive peace." [35] The Turkish minister who requested permission for his government to participate in the conference was turned down, as only the changes of territory between the Christian states was to be regulated.[36]

With this the much heralded meeting at Nish was killed. Not even the armistice was to be signed there. Sazonov's plan for a conference at St. Petersburg which had been changed into a conference at Nish, had now been supplanted by the conference at Bucharest, a conference which in conception or sponsorship had little to do with Russia.

The agreement to settle all questions at Bucharest still did not end nor give prospects of immediately ending the actual conflict. In order to hasten the armistice King Carol on July 24th addressed a personal plea to each of the allied sovereigns.[37] King Nikita and King Peter, temporarily satiated with their conquests and somewhat apprehensive of Greek designs, were willing to call a halt. King Constantine, however, was adamant and, in spite of all advice from his counsellors and from the great powers, still insisted on a simultaneous signature of the armistice and preliminaries of peace.[38] But by the time Venizelos reached Bucharest the position of the Greek army had become so unfavorable that King Constantine consented to signing an immediate armistice.[39] The Greek premier had been advising this for some days, but had always been refused by his sovereign, who desired to dictate peace as a military conqueror. At the

[34] *Rumanian Green Book*, nos. 218, 244, 248, 249, 250.
[35] *Ibid.*, no. 251.
[36] *Ibid.*, no. 246; S.D., I, nos. 348, 349; Ö-U.A., VI, no. 8040.
[37] D.D.F., 3d. ser., VII, no. 455; Ö-U.A., VI, no. 7986.
[38] D.D.F., 3d. ser., VII, no. 468; Ö-U.A., VI, no. 8007; see also no. 8009.
[39] Gibbons, *Venizelos*, p. 150; B.D., IX, ii, 1073.

first meeting of the conference at Bucharest on July 30th an armistice of five days was arranged for without any ado, and the delegates were able to turn their attention immediately to the territorial settlement.[40]

After a second plenary session on July 31st it was decided that Bulgaria should undertake private discussions with each of the allies. Bulgaria still had hopes of obtaining a separate peace with Rumania or at least that she might use this possibility as a lever in the other discussions. Maiorescu, however, definitely spiked that hope when he announced the Bulgarian-Rumanian settlement at the general session on August 4th, not as a separate accord, but simply as part of the work of the conference which would include all agreements.[41]

Serbia and Greece at first presented absurd territorial claims in order to have plenty of leeway for bartering. After all, they had told each other that they could have these territories in their secret military convention. Serbia claimed the Struma river as the boundary but finally agreed to the watershed of this river, giving Bulgaria possession of the region of Strumitza. She insisted on the towns of Kotchana and Shtip, both of which Austria thought should go to Bulgaria.[42] Berchtold's idea that Bulgaria should have territory on the right bank of the Vardar was laughed at. The Greeks claimed the Aegean coast up to Makri, with ample hinterland, and also insisted more than the others on a war indemnity. This would have left Bulgaria only about forty kilometers of Aegean coastline. Concessions were negotiated except in respect to the city of Kavala. Here "the Bulgarians were stubborn and M. Venizelos was quite uncompromising." [43] In fact this city was much more than a controversial point between Bulgaria and Greece. In it were cradled hopes

[40] *Le traité de paix de Bucarest du 28 juillet (10 août) 1913. Précédé des protocoles de la conférence*, ed. by the ministry of foreign affairs (Bucharest, 1913; hereafter cited as *Paix de Bucarest*), annexe au protocole, no. 1, pp. 6–7. The protocols of the peace conference are also to be found in Martens, *Traités*, 3d. ser., VIII, 19–60.

[41] *Paix de Bucarest*, protocole, no. 5, p. 16.

[42] Berchtold to Fürstenberg, July 25, 1913, Ö-U.A., VI, no. 8016.

[43] Barclay to Grey, Aug. 8, 1913, B.D., IX, ii, no. 1225, p. 972.

for future alliance relationships in the Balkans and a shift of the balance of power.

From the beginning of the Second Balkan War the great powers had assumed that whatever settlement the Balkan states might make among themselves, it would have to be ratified by the signatories of the Treaty of Berlin. Austria especially maintained that, in view of her "vital interests," she must have the right to review the final territorial arrangements. But at Berlin Jagow was tired of the necessity of supporting Austrian demands, which he often considered picayune, and did not relish the prospects of an international conference. The Kaiser was dead set against such an affair and the German foreign office systematically undertook to undermine the whole project.[44] In the first place, no available meeting place could be discovered. St. Petersburg and Vienna were too much involved in the whole Balkan problem; Rome was too hot at this time of the year; Grey, still struggling with the ambassadors' conference, could hardly be expected to preside over another one. Paris was out of the question because of a certain ambassador (Izvolsky) and Berlin was "ausgeschlossen" for here they did not wish to reap another harvest of hatred as in 1878. Therefore, Jagow had been glad to further the idea of the Conference at Bucharest, where all the great powers would have representatives who could more or less supervise the settlement. In the end the final settlement could be ratified by an exchange of notes between the capitals, but there would be no general revision.

Although both England and France had grave doubts if things could be settled as Jagow proposed, they were willing enough to fall in line with his policy. Never rejecting the theory of revision, they also never championed it. Austria and Russia, however, were united for once in maintaining that they would have to give their approval to the final settlement. An exchange of views between St. Petersburg and Vienna indicated that the two cabinets were not very far apart on how the future bounda-

[44] G.P., XXXV, no. 13554 note; D.D.F., 3d. ser., VII, no. 445.

ries were to be drawn.[45] Austria wanted Serbia's portion on the left bank of the Vardar cut smaller than did Russia. Both countries knew that the real difficulties would not arise in this section but rather over the amount of territory Bulgaria should receive on the Aegean. Although Russia at times had wavered on the question of Kavala,[46] she now united with Austria in insisting that this city should be given to Bulgaria. With an eye to future alignments in the Balkans each government felt that it could not permit the other to champion the Bulgarian cause without joining in. They were equally united, both in maintaining that Adrianople would have to be returned to Bulgaria and in their inability to suggest how the Turks should be put out of the city.

Grey, who felt that Bulgaria should have at least a port on the Aegean, originally thought Kavala should be the city. Nevertheless he was not inclined to insist and was quite willing to believe accounts of the great possibilities of Dedeagach as a Bulgarian seaway. France, not without a glance towards Berlin, warmed more and more to the idea of a Greek Kavala as the crisis developed. But the real exponent of Greek views was Germany. The conference at Bucharest was just getting under way when King Constantine had his wife telegraph to her dear brother, the Kaiser: "Tino [King Constantine] just wired begging me to telegraph you that most important would be ein gutes Wort einzulegen King Roumania to support claims Greece on Cavalla. Please excuse forwarding this important message. Sophy." [47] William II, ever gracious and willing to play dynastic politics, forwarded the telegram to King Carol with the question: "Could you do something about Kavala? I would be very sympathetic to this question. Sincere greetings and best wishes for your successes." [48]

[45] Ö-U.A., VI, nos. 8030, 8075, 8088, 8092, 8108, 8112, 8150; VII, nos. 8170, 8220, 8221 Anlage.

[46] S.D., I, nos. 344, 357; Izvolsky, III, no. 1010.

[47] July 31, 1913, G.P., XXXV, no. 13696. This telegram is quoted as given and is not translated.

[48] *Ibid.*, XXXV, no. 13696 note. Jagow, in answer to a personal request from King Constantine sent a similar telegram to the Rumanian sovereign (*ibid.*, no. 13698).

King Carol was in an equivocal position. Unwilling to see Bulgaria weakened too much, he was personally inclined to see Kavala with its rich tobacco fields go to Bulgaria. Moreover Austria was pressing him to use his influence in favor of Bulgaria, and, in a personal letter to King Ferdinand, Carol had promised him to further his cause, if it were possible.[49] Now Germany demanded just the opposite and the Rumanian king began to change sides. This was not difficult, for all he had to do was keep silent for the Greeks to win their point.

Before the Kaiser's telegram arrived, however, Maiorescu had thought it best to take steps to prevent the conference from collapsing because of Kavala. Venizelos, representing King Constantine, maintained an uncompromising attitude, but he did indicate that, although Greece would never voluntarily resign its claims to Kavala, she might bow to the decree of the great powers.[50] This would enable King Constantine and the Greek government to defend the loss of the city before the Greek populace. Maiorescu thereupon met the ministers of Austria, Italy, and England at the Russian legation on the evening of the second day of the conference. Here it was agreed that as a safeguard against a possible breakdown of negotiations each minister should ask his government for authorisation to declare to Maiorescu that, whatever the decision come to by the conference in regard to Kavala, the great powers reserved the right to revise the decision.[51]

This proposal had great possibilities. If things came to a deadlock it would be perhaps the only way to save the conference and to prevent the resumption of hostilities. This all the powers wished. On the other hand it did recognise the necessity of revision — if only on a single point — and this some powers, notably Germany and France, wanted at all cost to

[49] G.P., XXXV, nos. 13699, 13705, 13706.

[50] Ö-U.A., VI, no. 8141; G.P., XXXV, no. 13699; Izvolsky, III, no. 982.

[51] The idea of making such a declaration apparently originated with Jonescu (B.D., IX, ii, no. 1191; see also no. 1225). The French minister was not at the Russian legation but joined in the suggested action (D.D.F., 3d. ser., VII, no. 511); see also, G.P., XXXV, no. 13699; Ö-U.A., VII, no. 8161.

forestall. The Russian government submitted to each of the powers a uniform draft formula for a declaration to be made to Maiorescu.[52] This was sidetracked, and each cabinet submitted its own guarded statement to Bucharest.

Austria naturally enough accepted Maiorescu's proposal, but instructed her minister to make the declaration only if another power did so, and then to add that this declaration did not stand in the way of revision on other points.[53] Great Britain also wanted it understood that this did "not preclude the Powers from revising other points if they think it necessary." [54] Although the British minister was authorised to make the declaration only "if all your colleagues are similarly instructed" he deposited the declaration with the Rumanian minister with this reservation.[55] Soon it was noised about that Great Britain had agreed to the revision of Kavala. This incensed the Greeks, but influenced the Bulgarians to give way for the moment to the Greek demands. The French foreign office, desiring the conference to proceed to its end without the intervention of the powers, instructed Blondel to be very reserved in this matter. If a rupture was certain and if all the powers agreed, France did not object to the proposal.[56] Italy agreed *si omnes*.[57] The Russian minister's declaration apparently was without reservation, in line with the draft formula, but was delayed some days.[58]

At Berlin, where the proposal crossed with the Kaiser's telegrams to King Carol on behalf of his Greek brother-in-law, Maiorescu's efforts met with little sympathy. The Kaiser was

[52] Ö-U.A., VII, no. 8207. See G.P., XXXV, no. 13707 note, in regard to the controversy as to whether Izvolsky ever submitted this declaration to the French foreign office. That he did is clear from D.D.F., 3d. ser., VII, no. 529.

[53] Berchtold to Fürstenberg, Aug. 2, 1913, Ö-U.A., VII, no. 8177.

[54] B.D., IX, ii, no. 1191.

[55] *Ibid.*, IX, ii, no. 1210, see also no. 1204; D.D.F., 3d. ser., VII, no. 580. Hearing that the British minister had made the declaration the Austrian minister in accordance with his instructions submitted his statement to Maiorescu (Ö-U.A., VII, no. 8204).

[56] D.D.F., 3d. ser., VII, nos. 518, 526.

[57] Ö-U.A., VII, nos. 8217, 8293.

[58] *Ibid.*, VII, no. 8249; D.D.F., 3d. ser., VII, 562.

very much against the proposal. Only if King Carol desired the declaration and if it appeared that only this would prevent the reopening of hostilities — and then only *si omnes* — was the German minister empowered to join in the declaration as to Kavala.[59] Later instructions virtually withdrew this authorisation as Jagow hoped to get around all revision. In fact things had so picked up at the conference that Maiorescu on August 6th told the German minister to forget about his declaration.[60]

The position taken by the powers on Maiorescu's proposal indicated fairly well the part played by the different ministers at the conference. The Russian and Austrian ministers were particularly active, while the Italian, Fasciotti, more because of his personal nature than on account of his instructions from Rome, ran them a close second. The German, English, and French ministers held themselves very much in reserve. Only once did Blondel really intervene, and then apparently to good effect. On August 6th the agreement between Serbia and Bulgaria was announced at a plenary session, but a deadlock over some strategical positions still held up the Greek-Bulgarian settlement. Maiorescu adjourned the sitting. Venizelos chanced to meet the French minister, who happened to be at the foreign office awaiting the close of the session. Blondel pleaded with him to give way on his own responsibility and not to wait for authorisation from Athens.[61] After further assurances from the Rumanian side, Venizelos did assume this responsibility. Half an hour after the sitting had been adjourned it was reassembled and the Greek-Bulgarian accord was announced.[62]

While the treaty was being drafted and the detailed boundary protocols drawn up, the conference busied itself with various minor tasks. The original five-day armistice had been extended for three days and was now concluded *sine die*. Largely through Rumania's efforts the Greek demand for indemnity and compensations for "wanton destruction" were passed over. The Bul-

[59] G.P., XXXV, nos. 13707, 13708, 13709.
[60] *Ibid.*, XXXV, no. 13723.
[61] D.D.F., 3d. ser., VII, no. 572; B.D., IX, ii, 973.
[62] *Paix de Bucarest*, protocole, no. 7, pp. 27–32.

garians desired that the other states should recognise in their newly acquired territories the autonomy of religious communities and the liberty of schools. This demand was rejected under the pretext that their respective constitutions already guaranteed these things.[63] This gave the Bulgarians an excuse for turning down various Greek demands of a similar nature. Maiorescu's eagerness to forestall a rupture of the conference by inviting the powers to make a reservation on Kavala now came back to plague him. Having called the fiddler he now had to pay him. He was in duty bound to read the Austrian and Russian declarations on revision to the conference.[64] The declaration of the other powers having been hamstrung with the reservation *si omnes* (which condition was not met on account of the hostility of Germany and France) were not read. The Bulgarian delegates immediately announced that the above Russian and Austrian declarations "had contributed to determine their consent to accept the conditions of peace."[65] They returned to this idea again and issued a formal declaration stating:

> Out of deference to the wishes of the great powers the Bulgarian delegates have consented to establish a partition of territory acquired from Turkey based solely on considerations of facts. They express the hope that Bulgaria will find in the great powers support to improve her position in accordance with the necessities of her commercial and national development.[66]

[63] Tonchev to Genadiev, Aug. 8, 1913, Ministerstvo na vŭnshnite raboti i na ispovedaniyata, *Diplomaticheski dokumenti po namesata na Bŭlgariya v evropeĭskata voĭna* [Diplomatic documents on the entry of Bulgaria into the World War] (2 vols.; Sofia, 1920–1; hereafter cited as *Diplomaticheski dokumenti*), I, 3 (no. 7). Bulgaria's position was in line with a note from the United States to the conference requesting that such a statement be incorporated into the treaty (*The Annual Register*, 1913, p. 352). Rumania in an exchange of notes with Bulgaria, Greece, and Serbia had obtained guarantees from each that they would respect the autonomy of the Kutso-Vlach schools and churches in their territories and would permit the Rumanian government to subsidise them (*Paix de Bucarest*, pp. 83–85).

[64] This he did at the plenary session on August 8th (*Paix de Bucarest*, protocole, no. 10, p. 48; Ö-U.A., VI, no. 8319).

[65] *Paix de Bucarest*, protocole, no. 10, p. 48.

[66] *Ibid.*, protocole, no. 11, p. 60.

The other delegates violently protested this Bulgarian view and Maiorescu as president of the conference declared:

> In taking cognisance of the declaration of the allies he thought he was expressing a conviction shared by the entire assembly in saying that the terms of the statement made by the first Bulgarian delegate could neither weaken nor invalidate in any way whatever the juridical value of the treaty.[67]

The Bulgarians had hoped to have these declarations annexed to the treaty as protocols. This, however, was denied them and they were merely incorporated into the minutes of the conference. Bulgaria therefore had no legal foundation on which she might base a later claim for revision.

The treaty as signed on August 10th and sanctified by an official *Te Deum* in the cathedral was a very short and concise document. Optimistically it promised peace and amity from the date of ratification. Three protocols annexed to the treaty traced in detail the future boundary lines. Rumania was to have the Turtukaia-Balchik line drawn rather liberally on both ends; Serbia was to have the Vardar valley including Shtip and Kotchana, but no corridor to the Aegean as had been suggested in the military convention with Greece; Greece was to have the island of Crete,[68] Kavala and a northern boundary that ran just below Monastir approximately parallel with the coastline. Mixed commissions were to be appointed within fifteen days to delimit the boundaries on the spot. Should disagreement arise recourse was to be had to arbitration by a friendly government. Serbia and Bulgaria undertook to settle long pending differences over their old frontier. Several articles dealt with demobilisation, use of railways, evacuation of territories, exchange of prisoners, etc.[69]

[67] *Paix de Bucarest*, protocole, no. 11, p. 61.

[68] The editors of the French documents state that the mention of Crete in the treaty was an error and that Thasos was meant (D.D.F., 3d. ser., VII, no. 601 note). That Crete was meant, however, is clear from the reading of the tenth protocol of the conference (*Paix de Bucarest*, p. 49).

[69] The treaty, additional protocols, and maps showing in detail the future Bulgarian-Rumanian, Bulgarian-Serbian, and Bulgarian-Greek boundaries are

Peace was at hand. Congratulations were in order. Telegrams, some of them indeed solicited, showered upon the Rumanian capital. As early as August 7th when it was certain there would be no rupture of the conference, King Carol had telegraphed to the German emperor:

After overcoming grave difficulties the conclusion of peace is assured, which thanks to you remains definitive. In this moment so important for my Government my thoughts are with you and I thank you with all my heart for your friendship and warm sympathy which you have specially shown me in these serious times.[70]

The Kaiser had just returned from a Northland cruise and from on board the "Hohenzollern" answered as follows:

Your telegram which reached me this night is a great and true pleasure for me. I express to you my sincerest and heartiest congratulations on the fine success which not only your people, but also all the belligerent states, and with them the whole of Europe owe to your wise and truly statesmanlike policy. It is at the same time a great satisfaction to me that you mention that I have been able to contribute to what has now been achieved. May Almighty God graciously preserve you for a long time still for the welfare of your country, the wonderful development of which I shall continue to follow with hearty friendship and admiration. I rejoice in our coöperation in the work of peace.[71]

This evoked another telegram of heartfelt appreciation from King Carol.[72] Immediately the Kaiser had the brilliant idea that these telegrams should be published. The chancellor had some qualms of conscience because Vienna had just proclaimed the necessity of revising the treaty. However, on the insistence of the Kaiser and with the deliberate intention of curbing Vienna's zeal for revision, the telegrams were published in the *Lokal Anzeiger* on August 10th.[73] Later the foreign office offi-

---

to be found in *Paix de Bucarest*, pp. 67 ff. The treaty is also to be found: Martens, *Traités*, 3d. ser., VIII, 61–78; *British Foreign and State Papers*, CVII, 663–670; D.D.F., 3d. ser., VII, no. 601. See map, p. 454.

[70] As translated in B.D., IX, ii, no. 1229 enclosure; see also, G.P., XXXV, no. 13732. [71] B.D., IX, ii, no. 1229 enclosure no. 2; G.P., XXXV, no. 13733.

[72] B.D., IX, ii, no. 1229 enclosure no. 3; G.P., XXXV, no. 13734.

[73] G.P., XXXV, nos. 13736, 13737; Ö-U.A., VII, no. 8682.

cials tried to convince Berchtold that they had not known of the publication of the telegrams in advance. At the same time it was announced that the Kaiser had appointed the King of Greece "General Feldmarschall," and had bestowed the Grand Cross of the Red Eagle on the Greek crown prince and the Rumanian prime minister, Maiorescu.[74]

The Austrian statesmen were incensed at Germany's action. And rightly so, for it was nothing more nor less than a blunt public proclamation of the lack of harmony between the allies. After all, dirty linen need not be washed in public. For the past weeks each had been trying to convince the other about Kavala, but without success. Berchtold had intensified his efforts to convince Germany that Austria on account of Serbia would in the future have to base her Balkan policy on Bulgaria.[75] But nothing could be done at present, and the two allies continued their diverse Balkan policies for a while longer.

After the Kaiser's telegrams the chances of revising the Treaty of Bucharest were very slim. Obviously it was up to Austria and Russia to push the matter — if it were to be pushed — for they had been the only ones to demand revision. Berchtold with heavy heart fought on and proceeded to get in touch with St. Petersburg.[76] But here he met with the cold shoulder. Sazonov would not consider revision of the Bulgarian-Serbian frontier and was no longer concerned about Kavala either, for in this latter case he had concluded that he must consider the wishes of France.[77] Revision of Kavala alone without considering the Bulgarian-Serbian frontier was not to Berchtold's taste. He therefore dropped the matter, also, and after August 14th revision was a dead issue.[78]

[74] Granville to Grey, Aug. 10, 1913, B.D., IX, ii, no. 1229.

[75] Ö-U.A., VII, nos. 8157, 8158, 8159, 8226, 8279, 8345, 8346.

[76] Berchtold to Thurn, Aug. 12, 1913, *ibid.*, VII, no. 8356. Bulgaria at this time also attempted to get Russia to demand revision of the decision on Kavala (Bobchev to Genadiev, Aug. 11, 1912, *Diplomaticheski dokumenti*, I, 16 [no. 15]).

[77] Ö-U.A., VII, no. 8386, see also nos. 8270, 8336. That Russia had no intention of pressing for revision is clear from the French documents (D.D.F., 3d. ser., VII, nos. 552, 597, VIII, no. 5; see also, S.D., I, no. 357).

[78] Ö-U.A., VII, no. 8498; B.D., IX, ii, no. 1235. Even recognition of the Treaty of Bucharest by an exchange of notes between the powers, which von

On the battlefield, in the treaty, as well as in the matter of revision, Bulgaria was defeated. The opposing coalition stood victorious on all fronts, and rumor had it that these governments had bound themselves by a very secret treaty to maintain the territorial settlement as outlined in the treaty.[79] Whether or not there was a formal treaty, or "a formula of guarantee appended as a declaration annexed to the treaty of Bucharest,"[80] or only an understanding was a matter of conjecture. It now seems clear that there was no signed agreement of any kind and that the three countries were united only by a common interest in maintaining the peace settlement inviolate.

Revision of the Treaty of Bucharest had in no small part been sidetracked by an even more complicated and thorny problem which faced the powers. This was the task of dealing with Turkey, which by her advance across the Enos-Midia line had violated the frontier as guaranteed by the powers at the end of the First Balkan War. Should she be permitted to retain the city of Adrianople and thus set at naught the decision of the great Christian states? Could territory once freed be returned to the Moslem yoke?

The powers had been especially busy during the last months with Turkish affairs. In addition to all the problems arising directly out of the wars, negotiations in regard to navigation rights on the Persian Gulf and the Tigris and Euphrates, Mesopotamian oil, the Bagdad and other railway concessions were in full swing. These centered in London where Hakki Pasha had

---

Jagow thought would at least be necessary on account of the Treaty of Berlin, never took place (G.P., XXXV, no. 13550). In the spring of 1914 Grey attempted to get concerted action for a declaration to the Balkan states recognising the Bucharest Treaty. The replies from the different powers showed such divergent views that he went ahead alone and submitted a formal declaration to the different Balkan capitals accepting the terms of the Treaty of Bucharest (B.D., X, i, 292 ed. note; no. 359). The other powers apparently never formally recognised the new order of things in the Balkans.

[79] For example see the section, "Der Gedanke eines neuen Balkanbundes" in Nikolaides, *Griechenlands Anteil an den Balkankriegen*, pp. 413–18; D.D.F., 3d. ser., VIII, nos. 25, 43.

[80] Descos to Pichon, Aug. 23, 1913, D.D.F., 3d. ser., VIII, no. 76; see also, no. 254.

been sent by the Turkish government as a special representative to discuss these questions.[81] The British statesmen were especially eager to bring these negotiations to a successful conclusion. The perennial question of Armenian reforms was also very much on the carpet.

Russia had again raised the Armenian problem at Constantinople and the other powers feared that she might take steps leading to the break-up of Asiatic Turkey.[82] Turkey as usual had announced her intention of reforming her administration. Secretly she had made proposals to different states to aid in this work. Germany was to reorganise the army; Italy had prospects of controlling the gendarmerie in Syria; France had the reorganisation of finances, post and telegraph; England was to send officials for the reform of the gendarmerie, justice and public works in the Armenian vilayets.[83] Turkey apparently was quite willing to forego the aid of Russia and Austria in working out reforms. Sazonov, however, would not have it this way. He was soon at loggerheads with Great Britain over the sending of British officers into territory which bordered on Russia.[84] This situation was eased when the Turkish government announced (at the very start of the Second Balkan War) a project of reform not limited solely to Armenia but intended for the entire empire.[85] The ambassadors at Constantinople were authorised to study this project and a similar project advanced by Russia a few weeks earlier.

While the powers were bickering over Armenia, Turkey had decided to answer the solicitations of the Balkan allies, and to profit by the difficulties of Bulgaria. On July 8th she had very correctly requested the powers to take steps at Sofia to bring about the evacuation of the Bulgarian troops from the territory which had been guaranteed to Turkey by the Treaty of London. She threatened to send in her troops without waiting any longer

[81] See especially, B.D., X, ii, chs. xcii, xciii; G.P., XXXVII, i, ch. cclxxxv.
[82] G.P., XXXVIII, no. 15282 note.
[83] *Ibid.*, XXXVIII, no. 15439; B.D., X, i, no. 479.
[84] *Ibid.*, X, i, nos. 528, 531 minutes.
[85] *Ibid.*, X, i, nos. 535 minutes, 538 enclosures, 545.

for the Bulgarians to withdraw.[86] Bulgaria of course complied with this demand, and the Turkish armies filed into the territory. When, however, news of Turkish troops beyond the Enos-Midia line reached the capitals of Europe, protests poured in from every hand. Turkey, used to such admonitions and well aware of the disunity among the powers, went nonchalantly ahead.[87] On July 19th she announced that she must insist on bending the Enos-Midia line in such a fashion that Adrianople should fall to Turkey.[88] This territory would be occupied, but no more.

This announcement naturally caused a stir at the different capitals. At London the ambassadors at one of their conferences talked over what was to be done.[89] In the end each ambassador was invited to consult his government. A variety of schemes were now born.

Since each country had already individually taken steps at the Porte, Berchtold now proposed a collective *démarche*. Jagow was opposed to this procedure, as he rightly foresaw that it would do no good. Russia wanted a joint naval demonstration which France, Germany and England all turned down. Russia further proposed the restriction of credit to Turkey. The concession of the tobacco *régie*, which was under French domination, was renewed just at this time,[90] and Sazonov was particularly wrought up over the advances which this organisation made to Turkey. No doubt these, along with special advances of the Council of the Ottoman Debt, did provide the money for the recapture of Adrianople. However, not only the French but also the German and Austrian foreign offices felt that they could not restrict the tobacco *régie*, which was a "private concern"! [91] France likewise deprecated any other

[86] Ö-U.A., VI, nos. 7691, 7714. [87] Izzet Pascha, *Denkwürdigkeiten*, p. 212.

[88] Ö-U.A., VI, no. 7894; G.P., XXXV, no. 13560 Anlage; B.D., IX, ii, no. 1161 ed. note.

[89] D.D.F., 3d. ser., VII, no. 436.

[90] *Ibid.*, VII, no. 434.

[91] *Ibid.*, VII, no. 575, VIII, nos. 13, 92; B.D., IX, ii, no. 1248; G.P., XXXV, no. 13780; Ö-U.A., VII, no. 8421.

form of financial pressure, ostensibly because of the difficulty of getting all the powers to agree.[92] Opposed to plans suggested by others, the Quai d'Orsay advanced no plans to bring about Turkish evacuation of Adrianople. Italy suggested that perhaps Turkey could be induced to surrender the city in return for some concessions in respect to the Aegean Islands. Germany advanced Wangenheim's suggestions that Turkey might withdraw if she were offered: (1) a better frontier than the Enos-Midia line, possibly the Ergene river; (2) exemption from any indemnity; (3) an increase of 4% in Turkish custom dues; (4) a mudir (spiritual representative) in Adrianople; (5) revision of the capitulations; (6) a guarantee of the possession of those islands which Italy was to return to Turkey according to the provisions of the Treaty of Lausanne.[93] Grey, who "thought that Turkey must be induced to withdraw from Adrianople, but . . . had been from the beginning opposed to precipitate coercive measures," thought the German proposal offered a good basis for negotiations.[94] The powers no doubt would have had some difficulty in agreeing about the tariff, capitulations, and the islands, but the matter never came to a discussion. The German government was very soon "inclined to drop it, because it did not seem likely to be acceptable." [95] In fact Turkey bluntly informed Berlin that under no circumstances would she surrender Adrianople even for compensation.[96] The Kaiser, who favored a Turkish Adrianople, also

[92] D.D.F., 3d. ser., VIII, no. 16. "The attitude of the French government makes all action by the concert impossible even in the unlikely event of Germany and Russia coming to some agreement as to what is to be done to get the Turks out of Thrace. I imagine that the motive for this attitude is mainly financial (Minute by H. C. Norman, initialed by Nicolson and Grey, July 26, 1913, B.D., IX, ii, no. 1180).

[93] G.P., XXXV, nos. 13616, 13618; XXXVI, i, no. 13754 note; B.D., IX, ii, no. 1203.

[94] B.D., IX, ii, no. 1203, see also no. 1233; G.P., XXXV, no. 13758. Pichon and Sazonov also were pleased with the plan (G.P., XXXVI, i, nos. 13761, 13776). For Grey's attitude on the question of Adrianople on the day he signed a series of economic agreements with Turkey see, Grey to Marling, July 29, 1913, B.D., X, ii, no. 123.

[95] Grey to Granville, Aug. 13, 1913, B.D., IX, ii, no. 1233; see also, G.P., XXXVI, i, nos. 13772, 13773.

[96] G.P., XXXVI, i, nos. 13756, 13757.

gave direct orders to avoid mixing in this question if possible.[97]

In order to stir up the other powers Russia at various times indicated that she might be forced to take separate action. This would have raised the whole problem of Asiatic Turkey, already complicated by the discussion of Armenian reforms, and all the other powers hastened to curb Russian initiative. Berchtold gave notice that if Russia were forced to intervene in Turkey on behalf of Bulgaria, he would also feel free to take similar measures.[98] What these measures were to be was not stated, but it was hard to see how Austria could take such action without at least transporting troops across Serbia. And Austrian troops anywhere in Serbia was exactly what Sazonov wanted to prevent at any cost.

After much telegraphing hither and yon the concert of Europe finally produced on August 7th a collective *démarche* at the Porte. This had been recommended by the ambassadors' conference at London as early as July 24th.[99] The powers now at least outwardly thundered in unison: "Respect the Preliminaries of London!"; the grand vizier smiled and promised to refer the matter to the council of ministers. The day before Turkey had stolen a march on the powers and had presented each of them with a long memorandum as to why Turkey could not possibly leave Adrianople. The answer to the collective *démarche* was the same.[100] Meanwhile the Bulgarian officials informed the powers that they had decided to accept the conditions of the Treaty of Bucharest and to demobilise the troops. They did this because of the "profound conviction of the government that the great powers, who are working in favor of adoption of the Enos-Midia line, will be able to impose on Turkey respect for the Treaty of London arranged under their auspices." [101]

With the Treaty of Bucharest signed, Russia's willingness to

[97] *Ibid.*, XXXVI, i, nos. 13763, 13764.
[98] Ö-U.A., VI, nos. 8002, 8011.
[99] D.D.F., 3d. ser., VII, nos. 555, 568.
[100] G.P., XXXVI, i, nos. 13759 Anlage, 13774; D.D.F., 3d. ser., VIII, no. 8.
[101] Bax-Ironside to Grey, Aug. 7, 1913, B.D., IX, ii, no. 1213.

forego the revision of that document only heightened her sense of obligation to do something for Bulgaria in Thrace. Austria, not out of friendship but out of rivalry, appeared to be the only power willing to lend a "sympathetic" ear. Tisza worked out two long memoirs urging coöperation with Russia eventually even in a military way.[102] Berchtold and Francis Joseph were, however, disinclined to go so far as military coöperation.[103] When it was clear that Russia would permit no modification of the Serbian-Bulgarian frontier, Berchtold saw no reason for antagonising Turkey in order to further a project which would only restore the prestige of the big Slav brother at Sofia. About August 17th, reports of a new Turkish advance towards Mustafa Pasha and Dedeagach — officially justified by Bulgarian massacres — set Sazonov on edge.[104] He went to the tsar and obtained permission to withdraw the Russian ambassador from Constantinople. At London they were upset by this sudden burst of action and Nicolson in despair wrote: "It is impossible to foresee from one day to another what M. Sazonov will do." [105] Again the slow process of getting another collective admonition at Constantinople began. This time the step was welcomed by the Turkish officials for it would give them an opportunity to make some concessions which would help Russia to save her face.[106] It is quite clear that this new forward movement by the Turkish army was a deliberate scheme to enable the government to meet some of the demands of the powers without surrendering Adrianople. Thus on August 21st, even before the powers made any progress with the collective *démarche*, Turkey announced that under no circumstance would Turkish troops be permitted to occupy the right bank of the Maritza, except

[102] Ö-U.A., VII, nos. 8343, 8474.

[103] *Ibid.*, VII, nos. 8376, 8498, 8521.

[104] D.D.F., 3d. ser., VIII, nos. 44, 51. In London Hakki Pasha claimed that the King of Greece "issued a direct invitation to the Ottoman government to occupy Dedeagach" since he did not want to hand the territory over to the Bulgarians on the withdrawal of Greek troops (Minute, Mr. Parker, August 19, 1913, B.D., X, ii, no. 139).

[105] Minute, Aug. 19, 1913, B.D., IX, ii, no. 1242.

[106] G.P., XXXVI, i, nos. 13786, 13789.

for a few strategical points, or any territory in addition to that which was indicated by the declaration of July 19th.[107] The peril of a new advance being officially ended, the powers, as France had intimated to the Porte, were ready to close their eyes to the fate of Adrianople.[108] They willingly turned over to Bulgaria the difficult task of saving Adrianople from Mohammedan rule.

As early as August 12th the grand vizier had suggested to Germany that if the powers would only mind their own business for a couple of weeks he would be able to reach a direct settlement with Bulgaria. This idea had appealed to the Wilhelmstrasse for there the officials were having a difficult task to harmonise outward coöperation with the powers in maintaining the Preliminaries of London with the Kaiser's instruction that Turkey should have Adrianople.[109] They had sounded out the other powers on this scheme.[110] Now that Turkey had stopped its new advance and given promises about the right bank of the Maritza the plan of direct negotiations came more and more into the foreground. Nachovich, the Bulgarian representative who had been sent to Constantinople at the beginning of July and had remained there during the recent hostilities, tried to impress upon his government the wisdom and necessity of dealing directly with Turkey.[111] But Genadiev at Sofia was much opposed to this procedure, as he still had hopes that the powers would save Adrianople for Christian rule.[112]

Germany and Italy were especially active in forwarding a

[107] B.D., IX, ii, no. 1250; Ö-U.A., VII, no. 8439; G.P., XXXVI, i, nos. 13790, 13792. Repeated orders by the grand vizier to withdraw all troops from the right bank of the Maritza were not obeyed by the commanding officers. Since Adrianople was located on both sides of the stream it was necessary, if the city was to have any value as a fortress, to control both banks at certain places (Izzet Pascha, *Denkwürdigkeiten*, p. 213).

[108] Radowitz from Paris to foreign office, Aug. 21, 1913, G.P., XXXVI, i, no. 13793.

[109] *Ibid.*, XXXVI, i, nos. 13763, 13764, 13779.

[110] *Ibid.*, XXXVI, i, nos. 13774 note, 13777.

[111] Ö-U.A., VII, no. 8466; G.P., XXXVI, i, no. 13802; D.D.F., 3d. ser., VII, nos. 530, 544; VIII, no. 83 note.

[112] *Diplomaticheski dokumenti*, I, 18 (no. 37), 25 (no. 48), 27 (no. 53).

bilateral solution. No powers opposed it, and finally Russia advised the Bulgarian government that it was laying itself open to further attack if it did not enter upon direct *pourparlers*.[113] With an appeal for aid to anyone and everyone, the Bulgarian government on August 29th named its delegates and made ready to send them to Constantinople. Not only the Treaty of Bucharest, but also the question of Adrianople was now definitely out of the hands of the powers. This time it was possible to hand the problems of the Balkans back to the Balkan states; the following year the powers themselves were to be drawn in to participate not with the patter of discussions but with the roar of guns.

[113] Ö-U.A., VII, nos. 8483, 8506; D.D.F., 3d. ser., VIII, no. 96.

CHAPTER XIX

THE FINAL PEACE TREATIES

THE Preliminaries of London of May 30, 1913, though officially a treaty of peace between the Balkan allies and Turkey, had left many problems unsettled. The ambassadors' conference had, by the terms of the treaty, been explicitly entrusted with the task of settling certain outstanding territorial questions. These were the southern Albanian boundary and the Aegean Islands. The northern Albanian boundary and the question of Scutari had occupied the winter and spring sessions of that conference. Agreement had been reached as to the northern boundary, and Scutari had been occupied on behalf of the powers on May 14th. The summer sessions of the ambassadors' conference, following the Preliminaries of London, dealt with the southern boundary of Albania and came to a decision as to its general direction. The broad outlines of Albania's future government had been determined and the probable sovereign of that state had been tentatively selected.[1] But there was much yet to be done. A transitional government had to be created through the establishment of the International Control Commission, and the sovereign proclaimed. The northern and southern boundary commissions had to be appointed and started on their tasks of delimiting the actual boundaries. It was evident that these bodies would receive little coöperation from either Serbia or Greece. The future of the Aegean Islands was discussed by the ambassadors but even their general conclusions on this matter had not been ratified by the governments they represented.

The Turks had, as a matter of fact, completely upset the Preliminaries of London by their advance over the Enos-Midia line on July 12th, while the Balkan allies were fighting over their

[1] See above, pp. 332–34.

spoils. Under protest of the powers the Turkish advance ceased on August 21st, but the Bulgarians and Turks had to negotiate an entirely new treaty to cover the new territorial situation. Turkey now held Adrianople. The Treaty of Bucharest of August 10th settled the problems created by the Second Balkan War between Bulgaria and the allies, but Serbia and Montenegro had not yet agreed upon a partition of spoils. The future of the Aegean Islands was still uncertain and constituted the great obstacle to the reëstablishment of normal relations between Turkey and Greece. Serbia and Montenegro also had to regulate such matters as exchange of prisoners, protection of minorities, etc., with Turkey. Although no state of war existed, a treaty of peace was necessary between Turkey and each of the Balkan states separately.[2] The cession of Turkish territory to Christian states also raised problems of an international character concerning railways and finances.

Woven inextricably through the settlement of these difficulties was the greatest problem of all arising out of the wars of 1912–1913, namely the ordering of future alliance relationships in the Balkans. So delicately was the balance of power drawn that a shift one way or another might have the most serious consequences. In addition there were many less direct repercussions which needed solution. Renewed demands for reform in Turkey, the Liman von Sanders Mission,[3] a quickened scramble

[2] This was the result of the singular status of the Preliminaries of London. After the acceptance of that agreement, at subsequent conferences of the peace delegates it had been held that while the treaty was definitive as signed between Turkey and the bloc of allies, it necessarily had to be followed by "definitive treaties with each of the allies" dealing with pending questions which particularly concerned each one (Protocoles, June 2, 6, 1913, B.D., IX, ii, 1052–3). Ratifications of the Preliminaries (Treaty) of London had never been exchanged and so under international law it actually was technically without validity (Martens, *Traités*, 3d. ser., VIII, 16).

[3] In regard to the tense international situation at the close of 1913 arising out of the sending of a German military mission to Turkey headed by General Liman von Sanders see, Hans Herzfeld, "Die Liman-Krise und die Politik der Grossmächte in der Jahreswende 1913/14," *Berliner Monatshefte*, XI (1933), 837–58, 973–93; Fay, *Origins of the World War*, I, 498–524; Brandenburg, *Von Bismarck zum Weltkriege*, pp. 409–11; Carl Mühlmann, *Deutschland und die Türkei 1913–1914* (Berlin, 1929).

for concessions — this time even entered into by Italy and Austria-Hungary — in order to have an established stake in Asiatic Turkey when final dissolution came, all these helped to make the Near East the focal point of international politics. And finally, how was the spirit of imperialism, militarism, and nationalism, heightened throughout Europe by these conflicts, ever to be stilled? How was the argument started in October, 1912 as to whether Creusot or Krupp guns were superior ever to be settled? Europe was at peace and yet the cabinets, as they undertook to watch over the final settlements, were faced momentarily with a renewal of war in the Balkans.

The Bulgarian delegates who had been dispatched to Constantinople after the powers had washed their hands of the problem of settling the status of Adrianople, were faced with a most difficult task.[4] They were to salvage as much of Thrace as possible and at the same time lay the basis for a future understanding with Turkey. From the powers they could expect little effective support since Turkey was well aware of the disunity which existed among them, and acted accordingly. In addition the Bulgarian army was totally disorganised. The Bulgarian statesmen might threaten to break off negotiations if certain points were not met, but no one knew better than the Turks that this was mere bluff. Haggling and bazaar bargaining was to be expected, but it was clear that the Bulgarians would have to sign on the dotted line. On the other hand the Turkish officials, in view of the tense relations with Athens, were willing to concede some points for the sake of an Entente. The possibility of a Turkish-Bulgarian attack on Greece could not only be used to threaten Greece but also the powers, who had not yet decided the final fate of the islands and were longing for a period of quiet in the Balkans.

The Austrian ambassador at Constantinople thought it would not take long for Bulgaria, obsessed by a passion for the revision of the Treaty of Bucharest, and Turkey, dominated by the

[4] See above, pp. 405–6.

desire for the Aegean Islands, to get together.[5] Such was the case. On September 6th the peace commission held its first official session.[6] Each delegation advanced proposed boundary lines. The next days were spent in bargaining. On the 18th the boundary accord was signed. Starting at the mouth of the Maritza, and terminating at the mouth of the Rezvoya just north of Imaada on the Black Sea, the boundary was to leave Demoloho, Adrianople, and Kirk-Kilisse to Turkey.[7]

The Turkish government was much concerned over the protection of its nationals in the territory to be incorporated into Bulgaria. At the same time the Bulgarians pushed their idea of a Turkish-Bulgarian entente. On September 27th the Bulgarian minister of foreign affairs, over-optimistic, jubilantly informed the Austrian minister Tarnowski that a defensive alliance would be signed at Constantinople.[8] Negotiations to this end were making good progress but were not complete when the peace negotiations were concluded on September 30, 1913.

The Treaty of Constantinople between Bulgaria and Turkey was to serve as a model for the later treaties to be made between Turkey and the other Balkan states. In addition to the territorial settlement, it provided for the resumption of diplomatic and treaty relations, evacuation of territories, exchange of prisoners, amnesty, right of inhabitants of the newly acquired Bulgarian territory to opt for Ottoman citizenship, equal civil and political rights for Mohammedan and Christian, etc. Elaborate provisions were made in regard to religion. Prayers were still to be said in the name of the sultan, and special guarantees were inserted for the protection of mosques and the muftis. An annex to the treaty provided for settlement through the Hague Court of Arbitration of disputes which might arise over certain articles.[9]

[5] Pallavicini to foreign office, Sept. 6, 1913, Ö-U.A., VII, no. 8550.

[6] *Ibid.*, VII, no. 8562.

[7] *Ibid.*, VII, nos. 8642, 8659; G.P., XXXVI, i, no. 13825. See map, p. 454.

[8] Ö-U.A., VII, no. 8733.

[9] Martens, *Traités*, 3d. ser., VIII, 78–93. Portions of the treaty are similar to parts of "Treaty Drafts" presented by the allies and Turkey at the peace con-

Austria of all the powers had no doubt been the most helpful in bringing about the settlement. Indeed Genadiev had instructed the Bulgarian delegates: "Concerning the agreement with Turkey and the negotiations with Talaat and Jemal you may communicate frankly with Pallavicini but with absolutely none of the other ambassadors." [10] Austrian counsels of moderation at both Sofia and Constantinople helped the discussions over several difficult points.[11] With special interest the Ballhausplatz followed the course of the negotiations for an entente. The Bulgarians were advised not to push matters too much.[12] General Savov, chief of the Bulgarian delegation, was more inclined to the immediate conclusion of an entente than Genadiev.[13] Talaat Bey, minister of interior and chief Turkish negotiator, seemed disposed, however, to strike while the iron was hot. With the greatest secrecy the preliminary draft of a military convention was transmitted to Sofia.[14] The Austrian minister was at once permitted to see it and took it with him when he left for Vienna. The Bulgarian government now worked out a counter project.[15] The changes were for the most part acceptable to Turkey, but negotiations were protracted throughout November and December, 1913, over various details. On December 27th, Tarnowski was able to report the gratifying news that the accord was perfected, and the text was being sent to Sofia for signature.[16] However a change in the ministry at Constantinople and some changes in the ministry at Sofia "delayed" the completion of the agreement. Next the Bulgarian election intervened. Toward the end of January, 1914, when the powers were about ready to announce their decision on

---

ference in the sessions after the signature of the Preliminaries of London (Protocole 13, June 6, 1913, B.D., IX, ii, 1054–58).

[10] Genadiev to Savov, Sept. 2/15, 1913, *Diplomaticheski dokumenti*, I, 52.

[11] Ö-U.A., VII, nos. 8586, 8587, 8588, 8600, 8606, 8652, 8672. These Bulgarian-Turkish negotiations can be followed best in the Austrian documents, the other documentary collections adding little to the picture there presented.

[12] *Ibid.*, VII, no. 8645.

[13] Toshev, II, 461–2.

[14] Tarnowski to foreign office, Oct. 10, 1913, Ö-U.A., VII, no. 8821.

[15] *Ibid.*, VII, nos. 8827, 8858; see also, nos. 8930, 8942, 8986, 9065, 9095.

[16] *Ibid.*, VII, no. 9129.

the islands, Turkey, knowing the decision would be unfavorable to her, wanted to push the signature of the convention with Bulgaria. The Bulgarian government now showed hesitancy, and demanded the insertion of an additional clause assuring each country more freedom by binding each only to neutrality rather than to coöperation for the next two years.[17] Soon the harsh treatment by Bulgaria of Mohammedans in the newly acquired territory led to bitter recriminations between Sofia and Constantinople. Under these conditions nothing could be done about the military convention.

Changes in the ministry, Bulgarian elections, disputes over treatment of nationalities were of course only the ostensible reasons for failure to sign the agreement. In February, 1914, the Greek and Serbian premiers after a visit to St. Petersburg stopped off at Bucharest. Rumors of a Rumanian-Serbian-Greek alliance spread like wildfire. No definite agreement was signed but the new Rumanian cabinet of Bratianu did give Pašić and Venizelos definite assurances "that Rumania was determined to maintain the provisions of the Treaty of Bucharest . . . and in no case would tolerate an attack on the *status quo* no matter from what side it might arise." [18] Bulgaria was not anxious to be brought face to face with this combination by some rash step on the part of Turkey. Besides, Bulgaria always considered the arrangement with Turkey only as a step towards a rapprochement with the Triple Alliance.[19] Her renewed offers to Austria of an alliance had been sympathetically received, but that was all.[20] Berchtold, while willing to help Bulgaria in every respect, did not feel that he could assume any definite obligations. It was only after great difficulty that he was able to arrange an Austrian-German loan for Bulgaria in the spring of 1914.[21] After all, Bulgaria would have to make her alliance

[17] Ö-U.A., VII, no. 9224; see also nos. 9235, 9242, 9387.

[18] R.D., I Reihe, I, no. 315; D.D.F., 3d. ser., IX, nos. 253, 254, 283.

[19] Ö-U.A., VII, nos. 9281, 9393.

[20] For the original offer see, Tarnowski to foreign office, July 22, 1913, *ibid.*, VI, no. 7937; also, VIII, nos. 8647, 8688, 8702, 8735, 8775, 9098, 9108.

[21] See Ö-U.A., VII, nos. 9422, 9428, 9442 note, where the most important references on these negotiations are cited. Russia at this time attempted to

not only with Austria but with Austria's allies as well. Berlin still turned a cold shoulder to Sofia. Jagow, following the Kaiser's instructions, had from the very beginning of the negotiations done his best to sabotage the Turkish-Bulgarian entente and replace it with a Turkish-Greek one.[22] The possibility that Turkey might accept Germany's plan and settle with Greece, leaving the way clear for Turkish *revanche* in Thrace, led the Bulgarian statesmen to fear Turkish treachery. Bulgaria's relations with Rumania had not improved materially,[23] and this gave promise of forever halting Bulgaria's approach to Berlin and even to Vienna. And without that approach there was nothing of real value to Sofia in a military convention with Turkey. As long as it was left unsigned, the road was left clear for a possible rapprochement with the Triple Entente. Had Germany and Austria seen eye to eye on Balkan matters, the Turkish-Bulgarian entente could have been concluded overnight.[24] As it was, the negotiations still hung fire in July, 1914.[25]

Direct Turkish-Greek discussions which constantly had their bearing on the Bulgarian-Turkish relations just outlined did not progress smoothly. For several months after the Treaty of Bucharest the question of the Aegean Islands stalled all efforts to reëstablish normal peacetime relations between Athens and Constantinople. According to the Preliminaries of London the

---

bring about a change of ministries at Sofia and the installation of a pro-Russian cabinet by indicating the possibility of opening the Paris money market for a Bulgarian loan (R.D., I Reihe, I, no. 358; II, no. 207; III, nos. 29, 43, 93, 238, 242; Dr. V. Radoslavoff, "Die Rolle und die Ziele Bulgariens im Kriege," *Die Kreigsschuldfrage*, VI (1928), 1138–9). The last minute Russian-French efforts to forestall the German loan were of no avail (R.D., I Reihe, II, nos. 301, 316, 418; III, no. 162; IV, no. 189). For the terms of the loan granted in June, 1914 see, Henri Prost, *La Bulgarie de 1912 à 1930* (Paris, 1932), pp. 57–60; *The Near Eastern Year Book*, 1931–2, pp. 159–60.

[22] G.P., XXXVI, i, nos. 13813, 13816, 13821 marginal notes.

[23] D.D.F., 3d. ser., X, nos. 174, 181, 560; R.D., I Reihe, III, no. 369.

[24] This was the opinion of Wangenheim in May, 1914 (see his excellent analysis of Balkan policy in a private letter to Jagow, May 7, 1914, G.P., XXXVI, ii, no. 14587).

[25] The text of a Bulgarian-Turkish treaty of January 12/25, 1914 which was supplied to the Russian foreign office on May 13, 1915 by the French embassy is beyond doubt apocryphal (R.D., I Reihe, I, 449–450).

powers were to decide the future of the islands. This burning issue was tied hand in glove with the problem of satisfying Greek claims relative to the southern boundary of Albania and will be discussed later in that connection.[26] It will suffice here to deal with the conclusion of the Treaty of Athens of November 14, 1913.

After the end of the Second Balkan War, Germany did her best to bring Greece and Turkey together. But the leaders at Constantinople dallied and, instead of falling in with Germany's scheme, much to the delight of the Ballhausplatz struck up intimate relations with Bulgaria. It also seems certain that Italy encouraged the Turkish statesmen to press for certain islands which were in Greek possession.[27] This, of course, did anything but bring the two countries together. The Italian statesmen were hard at work trying to efface the effects of the Tripolitan War and establish themselves as friends of Turkey. By favoring Turkey at the cost of Greece they had hopes of obtaining economic concessions in the region of Adalia. It was Rumania which finally brought about the conclusion of the treaty between Greece and Turkey. Much to the Kaiser's satisfaction,[28] King Carol informed Constantinople and Athens that a Turkish-Bulgarian attack on Greece would result in Rumanian intervention because it would threaten the settlement made at Bucharest.[29] This had a calming influence, and Take Jonescu in a visit to both capitals was able to bring about the signature of the agreement.[30]

This Treaty of Athens of November 14, 1913 provided for the resumption of diplomatic and commercial relations, exchange of prisoners, religious rights of Mohammedans in the ceded territories, citizenship, etc.[31] Unfortunately no agreement was

[26] See below, pp. 431–42.

[27] G.P., XXXVI, i, nos. 13541, 13850.

[28] *Ibid.*, XXXVI, i, nos. 13865, 13866, 13872, 13885, marginal notes to 13887, 13891, 13896.

[29] Jonescu, *Some Personal Impressions*, pp. 191–3; Ö-U.A., VII, nos. 8971 note, 8978, 8979; D.D.F., 3d. ser., VIII, no. 454; G.P., XXXVI, i, no. 13891.

[30] G.P., XXXVI, i, nos. 13896, 13897; D.D.F., 3d. ser., VIII, nos. 462, 476, 486.

[31] Martens, *Traités*, 3d. ser., VIII, 93–101.

reached on the future of the Aegean Islands. This difficulty was glided over, with both countries agreeing to maintain the Treaty of London, especially Article V. This article was the one which placed the fate of the islands in the hands of the powers. *À propos* of the Greek-Turkish agreement, the German chargé at Athens reported:

> Whether the treaty can be used as a basis for further rapprochement with Turkey, which one desires here, will depend upon the solution of the question of the islands. Faith in the Turkish government after the experiences of the recent negotiations is not very great.[32]

While the Turkish government was negotiating with Sofia and Athens they also carried on desultory discussions with Belgrade. Since Turkey and Serbia had no territorial dispute — this matter having been settled as far as they were concerned by the Treaty of London — their differences were less immediate and provocative than those confronting the other countries. Yet neither government seemed disposed to hasten negotiations. Serbia at this time was chiefly occupied with northern Albanian affairs and with Austrian hostility to her actions in this region. When these Albanian difficulties grew less acute the discussions between Constantinople and Belgrade were accelerated. On November 23rd the Quai d'Orsay was informed that the terms of a treaty had been agreed upon.[33] However, the document remained unsigned. Although there were no serious differences, questions regarding nationality, schools, religious guarantees, property of the mosques afforded bountiful opportunities for bickering.[34] In February, 1914 the French and Russian ministers at Belgrade urged the Serbian government to hasten the negotiations.[35] Finally on March 14, 1914 the Treaty of Constantinople was signed.

This agreement was not unlike the peace treaties negotiated

[32] Bassewitz to Bethmann Hollweg, Nov. 14, 1913, G.P., XXXVI, i, no. 13898.

[33] Bompard to Pichon, Nov. 23, 1913, D.D.F., 3d. ser., VIII, no. 518.

[34] *Ibid.*, IX, nos. 9, 26, 163, 244, 328, 338.

[35] *Ibid.*, IX, nos. 227, 328, 368. Hartwig felt that Turkish-Bulgarian negotiations made the Turkish government reluctant to come to an agreement with Serbia (R.D., I Reihe, II, no. 88).

by Turkey with Bulgaria and Greece. Their desire "of consolidating the ties of peace and friendship happily reëstablished between them and to facilitate the resumption of normal relations between the two countries" was proclaimed. The Treaty (Preliminaries) of London of May 30, 1913 was reaffirmed, but to leave no doubt of the status of peace, they inserted a clause providing: "There will be from the date of signature of the present treaty peace and friendship between Serbia and Turkey." No such clause had been inserted in the Treaty of Athens, it being rather euphemistically held that the peace between the two countries really dated from the Treaty of London. As in the other treaties, provision was made for the resumption of diplomatic relations, exchange of prisoners, protection of religious property and rights of the Moslem priesthood, etc.[36]

There had thus been signed since the outbreak of the First Balkan War the following peace treaties. First the Preliminaries of London of May 30, 1913, which at times is called the Treaty of London. This was later to be declared a definitive treaty, but the ratifications had never been exchanged. Its provisions were accepted as binding among themselves by the signatories of the Treaty of Constantinople of September 29, 1913 between Bulgaria and Turkey; the Treaty of Athens of November 14, 1913 between Greece and Turkey; the Treaty of Constantinople of March 14, 1914 between Serbia and Turkey. No special treaty was ever negotiated between Montenegro and Turkey, nor were diplomatic relations ever resumed between the two countries.[37]

Although Montenegro might spurn negotiating with Turkey, she was forced to negotiate an agreement with Serbia. Neither the Preliminaries of London nor the Treaty of Bucharest had allotted any definite territory to Montenegro. This was left for direct settlement between Cetinje and Belgrade. Just exactly what arrangements had been made in their alliance treaty of October 6, 1912 is uncertain. At any rate after the Second

[36] Martens, *Traités*, 3d. ser., VIII, 643–8.

[37] Gustav von Hubka, "Diplomatentum in Montenegro," *Berliner Monatshefte*, XIV (1936), 657.

Balkan War Montenegro claimed the Sanjak of Novibazar, Djakova, Prizren, and a southern boundary constituted by the further watershed of the Drin. Hartwig, who was cognisant of these demands, was confident that the Serbian government would be very conciliatory and that there would be no difficulties except in regard to Prizren.[38] He was over-optimistic.

As early as September 1, 1913 the Austrian minister at Cetinje had reported that the agreement between Serbia and Montenegro was to be signed that day.[39] But this was not to be. The Albanian difficulties,[40] in which King Nikita also touchily put his fingers, delayed matters. On November 3rd the French minister was finally able to report the settlement of all differences and on November 7th the agreement was signed at Belgrade.[41] Montenegro received Djakova, Plevlje, and half of the Melokia plain. Her territory had been increased 2,129 square miles and her population doubled.

The Sanjak of Novibazar had been divided; Serbia and Montenegro now had common frontiers. Within a few months rumors of a Serbian-Montenegrin union began to cause uneasiness at Vienna.[42] This union — smiled upon at St. Petersburg — was something the Austrian officials felt they could not permit. Serbia would then have her Adriatic port and that was what Austria in the autumn of 1912 had decided should never be permitted. This question of the proposed union added its bit to the weight of the Serbian problem which pressed upon the Ballhausplatz in 1914.

[38] D.D.F., 3d. ser., VII, no. 590. King Nikita at this time was dissatisfied with Russia and did not like Hartwig's efforts at Belgrade. The French government attempted to better Russian-Montenegrin relations and also authorised the issuance of a loan to Montenegro (*ibid.*, VIII, nos. 109, 198, 281, 284, 291).

[39] Ö-U.A., VII, no. 8524.

[40] D.D.F., 3d. ser., VIII, no. 316; see below, pp. 419–27.

[41] *Ibid.*, VIII, no. 435 and note; *Statesmen's Yearbook*, 1914, p. 1090.

[42] On March 15, 1914 King Nikita on Sazonov's suggestion sent a letter to King Peter suggesting that while each state should retain its own rulers and government there might be a union based on military, diplomatic, and financial considerations (R.D., I Reihe, II, nos. 97, 119, 159, 160, 169 Anlagen; D.D.F., 3d. ser., X, nos, 141, 286; see also, *ibid.*, p. xiii; G.P., XXXVIII, ch. CCXCI). For a good account of the German and Austrian attitudes on these negotiations see, Gooss, *Das österreichisch-serbische Problem*, pp. 159–164.

CHAPTER XX

THE ALBANIAN BOUNDARIES AND THE AEGEAN ISLANDS

While Turkey and the Balkan states were negotiating their peace treaties the powers busied themselves with Albanian affairs. The ambassadors' conference had agreed upon a Statute of Albania which arranged for an international control commission. This was finally appointed and held its first meeting at Valona on October 16, 1913, where it began the task of supervising the organisation of a gendarmerie and the establishment of a semblance of government in Albania.[1] But for a long time after the conference of ambassadors had agreed upon the northern boundary of Albania, Serbian troops remained on Albanian soil, and the commission to delimit the actual boundary remained unconstituted. Although the latter body was first scheduled to begin its work on August 1st, it was not until September 23rd that all representatives met at Scutari. It was another month before work was actually begun at Lake Ochrida, from which point the commission wearily worked its way northward.[2]

Serbia had long been advised by the powers to evacuate territory which had definitely been awarded to Albania. On July 29th Grey had suggested at the conference of ambassadors that a joint *démarche* be made at Belgrade.[3] Serbia was to be forcefully reminded of her obligation to evacuate Albanian territory without delay, and at the same time the engagement of the powers guaranteeing Serbia a commercial outlet on the Adriatic was to be renewed and confirmed in writing. It was not until

[1] G.P., XXXVI, i, nos. 14025 note, 14053. This commission never established effective control over Albania. It later coöperated with the makeshift government under the Prince of Wied and continued to exercise nominal control after his departure in September, 1914 (*ibid.*, XXXVI, ii, no. 14552). For further details about the International Control Commission see, *ibid.*, XXXVI, i, ch. CCLXXIX; Stickney, *Southern Albania*, pp. 47–54; Swire, *Albania*, *passim*.

[2] B.D., X, i, no. 8, ed. note; G.P., XXXVI, i, nos. 13941, 13958.

[3] Ö-U.A., VI, no. 8103.

two days after the signature of the Treaty of Bucharest that all the ministers had their instructions and not until August 17th that the *démarche* was made.[4] Pašić graciously promised to withdraw the troops. Failure, however, to do this caused Berchtold on September 4th to request a further protest from the powers. This time it was impossible to obtain unanimous action. Neratov, who presided over the Russian foreign office while Sazonov vacationed in France, saw absolutely no need for new advice at Belgrade. In his opinion the Serbs were but maintaining law and order in territory rent by warfare and revolt.[5]

It is true that the tardiness of the powers in organising the boundary commissions and in establishing the provisional government of Albania contributed to the uncertainty of the situation. Some Albanian tribes rose in revolt against being transferred to Serbia and Montenegro. Exclusion from age-old market centers by the Serbians was also a cause of protest.[6] Thousands fled before the suppressive measures of the Serbian army.[7] The Belgrade government justified its action by charging the Austrians, Bulgarians, and Turks with stirring up trouble among the Albanians. It would be hard to substantiate such charges. The Austrian foreign office certainly desired peace in this region. On the other hand some Austrian rifles might well have found their way into the hands of Albanians.[8] There ap-

[4] *Ibid.*, VII, nos. 8344, 8410.

[5] *Ibid.*, VII, no. 8564; see also nos. 8634, 8656; D.D.F., 3d. ser., VIII, no. 173.

[6] Grey stated to the French and Russian ambassadors in May 1914: ". . . My recollection was that, according to independent information, the violations of the frontiers by Albanians, of which the Serbians had complained, had arisen from the fact that, when the Serbians evacuated Albanian soil in accordance with the decisions of the powers, they took with them the cattle belonging to the Albanians, and the Albanians had come over the frontier in pursuit of their cattle. There had been further trouble because the Albanians were denied access to places which had been allocated to Serbia but which were the natural markets for the Albanians to secure supplies from" (B.D., X, i, no. 128). In this connection see also material presented by Swire, *Albania*, pp. 175–8.

[7] See the reports of the German delegate on the boundary commission (G.P., XXXVI, i, nos. 13961, 13971, 13999).

[8] Crackanthorpe to Grey, Sept. 10, 1913, B.D., X, i, no. 6; D.D.F., 3d. ser., VIII, no. 247.

parently was some activity on the part of Bulgaria, or at least on the part of Bulgarian-Macedonians.[9] There is much evidence, however, that Serbia stirred up the tribes in order to fish in troubled waters.

The English minister at Belgrade held that "the basis of Serbian policy is to establish the fact that the new Principality cannot possibly become 'viable' and to encourage centrifugal tendencies for this purpose."[10] It is clear that Serbia planned to use the internal situation in Albania as a pretext for obtaining (1) boundary rectifications and (2) to obtain a government in Albania which would be friendly to Serbia and not subservient to Austria.[11] As the boundary commission had not yet laid down the boundary, actual occupation by Serbian troops might well constitute a strong influence on this body.[12] The second point of the program Serbia hoped to obtain by furthering the designs of Essad Pasha to become ruler of Albania. There is no question but that this sinister character — the German delegate on the Balkan boundary commission called him the greatest "Gauner" in Albania[13] — had his hand in the Albanian "uprising." Strandtmann, the Russian chargé at Belgrade, reported the Serbian plan to be:

> The impecunious Essad Pasha will be sent money, and the military plans call for the complete annihilation and dispersion of Ismael Kemal, Isa Boletin and their friends. Whereupon Essad Pasha will be set up as governor-general at Valona. The latter, with whom the Serbian government has been in touch for some time, is prepared to recognise the suzerainty of the sultan as is shown by his flag with the eagle and half-moon. He is also willing to undertake a boundary

[9] D.D.F., 3d. ser., VIII, nos. 193, 215, 234, 236, 242, 267, 323; IX, no. 182.

[10] B.D., X, i, no. 6; see also, no. 23.

[11] Strandtmann to Sazonov, Sept. 25, 1913, S.D., II, no. 854.

[12] When the French chargé inquired as to whether the Serbian government desired a prompt reunion of the boundary commission he was told: "Non certes, nos troupes occupent les territoires litigieux; cela vaut mieux ainsi nous pouvons en tirer profit" (Clément-Simon to Pichon, Sept. 20, 1913, D.D.F., 3d. ser., VIII, no. 173).

[13] Von Laffert to Bethmann Hollweg, Oct. 23, 1913, G.P., XXXV, i, no. 13961; see also, B.D., X, i, nos. 13, 32, 56; S.D., I, nos. 318, 322; II, no. 834; R.D., I Reihe, I, no. 316; M. E. Durham, "The Story of Essad Pasha," *The Contemporary Review*, CXVIII (1920), 212–3.

rectification in accordance with Serbia's wishes up to the Black Drin. At the request of Essad this surrendered territory will be occupied, supposedly temporarily, by Serbian troops in order to maintain order. After establishing his power Essad will have himself proclaimed Prince of Albania.[14]

Apparently it was largely these connections with Essad Pasha which led Sazonov a month later to tell the British chargé in strictest confidence:

. . . Serbia had been more to blame than was generally supposed in the events which had led up to the recent ultimatum from Austria. Mr. Spalaiković had held the most impudent language with regard to Serbia's coming to an understanding with Essad Pasha and combining with him to crush the Albanian Government provisionally established at Valona. The question of Serbian access to the Adriatic would thus, Mr. Spalaiković had said, be satisfactorily settled.[15]

Such a plan would indicate that Serbia never had any real intention of evacuating Albania.

There was no united protest of the powers at Belgrade, but the Serbian government notified the Austrian and Russian ministers again on September 15th that the troops would be withdrawn from Albania up to the Drin.[16] Yet on September 19th the Serbian government submitted a circular note to the powers explaining its position and indicating that it might be necessary to advance troops and reoccupy certain strategic positions.[17] As the French chargé reported: "but even before the withdrawal of the troops could be completely brought about, the Serbian government announced that it would be forced to advance anew." [18] In Clément-Simon's opinion Serbia was intent on facing the powers with a *fait accompli* and by the possession of territory to force a rectification of the projected frontiers.

About the same time the Serbian government aroused the ire of Austria by announcing the opening of several new customs

[14] Strandtmann to Sazonov, Sept. 25, 1913, S.D., II, no. 854.
[15] O'Beirne to Grey, Oct. 28, 1913, B.D., X, i, no. 56.
[16] Ö-U.A., VII, nos. 8635, 8706 Beilage.
[17] B.D., X, i, no. 12; D.D.F., 3d. ser., VIII, no. 175.
[18] Clément-Simon to Pichon, Sept. 20, 1913, D.D.F., 3d. ser., VIII, no. 173; see also, no. 267.

houses — which in effect would cut off certain Albanian tribes from their accustomed market places.[19] The English minister at Belgrade was pessimistic over the entire situation and found the acting minister of foreign affairs, Spalaiković (Pašić was abroad), very bellicose.[20] Apparently Serbia did withdraw some troops, but her army was never clear of Albanian soil. News of renewed uprisings and attacks on the Serbian forces led the Belgrade government towards the end of September to mobilise anew certain divisions of the army.[21] A telegram from the British chargé at St. Petersburg indicates the Russian attitude towards this action by Serbia:

> Acting Minister for Foreign Affairs is informed from Belgrade that Serbia intends to inflict a severe lesson on Albania for which purpose Serbian troops will cross frontier. He understands that after the operations against the Albanian forces have been carried out, Serbia will continue to hold some positions within Albania. He has informed Serbian government that he appreciates good reasons which they have for proposed actions. At the same time he has recommended them to proceed with the same prudence they have shown hitherto. He is aware that Serbian action is likely to give rise to objections from Austrian Government, but he considers that she is justified in taking precautionary measures against the recurrence of recent incidents.[22]

On October 3rd Pašić stopped off in Vienna on his return to Belgrade from Paris, and had a friendly conference with Berchtold. It was again made clear to him that the boundaries established by the ambassadors' conference would have to be respected.[23] Nevertheless, although continuing to promise that this boundary would be respected, Pašić a few days later spoke of the necessity of perhaps occupying provisionally some villages.[24] This was considered necessary as a means of safe-

[19] Ö-U.A., VII, no. 8649.

[20] B.D., X, i, nos. 9, 15, 20; see also, Ö-U.A., VII, nos. 8674, 8691, 8721; D.D.F., 3d. ser., VIII, no. 173.

[21] Crackanthorpe to Grey, Sept. 24, 25, 1913, B.D., X, i, nos. 18, 20; Ö-U.A., VII, no. 8705; D.D.F., 3d. ser., VIII, nos. 196, 328.

[22] O'Beirne to Grey, Sept. 27, 1913, B.D., X, i, no. 22.

[23] Ö-U.A., VII, no. 8813; B.D., X, i, no. 32.

[24] Ö-U.A., VII, nos. 8797, 8808.

guarding the Serbian forces from future attack by Albanian tribesmen.

The situation soon took a turn for the worse. In the first weeks of October, Serbian troops reoccupied certain Albanian towns. The ambassadors of the Triple Alliance thought that this less conciliatory attitude on Serbia's part coincided with Hartwig's return to Belgrade. Be that as it may, certainly the Serbian policy was not censored at the Russian foreign office where Neratov still directed affairs. The English chargé reported:

> . . . In the Serbian-Albanian question Neratov has shown himself disposed to support Serbia rather far, at any rate in theory. He approves of the Serbians penetrating into Albania in order to chastise the Albanians and of their retaining of strategical points after the military operations are concluded as a precautionary measure. He also considers that the Serbians are entitled to claim territorial compensation from Albania, and when I suggested that this would bring them into collision with the decisions of the London Conference he maintained that, since the powers were responsible for the existence of Albania as a neutral state under their guarantee, they would not dispute the right of another state which has been the object of unprovoked attack from Albania to recover compensation for the losses thereby caused. Thus he in theory sides with the Serbians and approves of their intentions, but how far he will support them in practice is of course a very different matter.[25]

At Vienna the conclusion was reached that very energetic measures would be required to get Serbia to evacuate Albanian soil. After all it took not only an international blockade but also a direct threat of force from Austria to get the Montenegrins out of Scutari. "United Europe" had failed to remove the Turks from Adrianople. On October 3rd at a crown council the Austrian statesmen came to the conclusion that they would either have to accommodate themselves to Serbia's getting additional territory, or confront Belgrade with an ultimatum in order to bring about the evacuation of Serbian troops. Tisza, Stürgkh, Conrad, and Bilinski all spoke for energetic steps. The chief

[25] O'Beirne to A. Nicolson, Oct. 2, 1913, B.D., X, i, no. 31.

of staff was delighted that so many others agreed with his views in respect to an active policy against Serbia.[26]

Reports continued to reach Vienna of new Serbian advances. On October 14th the Austrian chargé was instructed to inquire what was meant by "provisional occupation of Albanian territory." He was to question the Serbian government:

> . . . Was it prepared to stop its military preparations for a penetration into Albania, and was it also prepared to recall those troops which were in Albania within a definite short time limit? The monarchy would make its further action towards Serbia dependent on the way these questions were answered and on Serbia's fulfilling its earlier promises, for we have made up our minds to use all measures that we consider proper to bring about the complete recognition of the decisions reached at London.[27]

Berchtold immediately notified the governments at Berlin, Rome, and Bucharest of his step. He warned them that Austria was set on seeing things through this time and asked them for their support.[28]

From Berlin assurances came that "in the efforts to insure a viable Albania we stand firmly behind Austria." [29] The German foreign office immediately advised its chargé at Belgrade to support the Austrian demands.[30] Steps were taken to win Great Britain and France to do likewise and the British ambassador at Berlin found the German officials "much perturbed" over the seriousness of the situation.[31] Although the Italian minister at Belgrade was ordered to support the action of the Ballhausplatz, the Austrian chargé at Rome felt that the Italians were disinclined to do anything and would be glad to see the Dual Monarchy pull the Albanian chestnuts out of the fire.[32] However, even before these replies reached Vienna, an answer

[26] Ö-U.A., VII, no. 8779.

[27] Berchtold to von Storck, Oct. 14, 1913, *ibid.*, VII, no. 8828.

[28] *Ibid.*, VII, no. 8837; G.P., XXXVI, i, nos. 14160, 14161.

[29] Zimmermann to von Tschirschky, Oct. 16, 1913, G.P., XXXVI, i, no. 14162.

[30] Zimmermann to von Scharfenberg, Oct. 16, 1913, *ibid.*, XXXVI, i, no. 14163.

[31] Goschen to Grey, Oct. 16, 1913, B.D., X, i, no. 38; see also, G.P., XXXVI, i, nos. 14162, 14164; D.D.F., 3d. ser., VIII, no. 335.

[32] Ö-U.A., VII, nos. 8832, 8840, 8849.

had been received from Belgrade. To Berchtold's summation Pašić had retorted:

> The order to halt the further advance of the Serbian troops towards Albania has already been given. The question, as to when the Serbian troops already on Albanian soil would be withdrawn, would depend on the development of circumstances in Albania.[33]

The above telegraphic declaration was clarified by detailed reports.[34] From the beginning the Serbian reply was considered inadequate. Assured on the morning of October 17th, of Germany's general support, Berchtold at once took steps to bring Serbia to terms. Without consulting Berlin or Rome he dispatched that evening a verbal note to Belgrade:

> . . . Austria-Hungary could under no conditions consent to the modification of the international decision on the confines of Albania. The last reply on this subject by the Royal Serbian Government at the Imperial and Royal legation is as unsatisfactory as that contained in the notice submitted at the Imperial and Royal Ministry of Foreign Affairs by the Serbian minister. As a matter of fact the order authorising the Serbian troops to stop their march can not be considered sufficient. It is indispensable in the eyes of the Imperial and Royal Government that the Serbian Government proceed immediately to recall the troops which have passed the frontiers fixed by the conference of ambassadors at London and which consequently are occupying part of Albania. The Imperial and Royal Government expresses the hope that the Serbian Government will proceed immediately to the complete evacuation of all territory within eight days. If this is not done, the Imperial and Royal Government, to its great regret, will find it necessary to have recourse to appropriate means to assure the realisation of its demand.[35]

This note was presented at midday October 18th. The same day the other powers — Germany and Italy no sooner than any other country — were notified of the Austrian step. A cov-

[33] Von Storck to Berchtold, Oct. 15, 1913, *ibid.*, VII, no. 8834. The French chargé at Belgrade characterised Pašić's answer as "réponse vague et purement dilatoire" (D.D.F., 3d. ser., VIII, no. 350).

[34] Ö-U.A., VII, nos. 8835, 8836, 8844, 8845, 8846.

[35] Berchtold to von Storck, Oct. 17, 1913, *ibid.*, VII, no. 8850. On the drafting of this note and its presentation see, Alfred Rappaport, "Albaniens Werdegang," *Die Kriegsschuldfrage*, V (1927), 840.

ering note justified the actions of the Viennese Government.[36]

The whole procedure followed at this time was later duplicated in July, 1914: the warning to Serbia, the general promise of support from Germany, the independent presentation of the ultimatum, the subsequent notification of ally and rival. In October, 1913, the solution was easily reached. The desired end of Austrian action — Serbia's compliance with an international decision — was manifestly so correct that the danger of a general war was slight.

The "precipitate action of Austria" — although the record shows the powers had been trying for over two months to get Serbian troops out of Albanian territory — aroused consternation at the Entente capitals. There were protests from London, Paris, and St. Petersburg, but no one actually stepped up to defend Serbia.[37] On October 17th, e.g. before the Austrian action, Sazonov and Pichon had in fact called the Serbian minister at Paris to them and counselled him to advise his government to meet the Austrian wishes in order to forestall future demands and the possibility of a cheap diplomatic victory for the Ballhausplatz. In order to make it easier for Serbia to give in, they held forth a promise of the opening of the French money market to Serbia.[38] Even if Serbia had been inclined to follow this advice, the Austrian ultimatum came too soon for her to act upon it. The German government immediately gave its full support to the Austrian measure.[39] To Berchtold's expression of hope that the Serbian government would meet his demands, the Kaiser impulsively noted, "That would be very regrettable! Now or never! Something or another order and peace will have to be established down there." [40]

[36] Ö-U.A., VII, no. 8854.

[37] *Ibid.*, VII, nos. 8862, 8866, 8884; G.P., XXXVI, i, nos. 14177, 14188, 14191; B.D., X, i, nos. 38 minutes, 43; D.D.F., 3d. ser., VIII, nos. 342, 343, 346; S.D., I, no. 382.

[38] Izvolsky, III, nos. 1096, 1114; D.D.F., 3d. ser., VIII, nos. 343, 502. Serbia later did obtain a loan in Paris, but only after agreeing to place large orders for military supplies with French manufacturers (*ibid.*, no. 648; IX, nos. 28, 133).

[39] G.P., XXXVI, i, nos. 14175, 14178, 14181; Ö-U.A., VII, nos. 8861, 8872.

[40] G.P., XXXVI, i, no. 14176 marginal note.

There can be no doubt but that the Austrian diplomats meant business this time. Berchtold was careful to point out that the decisions taken had the full approval of Francis Joseph. The Serbian government immediately decided to meet the Austrian demands. Even Hartwig used his great influence to this end and was particularly instrumental in influencing the Serbian decision.[41] The notification from the Rumanian government that it could not support Serbia in a conflict with Austria over the question of North Albania no doubt also had a deciding influence both on Hartwig and on the Serbian cabinet.[42] On October 20th the Serbian government notified Vienna that the troops would be evacuated from Albanian soil within the prescribed eight days.[43] This was followed on October 25th by a formal notification that the troops had all been withdrawn.[44]

The Austrian-Serbian crisis of October, 1913 was now safely weathered. But angry passions smouldered on at Belgrade. The Entente capitals were incensed and even the moderate Kokovtsov, on a visit to Paris, assured the Serbian minister that "similar actions dare not be repeated." [45] At Rome the Austrian step had aroused displeasure. Although the ultimatum was perhaps not liked in Berlin, the firmness and decision of the Viennese government was welcome as a sign of strength. The German government seized this occasion to express its solidarity with Vienna. Events connected with the Treaty of Bucharest had shown how divergent the policies of the two allies had become in Balkan matters. Now this impression could be dispelled. Emperor William was especially careful to express his approval of Austrian action. At the dedication of the War Memorial at Leipzig, October 18, 1913, Conrad found him distinctly Serbophobe and willing to support Austria in action against Belgrade.[46] The day after the official notification of the Serbian

[41] Crackanthorpe to Grey, Oct. 22, 1913, B.D., X, i, no. 52; Ö-U.A., VII, no. 8882; D.D.F., 3d. ser., VIII, nos. 350, 369.

[42] D.D.F., 3d. ser., VIII, nos. 348, 390.

[43] Ö-U.A., VII, no. 8878.

[44] *Ibid.*, VII, nos. 8918, 8919.

[45] Vesnić to foreign office, Nov. 10, 1913, S.D., I, no. 382.

[46] Conrad, III, 469–70.

withdrawal of troops the Kaiser was in Vienna. It was a Sunday, October 26th, and the German embassy gave a tea in honor of its imperial guest. Here Count Berchtold had a long, fateful, political conversation with His Majesty. William II did most of the talking. Such assurances of coöperation and support from the fountain head of authority heartened the Austrian minister. Doubts of German coöperation vanished. Henceforward he was to feel himself certain of German aid. According to the Kaiser:

> Panslavism and with it Russia have played their rôle in the Balkans, but simultaneously the Slavic states have been strengthened in a fashion that gives Germany and Austria-Hungary pause to think. The war between East and West can not be avoided indefinitely and if Austria-Hungary is then open to an attack in the flank by a respectable military power, this could have a fateful influence on the struggle of the nations. . . . The Slavs were not born to rule but to serve. This they must be taught. . . .

His Majesty then sketched a scheme by which the Dual Monarchy should bind Serbia to its support. On Berchtold's protest that such a plan could not be realised, the Kaiser continued:

> When His Majesty Emperor Francis Joseph demands something the Serbian government must give way, and if it does not then Belgrade will be bombarded and occupied until the will of His Majesty is fulfilled. And of this you can be certain, that I stand behind you and am ready to draw the saber whenever your action makes it necessary.

His Majesty accompanied these words with a movement of his hand towards his saber. Other matters were discussed. The thread which ran through all the Kaiser's utterances however was that the Dual Monarchy "could fully and completely count on him and that whatever came to him from the Vienna foreign office would be considered a command." [47]

Different attitudes and different views on many subjects, it is true, smouldered on at the Wilhelmstrasse and the Ballhausplatz. Yet there is no question that from the time of the October

[47] Tagesbericht über eine am 26 Okt. 1913 mit dem deutschen Kaiser Wilhelm geführte Unterredung, Oct. 28, 1913, Ö-U.A., VII, no. 8934; see also, Cartwright to Grey, Oct. 29, 1913, B.D., X, i, no. 57.

crisis, 1913, the two allies came closer and closer together until they became "blood brothers" on the battlefields of the World War.

With the withdrawal of Serbian troops from Northern Albania the work of the northern boundary commission was simplified. The Serbians were incensed over the supposed hostility of the English delegate on the commission. Their protest at the foreign office received a curt answer.[48] There was indeed great animosity between the different delegates on the commission. Snow added to the difficulty. Typhus developed in the accompanying detachments of Italian and Austrian soldiers. The commission had many irritating encounters with the Serbian border guards. On December 12, 1913 the commission held its last meeting before adjourning for the winter months.[49] It reassembled in May, 1914, but its labors were cut short by the outbreak of the war.

With Serbia's acceptance of the Austrian ultimatum in October, 1913, the northern boundary of Albania surrendered its place in the spotlight to the southern boundary. After various delays the commission which was to settle that disputed issue met on October 4th at Monastir.[50] It immediately decided that all "Greek or Albanian delegations" were to be turned away. Various other rules designed to aid an impartial investigation were adopted.[51]

The actual field work had hardly begun before serious differences arose between the Triple Alliance and Triple Entente members. On this commission the German member had strict orders to support the views of his Austrian and Italian colleagues, but if possible to put in a good word for Greece.[52] The representatives of the Alliance were, however, pretty well agreed on giving certain villages to Albania. The French and Russian

[48] S.D., I, nos. 373, 378; G.P., XXXVI, i, nos. 13971, 13994.

[49] The work of this commission can be traced in the exceptionally interesting reports of the German member (G. P., XXXVI, i, nos. 13961, 13971, 13993, 13994, 13999, 14000, 14010, 14012, 14023).

[50] B.D., X, i, no. 8 ed. note.

[51] Stickney, *Southern Albania*, pp. 36–7.

[52] G.P., XXXVI, i, no. 13932.

delegates did not always receive as firm support from their British colleague as they desired. The latter was accompanied by his wife who was, according to the French, influential and very anti-Greek.[53]

The Greek government unceasingly bombarded the different capitals with its views on how the boundary was to be drawn. There was evidence that measures were being taken by Greece to hinder the work of the commission. Originally this commission had been scheduled to meet on September 1st and to complete its work by November 30th. Within a month of that date all Greek troops were to be withdrawn from territory assigned to Albania. Obviously it was now impossible for the commission to live up to this time table. Much to the consternation of the Entente powers, Austria and Italy nevertheless on October 30th warned the Greek government that Greek troops would have to be withdrawn from Albania by December 31st, the date originally set by the ambassadors' conference at London.[54]

Meanwhile the frontier commission made little progress working from village to village. It was clear that factors other than language would have to be considered in drawing the frontier. Winter was at hand and in order to hasten matters, Grey submitted to the powers a suggested frontier worked out by the British member of the commission.[55] It conformed fairly well to the views of the Triple Alliance since it had been worked out with the collaboration of the Italian and Austrian members of the commission. In the end the English proposal was substantially accepted as the southern boundary. Glad to forsake the wet and cold of the Albanian mountains, the commission retreated to the comforts of Florence and here the final decisions were reached. These were incorporated in the so-called "Proto-

[53] See the summary report of the work of the commission submitted by the French member, Lallemand to Doumergue, Dec. 19, 1913, D.D.F., 3d. ser., IX, no. 40 annexe.

[54] Ö-U.A., VII, no. 8941 note; D.D.F., 3d. ser., VIII, nos. 422 note, 425, 427, 439, 449, 457, 466.

[55] Aide-mémoire, Goschen to German foreign office, Nov. 19, 1913, G.P., XXXVI, i, no. 13990; see also, D.D.F., 3d. ser., VIII, no. 497; IX, no. 40 annexe.

col of Florence" of December 19, 1913. The boundary line was to run in a general southwest-northeast direction from Phtelia, near Cape Stylos to Lake Prespa, passing about forty kilometers from Janina. Both Koritza and Argyrocastro, the two focal points in dispute, were to go to Albania.[56]

The question now was, could the powers see that this boundary was respected? Would it come to a threat of arms as had been the case in the northern boundary? At the ambassadors' conference it had been generally admitted that the southern boundary was connected with the question of the islands. Clearly the Protocol of Florence was but one half of the solution of the Greek-Albanian-Turkish problem.

In the Preliminaries of London of May 30, 1913, both Turkey and Greece had agreed that the powers should decide the fate of the Aegean Islands. The conference of ambassadors had decided that when Italy, in accordance with the Lausanne Treaty, should return the Dodecanese to Turkey the powers would then decide what the ultimate status of these islands should be. As to the islands in Greek occupation, no formal decision was reached, although it was certainly the general understanding that they should go to Greece, with the exception of Tenedos and Imbros, which for strategical reasons were to be restored to Turkey. It should be pointed out, however, that the powers had in no way placed themselves under any obligations to Greece in this matter.[57]

Such ill-defined terrain provided the best possible field for political maneuvering. Turkey, having regained Adrianople in spite of the united will of Europe, had everything to win and nothing to lose in demanding the return of the islands. It was clear that if Greece could be moved to surrender them voluntarily, none of the powers would object.

Indeed, both before and after the Greek-Turkish Treaty of Athens was signed on November 14, 1913,[58] the grand vizier

[56] G.P., XXXVI, i, no. 14020; Stickney, *Southern Albania*, p. 40. See map, p. 256.

[57] Grey to Bertie, Nov. 26, 1913, B.D., X, i, no. 166. See above, pp. 338–39.

[58] See above, pp. 414–15.

threatened to fight if the powers did not award the islands to Turkey. Quite correctly the Kaiser once noted: "Donnerwetter, that is unbelievably fresh! Why that is a direct threat, and an attempt to influence the decision of the powers! That we dare not swallow; icy, sharp, cold settlement is necessary!" [59] But no country, least of all Germany, was ready to follow out the Kaiser's prescription. Such measures might jeopardise their position in Constantinople, and as the British ambassador noted: "All the Powers, including ourselves, are trying hard to get what they can out of Turkey. They all profess to wish the maintenance of Turkey's integrity but no one ever thinks of this in practice." [60] The energetic young Turk leaders — men of far different caliber from Abdul Hamid's underlings — now seemed more than ever bent on forcing the powers to show their colors. They continued to press for the acquisition of the islands; possession of Chios and Mytilene was a matter of life and death to them. Feeling that time worked in their favor and that sooner or later the powers would split over the question, the statesmen at the Sublime Porte did all they could to delay matters.

Venizelos wisely thought it was well to have the powers make their award on the islands at once. When it became clear that the decision as to the southern boundary of Albania would be adverse to Greek pretensions, he pressed for a decision on the Aegean Islands. The British minister at Athens reported:

> If he could show that the sacrifice of modern (sic: northern) Epirus was part of a general settlement which allotted to Greece the islands in Greek occupation except Imbros and Tenedos and secured withdrawal of Italy from the other islands and the grant to them of a large autonomy under Turkish sovereignty, he might obtain its acceptance here although nothing would prevent local resistance. But his position would not be tenable if after withdrawing from the disputed zone he was confronted with demands for further concessions in the islands and with Italian occupation tending to become permanent.[61]

[59] G.P., XXXVI, i, no. 13862 marginal note.
[60] Mallet to Grey, Dec. 17, 1913, B.D., X, i, no. 174.
[61] Elliot to Grey, Dec. 10, 1913, *ibid.*, X, i, no. 89.

Venizelos' request to have the problems of the southern boundary and the islands "settled simultaneously and at once" was not unreasonable. Grey undertook the thankless task of pressing for a general settlement. On December 12th he submitted a long memorandum to the powers. As the decision of the powers on the southern boundary was about to be announced, it was essential in view of previous declarations to come to some agreement as to the time limit for the evacuation of the disputed territories by Greece. Also since this boundary had always been linked at the ambassadors' conference with the problem of the islands it would be necessary to inform the Turkish and Greek governments of the decision that these islands should all remain in Greek possession except for Tenedos and Imbros. In order to make the decision of the powers "as easy and palatable as possible to Turkey" Grey thought it was "essential that definite arrangements should now be agreed upon by the powers, and communicated to the Porte respecting the fate of the islands in Italian occupation." Since Italy had given assurances that the islands would be returned when the Treaty of Lausanne was fulfilled, the powers might now, if they agreed to this solution, assure the sultan that they had decided that these islands should revert to Turkey — subject to certain conditions regarding autonomous administration. This would fulfill the decision of the ambassadors' conference of August 11th where it had been agreed that the powers should decide the ultimate fate of the Dodecanese.[62]

This "secret proposal" was at once known in Constantinople and the Turkish statesmen dispatched lengthy incriminations to London charging Grey with depriving them of the islands occupied by Greece.[63] In the Alliance capitals it was thought that Great Britain was trying to better its position at Athens. Von Jagow, totally misinterpreting Grey's proposal, suggested at Rome that indeed everything would be easier if Italy could decide on a simultaneous surrender of the occupied islands.[64]

[62] *Ibid.*, X, i, no. 91.

[63] *Ibid.*, X, i, nos. 173, 178, 186.

[64] G.P., XXXVI, ii, nos. 14219, 14230.

San Giuliano was particularly irritated at this "English attempt" to get him to set a date for Italian evacuation.[65] By this time the Italian statesmen had devised the theory that Turkey owed Italy for the cost of the occupation of the islands. Admittedly Turkey could never pay cash, and so the Dodecanese were to be held in pawn for a concession in the region of Adalia.[66] The desired Italian concessions conflicted with England's ambitions in Asia Minor, and consequently Germany and Austria were willing to lend San Giuliano support. Thus it took a little time to persuade the Italians that Grey had never intended to press for a definite date of Italian evacuation — that this was only Jagow's interpretation of the English note.

It was not until December 31st that the Alliance ambassadors finally submitted an answer to Grey.[67] This answer dealt only with the Albanian boundary, requesting that Greece be asked to withdraw her forces by January 18th, e.g., one month after the signature of the Protocol of Florence. But this did not help things along, for as everyone knew, the future of the islands was the important issue. Finally, on January 14th, having delayed a few days longer at the request of the Turkish government, the Alliance ambassadors handed in a second identical note.[68] It again demanded evacuation of the Greek troops by January 18th and only after such evacuation did Germany and Austria feel that Greece should be assured of the islands in her possession. The exception was, as usual, made as to Imbros, Tenedos and Casteloritza, which were to go to Turkey. Grey's proposal was nevertheless accepted in principle, and so he set about putting it in final form. He requested that a new date for evacuation be set and drew up a draft of the declaration that

[65] *Ibid.*, XXXVI, ii, nos. 14230, 14237.

[66] R.D., I Reihe, I, nos. 43, 74, 116; B.D., X, i, no. 201. On December 12, 1913 the British ambassador at Rome put in an energetic protest against connecting "schemes of Italian expansion on the mainland of Asiatic Turkey with the question of the islands" (*ibid.*, nos. 168, 170). Nicolson thought Italy would no more evacuate the islands than Great Britain would evacuate Egypt (*ibid.*, no. 147 minute).

[67] G.P., XXXVI, ii, no. 14229 Anlage; D.D.F., 3d. ser., IX, no. 2 annexe.

[68] G.P., XXXVI, ii, nos. 14249, 14252, 14253 Anlage; B.D., X, i, no. 203.

should be made at Constantinople and Athens. In this no mention was made of the Dodecanese, but in submitting it to the powers Grey wrote:

> I would, however, point out that, as long as one of the great powers remains in occupation of these Aegean Islands [Dodecanese] the situation will remain abnormal, and that, while it is primarily a matter for Italy and Turkey to arrange the return of these islands to the latter in accordance with the provisions of the Treaty of Lausanne, yet all the powers with whom, by the subsequent agreement of last August, it rested to decide the ultimate destination of the islands have an interest in their fate.[69]

Grey further added that he thought the declarations should be submitted to Greece and Turkey, only "on condition that it is formally acknowledged by the powers that they will in common accord take steps, if necessary, to make their decisions respected by each of the two countries concerned."

The statement that "the situation will remain abnormal" as long as Italy occupied the Dodecanese aroused protests and objections from the Triple Alliance which in this matter followed the leadership of Rome. These powers were also opposed to obligating themselves so far as coercive measures were concerned, if the decisions were not accepted. In this they were joined by France and Russia.[70] It was generally held that Greece and Turkey would meet the wishes of the powers, and if they did not, then it would be time enough to decide what measures should be taken. Consequently on February 13–14th, the powers collectively announced their decision at Athens and Constantinople.[71] Greece was to withdraw all troops from Albanian territory by March 31st and only then was she to obtain the islands, save Tenedos, Imbros, and Casteloritza. Further she was not to fortify them and she was to undertake to prevent smuggling from them into Turkey.

An unqualified acceptance of the award of the powers could hardly have been expected. The grand vizier was long accus-

[69] Grey to Lichnowsky, Jan. 23, 1913, B.D., X, i, no. 211.
[70] *Ibid.*, X, i, nos. 231, 233, 237, 269.
[71] *Ibid.*, X, i, nos. 252, 253.

tomed to collective *démarches* and was unimpressed by them. He "took note" of the decision, but regretted that the powers had not seen fit to take into consideration the vital necessities of Turkey, which were so important for future peace.[72] Greece agreed to evacuate Albanian territory by March 31st, but proposed certain boundary rectifications near Koritza and in the valley of the Argyrocastro. For the cession of certain towns in the latter region, Greece was willing to cede a small bit of territory along the coast and to pay 2,500,000 francs to the new Albanian state. Since the newly acquired islands were not to be fortified, she requested a guarantee of protection and neutrality by the powers. There were certain other demands such as guarantees for protection of property and religious and linguistic rights in the evacuated territories.[73]

On March 8th the Italian and Austrian ministers in the presence but not with the coöperation of the German minister gave an oral answer to the Greek note. They confined themselves entirely to Albanian matters and made no mention of the islands. As to the rights of minorities they pointed out that this was already being cared for by the International Control Commission which had adopted a program for the protection of minorities throughout Albania. On the whole Greek claims for boundary rectification were denied, although the possibility of slight changes in one or two districts as had been promised to Venizelos were reaffirmed.[74] This independent action irritated the Entente statesmen who thought Austria and Italy were separating themselves all too often from the concert in regard to Albania.[75] They thereupon agreed upon a draft formula for an official reply to be handed in at Athens. With minor changes this was approved by the Triple Alliance powers, but it was not until April 24th that identical notes were presented to the Greek government by the representatives of the

[72] *Ibid.*, X, i, no. 253 enclosure 2; R.D., I Reihe, I, no. 265.

[73] B.D., X, i, no. 255 enclosure.

[74] Elliot to Grey, March 8, 1914, *ibid.*, X, i, no. 123; R.D., I Reihe, I, no. 294.

[75] B.D., X, i, no. 123 minutes; R.D., I Reihe, I, nos. 394, 421, 429, 436; D.D.F., 3d. ser., IX, nos. 413, 418, 425, 435.

great powers.[76] So far as Albania was concerned this communication was not unlike the answer of the Austrian and Italian ministers. Now, however, the powers stated in addition that they would attempt to obtain minority guarantees for the population of the islands of Imbros, Tenedos and Casteloritza which were to be returned to Turkey. They promised further that they would use their "friendly" influence to obtain recognition by Turkey of the transfer of the other islands then in Greek occupation to Greece.

The southern boundary and Aegean Islands problems were however far from being settled. On February 28, 1914, Northern Epirus had declared its independence under the leadership of Zographos, former foreign minister of Greece. Mr. Lamb, the British representative on the International Control Commission, telegraphed from Valona:

> It is perfectly obvious that these measures could not have been adopted without the knowledge and connivance of the Greek authorities in occupation of Argyrocastro as well as of those in Corfu. . . . The Greek government would appear at last to have come to the conclusion that the force which they have organised in the occupied provinces can be trusted to "maintain itself unassisted against the Albanians" and is going to "allow them to try," but it required a remarkable degree of effrontery to permit the leaders of this force to communicate their intentions to the representatives of the guaranteeing powers in Albania, whilst the country is still officially administered by Greece.[77]

A Greek dominated state of Epirus was scarcely better from the Albanian point of view than official Greek occupation. On the other hand there can be no question that affairs were in a bad state in this region. Conflicts between "Greek Christians" and "Mohammedan Albanians" did not belong to the realm of legend. The Greek charge that the newly organised Albanian

[76] Identic note communicated to M. Venizelos, April 24, 1914, B.D., X, i, no. 268. There is an editorial note to this document which traces the history of its drafting.

[77] Lamb to Grey, Feb. 28, 1914, *ibid.*, X, i, no. 119. The British minister at Athens thought that Mr. Lamb's statement did not do justice "to the loyalty of Monsieur Venizelos's policy in regard to Epirus" (*ibid.*, no. 122).

gendarmerie was unable to cope with the situation was all too true. Nor did Prince William of Wied bring "law and protection" with him when he landed on Albanian soil March 7th. Nevertheless, continued occupation by Greek troops only aggravated the situation. It was not until the end of April that Greece officially announced complete withdrawal of her troops.[78] But if Greek troops ever were withdrawn, certainly Greek irregulars remained. The Dutch officers of the Albanian gendarmerie never ceased reporting that Greek troops were on Albanian soil.

Disorder was heightened at this time by another revolt in middle Albania. Essad Pasha, officially minister of interior in the Prince of Wied's government, was no doubt connected with this rebellion. Essad Pasha had played a sinister rôle in Albanian affairs ever since his surrender of Scutari. As has been pointed out, he was probably in touch with Serbia during the troubles over the northern boundary in the autumn of 1913.[79] It is possible that both the Greek and Turkish governments subsidised his activities in the south of Albania. At one time or another, various powers were suspected of furthering his designs.[80] He was not above taking bribes, and it is almost certain that he was in Italian pay in the spring of 1914. Just where he stood is hard to say, but it is clear that he was not a force working for stabilisation of Albania in coöperation with the powers. Finally on May 19, 1914, he was arrested on the insistence of one of the Dutch officers of the gendarmerie and exiled to Italy. Here he was welcomed, decorated, and "honored as a martyr." [81]

In order to bring about a semblance of order in South Albania, the International Control Commission decided to nego-

[78] Dragumis to von Jagow, April 29, 1914, G.P., XXXVI, ii, no. 14376.

[79] See above, pp. 420–21.

[80] B.D., X, i, nos. 107, 113, 202; R.D., I Reihe, III, no. 256; Conrad, III, 678, 681.

[81] Prince Wilhelm zu Wied, *Denkschrift*, p. 19; G.P., XXXVI, ii, no. 14441; Conrad, III, 687–8. Essad was finally assassinated in a Paris street on June 13, 1920 (M. E. Durham, "The Story of Essad Pasha," *The Contemporary Review*, CXVIII [1920], 213).

tiate with the leaders of the Epirot rebellion. On May 18, 1914 an accord was concluded on the island of Corfu.[82] This provided for a certain amount of autonomy for the Epirot provinces within the Albanian state. It was not until July 2, 1914, that the powers gave their approval to this accord.[83] Even then the Epirots refused to abide by it. On the eve of the outbreak of the World War, Prince William of Wied was still pleading with the powers to force Greece to withdraw its troops. The southern boundary remained to plague the powers at the Peace Conference in 1919, and in the early days of the League of Nations. When the final settlement was made, the powers, however, could do no better than accept the Protocol of Florence for the southern boundary. As a matter of fact this settlement was far more just than the whittled and compromised northern boundary. The statesmen of 1912–13 called into being an Albanian state; the statesmen of the post-war era recreated it on almost exactly the same lines.

The pronouncement of the powers on the Aegean Islands fared little better than the one on the southern boundary. It increased rather than settled the differences between Turkey and Greece. In April and May relations between these two opponents had been embittered by their treatment of subject nationals. Mutually they charged each other with massacres, arbitrary eviction, forced seizure of property. Turkish treatment of Greeks on the mainland opposite the islands of Chios and Mytilene, especially stirred the Greeks. These two islands the Turkish statesmen still insisted must be returned to Turkey. For them they would perhaps be willing to exchange some of the Dodecanese when Italy surrendered the latter. But to the Greeks a plump bird in the hand was worth more than a flock in the bush, especially when Italy kept inventing more and more reasons for retaining the Dodecanese.

When the Kaiser and Bethmann Hollweg visited Corfu in April, 1914, they made a real effort to bring about a settlement.

[82] G.P., XXXVI, ii, no. 14381.
[83] *Ibid.*, XXXVI, ii, no. 14398.

The Kaiser had often counselled Greece to be more conciliatory in matters relating to the southern boundary of Albania. He now urged an agreement with Turkey. Venizelos was willing to recognise Turkish suzerainty in Chios and Mytilene in return for an alliance mutually guaranteeing each other's possessions in Europe. At last there seemed some prospects of a settlement — autonomous islands administered and controlled by Greece but under nominal Turkish rule. The sultan would save face. The Turkish leaders agreed to negotiate on this basis, but insisted on Turkish sovereignty, not suzerainty, and that this solution should cover all the islands, not only Chios and Mytilene.[84] Greece was unable to accept these conditions and on May 28th the German minister at Athens concluded, "And therewith the Greek-Turkish negotiations appear to be completely ended."[85]

Each country talked of war; Turkey hastened to buy the Brazilian dreadnought "Rio de Janeiro" which was just leaving English yards. King Constantine felt that he must annihilate Turkish sea power before the dreadnought arrived. Meanwhile the Greek government sought hither and yon to purchase some dreadnoughts. Finally the United States consented to sell the "Idaho" and "Mississippi." With this the superiority of the Greek fleet was assured. King Constantine now felt safe and "peace," as he said, "was secure."[86] No doubt a far more important factor for peace was the refusal of Pašić to recognise the Greek-Turkish quarrel as a justification for Serbia's participation in another conflict. He advised the Greek government to moderate its demands.[87] Even King Carol of Rumania, at that very time acting as host to the Russian sovereign, also warned at Athens that he would not intervene to restrain Bulgaria in case of an unprovoked attack by Greece on Turkey.[88]

[84] *Ibid.*, XXXVI, ii, no. 14578.

[85] Quadt to foreign office, May 28, 1914, *ibid.*, XXXVI, ii, no. 14598.

[86] G.P., XXXVI, ii, nos. 14631, 14632; B.D., X, i, no. 291; R.D., I Reihe, III, no 352.

[87] Hartwig to Sazonov, June 1, 1914, R.D., I Reihe, III, no. 239; see also, no. 284; footnote 218c on p. 379.

[88] G.P., XXXVI, ii, nos. 14616, 14617, 14621.

Not to be outdone, the great powers as usual counselled moderation both at Constantinople and Athens. Supported by neither ally nor friends there was nothing left for the Greek government to do but to pull in its horns and continue negotiations with Turkey.

Rumania had at various times tried to further a rapprochement between Turkey and Greece, such as she had envisaged when she sponsored the Peace of Athens. Her attempts had always failed. The British chargé reported: "Monsieur Streit informed me that during the past months no fewer than four separate attempts at mediation had been made by Rumania, but all had fallen through." [89] Germany's plan of a Rumanian-Turkish-Greek combination remained as much of a day dream as ever. "No real scholar of the Orient will ever hold that it is possible to conciliate Hellenism and Ottomanism. Never will Greece surrender its hopes of a second Byzantium." [90] Such was the opinion of Germany's shrewd ambassador at Constantinople in May, 1914. And yet, because the Kaiser had suddenly become Grecophile and had insisted on a Greek Kavala, there was nothing for Wangenheim to do but to keep on trying to bring this impossible combination into being. To him Kiderlen's old plan of a Turkish-Bulgarian-Rumanian alliance — which was also the policy of the Ballhausplatz — was the only one worth aiming at; only such a combination would be of value against Russia.

With the failure of German and Rumanian mediation, Greece now showed interest in English offers of assistance. E. J. Dillon, correspondent of the *Daily Telegraph*, undertook to act as intermediary. He was "indefatigable in his efforts and made the journey between Athens and Smyrna, and Athens and Constantinople no less than five times within a period of less than three weeks." [91] As an old friend of Venizelos he had persuaded

[89] Erskine to Grey, July 25, 1914, B.D., X, i, no. 309.
[90] Wangenheim to Von Jagow, May 7, 1914, G.P., XXXVI, ii, no. 14587.
[91] Erskine to Grey, July 15, 1914, B.D., X, i, no. 302; see also, D.D.F., 3d. ser., X, no. 519; R.D., I Reihe, IV, no. 334.

the latter to make additional concessions. On July 13, the British ambassador at Constantinople optimistically reported:

> Dillon has just left Minister of the Interior. Cabinet have accepted Greek proposal for defensive treaty, including article providing for joint appointment of one of King's sons as Governor of these islands of Samos, Chios, and Mytilene. Meeting is to be arranged at Brussels between M. Venizelos and Turkish plenipotentiary, who will be Grand Vizier.[92]

It finally looked as if the long sought for Turkish-Greek settlement was at hand. It would surely have been a scoop for British diplomacy. However, on July 15, 1914 the report came that the Turkish government was "disposed to raise difficulties." Turkey now wanted to maintain an armed force in Mytilene and Chios, and also to retain control of the customs. Knowing that Greece would not accept these conditions, Dillon in despair rather precipitately broke off relations. Venizelos, anxious for relaxation, left for Munich to await news of the departure of the Ottoman delegates for the conference at Brussels. No one stirred at Constantinople, but Baron Giesl suddenly left Belgrade for Vienna. The World War was at hand. On August 15th Sir Eyre Crowe noted on a summary report from Athens: "This shows that even if war had not intervened there was little chance of the Dillon negotiations leading to a satisfactory issue." [93]

In spite of months of negotiating, one might in July, 1914, still have referred to "the future of the Aegean Islands."

[92] Mallet to Grey, July 13, 1914, B.D., X, i, no. 299.
[93] *Ibid.*, X, i, no. 309 minute.

CHAPTER XXI

THE FINANCIAL SETTLEMENT

IN THE Preliminaries of London the powers not only had assumed the burden of establishing the Albanian boundary and the future possession of the islands, but also they had contracted to supervise the settlement of financial questions arising out of the war.[1] From the very opening of hostilities the security of vested capital and economic concessions within the Turkish Empire caused concern among the powers. France with its great stake in Ottoman bonds, and Germany, deeply involved in the Bagdad Railway, were touched most directly. German experts busied themselves with the problem. The French government set up an interdepartmental commission to study the situation and see what could and should be done to protect European coupon-clippers. In the middle of November, 1912 the twelve-point report of this commission was transmitted by the Quai d'Orsay to the great powers for their consideration.[2] Russia and Germany were quick to respond. Both had some objections to offer, but the program was held to be an excellent basis for discussion.

The German foreign office was interested in the kilometer guarantees which had been given to the builders of the Bagdad Railway, and in the future strength of the Administration of the Ottoman Debt. Germany therefore wanted the share of the Turkish public debt which was to be taken over by the Balkan states to be based on the relative amounts contributed by the

[1] The German and French documents offer the best material for the study of the financial settlement. The Austrian collection is of little aid, because as a matter of editorial policy documents pertaining to economic and financial problems were eliminated in favor of those of greater political import.

[2] J. Cambon to Kiderlen, Nov. 21, 1912, G.P., XXXVII, ii, no. 15155. For the German answer see, *ibid.*, no. 15161 Anlage. Russia took this occasion to renew her demand for representation on the Council of the Ottoman Debt (D.D.F., 3d. ser., V, no. 10 annexe).

conquered provinces to certain revenues which had been earmarked for the Ottoman Debt. France, with great financial interests outside of the Ottoman Debt and uncovered by obligations assumed by that organisation, wanted the total share of the Balkan states to be based on the proportion of taxes contributed from the conquered area to the total Turkish state revenues. Discussion between German and French experts however showed that in all fundamental matters there was no great disagreement. Financial circles in both countries found it relatively easy to discover common ground.[3]

In the early days of January, 1913, when it looked as if negotiations might be concluded between the allies and Turkey, it became necessary to protect the claims of the powers by getting some clauses inserted into the proposed peace treaty. The French government on January 10th worked out three such articles.[4] The first provided for the recognition by the allied states of an obligation to take over a part of the Turkish debt. This was to be proportioned according to the existing relation between the revenues of these territories and the global revenue of the Empire, "calculated on the basis of the last three financial years." There were to be certain guarantees (designed to meet the German demands) to secure these funds for the protection of the creditors. These respective contributions of each state were to be converted into a capital obligation at the rate of 4%. The second article provided that the Balkan states should recognise and execute the contracts of concessions which had been granted for the exploitation of the territory which they were taking over. On the insistence of Austria an amend-

[3] G.P., XXXVII, ii, no. 15161 Anlage. For a good brief sketch of the Council of the Ottoman Debt see, Donald C. Blaisdell, *European Financial Control in the Ottoman Empire* (New York, 1929), ch. I. For tables showing the amount of the total indebtedness controlled by the "Administration of the Ottoman Public Debt" see, *Encyclopaedia Britannica*, 11th ed., XXVII, 436–39. See also the section "Finanzfragen" in Kurt Holdegel's, *Frankreichs Politik im Nahen Orient*, pp. 101–7.

[4] D.D.F., 3d. ser., V, no. 216 annexe II; G.P., XXXVII, ii, Anlage II. For a German-Austrian draft of the financial proposals to be incorporated into the final treaty see, *ibid.*, no. 15160.

ment was inserted especially recognising certain obligations in respect to the railway.[5] The third article provided that the details concerning the application and execution of the other two should be left to an international commission "where the six great powers would be represented."

By the time the powers had agreed upon these points, the St. James Peace Conference in London had been deserted. Of importance, however, was the fact that the powers had accepted the principle of settling the financial questions through an international commission; when and where this commission was to meet was not formally decided, but everybody knew it would be Paris. The French government on February 12th issued invitations to the powers to have the counsellors at their Paris legation sit with the French interdepartmental commission.[6] This body would then work out the plan of the international commission proposed under Article III above. This invitation was accepted and the French committee originally constituted in November now became an international committee. Poincaré, thwarted in his designs for a conference in October, was at last to have the satisfaction of seeing Paris become the center of deliberations. On the 6th of March, the ambassadors at London gladly adopted a resolution referring all financial matters to the Paris commission.[7] A later resolution recommended that the Balkan states and Turkey should also be represented at the Paris conference.[8]

This representation of the belligerent states had not been foreseen at first, and was a concession in order to get them to accept the propositions of the powers. At first the latter had been in agreement in opposing all demands for an indemnity from Turkey.[9] The Balkan allies however, continued to press their demands for financial compensation. They wanted to obtain sufficient indemnity to cover that portion of the Turkish

[5] B.D., IX, ii, no. 568; D.D.F., 3d. ser., V, no. 272.
[6] G.P., XXXVII, ii, no. 15183 Anlage.
[7] B.D., IX, ii, no. 686; G.P., XXXVII, ii, no. 15192 note.
[8] *Ibid.*, XXXVII, ii, no. 15193 note.
[9] B.D., IX, ii, nos. 534 ed. note, 541.

debt which the great powers would certainly place on their shoulders.[10] Russia tended to side with them.[11] This change in Russian attitude was due largely to a desire to hasten the conclusion of peace, and to prevent a Bulgarian advance on Constantinople.[12] Sazonov advanced the idea of indemnifying the Balkan states by using the 3% surtax on Turkish imports which had been set aside for seven years in 1907 for Macedonian reforms. With Macedonia in Christian hands this 3% surtax might well be devoted to some other purpose.[13] The powers however turned this scheme down. As a tactical maneuver Berchtold at one time promised Bulgaria to maintain a benevolent attitude on the question of an indemnity, but he never went beyond this.[14] Germany and England remained adamant in their opposition to an indemnity. They felt that the financial integrity and hence the very existence of Turkey was at stake. However, it was agreed that the question of compensations might be raised in the Paris commission. The German view is well portrayed by Zimmermann's statement: "In the end it is simply a problem in arithmetic if one apportions to the Balkan states 800 million francs as their part of the state debt and credits them with 100 million francs as a war indemnity,[15] or if you set as their portion of the state debt 700 million and in return demand the surrender of all claims to a war indemnity." With assurance of their representation on the Paris commission the Balkan states finally agreed to accept the proposals of the powers respecting finances. This became a regularly accepted article in the exchange of notes leading to the cessation of hostilities and the conclusion of peace. However, the original three-point program of January 10th, advanced by the French government, had been trimmed to one sentence by

[10] Izvolsky, III, no. 1044.

[11] B.D., IX, ii, nos. 777, 783.

[12] *Ibid.*, IX, ii, nos. 786, 814, 833, 836; D.D.F., 3d. ser., VI, no. 151.

[13] G.P., XXXVII, ii, no. 15211; B.D., IX, ii, no. 833; D.D.F., 3d. ser., VI, no. 254.

[14] G.P., XXXVII, ii, nos. 15218, 15251.

[15] Aufzeichnung des Stellvertretenden Staatssekretärs des Auswärtigen Amtes Zimmermann, May 13, 1913, *ibid.*, XXXVII, ii, no. 15211.

the time it was incorporated into the peace treaty. Article VI of the Preliminaries of London provided: "His Majesty the Ottoman Emperor and their Majesties the Allied Sovereigns remit the task of regulating the questions of a financial order resulting from the state of war which is now ended and from the above mentioned cessions of territory to the international commission to be called at Paris, to which they will delegate their representatives." [16]

The decision to permit the Balkan states to participate in the discussions at Paris raised various problems. The Triple Alliance powers had originally proposed that they should only have a consultative voice. France agreed, but on pressure from Russia and England reversed its position. A compromise was suggested by Grey: on certain questions the Balkan states and Turkey should be given a deliberative voice, and on others a consultative voice. It was to be left to the commission itself to decide when the statesmen from the Near East could only orate or when they could orate and vote as well. Such a plan provided too much opportunity for bickering. In the end all states large and small were given a deliberative vote, but in order to keep the four allied states from "majorising" the conference it was decided that the principle of unanimity was to hold for all decisions.[17] Originally Germany had agreed to the participation of the representatives of the small states only if the delegates of the great powers had a meeting first and here reached a decision on all important matters. Russia was loath to participate in such a preliminary conference, and in the end it was not held. When the conference did assemble and immediately ran into difficulties, the Germans had the consolation of saying "I told you so."

The Finance Conference finally met on June 4, 1913.[18] It immediately set up three major committees: (1) Comité de la dette, (2) Comité des concessions et contrats, (3) Comité des

[16] Martens, *Traités*, 3d. ser., VIII, 18.
[17] D.D.F., 3d. ser., VII, nos. 72, 92, 161; G.P., XXXVII, ii, no. 15245.
[18] G.P., XXXVII, ii, nos. 15238, 15252.

réclamations pécuniaires. Few plenary sessions were held and on July 18th the conference adjourned until September 30th. The reopening of hostilities on June 29/30th, the fact that the boundary of Albania was not yet settled, that definite treaties of peace had not been concluded between Turkey and the Balkan states, and not least of all the summer heat, were sufficient reasons to bring about a cessation of activity.[19]

The conference was well supplied with experts and data. The material with which to work was at hand, but little progress was made.[20] The first committee had the difficult task of proportioning the amount of debt which each of the states should shoulder. It apparently made the greatest progress. Although no definite figure was set, the English and German experts later agreed, on the basis of these negotiations, that the amount should be between 19½–20 million Turkish pounds. The second committee made little progress with its problem of concessions and contracts. The most thorny question of all — that of the railways — was hardly touched on, as this was reserved for the time being to direct negotiation between the states concerned. The third commission had to study the demands for compensation for war damages raised by the Balkan states. The word indemnity was avoided, but the meaning was the same. The Balkan states advanced exorbitant demands;[21] the Turks refused all payments. Much more than this was not accomplished.

The conference failed to reassemble on September 30th. During the winter there were a few exchanges between the cabinets on these questions. In April, 1914 the Turkish government requested the powers to reassemble and conclude the negotia-

[19] *Ibid.*, XXXVII, ii, no. 15256.

[20] The work of the commission can be judged from its published protocols (Ministère des affaires étrangères, Commission financière des affaires balkaniques, *Procès-verbaux des séances plénières et rapports présentés au nom des divers comités* [Paris, 1913]). Other pertinent documents are: Izvolsky, III, nos. 890, 944, 1044; G.P., XXXVII, ii, nos. 15245, 15252, 15255.

[21] See the "Recapitulatory Table of the Claims for Pecuniary Compensation made by the Balkan States as a Result of War Operations" *Carnegie Report*, p. 398.

tions.[22] At Constantinople they were naturally anxious to be relieved of part of the state debt. The French government made inquiries of the cabinets if a meeting in June would be acceptable. Vienna preferred to have the discussions postponed, since the negotiations with Serbia over the Oriental Railway had not been concluded.[23] At Berlin there were also certain negotiations pending with Turkey which they preferred to see concluded before the final settlement was made.[24] The Balkan states naturally were glad for any delay and so it was decided to postpone the conference until October, 1914.[25] The war at least spared the world this meeting. Ten years later the Lausanne Treaty of 1924 dealt anew with this hangover of the Balkan Wars.[26] Bonds have the happy faculty of being blessed by protectors of great pertinacity and eternal vigilance.

It has been mentioned that the regulation of the future status of the railways in the provinces conquered from Turkey was reserved by the Paris conference for direct negotiations among the states concerned. The railways in these territories had largely been under the administration of the Oriental Railways Company.[27] The majority of the shares of this organisation were originally owned by a consortium of German, Austrian, and Swiss banks.[28] In April, 1913, with the friendly aid of the Ballhausplatz and the Wilhelmstrasse, an Austro-Hungarian group of banks was able to acquire from German interests enough shares to give them majority control of the Oriental

[22] Türkische Note, April 21, 1914, G.P., XXXVII, ii, no. 15256.

[23] Notiz von der österreich-ungarischen Botschaft in Berlin, May 9, 1914, *ibid.*, XXXVII, ii, no. 15257.

[24] Memorandum für die österreich-ungarische Botschaft, May 9, 1914, *ibid.*, XXXVII, ii, no. 15258.

[25] Von Schoen to foreign office, May 26, 1914, *ibid.*, XXXVII, ii, no. 15259.

[26] Blaisdell, *European Financial Control in the Ottoman Empire*, pp. 203 ff.; for the final terms of the settlement see, *The Near East Year Book, 1931–1932*, pp. 693–4.

[27] For an excellent brief analysis of the financial control of these railways see, Herbert Feis, *Europe: The World's Banker, 1870–1914* (New Haven, 1930), ch. XIII.

[28] G.P., XXXVII, ii, no. 15115 note. In addition to its own lines the Oriental Railways Company had been granted a ninety-nine year concession of the Salonica-Monastir line in 1890 (*The Near East Year Book, 1931–1932*, p. 425).

Railways Company.[29] The Viennese government now felt that it was in a position to safeguard the way to Salonica. Guarantees would have to be obtained against discriminating tariff rates, and it would above all be necessary to see that Serbia and Greece extended certain privileges of transit similar to those contained in the railway convention of 1883.[30]

In 1908, when the declaration of independence by Bulgaria took a portion of the Oriental Railways out of Turkish suzerainty, the Bulgarian government had indemnified that company and Turkey by a payment of 21½ million francs.[31] The simplest solution now would have been to have Serbia, Greece, and Bulgaria do likewise. The officials at Vienna, however, were not eager to see this done, as it would mean losing all control over the operation of the railway to Salonica. They kept insisting that the Serbian government, which had seized the railways, should return them to the operation and control of the Oriental Railways Company. The Serbian military authorities, however, were not disposed to let the future means of mobilisation slip from their hands in this fashion. Greece escaped Austrian ire by returning at least part of the railways to the Oriental Railways Company, and with the reoccupation of Adrianople by Turkey, the portions of the Oriental Railways which remained in Bulgarian possession lost their significance. The settlement of the status of the railways in the Balkans therefore hinged upon direct Belgrade-Vienna negotiations with all the other powers adding their bits from the sidelines. As usual there were to be many words and few results.

In order to bridge the differences between the Serbian and

[29] G.P., XXXVII, ii, no. 15119 note. After the Second Balkan War, when it was clear that a goodly portion of the eastern network of the Oriental Railways would remain in Turkish hands, the Germans claimed a right to repurchase a number of shares from the Austro-Hungarian banks. These banks refused to resell the shares, but Germany was able to obtain certain guarantees as to their future control. Germany wanted to be safeguarded against these shares passing under the dominance of an unfriendly power (G.P., XXXVII, ii, nos. 15132, 15135, 15140, 15142).

[30] This was the so-called "convention à quatre": Austria-Hungary, Bulgaria, Serbia, and Turkey. See Martens, *Traités*, 2d. ser., IX, 720–6.

[31] G.P., XXXVII, ii, no. 15115 note; Feis, *Europe: The World's Banker*, p. 301.

Austrian demands and also to satisfy French financiers the French government as early as June, 1913 suggested a scheme for internationalising these Macedonian railways.[32] In December this plan was officially advanced.[33] It was proposed that the railways should pass to two international corporations — one for the Serbian portion, one for the Greek portion. The shares were to be divided three ways — one-third to France, one-third to Austria-Hungary, one-third to Serbia or Greece. Russia was to be allotted a certain portion of the French share. To the surprise of Izvolsky, the Ballhausplatz accepted the proposal.[34] The Austrians at this time were determined not to come to another clash with Serbia, and, moreover, were quite willing to be conciliatory to French financial circles. Undoubtedly the hope of obtaining access to the French money market had a deciding influence.[35]

However, this plan of internationalisation of the railways made little progress. Italy and Germany were none too friendly to the plan, since it left them out in the cold. Nor was Russia heart and soul behind it.[36] Serbia, although it was problematical whether it could raise the necessary credit, began to talk more and more about direct purchase. The Belgrade government expressed its willingness to give the Austrian government certain guarantees if direct purchase could be arranged.[37] At Vienna they adapted themselves to the situation and negotiations over the purchase price advanced. Austria first demanded 60, then 50 million francs in the name of the Oriental Railways Company; the Serbians raised their offer to 39.8 million francs. Finally the preliminary negotiations ended successfully by fix-

[32] Izvolsky to Sazonov, June 9, 1913, Izvolsky, III, no. 908.

[33] Izvolsky to Sazonov, Dec. 6, 1913, *ibid.*, III, no. 1155 Anlage; G.P., XXXVII, ii, nos. 15128, 15129, 15130; D.D.F., 3d. ser., VIII, nos. 558, 646, 656; IX, no. 50.

[34] Izvolsky, III, no. 1155.

[35] G.P., XXXVII, ii, no. 15130; D.D.F., 3d. ser., VIII, no. 151.

[36] By May, 1914 the plan of internationalising the railway was generally conceded to be dead (G.P., XXXVII, ii, no. 15147; Izvolsky, IV, no. 1328; R.D., I Reihe, II, no. 315; D.D.F., 3d. ser., X, nos. 199, 204).

[37] Von Griesinger to Bethmann Hollweg, April 30, 1914, G.P., XXXVII, ii, no. 15145; R.D., I Reihe, II, no. 387.

ing on a sum of 42 million francs.[38] There were good prospects of Serbia's obtaining the necessary credit — on burdensome conditions, it is true — on the French market. At the end of June, 1914, an Austrian delegation left for Belgrade to complete the negotiations, but was recalled almost immediately. The German minister at Belgrade reported: "It is no doubt correct as it is rumored here, that the negotiations were broken off as a result of the assassination." [39]

[38] Hartwig to Sazonov, June 16, 1914, R.D., I Reihe, III, no. 283; see also, G.P., XXXVII, ii, nos. 15147, 15148.

[39] Von Griesinger to Bethmann Hollweg, July 1, 1914, G.P., XXXVII, ii, no. 15149.

CHAPTER XXII

THE BALANCE SHEET

TURKISH debt, Balkan claims to war indemnity, regulation of railway concessions were the items which spread large across the financial balance sheet of the Balkan Wars. The great losses and disturbances to the economy of the Balkans can perhaps be subject to estimate, but can never be determined.[1] To consider the moral and social consequences of the war in each of the countries involved would require volumes, as is indicated by Professor Shotwell's great series on the "Economic and Social History of the World War." The territorial balance sheet, however, can be fairly well indicated by the following table and the accompanying map.

AREA AND POPULATION OF THE BALKAN STATES BEFORE AND AFTER THE BALKAN WARS[2]

	Area in square miles		Estimated Population	
	Before	After	Before	After
Albania	.....	11,317	....	850,000
Bulgaria	33,647	43,310	4,337,516	4,467,006
Greece	25,014	41,933	2,666,000	4,363,000
Montenegro	3,474	5,603	250,000	500,000
Rumania	50,720	53,489	7,230,418	7,516,418
Serbia	18,650	33,891	2,911,701	4,527,992
Turkey in Europe	65,350	10,882	6,130,200	1,891,000

But these shifts of boundary lines and of population did not bring a stable settlement. Deep seated animosities had been

[1] For discussions of the economic, moral, and social consequences of the Balkan Wars see, *Carnegie Report*, chs. VI, VII; Diplomatist, pp. 292–386. For estimates as to the total losses of the belligerents see, Samuel Dumas and K. O. Vedel-Petersen, *Losses of Life Caused by War* (Oxford, 1923), p. 59; Nikolaides, *Griechenlands Anteil an den Balkankriegen*, p. 401.

[2] *Carnegie Report*, p. 418; see also pp. 70, 419 for maps on which the accompanying map is largely based.

THE BALKAN SETTLEMENT OF 1913
Pre-war extent of the Ottoman Empire
Territory acquired by Rumania from Bulgaria
RUSSIA
AUSTRIA-HUNGARY
RUMANIA
Belgrade
Bucharest
Constantza
Silistria
Turtukaia
Danube R.
Balchik
Varna
SERBIA
Nish
Novibazar
MONTENEGRO
Cetinje
L. Scutari
Drin
Sofia
BULGARIA
Rujen
Maritza R.
Prizren
Scutari
Usküb
Perelik
Adrianople
Midia
TREATY OF LONDON MAY 30, 1913
Vardar R.
Struma R.
Strumitza
ALBANIA
Durazzo
Tirana
L. Ochrida
Monastir
L. Prespa
Ghevheli
Kavala
Dedeagach
Salonica
Enos
Constantinople
Thasos
Samothrace
Imbros
Lemnos
Tenedos
C. Stylos
Janina
GREECE
Mytilene
TURKEY
Athens
DODECANESE held by Italy since 1912
CRETE

aroused among the Balkan peoples and the spirit of persecution as well as of revenge had been kindled. "L'appetit vient en mangeant," and there were many in the enlarged but still small Balkan states who longed for still greater fields of glory.

The Treaty of Bucharest did not cure but only plastered up the sores of the Balkans and of Europe. It aggravated rather than soothed the Serbian problem for the Dual Monarchy. It whetted the appetites of Rumanian expansionists who now cast hungry eyes towards Transylvania. The Austrian general staff began to make plans for fortifications there. Indeed the peace treaty left Berchtold little prospect of putting through the Bulgarian-Triple Alliance rapprochement which he considered essential for the future protection and development of the monarchy against the Pan-Slav menace. For such an alignment he would have had to bring Bulgaria and Rumania together, which Germany apparently considered hopeless and which in truth did present difficulties. The Wilhelmstrasse was now intent on putting through a Rumanian-Greek-Turkish combination which Serbia might possibly join. This line-up meant overcoming what were probably even greater obstacles. But before anything could be accomplished it was most essential to bridge the differences which had developed between the two allies in the past months. The German opposition to revision of the Treaty of Bucharest had so nettled Conrad that he had cancelled his intention of attending the German maneuvers. It took the combined requests and commands of William II and Francis Joseph to bring his reconsideration and his presence on the maneuver fields of 1913.[3] Both governments realised the necessity of restoring closer coöperation in Balkan questions. This came about gradually in the winter and spring of 1913–14. By July, 1914 Germany was willing to work with rather than against Berchtold, which had not been true in the settlement of the Second Balkan War.

The Triple Entente had fared better than their adversaries.

[3] Conrad, III, 429–30; Ö-U.A., VII, no. 8495.

Great advances had been made in Rumania, and the British minister felt that "the time is passed when Austria might in case of a conflict with Russia have counted upon Rumania's armed assistance."[4] Russia, it is true, had lost its once dominant position at Sofia, but in turn Bulgaria had lost much of its alliance value. Moreover, there was still a large Russophile group in the country which was concentrated in the opposition parties. A change of ministries — not an unusual thing — might rapidly bring a strengthening of Russia's position there. Sazonov centered his Bulgarian policy on this objective in the spring of 1914. French influence in Greece and Turkey, all things considered, remained fairly strong.

The peace negotiations had, indeed, brought out some differences of opinion within the Entente. But these had never approached in seriousness those of the Triple Alliance. France differed from Russia on Kavala, but Russia never was set on this point, and Sazonov admitted that he favored Bulgaria simply because Austria did so. Especially at Belgrade and Bucharest there was close coöperation between the French and Russian ministers. If France ever opposed a Russian move, the opposition was very circumspect. There never was such a blunt and needless open contradiction of the policy of an ally as the Kaiser's insistence on the publication of his telegrams to King Carol. The world saw instead a French military mission in St. Petersburg, discussing the building of strategic railways, and holding public love-feasts with their brothers in arms.[5] Throughout the crisis England also followed a circumspect and even a reserved policy. It is clear that Downing Street was particularly concerned about maintaining good relations with St. Petersburg. True to England's traditional policy she recognised the correctness of the principle of revision as applied to the Treaty of Bucharest. Had Sazonov insisted on going through with this, he would have had more support from London than from Paris.

[4] Barclay to Grey, Aug. 25, 1913, B.D., IX, ii, no. 1251.
[5] D.D.F., 3d. ser., VIII, nos. 18, 62, 79; G.P., XXXIX, no. 15654.

The British statesmen were often much put out by what they termed Sazonov's vacillation. The same feeling existed in Germany with respect to Berchtold. The Kaiser labelled the latter an "alter Schauckelfritz" and used other unkind words about him.[6] But behind this vacillation lay a congenital inconsistency in the policy inherited from Austria's past. Indeed, both Sazonov and Berchtold were at this time carrying on a two-faced policy. Both of them, while willing to threaten separate action and use of troops — the ultimate support of all diplomacy —, were equally against war. Both their sovereigns, Francis Joseph more steadfast in his views than Nicholas II, placed a restraining hand on any rash measures. And yet Sazonov and Berchtold were supposed to further traditional policies which demanded active participation and domination in the Balkans. It is true that both put forth demands, proposed this thing and that and then had to withdraw. Both were attempting to bring about a peaceful solution of what were considered vital problems. Their efforts collapsed before the independent attitudes of the Balkan states and the lack of coöperation among the powers. Sazonov failed, it is true, to open the Straits, but he did improve his position in this matter. Berchtold not only failed to settle the Serbian question, but aggravated this cancer in the body of the monarchy.

Berchtold was less successful than Sazonov partly because he had less support, and partly because his problem was without doubt more difficult. In Austria it was a matter both of internal and external policy, and Berchtold as foreign minister could not really touch the source of his troubles. In the end it was not foreign policy but Austrian or rather Hungarian internal policy that cost the Triple Alliance Rumania's friendship and made Serbia so dangerous a foe. Whatever the limitations of a study in diplomacy may be, such a study of the Balkan Wars at least shows that the blame for Austria's position in 1914 cannot be placed entirely at the door of the foreign office. The foreign policy of Austria was as intelligent and as forbearing

[6] G.P., XXXV, no. 13635 marginal note.

as foreign policies are ever apt to be. The root of the difficulty lay elsewhere.

The loss of Rumanian support was a serious blow to the Triple Alliance. The Balkan Wars had given Russia an opportunity to prove herself Rumania's friend. Nor had the Triple Alliance been able to make this good by winning the friendship of Greece and Bulgaria. What the Triple Alliance lost, the Triple Entente gained. Russia, by constructing the Balkan League, had made the first move. The original League had been disrupted, but the Serbian-Greek-Rumanian-Montenegrin coalition with its interest in preserving the Peace of Bucharest had taken its place. Unfortunately the events of the Balkan Wars, which Europe successfully rode out amid endless conferences and notes, had upset the balance of power. No longer was it true, as the Kaiser had felt in 1913, that "the desire for peace was greater among the great powers than had been expected and that other poses could be designated as bluff." [7] The Balkans were officially at peace, but within a year the powers were to be at war among themselves about the Balkans.

[7] William II to foreign office, Aug. 16, 1913, *ibid.*, XXXVI, i, no. 13781.

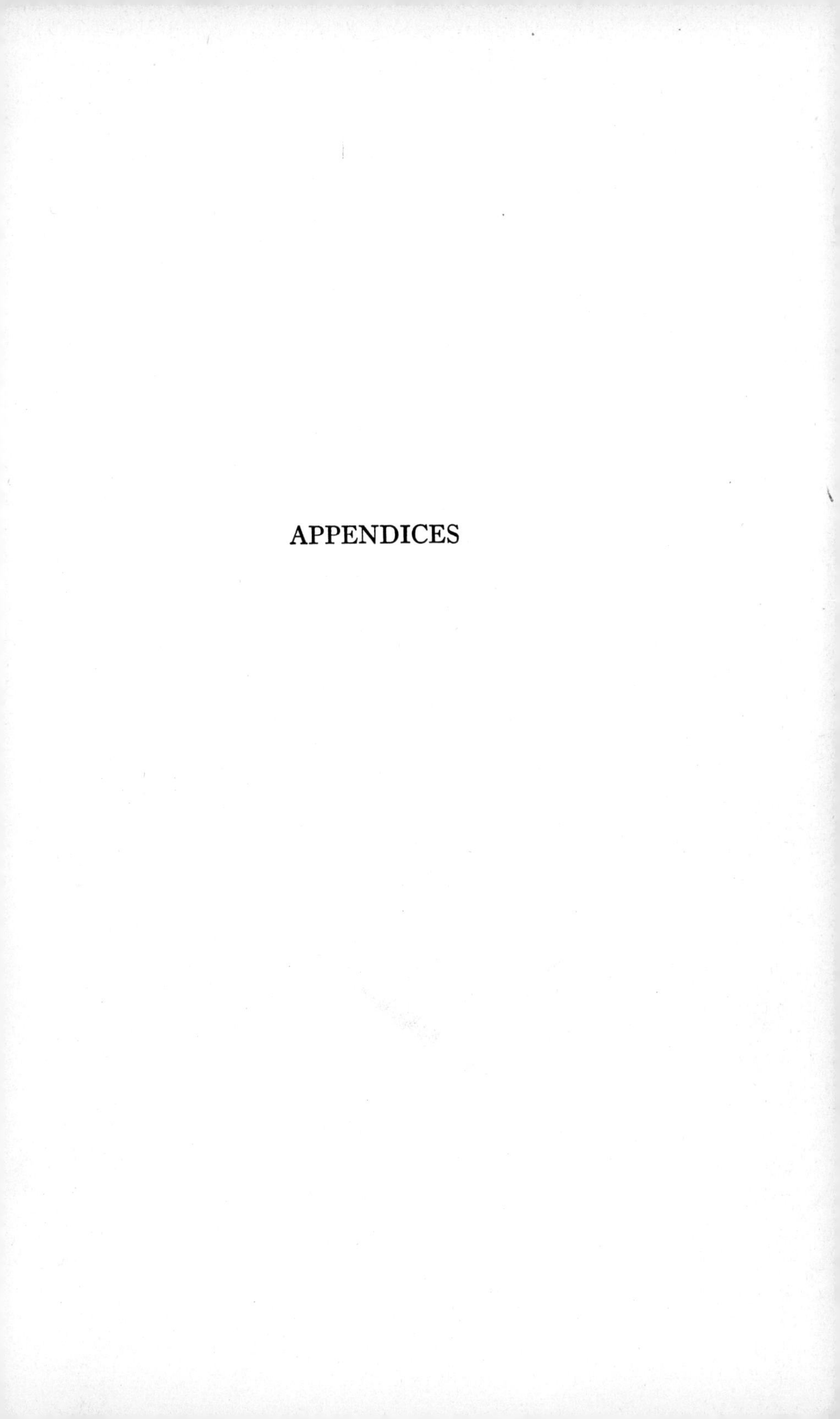

APPENDICES

APPENDIX I

AUSTRO-HUNGARIAN MILITARY MEASURES 1912–1913

I

Übersicht über die wichtigsten anlässlich der Balkankrise 1912–13 getroffenen militärischen Massnahmen.

Datum	Inhalt.
31/10/12	Absendung von ca 7000 Ers. Res. nach B.H.D. und Rückbehaltung des Präsenzjahrganges in B.H.D.
18/11/12	Errichtung der Grenzjägertruppe. (6 Komp. mit 23 Zügen a 70 mann)
21/11/12	Standeserhöhung der Territorialbereiche Krakau, Przemysl, Lemberg. (Nach den 88er Gesetzen)
24/11/12	Standeserhöhung der Territorialbereiche Temesvar, Agram. (Nach den 88er Gesetzen)
4/12/12	Standeserhöhung des I.R. Nr. 6 (Nach den 88er Gesetzen) [1 Bat. in B.H. already had *Standeserhöhung*.]
7/12/12	Standeserhöhung der Territorialbereiche Budapest und aller Art Zeugs- und Militärpflegsanstalten. (Nach den 88er Gesetzen)
7/12/12	Standesergänzung auf den vollen Kriegsstand in B.H.D.
16/12/12	Regelung des Einberufungstitels. [Classification of the different reserves then under arms. All were to be placed under paragraph 43 of point 2 of the *Wehrgesetz* of 1912.]
21/ 1/13	Ausnahmsweise Rückversetzungen in das Nichtaktiven Verhältnis. [This was to be granted on application (family needs), but was not to apply to more than 5% of the reserves.]
11/ 3/13	Rückversetzung des A.J. 1908 in das Nichtaktiven Verhältnis in 1–14 Kps.
29/ 4/13	Annahme voller Kriegsbereitschaft in B.H.D. (Voller Pferdekauf)
3/ 5/13 } 5/ 5/13 }	Einberufung aller B. H. Nichtaktiven.
8/ 5/13	Rückversetzung der B.H. Nichtaktiven in das n.a. Verhältnis.
16/ 5/13	Abrüstung in 1–14 Kps.

27/ 5/13 Austausch der 4 ältesten Assentjahrgänge in B.H.D.
31/ 7/13 Beurlaubung des A.J. 1906 in B.H.D.
11/ 8/13 Abrüstung in B.H.D.

II

Anzahl der zur ausnahmsweisen aktiven Dienstleistung einberufenen bzw, rückbehaltenen Reservisten und Ersatzreservisten in abgerundeten Zahlen. (Zu Abt. 10 Nr. 400 res von 1914, Beilage 7) [1]

K. & K. Heer	150,000
K. & K. Landwehr	31,000
K. U. Landwehr	21,500
K. & K. Kriegsmarine	6,500
	209,000
Hiezu Ers. Res des A.J. 1912 K. & K. Heer	15,000
Totale	224,000

III

Laufende Erhaltungskosten und einmalige Ausgaben anlässlich der Krise 1912/13 und 1908/09. (Zu Abt. 10 Nr. 400 res von 1914 Beilage 8)

	1912/13 (Kronen)	1908/09
A. Mehrerfordernis an Fortlaufenden Ausgaben, (Durch Neuaufstellungen, Erhöhung der Stände und Gebühren	106,104,000	35,775,000
B. Einmalige Ausgaben (Maschingewehre, Pulver, Karten, Reisen, Sanitätswesen, etc.)	202,989,000	144,225,000
Gesamtsumme	309,093,000	180,000,000

[1] Although separate tables are given only the sum-totals have been taken.

APPENDIX II

THE SERBIAN–BULGARIAN TREATIES OF 1904

Treaty of Alliance Between the Principality of Bulgaria and the Kingdom of Serbia [1]

The government of H. R. H. Prince Ferdinand I of Bulgaria and the government of H. M. King Peter I of Serbia, guided by the principle of "The Balkans for the Balkan nations," and inspired by a desire to safeguard the peace and security of their peoples, to preserve the territorial *status quo* on the Balkan peninsula, and to improve the condition of their fellow-countrymen in the Ottoman Empire, agree on the following:

I

Convinced of the utility of the program of reforms adopted at Mürzsteg for the vilayets of Salonica, Bitolya and Kossovo (Macedonia and Old Serbia), the two allied states hereby promise to promote jointly and by all peaceful means at their disposal the execution of these reforms in the said three vilayets, at the same time encouraging their introduction into the vilayet of Adrianople, thus safeguarding the lives, property and free development of their fellow-countrymen in these vilayets, on the basis of political and national equality in all respects.

II

Firmly resolved to apply all of their loyal efforts and goodwill for the preservation of peace on the Balkan peninsula, the two allied states hereby promise jointly to defend themselves with all the power and resources at their command, against any encroachment from whatever source, be it on the present territorial unity and independence of their respective states, or on the security and inviolability of the reigning dynasties.

III

Likewise the two allied states promise to oppose, with all the power and resources at their command, any hostile act or isolated occupation of the above-mentioned four vilayets, whatever nation may be responsible.

[1] I am indebted for the translation of these treaties to C. E. Black. They are taken from A. Toshev, *Balkanskite voini*, I, 153–8.

IV

In the circumstances foreseen in Articles II and III, the two allied states will conclude a special military convention, in which all possible eventualities and all their consequences will be provided for.

V

In the desire to prepare the ground for the full coöperation between the Slavs on the Balkan peninsula and to create favorable circumstances for an immediate agreement between the Kingdom of Serbia and the Principality of Montenegro, the two allied states hereby promise — whenever the question of Albania should arise — to support such a solution as would favor the interests of Montenegro.

VI

The two allied states hereby promise to discuss and decide jointly all questions which, by their nature and spirit, are within the sphere of this treaty.

VII

The two allied states hereby promise to submit to the final decision of His Imperial Majesty the Tsar of All Russians, all of those controversies which they are not able to decide among themselves. In case the Russian emperor declines to award a decision on such a controversial question, it will be placed in the hands of the Permanent Court of Arbitration at The Hague.

VIII

The present allied treaty remains secret. It may be communicated to a third party — in whole or in part — only after a preliminary agreement between the two allied governments.

After five years this treaty may be brought up for revision if the two allied states consider it desirable.

It becomes valid on the day of its ratification.

Concluded in Belgrade the thirtieth day of the month of March [O.S.] the one thousand nine hundred and fourth year after the birth of Christ, the third day of Easter.

In the name of the Principality of Bulgaria:

(s) D. Rizov
(s) Colonel of the General Staff Hesapchiev

In the name of the Kingdom of Serbia:

(s) General Sava Gruić
(s) Nikola Pašić

Treaty of Friendship between the Principality of Bulgaria and the Kingdom of Serbia

The government of His Royal Highness Prince Ferdinand I of Bulgaria and the government of His Majesty King Peter I of Serbia, deeply conscious of the common destinies of their neighboring and related states, and sincerely inspired by the desire of safeguarding the advantages of the regulated and peaceful political and cultural development of their nations through a friendly and brotherly union between them, agree on the following:

I

To permit the free importation of their respective products (of domestic origin), at the same time attempting to conduct similar customs policies with respect to other states, aiming at an eventual customs union (Zollverein).

II

To facilitate the mutual exchange and transit of their products by reducing the corresponding freight and passenger rates.

III

To equalise their telegraph and postal rates with their internal rates and to introduce the Cyrillic alphabet into their telegraphic communication.

IV

To abolish their frontier passports, and to remove all other hindrances to free communication between their peoples.

V

To conclude a judicial convention for the mutual execution of decisions under civil law as well as for the extradition of criminals according to common law (du droit commun), and of deserters.

VI

To conclude a monetary convention for the establishment of the free circulation of Serbian and Bulgarian money in their states, and thus to facilitate commercial relations.

VII

This treaty may be made public only after a preliminary agreement between the two states. It shall enter into force from the day of its ratification.

Concluded in Belgrade on the thirtieth of March [O.S.], 1904 (one thousand nine hundred fourth year) after the birth of Christ, the third day of the Resurrection.

In the name of the Kingdom of Serbia:

(s) General Sava Gruić
(s) Nikola Pašić

In the name of the Principality of Bulgaria:

(s) D. Rizov
(s) Colonel of the General Staff Hesapchiev

Approved: Chargé d'Affaires of the Agency, for the General Staff, Colonel Hesapchiev.

(By mutual consent the two allied states agree that this treaty be made public.)

Concluding Protocol

Today, March 31, 1904, we the undersigned: D. Rizov, Bulgarian diplomatic agent in Cetinje, and Hristofor Hesapchiev, Colonel of the General Staff, chargé d'affaires of the Bulgarian diplomatic agency in Belgrade, appointed by His Royal Highness Prince Ferdinand I of Bulgaria with plenipotentiary letters, issued in Plovdiv on March 22 [O.S.], as plenipotentiaries of the Principality of Bulgaria, and General Sava Gruić, president of the ministerial council, and N. P. Pašić, minister of foreign affairs of the Kingdom of Serbia, appointed by H. M. King Peter I of Serbia with a plenipotentiary letter, issued in Belgrade on March 28 [O.S.], as plenipotentiaries of the Kingdom of Serbia, with the aim of conducting negotiations for the drawing up and conclusion of a convention to guarantee the political and economic development of the said two states through joint action for protecting their national rights and interests, having exchanged our plenipotentiary letters which were found in good and due form, we proceeded to the execution of the mission entrusted to us.

After a long and varied exchange of opinions as to the foundations which should form the basis of such a convention, we decided:

I

That the convention should consist of two parts: the one, which may be made public after the condition foreseen in its text has been fulfilled, to be entitled: "A Treaty of Friendship between the Principality of Bulgaria and the Kingdom of Serbia" and to contain agreements of a cultural and economic character; the other, which is secret, to be entitled: "A Treaty of Alliance between the Principality of Bulgaria and the Kingdom of Serbia," and to contain agreements of a political and military character.

II

That, in order to avoid misinterpretations in the application of the said treaties, the following explanations are included in this protocol:

1

Concerning the Treaty of Friendship: (a) in Article I the phrase: "to conduct similar customs policies" is to be understood: as far as the existing commercial treaties of the two states permit this; and (b) as a supplement to Article III: the two states will agree upon making a joint proposal to the imperial Russian government for the immediate establishment of telegraphic communication between Russia and Bulgaria — if possible in the Cyrillic alphabet.

2

Concerning the Treaty of Alliance: (a) in Article I, the vilayet of Kossovo is understood to include the Sanjak of Novibazar. (b) in Article I, above the Serbian text of the Bulgarian-Serbian copy the last word *pogledu*, as synonymous with the word *otnoshtayu*, is not to be considered erroneous; (c) supplementary to Article I, the two allied states will promote mutual tolerance between their fellow-countrymen in the Ottoman Empire, and (d) in Article V "Albania" is to be understood within the boundaries of the vilayets of Scutari and Janina.

III

That the two treaties be written parallel and with two copies of each one, in the Serbian and Bulgarian languages; also that the copies for the Kingdom of Serbia should be in Bulgarian and Serbian, and the copies for the Principality of Bulgaria should be in Serbian and Bulgarian.

IV

That the original copies of the two treaties, duly ratified by the two sovereigns and their respective ministers, after the plenipotentiary letters and the present protocol have been attached, be kept in the private archives of H. M. King Peter I of Serbia and H. R. H. Prince Ferdinand I of Bulgaria. Only a copy of the Treaty of Friendship may be deposited in the archives of the Ministries of Foreign Affairs of the two states.

Concluded in Belgrade on March 31 [O.S.], the one thousand nine hundred and fourth year after the birth of Christ, the third day of Easter.

In the name of the Principality of Bulgaria:

(s) D. Rizov

(s) Colonel of the General Staff H. Hesapchiev

In the name of the Kingdom of Serbia:

(s) General S. Gruić

(s) Nikola P. Pašić

(Duly ratified by the sovereigns of the two allied states, the above treaties were exchanged in Sofia on April 29th [O.S.]).

BIBLIOGRAPHY

BIBLIOGRAPHY

I. Unpublished Sources; Bibliographical Note

One of the advantages of dealing with the history of the immediate past is that many of the leaders who helped shape the course of events can still be consulted. Many of the statesmen who were in power in 1912–13 graciously consented to see me. Some matters of detail had of course slipped their minds, and invariably I was referred to the great document collections. Unfortunately also the events of the Great War so overshadowed the Balkan Wars that problems in regard to the latter have been forgotten. Yet if the conversations did not always result in much factual gain they were extremely valuable for points of view and general orientation. In all cases I made extensive notes in my diary immediately after the conversations, and references which I have made in the footnotes always refer to these memoranda. I wish to express to these statesmen my appreciation and thanks for their willingness to help me, and it is primarily this desire which leads me to list their names.

Of those interviewed the following held governmental positions: Colonel V. I. Artamonov, Russian military attaché at Belgrade; Count Berchtold, Austro-Hungarian minister of foreign affairs; S. Bobchev, Bulgarian minister at St. Petersburg; M. Bogičević, Serbian chargé d'affaires at Berlin; S. Danev, president of the sobranje, Bulgarian minister-president, 1913; Colonel P. Dŭrvingov, Bulgarian officer in charge of the Macedonian Legion, member of the Macedonian Revolutionary Organisation; Dr. Milan Gavrilović, secretary to the Serbian minister of foreign affairs, member of the Black Hand, later editor of the *Politika*; Baron W. Giesl, Austrian minister at Cetinje (at Belgrade 1914), assigned as expert to aid the Austrian ambassador at the London Conference; Th. A. Ippen, Austrian consul in Albania, assigned as Albanian expert to aid the Austrian minister at the London Conference; Gottlieb von Jagow, German secretary of state for foreign affairs; Jovan M. Jovanović, first secretary at the Serbian foreign office, minister of foreign affairs 1912, Serbian minister at Vienna; Count Kokovtsov, Russian finance minister 1903–14, minister-president 1911–14; M. Majarov, Bulgarian minister at London; M. Peev-Plachkov, Bulgarian minister of instruction 1912–13, editor of the *Mir*; D. Popović, Serbian minister at St. Petersburg; S. Radev, Bulgarian minister at Bucharest, 1912, Bulgarian minister to the United States; Alfred Rappaport, Austrian consul in the Balkans, Balkan expert at the Ballhausplatz, 1909–; Count de Salis, British minister at Cetinje; N. N. Schebeko, Russian minister at Bucharest, ambassador at Vienna, 1914; Baron Maurice Schilling, "chef de cabinet" to the Russian foreign minister; Stanoje Stanojević, member of the Serbian general staff, professor at the University of Belgrade; D. Stanchov, Bulgarian minister at Paris; W. N. von

Strandtmann, first secretary to the Russian legation at Belgrade; Count Friedrich Szápáry, "Sektionschef" at the Austrian foreign office, ambassador to St. Petersburg, October 1913–14; D. Tonchev, Bulgarian finance minister 1913–17; A. Toshev, Bulgarian minister at Belgrade; Prince G. Trubetzkoi, director of the Near Eastern section of the Russian foreign office; Prince Leon Urussov, first secretary to the Russian legation at Sofia; Dr. Friedrich Ritter von Wiesner, "Sektionsrat" at the Ballhausplatz, December, 1913–.

I should, also, like to make special mention of the following scholars who very willingly granted me their aid. Although they were not in the diplomatic service, many of them were eye-witnesses, all of them students of the events with which I deal. I am especially grateful to Miss M. E. Durham for the material she placed at my disposal while in London, and for her continued interest and help. Professors Ludwig Bittner and Hans Uebersberger, whose seminar at the University of Vienna dealing with Austro-Hungarian foreign policy 1908–09 I was privileged to attend; Stephen Gaselee, librarian and director-general of the British foreign office archives; G. P. Gooch, joint editor of the British documents on the origins of the war; M. Jovanović, director of the Serbian archives; Professor Paul Milioukov, member of the Carnegie Commission to inquire into the causes and conduct of the Balkan Wars; Dr. William Miller, London *Times* correspondent at Athens, historian of the Near East; M. Moschopoulous, head of the press department at the foreign office at Athens, author of books dealing with Macedonia; Sir Bernard Pares, head of the School for Slavonic Studies at London; Professor Bogdan Popović of the University of Belgrade; Professor A. F. Pribram of the University of Vienna; Professor G. Salvemini, authority on Italian history; Karl Schwendemann, Legionsrat at the German foreign office; Dr. K. Stanishev, president of the Macedonian Revolutionary Organisation; J. Swire, historian of Albanian affairs; Alfred von Wegerer, editor of the *Berliner Monatshefte.*

In general the material in the major libraries of Europe is the same, with the exception of the newspaper files. One notable exception is the collection on Balkan affairs in the Gennadeion library at Athens. The magazine articles which were collected by M. Gennadius were especially useful.

At Constantinople the American chargé, David Williamson, generously permitted me to consult the archives of the embassy. My notes were submitted to the Department of State and one deletion was made. In general the department did not favor the use of American reports where the facts could be substantiated from other sources.

The material in the Kriegsarchiv in Vienna was of course more important for my work. I am especially indebted to Professor A. F. Pribram, who was instrumental in obtaining my admission to these records, the archive still being officially closed for this period. Director Glaise-Horstenau granted me permission to see all attaché reports and reports of the *Evidenzbureau*, 1912–13. Access to various other materials was also obtained. I was spared taking many notes for the period when Conrad was chief of staff by checking with the material presented in his memoirs. (*Aus Meiner Dienstzeit.*) His volumes are unusually complete. Many attaché reports were removed from the files by the *Evidenzbureau* and never returned. Yet it can be assumed that most of the pertinent parts were used in making up the reports of that bureau. The memoranda drawn up by Schemua and the papers grouped under "Nachlass Schemuas" were of special value. The account drawn up in 1914 of the Austrian military measures taken during the crisis was useful. Several of the summaries are given in Appendix I. The material obtained at the archive was a valuable supplement to the published Austrian documents.

II. Documents and Official Publications

ALBANIA

Resoconto e note sul Congresso Albanese di Trieste. 1–4 Marzo 1913 (Milan, 1913). Notes on the Albanian Congress held at Trieste. Albanian version in parallel column.

AUSTRIA-HUNGARY

Neisser, Karl (ed.), *Politische Chronik der österreichisch-ungarischen Monarchie* (Vienna, 1910–). A collection of news dispatches chronicling the events within the monarchy, and also in foreign countries. Neisser was director of the state archives of the Austrian chamber of deputies and used official sources in editing these volumes and those of the series listed below.

—— *Volkswirtschaftliche Chronik der österreichisch-ungarischen Monarchie* (Vienna, 1910–). Day by day reports on the Vienna bourse and summaries of the other leading continental exchanges are given.

—— *Parlamentarische Chronik. Beilage zur Politischen und Volkswirtschaftlichen Chronik der österreichisch-ungarischen Monarchie* (Vienna, 1911–). Reports of the meetings of the Delegations, the Austrian Reichsrat, the various Austrian Landtage, the Hungarian Reichstag, the Croatian-Slavonian Landtag, and the Bosnian-Herzegovinian Landtag.

Österreich-Ungarns Aussenpolitik von der Bosnischen Krise 1908 bis zum Kriegsausbruch 1914. Diplomatische Aktenstücke des Österreichisch-Ungarischen Ministeriums des Äussern. Ausgewählt von Ludwig Bittner, Alfred Francis Pribram, Heinrich Srbik, und Hans Uebersberger. Bearbeitet von Ludwig Bittner und Hans Uebersberger. 9 vol. (Vienna, 1930).

Pribram, A. F., *The Secret Treaties of Austria-Hungary 1879–1914*, English edition by Archibald Cary Coolidge, 2 vol. (Cambridge, Mass., 1920).

BELGIUM

Belgische Aktenstücke 1905–1914, ed. at the German Foreign Office (Berlin, 1915). This is the first edition of the Belgian documents captured by the German army. It contains the original telegrams of the ministers at London, Paris, and Berlin. There are therefore some differences from the documents published in the 1919 and 1925 editions, where the texts are those of circular telegrams sent out from the foreign office to inform the Belgian ministers at the different capitals. The documents of the 1915 edition are reprinted in the first supplementary volume of the 1925 edition.

Schwertfeger, Bernhard (ed.), *Die Belgischen Dokumente zur Vorgeschichte des Weltkrieges 1885–1914*, 5 Bände, mit 2 Ergänzungsbänden und 2 Kommentarwerken (Berlin, 1925).

—— *Zur europäischen Politik 1897–1914. Unveröffentliche Dokumente*, 5 vol. (Berlin, 1919).

BULGARIA

Doklad na parlamentarnata izpitatelna komisiya [Report of the parliamentary commission of inquiry], 4 vol. and 3 supplements (Sofia, 1918–19). This commission of inquiry was appointed by a decision of the seventeenth regular national assembly in its first extraordinary session at the sitting of May 10, 1914, for the investigation of the cabinets of I. E. Gueshov and Dr. St. Danev on their entire administration, including the preparation and conduct of the war. Vol. I, *The War, Its Diplomatic Preparation and the Diplomatic Negotiations*; vol. II, *Military Preparedness of the Army, the Sanitary Division and the General Headquarters*; vol. III, *Bidding and Supplies*; vol. IV, *Requisitions*. The verbatim transcription of testimony before the commission is to be found in the supplements.

Kesyakov, Dr. B. D., *Prinos kŭm diplomaticheskata istoriya na Bŭlgariya*, [Contribution to the diplomatic history of Bulgaria], 4 vol. (Sofia, 1925–35).

Miletich, Lubomir, *Dokumenti za protivoblgarskitie deĭstvia na srbskitie i na grtskitie vlasti v Makedonia prez 1912–1913 godina* [Documents regarding the anti-Bulgarian activities of the Serbian and Greek authorities in Macedonia 1912–1913], (Sofia, 1929).

Ministerstvo na vŭnshnite raboti i na izpovedaniyata, *Diplomaticheski dokumenti po namesata na Bŭlgariya v evropeĭskata voĭna* [Diplomatic documents on the entry of Bulgaria into the World War], 2 vol. (Sofia, 1920–21). This is usually known as the Bulgarian *Orange Book*. The documents begin with August 6, 1913 and continue into 1918. There are 240 documents (136 pages) on the period up to August 1, 1914.

Ministry of Foreign Affairs, *The Bulgarian Question and the Balkan States* (Sofia, 1919). Contains a convenient collection of documents and maps.

FRANCE

Ministère des affairs étrangères, *Documents diplomatiques. Les affaires balkaniques 1912–1914*, 3 vol. (Paris, 1922). Now superseded by the collection noted immediately below.

—— *Documents diplomatiques français 1871–1914* (Paris, 1929–).

These documents are divided into three series: I, 1871–1901; II, 1901–11; III, 1911–14.

—— Commission financière des affaires balkaniques, *Procès-verbaux des séances plenières et rapports présentés au nom des divers comités* (Paris, 1913).

GERMANY

Das Deutsche Weissbuch über die Schuld am Kriege, mit der Denkschrift der deutschen Viererkommission zum Schuldbericht der Alliierten und Assoziierten Mächte vom 29 März 1919 (Berlin, 1927). Contains many documents, especially Russian and Serbian, which have been reprinted in other collections, notably in the volumes published by M. Boghitschewitsch [Bogičević].

Die Deutschen Dokumente zum Kriegsausbruch 1914. Neue, durchgesehene, und vermehrte Ausgabe, ed. by Count Max Montgelas and Prof. Walter Schücking in consultation with Karl Kautsky (Berlin, 1927). A new edition of the so-called Kautsky documents.

Die Grosse Politik der Europäischen Kabinette 1871–1914, ed. by Johannes Lepsius, Albrecht Mendelssohn Bartholdy and Friedrich Thimme, 40 vol. (Berlin, 1927).

Goetz, Prof. Dr. Walter, *Briefe Wilhelms II an den Zaren 1894–1914* (Berlin, 1920).

GREAT BRITAIN

British Documents on the Origins of the War 1898–1914, ed. by G. P. Gooch and Harold Temperley, 12 vol. (London, 1927–).

A Handbook of Serbia, Montenegro, Albania and Adjacent Parts of Greece, ed. by the Geographical Section of the Naval Intelligence Division (London, 1920).

Prothero, G. W. (ed.), *History of the Eastern Question* (London, 1920). A handbook prepared for the information and use of the British delegates at the Paris Peace Conference, and published by the Foreign Office.

GREECE

The Vindication of Greek Policy 1912–1917, a Report of Speeches Delivered in the Greek Chamber August 23–26, 1917 by E. Venizelos and Others (London, 1918).

The Greek White Book. Diplomatic Documents, 1913–1917, translated by Theodore P. Ion (American Hellenic Society, New York, n.d.; French edition Paris, 1918). Published after the abdication of King Constantine to justify the entrance of Greece into the World War. It should be read in connection with M. Frangulis' *La Grèce et la crise mondiale*, who points out cases where the documents were edited.

RUMANIA

Ministère des affaires étrangères, *Documents diplomatiques. Les événements de la péninsule balkanique. L'action de la Roumanie septembre 1912–août 1913*. (Bucharest, 1913).

Ministère des affaires étrangères, *Le traité de paix de Bucarest du 28 juillet (10 août) 1913. Précédé des protocoles de la conférence* (Bucharest, 1913).

RUSSIA

Adamow, E., *Die Europäischen Mächte und die Türkei während des Weltkrieges*, 2 vol. (Dresden, 1930). A translation of a Russian publication dealing with the Straits Question. It has some valuable summary chapters on events before the World War. The documents range from August 20, 1914 to October 1, 1917.

Die Internationalen Beziehungen im Zeitalter des Imperialismus. Dokumente aus den Archiven der Zarischen und der Provisorischen Regierung, herausgegeben von der Kommission beim Zentralexekutivkomitee der Sowjetregierung unter dem Vorsitz von M. N. Pokrowski. Einzig berechtigte deutsche Ausgabe Namens der Deutschen Gesellschaft zum Studium Osteuropas herausgegeben von Otto Hoetzsch (Berlin, 1931–). This collection of documents is designed to cover the period 1878–1917. They are to appear in three series: I, 1878–1904; II, 1904–14; III, 1914–17. So far only volumes of the third series have appeared.

Laloy, E., *Les documents secrets des archives du ministère des affaires étrangères de Russie* (Paris, 1920).

Marchand, René (ed.), *Un livre noir. Diplomatie d'avant guerre d'après les documents des archives russes, novembre 1910–juillet 1914*, 3 vol. (Paris, 1922–34).

Marguerite, Victor (ed.), *Les alliés contre la Russie avant, pendant et après la guerre mondiale. Faits et Documents* (Paris, n.d.). A series of essays by various Russian military experts, dealing mostly with events since 1914. The Franco-Russian military and naval agreements receive full treatment. Many Russian documents are here reprinted in French translation.

Ministerstvo inostrannykh diel, *Sbornik diplomaticheskikh dokumentov kasayushchikhsia sobytii balkanskom poliostrovie* (August 1912–July 1913) [Collection of diplomatic documents concerning events in the Balkan peninsula] (St. Petersburg, 1914). This is usually known as the *Russian Orange Book on the Balkan Wars*. The most important of the documents can be found in German translation in *Zeitschrift für Internationales Recht*, XXV (1915), 130–168.

Ministerstvo inostrannykh diel, *Materialy po istorii franko-russkikh otnoshenii za 1910–14 g.* [Materials for the history of Franco-Russian Relations 1910–14] (Moscow, 1922). These documents have practically all been translated and are to be found in Stieve's *Der diplomatische Schriftwechsel Iswolskis*, and Marchand's *Un livre noir*.

Narodni komissariat po inostrannym dielam, *Sbornik sekretnikh dokumentov iz arkhiva bivshavo ministerstvo inostrannykh diel*, [Collection of secret documents from the archives of the former ministry of foreign affairs], 2nd ed. (Petrograd, 1917–18).

Popov, A. L., "Diplomaticheskaia Podgotovka Balkanskoi Voini 1912" [The Diplomatic Preparations of the Balkan War, 1912] *Krasny Arkhiv*, VIII, IX, XV, XVI. Published in part in German translation in *Berliner Monatshefte*, VII (1930), nos. 7–9; VIII (1930), nos. 5, 6, 10, 11, 12; IX (1931), no. 1. A very important selection of Russian documents covering the period from September 29, 1911 to November 9, 1912.

Siebert, B. von (ed.), *Diplomatische Aktenstücke zur Geschichte der Ententepolitik der Vorkriegsjahre* (Berlin, 1921). A collection of telegrams exchanged between the Russian foreign office and the Russian minister at London, 1908–14. Arranged by subject. This publication has been superseded by the new three volume edition, listed below.

—— *Graf Benckendorffs Diplomatischer Schriftwechsel*, 3 vol. (Berlin, 1928). Documents arranged chronologically.

Stieve, Friedrich (ed.), *Der Diplomatische Schriftwechsel Iswolskis 1911–1914. Aus dem Geheimakten der Russischen Staatsarchive*, 4 vol. (Berlin, 1925). In this same edition volume five is a commentary entitled *Iswolski und der Weltkrieg 1911–1914*; volume six contains documents from the period of the World War and bears the title, *Iswolski im Weltkriege. Der Diplomatische Schriftwechsel Iswolskis aus dem Jahren 1914–1917.*

SERBIA

Boghitschewitsch, Dr. M., *Die Auswärtige Politik Serbiens 1903–1914*, 3 vol. (Berlin, 1928, 1929, 1931). Vol. I, *Diplomatische Geheimakten aus serbischen Archiven*; vol. II, *Diplomatische Geheimakten aus russischen, montenegrinischen, und sonstigen Archiven*; vol. III, *Serbien und der Weltkrieg* (A commentary). Boghitschewitsch obtained many of the Serbian documents from Austrian sources, the result of the capture of the Serbian archives during the war. The second volume contains documents available in other collections. Only one or two Montenegrin documents are given, and these are published for the first time. In the commentary the author draws heavily on the Austrian documents.

GENERAL

Carnegie Endowment for International Peace, *Report of the International Commission to Inquire into the Causes and Conduct of the Balkan Wars* (Washington, D. C., 1914). The commission was made up of representatives from Austria, France, Germany, Great Britain, Russia, and the United States. The report was written largely by Prof. Paul Milioukov, the representative from Russia.

Martens, *Recueil général de traités* (Göttingen, 1817–97; Leipzig, 1897–).

Niemeyer, Th. and Strupp, K. (editors), "Die beiden Balkankriege; Politische Urkunden," *Jahrbuch des Völkerrechts*, II, i (Leipzig, 1914). Texts of treaties, notes, etc., pertaining to the Balkan Wars which appeared in the newspapers are here reprinted. Memoranda by the monks on Mt. Athos and practically all the documents of the *Rumanian Green Book* are given.

Saucerman, Sophia, *International Transfers of Territory in Europe with Names of the Affected Political Subdivisions as of 1910–1914 and the Present* (Government Printing Office; Washington, 1937).

Schwertfeger, Bernard, *Die Diplomatischen Akten des Auswärtigen Amtes 1871–1914. Ein Wegweiser durch das grosse Aktenwerk der Deutschen Regierung*, 8 vol. (Berlin, 1928).

III. Memoirs and Biographies

Auffenberg-Komarow, *Aus Österreichs Höhe und Niedergang — Eine Lebensschilderung* (Munich, 1927). Austro-Hungarian minister of war 1911–12.

Baernreither, Joseph Maria, *Fragmente eines politischen Tagebuches*, ed. Joseph Redlich (Berlin, 1928).

Balkanicus (Stojan Protić), *The Aspirations of Bulgaria* (London, 1915; French edition, Paris, 1915). Protić, Serbian finance minister 1912–13, minister of the interior 1913–14, was a close friend of Pašić and his account may be regarded as an official statement of the views of the Serbian government.

Beyens, Baron, *Deux années à Berlin 1912–1914*, 2 vol. (Paris, 1931).

Boghitschewitsch, Dr. M., *Kriegsursachen* (Zurich, 1919; English edition, Amsterdam, 1919; French edition, Paris, 1925). The French edition has some corrections and some additional material.

Bosdari, Alessandro, *Delle guerre balcaniche, della grande guerra e di alcuni fatti precedenti ad esse* (Milan, 1928).

Buchanan, Sir George, *My Mission to Russia and Other Diplomatic Memories*, 2 vol. (Boston, 1923).

Chlumecky, Leopold von, *Erzherzog Franz Ferdinands Wirken und Wollen* (Berlin, 1929).

Christoff, R. P. P., *Journal du siège d'Andrinople. Notes quotidiennes d'un siège* (Paris, 1914).

Conrad, Feldmarschall, *Aus meiner Dienstzeit 1906–1918*, 5 vol. (Vienna, 1921–25).

Constantine I, *A King's Private Letters. Letters of Constantine to Paola — Princess of Saxe-Weimar, 1912–1923*, Preface by Admiral Mark Kerr (London, 1925).

Danev, Stojan, *Balkanský svaz a válka s Tureckem, 1912–1913* (Prague, 1935).

Un Diplomate, *Paul Cambon. Ambassadeur de France* (Paris, 1937).

Driault, Edouard, *Le roi Constantin* (Versailles, 1930).

Durham, M. E., *The Struggle for Scutari* (London, 1914). Miss Durham was a newspaper correspondent who did relief work with the Montenegrin armies and was one of the first to enter Scutari. She is an eminent authority on all things Albanian.

Egli, Karl, *Drei Monate vor Skutari* (Bern, 1913). Egli was a lieutenant in the Swiss army attached to a Swiss Red Cross unit serving with the Montenegrin forces.

Eisenmenger, Victor, *Archduke Francis Ferdinand* (London, 1931).

Fabius, J., *Das Brutnest. Momentbilder aus dem Balkan vor dem Weltkriege* (Berlin, 1920). An account by a Dutch officer who acted as war correspondent, and who later went to Albania to help organise the gendarmerie.

Gibbons, Herbert Adams, *Venizelos* (London, 1921).

Giesl, Baron Wladimir, *Zwei Jahrzehnte im Nahen Orient*, herausgegeben von Generalmajor Ritter v. Steinitz (Berlin, 1927). Personal reminiscences of one of Austria's foremost Balkan diplomats.

Giolitti, Giovanni, *Memoirs of My Life*, translated from the Italian by Edward Storer (London, 1923).

Goltz, Generalfeldmarschall Colmar Freiherr von der, *Denkwürdigkeiten*, bearbeitet und herausgegeben von Friedrich Freiherr von der Goltz und Wolfgang Foerster (Berlin, 1929).

Grey, Viscount of Fallodon, K. G., *Twenty-Five Years 1892–1916*, 2 vol. (New York, 1925).

Grogan, (Ellinore) Lady, *The Life of J. D. Bourchier* (London, 1926). Bourchier was for many years the Near East correspondent of the London *Times*. The biography is based on diaries and other private papers.

Guéchoff, I. E., *La genèse de la guerre mondiale. La débâcle de l'alliance balkanique* (Berne, 1919).

Gueshoff, I. E., *The Balkan League*, translated by Constantin C. Mincoff (London, 1915; French edition, Paris, 1915). The most important source we have on the origins of the Balkan League. Gueshov was Bulgarian prime minister and minister of foreign affairs 1911–13.

Gueshov, I. E., *Prestŭpnoto bezumie i anketata po nego. Fakti i dokumenti* [The criminal folly and the investigation concerning it. Facts and documents] (Sofia, 1914). A defense of his policy against the attacks of his political opponents.

Gueshov, I. E., Danev, Dr. St., Teodorov, T., Majarov, M. I., Peev, I., and Abrashev, P., *Nashata duma* [Our case] (Sofia, 1925). A defense by a group of statesmen who were in office in 1912–13 against the accusations of treason levelled by the opposition parties in 1923.

Hoyos, Graf A., *Der deutsch-englische Gegensatz und sein Einfluss auf die Balkanpolitik Österreich-Ungarns* (Berlin, 1922). An essay by the *Chef de Cabinet* to Count Berchtold, emphasising the defensive character of Austrian policy.

Izzet Pascha, *Denkwürdigkeiten des Marschalls Izzet Pascha*, Aus dem Original-Manuskript übersetzt, eingeleitet und erstmalig herausgegeben von Karl Klinghardt (Leipzig, 1927). Chief of staff, minister of war, commander in chief, grand vizier, minister of foreign affairs, and minister of the interior, were some of the offices held by Izzet Pascha.

Jäckh, Ernst, *Kiderlen-Wächter. Der Staatsman und Mensch. Briefwechsel und Nachlass*, 2 vol. (Berlin, 1924).

Jonescu, Take, *Souvenirs* (Paris, 1919).

Jotzoff, Dimitri, *Zar Ferdinand von Bulgarien. Sein Lebenswerk im Orient* (Berlin, 1927).

Judet, Ernest, *Georges Louis* (Paris, 1925). M. Louis was French ambassador to St. Petersburg 1909–13.

Les Carnets de Georges Louis, 2 vol. (Paris, 1926).

Kalinkov, Dr. G., *Romŭniya i neĭnata politika spremo Bŭlgariya* [Rumania and her Bulgarian policy] (Sofia, 1917). Memoirs of the Bulgarian minister to Rumania during the Balkan Wars.

Kokovtsov, Count, *Out of My Past*, ed. H. H. Fisher (Stamford, 1935).

Kutschbach, A., *Der Brandherd Europas. 50 Jahre Balkan-Erinnerungen* (Leipzig, 1929). Memoirs of a German adventurer and newspaper correspondent in the Balkans 1875–1925.

Lee, Sir Sidney, *Edward VII. A Biography*, 2 vol. (London, 1925, 1927).

Lichnowsky, Karl Max, *Meine Londoner Mission 1912–1914* (Berlin, n.d.). Eng. ed. *The Guilt of Germany for the War of German Aggression* (New York, 1918).

—— *Auf dem Wege zum Abgrund. Londoner Berichte, Erinnerungen und sonstige Schriften*, 2 vol. (Dresden, 1927). English edition, *Heading for the Abyss; Reminiscences* (New York, 1928).

Lindenberg, Paul, *König Karl von Rumänien. Ein Lebensbild dargestellt unter Mitarbeit des Königs*, 2 vol. (Berlin, 1923).

Mach, Richard von, *Aus bewegter Balkanzeit 1879–1918; Erinnerungen* (Berlin, 1928). Most valuable part deals with the years 1885–1893.

Madol, Hans Roger, *Ferdinand von Bulgarien, der Traum von Byzanz* (Berlin, 1931).

Masaryk, Dr. Thomas Garrigue, *The Making of a State. Memories and Observations 1914–1918*, English version, arranged and prepared with an introduction by H. W. Steed (New York, 1927).

Melas, George, *L'Ex-roi Constantin* (*Souvenirs d'un ancien secrétaire*) (Paris, 1921).

Moltke, Helmuth von, *Erinnerungen, Briefe, Dokumente 1877–1916*, ed. by Eliza von Moltke (Stuttgart, 1922).

Mott, T. B. (trans.), *The Personal Memoirs of Joffre*, 2 vol. (New York, 1932).

Mouktar Pacha, M., *Mon commandant au cours de la campagne de Balkans* (Paris, 1913).

—— *La Turquie, l'Allemagne et l'Europe depuis le traité de Berlin jusqu'à la guerre mondiale* (Paris, 1924).

Muret, Maurice, *L'Archiduc François-Ferdinand* (Paris, 1932).

Musulin, Freiherr von, *Das Haus am Ballplatz. Erinnerungen eines österreichisch-ungarischen Diplomaten* (Munich, 1924).

Nekludoff, A., *Diplomatic Reminiscences Before and During the World War 1911–1917*, translated from the French by Alexandra Paget (London, 1920). Memoirs of the Russian minister to Bulgaria during the Balkan Wars.

Nicholas, Prince of Greece, *My Fifty Years* (London, 1927). Gives some interesting sidelights on inter-allied relations during the Balkan Wars.

Nicolson, Harold, *Portrait of a Diplomatist* (New York, 1930). A biography of Sir Arthur Nicolson, British ambassador at St. Petersburg, 1906–10, and permanent under-secretary of foreign affairs at the British foreign office 1910–16.

Peshev, P., *Istoricheskite sŭbitiya i deyateli ot navecherieto na osvobozhdenieto ni do dnes, s belezhki za ahivota mi* [Historical events and personalities from the eve of our liberation until today, with notes on my life] (Sofia, 1929). Memoirs of a prominent Bulgarian statesman, minister of justice and education in the Radoslavov cabinet 1913–18.

Poincaré, Raymond, *Au service de la France. Neuf années de souvenirs*, 10 vol. (Paris, 1926–33). Volume II, *Les Balkans en feu 1912*; volume III, *L'Europe sous les armes 1913.*

Pomiankowski, Joseph, *Der Zusammenbruch des Ottomanischen Reiches. Erinnerungen an die Türkei aus der Zeit des Weltkrieges* (Vienna, 1928). Pomiankowski was military attaché at Constantinople from 1909 on.

Porter, Charles W., *The Career of Theophile Delcassé* (Philadelphia, 1936).

Radoslawoff, Dr. Vasil, *Bulgarien und die Weltkrise* (Berlin, 1923). Bulgarian premier, July, 1913–18.

Rappaport, Alfred, *Au Pays des Martyrs* (Paris, 1927). Reminiscences of a former consul-general of Austria-Hungary in Macedonia, 1904–09. Contains an interesting chapter on Mt. Athos.

Redlich, Joseph, *Emperor Francis Joseph of Austria* (London, 1929).

Rodzianko, M. V., *The Reign of Rasputin* (London, 1912). Rodzianko was president of the duma.

San Giuliano, A., *Briefe über Albanien* (*Deutsch von D. Schulz und W. Wichmann*) (Leipzig, 1913). Letters written on a visit in 1902 and interesting for the description of the country.

Sazonov, Serge, *Fateful Years 1909–1916. Reminiscences* (New York, 1928).

Schebeko, N., *Souvenirs. Essai historique sur les origines de la guerre de 1914*, preface by Jules Cambon (Paris, 1936).

Schelking, Eugene de, *Recollections of a Russian Diplomat* (New York, 1918).

Schmiterlow, Bernhard von, Oberstleutnant a. D., *Aus dem Leben des Generalfeldmarschalls Freiherr von der Goltz-Pascha. Nach Briefen an seinen Freund* (Berlin, 1926).

Sforza, Comte, *Pachitch et l'union des yougoslaves* (Paris, 1938).

Sosnosky, Theodor von, *Franz Ferdinand, Der Erzherzog-Thronfolger* (Berlin, 1929).

Stancioff, Anna, *Recollections of a Bulgarian Diplomatist's Wife* (London, 1930).

Steed, H. W., *Through Thirty Years 1892–1922*, 2 vol. (London, 1924).
Steinitz, E. R. von, *Rings um Sasonow. Neue dokumentarische Darlegungen zum Ausbruch des grossen Krieges durch Kronzeugen* (Berlin, 1928). A series of essays by former diplomats (mostly Austrian), in answer to statements made by Sazonov in his memoirs.
Story, Sommerville (ed.), *The Memoirs of Ismail Kemal Bey* (London, 1920).
Suchomlinow, W. A., *Erinnerungen* (Berlin, 1924). Suchomlinov was Russian minister of war, 1909–15.
Szilassy, Baron J. von, *Der Untergang der Donau-Monarchie. Diplomatische Erinnerungen* (Berlin, 1921).
Taube, Freiherr von, *Der grossen Katastrophen entgegen. Erinnerungen* (Berlin, 1929).
Tommasini, Francesco, *L'Italia alla vigilia della guerra. La politica estera di Tommaso Tittoni*, 3 vol. (Bologna, 1934–8). The three volumes thus far published cover the period down to the annexation crisis of 1908.
Toshev, A., *Balkanskite voĭni* [The Balkan Wars], 2 vol. (Sofia, 1929–31). Toshev was Bulgarian minister at Belgrade 1908–13.
Trevelyan, George Macaulay, *Grey of Fallodon* (Boston, 1937).
Tschuppik, Karl, *Franz Joseph I., Der Untergang eines Reiches* (Hallerau bei Dresden, 1928).
Wilhelm, Fürst von Albanien, Prinz zu Wied, *Denkschrift über Albanien, Als Manuskript gedruckt! Nicht für die Öffentlichkeit!* (Berlin, 1917). Much stress is laid on the difficulties which faced him when he reached Albania in the spring of 1914, and the lack of support by the powers.
William II, *The Kaiser's Memoirs*, English translation by Thomas R. Ybarra (New York, 1922).
Zambaur, Hortense von, *Die Belagerung von Skutari (10 Oktober 1912 bis 22 April 1913). Ein Tagebuch* (Berlin, 1914). The diary of the wife of the Austrian consul at Scutari.

IV. Monographs and General Historical Works

Ancel, Jacques, *Peuples et nations des Balkans* (Paris, 1926).
Balcanicus (Stojan Protić) *Les Serbes et les Bulgares dans la guerre balkanique. Avec une carte des territoires occupés* (Paris, 1913).
—— *Le problème albanais. La Serbie et l'Autriche-Hongrie* (Paris, 1913).
Der Balkankrieg 1912/13 und die Oesterreichisch-Ungarische Politik (Vienna, 1913). A sharp criticism of Austro-Hungarian Balkan policy.
Bell, H. T. Montague (ed.), *The Near East Year Book 1931–32* (London, 1931).
Bernard, Roland, *Essai sur l'histoire de l'Albanie moderne* (Paris, 1935).
Bickel, Otto, *Russland und die Entstehung des Balkanbundes 1912. Ein Beitrag zur Vorgeschichte des Weltkrieges* (Berlin, 1933).
Blaisdell, Donald C., *European Financial Control in the Ottoman Empire* (New York, 1929).

Boghitchévitch, Dr. M., *Le procès de Salonique juin 1917* (Paris, 1927).
—— *Le colonel Dragoutine Dimitriévitch Apis* (Paris, 1928).
Boucabeille, Lt. colonel breveté, *La guerre turco-balkanique* (Paris, 1914).
—— *La guerre interbalkanique: événements militaires et politiques survenus dans la Péninsule des Balkans jusqu'en octobre, 1913* (Paris, 1913).
Brandenburg, Erich, *Von Bismarck zum Weltkriege* (Berlin, 1925). A standard German account of prewar diplomacy.
Butterfield, Paul R., *The Diplomacy of the Bagdad Railway 1890–1914* (Göttingen, 1932).
Cassavetti, D. J., *Hellas and the Balkan Wars* (London, 1914).
Chekrezi, Constantine, *Albania, Past and Present* (New York, 1919).
Chlumecky, Leopold Freiherr von, *Die Agonie des Dreibundes. Das letzte Jahrzehnt Italienischer Untreue* (Vienna, 1915). A reprint of newspaper articles published 1906–14.
Christowe, Stoyan, *Heroes and Assassins* (New York, 1935).
Colocotronis, V., *La Macédoine et l'hellénisme. Étude historique et ethnologique* (Paris, 1919).
Cvijić, Jovan, *La péninsule balkanique* (Paris, 1918). A geographical treatment of the Balkans.
—— *Questions balkaniques* (Paris, 1916).
Danev, Dr. S., *Ocherk na diplomaticheskata istoriya na balkanskite dŭrzhavi* [Outline of the diplomatic history of the Balkan states] (Sofia, 1931).
David, Wade Dewood, *Turkey and the Powers, 1907–1909. An Abstract of a thesis submitted at the University of Illinois, 1932.* (Urbana, 1932).
Dengler, Amalie, *Der englische Botschafter Sir George Buchanan und seine Stellung zu Deutschland* (Berlin, 1937).
Dickinson, G. L., *The International Anarchy 1904–1914* (New York, 1936).
Diplomatist, *Nationalism and War in the Near East* (Carnegie Endowment for International Peace), (Oxford, 1915).
Dreyer, Colonel, *La débâcle Bulgare. Deuxième guerre balkanique de 1913* (Paris, 1921). An account by a Russian officer.
Driault, Ed., *La grande idée — La renaissance de l'héllenisme* (Paris, 1920).
Driault, Ed. et Lhéritier, M., *Histoire diplomatique de la Grèce de 1821 à nos jours*, 5 vol. (Paris, 1926).
Drossos, Dem. J. D., *La fondation de l'alliance balkanique* (Athens, 1929).
Durham, M. Edith, *Through the Lands of the Serb* (London, 1904).
—— *The Burden of the Balkans* (London, 1905).
—— *High Albania* (London, 1909).
—— *The Struggle for Scutari* (London, 1914).
—— *Twenty Years of Balkan Tangle* (London, 1920).
—— *The Serajevo Crime* (London, 1925).
—— *Some Tribal Origins, Laws, and Customs of the Balkans* (London, 1928).
Dumas, S., and Vedel-Petersen, K. O., *Losses of Life Caused by War* (Oxford, 1923). A study undertaken under the direction of the Committee of Research of the Carnegie Endowment for International Peace.

Dŭrvingov, Colonel Peter, *Istoriya na Makedono-Odrinskoto opŭlchenie* [History of the Macedonian-Adrianople Legion], 2 vol., I, *Zhivotŭt i deĭstviata na opŭlchenieto v voĭnata s Turtsia,* [Life and activities of the legion during the war with Turkey], II, *Zhivotŭt i deĭstviata na opŭlchenieto v voĭnata s sŭyuznnitsite prez 1913 g.,* [Life and activities of the legion during the war with the allies in 1913] (Sofia, 1919–25). Colonel Dŭrvingov, a Macedonian resident in Bulgaria and an officer in the Bulgarian army, was placed in command of the Macedonian legion.

Earle, Edward Mead, *Turkey, The Great Powers and the Bagdad Railway* (New York, 1923).

Emin, Ahmed, *The Development of Modern Turkey as Measured by its Press* (New York, 1914).

Evelpedi, C., *Les états balkaniques. Étude comparée; politique, sociale, économique, et financière* (Paris, 1930). An excellent social study of present conditions, with a good bibliography.

Fay, Sidney B., *The Origins of the World War,* 2 vol. (New York, 1928).

Feis, Herbert, *Europe, The World's Banker 1870–1914. An Account of the European Investment and the Connection of World Finance With Diplomacy Before The War* (New Haven, 1930).

Frangulis, A. F., *La Grèce et la crise mondiale,* 2 vol. (Paris, 1926). A bitter indictment of Venizelos. The return of King Constantine in 1921 gave Frangulis and other "royalist historians" access to the Greek archives and enabled them to supplement the White Books published by Venizelos.

Frantz, Gunther, *Russlands Eintritt in den Weltkrieg* (Berlin, 1924). A study by a former member of the German general staff based largely on unpublished documents. The book deals primarily with Russian preparedness for war in 1914.

Frantz, Gunther, *Russland auf dem Wege zur Katastrophe* (Berlin, 1926).

Frascheri, Sami Bey, *Was war Albanien, was ist es, was wird es werden?* (Vienna, 1913). Translated from the Turkish translation of the original Albanian printed in 1899. Note especially Albanian attempts at a written alphabet.

Freundlich, Leo (ed.), *Albaniens Golgotha; Anklageakten gegen die Vernichter des Albanervolkes* (Vienna, 1913). A pamphlet containing tales of Serbian atrocities published at the time the Scutari crisis was at its height.

Friedjung, H., *Das Zeitalter des Imperialismus,* 3 vol. (Berlin, 1922). Volumes two and three were written by Professor Pribram after the death of Professor Friedjung.

Fuad, Ali, *La question des Détroits. Ses origines, son évolution, sa solution à la conférence de Lausanne* (Paris, 1928).

Gauvain, A., *L'Europe au jour le jour,* 14 vol. (Paris, 1917–1923). Articles reprinted from the *Journal des Débats,* 1908– .

Georgevitch, Dr. Vladan, *Die Albanesen und die Grossmächte* (Leipzig, 1913).

Giesche, Richard, *Der serbische Zugang zum Meer und die europäische Krise 1912* (Stuttgart, 1932).

Girginov, Dr. Al., *Narodnata katastrofa. Voĭnite 1912/13 g.*, [The national catastrophe. The wars of 1912–13] (Sofia, 1926). A brief history of the Balkan wars based almost exclusively upon the report of the Bulgarian Parliamentary Commission of Inquiry.

Goltz, Baron von der, *La défaite de la jeune Turquie et la possibilité de son relèvement*, traduit par Gaston Dietrich, (Paris, 1913).

Gooch, George P., *History of Modern Europe, 1878–1918* (New York, 1923).

—— *Before the War. Studies in Diplomacy*, 2 vol. (London, 1936, 1938).

Gooss, Roderich, "Das österreichisch-serbische Problem bis zur Kriegserklärung Osterreich-Ungarns an Serbien, 28 Juli 1914" (Berlin, 1930). Gutachten vor dem Untersuchungsausschuss des Deutschen Reichstages 1919–1930, *Die Vorgeschichte des Weltkrieges*, Reihe I, X. In the same volume Herman Wendel's article, "Die Habsburger und die Südslawenfrage."

Gopčević, Spiridion, *Geschichte von Montenegro und Albanien* (Gotha, 1914).

Grottie, Hugo, *Durch Albanien und Montenegro* (Munich, 1913). A travel account of a journey made in 1912.

Guide de Mont Athos, (Editions F. Perilla, Salonica, 1928). Contains a short historical introduction and a description of each of the monasteries.

Hanotaux, Gabriel, *La guerre des Balkans et l'Europe 1912–1913. Études diplomatiques, deuxième série* (Paris, 1914). A series of articles originally published in *La revue hebdomadaire* and *Le Figaro* during 1912–13.

Hasluck, F. W., *Athos and its monasteries* (London, 1924).

Helmreich, E. C., "The Conflict between Germany and Austria over Balkan Policy, 1913–1914," *Essays in the History of Modern Europe*, ed. by Donald C. McKay (New York, 1936).

Herre, Paul, *Die kleinen Staaten Europas und die Entstehung des Weltkrieges* (Munich, 1937).

Hertslet, Sir Edward, *The Map of Europe by Treaty*, 4 vol. (London, 1875–91).

Hiller, Gerhard, *Die Entwicklung des österreichisch-serbischen Gegensatzes 1908–1914* (Halle, 1934).

Holdegel, Kurt, *Frankreichs Politik im Nahen Orient und im Mittelmeer in der Zeit vom Ausbruch des italienisch-türkischen Krieges bis zum Zusammentritt der Londoner Botschafterkonferenz Oktober 1911–Dezember 1912* (Dresden, 1934).

Hosse, Carl, *Die englisch-belgischen Aufmarschpläne gegen Deutschland vor dem Weltkriege* (Vienna, 1930).

Howard, Harry N., *The Partition of Turkey. A Diplomatic History 1913–1923* (Norman, Oklahoma, 1931).

Iancovici, D., *Essai sur la crise balkanique 1912–1913* (Paris, 1916).

Ischirkov, A., *Les confins occidentaux des terres bulgares. (Notes et documents. Onze cartes.)* (Lausanne, 1916.)

Izzet-Fuad Pasha, General, *Paroles de vaincu; après désastre — avant la revanche* (Paris, 1913).

John, Willi, *Das Dardanellenproblem und die Grossen Mächte im Jahre 1911* (Breslau, 1934).

Jorga, M., *Histoire des états balkaniques jusqu'à 1925* (Paris, 1925).

Kanitz, Felix, *Das Königreich Serbien und das Serbenvolk, von der Römerzeit bis zur Gegenwart*, 3 vol., (Leipzig, 1914).

Kanner, Heinrich, *Kaiserliche Katastrophen-politik. Ein Stück zeitgenossischer Geschichte* (Leipzig, 1922).

Khristov, Polkovnik A., *Kratka istoriya na osvoboditelnata voĭna 1912–1913 godina* [A brief history of the war of liberation of 1912–1913] (Sofia, 1921). Primarily a military history.

Kiendl, Hans, *Russische Balkanpolitik von der Ernennung Sassonows bis zum Ende des zweiten Balkankrieges. Teildruck der Inauguraldissertation "Russische Balkanpolitik 1905–1913"* (Munich, 1925).

Klemti, Dr. D., *Darf Oesterreich auf den Sandschak von Novi-Bazar verzichten?* (Vienna, 1913). The author answers in the negative.

Korff, Baron S. A., *Russia's Foreign Relations during the last Half Century* (New York, 1922).

Krebs, Gunther, *Die Deutsche Bagdadbahnpolitik im Urteil der Entente-Publizistik* (Breslau, 1933).

Lamouche, Colonel, *Quinze ans d'histoire balkanique* (Paris, 1928).

Lončarević, Dušan, *Jugoslaviens Entstehung* (Vienna, 1929). A history of Serbia, 1903–1914, by the former head of the Austrian press bureau in Belgrade. Many excerpts from Serbian newspapers and parliamentary debates are given.

Louis, Herbert, *Albanien. Beiträge zur Landeskunde des Albanischen Epirus* (Stuttgart, 1927). A good geographical description, although in places rather technical.

Londres, Albert, *Terror in the Balkans* (London, 1935). A popular account of the Macedonian Revolutionary Organisation dealing mostly with the post-war period.

Luke, Harry, *The Making of Modern Turkey* (London, 1936).

Lutz, Hermann, *Lord Grey and the World War* (London, 1928).

Maccas, Léon, *La question Grèco-Albanaise* (Paris, 1921).

Mandelstam, André, *Le sort de l'empire ottoman* (Paris, 1917). A history of Turkey 1908–1917 by a professor of international law at the University of Petrograd. Mandelstam was at one time first dragoman to the Russian embassy at Constantinople.

Markovich, J. T. (ed.), *La Macédoine et les macédoniens* (Corfu, 1918).

Mary-Rousselière, André, *La Turquie constitutionnelle. Contribution à l'étude de la politique intérieure turque* (Rennes, 1925).

Mears, E. T., *Modern Turkey* (New York, 1924).

Meyer, Phillipp, *Die Haupturkunden für die Geschichte der Athosklöster. Grösstentheils zum ersten Male herausgegeben und mit Einleitungen versehen* (Leipzig, 1894). The standard work on the monasteries of Mount Athos.

Meyer, Alfred, *Der Balkankrieg 1912–13* (Berlin, 1913).

Michaelis, Herbert, *Die deutsche Politik während der Balkankriege 1912–13* (Waldenburg, 1929).

Michon, Georges, *L'alliance franco-russe 1891–1917* (Paris, 1927).

Miller, William, *The Ottoman Empire and its Successors, 1801–1927* (Cambridge, 1927). Being a revised and enlarged edition of *The Ottoman Empire 1801–1913*.

—— *Greece* (New York, 1928).

Mishew, D., *The Bulgarians in the Past* (Lausanne, 1919).

Mondesir, Piaron de, *Siège et prise d'Andrinople. (novembre 1912–mars 1913)* (Paris, 1914).

Montgelas, Count Max, *The Case for the Central Powers* (London, 1925).

Moschopoulos, Nicéphore, *La question de Thrace ou le mensonge bulgare* (Athens, 1922).

Mousset, Albert, *L'Albanie devant l'Europe 1912–1929* (Paris, 1930).

Mühlmann, Carl, *Deutschland und die Türkei 1913–14* (Berlin, 1929).

Mülinen, Dr. Graf von, *Die lateinische Kirche im Türkischen Reiche* (Berlin, 1901).

Nastić, *Wo ist die Wahrheit* (Serajevo, 1908).

—— *Finale* (Serajevo, 1908).

Newbigin, M. I., *Geographical Aspects of Balkan Problems in their Relation to the Great European War* (London, 1915).

Nicolaides, Cleanthes, *Griechenlands Anteil an den Balkankriegen. 1912–1913.* (Vienna, 1914).

Nikolitch, Dragutine, *Les différends de frontière de l'Albanie* (Paris, 1927).

Nintchitch, Momtchilo, *La crise bosniaque (1908–1909) et les puissances européennes*, 2 vol., (Paris, 1937). Written by a former minister of foreign affairs of Jugoslavia who has drawn on material from the Serbian archives.

Oesterreichisches Albanien Komitee, *Was will das Oesterreichische Albanien Komitee?* (Wien, 1914). This is a group of lectures given at the meeting of a committee created to spread propaganda in favor of Albania.

Oncken, Hermann, *Das Deutsche Reich und die Vorgeschichte des Weltkrieges*, 2 vol., (Leipzig, 1933).

Palat, General, *Guerres des Balkans 1912–13* (Paris, 1915).

Panaiotoff, I., *Vorgeschichte und Entstehung des Balkanbundes von 1912*, (Maschinenschreiben), (Göttingen, 1923).

Passadis, Augustin, *La question de l'Orient et la Grèce* (Paris, 1929).

Penennrun, Alain de, *40 jours de guerre dans les Balkans. La campagne serbo-bulgare en juillet 1913* (Paris, 1914).

Pinon, René, *L'Europe et la Jeune Turquie* (Paris, 1911).

Polyvious, Pericles J., *L'Albanie et la réunion d'ambassadeurs à Londres* (Paris, 1914).

Pribram, A. F., *Austrian Foreign Policy* (London, 1923).

Prost, Henri, *La Bulgarie de 1912 à 1930* (Paris, 1932).

Radeff, S., *La Macédoine et la renaissance bulgare au XIXe siècle* (Sofia, 1918).

Rankin, Lt. Colonel Reginald, *The Inner History of the Balkan War* (New York, n.d.). One of the best accounts of the First Balkan War written by the special correspondent of the London *Times.* For some of his chapters he relies entirely on current newspaper accounts and these are not always accurate. Bourchier furnished him with much material.

Redlich, Baron Marcellus D. A. R. von, *Albania, Yesterday and Today* (Worcester, Mass., 1936).

Rizoff, D., *The Bulgarians in their Historical, Ethnographical, and Political Frontiers* (Berlin, 1917). A very convenient collection of maps made by European scholars at different periods.

Sasse, H. G., *War das deutsche Eingreifen in die Bosnische Krise im März 1909 ein Ultimatum?* (Stuttgart, 1936).

Savadjian, L., *Bibliographie balkanique* (Paris, 1931–).

Schmitt, Bernadotte E., *The Coming of the War. 1914*, 2 vols. (New York, 1930).

—— *The Annexation of Bosnia 1908–1909* (Cambridge, 1937).

Schopoff, A., *Les États balcaniques et le principe confédératif* (Sofia, 1913).

—— *La confédération balcanique et la question macédonienne* (Sofia, 1915).

Schulthess' Europäischer Geschichtskalender (Munich, Annual).

Seiner, Franz, *Ergebnisse der Volkzählung in Albanien in den von den österreich-ungarischen Truppen, 1916–1918, besetzten Gebiete* (Vienna, 1922).

Seton-Watson, R. W., *The Southern Slav Question and the Habsburg Monarchy* (London, 1911).

—— *The Balkans, Italy, and the Adriatic* (London, 1916).

—— *German, Slav, and Magyar; A Study in the Origins of the Great War* (London, 1916).

—— *The Rise of Nationality in the Balkans* (London, 1917).

—— *Serajevo; A Study in the Origins of the Great War* (London, 1925).

—— *A History of the Roumanians from Roman Times to the Completion of Unity* (Cambridge, 1934).

Sieghart, Rudolf, *Die letzten Jahrzehnte einer Grossmacht. Menschen, Völker, Probleme des Habsburgerreichs* (Berlin, 1932).

Slivensky, Ivan, *La Bulgarie depuis le traité de Berlin et la paix dans les Balkans* (Paris, 1927).

Sosnosky, Theodor von, *Die Balkanpolitik Österreich-Ungarns seit 1866*, 2 vol. (Berlin, 1913, 1914).

Sousa, Nasim, *The Capitulatory Régime of Turkey. Its History, Origin, and Nature* (Baltimore, 1933).

Spender, Harold, *The Cauldron of Europe* (London, 1925).

Stambler, Bernard, *Les Roumains et les Bulgares; le traité de Bucarest (28 juillet/10 août, 1913)*, (Paris, 1914).

Stanojević, Stanoje, *Die Ermordung des Erzherzogs Franz Ferdinand. Ein*

Beitrag zur Entstehungsgeschichte des Weltkrieges, translated by Hermann Wendel (Frankfurt a. Main, 1923).
Stavron, M. S., *Études sur l'Albanie* (Paris, 1922).
Stephanopoli, Jeanne Z., *Les Îles de l'Égée, leurs privilèges. Avec documents et notes statistiques* (Athens, 1912).
Stevenson, F. S., *A History of Montenegro* (London, 1913).
Stickney, Edith P., *Southern Albania in European Affairs 1912–1923* (Stanford, 1926).
Stieve, Friedrich, *Deutschland und Europa 1890–1914. Ein Handbuch zur Vorgeschichte des Weltkrieges mit den wichtigsten Dokumenten und drei Karten* (Berlin, 1926). English edition, *Germany and Europe* (London, 1928).
—— *Die Tragödie der Bundesgenossen. Deutschland und Österreich-Ungarn 1908–1914* (Munich, 1930).
Stojanoff, Dr. A., *Die handelspolitische Situation der Balkanstaaten gegenüber Österreich-Ungarn. Dargestellt auf der Grundlage des bulgarisch-serbischen Zollunionvertrages vom 9 Juli 1905* (Vienna, 1914).
Strupp, Karl, *La situation juridique des Macédoniens en Jugoslavie* (Paris, 1929).
Swire, J., *Albania, The Rise of a Kingdom* (London, 1929).
—— *King Zog's Albania* (London, 1937).
Sydacoff, Bresnitz von, *Aus dem Geheimnissen des Balkankrieges* (Leipzig, 1913).
Szánto, Alexander, *Apis, der Führer der "Schwarzen Hand"* (Berlin, n.d.).
Tcharykow, N. V., *Glimpses of High Politics. Through War and Peace 1855–1929* (London, 1931).
Tukin, Cemal, *Die politischen Beziehungen zwischen Österreich-Ungarn und Bulgarien von 1908 bis zum Bukarester Frieden* (Hamburg, 1936).
Tyler, Mason Withing, *The European Powers and the Near East* (Minneapolis, 1925).
Union of Macedonian Political Organisations of the United States and Canada, *Pro Macedonia. Balkan Locarno and the Macedonian Question* (Indianapolis, 1928).
Van der Veen, J. Brandt, *De Voorgeschiedenis van de Balkanoorlog* (Utrecht, 1935).
Viallate, A., *La vie politique dans les deux mondes, 1906–1907* (Paris, 1907).
Voniovitch, Ilia, *La question de Scutari* (Paris, 1924).
Wedel, Oswald H., *Austro-German Diplomatic Relations 1908–1914* (Stanford University, 1932).
Wegerer, Alfred von, *Bibliographie zur Vorgeschichte des Weltkrieges* (Berlin, 1934).
Weigand, Prof. Dr. Gustav, *Ethnographie von Makedonien. Geschichtlich, nationaler, sprachlich, statistischer Teil* (Leipzig, 1924).
Wendel, Hermann, *Südslawien (Jugoslawien); Land und Leute, Geschichte, und Kultur, Produktion und Handel in Einzeldarstellungen* (Frankfurt am Main, 1922).

Wendel, Hermann, *Kreuz und quer durch den Südslawischen Süden* (Frankfurt am Main, 1922).

—— *Die Habsburger und die Südslawenfrage* (Leipzig, 1924).

—— *Der Kampf der Südslawen um Freiheit und Einheit* (Vienna, 1925).

Wolf, John B., *The Diplomatic History of the Bagdad Railroad* (Columbia, Missouri, 1936).

Woods, H. C., *War and Diplomacy in the Balkans* (London, 1915).

Zaionchkovskii, A., *Podgotovka rossii k mirovoi voine v mezhdunarodnom otnoshenii* [Russia's Preparation for the World War: International Relations] (Moscow, 1926).

V. Newspapers and Periodicals

Ancel, Jacques, "Races, langues, empires et églises dans les Balkans," *Le Monde Slave* (March, 1926), II, N.S., 382–405.

Ashton, George, "The Entente Cordiale and the Military Conversations," *The Quarterly Review* (April, 1932), CCLVIII, 363–83.

Auffenberg-Komarow, Baron M., "Indirekte Kriegsschuld," *Die Kriegsschuldfrage* (June, 1928), VI, 547–52.

—— "Zur Vorgeschichte des Weltkrieges. Das Krisenjahr 1912," *Die Kriegsschuldfrage* (August, 1927), V, 769–72.

Bach, August, "Die November und Dezemberkrise 1912. Ein Vorspiel zum Weltkrieg," *Berliner Monatshefte* (February, 1935), XIII, 101–22.

Baernreither, Dr. Joseph, "Aehrenthal und Milovanovitch, Ein Tagebuchblatt," *Deutsche Revue* (January, 1922), XLVII, 84–9.

—— "Unsere Handelsbeziehungen zu Serbien," *Österreichische Rundschau* (October–November, 1911), XXIX, 1–16; 105–21.

Bittner, Ludwig, "Die schwarze Hand," *Berliner Monatshefte* (January, 1932), X, 55–64.

—— "Graf Friedrich Szápáry," *Berliner Monatshefte* (December, 1936), XIV, 958–62.

—— "Österreich-Ungarn und Serbien," *Historische Zeitschrift* (October, 1931), CXLIV, 78–104.

Boghitschewitsch, Dr. M., "Mord und Justizmord. Aus der Vorgeschichte des Mordes von Sarajewo und des Königreichs Jugoslawien," *Süddeutsche Monatshefte* (February, 1929), XXV, 331–70.

—— "Die serbische Gesellschaft 'Vereinigung oder Tod,' genannt die 'Schwarze Hand' " (German and English), *Die Kriegsschuldfrage* (September, 1926), IV, 664–89.

Bourchier, J. D., "Articles on the Origin of the Balkan League," London *Times* (June 4, 5, 6, 11, 13, 1913).

Brauner, Josef, "Bosnien und Herzegowina. Politik, Verwaltung und leitende Personen," *Berliner Monatshefte* (April, 1929), VII, 313–44.

Brooks, Sydney, "British Policy in the Near East," *Fortnightly Review* (January, 1913), XCIII, N. S., 112–24.

Caclamanos, Demetrius, "Reminiscences of the Balkan Wars," *Slavonic Review* (July, 1937), XVI, 113–28.
Caraglieri, Dr., "Das Kretaproblem," *Jahrbuch des Völkerrechts* (1914), II, ii, 339–463.
Chlumecky, Leopold Freiherr von, "Franz Ferdinands Aussenpolitik (Aus persönlichen Erinnerungen)," *Berliner Monatshefte* (June, 1934), XII, 455–66.
Dietrich, Richard, "Die Bemühungen Frankreichs zur Festigung der Entente cordiale 1911–12," *Berliner Monatshefte* (September, 1934), XII, 767–84.
Diamandy, C. J., "La grande guerre vue du versante oriental," *Revue des deux mondes* (December 15, 1927), 7e. Per., XLII, 781–804; (January 1, 1928), 7e. Per., XLIII, 129–43.
"Das diplomatische Doppelspiel Russlands beim Ausbruch des ersten Balkankrieges," *Archiv für Politik und Geschichte* (1924), II, 405–17.
Dungern, Dr. Freiherr von, "Die Entstehung des Staates Albanien," *Jahrbuch des Völkerrechts* (1914), II, ii, 269–318.
—— "Die Bukarester Friedenskonferenz," *Jahrbuch des Völkerrechts* (1914), II, ii, 245–68.
Durham, M. E., "The Story of Essad Pasha," *Contemporary Review* (August, 1920), CXVIII, 206–15.
"The Eastern Question and European War," *Fortnightly Review* (December, 1912), XCII, N. S., 989–1000.
Florinsky, M. T., "Russia and Constantinople. Count Kokovtzov's Evidence," *Foreign Affairs* (October, 1929), VIII, 135–41.
Frantz, G., "Die Meerengenfrage in der Vorkriegspolitik Russlands," *Deutsche Rundschau* (February, 1927), LIII, 142–60.
Gottschalk, Egon, "Die Entrevue von Constanza," *Berliner Monatshefte* (June, 1934), XII, 466–85.
—— "Rumänien und der Dreibund bis zur Krise 1914," *Die Kriegsschuldfrage* (July, 1927), V, 632–65.
Helmreich, E. C., "Die tieferen Ursachen der Politik Berchtolds im Oktober 1912," *Berliner Monatshefte* (March, 1932), X, 218–44.
—— "Russlands Einfluss auf den Balkanbund im Oktober 1912," *Berliner Monatshefte* (March, 1933), XI, 217–45.
—— "Die serbisch-bulgarischen Verträge von 1904," *Berliner Monatshefte* (August, 1933), XI, 772–80.
—— "Die Haldane-Mission," *Berliner Monatshefte* (February, 1934), XII, 112–43.
—— "Ein Nachtrag zu dem serbisch-bulgarischen Abkommen von 1912," *Berliner Monatshefte* (December, 1935), XIII, 1073–76.
—— "An Unpublished Report on Austro-German Military Conversations of November, 1912," *Journal of Modern History* (June, 1933), V, 197–207. Reprinted in part, *Berliner Monatshefte* (September, 1933), XI, 893–97.
—— "Montenegro and the Formation of the Balkan League," *Slavonic Review* (January, 1937), XV, 426–34.

Helmreich, E. C. and Black, C. E., "The Russo-Bulgarian Military Convention of 1902," *Journal of Modern History* (December, 1937), IX, 471–82.

Herzfeld, Hans, "Die Liman-Krise und die Politik der Grossmächte in der Jahreswende 1913–14," *Berliner Monatshefte* (September, October, 1933), XI, 837–58; 973–93.

Hubka, Gustav von, "Kritische Tage in Montenegro," *Berliner Monatshefte* (January, 1931), IX, 27–45.

—— "Diplomatentum in Montenegro," *Berliner Monatshefte* (August, 1936), XIV, 657–62.

—— "König Nikolaus von Montenegro," *Deutsche Revue* (April, June, 1921), XLVI, 23–31; 174–84.

Ippen, Th. A., "Das religiöse Protectorat Österreich-Ungarns in der Türkei," *Die Kultur* (1902), III, 298–316.

Jánossy, Dionys, "Der handelspolitische Konflikt zwischen der österreichisch-ungarischen Monarchie und Serbien in den Jahren 1904–1910," *Jahrbuch des Wiener ungarischen historischen Instituts* (1932), II, 285–312.

Jorga, N., "Le mont Athos et le pays Roumaine," *Bulletin de la section historique, Académie Roumaine* (January, 1914), II, 149–213.

—— "Comment la Roumanie s'est détachée de la Triplice d'après les documents austro-hongrois et des souvenirs personnels," *Revue historique du Sud-Est européen* (July-September, 1932), IX, 235–307.

Jovanović, Slobodan, "Nicholas Pašić: After Ten Years," *Slavonic Review* (January, 1937), XV, 368–76.

Kabisch, Ernst, "Die Militär- und Marinekonventionen der Triple-Entente vor dem Ausbruch des Weltkrieges," *Die Kriegsschuldfrage* (April, 1927), V, 282–309.

Kiszling, Rudolf, "Russlands Kriegsvorbereitungen im Herbst 1912 und ihre Rückwirkungen auf Österreich-Ungarn," *Berliner Monatshefte* (March, 1935), XIII, 181–92.

Korostovetz, Wladimir von, "Graf Alexander Konstantinowitsch Benckendorff," *Berliner Monatshefte* (November, 1936), XIV, 887–901.

Laloy, Emile, "L'Autriche et la Serbie en juillet 1913," *Mercure de France* (February, 1934), CCL, 53–68.

Langer, W. L., "Russia, the Straits Question and the European Powers, 1904–1908," *The English Historical Review* (January, 1929), XLIV, 59–85.

—— "Russia, the Straits Question and the Origins of the Balkan League," *The Political Science Quarterly* (September, 1928), XLIII, 321–63.

Lawton, Lancelot, "A German View of the Turkish Defeat," *Fortnightly Review* (May, 1913), XCIII, N. S., 975–88.

Lutzow, Count, "Is Austria really the Disturber," *Fortnightly Review* (March, 1913), XCIII, N. S., 598–602.

M., "The Balkan League, History of its Formation," *The Fortnightly Review* (March, 1913), XCII, N. S., 430–40.

Marco, "Before the Battle of Kumanovo," *Nova Europa* (1927), XVI.

Marco, "Nikolaus Hartwig. Serbiens Aussenpolitik vor dem Weltkrieg," *Die Kriegsschuldfrage* (August, 1928), VI, 745–69.

"Montenegrinische Dokumente zur Annexionskrise," *Berliner Monatshefte* (August, 1937), XV, 702–06.

"Neue Montenegrinische Dokumente," *Berliner Monatshefte* (September, 1937), XV, 796–98.

Mousset, A., "Documents. La diplomatie française de la genèse des guerres balkaniques," *Le Monde Slave* (1932), III, 259–277.

"Mt. Athos. Relation of the monasteries to the Greek government," London *Times* (June 24, 27, 30, 1927).

Mutius, Gerhard von, "Die Türkei 1911–1914. Aus unveröffentlichen Lebenserinnerungen," *Preussische Jahrbücher* (June, 1934), CCXXXVI, 212–20.

"Die Narodna Odbrana," *Die Kriegsschuldfrage* (March, 1927), V, 192–225.

Neimeth, Josef, "Zur Geschichte des Balkanbundes," *Schmollers Jahrbuch* (1917), XLI, 87–133.

Niemeyer, Theodor, "Die Londoner Botschaftervereinigung," *Jahrbuch des Völkerrechts* (1914), II, ii, 487–523.

Novakovitsch, Dr. "Die Intervention der Grossmächte in der Skutarifrage," *Jahrbuch des Völkerrechts* (1914), II, ii, 222–38.

Peacock, Wadham, "The Future of Albania," *Fortnightly Review* (May, 1913), XCIII, N. S., 920–32.

Peritch, J., "Die politischen Folgen der Balkankriege insbesondere im Hinblick auf die Balkanslaven," *Jahrbuch des Völkerrechts* (1914) II, ii, 182–221.

Philalethes, "König Ferdinand erzählt aus seinem Leben. Unterhaltung mit dem ehemaligen bulgarischen Herrscher," *Neue Freie Presse* (February 22, 26, 1931).

Popović, Chedo A., "The Work of 'Union or Death' in Preparing for the Balkan War," *Nova Europa* (1927), XVI, nos. 10, and 11.

——"Das Sarajewoer Attentat und die Organisation 'Vereinigung oder Tod,'" *Berliner Monatshefte* (November, 1932), X, 1097–1121.

Popovitch, Professor Pavle, "Bulgaria and the Balkan Alliance," *The Balkan Review* (April, 1927), I, 174–187.

"Potiorek über die österreichisch-serbische Spannung 1913," *Die Kriegsschuldfrage* (March, 1928), VI, 260–4.

Radoslavoff, V., "Die Rolle und die Ziele Bulgariens im Kriege," *Die Kriegsschuldfrage* (December, 1928), VI, 1135–42.

Randi, Oscar, "Nicola P. Pašić," *L'Europa Orientale* (1927), VII; 1–41, 155–82, 231–55.

Rappaport, Alfred, "Albaniens Werdegang," *Die Kriegsschuldfrage* (September, 1927), V, 815–44.

——"Montenegros Eintritt in den Weltkrieg," *Berliner Monatshefte* (October, 1929), VII, 941–66.

——"Mazedonien und die Komitadschis," *Berliner Monatshefte* (August, 1930), VIII, 731–47.

Rappaport, Alfred, "Rund um den Friedjungprozess," *Berliner Monatshefte* (April, 1931), IX, 339–57.

—— "Spalajković," *Berliner Monatshefte* (July, 1935), XIII, 555–76.

Redlich, J., "Habsburg Policy in the Balkans Before the War," *Foreign Affairs* (July, 1928), VI, 645–57.

Roloff, Gustav, "Die Begründung des Balkan-Bundes nach den serbischen, englischen, und deutschen Akten und anderen Quellen," *Preussische Jahrbücher* (May, 1930), CCXX, 113–19.

Sasse, Heinz, "Nicola Pašić," *Berliner Monatshefte* (January, 1936), XIV, 23–42.

Schargl, Ludwig, "Die Affäre des österreichisch-ungarischen Konsuls Prohaska im ersten Balkankriege, 1912," *Berliner Monatshefte* (April, 1929), VII, 345–54.

Schultz, Maurice, "La politique économique d'Aehrenthal envers la Serbie," *Revue d'histoire de la guerre mondiale* (1935), XIII, 325–47; (1936), XIV, 23–42.

Schwendemann, Karl, "Grundzüge der Balkanpolitik Österreich-Ungarns von 1908–1914," *Berliner Monatshefte* (March, 1930), VIII, 203–26.

Schwertfeger, Bernhard, "Die Militärpolitischen Beziehungen Frankreichs und England zu Belgien nach 1912," *Berliner Monatshefte* (July, 1934), XII, 594–614.

—— "Die militärpolitischen Beziehungen Frankreichs und Englands zu Belgien im Jahre 1912," *Berliner Monatshefte* (June, 1933), XI, 541–64.

Seton-Watson, R. W., "Les relations diplomatiques austro-serbes," *Le Monde Slave* (1926), III, 273–88.

—— "William II's Balkan Policy," *The Slavonic Review* (June, 1928), VII, 1–29.

"Slovenski Jug," *Berliner Monatshefte* (December, 1930), VIII, 1142–56.

Steinitz, Edward Ritter von, "Berchtolds Politik zu Beginn der Balkan Krise 1912," *Berliner Monatshefte* (January, 1931), IX, 45–57.

—— "Berchtolds Politik während des ersten Balkankrieges," *Berliner Monatshefte* (March, 1931), IX, 229–48.

—— "Berchtolds Politik während des Waffenstillstandes auf dem Balkan," *Berliner Monatshefte* (August, 1931), IX, 723–46.

—— "Berchtolds Albanische Politik," *Berliner Monatshefte* (February, 1932), X, 153–67.

—— "Berchtolds Politik gegen den Balkanbund," *Berliner Monatshefte* (April, 1932), X, 331–45.

—— "Berchtolds Politik während des zweiten Balkankrieges," *Berliner Monatshefte* (July, 1932), X, 660–74.

Todoroff, Kosta, "The Macedonian Organization Yesterday and Today," *Foreign Affairs* (April, 1928), VI, 473–82.

Vivian, Herbert, "After the War," *Fortnightly Review* (February, 1913), XCIII, N. S., 312–21.

Wedel, O. H., "Austro-Hungarian Diplomatic Documents 1908–1914," *Journal of Modern History* (March, 1931), III, 84–108.

Wegerer, Alfred von, "Graf Berchtolds Interview über den Kriegsausbruch," *Berliner Monatshefte* (June, 1935), XIII, 518–28.

Woods, H. Charles, "The Armies of the Balkan League," *Fortnightly Review* (December, 1912), XCII, N. S., 1060–70.

Yovanovitch, M. Yovan, "How Austria Willed War," *The Balkan Review* (March 1919), I, 73–85.

Newspaper Clippings on the Balkan Wars, largely from the American Press, 2 vol. (Harvard College Library).

Frankfurter Zeitung

London *Times*

Münchener Allgemeine Zeitung

Vienna. *Fremdenblatt*

Vienna. *Neue Freie Presse*

Vienna. *Die Zeit*

INDEX

INDEX

For purposes of identification senders or receivers of telegrams mentioned in the footnotes are indexed in the case of those whose names do not appear at any time in the text.